UNDERSTANDING
PARENTING

UNDERSTANDING
PARENTING

Michael L. Jaffe

Kean College

 Wm. C. Brown Publishers

Book Team

Editor *Michael Lange*
Developmental Editor *Carla J. Aspelmeier*
Production Editor *C. Jeanne Patterson*
Designer *K. Wayne Harms*
Art Editor *Gayle A. Kane*
Photo Editor *Carrie Burger*
Permissions Editor *Vicki Krug*
Visuals Processor *Jodi Wagner*

Wm. C. Brown Publishers

President *G. Franklin Lewis*
Vice President, Publisher *George Wm. Bergquist*
Vice President, Publisher *Thomas E. Doran*
Vice President, Operations and Production *Beverly Kolz*
National Sales Manager *Virginia S. Moffat*
Advertising Manager *Ann M. Knepper*
Marketing Manager *Kathy Law Laube*
Production Editorial Manager *Colleen A. Yonda*
Production Editorial Manager *Julie A. Kennedy*
Publishing Services Manager *Karen J. Slaght*
Manager of Visuals and Design *Faye M. Schilling*

Cover photo © Pete Saloutos/After Image, Inc.

The credits section for this book begins on page 397, and is
considered an extension of the copyright page.

Library of Congress Catalog Card Number: 89-81451

ISBN 0-697-07890-6

Printed in the United States of America by Wm. C. Brown Publishers,
2460 Kerper Boulevard, Dubuque, IA 52001

10 9 8 7 6 5 4 3 2 1

*To my children
and all children*

Brief Contents

Contents

8 SELF-CONCEPT, SELF-ESTEEM, AND SEXUAL IDENTITY

9 ADJUSTMENT, STRESS, AND COPING

10 COMPETENCE AND ACHIEVEMENT

Preface

My primary goal in writing this text is to offer students a comprehensive, stimulating, and, I hope, well-written overview of the parenting process. Parents, prospective parents, and those who work with families require and deserve the best information about child rearing that is currently available.

Over the past 20 years, so much has been learned about parenting, yet so little of this information reaches those who need it most. Much of the advice offered to parents by "experts" on TV and in magazines reflects cultural biases and ideology more than the extensive research literature accumulating in professional journals (Young, 1990).

A major challenge in writing a text such as this one is to present accurate and useful information, without oversimplifying the topic or issue, in a format that is accessible to interested readers. I have tried to avoid the use of psychological jargon when possible, but sometimes the terminology used by researchers and theorists most precisely describes a point or concept.

In addition to reviewing well over a thousand recently published journal articles and books, I have included relevant clinical material from my own experiences in private practice as a family therapist. Working with and studying distressed families helps us understand the complexities and the vulnerabilities of the family system. Many of the child-rearing problems and issues discussed in this text are gleaned from the parenting workshops I have had the pleasure of conducting over the past 10 years. Raising 2 sons has provided my wife and me with a very realistic view of the ups and downs of parenting.

Parenting is a challenging, demanding role and an extremely fulfilling and enjoyable one. I hope this text conveys my respect for and fascination with the parenting process. I salute the remarkable investigators and theorists whose curiosity about family processes and child rearing has provided the raw material for this project. I would be very grateful for any suggestions, corrections, or feedback about this book that readers are willing to provide (Psychology Department, Kean College of New Jersey, 07083).

PLAN OF THIS BOOK

Chapter 1, Parenting in Perspective, reviews the history of childhood and the status of children today. Four parenting goals are suggested, and 4 contemporary issues in parenting are examined at length.

Chapter 2, Theoretical Perspectives, reviews 12 theories and models of development that clarify the parenting process. Chapter 3, The Roots of Personality, explores the basics of personality development, emphasizing biological factors. Chapter 4 presents useful information about pregnancy, birth, infancy, and the transition to parenthood.

Chapter 5 provides a broad context for understanding the relationship between parental authority, discipline styles, and children's noncompliant behavior. Chapters 6 and 7 review specific discipline and communication styles that support the 4 parenting goals cited in the first chapter. The nature of relationships in families is also addressed in chapter 7.

Chapter 8 examines parental influences on the development of children's self-concept, self-esteem, and sexual identity. Chapter 9 explores children's emotional development in families, emphasizing the role of stress and coping resources. Chapter 10 discusses home and family factors in the development of competence and achievement motivation.

Chapter 11 focuses on the special pleasures and problems of parenting adolescents. Chapter 12 reviews the effects of parental conflict, separation, and divorce on children; the nontraditional family configurations that follow divorce; and the fathering role. Chapter 13 discusses parenting children with special needs, and chapter 14 considers the effects on children of family violence, child abuse, and neglect. The epilogue summarizes some of the major conclusions of this book.

ACKNOWLEDGMENTS

I am extremely grateful to the many individuals who supported the writing of this text. I thank my colleagues and friends at Kean College of New Jersey for their support, particularly Bonnie M. Kind for providing a thoughtful review of an early draft. I thank Kean College for granting me a one-semester sabbatical to work on this book.

I would like to thank the following people who reviewed all or parts of this manuscript. Their suggestions and contributions have helped make this a better book.

Alice Atkinson
University of Iowa

Larry J. Cology
Owens Technical College

Robert K. Drummond
Mid-America Nazarene College

J. Eileen Gallagher Haugh
St. Mary's College

Bonnie M. Kind
Kean College

Phil Osborne
Hesston College

Sandy Osborne
Montana State University

I appreciate the efforts of all of those people at Wm. C. Brown Publishers who participated in this project. Their names are found on the bookteam/copyright page.

I thank Jeri Warhaftig and Lynne Federman for sharing their poignant, moving personal experiences as parents with the readers of this text. I thank my sons Justin and Eric for helping me become a better parent and for their help in illustrating this text. I thank my wife Gail for her love and patience over 20 years of marriage, and I thank my parents for their continued support.

Michael Jaffe

UNDERSTANDING
PARENTING

Parenting in Perspective

OBJECTIVES

After studying chapter 1, students should be able to

1. Explain what is meant by the "fulfillment-struggle" polarity of parenting
2. Describe at least five reasons for having children, and evaluate each one
3. Give a general overview of the history of childhood, tracing the emergence of modern conceptions of children
4. List five serious problems confronting large numbers of children in the United States today
5. Describe the four goals of parenting and the rationale for each
6. Describe the key issues surrounding the following topics
   a. Dual-career parenting
   b. Day-care programs for preschool children
   c. Day-care programs for infants
   d. Children in self-care
7. Describe three different approaches to parent training, and evaluate each one

INTRODUCTION

Meeting Mark's Mom

"Closing in on the next due date for his book report, I could feel the tension mounting. My mood was 'edgy' and demanding—bad start. When I realized I was cursing under my breath, I decided it was high time to change the course of things. So we worked at it as much as we could with the time that was left. This new book was less comprehensible to him. Two days after it was due, he's still not finished reading it.

"I'm taking a more laid-back approach to Mark and, also, his room. At this point, there are clothes, refuse, toys, blankets, drawings, everywhere. We can't move through the room without stepping on something. I've told him if he doesn't find the dirty clothes for me, they won't get done with the laundry. Do you think it's possible to be a discouraged parent? I feel like we're going nowhere and I want to give up! I know it won't do anyone any good if I do, though. I've thought about your stance of no punishment . . . how does one work up the courage and where does one begin?"* (Mark's mother).

THE DECISION TO PARENT

Throughout this text, we will have several opportunities to follow the progress of Mark and his mother, a single woman attending my undergraduate parenting class. This particular journal entry captures the occasional frustration, confusion, and discouragement of parenting.

When deciding whether to have children, we may envision the joyful, tender moments that we associate with child rearing. And such moments are plentiful. However, most parents discover that child rearing is more difficult than they anticipated. One father of three reported that parenting "changed our lives in a lot of ways. We don't have a lot of freedom; we don't have much time for each other. Every free minute we have, somebody needs something." But he added, "When they smile, it makes it all worthwhile."

The decision to parent should be based on realistic expectations about living with children, the burdens of child care, and about our own willingness and ability to place someone else's needs before our own. Deciding whether to parent raises many fascinating questions. Why have children in the first place? Will I be a good parent? In what ways will becoming a parent change my life? How will it affect my relationship with my partner? What will my children be like?

Upon further reflection, additional considerations arise. What are the financial implications? Who will take care of my children as infants and as toddlers? How will I discipline them? Though we may decide to have children to enrich our own lives, these questions remind us of the profound responsibilities associated with bringing a child into the world. These questions suggest a polarity: the potential fulfillment of parenting versus the daily challenge (and occasional struggle) to do it well.

FAMILY LIFE: CONTENTMENT AND CHAOS

Recent polls support this polarity. A parent survey conducted by the magazine *Better Homes and Gardens* (October, 1986; results summarized by Collins, 1986a) elicited responses from 30,000 readers. (Note: This was not a scientific survey, and the opinions expressed, although interesting, should not be considered representative of parents in general.) A majority reported believing that, compared to their own parents, they are better parents, they spank their children less, and they express more affection. In describing their family life, 70 percent depicted it as loving, 65 percent said it is fun, and only 4 percent characterized it as hostile.

Fifty-one percent of the respondents depicted family life as "chaotic," which the researchers did not interpret negatively. Sixty-one percent of the parents reported believing that communication among family members is better and more open today and 88 percent said they feel they are good parents. Most significantly, 90 percent said they believed that having children is worth all the sacrifices, and 80 percent reported that, if they could start the parenting process over, they would still have the same number of children.

On the other side of the polarity, 75 percent claimed that it is much harder to parent today than in the past, and 51 percent reported that they sometimes feel overwhelmed by their responsibilities. The most frequently cited problem was financial, even in middle-class families. Almost half reported having difficulty balancing work with home responsibilities. A third reported difficulties in disciplining their children.

Parents complained about disobedience and were disturbed by conflicts between their children. Though most respondents felt they were good parents, almost three-quarters were critical of *other* parents for not spending enough time with their children!

How do children feel about their parents' efforts? A poll of 1,000 children, conducted by the American Chicle Group (*New York Times,* March 12, 1987), found that the children sampled approve of how their parents are raising them. They endorse their parents' concerns about school grades, hobbies, friends, and TV. The children felt that their family life would be improved if they got along better with their siblings and if they could talk more openly with their parents. Teenagers felt home life would be improved if they were treated more like adults.

These statistics reinforce one of the themes of this textbook: parenting can be both fulfilling and overwhelming, sometimes on the same day! The more realistic our expectations about children and ourselves, and the more informed we are about child development and the parenting process, the more likely that we will fall closer to the fulfillment end of the continuum.

In this chapter, we review the history of childhood and some of the problems confronting children today. We look at reasons for having children and consider parenting goals that might guide the process of child rearing. We will also examine four contemporary issues related to parenting.

HISTORY OF CHILDHOOD

Study Question   *How has the concept of child-hood changed over the ages?*

Over the last few generations, a view of children and childhood has emerged that is strikingly different from that held by our ancestors (Cleverley & Phillips, 1986). Today we view children as innocent, vulnerable, young beings requiring loving care and protection. We have a better (though far from complete) understanding of the relationship between a child's potential, the conditions of rearing, and the child's eventual character and achievements.

A review of the history of childhood reveals that ignorance about children and prevailing economic conditions were the primary factors influencing their status in society. Recent archaeological evidence suggests, for example, that infanticide (killing infants or allowing them to die) and ritual slayings of children were common in ancient, crowded Carthage. Child sacrifice controlled population growth and also allowed families to maintain their fortunes over generations. It is estimated that about 20,000 children were sacrificed between 800 B.C. and 146 B.C., when Roman invaders destroyed Carthage (Browne, 1987).

Greek philosophers advocated that children be raised to be responsible and productive citizens and that children with special talents be groomed for public service. Plato suggested separating young children from their parents and having them be raised instead by the state. Presumably, these children would be free of the corruption that plagued Greek government. Aristotle contended that only those children with special abilities should be raised to become leaders. Aristotle was also one of the first to suggest that rearing strategies be adjusted to accommodate children's individual natures.

Advantaged children in ancient Rome fared well. Mother-infant bonding at birth was the norm. Boys and girls played with toys and

Painting portraying the child as a miniature adult. Aries used paintings such as this one to conclude that, historically, children often have been viewed and treated like miniature adults. More recent analyses suggest his conclusions were somewhat overdrawn.

learned how to read and write, and boys attended school. Roman views of childhood and family apparently resembled those of modern times and were quite enlightened compared to those that ensued during the Middle Ages (Luepnitz, 1988).

During the Middle Ages (approximately the fifth to fifteenth centuries), children apparently were treated very harshly, relative to modern standards (Aries, 1962). Children were often abandoned if their parents could not provide for them. Even infanticide was widespread. Females, illegitimate children, and children born with abnormalities were at greatest risk. Documentation about children's lives during this epoch is limited. Only the clergy were literate, and they didn't have children. Given the literature that has survived, there is little reason to believe that children were treated as humanely as most children are today.

Childhood as we think of it today did not exist until very recently in human history. In the preindustrial world, children were considered infants until about the age of 7 years, and then they were treated as miniature adults—working, dressing, drinking, and smoking like adults. If children violated laws, they were punished as harshly as adults (Aries, 1962). Documents reveal that children as young as 7 years were occasionally imprisoned or hanged for stealing.

As important to parents as survival in this world was salvation in the next. Calvinist and Puritan parents assumed that children were inherently sinful in their disobedience and defiance. Faith in God and firm discipline, rather than parental affection, were believed to be necessary for healthy development (Kagan, 1978). "Good habits were developed under a strict regime of controlled sleeping, fasting between meals, whispered requests for food at table, regular family prayers, and the judicious application of corporal punishment" (Cleverley & Phillips, 1986, p. 29). Many fundamentalist religions continue to advocate this model of family life.

Parents valued obedience and submission in their children, not independence or assertiveness. It was considered the parent's sacred duty to "beat the hell" out of the foolish, wicked child. Children who were disobedient received "correction," often a brutal beating. Though children were expected to display affection to their parents, it was considered counterproductive for parents to "spare the rod and spoil the child." (As we shall see, punitive discipline methods continue to be widely practiced to this day.)

With most families' daily priority being survival, children's labor was considered a necessity. There was little time for play, and there were few, if any, toys. Before the sixteenth century, children and adults were unschooled. Children as young as 6 or 7 years old lived as apprentices or servants. They often lived far away from their families, encountering even harsher circumstances than they faced at home.

Aries (1962) quotes the philosopher Montaigne: "I have lost two or three children in their infancy, not without regret, but without great sorrow." The lack of tenderness displayed to children strains our credibility until we consider the mortality rates of children during the Middle Ages. Historical records suggest that one-half to two-thirds of all children died during infancy! Think of the emotional risks parents would assume in forming strong attachments to children, only to watch them die, one after another. Today, we can assume that a newborn infant will survive birth, infancy, and childhood, and will do so without serious disability. Before this century, parents could make no such assumption.

The major causes of high mortality rates for children included ignorance about the importance of sterilization during birth and poor or nonexistent sanitation. These conditions fostered childhood diseases that devastated infants and children. There were no pediatricians, no hospitals, no intensive care, no immunization against contagious childhood illnesses, and no antibiotics to treat them. Fortunately, most childhood diseases have been tamed in this century.

By the sixteenth century, a new conception of children was emerging. There was greater uncertainty about whether children are inherently innocent or wicked. Renaissance essayist Michel de Montaigne (1533–1592) speculated that some children are good and some are evil (Synnott, 1988). Childhood began to be regarded by some as a separate and unique stage of life, crucial to the individual's later development.

John Locke (1632–1704), British philosopher and statesman, adopted an environmentalist stance in development. Locke suggested that children's minds are blank at birth, to be molded by their caretakers. He emphasized the importance of patient, parental instruction in shaping children's character. Locke suggested that children are neither innately good nor innately bad; the environment can lead them in either direction. He advocated that parents show affection to their children (Kagan, 1978).

Jean Jacques Rousseau (1712–1778), an influential French philosopher, admired some aspects of Locke's position. He agreed that children, who he believed are basically good, might be corrupted by ignorant or insensitive caretakers. Rousseau hypothesized that under optimal conditions, children's innate talents will emerge. He sometimes suggested minimal interference from adults. For example, he advocated giving children the freedom to follow their natural impulses. Other times he urged parents to carefully regulate their children's experiences and even use force if necessary (Synnott, 1988). Apparently, he himself was undecided on this issue (Cleverley & Phillips, 1986).

Rousseau recommended that mothers care for their children themselves, rather than rely on wet nurses or other caretakers. He was a strong advocate of a close mother-child bond, and his writings led to a period during which motherhood was romanticized. He had nothing to say about fathering. Rousseau eventually abandoned his own five children to an orphanage (Synnott, 1988).

Child-rearing values in Japan from the mid-seventeenth to the mid-nineteenth centuries reflect enlightened views about children and even have a contemporary flavor. Documents written for the public suggested that children "are innately good rather than evil, environmental factors rather than innate ones account for differences among children, and children are autonomous learning beings rather than passive to experience" (Kojima, 1986).

In the west, economic changes related to the industrial revolution encouraged additional changes in perspective. Increased use of machines allowed not only less dependence on child labor, but also leisure time for parents to spend with their children. The industrialization of work made society more complex. Less demand for child labor, combined with a greater need for literate citizens, led to the establishment of schools.

Let us not forget that during industrialization, countless children worked in factories under barbaric conditions. Reform came, but slowly. In Britain, the Factory Act of 1833 prohibited labor for children under 6 years. Children younger than 10 could not work more than 16 hours a day. In the United States, black children living in slavery had no protection at all (Synnott, 1988).

In schools, children were sheltered from the harsh demands of the adult work environment. They could spend time with other children in a relatively safe place. They could play and explore the world while developing valued skills. Many schooling traditions, such as the two months of "vacation" to help harvest summer crops, continue today with little awareness of their origins.

During the nineteenth century, in the industrial world, mothers became the central figures in parenting. Fathers worked in factories and offices rather than at home. Mass production replaced the homemade goods that traditionally occupied maternal time. By mid-nineteenth century, mothers were largely responsible for raising their children. "Mothers were to devote themselves exclusively to child care, and anything that might go wrong with the child was associated with her incompetence. What emerged, in fact, was a belief that behind every criminal, alcoholic, and madman was a mother who had not done her duty. Maternal guilt was born—or at least given a new lease on life" (Luepnitz, 1988, p. 127).

Housework became a full-time job (Margolis, 1984). As medical and health technology developed and mothers became more attentive to their infant's needs, infant mortality rates improved. It became less risky for parents to become attached to their young children. Reasoning and persuasion had joined strictness as tools of discipline. Around 1880, adolescence was conceived as yet another unique and crucial stage of development.

Significant changes in the late nineteenth and early twentieth centuries contributed to today's relatively enlightened view of children. Universal primary education, graded by age, was extended to the lower and working classes. Stronger child labor laws protected children from adult exploitation. Child psychologists such as Arnold Gesell began to use scientific methods to gather useful information about children's development. Intelligence tests were devised to identify children with special needs so that they could receive special attention.

Our present century has witnessed a wide range of attitudes about child rearing, from the so-called permissiveness (really flexibility) encouraged by the writings of Drs. Freud and Spock, to the strict conditioning approach advocated by behaviorist John Watson. Whereas Dr. Spock advocates maternal expressions of warmth and affection, Watson warned against overindulgence. Excessive coddling of children, according to Watson, would encourage dependency and weakness. Several modern perspectives that relate to parenting are presented in chapter 2.

Toward the end of this century, we find a renewed interest in, and concern about, parenting. Challenging issues confront many of today's parents and children. These include poverty, child abuse, balancing work and family life, day care, adolescent drug abuse, suicide, and sexual safety. In the pages that follow, these and many other topics will receive our full attention.

CHILDREN TODAY

Study Question What serious problems confront children in the United States today?

A review of the history of childhood reveals the sad, sometimes shocking treatment of children. It is not always easy to find progress in the pages of human history, but clearly most children are better off today than ever before. Nevertheless, countless children are still being raised under extreme conditions that threaten their development.

In 1985, a government report based on a demographic profile of the school-age population in the United States revealed that (1) one in five children live in poverty; (2) almost one-fourth of the children under the age of 6 in the United States are poor; (3) one in five is raised by a single mother; and (4) one-third of all households headed by women are poor (*New York Times,* February 17, 1985).

In the fall of 1987, the Committee for Economic Development reported that one-fourth of all children in the United States live in poverty (notice the trend since 1985). As many as one-third of all children entering elementary school may lack basic skills needed for successful schooling. Three-fourths of all black infants are born to unwed mothers, half of whom are teenagers (*New York Times,* April, 1988). In 1986, 42 percent of all black families and 13 percent of all white families were headed by females (*New York Times,* March 1, 1988).

According to United States government statistics, 40,000 babies die each year because of inadequate prenatal and neonatal care. About one out of five infants is born to a teenage mother. Two-thirds of these girls have not graduated from high school. Adolescent mothers are typically impatient, insensitive, and punitive, compared to older, more experienced mothers (Garcia Coll, Hoffman, & Oh, 1987).

Each day in the United States, an average of 2,753 teenagers get pregnant, over 1,000 have abortions, 367 miscarry, 1,287 give birth, 609 contract a venereal disease, and 5 commit suicide. *Each day,* almost 1,000 children are abused, over 3,000 run away from home, and 2,269 illegitimate children are born. *Each day,* almost 3,000 children experience their parents' divorce, and almost 50,000 children are in juvenile correction facilities (*U.S. News and World Report,* November 7, 1988).

Two million handicapped children are not receiving appropriate educational services, even though such services are mandated by law. Two million teenagers drop out of school each year. One-third to one-half of preschool children may not be properly immunized against childhood diseases.

All is not well in the United States as far as children are concerned. This is especially true of black children living in the inner cities where homicide, crime, drug addiction, AIDS, welfare dependency, bitterness, and resentment toward white society exist at epidemic proportions. Ninety-one percent of the children born with AIDS in New York City are black or Hispanic. Three times as many blacks as whites live below the poverty level (Bernstein, 1988).

Few, if any, of these problems have simple solutions. However, cost-effective prevention and treatment programs exist. If these programs were widely available, thousands of lives and billions of dollars would be saved. A one-dollar investment in prenatal care saves three dollars in short-term hospital costs. One dollar spent on childhood immunizations saves ten dollars in later medical costs. One dollar spent on preschool education saves six dollars in later social remediation (*New York Times* editorial, September 25, 1988). Most of these problems are preventable but, nevertheless, are getting worse.

WHY HAVE CHILDREN?

One of the ironies of human reproduction is that conceiving and bearing children do not have to be planned. In the absence of proper precautions, nature will take its course, regardless of our intentions. "Rather than *deciding* on the number and timing of children, some couples simply experience their pregnancies as happenings, unplanned events, occurrences, or the will of God" (Neal, Groat, & Wicks, 1989, p. 325).

The United States birth rate in 1987 was the highest in 23 years, according to a government study issued in 1988 (*New York Times,* August 16, 1988). The "baby boomers," having completed their schooling and starting families of their own, brought almost 4 million infants into the world in that one year. Apparently, most adults in the United States are enthusiastic about having and raising children. In addition, couples with good reasons for having children may end up having larger families (Hoffman & Manis, 1979).

Society considers the parenting role normal behavior for adults. It is childless couples who may be considered "deviant." Nevertheless, the decision to bear children is not always easily made. Birth control technology, allowing us to distinguish sex from reproduction, makes childbearing a matter of choice. "Choice, of course, implies a weighing of costs and benefits; a consideration of the pros and cons, the advantages and disadvantages; an acknowledgment that there are both 'good' and 'bad' attributes of children and parenthood" (Neal, Groat, & Wicks, 1989, p. 313).

It is estimated that it will cost about $130,000 to raise a child born in 1988 to the age of 18 years, and an additional $120,000 to cover the cost of a college education (*New York Times,* February 20, 1988). But the frustrations of parenting are not primarily economic. Parents are expected to sacrifice their own needs and comforts when they conflict with those of their

WHY HAVE CHILDREN?

⑦ ⑦ ⑦ ⑦ THE TOP SEVEN REASONS ⑦ ⑦ ⑦

① TO DO YOUR LABOR

② TO BOSS AROUND

③ TO YELL AT

④ TO BRAG ABOUT

⑤ TO OVERPROTECT

⑥ TO GROUND

⑦ TO SEND TO COLLEGE

WORLD'S WORST CHILD

Justin Jaffe

children. Potential stresses of parenthood include the coordination of infant and child care, the division of household labor between parents, handling misbehavior, and meeting the demands of employment (Ventura, 1987). Most adults receive almost no preparation for the daily challenges of living with children. Nevertheless, if a child misbehaves, it is the parents who are held responsible.

Despite the high birth rates cited earlier, adults are, and should be, cautious about bringing children into this complex and imperiled world. Adults are remaining single for longer periods, and an increasing number of single adults report that they expect to remain childless. An organization known as NON

(National Organization of Nonparents) maintains that parenthood is glamorized and commercialized in our culture and that the child-centered life is not for everyone. Divorce rates can intimidate young couples engaged in family planning, as marriage becomes a less-than-permanent arrangement between the sexes (Neal, Groat, & Wicks, 1989).

Single women who prefer to remain childless say they anticipate greater personal and financial freedom in their lives, more satisfying marriages, and fewer obstacles in pursuing professional careers (Houseknecht, 1979). Women who are voluntarily childless, whether single or married, "recognize fewer benefits and greater costs in having children than do similarly educated women who want to become parents or are already mothers" (Callan, 1986, p. 269).

All Kinds of Reasons for Having Children

Study Question What would be your reasons for deciding to have or not to have children? Try to list at least three reasons for and against your having children.

The traditional reason for bearing children (and still the case in many developing countries) was **labor**. Parents viewed children as "helping hands" for the family's economic benefit. Since the welcome introduction of child labor laws early in this century, the major economic benefit of having children has been as a tax deduction. It is hard enough to get today's children to wash the dishes or clean their rooms, let alone plow the fields or plant the crops. Our ancestors also depended upon their children to provide **financial security** and care in old age. Unfortunately, this need still exists today for many of our older citizens.

Some people enjoy **exercising authority**. Since other adults may resist "being pushed around," these individuals may decide to have children. Although I am slightly exaggerating

the point, exercising authority is a motive that can be satisfied in parenting. Unfortunately, power is a human motive that is often abused, most sadly at the expense of a dependent child. In chapter 5, we discuss punitive parenting and consider the dynamics of power in parent-child relationships.

Similarly, many adults value **competitive advantage** and may seek to gain prestige from the accomplishments of their children. This may not always be to the child's advantage, particularly when parents put intense pressure on their children to perform at the parent's high standards. If you attend Little League-type baseball games and listen to some of the more aggressive parents, you know what I mean. There is nothing wrong in being proud of our children's achievements, but when we derive satisfaction from comparing favorably our children to other children, we ignore what is special about them in their own right.

A fifth possible reason for having children (if you're counting), is to **please one's own parents**. Parents put pressure on their adult children (particulary daughters) to reproduce. Our parents, when they subtly hint about the patter of little feet, are not just acting as agents of society. They want their grandchildren. Without reproduction, society dwindles into oblivion. Many religions, for similar reasons, encourage us to "be fruitful and multiply."

A variation of this theme is that **childbearing is women's destiny**, or that a woman cannot be completely fulfilled unless she becomes a mother. No equivalent claim is made for men. On this overpopulated planet, some societies, such as those in China and India, pressure their citizens to limit reproduction.

Some adults, particularly those with unhappy childhoods, view having children as an **opportunity to compensate** for their own sad history. These parents may "live through their children." Some adults who have suffered deprivations wish to give their children a better life than they had. Even parents with happy childhoods enjoy participating in activities that they would otherwise forego if they were not parents. Without children, I might never roam the aisles of Toys-R-Us, visit Disneyland, read 3-D comic books, have a catch, play Monopoly, or go back to the second grade for a special assembly program.

There are adults who view child rearing as a **lifelong project**, with unlimited opportunities for creative expression. These parents enjoy planning, arranging, and designing their children's futures. They have a clear image of how they want their child to be. They invest their child-rearing years with strategies and tactics designed to fulfill their visions. Child rearing is, for most parents, a lifelong project, but much of it does not go according to plan. As we see in the next chapter, unforeseeable events can play a major role in a child's development and personality.

A seventh reason for having children (are the reasons improving?) is **personal growth**. Before I had children, I could stay out as late as I wanted and then sleep until 10 A.M. or later the next morning. I could go to the movies on the spur of the moment and travel to distant lands unencumbered by diapers and bottles (I hope this doesn't sound too nostalgic). As a parent, I learned to put another person's needs before my own. (Many of us get a little bit of practice doing this in marriage, even before we have children.)

Imagine waking up at 4 A.M. on a cold, wintry morning to the fervent cries of your hungry little one. Imagine stumbling downstairs to the refrigerator, searching for the milk, and pouring it through a tiny opening without spilling any (at 4 A.M.). Imagine warming the milk (without melting the bottle) and feeding the baby, who indicates its gratitude by belching and immediately falling back to sleep. Imagine changing the baby's splendidly soiled diaper and then stumbling back to bed. Out of such experiences does personal growth arise. The transition to parenthood brings unlimited opportunities to grow, to expand, and to fulfill our potential as complete, nurturant, caring individuals.

Perhaps the most common reason parents give for having children is "**because I like children.**" Companionship is a very sensible reason for having children. Children are great companions—warm, affectionate, funny. I have spent some of my best moments in their company, driving them to nursery school, waiting with them at bus stops, having a catch, taking a walk, riding bicycles, reading, or singing with them. They are so safe to be with, and so "in the moment." Great conversation, strange jokes, cute observations, intense sadness, warm hugs—companionship.

The best reason for having children, in my opinion, is **to have fun raising them**. It is sad that so many parents forget this reason. Many come to see parenting as a struggle, as one frustration after another (see "Meeting Mark's Mom" at the beginning of this chapter). And they often blame the child! Children cannot help being children. If we can't appreciate their "perfection," that's not their problem. Or it shouldn't be. I am not saying child rearing is easy. That would be absurd. But the challenge of raising a child can become an enormous source of fulfillment if we understand, accept, and enjoy them as they are and as they change.

FOUR GOALS OF PARENTING

Study Question If you were a parent, what values or priorities would guide your child-rearing methods?

All societies give parents the primary responsibility for raising their children. Parents are held responsible for their children's health, safety, and socialization until the time that they can live without adult supervision. Raising children to lead independent and fulfilling lives in a complex, technological society is certainly challenging. Parents must compete with other powerful sources of influence, such as their children's friends, siblings, TV, and movies.

Nature produces at birth roughly the same number of male and female infants. Researchers have reported that a majority of college students, men and women, express a preference for bearing a male first child. Many ethnic groups prize firstborn males. If technology eventually permits parents to exercise such preferences, society might experience a preponderance of firstborn males and laterborn females.

Hock and Levy (cited by Stark, 1985) interviewed 55 couples expecting their first child. Forty-five percent of the couples said they would take advantage of sex-choice technology if it existed, and if it was safe and free. Three-quarters of the women said they would choose to have a girl, and 68 percent of the men said they preferred a boy. If they could only have one child, 77 percent of the parents-to-be preferred to have a child of their own sex. Two-child families are more common than one-child families. Today's parent expresses a preference for having at least one boy and one girl (*New York Times,* August 24, 1989).

Many geneticists are providing prenatal diagnoses to women who will abort a fetus solely on the basis of its sex. A recent survey found that 20 percent of the nation's geneticists approve of the use of prenatal diagnosis for the purpose of selecting the sex of a child. Many others are disturbed by this practice (*New York Times,* December 25, 1988). As with most new technologies, it is difficult to anticipate how this practice would affect society. Do you think parents should be able to select the sex of their first child or of laterborn children?

Parenting does not occur in a vacuum. Parents are often preoccupied with the stresses and strains of their own lives. Unfortunately, adults are vulnerable to stress, illness, marital conflict, drug problems, and financial pressures. Amidst the poignant dramas of their daily lives, some parents lose direction. Many are relieved just to make it through another day. Parents who have one bad day after another, and who find that they are not enjoying raising their children, begin to wonder why they had children in the first place (and then feel guilty for having such nasty thoughts).

To parent effectively, we need considerable support, but we also need direction. We need to know what we're doing, but first we have to decide where we want to go. Many parents eagerly seek child-rearing techniques and strategies that they believe will help their children become well behaved. However, before we can make decisions about methods of child rearing, we have to be clear about our priorities. What types of outcomes are we seeking?

This book suggests four parenting goals. They are not the only parenting goals one could propose. LeVine (1974) studied child-rearing practices across cultures. He concluded that parents in all cultures share the following three goals: (1) the physical survival of the child, (2) teaching the child economic self-sufficiency, and (3) teaching the child self-actualization. A father of three young children expressed his parenting goals: "I want my kids to be self-sufficient, independent, free-thinking people with a lot of self-esteem and empathy for other people. I want them to be good and decent human beings."

The following goals are not based upon any theoretical model. They focus our attention, in my opinion, on important and desirable outcomes of parenting. They probably reflect a middle-class bias since most studies in the child development literature have investigated white, middle-class children. Parents in lower socioeconomic classes may have different goals and different approaches to child rearing (Maccoby, 1980).

What we consider to be a favorable outcome of parenting should take into account the environment in which the child will eventually function. The parenting styles advocated in this text are consistent with and support the following parenting goals.

Good Behavior

Parents enjoy the parenting role (and their children) more when their children are well behaved (Kochanska, Kuczynski, & Radke-Yarrow, 1989). Child rearing is more pleasurable when children cooperate with their parents and siblings instead of behaving defiantly. Hence, it is no surprise that most parents consider good behavior a high priority.

But how do we define good behavior? Just as there is no one correct way to raise children, there is no agreed upon set of "commandments" about how children should act. Mothers and fathers often do not even agree with each other on standards and expectations. They might disagree about what constitutes a proper bedtime, acceptable snacking, or choice of clothing. Though children can learn to accommodate the different rules or standards of each parent, it is preferable for the parents to negotiate one set of standards that is agreeable to both. This consistency in parental standards reduces children's confusion about what is expected of them.

In defining good behavior, it is tempting to cite the Boy or Girl Scout pledge and suggest that children should be helpful, friendly, courteous, kind, reverent, and so on. However, parents must decide for themselves what constitutes good behavior. Keep in mind that children benefit when they can please other people too, not just their family members. It is not to a child's advantage to be accepted at home but be perceived as obnoxious by a friend's parents or the kids in the schoolyard. Once parents can articulate what behaviors they value, they can adopt child-rearing strategies that encourage those behaviors.

Competence

Parents are expected to teach their children useful behavior, that is, behavior that accomplishes something that they or someone else values. Infants cannot be expected to solve any but the simplest problems. Toddlers are capable of exercising a wide range of self-help and other useful skills, such as cleaning, dressing, and toileting themselves.

One of the major accomplishments of childhood is mastering the physical environment. This often takes the form of problem-solving skills that allow a child to identify a problem, generate a possible solution, and test it. If an attempted solution fails, competent children learn to persist until they are successful.

Parents can contribute extensively to their children's cognitive development. Parents generally evaluate their children's intellectual skills as reflected in their record of academic achievement. Most parents highly value achievement in school and convey to their children that they take their schoolwork very seriously.

Self-reliance defines another important aspect of competence. Young children are usually closely supervised by parents and teachers. As they develop, they become more independent in their judgments, decisions, and actions. Adolescents are better at delaying gratification than younger children. They have more adultlike intellectual abilities and prefer to handle their problems themselves rather than seek assistance. Again, there is much that parents can do to promote good judgment, achievement, and independence in their children. Thus, our second parenting goal is competence, comprising cognitive and intellectual abilities, achievement motivation, and self-reliance.

Good Parent-Child Relationships

We inhabit a world of people. For most of us, other people provide us with much of the satisfaction life has to offer. One of the challenges of parenting is teaching children to get along with each other and with us. This is particularly challenging because children are very self-centered. Occasionally, children are selfish, impulsive, insensitive, and demanding. These qualities set the stage for parent-child conflict. Good parental judgment often stands in opposition to a child's demands for immediate gratification.

The family is a "training ground" for having relationships. We assume that what children learn about relationships from their family life will be reflected in their outside relationships. Children observe their parents (and siblings) closely and learn. The relationship skills or deficits that result may influence their relationships in adolescence and adulthood. Of the hundreds of factors that affect a child's development and personality, the quality of moment-to-moment parent-child interactions stands out as potentially the most important.

Thus, we socialize our children within the context of our relationship with them. This relationship, which must be cultivated throughout childhood, becomes the major source of our influence with our children when they become adolescents. A satisfying, supportive, parent-child relationship is our third parenting goal.

Self-Esteem and Self-Confidence

To some observers, such as Carl Rogers (see chapter 2), the nucleus of personality is self-esteem, that is, how we evaluate and feel about ourselves. People who don't like themselves are prone to anxiety, depression, and self-destructive behavior patterns. People who like and accept themselves tend to have more satisfying and productive lives and better relationships.

The ability to accept and like ourselves is rooted in the feedback we get from other people early in our lives and from our ongoing record of successes and failures. Parents can have considerable influence in both areas. Be-

cause self-esteem and self-confidence play such central roles in personality, we include them as our fourth parenting goal.

Our four parenting goals are (1) good behavior, (2) competence, (3) good parent-child relationships, and (4) self-esteem and self-confidence. In our interactions with our children, we can make all four goals priorities. It does not make sense, for example, to raise our children to be obedient at the expense of low self-esteem. Why pressure our children to achieve at the cost of a poor relationship? Throughout this text, we will examine ways of spending time with children and ways of disciplining them that are consistent with these four parenting goals.

CONTEMPORARY ISSUES IN PARENTING: A SELECTION

Having It All?: Dual-Career Parenting

Study Question *Do children suffer when both of their parents work?*

Is it possible for two adults to have a strong, supportive relationship, pursue satisfying full-time careers, and still be good parents? Absolutely, if they have the patience of a saint, boundless energy, team spirit, a sense of humor, and enough money. It also helps if they have a full-time, preferably live-in, sitter-house-keeper (or at least high-quality day care). In other words, it is possible, but far from easy to achieve. I think most of the 13 million two-worker families with children would agree.

Is dual-career parenting desirable? Most child-care experts agree that child rearing should be a priority, not an afterthought. The traditional division of labor, with fathers working and mothers homemaking, satisfied this priority. Today, fewer than one in ten families conform to the traditional pattern. More than half of new mothers remain at their jobs (*New York Times,* June 16, 1988).

More than half of today's mothers are coping with the demands of employment, parenting, and homemaking.

How might dual parental employment influence children's development? "Parental employment may influence children's lives . . . by altering men's and women's *investment* in parenting, by changing parents' *expectations* for their children's behavior, by modifying parental *styles* or *strategies of discipline and control,* or by affecting parents' *perceptions* and evaluations of their children" (Greenberger & Goldberg, 1989, p. 22). Parental investment refers to the "degree to which adults commit to their role as a parent and to the fostering of optimal child development" (p. 22).

Are dual-employed parents less committed to raising their children? Do they raise their children differently than parents in preceding generations? Greenberger and Goldberg

(1989) questioned 94 employed mothers and 104 employed fathers about their socialization practices and their perceptions of their children. Each parent questioned had an employed spouse and a young child. According to the parents' responses, their employment did not detract from their commitment to child rearing.

Not all employed women work because they want to. Today, many mothers seek employment out of financial necessity. (See fig. 1.1 for some statistics on working mothers.) Single mothers, those living in poverty, and those having husbands who earn less than $15,000 a year comprise two-thirds of all working mothers. A poll of 50,000 women by *Family Magazine* (October, 1988) revealed that two-thirds of the working mothers who responded would stay home if they could afford to. (Again, this poll should not be considered a scientific survey. The results may not be representative of most working women.) Some researchers contend that most employed mothers would continue to work even if they were not financially pressed (Cotton, Antill, & Cunningham, 1989; DeChick, 1988; Hiller & Dyehouse, 1987).

Many women say they work because they no longer find the housewife-mother role as fulfilling as their employment. "They have developed committed, permanent ties to the workplace that resemble the pattern once reserved for men alone. When they have had children, they have tried to combine careers with motherhood. In short, they have rejected the domestic path that places children, family, and home above all else" (Gerson, 1986, p. 32).

Some women may choose a domestic lifestyle because of their unsatisfactory work experiences, or they may reject the double burden of career and home responsibilities. Nevertheless, a majority of women are feeling the "tug" of employment. "At each domestic frustration, at each spurt in their baby's independence, young mothers are apt to question whether

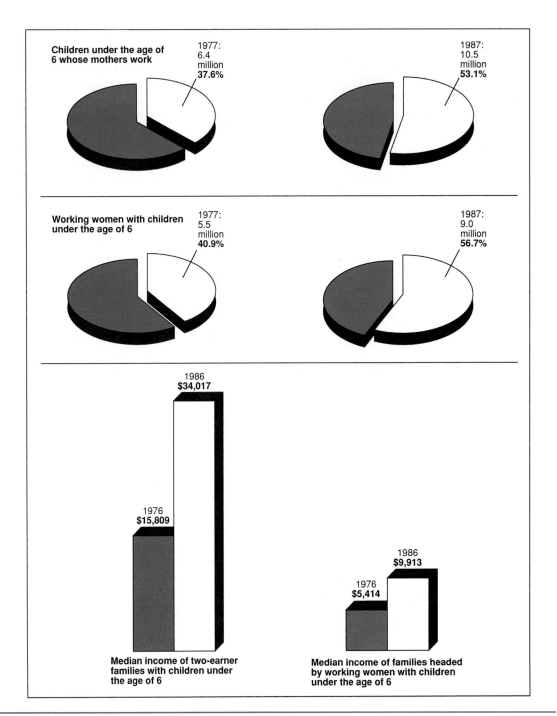

FIGURE 1.1
Increasing numbers of mothers are joining the work force.
Source: Bureau of Labor Statistics.

their baby's need to have them at home still outweighs their own need for an occupation outside the home" (Brazelton, 1986, p. 14).

The costs of dual-career parenting must be considered. Hertz (1987) interviewed successful dual-career couples. Most couples depended upon other, less-privileged individuals, usually women, to provide the housekeeping and child-care services that they were too busy to perform themselves. After satisfying their professional responsibilities, they usually had little time left for their partners. Their decisions about having children were based primarily on professional considerations. Childbearing was seen as a professional handicap. Many of these women returned to work within months of childbirth.

Even when working parents share the domestic responsibilities or hire housekeeping help, they have minimal leisure time and limited social lives. This outcome is accepted as part of the compromise they made for the economic and professional satisfactions of their dual-career life-style (J. H. Williams, 1987).

Husbands of employed women often express more child-related frustrations. Several studies (e.g., Russell & Radin, 1983) suggest that many husbands are not entirely comfortable in their role of house-father, though they may still support their wives' employment. "The increased participation of fathers in child care and household tasks that often results from maternal employment seems to have a positive effect on children, lessens the mother's role strain, and increases the father's self-esteem, but it has also been associated with marital discord" (L. W. Hoffman, 1989, p. 290). Men and women apparently have different expectations about how household labor should be shared (Benin & Agostinelli, 1988).

Children in Dual-Career Families

The traditional literature of developmental psychology (e.g., Bowlby, 1951; Spitz, 1946) emphasized the importance of attachment in development. Many theorists described the risks inherent in frequent or prolonged mother-infant separations. Research appeared to confirm the stability of the nuclear family configuration. It was widely accepted that mothers, through their sensitivity, nurturance, and full participation in their infant's life, play a critical role in the healthy development of their child.

Some recent studies (e.g., Barglow, Vaughn, & Molitor, 1987) have suggested that infants who experience daily separations from their working mothers may be at risk for developing insecure attachments. Other studies (e.g., Chase-Lansdale & Owen, 1987) find no such impairment. Hence, we have an issue: does maternal employment hinder the development of the infant's attachment to its mother? A recent, extensive review of the research literature concluded that there is no clear-cut difference between children in dual-career families and children in single-career families. "The data reveal primarily that the dual-wage family is not a single pattern, and parental attitudes seem more significant than the mother's employment status" (L. W. Hoffman, 1989, p. 290).

One of the problems in interpreting studies of maternal employment is that it is difficult to separate the effects of employment from other factors, including the personalities of parents who choose a dual-career life-style, the marital relationship, and the parents' hectic lives. The effects of employment presumably also depend upon the specific conditions of employment. These include the nature of the mother's work, her attitude about working, the child-care arrangements, the age and sex of her child, and whether employment is full or part time (L. W. Hoffman, 1974; McCartney & Galanopoulos, 1988; Schachere, 1990).

Easterbrooks and Goldberg (1985) found that mothers employed full time spent less weekday (but not weekend) time with their toddlers than mothers employed part time or not at all. Nonworking mothers spent an average of two hours a week more alone with their children than did working mothers. The number of hours spent together as a family did not vary with the mother's employment status. Importantly, maternal employment was not related to the children's security of attachment to either parent or to the child's ability to solve problems.

Guidubaldi and Nastasi (1987), in a national study of 573 elementary schoolchildren, found that children with working mothers scored higher on some measures of academic achievement and social adjustment. Children of mothers who stayed home reported better relationships with their mothers. The mothers who stayed home also reported greater satisfaction with their performance as parents than working mothers. The latter may have experienced greater stress from their conflicting roles.

Children of mothers who worked part time scored higher on several emotional and academic measures than children whose mothers worked full time. Children of divorced women who worked also did not appear to suffer from their mother's employment. Family income was a better predictor of children's social and academic adjustment than whether their mothers worked. This suggests that specific family circumstances and the mother's adjustment and state of mind are more powerful variables than her work status (Scarr, Phillips, & McCartney, 1989). Other studies have reported that children of working mothers are more independent, resourceful, and self-confident. Mothers who pursue professional careers may inspire their daughters to do the same.

The trade-off between greater role flexibility for women and less parental attention for young children is difficult to evaluate. If we believe that the best mother is a happy mother, and if mom is happier working than staying home, or if she must work out of financial necessity, then we must accept the current trends. We must help families find ways to compensate for decreased levels of parental involvement (Scarr et al., 1989). If we believe that mothers belong at home raising their children, and that children suffer when they are cared for by people who are not family members, then we must encourage families to reexamine their priorities.

Since society has traditionally been biased against maternal employment and does not support it institutionally, many employed women (and men) will probably continue to experience some conflict about their dual roles. We must also wonder to what extent society's lack of support of maternal employment contributes to working women's distress. We need to examine sexist role definitions that put the greater weight of this conflict on women's shoulders. Why should paternal employment always take precedence over maternal employment?

More generous parental leave or flexible work-time policies for new mothers by employers would help alleviate the considerable pressure on parents who are dependent on that second paycheck. The first four months following birth are critical in the development of trust and the emotional bond between parent and child. Swedish parents "can divide between themselves 12 months of leave and receive 90 percent of their prior income up to $20,000 for the first nine months" (B. Bower, 1988) Parents in the United States who work should have the same right that Swedish parents do to provide attention and care to their new infants.

Day-Care Programs

Study Question If you and your partner were both employed, who would provide care for your young child?

Nonparental child care has become the norm for a majority of children in the United States. Grandparents are not as available for caretaking as they used to be, and private sitters can be expensive. The arrangements made by working parents for their children's daily care

The quality of day care can influence children's cognitive and social development.

are likely to influence their development. High-quality day care exists but can be expensive. Low-quality day care is affordable but may compromise the physical and cognitive development of millions of children (Trotter, 1987a).

Studies support the role of stable and high-quality day care in promoting such positive outcomes as competence, self-confidence, and relationship skills (e.g., Howes & Stewart, 1987). Children in poor-quality programs are experiencing little more than custodial care, or "babysitting." Day-care facilities vary greatly in the quality of social interaction they offer (Jacobson & Owen, 1987).

There are over 60,000 licensed day-care centers in the United States and over 161,000 licensed day-care homes. Most children, however, are placed in unlicensed (though legal) family day-care homes where the staff and facilities are not regulated. Even licensing may mean little in some states where an application and fee might be sufficient to register a family day-care home (Kutner, 1988p). Licensing regulations provide only minimal guarantees of quality (Bogat & Gensheimer, 1986).

Yale psychologist Edward Zigler is one of the designers of the Head Start Program. He advocates a national child-care program. He believes "we must convince the nation that when a family selects a child-care center, they are not simply buying a service that allows them to work. They are buying an environment that determines, in large part, the development of their children. Remember, child care is a day in, day out, year in, year out phenomenon for a child" (Zigler, quoted by Trotter, 1987a).

Researchers have attempted to isolate those factors in the day-care environment that predict positive social outcomes. Phillips, McCartney, and Scarr (1987) studied 166 children attending representative child-care centers of varying quality. They found that the overall quality of the center, the caregiver-child verbal interactions, and the director's experience were good predictors of the children's social development in child care.

C. Peterson and R. Peterson (1986) compared groups of 3- to 5-year-old children from high- and low-quality day-care centers to same-aged children receiving home care. They observed the children interacting with their mothers in a laboratory setting. The children attending the low-quality facilities were less likely to follow task instructions and were less verbal. The home-care children were the most verbal. Children attending high-quality centers were intermediate. The researchers concluded that children attending day-care facilities are learning interaction patterns that affect their interactions with their mothers.

Parents read about sexual abuse, disease transmission, and accidents—including fires—in day-care settings. They are concerned about the vulnerability of their infants and toddlers. They know that they must carefully select their children's "substitute parents" (Kutner, 1988p). Parents considering day care for their children should start looking early, because some centers have extensive waiting lists. A nationwide survey by the United States Department of Health, Education, and Welfare (1976)

identified parental considerations about child care. Parents reported being most concerned about reliability, the warmth of the caregiver, cleanliness, safety, and the child's feelings about the facility.

Kutner suggests that if the center director does not invite parents to visit the center, or if they do not feel welcomed when visiting, they should look elsewhere. Parents should visit for at least one hour, preferably in the morning when the children are most active. Parents should observe whether the facilities are safe (capped electrical outlets, bars on first-floor windows, gates at stairways, fire exits). They should notice whether the rooms are nicely decorated for children. The most important factors are the training, qualifications, sensitivity, and responsiveness of the caregivers.

Parents should ask many questions about the quality of care. What is the staff-to-child ratio? What precautions are taken to prevent sexual abuse? Parents gain important information by watching how the staff handle conflicts among the children, episodes of crying, or toileting accidents. Parents can also interview the parents of children who have attended the center (Kutner, 1988p).

Bogat and Gensheimer (1986) administered structured telephone interviews to a predominantly white group of 167 married females in their late twenties who were employed part or full time, and who had called a day-care referral agency for information. They found that these parents valued most of the positive qualities of day-care facilities already cited. Sadly, most parents did not follow through in their actual search behaviors to locate the optimal facility.

Even though the parents could only evaluate the facilities through direct observation, they "rarely acted in ways to evaluate these characteristics within facilities and to make discriminative comparisons between alternatives. During their child-care search, these parents typically called only three providers, over one-fourth did not visit any facilities, and of those who did visit, most only visited one facility. . . . This points to a striking discrepancy between the attitudes of parents regarding quality day care and the behavior they use to secure such care" (p. 167).

Day Care for Infants

Half of the mothers of children 12 months or younger are working. Researchers, who generally accept the benefits of high-quality child care for older children, are debating the possible long-term effects of day care on young infants. Belsky and Rovine (1988) found evidence of less-secure attachment in infants who were placed in day care during their first year of life. Their research revealed that 12- and 13-month-old infants exposed to 20 or more hours of day care a week exhibited more avoidance when reuniting with their mothers in the Strange Situation test than children with less than 20 hours of day care a week. They were also more likely to be classified as insecurely attached. Sons receiving more than 20 hours a week of nonmaternal care were more likely to be insecurely attached to both parents.

Some studies have found that children who as infants had been in day care may be more aggressive with their peers and less compliant to their parents' instructions. Other studies have not confirmed these findings. In a longitudinal study of Swedish children, Andersson (1989) observed that children entering day care before their first birthday "were generally rated more favorably and performed better than children with late entrance or home care" cognitively and in their emotional development (p. 857). Andersson notes that Swedish day care is of exceptionally high quality.

We should not hastily conclude that infant day care is harmful. In Belsky and Rovine's study, a majority of the infants exposed to extensive day care revealed secure attachments to their mothers. Half of the sons with extensive day care showed secure relationships with their fathers and almost two-thirds of the boys

receiving extensive nonmaternal care show secure attachment to at least one parent. Characteristics of the mother, of the child, of the day-care arrangements, and the father's involvement all may mediate the effects of extensive nonmaternal care for infants.

One possible hazard of day care, particularly for infants and toddlers in diapers, is increased risk of infection for the children and, eventually, their families. "Centers that care for children still in diapers account for the vast majority of day-care–related illnesses that are often easily transmitted through saliva or stool. Toddlers tend to crowd together, making it easy to spread infections; their hygiene usually leaves much to be desired; their immune systems are not fully developed, and they have not yet had the opportunity to acquire immunity to common infectious organisms" (Brody, 1986a).

Easily transmitted illnesses include mild respiratory infections like colds, diarrhea, and ear infections. Ironically, children may benefit from contracting some infections, such as chickenpox, that only occur once and produce milder symptoms in childhood. In any case, routine parental visits to day-care facilities to ensure that sanitary and hygienic practices exist are desirable. Making sure that children are immunized at the right age is particularly important when they are in day care (Brody, 1986a).

High-quality, parental home care is preferable to day care. Many parents do not have this option; affordable high-quality day care becomes a necessity. High-quality day care is preferable to low-quality parental home care. Many parents who stay home with their children spend little time with them or have poor-quality interactions. "Maternal employment is a reality. The issue today, therefore, is not whether infants should be in day care but how to make their experiences there and at home supportive of their development and of their parents' peace of mind" (Clarke-Stewart, 1989a, pp. 271–272).

Children in self-care spend time at home alone or with a sibling without adult supervision.

Children in Self-Care

Study Question What problems might confront children who lack adult supervision after school?

Rodman, Pratto, and Nelson (1988) suggest the following definition of self-care: "A self-care child is one between the ages of approximately 6 and 13 years who spends time at home alone or with a younger sibling on a periodic basis" (p. 294). About a quarter of a million 5- to 7-year-olds are in self- or sibling-care after school (Cain & Hofferth, 1989).

Self-care children spend their before, after-school, or evening hours alone at home without adult supervision. Some of them may be responsible for the after-school care of their younger siblings. Many do chores; some prepare dinner for themselves or their families (Landers, 1988f).

The United States Department of Labor and the National P.T.A. estimate that 5 to 7 million children, a fourth of the elementary school population, are left alone at least 2 hours a day. Cain and Hofferth (1989) contend that "only" about 2½ million children either care for themselves after school or are cared for by a child (usually a sibling) under age 14.

Cain and Hofferth (1989) and a 1987 federal study by the National Institute of Child Health and Human Development concluded that most so-called "latchkey" children are white and middle class, 10 to 13 years old, and live in suburban or rural communities. Others contend that self-care children are not predominantly white or middle class (Collins, 1987b). Another issue is whether adolescents need after-school supervision (Steinberg, 1988b). Many teens play the role of parent-surrogate as baby-sitters. Others are susceptible to peer pressure and get into trouble.

How do self-care children feel about their time spent alone? Does a lack of supervision increase the risk of accidents or fire? Do these children feel isolated? Or do they benefit by becoming more independent, self-reliant, and responsible? The answers to these questions depend upon many factors. These include children's attitudes about being alone or caring for siblings, available activities, their age, sex, socioeconomic level, neighborhood, the length of time spent alone each day, whether the arrangement is voluntary or not, and the parent-child relationship (Galambos & Dixon, 1984; Lovko & Ullman, 1989).

Effects on Children

The research addressing self-care children is inconclusive. Family circumstances are so varied. A Louis Harris survey of 2,000 parents and 1,000 teachers conducted in 1987 found that 51 percent of the teachers polled cited lack of after-school supervision as the major cause of children's difficulty in school. Forty-one percent of the parents said their children were often alone between the end of school and 5:30 P.M. Most parents said they would enroll their children in after-school programs if they were available (*New York Times,* September 3, 1987).

Rodman, Pratto, and Nelson (1985) found no significant differences in self-esteem or social competence between matched samples of self-care and adult-care children. Vandell and Corasaniti (1988) found no difference between self-care third-grade children and those returning home to mothers on a variety of academic, self-esteem, and interpersonal variables. In fact, self-care children did better than children in after-school day-care programs on most measures. Many third graders attending the after-school program (designed for preschoolers) reported feeling embarrassed that they had to attend day care.

Cain and Hofferth suggest that parents decide whether to allow their children to remain unsupervised on the basis of their maturity and independence. Studies of inner-city children report that delinquent males and females have inadequate supervision after school (Galambos & Dixon, 1984). Long and Long (cited by Landers, 1986b) surveyed 362 parochial schoolchildren in Washington, D.C. Self-care children were more likely to suffer from mild depression, engage in solitary drinking, and be sexually active. These researchers suggest that the presumed benefits of self-care, such as increased independence and responsibility, could be achieved with less risk.

All investigators in this area agree that much more research is needed. It is safe to assume that some children probably suffer, that some children benefit, and that some children are not affected by the lack of adult supervision. Given the scope of the phenomenon, it is important to identify the factors that predict these outcomes.

Alternatives to Self-Care

Many parents report that they would have greater peace of mind regarding their children's safety and well-being (and experience fewer interruptions at work) if their children were receiving competent adult supervision. Most self-care children seem to prefer spending their before- or after-school hours with other people rather than with a TV set. Having parents "psychologically" available via phone calls also appears to alleviate feelings of isolation or loneliness. There are about 365 Phone Friend programs available nationwide, allowing children to communicate with adults who can advise them through a minor crisis.

In Virginia, the Family Day Care Check-In Program for 10- to 14-year-olds provides children with a neighbor who is designated as their check-in person. After checking in, children can go out and play or stay in the neighbor's house. Other communities have telephone "hot lines" that self-care children can call when lonely, bored, or afraid (Landers, 1986b). Teenagers occasionally call with school- or sex-related problems. Other programs have volunteers who call children at home to check up and chat briefly.

Unfortunately, high-quality, affordable programs are not abundant. California, the leading state in providing after-school care, serves only 14,000 of its estimated 800,000 self-care children. The state contributes $16 million a year to local school districts, park departments, and nonprofit agencies to support child-care centers, which offer arts and crafts, help with homework, games, sports, field trips, and transportation (Reinhold, 1987). Indiana, New York, New Jersey, and Massachusetts have also initiated programs for self-care children.

In the absence of such programs, there is still much that parents can do to prepare their children for the self-care experience. Parents should know where their children are and have clear-cut rules about their conduct. They should maintain telephone contact and teach their children self-help skills, including cooking, answering the phone cautiously, and household safety (Peterson, 1989). It is also important that when they arrive home, parents convey interest about the child's day.

Parent-Support and Training Programs

Study Question *How do most parents learn to parent?*

Given the importance of parenting, it is remarkable that most mothers and fathers receive so little preparation for this role. Most learn to parent "on the job," an inefficient and often discouraging process. It is also odd that society has provided so little support to families. Fortunately, family-support, education, and training programs are becoming more available (L. Williams, 1989). Whereas parent *education* programs, such as Parent Effectiveness Training (T. Gordon, 1970), help parents prevent the development of behavior problems, parent *training* programs help parents resolve already present, troublesome behaviors. "Both the parent training and parent education approaches are aimed at assisting parents at helping their children by providing the parents with practical information, by teaching them principles of learning and behavior modification, building parenting and communication skills, and the development of problem-solving skills" (Schaefer & Briesmeister, 1989, p. 2).

One of the best ways to support children is to support their families. Almost any serious family problem, such as chronic illness, unemployment, divorce, or drug abuse, will directly or indirectly affect its children. Centers have been established across the country that provide needed support to both parents and children. Most programs provide parent assistance in such areas as prenatal care, immunizations, parenting skills and day care (L. Williams, 1989).

Programs such as Head Start may have had mixed results because children had to return to their disadvantaged environments each day. Programs that change the family environment during the first years of life seem to hold greater promise. Family-support programs now exist in Connecticut, Kentucky, Maryland, Missouri, Minnesota, and Oregon. Most are open to everyone who applies, but they are usually located in poor neighborhoods (Lewin, 1988b). Research tentatively supports the efficacy of well-run programs in reducing child abuse, academic problems, delinquency, and teenage pregnancies.

Kentucky's Parent and Child Education Project works separately with young children and their parents. Parents are tutored three days a week toward a high school equivalency diploma. While adults learn parenting skills, children participate in preschool classes. Maryland's Friends of the Family center offers courses on child care, provides literacy tutoring, and offers groups for teenagers that help avoid unwanted pregnancies. Chicago's Beethoven Project offers free prenatal care, counseling, home visits, and access to day care and health care.

"All the new family-support programs share a conviction that it makes more sense, both socially and economically, to give high-risk children preventive help early in life, rather than wait and pay the higher costs of remedial education, foster care, delinquency, malnutrition, or emergency medical care" (Lewin, 1988b).

A model parent training program instituted in Missouri in 1982, the New Parents as Teachers Project, began by studying parents who displayed impressive parenting skills. They found that these parents provided their infants and toddlers with easy access to interesting environments that they could explore. Rather than restrict their movements, parents of competent children redesigned their homes to encourage their youngsters to have interesting, educational experiences (Meyerhoff & White, 1986).

Between 1982 and 1985, 380 families located in four very different socioeconomic communities in Missouri received a variety of services. The resultant cost of $800 per family each year was publicly and privately funded. Groups of 10 to 20 parents met with parent educators once a month for 1½-hour sessions. Assistance began during the last three months of pregnancy and continued until the child's third birthday. Fathers, grandparents, and sitters were also encouraged to attend.

Trainers visited each home once a month. Children were evaluated for social, language,

and intellectual progress. If problems were identified, prompt assistance was offered. If problems not related to the child's educational progress were identified, such as parental unemployment or illness, referrals to appropriate agencies were made. Parents watched videotaped demonstrations of typical behavior of infants and toddlers. Age-appropriate activities were suggested, and books, magazines, and advice were available (Meyerhoff & White, 1986).

Parents were encouraged to talk to their children. They learned how to use simple language and respond to the child's current motivational state. Parents were taught how to set realistic, but firm, limits and how to enforce them. They were encouraged to display unconditional love and to use discipline techniques appropriate to the child's level of development. These were the patterns identified in the rearing techniques of the parents of competent children. An evaluation team reported, "Children of parents participating in the New Parents as Teachers Project consistently scored significantly higher on all measures of intelligence, achievement, auditory comprehension, verbal ability, and language ability than did comparison children" (Maeroff, 1985).

The Addison County Parent-Child Center in Middlebury, Vermont, trains and pays 12 parents for 6-month periods. The center seeks out new parents who are at high risk for raising children with problems. Such parents are often young, high school dropouts. They are socially isolated, many have drug problems, and most were abused as children. This multifaceted program provides assertiveness training, practical experience with child care, home visitation, and basic parenting skills.

The director, Susan Harding, explained that "We have some clear rules. It's not O.K. to hit children or yell at them or call them names. A lot of young women come here with no idea that there is an alternative to hitting children" (S. Johnson, 1988a). The Vermont Department of Health compiled data indicating that Addison County had the lowest teenage pregnancy rate in the state. A federal report indicated a drop in welfare dependency in the families served by the center. Incidents of child abuse were significantly reduced, and employment significantly increased in the county.

The best parent-training programs do not present parents with rigid sets of procedures, but rather encourage them to provide their own solutions to everyday problems. Parents need to learn to recognize the causes of misbehavior and take corrective actions. Programs that allow groups of parents to share their observations and experiences also help them see that their child-rearing problems are not unique. The critical lesson for parents is that to get behavior change in children, the parents must first change their own behaviors (Jaffe, 1990).

SUMMARY

The process of parenting suggests a polarity: the potential fullfillment of child rearing versus the challenge (or struggle) to do it well. There are many reasons for deciding to have children. Among the best reasons for becoming a parent are personal growth, companionship, and the enjoyment of raising children. Unfortunately, many parents, with their hectic, stressful life-styles, lose perspective. Child rearing is not easy, but the better we understand children, the more likely we are to appreciate and enjoy raising them.

The history of childhood reveals that economics and ignorance about children were major factors influencing children's status in society. Given the high mortality rate for infants and children, our ancestors may have been reluctant to form the strong emotional attachments to their children that we take for granted today. Brutal treatment of children, infanticide, and abandonment were not rare occurrences. Since the sixteenth century, more enlightened views of children and childhood have gradually emerged. Children are now seen as innocent and vulnerable, and childhood is considered a separate and unique stage of life.

Despite overall progress in children's status, many children in the United States are raised under extreme conditions. Millions live in poverty. Large numbers experience physical, emotional, or sexual abuse. Too many receive inadequate health care and inferior education.

Four parenting goals are stated that indicate desirable outcomes of parenting. They include (1) good behavior, (2) competence, (3) good parent-child relationships, and (4) self-esteem and self-confidence. The parenting styles advocated in this book support these four goals.

Four topics that relate to parenting today are discussed. When both mothers and fathers work, other caretakers must be found. Many children of school age must care for themselves or their younger siblings after school because their parents are working. It is not yet clear how self-care, day care, and other arrangements affect young children's development. It is clear that families today require considerable support from the community. Parent-support and training programs are becoming more available and appear to promote more competent parenting.

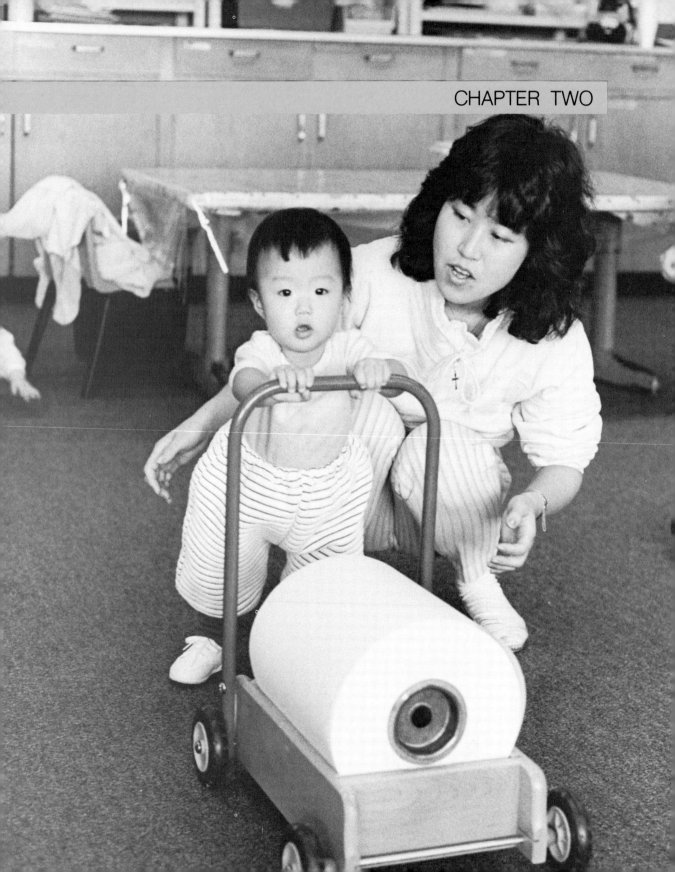

Theoretical Perspectives

OBJECTIVES

After reading chapter 2, students should be able to

1. Describe the obstacles to composing a comprehensive theory of parenting
2. Describe and give an example of a functional analysis
3. List the characteristics of stage theories of development and compare stage theories to cumulative models
4. Describe how each of the following Freudian concepts helps parents understand children's behavior: id, ego, superego, pleasure principle, reality principle, unconscious conflicts, defense mechanisms, and psychosexual stages
5. Describe the essential challenge, or crisis, for each of Erikson's psychosocial stages, and the positive and negative outcome for each: basic trust versus mistrust; autonomy versus shame and doubt; initiative versus guilt; industry versus role confusion; intimacy versus isolation; generativity versus self-absorption; and integrity versus despair
6. Speculate about the parenting styles of Freud and Erikson if they raised their children according to their own theories
7. Describe the challenges facing parents during each of Galinsky's six stages of parenthood
8. Describe the role of conditional regard, positive regard, feelings of worth, self-concept, and self-esteem in Rogers's model of personality, and their relevance to child-rearing practices
9. Define and describe the role of the following concepts in Piaget's model of cognitive development: justification, assimilation, accommodation, schema, egocentrism, sensorimotor stage, preoperational stage, concrete operational stage, and the stage of formal operations
10. Describe the major concepts of operant conditioning and how they help parents understand children's behavior
11. Define and describe the potential role of observational learning in parenting
12. Describe how the concept of boundaries is used in family systems theory
13. Describe the nature and effects of "small moments" in parent-children interactions
14. Explain what is meant by "domain-specific" parenting
15. Describe what is meant by "nonshared family environments," and use this concept to explain why siblings' personalities are usually so different
16. Discuss the factors that make children less susceptible to the effects of negative chance encounters

THEORETICAL PERSPECTIVES ON PARENTING

"I can't believe how three children from the same family can be so different. I'm sure there must be similarities. I just can't think of any off the top of my head" (parent of three children).

Like parents, scientists have difficulty making sense of individual children's personalities and development. After all, shouldn't children in the same family, with similar genetic makeup, the same parents, who are being raised in the same home, be alike? Most parents will tell you that their children are complete opposites. Unfortunately, when we study development, we rarely find that events are related to each other in simple or predictable ways.

One problem is that the effects of most life events are difficult to evaluate. Can one really understand the impact of a bitter parental divorce on a sensitive preschooler? Is anything of lasting importance happening when two siblings bicker or exchange sarcastic comments? How does one assess a hug or a smile from

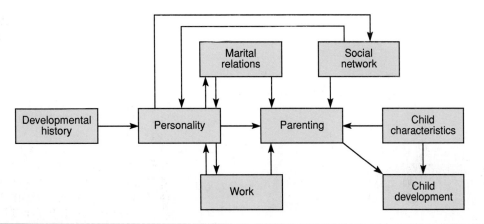

FIGURE 2.1
A process model of the determinants of parenting.

From Jay Belsky, "The Determinants of Parenting: A Process Model" in *Child Development,* 55, page 84, 1984. © The Society for Research in Child Development, Inc. Reprinted by permission of the publisher and author.

Grandma? Social scientists use carefully gathered information, or data, to speculate about real-life events. We sometimes call these speculations theories.

Psychological theories try to summarize current knowledge about behavior and development. Good theories generate testable predictions or hypotheses for further research. Theories are tentative, but they can provide us with useful perspectives that we might otherwise overlook.

What would a theory of parenting look like? It might begin by posing desirable child-rearing outcomes (such as the parenting goals cited in chapter 1). It might analyze child-rearing practices that encourage these outcomes and the processes involved in these practices (e.g., rewards, punishment, modeling). A plausible parenting theory must take into account the nature of children (their temperament, dispositions, needs), the influence of parental personality, and the marital relationship.

Additional topics might include the interaction between the infant's disposition and parental behavior, the effects of family experience on the development of personality, the significance of different family configurations, and the origins of self-regulation and competent behavior (see fig. 2.1). The actual list of topics addressed by a parenting theory would be much longer than this one. Lacking a theory of parenting, we look to theories of personality and development. They offer the broad perspectives we need to interpret research findings and our own observations of parent-child interactions.

Another way of understanding behavior is the experimental derivation of "functional analyses." An observable behavior, such as an infant's crying when a stranger approaches, is said to be functionally related to the variables that control its occurrence. Stranger distress is influenced by the age of the child, whether a parent is present, the number of caretakers the infant has experienced, the physical appearance of the stranger, his or her distance from the child, and other situational factors.

Most of the parenting-related phenomena we study are tentatively "explained" by relating them to the variables that determine their occurrence. We cite experimental data when

Sigmund Freud, Jean Piaget, and Erik Erikson.

available. However, much of the parenting research literature takes the form of surveys, interviews, naturalistic observations, and correlational studies. Because of the limitations inherent in all research methods, we remain wary of drawing hasty conclusions about cause and effect.

The theories and models presented in this chapter attempt to answer questions that parents might ask. What motivates children's behavior? See Freud. What challenges face children at different stages of development? See Erikson. What challenges confront parents at different stages of their children's development? See Galinsky. How do children try to make sense of their experiences? See Piaget. How do children come to like or dislike themselves? See Rogers. Why do children misbehave? See Skinner. How do children learn from watching their parents? See Bandura. Does personality change in large or small steps? See "Small Moments Model of Development." Why are siblings so different from each other? See "Nonshared Family Environments." These and other questions are addressed by the theories and models presented in this chapter.

THEORIES OF DEVELOPMENT

Freud, Piaget, and Erikson, like many parents, viewed children's development as a succession of distinct stages. Stages entail extended periods of stability surrounded by sudden or gradual transitions. The stable periods are usually associated with the emergence of a new skill or competency, such as walking, speaking, thinking logically, or being toilet trained.

Transitions from one stage to the next presumably reflect the maturation of anatomical or neurological structures that allow a new competency to develop, perhaps even independently of previous abilities (Kagan, 1984). All stage theories assume a fixed sequence of essentially biologically determined stages. Children sharing a particular stage may differ in age. Thus, the *rate* of development may reflect a child's unique experiences.

For example, we see the following predictable motor sequence in all normal infants: crawling, creeping, standing, walking. However, the ages at which these abilities emerge are quite varied. Although the average age at which creeping (hands and knees on floor) begins is 10 months, the normal range is from 5 to 12 months.

Most psychologists agree that development is orderly and that sequential patterns of development are the rule. However, not all psychologists find the concept of stages useful. Many view personality and cognitive development as a continuous process "in which learning experiences may accumulate in a variety of sequences, depending upon the specific learning opportunities the child happens to be exposed to" (Mischel, 1976, p. 292).

Thus, behavioral theories of development emphasize the child's day-to-day, accumulating changes in behavior (what we call learning) rather than biologically rooted maturational sequences. It is assumed by behavioral theorists, for example, that almost every parent-child interaction changes the child (and the parent) in some small way. If toddlers nag to get a cookie, it is because this behavior is occasionally rewarded, not because they are going through a "nagging stage."

Students of development examine both types of influence, the maturational dispositions and the complex contingencies of daily life, and their sometimes unexpected interactions. The following theories are of interest to parents for the light they may shed on the nature of children and their development.

FREUD'S PSYCHODYNAMIC THEORY

Study Question What motivates children's behavior?

It would be difficult to exaggerate the contributions of Sigmund Freud (1856–1939) to our understanding of human personality and development. In so many different areas of human functioning, Freud boldly went where no man or woman had gone before. Freud was trained as a physician in Vienna in the late nineteenth century. Based on his analysis of himself and many of his neurotic patients, Freud originated

a very biological theory of human personality and psychopathology. His influential theory emphasizes our animal nature and, therefore, our primitive, irrational impulses.

Because of the radical nature of many of his ideas, particularly about children's sexuality, Freud's views were ridiculed in Europe. In the United States, the more open-minded people of the 1920s considered his views with interest. From a contemporary perspective, Freud's interpretational methods and some of his conclusions are quite flawed. However, by investigating such topics as sexuality, dreams, conflict, and the unconscious, Freud stimulated research in these areas and furthered our understanding of them.

We will concentrate on those aspects of Freudian theory that contribute to our understanding of children. In essence, Freud argued that a child's unconscious conflicts and defenses are based upon child-parent interactions. Parents contribute immensely to children's psychological makeup, according to Freud, by gratifying or frustrating their needs and desires (Christenson, 1983).

The Id: Our Animal Nature

Philosophers and theologians have had difficulty coming to terms with our irrational nature. Freud, like Darwin, appreciated or, at least, accepted our irrational, animal nature because, well, we *are* animals! An objective view of human history must encompass not only our human achievements but also our species' history of war, brutality, intolerance, and oppression. (History demonstrates that humans are capable of far more brutal behavior than are members of other species.) After reading a daily newspaper, defending rationality and altruism as definitive human traits becomes difficult. It sometimes seems as though there are two vastly different sides to our human nature—our rational intellect and our irrational desires—both competing for control of our personality and behavior.

Freud portrayed our impulsive, demanding nature as the "id." This primitive basis of personality is an irrational, survival-oriented "energy source." The id supplies all psychic energy and is the driving force of personality. It is the biological component of our personality, one that we share with other animals. Throughout life, it remains the embodiment of our psychological needs, drives, impulses, urges, and desires.

The id operates according to the *pleasure principle,* which Freud considered the "primary process" of human motivation. Anything that provides gratification is good, and anything that is painful or annoying is bad. When the infant's needs or appetites are not satisfied, it becomes irritable and demands immediate gratification.

Is Freud telling us that humans (and other animals) are basically selfish, irrational, and driven by primitive impulses? In effect, he is. We see this aspect of human nature most clearly in the young child's impulsive, demanding temperament. The id consists of many powerful drives, including sexual and aggressive impulses. Freud felt that these two drives become frustrated when society attempts to place powerful constraints on their expression (e.g., "Keep your hands to yourself").

Enlightened Self-Interest: The Ego

Obviously, human personality is not all id; if it were, society as we know it could not exist. The ego, representing enlightened self-interest, gradually emerges from the id during the school years, using logical and realistic thinking to solve practical problems. However, its major function is to satisfy the id's urges and desires. The ego obeys the *reality principle,* which Freud considered the "secondary process" of human motivation. Unlike the id, the ego considers the consequences of its actions. The ego, in effect, admonishes the id, "I know what you want, and I'll get it for you, but we have to do it my way."

In other words, the ego serves the id by seeking socially approved means of satisfying needs and desires. Marriage, for example, becomes the socially sanctioned convention for satisfying our sexual appetites. Sports may provide an acceptable outlet for aggressive impulses. Those who impulsively satisfy their desires at another person's expense risk serious consequences that the ego tries to avoid. The ego "understands" that there is little gratification to be obtained if one becomes a social outcast. We can see that the ego has its hands full dealing with the irrational, impulsive id and its primitive pleasure principle. All it needs now is a third component of personality to deal with.

Guilt and Shame: The Superego

Yes, you guessed it. Along comes the superego, the internalization of our parents' standards of acceptable behavior. "The part which is later taken on by the superego is played to begin with by an external power, by parental authority. Parental influence governs the child by offering proofs of love and by threatening punishments which are signs to the child of loss of love and are bound to be feared on their own account . . . subsequently the superego takes the place of the parental agency and observes, directs, and threatens the ego in exactly the same way as earlier the parents did with the child" (Freud, 1933/1965, p. 62).

The superego, then, is essentially a built-in parent/judge that attempts to guide our conduct through guilt and shame. Because morality is relative (people often disagree about what is right and wrong), the superego, like the id, is said to be irrational. (The term "irrational" doesn't mean bad. It simply implies that reason or logic are not necessarily involved in the "judgments" of the id and superego.) As you may have assumed, the id and the superego are in perpetual conflict, and yes, the ego must mediate between them to arrive at an

Justin Jaffe

acceptable compromise. Hence, Freud is suggesting a conflict model of human personality as brilliantly depicted in Shakespeare's classic play *Hamlet.*

Unconscious Motivation

In addition, these forces usually operate outside of our awareness. To Freud, the conscious mind is a tiny part of the psyche because it consists only of material in our immediate awareness. The preconscious contains our normal, everyday thoughts, feelings, and memories when they are not in consciousness. The unconscious, however, is an enormous repository of repressed urges, desires, wishes, needs, and fantasies. Why are they repressed? Because, according to Freud, they are threatening to us (or at least to "society"). If we were aware of them, they would elicit considerable discomfort.

For example, Freud observed that infants and young children have a primitive sexuality. Most parents know this, because little girls and boys have considerable sexual and anatomical curiosity. They also get pleasure from touching their sex organs, and they sometimes make subtle comments like, "Daddy, when I grow up I want to marry you." Freud referred to this attraction to the parent of the opposite sex as the Oedipus (for boys) or Electra (for girls) complex. Most of us would find it quite disturbing to experience an erotic attraction to one of our parents. So Freud explains that these fantasies are repressed into the unconscious part of our minds, allowing us to avoid considerable anxiety.

An exception is the castration anxiety experienced by boys, their fantasized punishment by their fathers for being in love with their mothers. Freud believed that girls experience an equivalent fear of "loss of love" by their mothers for being in love with their fathers and for feeling hostile toward, or competitive with, their mothers.

"In a boy, the Oedipus complex, in which he desires his mother and would like to get rid of his father as being a rival, develops naturally from the phase of his phallic sexuality. The threat of castration compels him, however, to give up that attitude. Under the impression of the danger of losing his penis, the Oedipus complex is abandoned, repressed, and, in the most normal cases, entirely destroyed, and a severe superego is set up as its heir. What happens with a girl is almost the opposite . . . the girl is driven out of her attachment to her mother through the influence of her envy for the penis and she enters the Oedipus situation as though into a haven of refuge" (Freud, 1933/1965, p. 129).

What is one to make of this? Freud's ideas about male and female sexuality remain provocative and controversial at a time when new conceptions of sex roles and gender are still emerging. Today, enlightened parents are aware of and accept their children's sexuality and respond to their curiosity and expressions of sexual feelings in a supportive, informed, and matter-of-fact way.

Defense Mechanisms

The major result of the conflict between the id, ego, and superego is anxiety. To alleviate anxiety, the ego uses defense mechanisms to distort reality. One can distort reality by *denial,* pretending a problem does not exist; by *projection,* blaming it on someone else; by *repression,* not thinking about or forgetting the problem; by *rationalization,* making excuses; or by *reaction formation,* expressing a feeling that is the opposite of the unacceptable one. Freud's depiction of these and other defense mechanisms is one of his greatest contributions to our understanding of personality.

Denial is heavily practiced by adults and children alike. When my younger son was about 3½ years old, he was carrying a glass of milk through the living room and, in front of everyone, spilled it all over the carpet. His immediate reaction was, "I didn't do it." Now that's denial. My favorite example of projection in children is the often-sobbed "he started it." Forgetting to show one's parent a bad report card exemplifies repression. Alcoholics and cigarette smokers become experts at rationalizing their drug habits ("Nobody lives forever"). An example of reaction formation would be a little boy hitting or chasing a little girl he likes. He can't admit he likes her (it is a threatening feeling), so he expresses it through an opposite (and more comfortable) reaction.

The Psychosexual Stages of Development

Freud emphasized the role of pleasure in human personality. Many people, including several of his "disciples," believed he overemphasized biological factors and didn't give adequate attention to social factors in development. Nevertheless, he felt that as children develop, different *erogenous zones* in their bodies become the major source of gratification.

Freud proposed five psychosexual stages of personality development corresponding to various parts of the body. If a child were either deprived or overly indulged during any of these stages, *fixation,* or arrested development, might occur. Fixation reflects conflicts that have not been properly resolved. "During the critical psychosexual stages, particularly during the oral, anal, and phallic periods, the child either achieves sufficient need satisfaction to advance to new levels of development or is fixated so that future activity is affected by unresolved needs from the past" (Christenson, 1983, p. 409).

The first psychosexual stage (psychosexual really means bodily pleasure in this context) is the **oral stage** of infancy. The infant derives gratification mainly by sucking and eating. The **anal stage** corresponds to the toddler years, during which most children are toilet trained. This psychosexual stage reflects the gratification that children get from bowel movements and from the appreciation of one's parents when one performs one's toileting duties successfully (no pun intended).

At about the age of 5 years, children are in the **phallic stage**. Gratification is derived from genital stimulation, but not in a mature heterosexual form. This was considered the oedipal period by Freud. "During the oedipal period . . . the child experiences both heterosexual attachment to the opposite-sex parent and interpersonal competition with the same-sex parent. If these first intimate contacts are resolved satisfactorily, the child identifies with the same-sex parent and releases his or her attachment to the opposite-sex parent. If the relationships are not resolved satisfactorily, the child's subsequent ability to relate to both sexes can be seriously damaged" (Christensen, 1983, p. 409).

From about 5 to 11 years, children are in the **latency stage**. No particular bodily area is the focus of pleasure. The final **genital stage** represents mature heterosexual interest and activity. Freud suggested that fixation during any of these stages would produce characteristic personality traits associated with the particular stage.

Evaluation

Many of Freud's ideas have been supported by research and many have not (Kline, 1972). Though he brought to our attention important topics that need to be addressed, he exaggerated the influence of some factors and ignored others. For example, he felt that personality is essentially formed during early childhood. There is good reason to appreciate early influences, particularly parent-child interactions, but personality is never fixed and unmodifiable. Freud virtually ignored the influence of so many environmental factors that clearly affect development, such as the influence of peers and siblings.

His proposal that adult neurosis is rooted in early childhood conflicts profoundly influenced clinical psychology. Whether Freud's influence is ultimately positive or negative is still being debated. By suggesting a possible relationship between early experiences and adult pathology, Freud's work encourages parents to be more understanding and sympathetic in raising their children. It certainly helps parents appreciate the powerful role that gratification (the pleasure principle) plays in motivating children's behavior and misbehavior.

ERIKSON'S PSYCHOSOCIAL THEORY

Like Freud, Erik Erikson (b. 1902) postulated a stage theory of development (Erikson, 1963). Unlike Freud, he emphasized social as well as maturational factors. The stages of development, in the form of conflicts or challenges, are predetermined by biology. The child's ability to meet these challenges is determined largely by the social support provided by caretakers. Erikson also contends that personality develops over the life span, mainly through social interactions. Unlike Freud, Erikson does not attribute absolute influence to the earliest years of life.

Phases of the life cycle	1	2	3	4	5	6	7	8
Late adulthood								Integrity vs. despair
Middle adulthood							Generativity vs. stagnation	
Young adulthood						Intimacy vs. isolation		
Adolescence					Identity vs. identity confusion			
Middle and late childhood				Industry vs. inferiority				
Early childhood			Initiative vs. guilt					
Infancy		Autonomy vs. shame, doubt						
Infancy	Trust vs. mistrust							

FIGURE 2.2
Erikson's stages of development.

From John W. Santrock, *Life-Span Development,* 3d ed. Copyright © 1989 Wm. C. Brown Publishers, Dubuque, Iowa. All Rights Reserved. Reprinted by permission.

Erikson's theory postulates eight psychosocial stages of development. Four stages span childhood, one stage is associated with adolescence, and three stages correspond to early, middle, and late adulthood (see fig. 2.2). At each stage, a developmental challenge or crisis has to be faced and resolved. Each stage will have a positive, negative, or mixed resolution. The positive resolution leads to a healthy relationship with the world and with oneself. The negative resolution results in maladjustment. Few, if any, resolutions are completely positive or negative. The resolution of each stage partially depends upon the outcomes of the previous stages. We will briefly examine each stage.

Childhood

The first stage of psychosocial development, **basic trust versus basic mistrust**, occurs during the first year of life. This stage addresses the infant's vulnerability. The infant is completely dependent upon its parents to satisfy its needs. If parents provide sensitive and nurturant care, the infant experiences feelings of safety, pleasure, and hope. If the infant's needs are not satisfied, it experiences fear and mistrust. Unlike Freud, who emphasized the role of gratification during infancy, Erikson's first stage highlights the importance of trust. Infants who cannot trust their parents to care for them adequately will have difficulty facing later challenges.

The second psychosocial stage, **autonomy versus shame and doubt**, spans the second and third years of life. During this stage, infants are less dependent upon caretakers. Their challenge is to acquire a sense of autonomy by practicing their developing abilities. Parents can provide the child with opportunities to explore the world and demonstrate competence. In doing so, they encourage the infant-toddler to become more confident and self-sufficient. Parents who belittle a child through excessive punishment or ridicule sow the seeds of shame and self-doubt. They encourage feelings of incompetence and inadequacy.

The third stage of psychosocial development, **initiative versus guilt**, spans the ages 3 to 5 years. Children who are confident in their abilities initiate and enjoy new activities. Through play, exploration of the environment, and imitation of adults, children learn about the purpose of things. They learn how events are related. Again, punitive and insensitive parenting may encourage feelings of resignation and guilt and, later in life, feelings of unworthiness and lack of responsibility.

Spanning 6 years of age to puberty is the stage Erikson called **industry versus inferiority**. The positive outcome of this fourth stage is the fulfillment the child can obtain through competence and achievement, particularly in school. The negative outcome is the sense of inferiority that develops when his work does not satisfy the standards of his teachers or parents. "Work, in this sense, includes many and varied forms, such as attending school, doing chores at home, assuming responsibilities, studying music, learning manual skills, as well as participating in skillful games and sports. The important thing is that the child must apply its intelligence and abounding energy to *some* undertaking and direction" (Hall & Lindzey, 1978, p. 95).

Adolescence

Erikson viewed adolescence as a period of transition from childhood to adulthood. During this stage, **identity versus role confusion**, the child's identity begins to emerge. It arises from the conflict and confusion surrounding the various roles and life-styles from which he is expected to choose. The question is not so much, "Who am I?" as, "Who do I want to be?" Successful resolution of this stage is indicated by a fully functioning, competent, adult personality. The negative outcome is indicated by continuing role confusion and aimlessness. Without adequate parental support, adolescents may overidentify with popular heroes or peers, or escape through sex, drugs, delinquency, or even suicide.

Adulthood

Erikson's sixth psychosocial stage, **intimacy versus isolation**, corresponds to young adulthood. It is during this stage that most people start their own families. The major challenge of the young adult is to establish an intimate, caring relationship with another person. A positive outcome would be the ability to maintain sexual intimacy and trust in a marriage relationship. One can also achieve closeness and trust in friendships. Those who fear commitment or who are unable to share their lives experience isolation and loneliness.

The seventh stage, **generativity versus stagnation**, corresponds to middle age. Generativity refers to the ability to give of oneself to another person. This is ideally expressed in the parent-child relationship (although it can also be achieved in other ways, such as teaching). Parents can derive fulfillment by investing themselves in their children's lives, by guiding and teaching them, and by sharing their life experiences. Stagnation, the negative outcome of this stage, reflects self-absorption or a lack of giving.

The eighth stage, **integrity versus despair**, describes late adulthood. It reflects either satisfaction with the life one has led or bitterness about wasted opportunities. To a large extent, evaluation of one's life in old age will reflect the outcomes of the previous seven life stages (Kaplan, 1988).

Evaluation

Study Question *In what ways might Freud and Erikson differ as parents if they raised their own children in accordance with their theories?*

Like Freud, Erikson presents us with a conflict model of personality. However, Erikson is more optimistic than Freud. Freud assumed that neurosis is an almost inevitable by-product of rearing. Erikson, on the other hand, suggests that with parental sensitivity and encouragement, children can meet successfully the challenges of daily life.

Whereas Papa Freud might worry about being too strict and fixating Sigmund, Jr., at the oral stage, Papa Erikson would surely provide little Erica with sensitive and nurturant care and countless opportunities to demonstrate her competence. To Erikson, successful resolution of the early stages reflects the quality of parenting. Inadequate, insensitive parenting promotes the negative outcomes of mistrust, shame, guilt, and inferiority. Nurturant, supportive parenting encourages the positive outcomes of trust, autonomy, achievement, and self-esteem.

Erikson's theory, unlike Freud's, also acknowledges the special challenges of adolescence and adulthood. Each stage of life, from infancy through old age, presents opportunities for growth or stagnation. The nurturance we receive from our parents disposes us to nourish our children. Although Erikson does not present a theory of parenting, the implications of his life-cycle theory for parenting are considerable. How we evaluate our lives in late adulthood will reflect to a large extent the satisfaction we have derived from raising our own children.

GALINSKY'S STAGES OF PARENTHOOD

Study Question *How might the challenges of parenting change as children mature?*

Erikson's theory makes it very clear that developmental change does not end with adolescence. We spend far more lifetime as adults than we do as children. Adulthood provides us with countless opportunities to grow, to expand, and to see things differently. Life experiences provide the fuel for this growth. Few life experiences provide as much opportunity to realize our potential as nurturant, social beings as child rearing.

The seventh stage Erikson described, generativity versus stagnation, acknowledges the opportunities for growth inherent in the parenting role. Erikson's model, however, gives little detailed information about the specific changes in the parenting role over time and the challenges that accompany these changes. Galinsky (1981) describes such challenges in a six-stage model of parenting.

During the first stage, the **image-making stage**, parents-to-be face several tasks or challenges. The major challenge is preparing for birth and parenthood. "This includes preparing for a changing sense of self and changing relationships with one's partner and one's own parents. Parents-to-be begin to get attached to the unborn baby, begin to understand that the baby will be a separate person, and they ready themselves for the actual birth" (p. 14). Emotionally, this stage contains many highs and lows. Most expectant parents are both excited about the birth and concerned about their ability to parent well. Before birth, however, all they have to go on are "images,"—hence, the image-making stage.

The second or **nurturing stage** corresponds to infancy. During this stage, "parents compare their images of birth, of their child, and of themselves as parents with their actual experience" (p. 9). The major challenge of this stage is to become attached to the infant. This requires adjusting to the difference between the imagined and the real infant and accepting that this infant is theirs. Relationships among all family members, including grandparents, must be redefined. As they become more attached to the baby, parents' priorities change. "How much time should I give to the baby and how much to the other aspects of my life?" (p. 9).

The third or **authority stage** spans the preschool years. Parents must decide how to convey their authority and how to establish and enforce rules. Parents also must learn how to communicate with their children and how to communicate with each other about their children. "In the authority stage, parents are grappling with fundamental issues of power. Out of the welter of these issues, self-concepts are beginning to be shaped—both for the parent and the child" (p. 177).

The fourth or **interpretive stage** corresponds to the school years. The major challenge for parents in this stage is interpreting the world to their children. In the process of explaining, parents teach their children skills and values and shape their self-concept. In the process of answering children's questions, parents are clarifying their own views and values and revising their theories of child rearing. As in previous stages, parents wonder how involved they want to be in their children's lives. When does one hold on? When does one let go?

The fifth or **interdependent stage** spans adolescence. Authority and communication issues arise again. "The same questions are asked be-cause the child's growth often renders the old solutions obsolete" (p. 237). As the problems grow larger, the parents' authority declines. Children's sexuality must be acknowledged and accepted. "While teenagers are pursuing questions of identity, so are parents. Many are sizing themselves up, seeing how they have measured up to their dreams, how close or how far they are from the marks they set for themselves" (p. 273).

The final or **departure stage** occurs when grown children leave home. Parents must prepare for and adapt to a child's departure. Parents take stock of their successes and failures. The major challenge of this stage is "accepting one's grown child's separateness and individuality, while maintaining the connections" (p. 307). When the last child leaves, parents have to redefine their identity as a couple.

Evaluation

Galinsky's stage model of parenting reminds us that raising children changes parents as well as children. Each day provides new challenges, conflicts, and crises. We may rise to the occasion, or we may throw in the towel. The stakes are high for our children as well as for ourselves. Erikson highlights the challenges confronting children as they move from stage to stage. Galinsky's model does the same for parents, giving us perspective and courage to accept the challenge and, perhaps, to welcome it. I find myself experiencing both apprehension and excitement as my older son enters puberty. As the difference in our sizes diminishes, we both share an identity crisis. How do we relate to each other in a way that is comfortable for both of us?

"Taking care of a small, dependent, growing person is transforming, because it brings us in touch with our baser side, it exposes our vulnerabilities as well as our nobility. We lose our sense of self, only to find it and have it change again and again" (Galinsky, 1981, p. 317).

ROGERS'S SELF-ACTUALIZATION THEORY

Study Question *What, if any, obstacles have prevented you from realizing your full potential as an individual?*

Carl Rogers (1902–1987) and his colleagues have contributed what is sometimes called a "third force" model of personality development. Freudian psychology and behaviorism are the first two forces. Rogers's approach, known as humanistic or existential psychology, describes the conditions that allow the fulfillment of one's potential for growth, or what Rogers called actualization.

Actualizing tendencies represent an innate force inside all living things to become whatever we are capable of becoming. Most of us have experienced wanting to change, to expand, to excel at something. Rogers rejected Freud's conflict model of personality. To Rogers, when selfish or competitive impulses occur, they reflect a distortion of human nature imposed by a restrictive environment (Rogers, 1961).

Rogers believed that children's self-concepts largely reflect the feedback they receive from other people. Children tend to get diverse reactions from adults, but they are not always positive or encouraging (e.g., the common parental retort, "What's wrong with you?"). Some children will fail to realize their full potential because of the "constricting and distorting influences of parental training, education, and other social pressures" (Hall & Lindzey, 1978, p. 279). For example, parents who frequently criticize or disapprove of their children may encourage feelings of inadequacy or unworthiness that stifle the actualizing tendency.

Unconditional Acceptance

Rogers maintained that children require unconditional acceptance (or positive regard) from their caretakers. Parental acceptance and affection are often expressed conditionally. "Children learn when they are 'good' and when they are 'bad.' These values are incorporated by them as their 'conditions of worth.' They feel worthwhile only when engaging in certain activities and avoiding others. If these conditions of worth are few and reasonable, children can be open to a variety of experiences and learn from them. If there are many conditions of worth and if these conditions have to do with inevitable human feelings, such as sexual arousal and anger, children may deny or distort large portions of their lives to maintain a sense of worth. This denial and distortion, meant to gain parental and ultimately self-acceptance, actually deprives them of necessary information to guide their behavior. Self-actualization is thus impeded" (Christenson, 1983, p. 426–427).

When parents convey that the child's expression of anger toward them is unacceptable, the child must adapt by suppressing or even denying such feelings when they occur. This prevents the child from learning how to handle such feelings and results, ultimately, in his or her being controlled by them. The supportive parental message is, "I love you, no matter what." This does not mean that parents accept or condone misbehavior. Rather, they distinguish between who the child is (which they love no matter what) and what the child does (which may or may not be acceptable).

Positive regard from others leads to positive self-regard and then to the ability to care for others. In other words, children who feel accepted, valued, and loved by their caretakers can accept and love themselves. They can then learn how to accept and show love to other people, including, eventually, their own children.

Self-Esteem

Like most clinicians, Rogers observed that clients in therapy who are anxious and depressed usually have low self-esteem and difficult relationships. Personality problems arise, according to Rogers, when individuals receive conditional regard. The message is, "If you are good (or smart, strong, rich, beautiful), then I will accept and love you." Because it is often difficult or impossible to satisfy other people's conditions, we become wrapped up in our own perceived inadequacies. We may suffer from crippling defenses and fail to thrive. We may try to become what we think other people want us to be instead of being and accepting ourselves.

Feelings

Rogers advocated that parents should encourage their children to have feelings and express them freely. Some parents find the expression of negative feelings threatening and may attempt to suppress such displays. For example, if 3-year-old Katie falls and hurts herself, and Daddy says, "Oh Katie, come on, that doesn't hurt," what is Katie to think of her direct experience of pain? Daddy is denying the reality of her feelings. The implied message is, "Your feelings are not acceptable" or perhaps, "Keep your feelings to yourself."

If little Jason says, "Mommy, I hate you," will Mom respond angrily? "How dare you!" Or will she react sensitively and help him clarify and cope with his strong feelings? "Why are you so angry at me?" In other words, will Mom show caring? Many, if not most, children learn to keep their feelings to themselves. They have learned that it is not always safe to express them.

Evaluation

Carl Rogers emphasized our human disposition to grow, to feel, to love, and to fulfill our individual potential. He described the relationship between the feedback we get from our caretakers, how we feel about ourselves, how we feel about other people, and our willingness to be complete, loving, feeling individuals. Personality problems, according to Rogers, reflect distortions of our true nature, rooted in critical, unsupportive family environments. There is much that Rogers's theory has in common with Erikson's, although Rogers's is neither a stage nor a conflict theory. Both theories relate nurturant parenting to the development of a healthy personality.

Of all the models we examine, Rogers's presents the most optimistic view of human personality and development. Critics point out that his model is often vague and lacks scientific precision. To some extent, this reflects the subjective domain of personality that Rogers addressed. Carl Rogers's views about communicating with children are personified in the television personality Mr. Rogers (no relation). Mr. Rogers conveys a message to children that, sadly, some children rarely get from their own parents: that they are special.

PIAGET'S THEORY OF COGNITIVE DEVELOPMENT

Study Question *Why do some parents become frustrated when they try to reason with their young children?*

Like Freud, Jean Piaget (1896–1980) proposed a comprehensive stage theory of development that is strongly rooted in biology. Although trained in biology, Piaget considered himself an epistemologist (someone who studies the nature and source of knowledge). He wanted to know how a child comes to make sense of himself and his experiences. He observed children (including his own) of various ages solving problems, and he asked them questions about their reasoning. He called this method *justification*.

How Children "Know"

Piaget observed that children come up with solutions to problems that are age-related. You have probably noticed that when young children are learning language, they make predictable errors: "I goed outside and hurted myself." Children of different ages seem to have characteristic ways of thinking about events and objects. He proposed that as children mature, they display, in turn, four distinctive stages of "knowing." Cognitive abilities arise, Piaget claimed, through an interaction of maturation and active involvement with the world of people and objects.

In contrast to models of learning that depict children as passive recipients of knowledge, Piaget asserted that children create or construct their own knowledge. They integrate new information with what they already know, a process he called *assimilation.* This can be seen in the young infant's attempts to suck on any new object. In other words, the infant "knows" an object by sucking on it. Therefore, when finding a new object, the child uses an existing "schema," sucking, to know and experience it. (A schema is a way of knowing something, usually an action or a mental representation.)

If what the child already knows cannot encompass new information, the child's knowledge base must expand to incorporate the new information, a process called *accommodation.* If, for example, an object is too big to be placed in its mouth, the infant must find a new way of knowing the object—perhaps banging or throwing it. Piaget emphasized the importance of activity, or acting upon objects, in promoting learning and understanding. He believed that for children, verbal instruction is not as effective as learning by doing. For optimal learning, new information should be somewhat familiar to allow assimilation and somewhat challenging to promote accommodation.

Stages of Cognitive Development

As in the models of Freud and Erikson, each new Piagetian stage of cognitive development is derived from and builds upon earlier stages. Each advance leads to a broader, richer form of understanding the world. The sequence of stages is fixed: (1) the sensorimotor stage, (2) the preoperational stage, (3) the concrete operational stage, and (4) the formal operational stage.

The **sensorimotor stage** begins with the infant having no awareness of itself or of the world. Everything it experiences can only be known by its inborn ability to act upon the world of objects. In Piaget's (1954) model, it is cognitive structures that are acquired during learning, not information or responses. The term *sensorimotor* conveys that the major accomplishment of this stage (which lasts from birth to about 2 years of age) is the coordination of the infant's movements with its perceptions. Other acccomplishments of the infant include a primitive grasp of causality (in effect, "I can make things happen"), knowledge of the properties of familiar people and objects ("doggy bark"), a sense of separate identity, and the understanding that objects and people have a permanent existence.

The **preoperational stage** begins at about the age of 2 years and persists until 5 or 6. Cognitive abilities emerge at different ages for different children. During the preschool years, children continue to have many misconceptions about the world. Ask preschool children questions like, "Are trees alive?" or "Why is mommy your mommy?" Their answers are clever, but often inaccurate. They do not necessarily think logically about events, and they act as though everything in the world revolves around them (egocentric thought).

One day on the way home from nursery school, my younger son Eric and I were discussing his future. I was explaining that when children grow up, they leave their parents and live on their own. He considered this information for a few minutes and then asked, "When I grow up, can I still live with you?" I realized that the thought of living apart from his parents was somewhat threatening to him.

I assured him that he could stay with us as long as he wished. A few minutes later, he surprised me by saying, "Maybe I'll stay in the house, and you and Mom will move out." That is egocentric thinking. "I'll keep your house, Dad. You and Mom can work it out." The major achievement of this second stage is the ability to think symbolically, which is manifested in play and imaginative behavior but most impressively in speech.

Preschool children depend heavily on impressions, intuition, and partial logic to understand events. For example, ask a 2- or 3-year-old child where her dreams occur. She'll probably tell you her dreams are on the wall, the ceiling, or the pillow. Her reasoning is that since she can see the dream, her eyes must be open. Although parents often do appreciate children's charming conceptions of the world, Piaget's theory helps them understand how their young children think. This may improve parent-child communication.

The **concrete operational stage** is characterized by the development of logical thought. In this stage, logical thought is only applied to objects and events that are directly experienced (hence, the term "concrete"). In the early school years, children's thought becomes much more adultlike. School-age children are less deceived by misleading appearances. They have a much better understanding of causality, of how events are related. Like most parents, I can remember moments when my children finally connected on such a relationship—"Grandma is *your* mother?"

Another important characteristic of this stage is that children's thinking becomes less egocentric and more relativistic. Children are able to understand and appreciate that other people interpret events differently, and that one's point of view is subjective. "When one child talks to another, he comes to realize that his way of viewing things is not the only perspective. The

child sees that other people do not necessarily share his opinions. Social interactions inevitably lead to arguments and discussions; the child's views are questioned, and he must defend and justify his opinions. This action forces the child to clarify his thoughts . . ." (Ginsburg & Opper, 1988, p. 246).

The final stage is called the **formal operational stage**. Adolescents can think logically not only about concrete, tangible events but also about abstract, hypothetical events. Adolescents can speculate, and they can appreciate irony, metaphor, and analogy (and, therefore, poetry and literature). Such adultlike thinking frees us from immediate circumstances. It allows us to anticipate and plan future events. These are useful abilities for adolescents, who are making important decisions about their future. Sophisticated cognitive abilities allow them to appreciate abstract topics such as love, morality, politics, and religion. Some individuals, particularly those denied formal education, may never reach this final stage of cognitive development (Muuss, 1982).

Evaluation

For parents, Piaget's major contribution is helping us see that children, with distinctive mental structures, view the world quite differently from adults. Children have a unique perspective. They can easily be misled by perceptual cues, they are not committed to logical thought, and they are egocentric in their thinking and actions.

"One result of the child's cognitive structure is a view of reality which to the adult seems chaotic and unnatural. Another consequence is that the young child's use of language is different from that of the adult. That is, the words that the child uses do not hold the same meaning for him as they do for the adult" (Ginsburg & Opper, 1988, p. 238).

SKINNER'S OPERANT CONDITIONING MODEL

Study Question *What role do rewards and punishments play in socializing children's behavior?*

B. F. Skinner (b. 1904) is one of the towering figures of twentieth century psychology. He is best known for emphasizing the importance of environmental factors that shape behavior and personality. Most psychological theories, in explaining behavior, speculate about events *inside* of the person, such as the id, schema, self, feelings, conflicts, and motives. Skinner (1953) argues that *environmental* events shape and control our behavior. We are products of our learning histories.

As a determinist, Skinner assumes that behavior is controlled by identifiable variables. Scientists cannot gain direct access to events inside our skin, such as feelings or ideas. Skinner looks, therefore, to the environment to find controlling variables. Rather than speculating about inner causes of behavior, Skinner prefers the functional analysis approach described earlier in this chapter.

The systematic research of Skinner and his colleagues has given rise to one of the few behavioral technologies. Behavior modification consists of the application of positive reinforcement contingencies to encourage desirable behavior. Extinction and punishment contingencies, which are defined and discussed in chapter 6, may be used to discourage inappropriate or annoying behavior. Partly because of its effectiveness, behavior modification has stirred controversy. It has gradually become assimilated into mainstream applications in education, industry, clinical psychology, and child rearing (e.g., Baldwin & Baldwin, 1986).

Although Skinner does not deny the importance of biological factors and maturation, he contends that one's personality largely reflects one's individual reinforcement history. From infancy, our caretakers, through their responses to our behavior, encourage certain responses and discourage others. Each day, responses are shaped, strengthened, or maintained through their positive consequences, or weakened through negative consequences or extinction.

Effective parenting requires awareness of how our parental behaviors, such as attention and approval, influence our children's actions. In chapter 6, Skinner's operant conditioning model is used to clarify the topic of discipline. We will see how some parents inadvertently reinforce the very behaviors they complain about.

Evaluation

Skinner's research approach, known as the experimental analysis of behavior, has explained how positive and negative outcomes influence behavior. It remains to be seen whether a complete account of human behavior is possible and, if so, whether it can be accomplished without resorting to cognitive factors.

Skinner's critics claim his behavioral model is too simplistic to account for the complexities of human behavior, yet his research has led to a powerful technology of behavior change. There is no question that parents become more effective as behavior changers when they can understand and arrange outcomes that shape and maintain their children's behavior.

BANDURA'S SOCIAL-COGNITIVE THEORY

Study Question *What motivates children to observe their parents' behavior and occasionally imitate them?*

Albert Bandura (b. 1925) has proposed a comprehensive and influential theory of human learning and motivation from a social-cognitive perspective (Bandura, 1986). Although there are many ways that parents can influence children, one of the most powerful is through modeling.

Much of what children learn seems to result from simple observation. Children observe a parent's behavior and may mentally represent (in words or images) what the parent did or said. Bandura calls this phenomenon *observational learning*. At some future time, the child can use the mental representation to guide his behavior. Parents and teachers take advantage of this ability when they say to a child, "Watch how I do it and then you try." Bandura suggests that by observing other people behave and noticing the consequences of their actions, we form beliefs about the possible outcomes of our own behaviors.

We consider several aspects of Bandura's theory and research in this text. These include the variables that promote observational learning, the use of observational learning in discipline, the development of self-efficacy or self-confidence, the formation of gender identity, and, later in this chapter, the role of chance encounters.

Evaluation

It is possible that much, if not most, of what children learn, they learn from observing other people. When children are young, their parents are likely to be their most influential models. This may intimidate some parents ("Do as I say, not as I do"). Research performed by Bandura and others has revealed many of the factors that influence observational learning (discussed in ch. 6).

Bandura's social-cognitive theory is one of the most influential contemporary theories of learning and personality development. Many psychologists have eagerly awaited a plausible integration of behavioral and cognitive concepts. Bandura has come closest to realizing this goal. In a sense, Bandura and Skinner have generated complementary models. Together,

they have increased our understanding of rewards, punishments, and modeling as important mechanisms in socialization. Both men are environmentalists. Skinner contends that the environment (particularly the social environment) directly shapes our behavior. Bandura believes it is the environment as cognitively represented (e.g., beliefs, expectations) that influences our behavior. Both points of view have stimulated important research.

FAMILY SYSTEMS THEORY

Study Question My grandparents were profoundly influenced by the Great Depression, my parents by the Second World War, and I, to some extent, by the sixties. Today's children inhabit an electronic, materialistic culture with hazards that are quite different from those confronting their parents, grandparents, and great-grandparents. How might the ways in which we relate to each other as family members be influenced by (1) our different generational experiences, and (2) the different stages of the life cycle in which we find ourselves?

Erikson has described the challenges that confront individuals as they move from one developmental period to the next. Galinsky described the unique challenges that confront adults during their parenting years. Family systems theorists introduce a broader perspective. They contend that the multigenerational family system of relationships is the most important social environment for its members.

"While one generation is moving toward old age, the next is contending with the empty nest, the third with young adulthood, forming careers and intimate peer relationships and having children, and the fourth with being inducted into the system. Naturally there is an intermingling of the generations, and events at one level have a powerful effect on relationships at each other level" (Carter & Mc-Goldrick, 1988, p. 7).

Salvador Minuchin (1974), Murray Bowen (1978), J. Framo (1976), Jay Haley (1976), and others have formulated a therapeutic approach based on the assumption that the causes of maladjustment are not in the individual. Rather, they are contained in the family system of relationships. A variation of the family systems approach is the family life cycle model, which emphasizes the connectedness between generations and the stresses and strains associated with each stage in the life cycle. Carter and McGoldrick (1988, pp. 13–20) describe six family life cycle stages: (1) single young adults leaving home, (2) the joining of families through marriage, (3) families with young children, (4) families with adolescents, (5) launching children, and (6) families in later life.

A family unit includes anyone who lives with or cares for family members. This includes live-in grandparents or visiting baby-sitters. A critical assumption of this model is that marital conflict and parent-child problems are inextricably related. Framo has claimed that "whenever you have a disturbed child, you have a disturbed marriage" (Christenson, 1983).

Minuchin (1974) uses the concept of "boundary" as the basic unit of family organization and as a way of understanding maladaptive family behavior. Boundaries may be rigid or diffuse. Families in which members avoid meaningful contact with each other are said to have rigid boundaries. Families in which members are overly involved in each others' lives are said to have diffuse boundaries. "Between these extremes are clear boundaries, in which families have considerable room for interaction with one another but in which clear rules for this interaction exist" (Christenson, 1983, p. 432).

Various family members can be disengaged from, or enmeshed with, other family members. Complex combinations of alliances and exclusions are possible. Symptoms and conflicts can only be understood by observing how family members interact with each other.

I am currently working with a family that exemplifies these problems. A professional couple who had attended a parenting workshop of mine came in with various complaints about their 3-year-old son. They portrayed him as a difficult only child who is quiet and withdrawn with unfamiliar people. He behaves very aggressively with his parents and their full-time housekeeper. He has temper tantrums, is defiant, does what he wants to do, and occasionally hits them. He will not let his parents speak to each other in his presence. They can only speak to him. They must wait until he is asleep to communicate with each other. The parents were particularly eager to toilet train him and dispense with diapers. The housekeeper was resisting such training because she would have to clean up his "accidents."

In describing their problems with their son, both parents seemed somewhat bewildered by their ineffective parenting. The mother believed it was a mistake for them to have a child, given their personal inadequacies. She expressed intense guilt about her poor mothering. She very much resented her husband's criticisms of her yelling and of her displays of anger toward him and their son.

Over the first few sessions, it became clear that their marriage was not working. The wife described her husband as totally unsupportive, a liar, undependable, unambitious, and antisocial. He characterized her as loud, occasionally physically abusive, very negative, and critical; and he felt unappreciated. Both were overweight and implied that their partner was partly responsible. Both reported coming from dysfunctional families that encouraged extreme dependency in both of them.

Despite their problems, they felt they were "lucky" to find each other; no one else would want them. Most of their conflict centered around their handling of their son's misbehavior. In a typical situation, the child would behave defiantly. The mother would threaten and yell at him. The father would then "protect" the child from the mother by yelling at her for yelling at the boy. No wonder the 3-year-old didn't want them to speak to each other!

In family systems terms, the father was overly involved in his son's life, and the mother was disengaged from both her husband and son. The father's closeness with his son was at the expense of his closeness with his wife (Christenson, 1983). The mother felt left out and actually threatened to leave several times. The live-in housekeeper was a very powerful figure in this family. Both parents lacked the assertiveness to guide the caretaking behaviors of their employee ("What would she think?" or "She would never agree to that").

As marital therapy progressed, both learned how to support each other's parenting efforts. They realized that their son would benefit more from a "unified parental front" than from the divide-and-conquer strategy he was learning. They learned how to avoid conflict by using effective communication and problem-solving skills. They discussed effective ways of handling their son's misbehavior. It was also important that they learn to treat each other well and spend time with each other away from their son. The main point is that their son's problems were rooted in their dysfunctional relationship.

Evaluation

Family systems is a powerful model because it views family conflict in relationship terms rather than as individual maladjustment. It treats the family system rather than its individual members. A major problem confronting this model is the enormous complexity of the family system, particularly when several generations are included in the analysis.

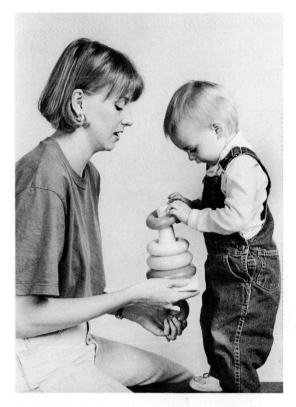

According to the small moments model, personality development reflects daily moment-to-moment interactions between children and their caretakers.

SMALL MOMENTS MODEL OF DEVELOPMENT

Study Question *Every day, children have dozens of interactions with their parents. What cumulative effect do these interactions have on the child's behavior and personality?*

Most of the theories so far discussed in this chapter portray development as reflecting critical events or stages. Cognitive theories, such as Piaget's (1954) and Bandura's (1986), also highlight commonalities in development, since most children share common cognitive structures and abilities. The behavioral learning theories, such as Skinner's (1953) operant conditioning model, offer cumulative models of development. Personality develops daily in small increments rather than in leaps and bounds.

The "small moments" model is in the tradition of the cumulative learning theories. Personality development is attributed to the daily, moment-by-moment interactions between children and their caretakers. Proponents of this model contend that "there are no critical phases in a child's life—the oral and anal periods of psychoanalysis, for example—but rather a long continuum of important moments" (Goleman, 1986a). Virtually every time parents and children interact, both parties are changing slightly. In this model, no period of life is attributed greater importance for development than any other period.

Researchers have carefully analyzed videotaped parent-child interactions. They observe distinctive ways in which mothers, for example, through their "countless small exchanges" with their children, shape "the child's pattern of interaction in later relationships in life" (Goleman, 1986a).

In one instance, all of the interactions between a mother and her twin sons were videotaped in periodic 3-hour sessions until the children were 15 months old. "At three-and-a-half months there were repeated exchanges in which the mother and Fred would gaze at each other. Fred would avert his face, his mother would respond by trying to engage eye contact again, and Fred would respond with a more exaggerated aversion of his face. As soon as the mother looked away, though, Fred would look back at her, and the cycle would begin all over, until Fred was in tears. With Mark, the other twin, the mother virtually never tried to force continued eye contact. Mark could end contact with his mother when he wanted" (Goleman, 1986a). When the infants were observed at later dates, Fred appeared more fearful and dependent than Mark. Fred continued to use gaze aversion to break off contact with other people. Mark looked people straight in the eye, usually with a smile.

This type of research has revealed subtle patterns in parental responsiveness that encourage or discourage specific behaviors in children. Children benefit when their parent's response is "attuned" to their actions. This lets an infant know that it is affecting another person, and that it is being understood. When parents were instructed to over- or under-respond to their infants, rather than matching their actions, the babies reacted with surprise or dismay.

One of the implications of the small moments model is that early experiences do not necessarily exert greater influence on development than later experiences. Rather, in the event of early abuse or deprivation, corrective experiences later in life can produce well-adjusted individuals. "An imbalance at one point can be corrected later; there is no crucial period early in life—it's an ongoing, lifelong process" (Stern, quoted by Goleman, 1986a).

Evaluation

The small moments model encourages a fine-grained analysis of the parent-child relationship. Distinctive patterns of parental responsiveness influence the child's behavior patterns and dispositions (e.g., Dadds, 1987). The child's momentary actions and reactions, in turn, influence parental behavior. The fine-grained small moments perspective challenges traditional, global stage theories of development that attribute greater influence to maturation than to the accumulated effects of daily encounters. Do not feel compelled to choose between the two approaches. Both models clarify important processes in development.

DOMAIN-SPECIFIC PARENTING STYLES

Study Question   Are parents consistent in how they respond to their children, or do they vary their behavior according to specific circumstances?

It is tempting to view individual parents as warm, strict, affectionate, critical, involved, accepting, or anxious. Many studies have indeed characterized parents in these ways to see whether children's characteristics are predicted by these specific parenting styles. Most parents, however, do not easily fit into the aforementioned categories.

Recent evidence suggests that parents do not necessarily respond in a consistent manner to their children's behavior (Costanzo & Woody, 1985). I confess that I fall, at different times, into all of these categories. Although I would like to think of myself as an affectionate and involved parent, my parenting style depends partly upon what is happening at the moment. It also depends upon which child I am with. I have noticed, for example, that I am more competitive in games with my older son than I am with my younger son. I am more "strict" about the food they eat than the TV shows they watch. I am "warmer" in the evening than I am upon awakening. I can, as a parent, be patient or impatient, affectionate or annoyed, anxious or relaxed. My reactions depend to some extent upon the specific circumstances and the domain of parenting at hand.

"Parents' impact on their children is not monolithic, but may be specifically tailored to particular problem areas and particular children in important ways" (Costanzo & Woody, 1985, p. 427–428). Thus, rather than comparing how parents differ from each other on various parenting dimensions, it may be more informative to examine how individual parents vary their parenting styles according to the particular domain, or child, they are addressing.

Example: Domain-Specific Parental Involvement

Parents are expected to be involved in their children's lives, but in what ways and to what extent? Parents vary their involvement in certain areas of their children's lives according to the importance they attribute to the particular domain. I am more likely to offer assistance to my children when they are doing their homework than when they are practicing the piano. As my children grow, the amount and type of my involvement in their lives change.

Having made this distinction, what does it mean to be an "involved parent"? And, can parents become too involved in some aspects of their children's lives? Parents who are too involved may hinder their children's development. "A parent is more likely to constrain and control a child's behavior when the particular content area is high in importance and strongly valued by the parent, and when the parent distrusts the child's naturally occurring learning in the area, because the appropriate skills are not readily acquired or discoverable" (Costanzo & Woody, 1985, p. 430).

The main point is that parental involvement is, and should be, domain specific. There are times when children require parental involvement, and there are times when involvement discourages self-reliance. Characterizing parents as involved or uninvolved is too simplistic. It is more helpful to ask, In what ways is a parent involved? and, Is the child's development being enhanced as a result?

Evaluation

The model of "domain-specific" parenting acknowledges the complexity of human interaction. It also underscores the hazards of generalizing about an individual's parenting style. Warmth, acceptance, and support are desirable parenting qualities. However, the specific ways parents respond to their children's behavior reflect many factors, including their momentary interpretation of the child's behavior and competencies. The more fine-grained our analysis of parent-child interactions, the less willing we become to classify parents using broad categories that ignore the richness and complexity of parent-child encounters.

NONSHARED FAMILY ENVIRONMENTS

Study Question *Why are siblings, who share half their genes and who seem to share common family experiences, usually so different from each other?*

Parents who have only one child might assume that all children are more or less like theirs. Having a second child cures them of this misconception. Second children are often described by parents as the "complete opposite" of the first. Children in the same family are only slightly more alike in personality than children from different families! Knowing one child in a family tells you almost nothing about what the other children are like. A study of brothers attending the same school found that their personalities were hardly more similar to each other than they were to boys whose lives were completely different (Scarr & Grajek, 1982).

"This low sibling resemblance is unsettling when one reflects that, on the average, siblings share 50 percent of the same genes, they are part of the same family, they are brought up by the same parents, and they grow up in the same community environments" (Daniels, 1986, p. 339). The slight similarities we observe in sibling personality appear to be due to their shared genes, not to their common experiences. The differences in sibling personalities, which are far greater than the similarities, seem to reflect aspects of the environment that are not shared (Loehlin, Willerman, & Horn, 1987; Rowe & Plomin, 1981).

Family, adoption, and twin studies have indeed found that children in the same family may experience "subtle disparities" in their home environments that make them increasingly different from each other (Goleman, 1987b; Rowe & Plomin, 1981). This is not to say that siblings are exposed to completely different family influences. They do share many features of their common environment, including parents, school system, food, neighborhood, housing, and vacations. However, the common experiences do not necessarily make them more alike. "Environmental factors make siblings in a family different from, not similar to, one another" (Daniels, Dunn, Furstenberg, & Plomin, 1985, p. 764).

One reason for this is that common experiences are not necessarily shared experiences. Siblings have the same parents, but this does not mean that their parents react to them in the same way. Parents may smile or talk more to one child than to another. They may be more lenient with a younger child and more strict with the older. Daughters may be treated differently than sons. Children seem to be more aware of differential parental treatment than are parents themselves. Children often resent what they consider to be unfair or preferential parental treatment. (The perception of favoritism, whether it exists or not, may increase hostility. The hostility is not usually expressed toward the parent, but rather toward the sibling who is perceived as receiving preferential treatment.)

The fact that parents generally treat their children differently is inevitable. Children of varied ages, temperaments, and abilities have diverse needs that require different parental reactions. The point is that we assume that sharing the same parents will make siblings more similar. In fact, children do not experience their parents in exactly the same way. Differential parental treatment appears to reinforce the somewhat different dispositions that already exist among siblings.

A good example of this involves infants' temperaments. Parents probably relate differently to a difficult infant (one who is moody and slow to adjust to change) than to one with a pleasant disposition. This is particularly likely if the difficult infant is a firstborn, and the parents are inexperienced.

Conversely, parents may try to treat two siblings with different temperaments alike. They would be surprised to find that the common parenting style leads to a very different outcome for the two children. Because siblings are different to begin with, common experiences may have different effects.

Another likely source of variation in sibling personality is the "sibling environment." "On the average, siblings experience quite different environments, especially in the areas of differential sibling interactions and differential peer characteristics" (Daniels & Plomin, 1985a, p. 747). For example, one of my sons has an "easy" brother and the other has a "difficult" brother. Hence, they learn different things from each other.

The number of diverse "mini-environments" that siblings inhabit is extremely large, in and outside of the family. They may have different friends, different teachers, and watch different TV programs. They are also likely to differ regarding accidents and illnesses. Thus, it is misguided to imagine that children, simply because they belong to the same family, have similar life experiences (Plomin, 1989).

Evaluation

Research is supporting the validity of the nonshared family environment concept. It remains to be seen whether nonshared environments are largely responsible for the substantial diversity we find in sibling personalities. Thus far, it does not appear likely that genetic differences between siblings can account for the personality differences (e.g., Daniels & Plomin,

1985b). In the next chapter, we will see how heredity may mediate the effects of nonshared experiences in siblings.

We have considered three relatively new areas of research that clarify the parenting process—"small moments," "domain-specificity," and now, "nonshared family environments." They have in common a finer-grained analysis of parent-child interaction than traditional global theories. They also reflect an increased appreciation of the complexity of the events that influence children's personalities. "We suggest that behavioral scientists may have to settle for a large number of environmental explanations of behavior, each with fairly circumscribed applicability" (Rowe & Plomin, 1981).

CHANCE ENCOUNTERS

Study Question What role does "fate" play over the course of one's life?

Social scientists face serious challenges when they try to predict the course of human personality over the life span. One major challenge is anticipating the effects of chance encounters (Bandura, 1986). Each day we make many decisions. We may decide to buy a lottery ticket, go to a dance, or have a physical checkup. Such ordinary actions can have consequences that drastically alter our life paths. Consider how you met your current life partner or best friend, or decided which college to attend. What unforeseen factors led you to choose your present major or career?

People's lives have been significantly altered by a book, a blind date, a car accident, a phone call, or a college course taken because others were not available. A few years ago, a student in my child psychology class inquired about a parenting course that was being offered the following semester. I wasn't aware that my school offered such a course. I thought I would enjoy teaching such a course, and I was right.

While teaching the parenting course, I decided to write a parenting textbook. If not for that student's chance inquiry, I doubt that I would have spent the last 24 months composing this text.

People are not equally susceptible to chance encounters, and not all such encounters have the same effects. Individuals who are successfully recruited by religious cults, for example, are typically lonely, isolated, and have low self-esteem. When they are exposed to a "closed system" of rigid beliefs, they might accept what they are taught without question. "Some chance encounters touch people only lightly, others leave more lasting effects, and still others branch people into new trajectories of life. Psychology cannot foretell the occurrence of particular fortuitous intersects, however sophisticated its knowledge of human behavior" (Bandura, 1986, p. 33).

Parents are naturally concerned about how their children will turn out. Most try to satisfy their children's physical and emotional needs. They hope their children will be happy, well adjusted, and productive. In reality, parental influence competes with countless other influences. Many are known; some cannot be anticipated. It is therefore reassuring that we can lessen children's susceptibility to potentially harmful chance encounters. We do so by encouraging the good judgment, positive self-esteem, autonomy, evaluative skills, and emotional resources comprised by our parenting goals.

SUMMARY

In the absence of a theory of parenting, we must turn instead to theories of personality and development to gain perspective on the parenting process. Each of the theories or models examined in this chapter brings our attention to some aspect of child rearing.

Freud's psychodynamic theory highlights the role of gratification, conflict, and early experiences in development. Freud's theory helps parents understand children's impulsive, demanding nature and the conflicts that might arise from a harsh parenting style. Psychodynamic theory implies that to minimize children's anxiety, parents should be patient and understanding.

Erikson proposed a theory of development emphasizing the importance of parental nurturance and sensitivity. Each of Erikson's psychosocial stages poses a developmental challenge, or crisis, that has either a positive, negative, or mixed outcome. Galinsky describes the developmental challenges encountered during six stages of parenthood. Child rearing changes parents as well as children.

Rogers emphasized the importance of unconditional acceptance and positive regard in the development of self-concept and self-esteem. The more accepting parents are of their children, the more accepting children will be of themselves and others.

Piaget's stage theory of cognitive development analyzes age-related changes in children's cognitive abilities. He found that, over the course of infancy and childhood, children develop more logical ways of understanding and explaining their experiences. Parents who assume young children think like adults may become frustrated and confused by their children's peculiar reasoning. Parents familiar with Piaget's model will be fascinated by the creative way young children interpret their world.

Skinner stresses the importance of one's history of reinforcement in the development of competent behavior. Parents familiar with the principles of operant conditioning are less likely to inadvertently encourage misbehavior and are more likely to promote desirable behavior patterns.

Bandura acknowledges both cognitive and behavioral factors in socialization. Learning occurs when children observe a model, cognitively represent the model's actions, and use the cognitive representation to guide their future behavior. Modeling is one of the most powerful ways parents can influence their children. Bandura also analyzes how chance encounters influence the life path.

Family systems theory views the family as a system of relationships that exerts considerable influence on family members. The small moments model emphasizes the moment-to-moment interactions between parents and children. It rejects the idea of critical phases or stages of development in favor of accumulated influences.

The model of domain-specific parenting is based on the observation that parents do not react consistently to different domains of their children's behavior. Parental reactions reflect many situational factors, including the importance attributed by the parent to a specific behavior. It is misleading to characterize parenting styles in global ways without taking the particular situation into account.

Children in the same families are quite different in their personalities, despite their shared genes and common environments. Their differences seem to reflect how they react to different mini-environments. Nonshared experiences appear to play a much greater role in personality development than shared experiences.

The Roots of Personality

OBJECTIVES

After studying chapter 3, students should be able to

1. Describe and give examples of how biological and environmental factors interact in the development of personality
2. Give examples for each of the four categories of influence on personality development
3. List several physical features that are transmitted genetically from parent to child
4. Define heritability; distinguish between traits with high, moderate, and low heritability; and give examples of each
5. Define temperament and list the distinctive behaviors that comprise it
6. Distinguish between "difficult," "easy," and "slow-to-warm-up" infants
7. Describe the possible interaction between temperament and nonshared family environments
8. List at least four broad temperamental dispositions that appear to have at least some heritability, and describe how they might influence personality development
9. Describe the possible contribution of both dispositional and environmental influences to a child's shyness
10. Describe how inherited characteristics, such as one's sex, race, or appearance, can indirectly influence the development of personality
11. Describe three ways through which genetic dispositions can mediate environmental influences on personality
12. Describe Bloom's model of the origin of special abilities
13. Discuss possible genetic and family influences on the development of alcoholism

Linda and Chuck

Linda, a 30-year-old graduate student, had first entered a rehabilitation project for her alcoholism when she was 19. During our first therapy session, she told me she had been in therapy "forever." She also said that she was dying for a drink.

She had started attending group meetings at Alcoholics Anonymous about 5 months previously and had been sober since. She was entering therapy again, she said, because she hated herself and because her family was "crazy." When she had been drinking, Linda would occasionally nick her skin with a razor blade. She recounted a history of disastrous relationships and self-destructive behaviors.

Alternating between laughter and tears, Linda related that almost everyone in her family was an alcoholic, including her parents and most of her six sisters and five brothers. One of those brothers, whom Linda said she hated, had just been killed in an alcohol-related automobile accident. Another despised brother, who had sexually abused Linda when she was a young girl, was in and out of alcohol rehabilitation centers. Linda, who hadn't spoken to most of her siblings for years, felt close to only one younger sister. Linda told me that, as a child, she had raised herself and her two younger sisters.

Chuck, a 32-year-old accounting major, lives with his parents. He had left home at 18 years of age and began a 10-year period of alcohol and drug abuse. His father and all three of his uncles were alcoholics. Chuck doesn't remember much about his family life during childhood, but he remembers that when there were fights, he would be the one who called the police. Tension was always high, and he was frequently humiliated by his parents' and uncles' behavior when they were drunk. Chuck also recalls that, when he was a child, his father spoiled him one moment and ignored him the next.

While Chuck was drinking, he flunked out of his senior year of college, went through a series of abusive relationships, and could not hold a job. He was arrested three times for possessing marijuana or drunk driving. In an early therapy session, Chuck told me that he feels lonely all the time, has no close friends, and sees himself as a failure. He has recently graduated from college and is struggling to remain faithful to his girlfriend, who is also an adult child of alcoholic parents. He is almost always angry at his parents, particularly his father, who, Chuck claims, still tries to control Chuck's life. (Chuck and I explore why he is back living with his parents.) Chuck attends three meetings of Alcoholics Anonymous a week. Although he has been sober for 5 years, he still thinks about drinking and getting high.

How do we understand such self-destructive behaviors in intelligent men and women? Both Chuck and Linda are appalled at the messes they have created of their lives. They are willing to accept some responsibility for their shattered lives, yet they constantly blame their families, particularly their parents, for their seeming inability to function normally.

Psychologists struggle to understand the complexities of human personality. In the cases of Chuck and Linda, we assume that growing up in severely dysfunctional families has permanently scarred them, emotionally and socially. Because so many children of alcoholic parents become alcoholics themselves, we might also wonder whether inherited dispositions toward addictive behaviors increased their susceptibility to alcoholism.

Given that alcoholism is an intergenerational problem, another question comes to mind. When people like Linda and Chuck have children, what kind of parents will they be? We are just beginning to understand the mechanisms by which alcoholism is transmitted from one generation to the next (Brown, 1988). Later in this chapter, we will return to the topic of growing up in alcoholic families.

NATURE AND NURTURE

Study Question How do biological and environmental factors interact to influence personality development?

Philosophers, psychologists, and parents all wonder about the relative contributions to personality of biology (heredity, nature) and rearing (environment, nurture). Parents contribute to their children's development in both ways. The biological contribution largely ends at birth, although it manifests itself throughout the life span.

The nature-nurture pendulum has swung both ways many times. Some psychologists, like Arnold Gesell (1928), emphasized biological factors in development. Others, like John B. Watson (1924), argued that personality almost exclusively reflects environmental influences. Today there is a consensus that personality development reflects a complex interaction between nature and nurture. The relative contributions of each depend upon the specific area of development we are considering.

For example, during infancy, biology dominates motor, perceptual, and emotional development. The environment overshadows maturation only when it takes such extreme forms as child abuse, neglect, and malnutrition. After infancy, the development of most abilities appears to reflect complex interactions between subtle biological dispositions and the conditions of rearing. The social environment plays a crucial role in shaping a child's character.

Language acquisition provides an excellent example of how biological dispositions interact with learning. Human infants are born with language centers in their brains that are neurologically programmed, if given proper stimulation, to comprehend and generate speech. However, the language that children eventually understand and speak is the one they are exposed to. Language abilities could not exist as we know them without both a biological and experiential foundation.

CATEGORIES OF INFLUENCE

It is helpful for parents to consider the following four categories of influence in development:

Category 1. Genetic biological variables (conception and heredity)
Category 2. Nongenetic biological variables (e.g., nutrition, disease, drugs)
Category 3. Learning history (e.g., conditions of rearing)
Category 4. Physical, social, and cultural environments

These are categories of convenience. They are not based on any particular theory or research model. They are intended to help organize the almost countless variables that influence human development. Developmental outcomes are rarely determined by single factors acting alone, such as birth order, family size, or father absence. Rather, large numbers of factors interact with each other in complex ways that almost defy our ability to measure their individual effects.

For example, children of alcoholic parents may inherit addictive dispositions or sensitivities (category 1). Prenatally, they may be exposed to, and damaged by, the alcohol consumed by their pregnant, drinking mother (category 2). Like Chuck and Linda, they will be raised in disorganized, chaotic, and perhaps abusive family environments (categories 3 and 4). Each of these categories represents hundreds of factors that can influence the development of personality.

Category 1. Genetic Biological Variables

Physical Resemblance

Study Question   What is the basis of children's physical resemblance to their parents?

Most children have at least some physical resemblance to one or both parents. Some children strikingly resemble one parent, and the other only slightly. Some children show almost no physical resemblance to either biological parent, although there might be some resemblance to a sibling, grandparent, uncle, or aunt. These varied outcomes reflect the random processes by which different combinations of parental genes are contributed to offspring.

Family resemblance is not surprising since children inherit their parents' genetic "blueprints" for the design and construction of their bodies. A child who resembles its father, for example, probably has inherited many dominant genes on its father's side that are expressed in facial and other noticeable features. About half of a child's inheritance is from its mother,* but many maternal genes may be recessive and therefore not expresssed in the child's features.

Examining any child, we could probably identify traits or features derived from both maternal and paternal genes. The big puzzle concerns children with little or no obvious physical resemblance to either parent. The distinction between genotype and phenotype reminds us that many of our parents' genes (genotype) may not be expressed in their appearance (phenotype), but might be expressed in ours. For example, two brown-eyed parents can have a blue-eyed child. Similarly,

---

*Siblings do share, on the average, about half their genes. Due to the random nature of the process, however, the range of similarity is between 40 percent and 60 percent. Thus, some siblings are more genetically alike than others. Siblings may be more similar to each other genetically than they are to their parents (Dunn, 1985).

other traits that our parents might be "carrying," but not showing, can become evident in our appearance or biological structure.

Whose Genes Are These, Anyway?

In 1773, a French zoologist named Jean Baptiste Lamarck proposed the doctrine of the inheritance of acquired characteristics. Lamarck suggested that characteristics and abilities acquired during one's lifetime could be transmitted to one's children through heredity. If this were true, a bodybuilder like Arnold Schwarzenegger would bear children who could, through heredity, enjoy the benefits of a more muscular and powerful body. Parents who cultivate their voices or who learn to play musical instruments would transmit musical abilities to their children. Lamarck was wrong, not in principle, but in mechanism. Acquired abilities and interests can be transmitted from parent to child, but not through heredity.

Study Question *How can parental abilities or characteristics be transmitted to children, if not through heredity?*

Lamarck's proposed mechanism of transmission—heredity—was incorrect because genes are immutable. That is, they do not change during our lifetime (unless they are damaged or mutate, in which case the result is almost certainly undesirable). Nothing that you do to improve yourself during your lifetime will change your genes. In fact, they are not really *your* genes! After all, you inherited them from your parents, who inherited them from their parents, and so on. The genes in our bodies today are probably at least hundreds of thousands of years old. There has been little genetic change in our species over this period.

All of our physical features are essentially inherited. This includes the size and shape of our bodies; our eye, skin, and hair color; blood type; sex; handedness; rate of physical and motor development; height; and facial appearance. Now let's qualify this statement. First,

most physical features are polygenetic. That means that many genes are responsible for the particular feature. There is no gene for a cute face, or even a cute nose! The size and shape of one's nose is determined by many genes, not a "nose gene." Genes from both parents determine most of our features.

A second qualification concerns heritability, the degree to which a trait is inherited. Most physical traits, such as those listed previously, have high or complete heritability. Other traits have moderate, low, or no heritability. An example of the latter would be musical preferences. It is very unlikely that our ancient genes predispose us to favor rock, folk, or classical music. Handedness, which refers to our preferred use of right or left hands, has moderate heritability, depending upon whether you are right- or left-handed. Right-handedness apparently has higher heritability than left-handedness. High heritability does not mean a trait cannot be modified. Changing the environment can change the ways in which genes express themselves.

A third qualification involves features such as height. We inherit not a specific height, but rather a range of possible heights. For example one person may inherit the range of 5 ft. 2 in. to 5 ft. 11 in. Another person may inherit a smaller range of 5 ft. 3 in. to 5 ft. 7 in. Where one's height actually falls in this range depends upon other variables, particularly nutritional and hormonal factors. This concept of an inherited range of possible values also applies to intelligence.

Temperament

Study Question *To what extent might "temperamental" dispositions be inherited?*

To the untrained eye, newborns look and sound alike. They seem to be remarkably similar in their behavior. Research confirms, however, that even newborns respond in distinctive ways that are believed to be at least partly inherited.

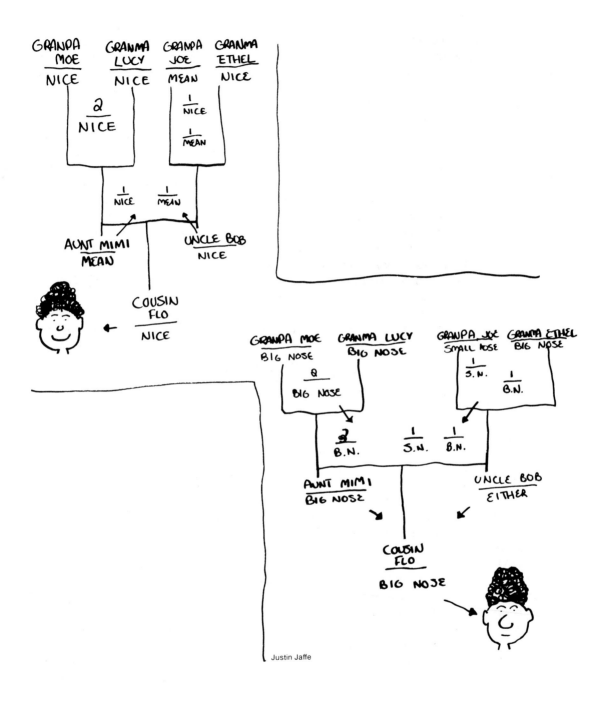

Justin Jaffe

The term temperament has been applied to the following response patterns (Thomas, Chess, & Birch, 1970):

1. Activity level (high or low)
2. Rhythmicity or regularity of biological functions such as sleep and hunger (regular or irregular)
3. Distractibility (distractible or not distractible)
4. Approach/withdrawal or the tendency to seek or avoid stimuli (positive or negative)
5. Adaptability to new situations (adaptive or not adaptive)
6. Attention span/persistence (long or short)
7. Intensity of reaction to stimuli (intense or mild)
8. Threshold of responsiveness to stimuli (low or high)
9. Quality of mood (positive or negative)

On the basis of these characteristics, children were classified as "easy," (about 40% of Thomas's sample), "difficult," (about 10%) and "slow-to-warm-up" (about 15%). Slow-to-warm-up children do not adjust well to changes. They are not particularly active and respond with less intensity than do difficult children. About 35% of Thomas's sample did not fit easily into any of the three categories.* We will see that an infant's temperamental dispositions may influence the direction in which its personality develops.

Heredity and Personality

The branch of psychology known as personality examines individual similarities and differences. In what ways are we different from and

---

*Difficult children may be at greater risk for psychological problems (Thomas, Chess, & Birch, 1968). Thomas and Chess (1977) suggested that parents adjust their parenting styles to accommodate their child's temperament. If temperament is inherited, how can we blame difficult infants for their moodiness?

similar to each other? What accounts for these differences and similarities? Various methods, including adoption and twin studies, have been used to study the origins of individual similarities and differences. Many theories of personality have been proposed. For our present purposes, let's define personality as all of those behaviors, thoughts, and feelings that are characteristic of an individual.

Thus, personality includes a person's beliefs, ideas, opinions, values, thoughts, skills, biases, preferences, moods, dreams, feelings, and desires. Thus, we tentatively conclude that personality is *not* inherited. That is, specific thoughts and behaviors (with the exception of reflexes) are not inherited. There is considerable evidence, however, that certain dispositions are at least partly inherited.

Many parents believe that specific behavior patterns and abilities can be inherited. "He has his father's sense of humor," or "She has her mother's ear for music." Since we know physical resemblance is inherited, it is natural for parents to assume that behavioral similarities are also inherited. Logically, it is not likely that these traits are passed on genetically. For a behavior to have heritability, there must be genes for that behavior. Genes would only have evolved for traits or behaviors that promoted our ancestors' survival. A sense of humor and musical ability are considered desirable traits today, but it is quite unlikely that they had survival value in our ancient past.

We can conclude that there are no genes for musical ability per se. However (here come the qualifications), there are inherited features and traits that support musical talent, such as good hearing, vocal cords that make pleasing sounds, long fingers (useful for playing many instruments), and manual dexterity. Thus, musical talent cannot be inherited (genes for such a trait would not have evolved), but characteristics that contribute to such talent may have evolved for reasons *having nothing to do with*

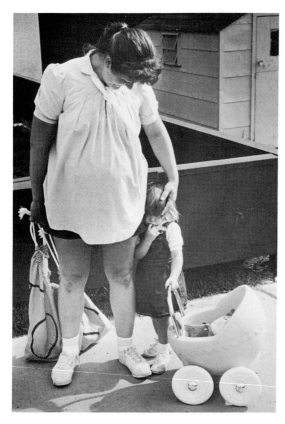

Extreme shyness and extreme sociability appear to have high heritability.

music. Society seeks and selects already existing traits that are valued (like athletic ability or "beauty"), although these qualities evolved for quite different reasons.

Stability of Personality Traits and Dispositions

Most parents have little difficulty recognizing predictable patterns of behavior in their infants and toddlers and label their children accordingly as cranky, easygoing, irritable, or happy. Recent research has confirmed the existence of stable dispositions in temperament.

Kagan, for example, has observed considerable stability over time in the personalities of children who are either very sociable or extremely shy. Children were rated as either very inhibited or very uninhibited when they were

21 months old. The inhibited children were particularly cautious in unfamiliar settings and very shy with strangers. Both groups of children were observed again when they were 4 to 5½ years old, and then again at 7½ years. Most of the children who were shy and timid as infants were still quiet and socially avoidant in unfamiliar social situations five years later. Most of the sociable infants remained talkative and outgoing with peers and adults at the age of 7½ years (Kagan, Reznick, & Gibbons, 1989; Kagan, Reznick, Snidman, Gibbons, & Johnson, 1988).

Both traits are accompanied by distinctive physiological profiles during stress (Kagan, Reznick, & Snidman, 1987). "Very shy children tend to become 'uncertain' when placed in an unfamiliar situation—a predisposition that may be related to their easily aroused stress circuit. Inhibited toddlers typically cling to their mothers and are very slow to venture into a strange playroom" (Asher, 1987, p. 58). Based on interviews with their mothers, Kagan reported that timid children, as infants, are also more colicky and irritable than less timid children.

Kagan suspects that these extreme patterns of sociability have significant heritability. He estimates that 10 to 15 percent of infants are genetically disposed to extreme shyness. Child rearing, according to Kagan, can alter this inherited disposition, but only slightly.

The direction in which children's personality evolves reflects the complex interplay between inherited dispositions, which may be strong or weak (stable or unstable), and conditions of rearing, which also can be strong or weak. "Nature gives the infant just a very small temperamental bias. The proper environmental context can change it profoundly" (Kagan, quoted by Asher, 1987, p. 64). Thus, a powerful parenting style can inhibit or modify a moderately strong disposition.

Let us use shyness as an example of how an inherited disposition might interact with family influences. Daniels and Plomin (1985b)

studied shyness in adopted and nonadopted children and their parents. They found both genetic and family influences. There was a remarkable resemblance between the degree of shyness of the biological mothers and their infants, whom they had given up for adoption within 3 months of birth. This observation supports the role of heredity. But shy adoptive parents also tended to have shy children. Given the absence of a genetic relationship, this supports the influence of rearing.

One rearing mechanism may be lack of exposure to novel social situations. "Shy and unsociable mothers expose neither themselves nor their infants to such experiences" (Daniels & Plomin, 1985b, p. 119). Let's suppose a shy mother is raising two daughters, one bashful and one more outgoing. The timid mother can contribute to the one daughter's shyness in two ways, genetically and through rearing (Daniels & Plomin, 1985b). By limiting their social contacts outside the family, the mother is depriving both daughters of opportunities to develop social skills and self-confidence. Thus deprived, the shy daughter's disposition continues to exert considerable influence on her subsequent personality development.

The sociable daughter has not inherited her mother's shy disposition; she is less socially inhibited. She is still being reared by a shy mother, but she may prefer contact and spend more time with, let's say, her nonshy father. She may also "demand" more contact with her peers than will her shy sibling. In other words, the sociable daughter, having inherited fewer social inhibitions, may create for herself social mini-environments that will promote her sociability despite her mother's shyness.

We can see that a child's temperament, mediated by inherited dispositions, can act as a "filter" through which social experience influences personality. If a parent remains fatalistic about a child's temperament and does little to change it, the dispositions may continue to exert their effects. But Kagan found that 40 percent of the moderately inhibited children became much less inhibited by the age of 5½ years, while fewer than 10 percent became more timid. Some parents encouraged sociability by encouraging other children to visit their home and by teaching their children how to cope with interpersonal stress. "Parents need to push their children—gently and not too much—into doing the things they fear" (Kagan, quoted by Asher, 1987, p. 64).

"In short, temperament may be conceptualized as the foundation for later personality" (Goldsmith, 1983, p. 341). Researchers have also reported stability in personality over the life span for anxiety level, friendliness, and eagerness for novel experiences (Goleman, 1987d). Twin and adoption studies reveal significant heritability for altruism, aggressiveness, empathy, nurturance, and assertiveness (Rushton, 1986). Other broad temperamental dispositions, including emotionality, reactivity, impulsivity, and activity level, may also have at least some heritability (Goldsmith, 1983).

Indirect Effects of Heredity on Personality
There is another link between heredity and personality. Many inherited characteristics, including one's gender, race, temperament, and facial appearance, influence people's reactions to us. How people (particularly family members) respond to us is a major determinant, over time, of our personality. So, we can see that heredity does influence personality development, but, in this case, in an indirect manner. Personality development is affected by people's reactions to our inherited characteristics.

We have seen, for example, that infant temperament apparently has substantial heritability. Let's consider it an inherited characteristic. Let's also assume that a difficult infant—irritable, overly active, and unhappy—is born to inexperienced, insecure parents. They have difficulty coping with the almost constant crying, the sleepless nights, and the demands of caretaking. Suppose these distressed parents reject this child; they become increasingly distant and hostile. (There is plenty of evidence that supports this pattern [e.g., Sirignano & Lachman, 1985]).

Clearly, intense parental rejection and hostility are going to affect this child's personality. For example, he is likely to develop emotional problems. Was it his difficult temperament that may have doomed him to neurosis? Not really. It was his parents' inability to cope with his difficult temperament, and their resulting hostility. Had the infant displayed an "easier" temperament, the parents would probably have been much more accepting. Several studies (e.g., Sprunger, Boyce, & Gaines, 1985) have confirmed that discrepancies between the behavioral styles of parents and infants can impair a family's adjustment to a new baby.

Scarr and McCartney (1983; see also Guillen, 1984) have suggested that children, in effect, create or seek environments that conform to their genetic dispositions. They suggest three types of influence that can occur.

1. *Passive influence* occurs when parents and children share common dispositions. For example, verbally disposed parents speak often to their verbally disposed children. The parents thus provide a stimulating language environment that conforms to and further encourages the child's dispositions.

2. *Evocative influence* occurs when children elicit characteristic responses from those who may or may not share their dispositions. "Cooperative, attentive preschoolers receive more pleasant and instructional interactions from the adults around them than the uncooperative, distractible children" (Scarr & McCartney, quoted by Guillen, 1984, p. 72). According to the model, parental behavior will gradually conform (positively or negatively) to the child's dispositional nature.

3. *Active influence* occurs when older children seek or create environmental conditions that satisfy their dispositions. "Some genotypes are more likely to receive and select certain environments than others" (Scarr & McCartney, quoted by Guillen, 1984, p. 73). Aggressive children, for example, may seek contact with other aggressive children or seek out violent TV programs or movies. These experiences, in turn, may encourage their aggressiveness. Inhibited children may create or select environments that ensure their privacy and, perhaps, their continued isolation.

Supporting this model of self-perpetuating dispositions, Caspi, Elder, and Bem (1987) found that ill-tempered children tend to become ill-tempered adults. "Men with histories of childhood tantrums experienced downward occupational mobility, erratic work lives, and were likely to divorce. Women with such histories married men with lower occupational status, were likely to divorce, and became ill-tempered mothers" (p. 308). Similarly, these investigators found that for males, shyness in childhood predicts a shy interactional style in adulthood (Caspi, Elder, & Bem, 1988).

They suggest a model whereby the interactional patterns of these individuals sustain their ill-tempered or shy behavioral styles via the consequences their behavior evokes in others. According to Scarr and McCartney's model, obnoxious children and bullies evoke reactions in other people that sustain their unpleasant interactional styles over long periods. Additional research is necessary to identify both child and parent behaviors that "mediate genetic influence on environmental measures" (Plomin, McClearn, Pederson, Nesselroade, & Bergeman, 1988, p. 744).

We have maintained that personality is not inherited, although broad temperamental dispositions appear to be. We have also seen how inherited characteristics can influence, albeit indirectly, personality development. It is also likely that powerful parenting styles can inhibit or modify inherited dispositions. The situation is complex. Inherited characteristics, including broad dispositions such as aggressiveness, sociability, and emotionality, interact with conditions of rearing and other environmental influences to determine the ebb and flow of personality.

Study Question *What can the study of identical twins tell us about the role of heredity in personality?*

Twins: Genetic and Environmental Factors in Personality Development Thomas Bouchard directs the Minnesota Center for Twin and Adoption Research at the University of Minnesota. He has studied more than 50 pairs of identical twins reared apart, 25 pairs of fraternal twins reared apart, hundreds of pairs of twins reared together, and a few reunited triplets. All of these people voluntarily participated in six days of extensive testing.

Bouchard was most impressed by the similarities in posture and expressive style in identical twins who were reared apart. They often displayed similar habits, jokes, mannerisms, gestures, and speed and tempo in their speech (C. Holden, 1987). The striking similarities in so many aspects of these people's lives were widely reported on TV and in newspapers.

Bouchard claimed that he identified 11 personality traits that have moderate heritability. They include leadership ability, capacity for imaginative experience, vulnerability to stress, alienation, and a desire to avoid risks. Bouchard also found that identical twins reared apart often have similar fears and phobias.

But could the following similarities be rooted in heredity: brand of toothpaste used, type of job, hobbies, spouses' names, type of car owned, and so on? The famous identical Jim twins, Jim Springer and Jim Lewis, were separated four days after birth and were reunited 39 years later. They discovered that they "had married and divorced women named Linda, married second wives named Betty and named

their first sons James Allan and James Alan, respectively . . . they both drove the same model of blue Chevrolet and they both enjoyed woodworking . . . they often vacationed on the same small beach in St. Petersburg, Fla., and owned dogs named Troy" (*Newsweek,* November 23, 1987, p. 58).

The public wondered, Is this coincidence, or some strange manifestation of genetics? Despite the remarkable similarities, logic suggests coincidence. Interview any two totally *unrelated* adults, and ask them hundreds of questions about their lives, tastes, food and music preferences, employment, and children. You will find dozens of surprising matches in their responses, simply due to coincidence.

The Minnesota research on twins has confirmed the findings of hundreds of studies performed over this century. What we call intelligence has at least moderate heritability. "Identical twins reared in the same family usually have about an 86 percent level of correspondence [in IQ scores]. Fraternal twins hover at about 60 percent. But identical twins reared apart are generally much more similar than same-nest fraternals, with a 72 percent match" (Rosen, 1987, p. 42). Ordinary siblings reared together have a 47 percent correspondence, and adopted children have a 32 percent correspondence with their nonblood siblings.

In the Minnesota study, "twins with very different schooling came out only a few points apart in intelligence" (Rosen, 1987, p. 42), suggesting a relatively minor role for environmental control of gene expression. This is not to say that the environment plays a minimal role in intelligence. There is a growing consensus that intelligence, as measured by IQ tests, receives approximately equal contributions from heredity and environment. However, the definition, measurement, and origins of intelligence remain controversial. If intelligence is viewed as a collection of abilities, such as in Gardner's (1983) model of multiple intelligences, heritability will probably vary across abilities.

The psychological-behavioral resemblance between parents and children includes the domain of "talent." The term talent is not neutral. It implies a natural rather than an acquired ability, though it can mean either. We often notice that certain abilities run in families. Musical parents tend to have musical children, achieving parents tend to have achieving children, and so on. We do not challenge this observation, but rather the tendency to assume that the talent or ability is transmitted genetically.

Professor Benjamin Bloom, an educational researcher, has studied the life histories of over a hundred of the best tennis players, Olympic swimmers, concert pianists, and research mathematicians. They are all world-famous, prize-winning individuals, the best in their fields (Pines, 1982). Dr. Bloom concludes, based on his research, that great skills reflect parenting involvement and encouragement more than inherited dispositions.

Dr. Bloom studied people who were not child prodigies, and who did not necessarily show exceptional ability as children. Most, according to their parents, were not even more talented than their siblings. The children who excelled were the ones who were the most motivated to succeed. Their motivation seems to reflect parental encouragement and involvement in their training.

The parents of these exceptional individuals greatly valued the field that their child eventually pursued and viewed it as a natural part of their lives. Their young children imitated them as they sang or played an instrument. The children received considerable attention and encouragement for doing so. When the children were about 5 or 6, the parents provided a first teacher who was not highly skilled, but who was kind and made lessons into games. Both parents and teacher lavished the child with rewards and praise.

These children received one-to-one tutoring, and the parents were involved in every step of the process. As the children's motivation increased, greater progress was made. Teachers gave these children extra attention, making them feel even more special. A more highly skilled teacher or coach was eventually hired, who told the children they had great potential. The parents attended lessons and supervised practice.

Many parents made enormous sacrifices in time and money on behalf of their child's ability. By early adolescence, the child was committed to his talent, seeking better teachers and equipment. Eventually, the parents sought the "master teacher" in the child's field. As teens, they practiced about 20 hours a week, with little or no social life or leisure time.

Initially, Dr. Bloom had assumed that talented young children would be selected for special instruction. He found the opposite, that children who received the attention and encouragement were the ones who *developed* the talent. The implications of these findings for our understanding of human potential are considerable. It is possible that most people are born with great potential to succeed in one field or another. The realization of this potential largely depends upon the parent's ability to entice the child into the field of study.

"Parents of successful pianists liked listening to music, and bought their children records and musical toys. They sang together. They showed their children how to play and read notes . . . As soon as the children began to show such proficiency, members of their families made a great fuss about it. And the children realized they were on the surest road to attention and praise" (Pines, 1982, p. C2). Other siblings may have shown more talent and certainly were exposed to the music or sporting activities pursued by the family. Nevertheless, the child who became the "star" had the greatest desire to succeed.

Children who excel may not always be the most talented, but they are usually highly motivated.

What light do Dr. Bloom's findings shed on our understanding of heredity and personality? How do these accomplished individuals become special? Or, are their parents the ones who are special? The combination of factors that Dr. Bloom describes includes children who are enticed into some field of study; who are willing to work hard (is there a genetic disposition working here?); parents who are willing to make great sacrifices toward a highly desired goal; and a society that highly values these individuals' abilities.

The Minnesota study found some evidence for the heritability of sexual preference in males, but not in females. Some studies have found high heritability for homosexuality in identical twins reared apart. Other studies have not. The origins of sexual preference are not known, but researchers are currently studying the role of hormonal events during prenatal development. (See Green [1987] for a discussion of the possible origins of homosexuality.)

The transmission of alcoholism from parent to child has been heavily studied. At least 25 percent of the sons of alcoholic fathers* are dependent on alcohol, compared to "only" 10 percent of the general population. Recent studies of adopted children suggest that as many as 40 percent of the children of alcoholics may suffer from the disorder. The best predictor of a son's becoming an alcoholic is having an alcoholic father (C. Holden, 1985). Other family factors, such as maternal acceptance of the alcoholic father's intoxicated behavior, may also increase the risk (McCord, 1988a).

When children of alcoholics develop the disorder themselves, heredity and rearing both become suspected influences (See Spotlight: Alcoholic Families). In the 1970s, studies conducted in Denmark and Sweden revealed that when sons of alcoholics are adopted by other families, they are just as likely to develop alcoholism as sons reared by their biological parents. This suggests that some individuals may inherit a propensity toward alcoholism (C. Holden, 1985).

Researchers have begun to identify inherited physiological and biochemical factors in children that may indicate a predisposition toward alcoholism. There is a low rate of recovery for alcoholics. Identifying children at risk, including adult children of alcoholics

(ACOAs), may enhance prevention of alcohol abuse. As of now, virtually all ACOAs are considered at risk.

Category 2. Nongenetic Biological Variables

Not all biological factors that influence development are genetically based. During the prenatal period, the fetus is vulnerable to a variety of *teratogens,* that is, external agents or events that can cause permanent harm. For example, pregnant women with inadequate diets may suffer from malnutrition, which deprives the fetus of the essential raw materials it needs for the normal growth and development of its organs. Drugs, such as alcohol, cigarettes (which contain nicotine and carbon monoxide), and caffeine, when ingested by a pregnant woman, have been proven to be harmful to the embryo, fetus, and, eventually, the child (e.g., Rosenthal, 1990; Streissguth, Barr, Sampson, Darby, & Martin, 1989).

Bacterial and viral infections can have devastating effects on the fetus, depending upon which period of pregnancy the mother contracts the disease. Complications during birth such as anoxia, an inadequate supply of oxygen to the infant's brain, can cause permanent brain damage and disability (see chapter 4). Thus, we distinguish between two types of biological influences, genetic (heredity) and nongenetic (teratogens).

Category 3. Learning History

If the specific behaviors that comprise personality are not inherited, what is their source? Specific behaviors, beliefs, opinions, attitudes, and so on are essentially *learned* over the life span through reinforcement, modeling, instruction, and other social-cognitive mechanisms we examine in succeeding chapters. The implications of this for parenting are obvious. Involved, effective parents can exert considerable, though far from total, influence on the development of their children's personalities.

---

*Researchers tend to study children of alcoholic fathers rather than mothers because alcoholic mothers can influence their children by drinking when they are pregnant.

About 28 million people in the United States have been raised by alcoholic parents. Every member of an alcoholic family contracts what some consider to be a family "disease," characterized by denial, co-dependence, and the need to control others. Alcoholic parents train their children to deny that alcohol is a serious family problem, although the effects of alcohol dominate and distort family life. Codependence refers to the preoccupation of other family members with the welfare and behavior of the alcoholic and the maladaptive ways in which they try to adjust (Brown, 1988).

The research literature portrays the alcoholic family environment as one of "chaos, inconsistency, unpredictability, unclear roles, arbitrariness, changing limits, arguments, repetitious and illogical thinking, and perhaps violence and incest. The family is dominated by the presence of alcoholism and its denial" (Brown, 1988, p. 27).

Children require stable, predictable environments, but children in alcoholic families grow up in a chaotic, disorganized environment where the *appearance* of normality becomes a major goal. Children must remain constantly on guard for unpredictable, embarrassing, and even dangerous parental behaviors (like driving while intoxicated). They have little opportunity to learn normal standards of behavior or even logical thinking.

"Parents may take turns, with one assuming responsibility while the other one drinks and vice versa. Both parents offer confusing and erratic models for their children as well as unpredictable emotional availability. The consequences of the lack of any consistent, stable parental figure are severe" (Brown, 1988, p. 53).

Linda and Chuck, described at the beginning of this chapter, were raised in families that were alcohol-focused, not child-focused. They both lacked the opportunity as children to observe or participate in healthy family relationships. Like many adult children of alcoholics, they had no basis in their early family lives for understanding how people relate to each other in supportive and healthy ways. As adults, they must learn from scratch how to trust, how to communicate, and how to live.

"Adult children of alcoholics often find themselves replicating their relationship with the alcoholic parent by choosing a dependent or alcoholic mate. Some avoid close relationships altogether, finding themselves more and more isolated and less and less able to trust. Those who marry and have children frequently feel that their main commitment is still to their parents. They feel frightened of needing to depend on another person and often feel inadequate as parents" (Brown, 1988, p. 66).

From the moment of birth, and possibly before, the infant is susceptible to learning, that is, to having its behavior changed by experience. Many studies have demonstrated that newborns, and even prematurely born infants who technically should still be fetuses, can be conditioned. Although newborns are not easily classically conditioned, operant conditioning of the newborn is not difficult to accomplish. For example, if every time the newborn turns its head to the right, it is given the opportunity to suck on a nipple for milk, but never when it turns its head to the left, the rate of head-turning to the right increases.

Although the extent to which personality may be influenced by inherited dispositions is still not clear, no behavioral scientist would deny the importance of our history of daily interactions with the environment in shaping our personality (i.e., the small moments model). Theorists may disagree about the nature of the learning processes that create and modify our behavioral repertoires, but the cumulative effects of our daily experiences on our personalities cannot be denied. Every evening we are slightly different than we were that morning, not that anyone, including ourselves, would notice the subtle changes. We will have many opportunities in this text, particularly in chapters 5 and 6, to examine the role that learning plays in the parenting process.

Category 4. Physical, Social, and Cultural Environments

Physical Environment

Because learning always occurs in some environment, it is helpful to consider the various environments we inhabit when we learn. We are always occupying some physical environment, whether it be a car, our room, a playground, a library, or an ocean. We begin life in our mother's uterus, tightly bound in the amniotic sac surrounded by amniotic fluid. As we grow, sensory systems begin to channel information to the developing brain through various sensory modalities, including sound, pressure, and movement. What the fetus might be learning before birth is anyone's guess.

We are born into a different physical environment, usually a hospital delivery room that is typically noisy and has bright lights, lots of commotion, and poking of the newborn. When we leave the hospital, we breathe the (polluted?) air, hear the noise of traffic, see lights and shadows, experience the motion of the vehicle we are traveling in, and are held tightly. We go home—to what? A house? An apartment? A shack? An igloo? Does the infant have its own room? Is it clean? Is it safe? Is there a play area and play equipment? Is the room well lit? Does traffic noise or loud music incessantly impose itself into the child's room? Infants and children inhabit incredibly different environments, and it would be naive to conclude that one's physical environment is irrelevant in one's development.

Social Environment

We are also born into a social environment— one inhabited by other people. What is our family configuration? Are both parents present? Are they our biological parents? Do they get along with each other? Are they both healthy, employed, and sane? Do we have siblings? How many? What is their birth order, their age spacing, their sex? How do they feel about our entry into their territory? The social environment also includes other family members, babysitters, neighbors, teachers, schoolmates, and friends. Will our friends be supportive, competitive, kind, sharing, aggressive? Children inhabit a complex social environment that exerts enormous influence over their development. The specific mechanisms and processes of social influence remain unclear (Rutter, 1985a).

Community We are born into levels of community, including neighborhood, local community (village, town, or city), state, national, and international levels. "From the preschool years through adulthood, the human being uses the neighborhood and community setting as a primary arena for the use of unstructured time. The neighborhood provides the setting for the child's development of competence in naturally occurring social and physical experiences . . . Through exploration of the neighborhood, children gain an understanding of the social and physical characteristics of the community, as well as its characteristics as a setting for play" (Schiamberg, 1988, p. 85–86).

What is your neighborhood like? Are there homes, front and backyards for children to play in, and any other children their age? Are there parks and community centers with play equipment and adequate supervision? Is your neighborhood a city block—noisy, dirty, threatening? Can children go outside by themselves? Do they have friends nearby? How far does their neighborhood extend? Our concept of community has been expanding in the twentieth century. But all "levels" of community can affect development.

Educational Setting School is an environment designed by the culture to provide basic skills and transmit cultural values and traditions. There is a specific curriculum to be taught that depends upon the child's age and cognitive abilities. School is also an environment in which socialization occurs, though, as with the formal curriculum, some schools are more effective than others. School environments are successful when they accomplish their stated curriculum and socialization goals so that children become educated and, at the same time, learn to treat each other well.

Media Children spend about a quarter of their waking hours watching television. Studies support the observation that TV can have a profound influence on children's development, more so for some children than others. Development is affected by the media primarily through the information provided to children through the TV programming and movies they watch. We examine the role that television plays in development in chapter 10.

Cultural Environment

The culture and subculture we inhabit determine our dress, food preferences, language, traditions, values, roles, and beliefs. Western culture is materialistic, goal-directed, and individualistic compared to other cultures—say Oriental. Of the various environments we inhabit, culture is the most profound and the most invisible. It is not until we leave our culture, in books or in travel, that we can appreciate how differently people live. Our understanding of development and personality requires a perspective that encompasses the many levels of environment we inhabit, their enormous complexity, and their interaction.

SUMMARY

Chapters 2 and 3 review our present understanding of personality development. We are biological beings who are very susceptible to environmental influences. Virtually every aspect of our nature reflects the complex interaction of biological and experiential factors.

Four categories of influence on personality are considered. This chapter focuses on influence category 1, genetic biological variables, and its interaction with category 3, learning history. Development begins at the moment of conception, when the 23 paternal chromosomes join the 23 maternal chromosomes. Thus, children inherit roughly half their genes from each parent. However, each child inherits a different, and random, sample of each parent's genes.

When we ask the important question, "what is inherited," we are inquiring about the heritability of our various features. Heritability refers to the degree to which particular traits are inherited. Most of our physical traits, such as eye, hair, and skin color, have high heritability. Most of the specific behaviors that comprise our personality have very low or zero heritability. Some traits, such as intelligence and susceptibility to disease, have moderate heritability. This means they will also reflect at least some environmental influence.

One of the most controversial issues in the history of personality study concerns the existence of inherited dispositions. There is considerable evidence that temperamental dispositions have high heritability. They can interact with environmental factors to influence personality development. Inherited dispositions seem to exist in the areas of emotionality, language development, cognition, and sociability. Several dispositions with moderate heritability were described. Various ways in which rearing interacts with such dispositions were also discussed.

Sex, race, facial appearance, and certain disabilities are inherited. They can exert an *indirect* influence on personality, mediated by how people react to these characteristics. To the extent that people treat males and females differently, for example, one's sex may predict certain personality traits.

Children who develop exceptional abilities are often "seduced" into a field of study or performance by their parents. Bloom describes the pattern in which highly motivated children, with extensive parental involvement, devote themselves to a discipline and eventually gain societal recognition for their valued abilities.

Much of what has been learned about the contributions of heredity and environment in personality development has reflected the study of adopted children and the study of twins, particularly identical twins, who have identical heredity. These studies have shed light on the contributions of nature and nurture to sexual preference, intelligence, and alcoholism.

Nongenetic biological influences on development include teratogens, external agents that can permanently harm the fetus. Personality, as defined in this chapter, is very much influenced by a child's learning and rearing history, including the moment-to-moment encounters in a variety of environments.

CHAPTER FOUR

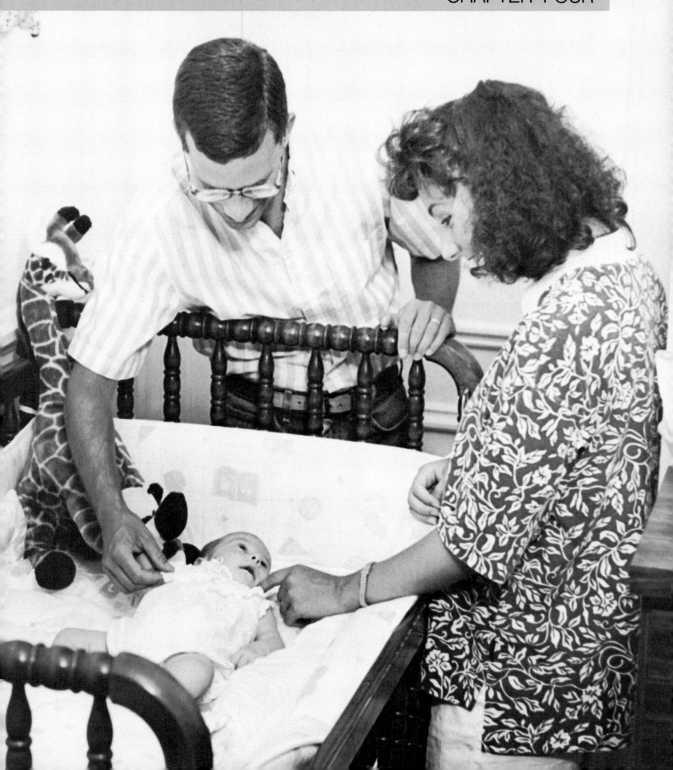

The Transition to Parenthood

OBJECTIVES

After studying chapter 4, students should be able to

1. Describe the physical and psychological sources of stress and discomfort for pregnant women
2. Discuss the standard delivery, the complications that can occur during birth, and the controversial aspects of cesarean sections
3. Present the key features of prepared childbirth and Leboyer's gentle birthing procedure
4. Describe the risk factors and problems associated with premature and postmature deliveries
5. Describe how various aspects of the birth situation and the characteristics of the infant can influence parent-child bonding
6. Distinguish between "maternal blues," postpartum depression, and postpartum psychosis
7. Describe the characteristics of Sudden Infant Death Syndrome
8. Describe the function of the infant's cry and how parents can cope with prolonged or inappropriate crying
9. Compare the advantages and disadvantages of breast- and bottle-feeding
10. Describe some of the adjustment problems facing new parents

INTRODUCTION TO PARENTHOOD

"My life changed when I became a parent. I slowly came to see my wife differently, as mother to my child. I began to view myself differently. Like so many men, the almost obsessive thought, 'I'm a father' continually echoed in my consciousness. But what does it mean to be a father? I was committed to full, equitable participation in the raising of my children, not out of obligation, but really, for the joy I anticipated in spending time with 'little kids.'

"I observed that my wife and I both became more nurturant, more caring, and mainly, more tired. When we had been childless, our marital relationship allowed for greater spontaneity and independence in time and place. As parents, our new responsibilities were clearly defined, and our dependence on each other was more clear-cut. Someone always had to be there as caretaker. Our infant son was difficult, issues arose daily on how to handle him, and our confidence wavered from day to day. Thirteen years later, we still waver a bit, but we are still enjoying" (father of two boys).

The transition to parenthood begins with the awareness of pregnancy and spans the prenatal period, birth, and the early years of child rearing. Chapter 4 examines this unique, exciting, and challenging time of life.

PREGNANCY

Pregnancy is usually a very special period in a couple's life. Pregnant women and their partners are said to be "expecting," and expectations are plentiful. Parents-to-be, especially for first births, are usually both excited and concerned about what lies ahead. Some women report never feeling better, healthier, and happier than during their pregnancy. Other women report the opposite. They find pregnancy extremely uncomfortable and discouraging. Most women fall between the two extremes, having good and bad days.

Physical Discomfort and Psychological Stress

Study Question   What sources of physical discomfort and psychological stress do women commonly report during pregnancy?

Many complex changes occur inside a pregnant woman's body. They require both physical and psychological adjustments. As the size of the fetus increases, a woman's internal organs become increasingly crowded. This may be reflected in gastrointestinal distress and, as bladder capacity is intruded upon, more frequent visits to the bathroom. Because the growing fetus changes a woman's center of gravity, she finds herself making postural adjustments.

The added weight of the fetus and difficulty sleeping may also contribute to the fatigue about which many pregnant women complain. About three-quarters of pregnant women report experiencing "morning sickness," usually early in pregnancy. High levels of estrogen are responsible. In late pregnancy, the breasts swell and become increasingly sensitive.

Pregnancy can also cause psychological distress. This is unfortunate for two reasons. Both mother-to-be *and* the fetus suffer when the mother's body creates excessive amounts of the stress hormone epinephrine (adrenaline). The hormone arouses the mother's body, irritates the fetus, and reduces its oxygen supply. Psychological stress usually reflects the physical discomforts already described and the woman's concern about how her partner will react to the changes in her appearance. Pregnant women are also apprehensive about losing mobility and independence as pregnancy progresses. Most of all, they are concerned about the health of the fetus and its eventual birth.

It is not unusual for husbands to feel threatened by some aspects of pregnancy. Many husbands express financial concerns. Since the average cost of pregnancy is $4,300 (or one-fifth of the average income of young couples in their twenties), financial pressures on the family are likely to increase. An insecure man may also fear having to compete with the newborn for his wife's attention. Fortunately, many men who are initially apprehensive find the parenting role more rewarding than they anticipated.

Men who feel neglected before or after the birth may act in ways that destabilize their marriages. They may not provide their partners with needed support, or they may express resentment in other ways. Pregnancy usually brings partners closer together. Most men behave in an increasingly protective and caring fashion.

During this time of heightened vulnerability, pregnant women depend heavily on the support of their partners, friends, and relatives. Good information about pregnancy and birth, as well as an active social support system, helps women cope with pregnancy-related stress. Creating a family, wondering what the baby will be like, and preparing for parenthood all contribute to this special period of life.

"As prospective parents contemplate these themes, they often turn into themselves, wondering about the knowns and the unknowns: that they are changing, but they don't know quite how; that the baby is made from them and yet distinct; that the baby will be an enormous part of their lives, but they don't know what it will look like; that they are anticipating the actual birth with excitement and fear" (Galinsky, 1981, p. 30).

Labor Day

Toward the end of gestation, the fetus orients toward the face-down, head-first position it will adopt during the passage through the birth canal (this adjustment in position is called "lightening"). Before true labor begins, many women experience the "false labor" of Braxton Hicks contractions. When women tell their obstetricians that they think they are in labor, the doctor usually responds, "If you only think you're in labor, you're not. When you are in real labor, you'll know." Labor gets its name from the considerable effort most women must exert in expelling the fetus from the uterus. Labor lasts an average of 14 hours for first births (but could be much shorter), with contractions increasing in frequency, duration, and sharpness of pain.

During the first stage of labor, which lasts from 7 to 12 hours on the average, the contractions of the uterus push the fetus against the cervix, which stretches from about 1/5 of an inch to about 4 inches in diameter. The onset of labor is also marked by the "water breaking." The amniotic sac ruptures, releasing the amniotic fluid.

The first stage of labor ends with the head of the fetus passing through the dilating cervix. This is likely to be painful. Transition to the second stage of labor is defined by a fully dilated cervix. At this point, contractions are occurring about once per minute. Transition lasts about one hour.

The second stage of labor is defined by the passage of the fetus through the vaginal canal to the outside world. The vaginal tissues must stretch considerably. If there is danger of tearing, an episiotomy (small incision) is performed to enlarge the opening. Stage two of labor typically lasts from 20 minutes to 2 hours.

After the newborn's head passes through the vaginal canal, with much maternal pushing, the rest of its body slips out easily. The infant may be slapped on its behind to encourage the first breath, and drops are usually placed in its eyes to prevent infection. An identifying band is placed around its wrist or ankle. Mucus and amniotic fluid are removed from its breathing passages by suction tubes.

Parents may be shocked upon first glimpsing their newborn. They see a puffy face and eyes, wrinkled skin, a red face, misshapen head, and a white greasy fluid (a lubricant and disinfectant called vernix caseosa) covering its body. In stage three of labor, the "afterbirth" (placenta and umbilical cord) is delivered. It is inspected for abnormalities and saved as evidence in case problems develop. Women may be given hormone injections to shrink the uterus and stimulate milk production.

SPECIAL DELIVERIES

"Birth is one of life's important moments. Parents have often seen pictures, read or been told of births with radiant parents. Sometimes those parents who have difficult births feel cheated, they feel they have missed out, been deprived or robbed of what they might have had . . . Parents see birth as an early indicator of what kind of parents they will be. They look at how they have handled the birth and judge themselves" (Galinsky, 1981, p. 53).

Delivering infants in hospitals, rather than at home, is a relatively new cultural practice. What we accept today as a "standard" delivery began to evolve in the mid-nineteenth century. In the year 1900, fewer than 5 percent of women delivered their infants in hospitals! Before the importance of sterilization was recognized in the mid-nineteenth century, the mortality rates of mothers and infants were very high. Doctors might leave the morgue where they had been performing autopsies, then deliver infants without first sterilizing their hands and instruments. Naturally, this practice promoted the spread of infections, leading to stillbirths and other complications. Perhaps 10 percent of newborns did not survive birth (McQuarrie, 1980).

At about the same time that the importance of sterilization began to be appreciated, anesthetics were discovered that lessened suffering during surgical interventions and labor. Blood transfusion technology also improved mortality rates. A twentieth century invention that provided speedy transportation to hospitals was the automobile.

In the 1960s and 1970s, more natural, and less medical, approaches to birth were becoming available. A relatively small number of couples opted to deliver their infants at home rather than in a hospital. They sometimes selected midwives rather than physicians to deliver their infants. More recently, the threat of litigation and high insurance rates has slowed this trend.

The use of anesthetic drugs to dull the pain of delivery is controversial. Powerful anesthetic drugs do lessen the pain, but at the cost of diminishing a mother's awareness of the birth. Most women in the United States decide to use pain-killing anesthetics during delivery, and some are given no choice. One mother recalls, "At the very beginning I was upset because my husband couldn't be in the delivery room. They put me out. I was groggy when they told me I had a daughter. I didn't get to see her when she was born. I didn't get to hold her. My gynecologist was very timid when he came in. He knew I was very upset. He knew I wanted to be awake."

Obstetric drugs cross the placenta to the fetus. Unfortunately, they enter the fetus's bloodstream and produce short- and possibly long-term effects on the infant (e.g., Sanders-Phillips, Strauss, & Gutberlet, 1988). Even local anesthetics (epidurals) may have noticeable effects on mother and child. Infants born to mothers who do not use powerful anesthetics are usually more alert and active (Murray, Dolby, Nation, & Thomas, 1981).

Emergency interventions are available if the fetus's head is too large to allow fetal passage through the birth canal. Similarly, if the placenta is blocking the cervical opening, if the fetus is not in the proper position to be delivered (breech birth), or if the fetal oxygen supply to the brain is impaired, speedy interventions ensue. If there is evidence that the fetus is distressed for any of these reasons, obstetricians can hastily perform a cesarean section. Because of the risks to the fetus's brain, obstetricians limit their use of forceps (metal clamps) to the last stages of delivery.

By 1986, almost a quarter of all births in this country were cesareans (compared to about 5% in 1970), some anticipated, some emergency. Cesarean births remain controversial because of the risks inherent in surgery and the extensive recuperation period. Surgery is also expensive. Those who believe the procedure is used excessively suggest that many doctors perform cesarean sections in difficult deliveries to avoid being sued if complications arise. Mothers might prefer the surgical procedure because they avoid the pain of labor. Women who have emergency cesareans often report being more dissatisfied with their deliveries than women receiving either elective cesareans or vaginal deliveries (Cranley, Hadahl, & Pegg, 1983).

A report by Ralph Nader's Public Citizen Research Group claimed that half of all cesarean deliveries are unnecessary. Their study revealed that such deliveries increase the risk of death or illness for the mother, raise the cost of delivering infants, and exact a "psychological toll" on the mother. It is accepted today that women who have previously had cesareans do not necessarily require them for subsequent births. Up to 80 percent of women who have had cesareans can subsequently deliver babies vaginally (*New York Times,* October 27, 1988; November 3, 1987).

Prepared Childbirth

For thousands of years, women have borne children under dreadful, unsterile, often terrifying conditions, reflecting ignorance of the birth process. Enlightened attitudes about birth developed in this century largely due to the pioneering efforts of Grantly Dick-Read (1933) and Fernand Lamaze (1972). Only in recent generations have we begun to appreciate the importance of involving the parents-to-be in the birth process. In the past, pregnant woman

Prepared childbirth classes demystify the birth process and provide needed support to expecting parents.

were treated as obstacles to be overcome in the delivery of their children. There are many birth options available to parents today. Prepared childbirth is one of the most popular.

Because my older son experienced a forceps delivery, I was not allowed to observe and participate in his delivery. My wife and I had gone through the Lamaze training, and we were very disappointed. Five years later, I was present for and participated in the birth of my second child. With all due credit to my wife's efforts, I never worked so hard in my life!

I was massaging, comforting, watching the fetal monitor, reminding my wife to use the proper breathing or relaxation routine, and (yes, I admit it) taking pictures. Being present for the birth of one's child and the opportunity to participate in its delivery is "totally awesome." Holding your newborn moments after its birth is an incredibly moving and memorable experience.

Prepared childbirth is based on the premise that birth should not be a mysterious and threatening process to new parents (Lamaze,

1972). Parents-to-be attend six weekly classes beginning during the seventh month of pregnancy. They are given accurate information about the anatomy and physiology of pregnancy and birth. All of the questions and concerns that pregnant parents have are addressed in an informal and supportive manner. Fathers are trained to coach and monitor their wives during the delivery. (Bringing fathers into the parenting process at this early point has benefits we will examine in a later chapter.)

Pregnant women are taught how to relax their bodies. They learn various exercises and breathing techniques that can be used during different stages of labor. Because she is preparing to participate in her delivery, it is important for a pregnant woman to exercise the muscles she will be using to expel the infant. Without this preparation, these muscles might become strained during labor (which can last up to 20 hours or more).

Exercising and being fit help during the delivery. A study published in the *Journal of the American Medical Association* (May, 1988)

found that moderate physical activity, including jogging, swimming, cycling, and playing tennis, does not endanger the fetus of a healthy woman who has a normal pregnancy, as long as she does not push herself to her limits.

Thus, prepared childbirth emphasizes father involvement, good information about the birth process, and minimal dependence on drugs that could harm the fetus during delivery.* A mother's ultimate reward for her efforts is seeing the birth of her child and holding it moments later.

Studies comparing women who have had successful Lamaze deliveries with those who preferred medicated deliveries are difficult to interpret. Both groups are "self-selected" rather than randomly assigned to the method of birthing and may differ in several ways. Nevertheless, some studies report that women who feel in control of their labor and who have their partners present during the delivery relate more positive experiences (Entwisle & Doering, 1981; Sosa, Kennell, Klaus, Robertson, & Urrutia, 1980).

Gentle Birth

Frederick Leboyer, a French obstetrician influenced by the works of Lamaze and Dick-Read, suggested that increasing the comfort of the mother during the birth process is addressing only half the problem (Leboyer, 1975). What about the comfort of the newborn? The fetus leaves a dark, warm, quiet, fluid-filled uterus to enter a bright, noisy, cold, hospital delivery room. Adding insult to injury, he is turned upside down and slapped on the behind. Welcome to Earth.

In an effort to minimize the "transition shock" from uterus to delivery room, Leboyer urges that the conditions of the delivery room

(which can be in the parents' home) be adjusted to approximate those of the uterus. He advocates that there be dim light, low noise (whispers), and gentle handling of the newborn as it is given to its mother. The infant should then be placed in a warm bath that not only cleans its body but is reminiscent of the warm, amniotic fluid in which it was recently immersed.

Research has not demonstrated that gentle handling produces measurable long-term benefits, but several of Leboyer's suggestions have become part of mainstream obstetrical care (Evans, 1989). Some critics worry about the potential danger of working in dim light and the possibility of infection in nonhospital deliveries. However, such procedures, in their gentleness, appear to be more humane than the traditional hospital delivery. What do you think?

Premature Deliveries

Study Question What is a premature delivery, and why is it considered hazardous to the newborn?

The best predictor of an infant's mortality is the timing of its birth. Maternal illness, malnutrition, multiple births, and other problems can lead to a premature delivery. Prematurity increases the risk of birth complications, particularly for males. Prematurity is defined either by a gestation period of 36 weeks or less, or by a birth weight of less than 5½ pounds (the average weight for a full-term newborn is about 7½ pounds).

Defined this way, about 10 percent of all live deliveries are premature. A recent government study found that about 17,000 infants, each weighing less than 2 pounds, are admitted to intensive care nurseries each year in this country. They have about a 70 percent chance of survival. Those weighing 2 to 3 pounds have a 90 percent survival rate (*Newsweek,* May 16,

---

*Low-dosage local anesthetics may be requested by the mother.

1988). Up to 100,000 newborns are placed in intensive care annually, with birth weights less than 5½ pounds. The mortality rate of prematurely delivered infants is about eleven times the normal rate.

"The most troubled babies are born at the current limit of viability, about 24 weeks old with a weight of about 500 grams (just over a pound). They bear little resemblance to full-term newborns. Their ear lobes are often just skin flaps at the sides of their heads and their eyes may be fused shut. Their skin is a dusky red color no matter what their race . . . Their lungs have developed to the point where they can breathe with the help of a machine called a ventilator; the lungs of babies any younger than this are so rudimentary that the infants have virtually no chance of survival" (*Newsweek,* May 16, 1988).

Parents and doctors must often make difficult decisions about how aggressively they will pursue treatment, particularly when serious birth defects are a likely outcome. "Is it right to continue aggressive treatment for infants who may not have much of a chance at normal life? And who should decide what is an acceptable quality of life? Should such extensive financial and technological resources be devoted to a relatively few patients? Wouldn't the money be better spent providing prenatal care and thus preventing many premature births?" (*Newsweek,* May 16, 1988).

Healthy women with good eating habits and good prenatal care are unlikely to bear premature infants. Women in poor health, who are malnourished, who are very young when they bear children, or who have multiple pregnancies, are at higher risk for premature delivery. A recent government study found that women with inadequate prenatal care are 30 percent more likely to bear a child prematurely. Prematurity and poverty are related. Women in lower socioeconomic groups have four times as many pregnancy and delivery problems as women who are economically better off.

Fortunately, at least half of all cases of prematurity are avoidable. Preventing premature births by providing poor pregnant women with good prenatal care is a very cost-effective and humane solution to this painful and expensive problem. A government study found that the United States health care system saves between $14,000 and $30,000 for every low-birth-weight delivery avoided. Adolescent females (a high-risk group for premature births) should be taught the signs of premature labor, which can often be arrested. According to a recent study, a new, inexpensive device that monitors uterine contractions may predict premature births (*New York Times,* August 2, 1988).

One of the unfortunate outcomes of a premature delivery is that the parents lose the opportunity for early contact with their newborn, who may spend many days or weeks in intensive care. Women who bear healthy children without complications usually have the option of "rooming-in." In this arrangement, the newborn shares its mother's hospital room for the standard 3-day recuperation interval before they leave the hospital together. Mothers who bear their children prematurely typically leave the hospital without their children and are usually very disappointed. Then there is the shock of seeing the newborn in intensive care—"a completely sedated infant with IV lines in the umbilicus, in the arm, maybe in the scalp, a tube in the nose, a baby hooked up to a respirator" (Klass, 1988).

Parents have difficulty interacting with premature infants, given the infants' weakness and very short attention spans. "Preemies" also tend to be underactive and have a weak cry (Trotter, 1987c). Parenting prematurely born infants, who tend to be born into low-income households, presents unique problems and challenges. Parents of these infants need special training and support. Some preterm infants who test normally at birth may have behavioral and cognitive problems later on and might require special education (T. Adler, 1989b).

Postmaturity

Infants are considered postmature if they are delivered more than 2 weeks past the mother's due date (that is, after the 42nd week of pregnancy). This happens in about 7 percent of all pregnancies. Some women have not yet experienced labor up to 5 weeks past their due dates, increasing the risk of brain damage and fetal death. "The baby can have problems with its oxygen or food supply. It may lose weight in utero and there may be fetal distress in labor. The baby has a higher risk of dying before or during delivery" (Witter, quoted by Kolata, 1988a). The fetus continues to grow, making vaginal delivery of the larger fetus more hazardous.

Obstetricians do not yet know when it is best to wait for a natural delivery, to induce labor artificially, or to perform a cesarean section. It is difficult to distinguish between true postmaturity and situations where a fetus requires more time to mature. If labor is induced and the mother's cervix is not ready for delivery, a cesarean must be performed. This is most frustrating for women who endure a long labor and then discover they must have a cesarean. It is even possible that the due date was miscalculated, and a premature, rather than a postmature, infant ends up being delivered (Kolata, 1988b).

Like premature infants, postmature infants require special handling. They tend to be "overactive, fussy and have a cry like a donkey bray. These difficulties limit the playfulness of the parents, which further limits the responsiveness of the infants" (Trotter, 1987c).

PARENT-INFANT BONDING

Study Question Is there a critical period soon after birth during which parents become strongly bonded to their newborn?

"Although I could intellectually relate to my wife's pregnancy and see that she was bonding with this unborn child, I had very little emotional attachment. I was getting anxious and excited about the birth—but I had no emotional attachment to the baby. I was curious about why I felt none. It didn't really bother me that much. But there was a striking change the minute she was born. I underwent such a change. All of a sudden, I was emotionally attached to this 'thing' " (father of two children).

Most parents develop powerful nurturant and affectionate feelings toward their children, some quickly, some gradually. The term "bonding" is used to describe the process by which these feelings arise and intensify following a child's birth. The nature of the bonding process is not completely understood, though it is assumed that both biology and learning are involved. The father quoted above seems to be implying that his attachment to his newborn daughter was immediate. It is important to remember that bonding is a gradual and complex process (Smolak, 1986).

Parents who have nurturant feelings toward their children will be concerned about their welfare and generally treat them well. The bonding process therefore increases the likelihood that the infant will survive and prosper. Affectionate feelings also help parents cope with the occasional frustrations that accompany child rearing. Parents who have ambivalent or negative feelings about their children, or no feelings at all, are not as likely to take good care of them. Many parents who are ambivalent at first eventually become strongly attached to their child. Children of parents who never become bonded may be at risk for a variety of developmental problems, including child abuse or neglect.

Circumstances surrounding the birth may enhance or weaken the bonding process. Bonding will probably be inhibited if the child is not wanted. Similarly, after birth, parents may have ambivalent feelings if the newborn is the "wrong" sex. Some parents may be slower to bond to children who are hard to care for, including cranky, premature, and handicapped infants.

Other conditions of birth may influence bonding. When couples attend prepared childbirth classes, the father is permitted to be present during the delivery to "coach" his wife and share the moment of birth. In a home delivery, other family members, including children, may be present for the birth.

Anesthetics that allow women to sleep through their delivery prevent them from participating in the birth and from holding the newborn moments later. Infants born to anesthetized women are also less alert and less active. Many women decide not to use general anesthetics during their deliveries. The combination of alert mother and responsive infant makes it more likely that there will be early, successful mother-infant interactions, probably enhancing the bonding process (Murray, Dolby, Nation, & Thomas, 1981). Women who have cesarean or premature deliveries are not likely to have early contact with their infants. This lack of early contact may or may not temporarily inhibit bonding.

The most dramatic moment in the bonding process occurs when proud parents first hold their newborn. "The first time that parents do, in fact, hold their child can be a powerful experience. Perhaps they feel the baby's skin on theirs, nestle the baby against them, cover the baby's tiny fingers with their hand, rub their mouths over the fuzz of the baby's hair, and look into the baby's eyes. Perhaps the mother offers the newborn her breast and the baby licks the nipple. Or perhaps the mother or father gives the baby a bottle" (Galinsky, 1981, p. 59).

How important is early parental contact with the newborn in the development of parent-infant attachment? Do humans, like many other species, have a critical period for bonding soon after birth? In the absence of sufficient early contact, will affectionate feelings fail to develop? These and other questions about bonding have been investigated.

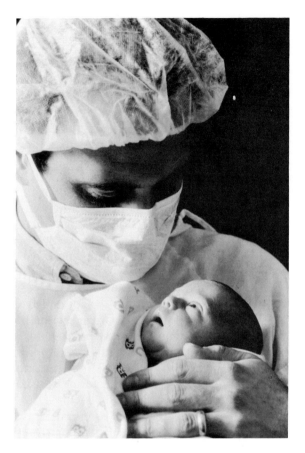

The bonding process begins between father and child.

Klaus and Kennel (1976) wondered whether different amounts of mother-infant contact soon after birth influence the bonding process. Two groups of low-income, first-time mothers were given different amounts of "extra cuddling" with their newborns. The two groups were matched on several demographic and cultural variables so they could be considered comparable. They were treated alike in all respects, except that one group of mothers received five hours a day of extra contact with their newborns. The extra contact began within three hours of birth and lasted throughout the three days until mother and child left the hospital. Both groups had a glimpse of the newborn at birth, a short visit 6 to 12 hours after the birth, and fed their infants every 4 hours.

The researchers interviewed the mothers and filmed them feeding their infants one month and twelve months after the birth. They found that the extra-cuddling mothers appeared to be more strongly attached to their infants than the control mothers, both one month and one year later. They held their infants closer while feeding them and stayed closer when the infants were being examined by a pediatrician. They also responded more quickly if the infant cried. The extra-cuddling mothers displayed greater concern and interest in their babies than did the mothers in the control group.

Studies like this one raised questions about traditional hospital practices that separated newborns from their mothers after birth. They led to innovative procedures such as allowing the infant to room-in with its mother during the hospital stay. Studies like Klaus and Kennel's imply that early contact and interaction between parent and infant foster the bonding process.

Klaus and Kennel concluded that there is a critical period soon after birth during which parents establish an initial relationship with the newborn. Goldberg (1983) and others criticized the methodology of the Klaus and Kennel study and disagreed with its conclusion. One criticism was that Klaus and Kennel studied poorer, minority women, whereas most studies of bonding have involved middle-class women. Perhaps the bonding process proceeds differently for these two groups.

At the present time, there is no convincing evidence of a critical period in the formation of parent-infant bonds. Parents who are separated from their infants do not appear to have weaker emotional bonds. Adoption studies also remind us that parents can become strongly bonded to children whom they first meet many years after these children's births. The parent-child bonding process apparently can tolerate less-than-perfect conditions of birth or early contact.

"We need to emphasize that we are talking about a *sensitive period* here rather than a critical period. A sensitive period means that conditions for the mother-to-infant attachment are optimal. In other words, the attachment can be formed more easily now than during some other period of development. Although the failure to bond may have permanent effects, those effects are not necessarily irreversible" (Smolak, 1986, p. 56).

Research does suggest that there may be mild short-term effects of early contact. Mothers with early or extra contact report more tender feelings toward their young infants and may breast-feed them for longer periods. It is not likely that these differences will have a noticeable impact on children's development. Mothers who are at risk for becoming abusive or neglecting, however, may benefit from early and extra contact. Society should support the bonding process for these parents in as many ways as possible.

Other Factors That Influence Bonding

The infant's appearance may enhance bonding. Most parents find their newborns physically appealing. The infant's "cute" features include a relatively large head with a protruding forehead and a small face, large dark eyes, chubby cheeks, and a small mouth. These features seem to elicit an almost instinctive attraction (Lorenz, 1943). It is not surprising that we find them duplicated in cartoon stars such as Mickey Mouse, teddy bears, and stuffed animals (E.T., like most aliens, is an exception to the rule).

In addition to infants' appearance, infant behaviors such as smiling, laughing, and cooing also promote bonding. The most potent influence is probably the reciprocal pattern of parent-infant behavior that emerges during the first year of life. Parents and infants enjoy countless opportunities for mutually satisfying interactions. One broad smile with eye contact

Most parents are happy and excited following the long-anticipated birth of a healthy child. Birth, however, brings both positive and negative changes. A significant number of new mothers suffer from a variety of depressive syndromes.

The so-called maternity blues syndrome is the most common alteration in mood following pregnancy. It is reported by a majority of new mothers. Lasting only a couple of days, it is characterized by frequent episodes of tearfulness and crying. Although moodiness may be considered a normal element of postpartum adjustment, it may signal the beginning of severe depression for a few women (Hopkins, Marcus, & Campbell, 1984).

Postpartum psychosis has received considerable attention recently. New mothers suffering from hallucinations and delusions have killed their young infants. Some employ a legal defense based on postpartum mental illness (*New York Times,* October 12, 1988). Fortunately, instances where mothers actually harm their babies are rare.

Mild to moderate postpartum depression is fairly common, affecting up to 20 percent of postpartum mothers. Depressed mothers may report the following symptoms: tearfulness; feeling sad, irritable, and lethargic; a loss of appetite; various sleep disturbances; and lessened sexual interest. They report feeling inadequate in their ability to provide infant care. Such depressive episodes last an average of 6 to 8 weeks. Some women report feeling depressed as much as one year following birth (Hopkins, Marcus, & Campbell, 1984), but positive feelings about the baby gradually increase over the first 16 months postpartum (Fleming, Ruble, Flett, & Van Wagner, 1990).

The causes of postpartum depression are not known. It may be precipitated by the physical discomforts associated with pregnancy, the stress of labor and delivery, the hormonal changes associated with pregnancy and lactation (milk production), or medications that may be administered throughout this period. With pregnancy and birth come the significant life changes that accompany the parenting role. These include financial pressures, possible marital tensions, and a loss of freedom. Women who had been working might feel pressured to return to their jobs. And, of course, caring for a new infant, particularly one with a difficult temperament, is a tremendous challenge. (How many men would become depressed if they gave up as much freedom and took on as many responsibilities as the average new mother?)

The link between infant temperament and depression may be mediated by the woman's feelings of inadequacy as a mother (Cutrona & Troutman, 1986). Women may feel pressured "to do all this childbearing perfectly; have a truly 'natural' birth, breast-feed (with no supplements), get a flat stomach, bond with the baby (without ambivalence) and prove that the baby won't have an adverse impact on her career and marriage" (Henshaw, 1988).

Positive postpartum adjustment is predicted by positive prenatal adjustment, the quality of the marital relationship, positive attitudes about pregnancy, the infant's health and behavior, and the mother's social support system (Cutrona & Troutman, 1986; Hopkins, Marcus, & Campbell, 1984; Stemp, Turner, & Noh, 1986). Women in unhappy marriages who are experiencing other life stresses and who lack social support are at greatest risk.

Unfortunately, not very much is known about the effects of a mother's postpartum depression on a child's development. Children of psychologically disturbed mothers do seem to have more than their share of adjustment problems (Lee & Gotlib, 1989). Postpartum depression in mothers seems to distort the normal patterns of mother-infant interaction (Cohn, Campbell, Matias, & Hopkins, 1990). "As a group, depressed mothers look away from their infants more, are angrier and more intrusive, and display less positive affect than normal mothers" (Tronick, 1989, p. 116). As a result, many of these children may learn maladaptive ways of interacting with other people (Dodge, 1990; Rutter, 1990).

from an infant can compensate for about six hours of parental weariness, fatigue, and frustration.

Observing parents exchanging smiles and vocalizations with their infants convinces us of the mutually reinforcing nature of such encounters. As already noted, parents of children who are difficult to care for may have fewer enjoyable interactions with their children, and the bonding process might suffer. However, parents of premature or sick infants should not fear that their lack of early contact with the infant soon after birth will impair their relationship (Galinsky, 1981). The ongoing, mutually satisfying interactions of parent and child can usually compensate for less-than-optimal conditions soon after birth.

Studies on father-to-infant bonding have produced inconsistent findings. It does not appear that early father-infant contact improves fathering. It seems likely, however, that early father participation in child care improves the mother-father relationship, which, in turn, promotes greater father involvement in child rearing (Palkovitz, 1985). Maternal characteristics—particularly a woman's adjustment to her status as a new mother (see Spotlight: Postpartum Adjustment and Depression)—also influence the course of bonding.

PARENTING INFANTS

Sleep

Study Question How do infants spend their time?

Infants, on the average, spend about 16 hours a day asleep, an additional 2 hours in a drowsy state, and almost 2 hours a day crying. They spend about 2 hours in a state called alert inactivity, which is the optimal time to play or interact with an infant, and about 2 hours a day awake and active (Wolff, 1966). By the time infants are a year old, they are "only" sleeping about 12 hours a day. Sleep time gradually decreases over childhood, stabilizing at about 8 hours by the teenage years.

Newborns do not sleep for 16 hours in a row, but rather divide their sleep into about 7 or 8 shorter naps, about once every 2 hours. By about 7 months of age, to their parents' delight, most infants sleep through the night. One of nature's cruel tricks on parents is that during the preschool years, children are early risers (like 6 A.M.!). As soon as they start school, in some cases, you cannot awaken them with a cannon. Newborns appear to dream about half the time they sleep. By the age of 1 year, like their parents, they spend only about a quarter of their sleep time dreaming.

Between 20 and 30 percent of infants have problems sleeping, and as many as one-third of children between the ages of 1 and 5 years may awaken during the night (Brody, 1986c). In effect, children have to learn how to fall asleep and how to stay asleep when a parent is not present. Infants can be trained to sleep through the night by increasing the time between daytime feedings. By gradually giving the infant fewer meals, it learns to tolerate longer delays between feeding periods. During nighttime feedings, infants can be given diminishing amounts of food. They do not need to eat at night.

Most children (and adults) benefit from a predictable sleep ritual of preparation for bed and quiet presleep activities. Children with bedtime-related fears can be given a sense of mastery over the situation (e.g., a flashlight or an antiburglar alarm). Older children who complain that they cannot fall asleep can be allowed to read or listen to quiet music until they feel drowsy.

Crying

Birth is followed by testing, cleaning, and draining the breathing passages, and, for the first time, states of deprivation and discomfort. These presumably stressful events elicit innate reactions in the infant—most noticeably, crying.

About 6,000 times a year, an apparently healthy infant stops breathing, usually late at night, without warning. The infant is found dead in its crib by its parents. This still mysterious phenomenon used to be called crib death and is now known as Sudden Infant Death Syndrome, or SIDS. SIDS is the most common "cause" of infant death during the first year, not including the first week after birth. SIDS is not really a determinant of death at all, but a diagnosis given when all other suspected causes have been ruled out (Cantor, 1988).

SIDS is most likely to occur between 2 and 4 months following birth, but can occur up to 9 months of age (*Science News,* October 15, 1988). Three quarters of the babies who die have had good prenatal care and have well-to-do parents. Naturally, parents are devastated by the loss and often feel guilty about not having prevented the death. (Coping with the death of a child is discussed in chapter 9.) Until recently, SIDS was considered a breathing

disorder, leading to chronic oxygen deficit. At this writing, scientists speculate that a subtle brain abnormality may cause the disorder (*New York Times,* February 14, 1989).

Infants identified as being at high risk for SIDS have been connected to breathing monitors. These devices, used at home, will sound an alarm if the infant does not breathe for a designated amount of time, alerting parents to the danger. Research has not yet proven the effectiveness of such monitors. The SIDS mortality rate has not improved with the use of these monitors. A New Jersey poll revealed that 15 percent of the parents of such infants believed their infants would have died without them. There are no other preventative steps that parents can take. "Babies with no apparent symptoms have died in their mother's arms while nursing and on doctor's examining tables. Death is apparently instantaneous and painless and cannot be reversed . . ." (Cantor, 1988).

The young infant's cry is an involuntary response to pain or deprivation. It is usually, though not always, a signal that some need is not being met. Infants cry when they are tired or hungry. The primary function of this loud, irritating noise is to elicit caretaking behaviors that will eliminate the source of their distress. Skinner would characterize crying as a negative reinforcer (to the parent) because it motivates caretaking behavior that leads to its removal.

When a young infant cries, a mother (as well as those who are not mothers) approaches and picks up the infant, puts it on her shoulder, talks to and strokes the infant, and rocks it back and forth or moves in a swaying pattern. Thus, initial reactions to crying are nonspecific attempts to comfort the distressed infant. Further responses are more specific and aimed at relieving the source of the infant's distress—for example, checking its diaper or offering a bottle (Gustafson & Harris, 1990).

Those who care for infants claim that they eventually come to distinguish among different types of cries, reflecting different levels of distress. Some parents may overinterpret the different cries when they label them as the hunger cry, the mad cry, the "I want attention" cry, or the sick cry. Parents learn to interpret the causes of infants' crying on the basis of situational cues, such as food or sleep deprivation (Reich, 1986), and behavioral cues, such as eye rubbing ("he's tired") or sucking movements ("she's hungry") (Gustafson & Harris, 1990).

For example, if the infant hasn't eaten for several hours and cries, the parent interprets the behavior as a hunger cry. If the infant has just eaten but hasn't slept for several hours, the distressed reaction is considered a "tired" cry. Others believe that there really are distinctive cries that parents eventually learn to recognize. Thompson analyzed recordings of infant cries for their acoustic properties. He found that

Justin Jaffe

the cries of very young infants resulting from different needs do sound different. When situational cues were eliminated, both experienced and naive adults accurately judged cries for *levels* of anger, fear, and distress (Hostetler, 1988b).

Zeskind (1980) found that as the pitch of the infant's cry increases, so does the urgency of the parent's need to respond. "If a baby is just a little distressed, say by being a bit hungry, he gives a regular, rhythmic, lower-pitched cry. Parents, we find, are not very bothered by that cry. But as the baby gets more distressed, his crying becomes higher pitched, the rhythm becomes faster paced, and the 'wah wah' segments get shorter. Parents get more distressed themselves as this happens" (Zeskind, quoted by Goleman, 1988f).

Frequent or prolonged crying disturbs parents. In their frustration, they may argue with each other about how to handle the situation. Worse, they may direct their anger at the already distressed infant. Since crying occurs reflexively for most of the first year, it makes little sense either to blame the infant or to ignore the crying. Psychologists usually suggest that parents hold and comfort crying infants. Toward the end of the first year, crying comes under voluntary control, and language skills begin to emerge. At this point, parents should respond according to their interpretation of why the infant is crying, sometimes comforting it, sometimes ignoring it (St. James-Roberts, 1989).

Some babies that awaken at night have been trained to "expect" to be held or rocked back to sleep. "The treatment for trained night crying is to let the baby cry. Otherwise, children will demand attention nightly until age 3 or 4" (Brody, 1986c). Parents can respond to the infant's cries about once every 20 minutes, but should only go in for a minute, make a reassuring comment, and then leave. If applied consistently, the crying should cease within a week. The more minimal the parental response, the less payoff for all the infant's efforts to gain attention (Chadez & Nurius, 1987). Ultimately, parents must trust their own judgment in handling their children's crying.

Toilet Training

Toilet training can begin whenever the infant or toddler is ready. Is readiness largely in the eyes of the beholder? Chinese parents believe that infants can be trained at about 12 months. They seem to be successful in their efforts. Western parents believe that children are not ready to be trained until they are between 2 and 3 years of age, so this is when most Western children are toilet trained.

Children who can dress and undress themselves, who can label the parts of their bodies, and who are highly motivated are usually ready (Azrin & Foxx, 1976). Some children are ready before their parents. Some toddlers are prepared to give up their diapers before their parents think they are. In any case, parents who have realistic expectations about their child's abilities, who know how to teach toileting skills, and who are patient will be successful (eventually).

"Children need to experience the natural consequences of poor toileting habits, and parents need to interfere less in what should be a self-managed body function. Most children learn toileting without any intervention, or with minimal intervention, by their parents" (Blechman, 1985, p. 76). Blechman suggests the following steps in toilet training:

1. Let children be responsible for cleaning up after an accident, teaching them the skills they will need to change their clothes, change the sheets, wash them, and so on. Self-reliance is promoted when children are given responsibility for toileting themselves, within their capabilities.
2. Increase the likelihood of bowel movements in the toilet, making the toileting situation as comfortable and private as possible.
3. Reward the child for bowel movements in the toilet, making sure you explain that you are using the rewards to help the child learn this skill. Many forms of positive reinforcement are available: praise, charts, stickers, prizes.
4. Make dry days and nights more likely by using these steps, by purchasing a conditioning device (such as Sears Lite Alarm) if necessary, and by frequently rewarding the child for being dry.

Feeding

Study Question   In what ways is mother's milk superior to formula for an infant?

"The closeness you feel with that baby is unbelievable. But you have to be willing to feed on demand. Some mothers say to me, 'Are you nuts?' It depends upon the type of mother you are. You really have to want to do it, or forget it" (mother who nursed all three of her children).

Healthy mothers with good diets can promote their infant's health through breast-feeding. Only a small minority of women in the United States chose to breast-feed rather than bottle-feed their infants before the 1960s. Today, two-thirds of United States women prefer nursing their children (Martinez & Krieger, 1985).

The advantages to the young child are many (Eiger & Olds, 1986). Breast milk is easier to digest than formula. It is high in good cholesterol, which stimulates metabolism, and in lactose, which stimulates the growth of "good"

The intimacy of breast-feeding may encourage maternal bonding.

bacteria in the child's intestinal tract. Breast-feeding confers to the child the mother's immunologic protection against colds, allergies, and minor infections, at least during the first three months of life. Mother's milk can be fortified with minerals, proteins, and calories for premature infants, increasing their likelihood of surviving (*New York Times*, October 11, 1988).

Infants who are nursed are less likely to be overfed compared to infants who are bottle-fed. However, they are not at lower risk for obesity, as previously believed. They consume fewer calories than bottle-fed infants, but their metabolism is slower. Breast-fed infants have healthier, straighter teeth and are less likely to

have diarrhea than bottle-fed infants (Brody, 1989). The intimate, skin-on-skin contact that occurs during nursing may enhance the mother-child bond. Nevertheless, women who are uncomfortable about nursing should understand that bottle-feeding is a very acceptable substitute.

Breast milk is not perfect. It has very little vitamin D compared to formula. Some mother's milk may be deficient in zinc, a deficiency that may cause skin disorders and delayed growth (Brody, 1989). Bottle-feeding frees mothers to be elsewhere at baby's mealtime and encourages fathers to be involved in caretaking. (Mothers don't have to be present to breast-feed. They can "express" breast milk when they are home and refrigerate it until feeding time.) A small percentage of women cannot nurse for physical reasons. Women who use drugs (including cigarettes and alcohol) should not breast-feed. The infant will ingest substantial amounts of harmful chemicals. Women who choose to breast-feed also must accept bland diets to avoid passing foods that are not easily digestible to their infants.

Jones (1987) surveyed 1,525 mothers regarding their decision to breast- or bottle-feed. Breast-feeding was associated with a woman's age, social class, and parity (number of previous children). Women were strongly influenced by their husbands' preferences. They were also influenced by the feeding method used by their own mothers. The most frequent reasons given for preferring breast-feeding were that it "was better for the baby" and that it was "natural." Bottle-feeding was chosen if breast-feeding was considered inconvenient or embarrassing, or if the woman had previously been unable to nurse. Ultimately, a woman should select the manner of feeding with which she is most comfortable.

THE TRANSITION TO PARENTHOOD

Study Question How does marital satisfaction influence the quality of parenting?

"Even though you think you are ready for a child, you don't realize how drastically your life changes. You don't have time for yourself anymore. I never really had a family to help me out with my babies. My husband and I simply stopped socializing with other couples for many months after the delivery" (mother of three).

In chapter 2, we considered a model that views the family as a complex social system. The organization of a family system changes drastically when a new member is added. The positive and negative life changes that accompany the transition to parenthood will probably affect the marital relationship (Sollie & Miller, 1980). Conversely, marital satisfaction before and during pregnancy are likely to influence how well the couple adjusts to the stresses and strains of child rearing (Snowden, Schott, Awalt, & Gillis-Knox, 1988).

Today's parents are very busy people, yet the infant's needs (and one's partner's needs) must be met. Where will the time come from? How will the new parents, who had sufficient time for each other until now, cope with their changing priorities? Will there be an equitable division of labor between husband and wife? How will the physically exhausted parents find the time and energy to satisfy each other's needs for intimacy and companionship (Sollie & Miller, 1980)?

New parents also ask, Are we good parents? and How can we tell? They realize that their responsibility for this new family member is virtually lifelong. And, as described by the mother quoted at the beginning of this section, they become intensely aware of their loss of freedom. New parents must adjust to the physical demands of caring for a newborn. "Having a baby launches a couple into the responsibilities of continuous coverage for that baby: someone, either the couple themselves or their representative must always be on call . . . It is the loss of free time accompanying parenthood that surprises and bothers new parents more than anything else" (Larossa & Larossa, 1989, p. 139).

Baby-sitters dominate their social lives. Travel is encumbered by diapers, bottles, and changes of clothing. Money is in short supply. These and other stresses test the marital relationship. It is usually the mother who wakes up several times a night to feed the infant. Many modern mothers must cope with four demanding roles: spouse, homemaker, mother, and employee (Belsky, Lerner, & Spanier, 1984). The increased work load and resultant scarcity of free time often produce tension between the new parents. Some fathers still resist an equitable distribution of household labor even if their wives are employed. Yet, they resent the lessening availability of sex and affection provided by their exhausted spouses (Rubenstein, 1989).

"When Adrienne was an infant, it was a chore for my husband to take care of her needs. I don't think he enjoyed giving her a bottle or changing her diaper. As she grew and developed a personality, he enjoyed her alot more. But we never shared the responsibilities. My contributions compared to his were always 80:20 or 90:10" (mother of two). Following the birth, men continue to see themselves as workers and husbands whereas women view themselves primarily as mothers. Unless an acceptable division of chores is arranged, conflict is likely.

Some couples grow together following birth; some grow apart. We do not yet understand why pregnancy and parenthood cement some relationships and destabilize others. Couples who view their relationship as a partnership and who have "easier" babies seem to be happier as parents. Women who reject the traditional division of household labor but who have husbands who do not pull their weight evaluate their marriages more negatively (Belsky, Lang, & Huston, 1986).

The effects of marital transitions on the quality of parenting are also poorly understood. Marital closeness and good communication skills are associated with better parenting, perhaps because the mother's emotional needs are being satisfied (Cox, Owen, Lewis, & Henderson, 1989). Some parents apparently compensate for their unhappy marriages by becoming more involved with their children (Brody, Pillegrini, & Sigel, 1986).

Maritally unhappy men may withdraw from both their wives and children (Dickstein & Parke, 1988).

There is evidence that relationship satisfaction remains stable over the course of pregnancy and into the early child-rearing years (Snowden, Schott, Awalt, & Gillis-Knox, 1988). Satisfying relationships usually remain satisfying after the birth of a child, and poor relationships often deteriorate even further (J. M. Lewis, 1988b). Some investigators observe a decline in marital satisfaction throughout the early child-rearing years. The most unhappy couples divorce (Belsky, Lerner, & Spanier, 1984). Couples in good relationships during the prenatal period are more likely to "show greater investment, sensitivity, and warmth in discussing and interacting with their child than are parents from dysfunctional marriages" (J. M. Lewis, 1988c, p. 419).

Erikson's model of adult development views parenthood as an opportunity for personal growth. New parents do report changes in their personalities following their child's birth (P. A. Cowan, 1988). Whether these changes are positive or negative may depend upon many of the factors we've considered, including the marital relationship and the infant's temperament (Sirignano & Lachman, 1985).

Parenthood brings enormous satisfaction and happiness to most parents. The presence of children usually increases family cohesiveness, that is, a "sense of family." Most parents feel needed and loved by their infants and children. Life is more unpredictable, which is exciting and occasionally intimidating. "It's a wonderful experience. There's nothing like the feeling of that little person who loves you so much and depends on you. It's a full-time job—it's very exhausting. It's much more tiring than work. You're mentally tied up all day long. But it's worth it when she kisses you goodnight and gives you a hug and gives you back that love" (mother of a 3-year-old girl).

SUMMARY

Pregnancy is an exciting time in a couple's life, but there are also new problems that require adjustment. Most, though not all, pregnant women report physical discomforts and psychological stresses. Good information about pregnancy and birth, together with a strong social support system, usually makes pregnancy a more positive experience.

Many couples choose a "prepared" childbirth and receive special training. Parents-to-be can also select a gentle birth delivery. The best predictor of infant mortality is the timing of the birth. The longer the fetus is in the uterus, the better. At least half the instances of premature delivery could be avoided by proper prenatal care.

Parent-infant bonding may be strengthened by approaches to birth that encourage the father's participation, that allow the infant to "room-in" with its mother during her recovery, and that give a mother plenty of early contact with her new infant. However, early contact with the infant is not necessary for normal bonding. The bonding process apparently can proceed normally with less than optimal conditions of birth or early parent-child contact.

Infants have relatively few biological needs and spend most of their days asleep. Sudden Infant Death Syndrome claims about 6,000 young infants each year. Although it is considered a respiratory disorder, its cause is not yet known. Children considered at risk can be attached to monitors that signal the parent when the infant's breathing is disrupted.

Parents who understand both the sleep and crying patterns of their infants can respond more appropriately. Toilet training can begin when both the child and parents are ready. The two most important parental ingredients in toilet training are realistic expectations and patience. The advantages and disadvantages of breast- and bottle-feeding were also discussed. Women should be guided primarily by their own comfort in using either method.

Relationship satisfaction appears to remain fairly stable through pregnancy and the early child-rearing years. Good relationships may become better, and poor relationships may deteriorate. The presence of children usually increases family tensions, but it also increases family cohesiveness and gives parents a new sense of belonging and importance.

CHAPTER FIVE

HOW DO PARENTS PERCEIVE THEIR CHILDREN?

Over time, parents formulate a model of their child's personality. These models are important because they guide parents' interactions with their children. Chances are, if you instruct a parent, "Tell me about your little girl," you will hear something like the preceding description of Carla. Parental models usually do not resemble those described in chapter 2. The models parents develop are much simpler, and they are not impartial. Parents come to know their children, not through systematic study, but through everyday informal observation and interaction.

Most of what parents know and learn about children and child rearing comes from daily contact. G. W. Holden (1988) asked 192 adults—mothers, fathers, and nonparents—to figure out why an infant was crying, based on clues they were given. "Women were more efficient and accurate than men in solving the problem, and nonparents, particularly males, had more difficulty in solving the problem than parents" (p. 1623). It is reassuring that practical experience with infants leads to better problem solving. To a large extent, in solving caretaking problems, parents learn to do what works.

Do parents view their children objectively? Apparently not. A Baptist minister, the Rev. Consuela York, quoted family members of inmates in a Chicago prison: "They'll say, 'He's in there for rape, Mother York, but he's a good boy.' Or 'He killed four or five people, but he didn't mean to' " (*New York Times,* January 30, 1989). Parents have very strong feelings about their children. We would be surprised, and perhaps even disturbed, to meet parents who viewed their child with complete objectivity.

We expect parents to express a positive bias toward their children. (Parents of different children often complain to each other about their children's behavior, but complaining about one's children is more socially acceptable than bragging.) We expect most parents to credit their children for their achievements, to rationalize their failings, and, occasionally, to overestimate their children's abilities (e.g., S. A. Miller, 1986).

The existence of such parental biases is supported by research. Gretarsson and Gelfand (1988) interviewed 60 mothers regarding their perceptions of their children's social behavior. "Mothers will see their children's praiseworthy social behavior as innate, stable, and dispositional, and their negative behavior as temporary and situationally caused" (p. 264). Thus, good behavior is credited to the child, and bad behavior is blamed on the situation. The parent's model of the child's personality can therefore be based mostly on good behavior. The bad behavior can be dismissed as temporary and atypical.

This perceptual bias serves at least two useful functions for parents. First, it reassures them that they are good parents. After all, they have good children. Second, it promotes more harmonious parent-child relationships. Parents of generally well-behaved children can view them as "basically good," even when they misbehave. Gretarsson and Gelfand suggest that this positive bias may reflect parents perceiving their children as dispositionally similar to themselves. Parents make this assumption because "offspring are similar genetically, are reared by the parents, and are viewed by others as extensions of their parents" (p. 267).

Parents of difficult children like Carla see them as dispositionally difficult. Viewing the oppositional child this way "relieves parents of responsibility for the child's condition and for improving it" (p. 268). It protects parental self-esteem. It also justifies spending more time with their better-behaved children. With difficult children, this type of bias may discourage parents from taking corrective actions. They may believe that such attempts are bound to fail.

How parents evaluate their children's behavior is also affected by their judgment of the behavior's desirability (Dix, Ruble, Grusec, & Nixon, 1986). Mothers may attribute children's helpful behavior to good intentions and dispositions. They may attribute misconduct to situational factors (e.g., temptation or peer pressure) or to developmental limitations (e.g., short attention span). As children get older, their parents become more likely to attribute their behavior to personal dispositions and intentions.

Parents are more likely to hold a child responsible for misconduct, and possibly punish, if the parent believes the child understood the violated rule and could have acted more appropriately (Dix, Ruble, & Zambarano, 1989). Parents assume that when their older children misbehave, they understand that what they are doing is wrong (Goodnow, Knight, & Cashmore, 1983). Therefore, the parents become increasingly annoyed by misbehavior ("At your age, you should know better"). If a younger child is perceived as not intending to break a rule or not able to inhibit the misbehavior, parents are less upset and less likely to punish (Dix & Grusec, 1985).

Parents also attribute, often erroneously, particular significance to certain traits or behaviors that they consider important. I have counseled parents who were very worried about toileting problems, thumb sucking, crying, or their child's resistance to going to sleep. More often than not, the behavior perceived as a problem is quite normal for a child of that age.

Sibling conflict, another source of worry to parents, is very common and even healthy. Some parents find any form of family friction unacceptable. If they are unduly worried about it, they might pressure the child (or children) to change. Children usually resist direct attempts to change their behavior, and unnecessary parent-child conflict may arise. In this example, if parents could appreciate how sibling conflict contributes to their children's development, they might be able to inhibit their premature interventions.

Parental models are revised as children grow. Parents look for "predictive signs" of their children's progress. Because they usually lack an objective basis for evaluation, they will compare their children to other children they know. Thus, children may be compared to their siblings or friends. Parents will also assess a child's progress over time (in effect, comparing the child to himself—"He's a lot calmer than he used to be"). I have always looked forward to conferences with my children's teachers. Teachers naturally spend a lot of time observing and interacting with children. I enjoy comparing their opinions about my children to mine. They are usually quite similar.

Why are we so interested in parental perceptions of children? These perceptions guide their reactions to their children. Parents do not view their children objectively, nor do they react to their children objectively. Parenting behavior is usually guided by parents' perceptions of their children, their values, and what they consider to be positive outcomes (Luster, Rhoades, & Haas, 1989). Parental beliefs about sex differences or other child qualities also guide their parenting behaviors (Mills & Rubin, 1990; Stern & Karraker, 1988).

In formulating and revising their models, parents are a little like scientists, "actively observing, framing sometimes far-reaching hypotheses, acting so as to foster some outcomes and thwart others, and continually revising their internal models of their children" (Costanzo & Woody, 1985, pp. 429–430).

Realistic Expectations about Children

Socialization of children has two primary goals: discouraging unacceptable behavior and teaching desirable behaviors, beliefs, and attitudes. If you choose to parent, this is your job.

THE OBNOXIOUS CHILD

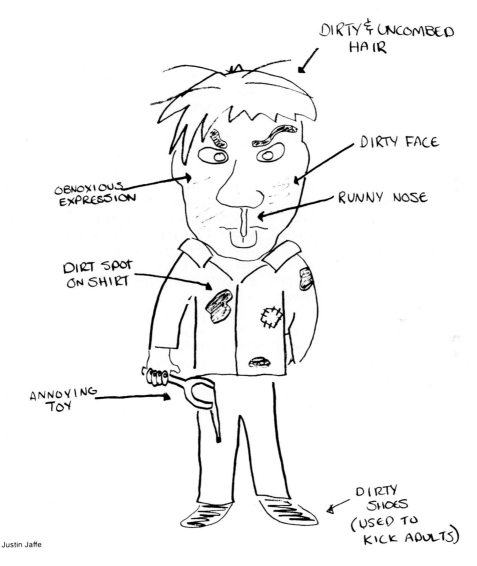

DIRTY & UNCOMBED HAIR

DIRTY FACE

RUNNY NOSE

OBNOXIOUS EXPRESSION

DIRT SPOT ON SHIRT

ANNOYING TOY

DIRTY SHOES (USED TO KICK ADULTS)

Justin Jaffe

The process of socialization requires years of persistent parental effort. This is not always well understood. Parents of young children, in particular, are often impatient when their children misbehave or are oppositional. Parental impatience during discipline encounters is likely to interfere with effective socialization, not enhance it.

That parents have unrealistic expectations about children and child rearing is understandable. Few parents have studied child development, undergone parent training, or had extensive experience with children before they had their own. New parents, for example, may be surprised (and dismayed) when they discover that infants do not sleep through the night until they are about 7 or 8 months old. They may also become frustrated by their inability to comfort a crying or cranky infant. (My "older" children still lose new sweatshirts and forget to give us phone messages.)

Parents also may have unrealistic expectations about the influence they can exert on their children's character. "Before they had children, they have spent time with what they have often regarded as 'obnoxious' children, children who monopolized adult conversations, who were rude, insolent, demanding, who seemed to have a remote-control switch on their parents, monitoring their moves. Before they had children, many parents have built their images of themselves in opposition to this kind of parenting in favor of a humane, respectful, peaceful relationship . . . Now they have the role of parent—they have the child whining at the circus, demanding crackers, cookies, candy, gum at the supermarket, jumping off the curb into the street, interrupting when they are in conversation. And almost by surprise, some hear themselves speak their own parents' words or act the part of the resentful, angry, or complaining parent" (Galinsky, 1981, p. 123).

Galinsky cites several unrealistic expectations that parents may hold. Good parents never get angry at their children. Good parents always feel unconditional love toward their children. We must be better parents than our parents were. My children must always be obedient and nice. My little baby will remain my little baby forever. Each of these unrealistic beliefs can sabotage the parent-child relationship by promoting parental guilt, disappointment, and discouragement.

Perhaps the biggest surprise for new parents is the amount of work required to care for an infant. Feelings of irritation and frustration toward the young infant are common. The combination of interrupted sleep (for the parent) and seemingly endless crying by the infant can produce angry, hostile, and then guilty feelings that make many parents uncomfortable.

At least our children are enormously grateful for all of our parental efforts and sacrifices. Aren't they? Parents who expect gratitude will be lucky to get an occasional hug or scribbled card on mothers' or fathers' day. Fortunately, children comply with most of their parents' requests. However, parents who expect immediate compliance or unquestioning obedience may, through their unrealistic expectations or demands, expose their children (and themselves) to considerable stress.

Some parents expect perfection. Children who learn that they can never satisfy their parents become discouraged and eventually stop trying. Overprotective parents, in treating their children as incompetent, may weaken their self-esteem and sense of autonomy. They may discourage accomplishment and encourage a lack of responsibility (Zimbardo & Radl, 1981). Finally, as Piaget taught, having realistic expectations about children requires our remembering that they do not perceive the world as we do. Good parenting requires that we accommodate our children's needs as well as our own (Bettelheim, 1987).

Realistic Expectations about Ourselves

Guilt is not an uncommon parental emotion. Parents may feel guilty because their children are poorly behaved, or because they feel inadequate about how they handle misbehavior. Raising children is an enormous undertaking. Child-rearing problems are inevitable. "If you feel that you constantly have to be the perfect parent and love your child totally, it complicates your job as a parent. If there's one thing we know about parenting, it's a humbling experience. There are no perfect parents, only real parents" (Yogman, quoted by Kutner, 1988v).

Enjoying child rearing requires not only a good grasp of the nature of children, but also an accurate assessment of our own strengths and weaknesses. Parents are human. We have emotions, we make mistakes, and we have been known to be unreasonable. My favorite parental contradiction is the oft-shouted, "STOP YELLING!!!" Acknowledging our limitations makes us less susceptible to guilt. It also demonstrates to our children that they do not have to be perfect either.

ROOTS OF PARENT-CHILD CONFLICT

Study Question   What is usually the source of parent-child conflict?

What do children want? Children are strongly motivated by what Freud called the pleasure principle, the immediate gratification obtained when their senses are stimulated or their desires are satisfied. Pleasure is a powerful (though invisible) reinforcer. What parents consider misbehavior usually produces gratification for children. They call it "fun." Children are not usually intentionally bad. They are disposed to do whatever produces positive (or avoids negative) outcomes.

Table 5.1 States Make Parents Responsible

Several states have passed laws that hold parents legally responsible for their kids' misbehavior; others have similar laws pending.
  Among laws now in place—
▸ *Arkansas:* Parents can be fined when their children skip school.
▸ *California:* Parents can be fined or jailed for allowing their children to participate in gangs.
▸ *Florida:* Parents can be jailed if they leave a gun accessible and their child hurts someone with it.
▸ *Hawaii, Wisconsin:* Parents can be forced to pay child support when their child has a baby.
▸ *Lucas County, Ohio:* The juvenile court will fine or jail parents for encouraging drug use or when their children skip school.
▸ *29 states and the District of Columbia (plus many local jurisdictions):* A federal waiver permits public housing projects to evict any family in which one child is found to be using or selling drugs.

From *NEA Today,* December 1989, National Education Association. Reprinted by permission.

Parental behavior is usually guided not by gratification but by responsibility for the child's welfare. Society holds parents responsible for their children's health, safety, socialization, and general development (see table 5.1). Responsibility begins with pregnancy, when a woman is sharing her body with the developing fetus. In fact, maternal responsibility begins well before pregnancy, when a female acts in ways to promote the health of her reproductive system.

Legal responsibility is assigned to parents until their child is 18 years old. Society, therefore, gives us about 18 years to attain our parenting goals. We have 18 years to raise children who will be responsible, honest, sensitive, productive, and loving. Personally, I feel I will need every minute.

Parents hold their children accountable for their actions after the first year. Parents begin setting limits on their infant's behavior. And children will test these limits, from simple refusal to bold defiance. We have noted the importance of having realistic expectations about children. We should not be surprised when children hit, lie, take what is not theirs, plead for a cookie, beg to stay up until the TV program is over, or seek gratification in other ways. These behaviors are quite common in young children. It is not the behavior but the parental response to it that determines the course of development.

Understanding Noncompliance

Effective parenting requires a multilevel perspective on parent-child interactions. Defiant behavior is best understood in the context of biological factors (such as the infant's temperament), the personal and marital resources of the parents, and the style of discipline adopted by each parent. Difficult children who have coercive parents in an unhappy marriage are at highest risk for behavior problems (Dadds, 1987).

Discipline encounters are best guided by long-term perspectives. These include the child's legitimate striving for autonomy, our ongoing relationship with the child (parenting goal #3) and the child's self-esteem (parenting goal #4). For these reasons, our attention is directed to the interactive nature of the child's resistance style and the parent's discipline style (Schaffer & Crook, 1980).

When we make a request or give an instruction to a child, we desire compliance. Most of the time, children do comply. As children develop, the consequences of their actions and parental standards of conduct temper the power of immediate gratification. Freud used the terms ego and superego to represent these two processes. Behaviorists cite reinforcement and observational learning.

"Parents who understand the subtext of a toddler's defiance do not take her negative behavior personally. They realize it is not a rejection of their love or authority. It is simply a way the child prepares herself for independence . . . the child is developing an awareness of herself as an individual. She is also trying to figure out the difference between what she can do and what she should do" (Kutner, 1988t).

How do children test parental authority? Kuczynski, Kochanska, Radke-Yarrow, and Girnius-Brown (1987) describe four distinct forms of children's resistance or noncompliance. Each elicits a different parental reaction. (1) *Passive noncompliance,* ignoring a parental request, decreases between the ages of 2 to 3 years. It usually elicits another (often louder) parental request. (2) *Direct defiance* by children, often expressed angrily, also decreases with age. It usually elicits coercion and punitive responding from parents. (3) *Simple refusal* does not vary with age and is less aversive to parents than is direct defiance. (4) *Negotiation, bargaining, and persuasion* comprise the fourth type of resistance. This is the most advanced form of resistance. It increases with age and is the least objectionable to parents. Parents may interpret these attempts as a display of autonomy and assertion, which many parents value.

Mothers tend to increase their use of verbal-persuasive control strategies—commands, explanations, bargaining, reprimands, suggesting alternatives—as children mature and such parental strategies become more effective. Parents gradually abandon physical strategies—touching, distraction, or physically guiding desirable behavior—as children become more skillful in resisting (Kuczynski et al., 1987).

As a child's style of resistance changes, so does parental control. Both parties usually prefer persuasive strategies over power struggles. Parents also lessen control as their children display more autonomy. Parents influence their children's interactive styles by negotiating with them. Both parental modeling and reinforcement of negotiation strategies encourage this process (Kuczynski et al., 1987).

Analysis of Misbehavior

The functional analysis model of "explaining" behavior was described in chapter 2. Instead of asking why a particular behavior occurs, behavioral psychologists prefer to ask, "Under what conditions does the behavior occur?" This question stresses the situational context of the behavior, which is observable, rather than the child's history, inner feelings, or intentions, which are not observable.

Some parents and psychologists, when considering why a particular behavior occurs, are drawn to historical analyses. When I am working with parents who are upset about a particular behavior pattern, I will surely ask them at some point to describe its first occurrence. A historical assessment may indeed improve one's understanding of a behavior's origins. However, parents' perception, memory, and interpretation of events are fallible. We can almost never know with certainty how or why a particular behavior pattern arose.

Children basically do what they have learned to do. They generally learn to do what pleases them. Terms like "pleasure" and "gratification" refer to subjective states that are not accessible to observation. Therefore, behavioral psychologists depend upon the *law of effect* or *reinforcement principle* to characterize lawful relations between the situation, the child's behavior, and observable consequences.

If children learn, for example, that they can provoke us by saying a "bad" word or talking freshly, then our angry reaction itself (verbal and nonverbal) may reinforce the child's utterance. Why would a child *want* to provoke us? Why would they find our display of anger reinforcing? It seems to be the nature of human interaction that when we feel hurt by someone, we return the suffering "in kind." The basic, unverbalized philosophy is something like, "If you hurt me, I'll hurt you back." Because parents know they are physically more powerful than their children, they might assume a pose of "I can hurt you more than you can hurt me." Even if true, this attitude is likely to engender resentment and further provoke the child.

When we either provide an aversive stimulus to a child (e.g., criticism) or remove a positive reinforcer (e.g., take away TV for the day), the child, in his frustrated state, may become disposed to retaliate. He may use any provocative tactic that "worked" in the past. Parents inadvertently teach their children the best ways of "hurting them back" through the intensity of their reactions to their children's provocations. Escalating power struggles often follow. Once a child has developed a repertoire of defiant or oppositional behaviors, it is that much more difficult to teach prosocial behaviors (Dadds, 1987).

Although children's behavior problems are often attributed to such negative parental behaviors as punishment, coercion, criticism, and inconsistent discipline, it is plausible that the absence of positive parenting may also be a contributing factor. Positive parenting strategies include guiding and monitoring children's behavior, expressing affection, and modeling appropriate behavior. Pettit and Bates (1989) observed family interaction patterns of 29 4-year-olds and their mothers and concluded that positive maternal behaviors predicted fewer behavior problems in the children. Negative parental behaviors, such as coercion, also predicted behavior problems in these children, but not as strongly as the absence of positive parenting strategies.

Western visitors to China and Japan are often impressed by the good behavior of Oriental infants and children. They wonder whether the differences they observe between Oriental and Western children reflect innate dispositions or different rearing practices (Kessen, 1975).

One observer (Butterfield, 1981) reported that Chinese children are "quiet, obedient, quick to follow their teacher's instructions, and they seldom exhibit the boisterous aggressiveness or selfishness of American children . . . The Chinese children do not cry, whine, throw tantrums or suck their thumbs." To those of us who are intimately familiar with children in the United States, this description strains our credibility. How do Oriental parents and teachers manage (if their socialization practices are responsible) to achieve these results? And, is there a trade-off between Oriental children's good behavior and other personal attributes that people in the United States value?

Butterfield cites several differences in how Oriental and Western parents and teachers approach caretaking. Chinese parents strive to promote intense closeness between themselves and their children. They swaddle their infants, binding their legs tightly in cloth. Chinese infants sleep in the same bed with their parents or grandparents.

"Part of the explanation for Chinese children's good behavior, some American psychologists who have visited China feel, is that Chinese parents and the teachers in nurseries and kindergartens tend to be warm, kind and attentive. During a day in the factory nursery school, this correspondent did not witness a single incident of physical punishment or harsh verbal rebuke by a teacher" (Butterfield, 1981). The school's director insisted that they never spank a naughty child. Rather, they use persuasion to correct misbehavior. If one child pushes another down, he is asked to help the child up and then apologize.

Some Chinese parents expressed concern that the regimentation their children face in nursery school and kindergarten makes them too placid and uncreative. "For the Chinese, the first twelve years of life are not a time to raise questions about autonomy, fairness, or the right of choice. They concentrate on learning, playing, and living, and think it strange that anyone should ask them whether they are happy or bored. Life is straightforward and plain. There are simple rules to obey, but compliance does not mean that they are obedient. It is the way things are, and they are only children" (Chin, 1988).

Japanese children are raised similarly. They sleep, as infants, at their mothers' breasts, and are carried during the day on their mothers' backs. "American mothers stimulate their infants and encourage them to be active. Most infant vocalizations are greeted with further encouragement. Japanese mothers tend to pacify and soothe their children" (Dworetzsky, 1984, p. 494). Japanese children are strongly encouraged to develop a dependency on their families and eventually on their peers, teachers, and employers.

Oriental children develop a much stronger group orientation than Western children. Children in the United States learn to value autonomy more than Oriental children. They value group participation, but not as much as they value individual achievement. There appear to be substantial differences in rearing practices between Western and Oriental children. We also observe different values and behaviors in the two cultures. The relationship between rearing and behavior remains unclear.

Children's Conceptions of Adult Authority

Study Question In what ways must parents adjust their discipline styles as their children mature?

Younger children usually accept the legitimacy of parental authority without question, partially because they lack the cognitive abilities to challenge it. When young children say "No—I don't want to," they are not challenging the *legitimacy* of the parent's authority. Rather, their noncompliance reflects their unwillingness to delay gratification. The noncompliant child is not saying, "You have no right to tell me what to do." Rather, he is saying, "I don't want to do it now (or ever)."

Older children and adolescents who ask, indignantly, "Why should I?" may indeed be challenging power-based authority as practiced by most parents. This is often seen, for example, in stepfamilies when an adolescent declares to a stepparent, "I don't have to listen to you. You're not my real father." We will see shortly how parents adjust their discipline styles as children mature and assert their autonomy.

Infants and toddlers, however, are guided largely by gratification. Many parental requests or demands delay or prevent pleasurable outcomes. A good example of this is the parental request that a child prepare for bed. Typically, the child is playing or watching TV. The request interferes with his immediate enjoyment. In addition, it requires effort (washing, brushing, undressing) toward an unwanted outcome (sleep). The resistance we encounter in this situation is predictable and understandable. Asking "Do I have to do it now," saying "I don't want to," or simply ignoring the parental request are common reactions.

Adults set limits, which children test. Parents establish rules, which children occasionally violate. In effect, children are testing the parents' willingness to enforce standards of behavior. This is normal. Even adults occasionally challenge society's ability to enforce its rules (called laws). For example, do all drivers come to a full stop at a stop sign when no officer is in sight? When parental authority is challenged by a child, there is no one correct way of responding. Parents should encourage compliance with the least "controlling" means available. (Specific discipline methods that support our parenting goals are described in the next chapter.)

As children develop, we notice changes in how they view their obligations to obey requests and commands, to report violations of rules, or to make their own decisions about their conduct. These changes reflect changes in how they interpret their own behavior and its possible consequences.

Tisak (1986) interviewed 120 children from ages 6 to 10 years to assess their perceptions of the boundaries of adult authority. She found that children feel justified in reporting a rule violation by another child if someone is harmed. This would not be considered "tattling." Children felt their parents have the right to establish rules that prohibit stealing and that require them to report observed violations. Children also reported feeling obligated to obey such rules, though less so for rules whose violation would not harm others. This would include rules involving household chores and choice of friendship. Reporting other children's rule violations for these less serious acts would be considered "tattling."

Thus, children set boundaries on adult authority that are related to the content of the violation. The children's rationales were based on their perception of how the rule violations affect the welfare of others. Older children granted themselves, not their parents, the right to make choices about actions that primarily affect themselves, such as their choice of friends. If the violation was not serious, children also preferred to remind the violator about the consequences of his actions, rather than report it to an adult.

Children are usually encouraged to obey authority. It is not always clear to children what constitutes a legitimate authority. Laupa and Turiel (1986) found that children consider the age and social position of the person as well as the type of instruction given. Children gave priority to adult authority over peer authority and gave priority to peer authority over adult nonauthority. In the "old days," parents may have felt comfortable urging their children to respect and obey all "grown-ups." Today, cautious parents teach their children how to say no to certain unacceptable behaviors in others regardless of their age.

Adolescents' Conceptions of Parental Authority

Study Question   How do adolescents view parental authority differently from younger children?

One of the major sources of conflict between parents and adolescents involves the degree of control parents retain over their children's activities. Parents usually grant greater autonomy as their children mature, but younger adolescents in particular report dissatisfaction with parental control in certain domains. "Adolescents appear to view an increasing range of issues that were once viewed as legitimately subject to parental control as now under personal jurisdiction" (Smetana, 1988, p. 321). Such issues include their eating habits, the movies or TV shows they watch, social activities they wish to attend, how they dress, and their choice of friends.

Smetana (1988) studied how adolescents and their parents view the domains of parental authority. She interviewed 102 adolescents, ranging in age from 10 to 18 years, and their parents. She found that parents of preadolescents and young adolescents view all events in their children's lives as being under their jurisdiction. As their children matured, however, parents became more willing to lessen their control regarding *personal* issues, but not over *moral* issues (entailing fairness, the child's welfare, and obligations) or *conventional* issues (including social coordination and responsibility).

Children and adolescents agreed that parents should maintain jurisdiction over moral and conventional issues throughout adolescence. However, adolescents often differed from parents in whether they viewed an issue as personal or conventional. Smetana also found that whereas mothers were more likely to reason about justice (or fairness) than fathers, fathers were more likely to reason about responsibility. Who do you think adolescents will be more likely to approach for such negotiations, mothers or fathers? And why?

INTERNALIZATION OF PARENTAL STANDARDS

Over the course of development, children's behavior becomes increasingly guided by their own internal standards rather than by parental command (C. C. Lewis, 1981). Baumrind and others have argued that internalization of parental values is supported by firm parental control. Attribution theory (Lepper, 1981), on the other hand, implies that the acceptance of parental standards is best served by minimizing external pressure.

"The least pressure that is sufficient to obtain a child's compliance will promote the greatest internalization of values by the child" (C. C. Lewis, 1981, p. 548). In other words, the least conspicuous ways of gaining compliance foster the greatest acceptance of parental values. "The child who obeys under only mild adult pressure cannot as easily attribute his or her own compliance to external pressure and must draw another conclusion, such as the following: 'I am obeying, so I must be the kind of kid who obeys rules' or 'I am obeying, so it must be because I believe in this rule'" (C. C. Lewis, 1981, p. 548). The key point is that giving children the sense that they are choosing to behave well, rather than being forced to behave well, increases their acceptance of parental standards.

NO SIMPLE FORMULA FOR HANDLING DISCIPLINE ENCOUNTERS

I usually begin my parenting workshops by taking questions. The most frequent questions are of the "How do I deal with . . . " variety. Parents ask about crying, bedtime, feeding, dressing, sibling conflicts, school-related problems, bed-wetting, and shyness. Such questions imply that there are formulas for dealing effectively with childhood problems. "All you have to do when she wets her bed is. . . . " Such miracle cures are presumably independent of the particular child's history, family circumstances, situational factors, and so on.

Although there are predictable patterns in each of these situations, there is no simple, guaranteed formulation that applies to all children in all situations. "In parenthood, there are no such systems, no easy step one, step two plan to follow. Not only that, the child will probably test any strictures to see how steadfast they are, if they'll sway. The child wants and needs to know what the real ground rules are and how his or her parents react to pressure" (Galinsky, 1981, p. 120).

Children are so different from each other. A discipline encounter must be tailored to the particular child and to the specific circumstances. Thoughtful parents, when motivating children, take into account their children's characteristics. For example, children who are competitive will dress quickly when we are having a fast-dressing contest. Children who are picky about food might be more willing to try something they have helped to prepare themselves.

Parents should also adopt a parenting style with which they and their partners are comfortable. Parents may differ from their partners in their philosophies of child rearing, their patience, their perceptions of their child, and their resourcefulness. An effective, mutually supportive style of discipline evolves gradually, as parents increase their understanding of their child and child rearing (See Spotlight: A Team Approach to Parental Discipline).

Reciprocal Effects or How Parents and Children Raise Each Other

Parents have the opportunity to exercise considerable influence over their children, but they do not remain unaffected by the daily flow of parent-child interactions (Belsky, 1981). The reciprocal nature of influence in parent-child relationships is now well documented (Bell & Harper, 1977; Lewis & Rosenblum, 1974). Family systems theory, discussed in chapter 2, stresses the reciprocal nature of family influences.

We have also seen in chapter 4 how infant behavior influences the course of parental bonding. Further, infants provide cues (e.g., crying), about their momentary needs, and they reinforce successful parental interventions (e.g., by smiling). They initiate and respond to social encounters. Infants may exert greater influence on their caretakers than the other way around (Bell, 1968; 1979; Mohar, 1988).

"The capacity of infants to control our lives can be very unsettling. Who else can get adults to change their entire pattern of activity and sleep?" (Silberman & Wheelan, 1980, p. 116). Even parents' personalities may change as a

SPOTLIGHT: A Team Approach to Parental Discipline

It is desirable for parents to be in agreement when children are being disciplined. Parental agreement appears to be related to healthy family functioning (Deal, Halverson, & Wampler, 1989). Yet, one of the most frequent sources of marital conflict is disagreement about how and when to discipline.

It is all too common, in the heat of battle, for frustrated parents to lash out at each other's floundering attempts to improve a deteriorating situation. "A lack of agreement about child rearing may indicate a more general lack of communication between parents" (Deal, Halverson, & Wampler, 1989).

Couples who are dissatisfied with their marriages have more marital conflict, which spills into parent-child relationships. Marital friction is associated with inconsistent parental discipline, at least between fathers and daughters (Stoneman, Brody & Burke, 1989). Fathers who are dissatisfied with their marriages are more punitive when disciplining their children.

Parents may disagree with each other about how to manage a discipline encounter for several reasons. They may have different standards of behavior. Typically, one parent is more lenient than the other. Parents differ about what they believe constitutes normal development or effective discipline. They may interpret the situation differently (Blechman, 1985). Ironically, children suffer the most when parents argue with each other about discipline, particularly in their presence. Children of divorce are particularly likely to test their parents' ability to impose consistent guidelines.

Children benefit when their parents support each other's discipline interventions (Vaughn, Block, & Block, 1988). A "team approach" to discipline is less confusing to children who would otherwise have to learn two different sets of standards to satisfy both parents. A team approach also discourages children from using a "divide and conquer" strategy for getting what they want by playing one parent against the other. Some children learn to get what they want by approaching the more lenient parent first. Or, if one parent refuses a request they approach the other parent for satisfaction. These tactics undermine parental authority and could instigate marital conflict.

In marriage counseling, I sometimes hear spouses complain, "She always makes me the bad guy" or "He's worse than the kids." Learning to use parental conflict to their advantage is not healthy for children's adjustment. Nor do they benefit when their mothers avoid parental responsibility by adopting the "Wait till your father comes home" strategy. This threat encourages children to fear their father's arrival, as well as suggesting that women cannot take charge in difficult situations.

Most discipline situations are predictable. Parents who relate well to each other should be able to discuss alternatives and then agree upon an acceptable strategy for handling specific discipline problems. It helps if they work on one problem or issue at a time. Importantly, they should take seriously each other's point of view. If they disagree, they should do so privately.

Ideally, parents will negotiate a tentative strategy, try it out, and then evaluate its success at a later time. With older children, parents can develop strategies for handling conflict during regularly scheduled family meetings. At such times, the child's point of view should be solicited and respected (Silberman & Wheelan, 1980).

function of children's temperaments and child-rearing experiences (Mulhern & Passman, 1981; Patterson, 1982).

One of the most important themes of discipline is that parents be *responsive* rather than *reactive* to their children's behavior. Anticipating and avoiding opportunities for misbehavior has been shown to be a more effective discipline strategy than reacting to misbehavior (Holden & West, 1989).

When parents are reactive, difficult children will bring out the worst in them. Anderson, Lytton, and Romney (1986) had mothers of either normal or conduct-disordered boys (boys who are defiant and aggressive) supervise both types of children on a simple computational task. Whether they were working with their own sons or not, mothers were more demanding and coercive when they worked with the difficult boys than when they worked with the normal boys. The conduct-disordered boys, through their noncompliance and lack of cooperation, provoked punitive responses from every mother with whom they interacted.

This study helps us see how parents accommodate their style of discipline to the child's behavior and temperament. It is possible that punitive parenting makes difficult children more difficult. The present study demonstrates that difficult children elicit punitive, coercive parenting. It is important that we recognize how these two processes may generate an escalating cycle of coercive parenting and defiant reactions in children.

Children quickly learn to identify their parent's vulnerabilities and exploit them when possible. "In the course of their interaction, children, randomly at first, hit upon something sooner or later that is their mother's and/or father's Achilles' heel, a kind of behavior that especially upsets, offends, irritates, or embarrasses them. One parent dislikes name-calling, another teasing, another food eaten sloppily, or smeared on the face, another bathroom jokes" (Galinsky, 1981, p. 122). Parents who are easily provoked by such actions give their children enormous manipulative power over them, a serious error.

The ultimate feedback parents receive regarding the effectiveness of their style of discipline is the child's behavior. The child's responses to discipline encounters gradually modify the parent's discipline style (Mulhern & Passman, 1981). A feedback loop emerges that, under optimal conditions, encourages flexible and experimental parenting strategies. Competent parents continually adjust their strategies according to their effectiveness. The child is teaching the parent how to teach the child. (At the same time, the parent may be teaching the child how to parent!) Parents, not children, will ultimately decide whether the discipline cycle that develops is coercive or flexible.

Competing Influences

Parental influence does not occur in a vacuum. Parents compete in teaching values, attitudes, and behaviors with baby-sitters, siblings, teachers, neighbors, peers, TV, movies, and popular music. Parents have the advantage of greater contact during the child's formulative years. Nevertheless, some parents will still be more influential than others. The primary factors determining how much constructive influence parents have are the quality of the parent-child relationship (see chapter 7) and parental style of discipline. A strong parent-child relationship also lessens the impact of negative peer influences and chance encounters.

Children's behavior reflects peer and other influences but the parent-child relationship is potentially the most significant.

Dimensions of Discipline

Do parents differ in how they raise their children? Can we identify different parenting styles? If we can, is parenting style related to children's behavior and personality? To answer these questions, researchers interview parents and observe their interactions with their children. A number of presumably independent dimensions of discipline style have been proposed and investigated. Examples of such dimensions are

1. Acceptance-rejection or warmth-hostility (Becker, 1964; Maccoby, 1980)
2. Restrictive-permissive or parental control (Sears, Maccoby, & Levin, 1957)

3. Competence-incompetence (B. L. White, 1971)
4. High involvement-low involvement (Maccoby & Martin, 1983)

Erikson (1963), in his psychosocial theory, emphasized two of these dimensions, parental warmth and parental control. Parental warmth is usually defined as the expression of affection and approval toward one's children. Maccoby (1980) defines warmth as the parent's commitment to children's welfare, and sensitivity and responsivity to their needs. Warmth is also expressed as willingness to spend time with children and showing enthusiasm for their accomplishments.

Hostile or rejecting parents are generally punitive, using coercion rather than approval to motivate compliance. They are likely to ridicule or criticize misbehavior. Fortunately, the vast majority of parents are generally affectionate rather than hostile. Nevertheless, most parents are occasionally hostile. Few parents are either always warm or always hostile.

Let's consider the restrictive-permissive continuum. Parents are considered restrictive if they discourage independence, establish firm and narrow rules, and punish children vigorously. Restrictive parents are generally demanding and impose strict limits on their children's autonomy. Most parents become less restrictive as their children mature. Permissive parents make few demands on their children and are lax in stating or enforcing rules. They encourage their children to express their opinions and to make their own decisions (Sears et al., 1957).

After distinguishing parental discipline styles, researchers assess children's behavior and personality. Global personality measures are obtained such as assertiveness, aggressiveness, hostility, achievement, self-esteem, and dependency. These measures are based on parental interviews and observation of children in varied settings.

Do different parenting styles predict different personality characteristics in children? Research confirms that parental warmth is associated with secure attachment, good behavior, academic achievement, and positive self-esteem (Coopersmith, 1967; Estrada, Arsenio, Hess, & Holloway, 1987). Parental rejection during childhood predicts depression during adolescence (Lefkowitz & Tesiny, 1984). Is warmth by itself enough to promote optimal development? It's not likely. Permissive parents are warm, but as we will see, their children may be less competent socially and cognitively.

Weisz (1980) analyzed 244 letters that children submitted to a newspaper contest entitled, "Why Mom Is The Greatest." Note that only children who like their mothers would respond to such a contest. Weisz concluded that children evaluate their parents largely on the basis of warmth and affection. Children and adolescents both viewed parental control as a sign of caring. Children of excessively permissive parents might feel uncared for.

BAUMRIND'S MODEL OF DISCIPLINE STYLES

Diana Baumrind (1966; 1967; 1968; 1971; 1975) distinguishes three styles of parental discipline. She contends that each parenting style predicts distinctive behavioral patterns in children. The three styles are labeled authoritative (also known as democratic), permissive, and authoritarian (also known as punitive). See table 5.2.

Authoritative parents are warm, but firm. They use reason and persuasion to gain compliance. They explain rules and encourage verbal give-and-take with their children. They are flexible in setting limits and are responsive to their children's needs. They encourage independent thinking in their children and are accepting of opposing points of view. They are not permissive; when reason does not prevail, they are willing to use power to gain compliance.

Permissive parents are also accepting and nonpunitive. They consult with their children, explain family rules, encourage autonomy, and use reasoning. They differ from authoritative parents primarily in their avoidance of supervision and control. They either do not establish standards of conduct or set standards that are below what their children could meet. They may indulge or ignore their children's needs.

Table 5.2 Parenting Styles and Children's Behavior

Parental Type	Children's Behavior
Permissive-indulgent parent	*Impulsive-aggressive children*
Rules not enforced	Resistive, noncompliant to adults
Rules not clearly communicated	Low in self-reliance
Yields to coercion, whining, nagging, crying by the child	Low in achievement orientation
Inconsistent discipline	Lacking in self-control
Few demands or expectations for mature, independent behavior	Aggressive
Ignores or accepts bad behavior	Quick to anger but fast to recover cheerful mood
Hides impatience, anger, and annoyance	Impulsive
Moderate warmth	Aimless, low in goal-directed activities
Glorification of importance of free expression of impulses and desires	Domineering
Authoritarian parent	*Conflicted-irritable children*
Rigid enforcement of rules	Fearful, apprehensive
Confronts and punishes bad behavior	Moody, unhappy
Shows anger and displeasure	Easily annoyed
Rules not clearly explained	Passively hostile and guileful
View of child as dominated by uncontrolled antisocial impulses	Vulnerable to stress
Child's desires and opinions not considered or solicited	Alternates between aggressive unfriendly behavior and sulky withdrawal
Persistent in enforcement of rules in the face of opposition and coercion	Aimless
Harsh, punitive discipline	
Low in warmth and positive involvement	
No cultural events or mutual activities planned	
No educational demands or standards	
Authoritative parent	*Energetic-friendly children*
Firm enforcement of rules	Self-reliant
Does not yield to child coercion	Self-controlled
Confronts disobedient child	High-energy level
Shows displeasure and annoyance in response to child's bad behavior	Cheerful
Shows pleasure and support of child's constructive behavior	Friendly relations with peers
Rules clearly communicated	Copes well with stress
Considers child's wishes and solicits child's opinions	Interest and curiosity in novel situations
Alternatives offered	Cooperative with adults
Warm, involved, responsive	Tractable
Expects mature, independent behavior appropriate for the child's age	Purposive
Cultural events and joint activities planned	Achievement-oriented
Educational standards set and enforced	

From Baumrind, 1967, pp. 43–88.

THE FAR SIDE

By GARY LARSON

"You want me to stop the car, Larry, or do you want to take your brother off the rack this instant?"

Authoritarian, or punitive, parents value obedience above all. They limit their children's freedom by imposing many rules, which they strictly enforce. They favor punitive, forceful measures and mainly use power to gain compliance. They value preservation of order and tradition and are uncompromising. They do not encourage verbal give-and-take with their children.

Baumrind concluded that observed differences in children's self-reliance, self-control, achievement, mood, and aggressiveness are predicted by these parenting styles. Authoritative parents, combining warmth with firmness, have children who are the most self-reliant, self-controlled, socially responsible, achievement-oriented (particularly girls), friendly (particularly boys), and happy.

Permissive parents, avoiding control, have children (particularly sons) who are rebellious and the least self-reliant and self-controlled. Their children are also the least independent and are the least achieving of the three groups. Authoritarian (punitive) parents, who are the most restrictive, have children (particularly sons) who are the most unhappy, unfriendly, fearful, and moody (Baumrind, 1968). Baumrind has observed that children's characteristics associated with parenting style tend to persist throughout childhood into adolescence.

Based on these observations, Baumrind endorses the authoritative or democratic style of parenting. Notice that both authoritative and authoritarian parents are more controlling than permissive parents. They differ, however, in how they control. Authoritative parents are firm, but they prefer to control through discussion, reason, and persuasion. Authoritarian parents are strict and punitive. They demand obedience and discourage verbal expression from their children.

Maccoby and Martin (1983) have studied the "uninvolved" parent. Such parents expend minimal effort toward the care and socialization of their children. They have little interest in their children's development. They may satisfy the basic needs of the child for food and shelter, but they are emotionally distant. They neglect their children's social and emotional needs. (The topic of child neglect is covered in chapter 14.) As we would expect, children of such parents show social, cognitive, and emotional impairments, even by the age of 2 years (Egeland & Sroufe, 1981).

Because these studies are correlational in nature, we cannot infer causality between parenting style and child characteristics. That is, we can conclude that parenting style *is related to* patterns of children's behavior, but we can't *attribute* children's behavior patterns to the specific parenting style. As previously noted, parenting style might reflect the child's behavior and temperament. The reciprocal influences between parent and child make it difficult to distinguish cause from effect.

Parents who practice different rearing strategies probably differ in other ways that could affect their children. Parents from lower socioeconomic classes, for example, value different traits and have more punitive and restrictive parenting styles than middle-class parents (Maccoby, 1980). They probably also differ in their level of education, marital satisfaction, and life stress. It might be these moderator variables that are influencing children's personalities and behavior rather than (or in addition to) parenting style.

C. C. Lewis (1981) has argued that the authoritative parenting style is a reaction to a child's personality rather than a cause of it. Baumrind disagrees. She contends that authoritative parents model caring and assertiveness, which their children eventually imitate. Such parents are more adept at reinforcing prosocial and competent behaviors in their children than punitive or permissive parents. Their children perceive them as fair and understanding and therefore internalize their values. Further research is needed to shed light on the direction of causality between parenting style and children's personalities.

DOMAIN-SPECIFIC PARENTING STYLES REVISITED

To be useful, any general depiction of a parenting style must be translatable into specific parental actions that relate to the situation at hand. According to the domain-specific model of parenting, characterizing parenting styles broadly belies the complexities of specific, daily, parent-child interactions.

Parents may be "warm" at bedtime but "restrictive" if the child requests another hour of TV time. Parents may be fair on Tuesday, when they agree to buy the sneakers they promised, and unreasonable on Wednesday, when they are too tired to go to the mall. Parents may be involved on Saturday afternoon, coaching the soccer game, but away on Sunday, missing the school picnic. Parenting style usually reflects the specific situation, or domain, at hand. When we characterize parents or children in global ways, we ignore the key situational factors that so often determine our actions.

Costanzo and Woody (1985) acknowledge that there may be some basis for generalizing about parenting styles. After all, some parents *are* more controlling, anxious, competent, or more involved than others. These dispositions could very well influence their children's behavior. The key point is that when we examine effective parent-child discipline encounters, we are likely to observe considerable variation in the particular parent's response across situations.

Many studies of personality traits, intellect, and psychopathology reveal that *within*-family environmental variables are considerably more influential than *between*-family factors (Goldsmith, 1983; Rowe & Plomin, 1981). In other words, the ways in which parents differ in child-rearing practices are not as influential in personality development as the day-to-day variation within a particular parent's style.

POWER AND PUNISHMENT IN PARENTING

Children today have rights, including the right to be protected from their own parents, if necessary. Nevertheless, society gives parents wide latitude regarding the choice of child-rearing practices (see Spotlight: Should Children Have The Same Rights As Adults?). I have been counseling a single mother and her two young adolescent children. The mother regularly slapped or spanked her son and daughter. She

Rubinstein and Slife (1984) raise this provocative question in their book on controversial psychological issues. In this century, many oppressed groups have sought full equality in United States society. What about children who, some would argue, are the most powerless and oppressed of all social groups?

Rubinstein and Slife present two contrasting points of view. Richard Farson, in his book *Birthrights* (1974), contends that children should have exactly the same rights that adults have, including the right to self-determination, that is, to make their own decisions. Diane Baumrind (1978) agrees that children have fundamental rights. These include the right to be protected from abusive or neglecting parents. She argues, however, that children do not have the right to self-determination, because they have not yet developed the ability to make good choices.

Farson desires "a single standard of morals and behavior for children and adults. No more double standard . . . Children would have the right to engage in acts which are now acceptable for adults but not for children, and they would not be required to gain permission to do something. . . ." According to Farson, children deserve the right to "exercise self-determination in decisions about eating, sleeping, playing, listening, reading, washing, and dressing. They would have the right to choose their associates, the opportunity to decide what life goals they wish to pursue, and the freedom to engage in whatever activities are permissible for adults."

When adults voluntarily abandon their authority, Farson contends, children can learn good judgment the same way that adults do—from their mistakes. Let children experience the natural consequences of their actions. If they are not forced to go to bed at a particular time, children will have to learn to regulate their need for sleep the way adults do. If they stay up too late, they will not be able to function well the next day. Like most adults, they will develop good judgment about a sensible sleep time.

Diane Baumrind (1978) considers Farson's "child liberation" model naive. Self-determination for children, according to Baumrind, is a capacity to be developed, not a right to be granted. "Self-determination assumes the ability to choose among known alternatives whose consequences are also known and embraced. It is precisely this ability to make choices knowledgeably that the young child and unemancipated adolescent lack . . . Conventional and scientific wisdom dictates that rational authority is a natural and legitimate right of adult caretakers."

Baumrind asserts that the privileges and responsibilities of parents and children are not equal. Instead, they are reciprocal. They reflect the differing capacities and statuses of adults and children. As children develop the abilities we associate with adult wisdom and judgment, they earn the right to self-determination. Do you agree?

---

sometimes used switches on their ankles when they were disrespectful or defiant. Since the switches left marks on her daughter's legs and ankles, the mother was reported anonymously to a state agency that investigated the complaint.

Although concern was expressed by a social worker about the mother's harsh treatment of her children, no charges were filed. The daughter began to threaten that she would report her mother to the police if her mother hit her. The daughter did, in fact, call the police once. The lieutenant who handled the case told the girl that her mother had the right to spank her. In fact, he spanked his own children!

It is not easy to distinguish, sometimes, between very harsh parenting and abuse. Both are usually administered in a state of anger. Although our society condemns child abuse, it accepts punishment as a necessary tool of discipline. Most parents use punishment in disciplining their children (Sears, Maccoby & Levin, 1957).

Hoffman's Model of Parental Power Assertion

M. L. Hoffman (1967) investigated the effects of excessive parental power assertion on children. He defined power as the "potential an individual has for compelling another person to act in ways contrary to his own desires" (p. 128). He defined power assertion techniques as those that "put direct coercive pressure on the child to change his entire ongoing pattern of behavior immediately" (p. 129). Children, because of their low power status, cannot avoid power assertion by adults.

"The parent possesses and controls the material and emotional supplies needed by the child. As the controller of these supplies, and with his greater physical strength, he is in the position to punish the child at will, either physically or through deprivation . . . Furthermore, the parent's treatment of the child—outside of extreme neglect and cruelty—is subject to little, if any, legal restraint. Probably in no other relationship does a person in our society have such complete power over another" (M. L. Hoffman, 1967, p. 129).

When parents use threats to gain compliance, according to Hoffman, they are imposing their parental will on the child. They do so without any explanation or compensation to the child for their compliance. Gerald Patterson (1982) has observed that parents of aggressive children punish according to their mood, rather than the child's actions. Hoffman suggests that excessive use of power-assertive techniques frustrates children. It also weakens their sense of autonomy. They develop feelings of hostility and resistance and may display poor impulse control. Heavily punished children often treat other children abusively. These characteristics are most dramatically observed in the behavior of bullies (see chapter 14).

Hoffman tested his model using a sample of 12 middle-class and 10 working-class families with a child attending a half-day nursery school.

He found that working-class fathers used more power assertions than middle-class fathers. Working-class mothers showed more frequent initial power assertions than middle-class mothers. Hoffman concluded that the frequent use of power assertions by mothers leads to the development of hostile feelings, which children then direct toward their peers.

A father's power assertions can have an indirect but powerful effect on the child, mediated by his treatment of his wife. Thus, a mother's harsh rearing of her children often reflects her husband's harsh treatment of her. Crockenberg (1987) found that angry and punitive mothers tended to have children who were "angry and noncompliant and who distanced themselves from their mothers." Researchers have also observed differences in how mothers and fathers are affected by their sons and daughters during discipline encounters. Boys appear to exert more influence over mothers' discipline strategies, and girls exert more influence over fathers' (Cowan & Avants, 1988; Mulhern & Passman, 1981).

Punishment

Parents are in a position of authority. Authority implies power. The traditional model of parental discipline has been punitive, that is, based on the power to punish. Traditionally, it was assumed that punishment was necessary to save the child's soul ("Spare the rod, spoil the child"). As described in chapter 1, children were assumed to be innately mischievous, if not downright wicked. If parents spared the rod, it was assumed, their children would be unmanageable.

Over the course of human history, and particularly in this century, there has been a gradual shift away from punishment and coercion to motivate behavior change. This shift from aversive control has been accompanied by a trend toward greater individual freedom (Skinner, 1971). Parents are becoming wary

Punishment often leaves children feeling sad, angry, and alienated.

about using punitive authority although at times they attempt to rationalize it. They might say, "This will hurt me more than it hurts you" or "I do it for your own good." Thus, punishment can be depicted as a reflection of parental concern and even affection.

Today, thanks to people like Darwin and Freud, we are more aware of the relationship between frustration and aggressive behavior. Parents are more likely to punish when they are frustrated by their children's misbehavior or by their own life problems. It is well documented that abusive parents tend to strike in anger. Oldershaw, Walters, and Hall (1986), for example, found that, compared to nonabusive mothers, abusive mothers "used more com-

mands, and more power-assertive and less positively oriented control strategies . . ." (p. 722).

There are probably many parents who punish strategically. (Using punishment effectively is discussed in the next chapter.) They remain calm and thoughtful and punish to accomplish specific discipline goals. Most parents appear to punish nonstrategically, when they are frustrated and angry. Perhaps their emotional needs are temporarily satisfied by "venting."

Excessive punishment does not support our four parenting goals. Rather, it thwarts our attempts to promote good behavior and competent behavior. When children's failures are criticized, they may develop a fear of failure.

The role that grandparents play in the lives of their children has changed considerably over time. Grandparents today, particularly maternal grandmothers, may exercise considerable responsibility in rearing and disciplining children. Increasing numbers of grandparents are raising their grandchildren (Kennedy & Keeney, 1988).

Before this century, "there were few living grandparents and most grandchildren never knew their grandparents. Now, for the first time in history, most adults live long enough to get to know most of their grandchildren, and most children have the opportunity to know most of their grandparents . . . A new role as protector has emerged for grandparents due to the growing affluence of the elderly, the rise in divorce, and declining numbers of grandchildren (Kennedy & Keeney, 1988, p. 27).

Grandparents today report that they enjoy regular visits with their grandchildren. Children report that relationships with their grandparents are special. Children still become particularly attached to their grandmothers. However, in the presence of a stranger, they will prefer their mother to their grandmother (Myers, Jarvis, & Creasey, 1987). Some grandparents, particularly in old age, have little involvement with their grandchildren. Tension between parent and grandparent about how to raise the child also lessens child-grandparent contact.

In the domain of discipline, grandparents are stereotyped as being permissive in setting or enforcing limits and indulgent regarding children's requests. Blackwelder and Passman (1986) compared 24 mothers' and 24 maternal grandmothers' disciplinary interventions under identical circumstances. The investigators were able to gradually lessen the number of correct responses that the children scored on a task. As the children's performance worsened, both mothers and grandmothers increased the amount of both reward and punishment.

With further decrements in performance, mothers continued to increase the intensities of reward and punishment, but grandmothers leveled off. The investigators found that the disciplinary styles of mothers and grandmothers were more similar than different. Maternal grandmothers "act as role models and advisors" to their daughters. Both mothers and grandmothers were somewhat likely to overlook errors, but rarely overlooked opportunities to dispense rewards.

There were some differences in discipline style between the two groups. When the children were performing well, grandmothers dispensed significantly more rewards than did mothers. By the end of the session, when the children were performing most poorly, grandmothers were less punitive than were mothers. Three grandmothers refused to punish at all. No mother chose to withhold punishment.

The differences supported the stereotype that grandmothers "are more giving, less punitive, and more forgiving than are mothers" (p. 80). However, the more responsibility the grandmothers felt they had for teaching, socializing, raising, and disciplining the children, the more intensely they punished. "Grandmothers who more closely approximated the conventional maternal role were found to discipline more intensely than did less involved grandmothers" (p. 86).

Children confirm that relationships with their grandparents are special.

When children are praised, they are more likely to develop a need for achievement (Cordes, 1985). Harsh punishment threatens parent-child relationships ("Wait till your father comes home"). It can also encourage negative self-esteem (for the children *and* the parents).

Punitive parents highly value obedience. They are willing to use power and pain to promote compliance. Rather than engage in verbal give-and-take with their children, they are more likely to respond to resistance with a "because I said so" power assertion. As already cited, children of punitive parents are more aggressive, unhappy, and withdrawn than children of parents with nonpunitive styles. Those who are victims of the abuse of power may learn to value power and, eventually, struggle to achieve it.

"Children who struggle for power are defiant and rebellious. They may argue about all requests from their parents, they may ignore them, or they may comply in a way other than the parent wanted . . . If the struggle for power continues and children feel they cannot defeat the parents, they may seek retaliation and revenge. Children who pursue revenge feel they are not lovable; that they are significant only when they can hurt others as they believe they were hurt" (Berns, 1985, pp. 133, 135).

Children who are obedient may also be fearful. Some learn antisocial ways of avoiding detection, such as lying. Ironically, parents who use physical punishment are more likely than nonpunitive parents to have children who misbehave and violate rules (M. L. Hoffman, 1970; Power & Chapieski, 1986). Adams and Tidwell (1988), for example, questioned parents of hearing-impaired children about how they handled their children's misbehavior. Parents who felt they were successful in handling misbehavior said they mainly used discussion and explanation, whereas parents who felt they were unsuccessful in discipline relied mainly on scolding.

Let's remember that rule-breaking children may put pressure on their parents to punish (Bell, 1968). Thus, the direction of causality is not clear. Nevertheless, parental use of punishment is to some extent determined by its effectiveness in changing children's behavior (Mulhern & Passman, 1981).

Silberman and Wheelan (1980) observe that children can profit from adult wisdom and still challenge adult authority (p. 17). Adults have power over children and should exercise it judiciously. Most parents continue to punish. The discipline strategy advocated in this book suggests that if punishment is used at all, it should be used as a last resort (that is, when all else fails).

SUMMARY

Child-rearing strategies are guided by parents' practical experiences with children, but also by parental biases and beliefs. Parents who consider their children well behaved may attribute their good behavior to the child's disposition. They may blame misbehavior on situational or other factors. Parents who perceive their children as difficult or oppositional also tend to view such behavior as dispositional. This may discourage attempts to improve their behavior.

Parental frustration often reflects unrealistic expectations about children. Realistic expectations allow parents to be more patient and understanding when in conflict with children. New parents have the greatest number of unrealistic expectations, particularly regarding the amount of work involved in caring for an infant. Parental stress and guilt are lessened when parents have realistic expectations about their own resources and limitations.

Much conflict between parents and children reflects children's difficulty in delaying gratification. Children strive for pleasure; parents set limits on their behavior. When their desires are not appeased, children become frustrated and repeatedly attempt to attain their goal. They learn to repeat whatever actions lead to satisfaction. If being annoying achieves their goal, this is what they will learn to do. Parents often encourage, unintentionally, the very behaviors they complain about.

Children and young adolescents generally accept their parent's authority, but will challenge the boundaries set for their conduct. As children mature, they desire greater autonomy over personal decisions. They accept parental control in moral and conventional matters. When children resist established limits, parents should adopt a discipline strategy consistent with our four parenting goals.

Parents compete in raising their children with many other sources of influence, including their partners. Children profit when parents adopt a "team approach" to discipline. Most parents learn to adjust their discipline strategies to the age and stage of development of the child. They become more flexible and more willing to negotiate and reason as children mature. There is no simple formula for handling a discipline encounter. Parental strategy should reflect a good understanding of the particular child and the dynamics of the situation at hand.

Various dimensions and styles of discipline are discussed, including Baumrind's influential model. She distinguishes between three discipline styles: authoritative (democratic), authoritarian (punitive), and permissive. She contends that children's personalities may reflect their parents' style of discipline. Punitive parenting does not generally support our four parenting goals.

Changing Children's Behavior

OBJECTIVES

After studying chapter 6, students should be able to

1. Explain why rules are useful and what parents can do to encourage rule-following behavior
2. Describe discipline strategies that are appropriate for infants and toddlers
3. Describe how operant conditioning principles can be used to change children's behavior
4. Describe how parents sometimes unintentionally encourage such undesirable behaviors as temper tantrums
5. Describe how the extinction procedure, in general, and ignoring, in particular, can be used to discourage unacceptable behavior
6. Evaluate the reservations that have been expressed about the use of rewards in discipline
7. Distinguish between intrinsic and extrinsic reinforcers and their role in teaching new behavior
8. Distinguish between social, activity, and token reinforcers, and give examples of each
9. Define natural and logical consequences and how their use helps parents avoid power struggles
10. Describe how some parents inadvertently discourage self-reliance
11. Define observational learning, and explain why it is a powerful learning process
12. Distinguish between two types of punishment
13. Describe how to use punishment effectively
14. List and explain the possible side effects of punishment
15. Describe how overcorrection may be applied in child rearing
16. Evaluate the advantages and disadvantages of the time-out procedure

INTRODUCTION

Mark # 1

"My parenting definitely needs more structure. In the area of motivation, for instance, I erroneously approached this from the negative angle. I'd set high standards and tell Mark how I knew he could do better than he was doing. B's and C's had to become A's in schoolwork. I realize now that I must reinforce all positive efforts rather than complaining about half-measures. At times though, I feel blinded by my first perceptions. I'm hasty and harsh in my judgments. Then it is too late for me to renege.

"When Mark seems completely indifferent about sports, culture, grades, and achievements, I get so frustrated! He seems to be self-centered and 'one-track-minded.' Play and his friends seem to be the only things that matter. I've been trying to acknowledge all of his efforts lately, at homework and being responsible. It looks as though he senses more encouragement from me and likes it. I'm trying to be less domineering and meddling. I can't help myself, though, when it comes to homework. Everyday without fail, I go through his book bag checking for homework assignments, memos, etc. Somehow I don't feel it's invading his privacy, but rather keeping tabs on him. Uninvolved and unconcerned parents end up with unpleasant surprises, don't they?"

Mark's mother is a single parent who was attending my undergraduate parenting class. We will have the opportunity to share additional entries in her journal and trace her efforts to improve her communication and relationship with Mark, her 9-year-old son. Mark's mother is expressing a common parental dilemma—how involved should parents be in regulating their child's behavior? On the one hand, children provide numerous instances of irresponsibility and selfishness that are difficult to overlook.

Unconcerned parents end up with unpleasant surprises, don't they? On the other hand, becoming upset about misbehavior rarely improves things.

Of the four parenting goals emphasized in this book, parenting goal #1, good behavior, seems to be of greatest immediate concern to parents. It is helpful, however, to view good behavior in a broader context that includes the other three parenting goals described in chapter 1. The proper focus of a discipline encounter is not the child's misconduct, but the parent's response to it.

Effective discipline requires that parents be responsive, not reactive, to their children's misbehavior. This means that, during discipline encounters, parents should try to act in ways that support all four parenting goals, rather than respond impulsively to the child's misconduct. Reactive parents take the child's behavior at face value—they are annoyed and they criticize. Like Mark's mother noted, they are blinded by their first impressions. But their disapproval has minimal effect ("I've told you a hundred times . . ."). Responsive parents view a discipline encounter as an opportunity to teach the child something rather than as an opportunity to vent their anger. This chapter examines the strategic use of learning principles to change children's behavior.

INFANT DISTRESS

Study Question   Can infants be spoiled?

Parents of infants wonder when effective discipline strategies can and should be applied. Practical questions arise about feeding or holding distressed infants, whether infants should be allowed to cry themselves to sleep, and how to respond when infants solicit attention and care. Because infants cry or fret reflexively for much of the first year, it does not make sense to ignore their distress. Parents should follow their natural impulses and comfort a crying infant. Failing to respond to a distressed infant may have an unintended outcome—a child with a heightened need for attention and reassurance.

"Put yourself in the baby's position. If you were unable for whatever reason to correct a situation you were in, and the best you could do was scream in the hope that something would happen to improve your condition, how would you feel if no one came to help you? . . . If you're ignored and left alone to cry, you're always going to feel deprived and you'll probably be *more* likely to turn out a brat" (Balter, quoted by Winn, 1989).

Responsive parents allow their children to learn that they can have an effect on their environment. They respond promptly and *appropriately* to their infant's actions. They are also careful not to "spoil" their child—that is, not to lavish the infant with unwanted or unneeded attention. Infants of responsive parents learn that they can "trust" their parents to care for them when they are truly in need (Erikson, 1964). Psychologists thus advocate that parents comfort their distressed infants. When possible, they should remove the source of the infants' discomfort by feeding or holding them or by taking other appropriate actions.

SETTING LIMITS FOR OLDER INFANTS AND TODDLERS

Study Question   How does one "discipline" older infants and toddlers?

Since the older infant and young toddler are not yet able to grasp such abstract concepts as "good behavior" and "bad behavior," parents define limits by consistently responding to specific acts in specific situations. Silberman and Wheelan (1980) suggest "brief, firm statements and physical restraint. If the child is doing something that we want to stop, it is best to say 'no' and name the object involved and the possible consequences of the child's action (such as "no—dishes break") and, if that does not suffice, to remove the child from the situation" (p. 117). Because many months or years may be necessary for children to learn to inhibit unacceptable behaviors, consistency and patience become necessary ingredients of good parenting.

Standards of Acceptable Behavior

What is "unacceptable behavior?" That is for parents, other caretakers, and the community to decide. They should take into account a child's ability to understand and follow rules. We try to provide our children with skills that will gain them both personal satisfaction and acceptance from the community-at-large. We try to discourage behaviors that are considered obnoxious or annoying and that may lead to social rejection.

Parents residing in most middle-class communities have fairly similar values regarding child rearing. Most encourage their children to be friendly, cooperative, helpful, and so on. Similarly, most parents discourage hitting, teasing, bullying, stealing, lying, and cheating. Such behaviors are not uncommon among young children. To some extent, they reflect limitations in children's understanding of rules and insensitivity to other people's feelings.

Nevertheless, parents must set and enforce limits on these behaviors beginning in infancy. During the second year, children become more sensitive to the emotional states of other family members and begin to modify their behavior accordingly. Kagan (1981) has demonstrated that during their second year, children become interested in discrepancies between what is expected and what actually occurs. They show distress when they cannot satisfy goals set by adults. Kagan interprets these observations to mean that children are beginning to understand and become concerned about adult standards.

Promoting Rule-Following Behavior

Sometimes parents express desired behavior patterns or performance standards as rules. Rules specify what behaviors are expected, in what situations, and what will happen if the rule is satisfied or violated (Baldwin & Baldwin, 1986, ch. 11). For example, consider the rule: "As soon as your hands are clean, you can sit down at the table for dinner." This rule states a positive outcome, but implies a negative consequence (no dinner) if the desired behavior does not occur. Children eventually learn to appreciate the need for rules. They help guide our behavior, and their adherence minimizes social conflict.

Children resist rules that they consider unfair. Such rules seem to serve other people's interests at their expense. Children benefit when parents give a reason that the child can understand for obeying the rule. Parents should remind children about rules ("What is the rule about washing your hands before dinner?") and reinforce rule-following behavior rather than criticize transgressions. Verbal reminders should gradually be replaced by situational cues. For example, instead of telling children to put on their seatbelts, a parent can sit silently in the driver's seat until all seatbelts are fastened.

Parke (1969; 1973) advocates the use of cognitive structuring procedures in discipline, such as providing reasons for not breaking rules. Children may not automatically understand a rule, its value, or the consequences of disobeying it. Parke found that providing children with a simple reason for following a rule combined with a punishing buzzer resulted in more rule following than punishment alone. Parke suggests that providing cognitive guides to children makes more sense than a display of power. Rule-following behavior is also encouraged by giving children responsibility for enforcing the rule, by encouraging them to see themselves as "honest," and by teaching specific self-instructions for resisting temptation (Toner, 1986).

It is helpful to have young children repeat a rule so that we know they can at least verbalize it ("What is the rule about holding scissors?"). One of the earliest rules that parents teach (the so-called Golden Rule) is, "Treat other people the way you want them to treat you." To a young child, this might be expressed, "If you are nice to other people, they will be nice to you." The converse should also be noted. "If you are mean to other people, how will they treat you?" This simple rule is very useful because it is a generally valid description of human interaction. However, it requires many years of interpersonal experience and cognitive maturation before children can grasp its full meaning and implications.

An obstacle to rule learning is that exceptions to rules may impede one's ability to appreciate their usefulness. For example, even when 2-year-old Brian is mean to Grandma, she may still be nice to him. In any case, we remind children about these relationships, when appropriate, so that they eventually become internalized rules (self-statements) that will guide their behavior.

"The rules we have, however, need to be stated and restated until they are internalized. Beginning statements over and over again with the simple phrase, 'The rule is . . .' helps a child focus on what we are saying. It is also important to show young children what we expect, not just tell them. And this is a good time to start accompanying directives with brief, understandable reasons, such as, 'Push your cup away from the edge of the table. The juice won't spill if you do that.' By doing this a child begins to sense that our authority is more rational than arbitrary" (Silberman & Wheelan, 1980, p. 121).

Discipline Strategies

Parental attempts to gain compliance from children begin during infancy (Dunn & Munn, 1985), usually in the form of directive questions ("Where is the spoon?") and contextual cues. Parents also learn crucial verbal and nonverbal strategies for bringing infants' attention to the task at hand and then encouraging their involvement in it. "By successfully manipulating [the infant's state], the parent can avoid the clash-of-wills that is so often portrayed as typical of all socialization efforts, whereby compliance is supposedly extracted from an invariably reluctant child" (Schaffer & Crook, 1980, p. 60). The key point is that responsive parenting can usually avoid child noncompliance.

Power and Chapieski (1986) found that infants complied with their mothers' initial attempts to restrict their handling of objects about half the time. When infants did not comply, the mothers usually repeated the rule, and the infants eventually did obey. Infants of physically punishing mothers showed the *least* amount of compliance and were the most likely to grab breakable objects! Physically punitive mothers also had the fewest number of objects available at home for infant play.

This study, like many others, implies that punishment is an ineffective long-term discipline strategy. Infants and young children respond to gentle strategies that bring their attention to the task and that use directive questions and nonverbal cues to motivate compliance. Reactive, punitive parenting styles seem to provoke defiant, limit-testing behaviors.

Occasionally, parents must physically prevent the child from biting the dog, grabbing a knife, or leaning out a window. This gentle restraint should be accompanied by an authoritative "No—you'll hurt yourself." Physical restraint should be accompanied by an explanation, even if the reason cannot yet be grasped by the young child. Distracting young children from dangerous situations or objects often works.

Perhaps the most efficient long-term "discipline" strategy for very young children is to arrange a safe and stimulating environment with minimal opportunities for mischief and mayhem. "Babyproofing" rooms and homes typically occurs by the age of 6 months, when infants begin to crawl and then creep from room to room. Play areas should be arranged to encourage desirable play activity with attractive, age-appropriate toys or play materials that challenge and entertain. Caretakers should always be present or nearby, not only for the child's safety. Vigilant caretakers use positive reinforcement and arrange natural consequences that are interesting and stimulating outcomes for the infant's behavior.

THE ROLE OF OPERANT CONDITIONING

Study Question What role do rewards and punishments play in changing children's behavior?

Operant conditioning refers to a type of learning in which the consequences of a behavior lead to changes in its frequency of occurrence. Certain consequences make a particular behavior more likely to occur. Parents usually call these consequences rewards, but behavioral scientists call them reinforcers.

Other types of consequences lessen the frequency of the behavior they follow. The processes involved are called punishment and extinction. *Punishment* is said to occur when a behavior is weakened by the presentation of an aversive stimulus (something "bad") or the removal of a positive reinforcer (something "good"). *Extinction* refers to the weakening of a behavior when the reinforcer that motivated the behavior is removed. All of these consequences are defined by their effects on behavior.

Behavior modification refers to the use of operant conditioning principles in practical situations, including education and child rearing. Using positive reinforcers to encourage desirable behavior is not only more effective but also more practical and more humane than using coercion, threat, or punishment (Baldwin & Baldwin, 1986; Kazdin, 1984).

Behavior modification approaches usually advocate the following: think behavior, think solution, think positive, think small steps, think flexible, and think future (Kanfer & Schefft, 1988). Parents are encouraged to view discipline in terms of changing children's behavior rather than changing personality traits or dispositions. Solutions usually require changing the consequences of children's behavior. This usually means that the parents must change their own way of responding to the misbehavior. Positive outcomes are preferred to criticism or punishment.

Parents are encouraged to notice and reinforce improvement, no matter how slight. Setting realistic goals enhances the likelihood of success, building both the parent's and the child's self-confidence. Flexibility means that there are many ways to achieve a positive change. If one strategy doesn't succeed, plan another. Thinking about the future allows parents to concentrate on how they want their child to be, not how he has been in the past.

Parents occasionally violate basic principles of learning in their attempts to reward or punish their children's behavior. For example, they may ignore good behavior and, instead, "catch the child being bad." Ironically, even negative attention to misbehavior may encourage future occurrences. Parents can learn to analyze their children's behavior in everyday situations such as bedtime, dinnertime, or homework time. They can learn how to use positive means to motivate compliance. Understanding how

Bedtime provides opportunities for moments of closeness between parents and children.

children's behavior is influenced by situational factors and behavioral outcomes dramatically enhances parents' ability to encourage good behavior while avoiding unnecessary family conflict.

Children naturally resist bedtime, for example. It interferes with their play and requires considerable effort with little immediate payoff. The bedtime sequence eventually leaves them in bed in a darkened room with nothing to do but sleep. Sleep is a positive reinforcer for adults, but children may treat bedtime as an aversive stimulus.* By encouraging a predictable sleeptime routine leading to a reinforcing outcome, parents may avoid or lessen children's resistance.

*A stimulus is considered aversive if we would try to avoid or escape from it.

For example, the child might be read an interesting story or be entertained by a brief but amusing puppet show when he is in bed and prepared for sleep. Letting older children read in bed by themselves for 10 to 15 minutes takes advantage of the sedative effects of reading. Many parents encourage their children to discuss their day at bedtime as a way of staying in touch ("What was the best thing that happened today? What was the worst thing?"). It is thoughtful parenting to arrange an attractive, but not arousing, incentive at the end of the bedtime routine that motivates the entire sequence.

Anticipating children's reactions to requests or demands gives us the opportunity to apply other strategies as needed. For example, rather than telling Jennifer in the middle of a TV program to get ready for bed, we can give her a 10-minute "warning" to finish what she's doing.

Even better, we can remind her that her agreed-upon bedtime is approaching. (Ideally, we would not even have to remind her.)

Rather than pleading with Ben to get dressed every morning, we can reach an understanding whereby the first thing he does each morning is get dressed. After he is dressed, he can watch TV. If Diane isn't giving us her full attention, we maintain eye contact with her and speak firmly until she does. Many conflicts with children can be avoided if we acknowledge the child's point of view and still firmly assert our legitimate authority.

One of the most difficult skills for parents to learn is ignoring misbehavior. Parental attention is a subtle but powerful reinforcer for children's behavior. Misbehavior is inherently "attention-getting." Most parents understand the power of attention. They even teach their children to ignore another child's teasing behavior because "if he sees it upsets you, he'll continue to do it." The problem is that misbehavior is often provocative. Parents react impulsively rather than strategically. Sometimes, the best response is selective ignoring.

Carol and the Cookie

Let's examine a common parent-child interaction. Right before dinner, Carol asks her father for a cookie. Her father naturally refuses for good reasons. He has invested a considerable amount of time preparing dinner, and, like most parents, he will find it reinforcing to see Carol eat healthy food. Father knows that if Carol eats a cookie now, she will be less interested in eating dinner. Therefore, Father gently refuses Carol's request.

But Carol really wants this cookie! She pleads; she whines; she begs; she *demands* a cookie. Notice that Carol has already learned that if initial requests are not granted, try, try again. Many children, like Carol, have learned to impose upon Mom and Dad an annoying situation (nagging) from which they can easily escape by giving in. Very clever, these children. All Dad has to do to escape from Carol's harangue is to give her the cookie.

Because Dad has previously been (negatively) reinforced for relenting, he gives Carol the cookie.* He adds a brief warning about how Carol had better eat her dinner when it is ready. Dad's strategic error, of course, is reinforcing Carol's nagging behavior by giving her the cookie. Next time Dad refuses a request, Carol will be more likely to nag.

What has Dad learned? Giving in "works" for Dad in the short run. Carol's nagging stops, but, because Dad's giving in has been reinforced, he becomes more likely to relent in the future. If Carol doesn't eat her dinner, Dad may hold out longer next time before giving in, or perhaps Dad may not give in at all. It is exactly Dad's unpredictable behavior, either waiting longer before giving in or sometimes not giving in, that encourages persistence in Carol's nagging. Nagging is like gambling; sometimes it pays off, and sometimes it doesn't. Since Carol never knows the outcome ahead of time, she makes the effort. In the long run, giving in to Carol doesn't work for Dad, because, periodically, he will have to put up with her nagging.

It is almost certain that if Dad strategically withheld these payoffs, Carol's nagging would eventually cease. Withholding reinforcement from an established behavior is called extinction. When it is clear that our parental attention is reinforcing the annoying response, withholding our attention will discourage further occurrences. Notice that in extinction, nothing is being taken away from the child. Rather, the usual reinforcer, in this case attention or a cookie, is being withheld. It is easy to see how parents who are not aware of behavior principles often encourage the very behaviors they disdain.

---

*Negative reinforcement involves escaping from or avoiding something bad. Dad is escaping from Carol's nagging.

Dad should also know that extinction often elicits increased or exaggerated arousal before the gradual reduction in nagging begins. Initially, Carol may escalate her efforts to get her cookie; she may even have a tantrum. Dad should also anticipate "spontaneous recovery" of nagging behavior in the future and remember how to respond accordingly. ("Carol, what is the rule about snacks before dinner?")

Mark #2

"About a week ago, the counselors from Mark's after-school program told me that he had to leave the activities because he was misbehaving. He was singing silly songs or making unpleasant noises and would not stop when asked to. On these occasions, I apologized to the counselors and talked to Mark. I explained to him that his behavior is rude and how difficult it must be for the counselors. Then I asked him to please try to behave himself. The other day, there was another incident.

"He was disrupting art lessons by making animal-type noises. When the counselor told me, I told Mark to apologize and promise to try to not misbehave again. He said 'I'm sorry' softly and quickly, leaving it at that. All three of us knew it meant nothing at all. In the car, he proceeded to be loud, unruly and continued making noises. I asked him to calm down and told him to stop. He still kept it up. I tried to get him to stop again, but he couldn't even hear me. As I realized how he must be enjoying this power, I dropped out. I simply ignored his behavior; shortly after, he lost interest and stopped."

Strategic Use of Reinforcers

Reinforcers are most effective in teaching new behavior when they are presented immediately following the desirable response. Sometimes, caretakers assume a stimulus is a positive reinforcer, when it is actually a neutral or even an aversive stimulus. We can only be sure a stimulus is a reinforcer if it encourages the response it follows. Keep in mind that repeated presentations of the reinforcer may lead to satiation. That is, the stimulus may eventually lose its reinforcing properties ("too much of a good thing").

The ways in which parents schedule reinforcers may encourage persistent, objectionable behavior in their children. Tantrum behavior (see Spotlight: Anatomy of A Tantrum) is encouraged by parents' waiting longer and longer before they give in to their children's demands. As we have seen, parents encourage children to escalate their efforts by occasionally giving in. (Dramatic displays of temper and tantrums are more likely to "succeed" in public settings, when parents submit rather than endure public embarrassment.)

Let's visit Carol's home two nights later. Before dinner, Carol asks Dad for a chocolate cupcake. Dad remembers that Carol did not finish her dinner two nights ago and turns down Carol's request. Because of Carol's previous "success," her nagging behavior is even more persistent than it was before. And Dad is confronted with an even more unpleasant situation. All he has to do to escape from Carol's outburst is give in. If Dad waits a little longer tonight before he submits, Carol's nagging may escalate into a tantrum. Get the picture?

Study Question How can parents get their children to take their "No" seriously?

What's a father to do? By stating a rule, such as "No snacks before dinner," and explaining the reason for the rule, "If you eat sweets before dinner, you won't feel like eating the healthy stuff," Dad finally takes control of the situation. When Dad enforces the rule, Carol learns two things: why there are no snacks before dinner and that Dad means what he says. Parental responsibility, not Carol's desire for sweets or resultant nagging, should guide Dad's behavior in this situation.

My older son threw his one and only temper tantrum when he was about 3 years old, on our living room floor. I do not recall the details, but I was sitting on the couch, *New York Times* in hand, and probably refusing a request to visit the toy store.

Since I had never witnessed a tantrum at close range, I was enormously curious and would have liked to scrutinize his every action and perhaps even take notes. The drama of the event was impressive. Sounds of screaming, crying, and floor pounding filled the house. I realized that paying even the slightest attention to his behavior might encourage a repetition at some future time. I continued reading my paper, with barely a glance in his direction. Fortunately, I have not yet had another opportunity to observe this fascinating phenomenon.

According to Blechman (1985), "A temper tantrum takes place when a child, who has not been mistreated, is out-of-control for at least 1 minute, screaming, crying, throwing things, or hitting . . . Usually tantrums occur when a child has been told no or when a child is very tired" (p. 89). The dramatic display of frustration and anger is the ultimate expression of Freud's concept of the id: "Give me what I want immediately or I will rant and rave." Ironically, toy stores and birthday parties are common settings for tantrums. Placing young children near toys they cannot have is like striking a match on a can of gasoline.

Unlike psychologists, most parents do not find tantrum behavior exotic and fascinating. They find tantrums extremely annoying and, if they are occurring publicly, very embarrassing. "At first I felt angry. I felt that the people in the store would think I'm a horrible mother, that I can't control my child. I knew it was going to be a real battle . . . Those people in the store are strangers. You have to take care of your child first" (Sternberg, quoted by Kutner, 1987b).

Because the tantrum is aversive to parents, they are tempted to give in to the child. This usually stops the tantrum. As you supposed, this is a poor way of handling a tantrum. Children have tantrums to get what they want! By reinforcing the outburst, a parent almost guarantees a repeat performance.

Many parents have found that removing the child from the immediate setting in which the tantrum is occurring alleviates the child's distress. It also demonstrates the parent's control of the situation. Responding in a matter-of-fact way rather than "losing it" also prevents the incident from escalating into a power struggle. At home, responding to the child's frustration, but not reacting to the tantrum, may comfort the child without encouraging an inappropriate display of temper. For persistent tantrum behavior, the time out procedure may be used (see Spotlight: Time Out from Reinforcement).

Parents should encourage children to express their disappointment or anger in words rather than through out-of-control behavior. As reported in chapter 3, Caspi, Elder, and Bem (1987) studied adults who had had temper tantrums in late childhood (ages 8 to 10 years). They found that men who had tantrums in childhood had adjustment and relationship problems as adults. Women who had histories of tantrum behavior were ill-tempered mothers and prone to divorce. Fascinating.

The researchers suggest that individuals who as children adopt explosive interpersonal styles come to evoke responses in other people that perpetuate this maladaptive pattern. This is all the more reason to discourage such high-arousal states in children.

THE TANTRUM

THE THREE STEPS TO A TANTRUM

STEP ①   STEP ②   STEP ③

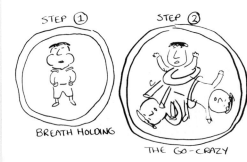

BREATH HOLDING

THE GO-CRAZY

THE NEVER-ENDING SCREAM

STEP ④

DO NOT FEED THE KID

LOCKED-UP IN THE ROOM

Justin Jaffe

How should Dad respond to Carol's inevitable nagging? He should use the extinction procedure. If, after explaining the "no snacks before dinner" rule to Carol, she still continues whining, another rule is stated: "I will not listen to you when you whine." If Dad's attention and arguing are reinforcing Carol's nagging and they are now consistently withheld, we can expect a gradual lessening of this behavior over time.

Punitive parents often respond to a child's "why should I?" question with the famous angry retort, "because I said so." This thoughtless response is the clearest invitation to a power struggle I can imagine. Children deserve to be reminded of the relevant rule, and they deserve a decent explanation of the rule's rationale. If Carol, in the preceding example, was open to a discussion of the nutritional facts of life, Dad should welcome such an exchange of information. Once we are confident that Carol understands both the rule and its rationale, however, we are not obligated to continually repeat either.

It is more helpful to ask, "Carol, what is the rule?" Children will argue indefinitely if we let them, and this wears parents down. "But why . . . but why?" Parental responsibility requires clearly stating the rule, explaining it once at a level a child can understand, and firmly refusing to participate in a coercive, nagging ritual. Although children resist the logic of "I'm doing it for your own good," they ultimately gain from hearing the sensible reasons behind our decisions.

Differential Reinforcement of Other Behavior (DRO)

Attempting to weaken a behavior, through extinction or punishment, can be tedious. We should first consider replacing the unwanted behavior with one that is more desirable. Remember, strategies that weaken behaviors do not teach a child what to do. Rather, they teach what *not* to do in that situation.

A schedule of reinforcement that encourages any response other than the undesirable one is called differential reinforcement of other behavior or DRO. For example, we can discourage thumb-sucking behavior by reinforcing "hand-out-of-mouth" behavior. Contingent praise, or using material incentives, can increase the frequency of hand-out-of-mouth behavior, thereby reducing hand-in-mouth behavior. "Linda, I'm so proud of you when your fingers are not in your mouth, and you look so grown-up."

Parents and teachers can also learn to identify "competing" responses, that is, behaviors that are incompatible with the offensive behavior. For example, I have learned to offer my children sliced apples or other fruit several minutes before their anticipated visit to the kitchen for a sweet snack. The "law of least effort" suggests that an apple in hand is worth a cookie in the kitchen.

I also try to catch the rare instances when they are nice to each other and express my appreciation. "Thank you for being patient with Eric. I know he asks a lot of questions." Increasing the frequency of more desirable responses automatically reduces the occurrence of the misbehaviors we are trying to discourage. "Catching the child being good" is preferable to the perpetual critical stance of some parents.

". . . When a loud unruly child plays quietly, that is the perfect time for parents to use praise, rewards and privileges, or suggestive praise. At first, some parents find it difficult to give this attention. When their children behave well, they are relieved that there are no problems and hope the quiet, desirable behavior continues. They may even stay away from the well-behaved children, afraid their presence will upset the pleasant behavior. If parents do not use their positive skills when their children behave well and, instead, respond to their children for misbehaving, they create an escalating cycle of punishment and misbehavior that is sustained by parental attention" (Dangel & Polster, 1988, p. 24).

RESERVATIONS ABOUT THE USE OF OPERANT CONDITIONING

Behavioral strategies based on the thoughtful application of positive outcomes can be a powerful parenting tool. Nevertheless, there are critics who question the wisdom, the usefulness, and even the ethics of rewarding children's behavior. Criticisms include the assertion that parents who use rewards are "bribing" their children to behave well, that special incentives deprive children of the opportunity to take responsibility for their duties and make the parent responsible instead, and that children will become "spoiled" in that they will always expect or demand to be rewarded for their good behavior.

Some have claimed that children can become "dependent" on rewards. A desirable behavior may cease when the reward is withdrawn or might occur only in the presence of authority figures, that is, those with the power to reward or punish (Dinkmeyer & McKay, 1982; Kazdin, 1984). There is increasing evidence that reward can undermine prosocial behavior in that such behavior may cease when the rewards are terminated (Fabes, Fultz, Eisenberg, May-Plumlee, & Christopher, 1989). This seems especially true for children whose parents depend heavily on the use of incentives. Such children may help when rewards are available and refuse to help otherwise. Schwartz (1986) contends that the use of incentives may be at the expense of rule finding, hypothesis testing and other cognitive operations.

It is misguided, however, to equate the use of rewards with bribery. Bribery is usually defined as offering someone an incentive to act illegally or immorally. Offering children incentives for good behavior does not satisfy such a definition. I agree, however, that the "if-then" approach ("If you brush your teeth, then you can read for 5 minutes"), which does motivate young children (Boggiano & Main, 1986), encourages cooperation for the "wrong" reason (Ginott, 1965).

Rewards can be a powerful child-rearing tool when used judiciously. Appreciating the strategic use of incentives requires a distinction between intrinsic and extrinsic reinforcers. Extrinsic reinforcers, such as money, grades, and awards, are arbitrarily related to the activity being encouraged. Gold stars or "happy faces" can be used to reward cooperative behavior in kindergarten, but the payoff has no obvious connection with the behavior that produced it. Money is a highly valued, extrinsic reinforcer that governs much of our working lives.

Intrinsic reinforcers are inherent in the activity itself. Consider the enjoyment we get from hearing ourselves play the piano well or seeing our well-hit tennis ball return over the net. Nobody has to reward us for eating, reading, sexual activity, taking a bath, or brushing our teeth. These activities are intrinsically reinforcing; that is, they are reinforcing in their own right. In education, unfortunately, the use of extrinsic reinforcers, particularly exam and course grades, has undermined the traditional intrinsic reinforcers that motivated scholars of the past, particularly knowledge for "its own sake."

When teaching children new behaviors, we initially rely on extrinsic reinforcers such as toys, candy, or, preferably, social reinforcers (discussion follows) such as praise and approval, because without these incentives the desired behavior would probably not occur. Children say, often with good reason, "I don't want to," or ask, justifiably, "Why should I?" Punitive parents might respond, less justifiably, "Because I said so."

Parents can ease the transition into new habit patterns, such as toileting skills, by offering children extrinsic reinforcers for the new behaviors. However, once the new behavior is occurring at some strength, the extrinsic reinforcers should be gradually faded out, so that the intrinsic, or natural, reinforcers can assume control. We avoid the risk of extinguishing the new response pattern by not withdrawing the external incentives prematurely.

It is usually a mistake to offer a reward for an established behavior pattern that is intrinsically reinforcing. If a child enjoys dressing herself, and this ability enhances her self-esteem, it would be misguided to offer her an incentive for the same activity. Occasionally acknowledging or appreciating self-reliance is appropriate, but offering someone a reward for something they are doing for a more natural outcome is counterproductive.

TYPES OF REINFORCERS

It is useful to distinguish between different categories of reinforcers. *Primary (unconditioned) reinforcers* such as food, water, and sleep acquired reinforcing properties over the course of evolution because of their role in survival. These stimuli are reinforcers at birth; no learning is required.

Secondary (conditioned) reinforcers acquire their reinforcing properties by becoming signals for subsequent reinforcement. The odor of food cooking acquires its reinforcing properties by signaling food is near. Seeing Dad's car pull into the driveway becomes reinforcing because it signals that soon we will be having fun with him. Our employer's scowl becomes a negative reinforcer because it may predict a "chewing out" or worse. We will consider three categories of conditioned reinforcers: social, activity, and token.

Using Social Reinforcement

Mark #3

"Well, he finished the book and book report, not exactly on time. Left to his own devices on my school night, he chose to ride his bike instead of starting his report. My unsuspecting landlady reminded him (once he was in for the night) that he should do his homework. At 10:30 P.M. when I came home, he was just beginning his second draft. When I realized his ploy to 'have it his way,' I was

very annoyed. I rapidly began reading over his first draft and criticized how it 'told too much for a summary.' Many words and minutes later, I saw my poor parenting in motion. I finished reading it, told him more fairly that it really was a good book report and that he could finish tomorrow. (He ended up finishing it at lunchtime the next day.) I asked him whether he felt good and proud that he finished the book. I told him I was proud of him. Mark immediately seemed relieved that I had let up on the pressure, and admitted he was happy and proud too."

For most of us, negative reactions from others can be very discouraging. Positive feedback has become a major incentive to us to behave well. Mark's mother caught herself in mid-lecture and decided to reinforce what Mark had accomplished rather than criticize what he had not. Social reinforcers, such as attention, praise, approval, hugs, kisses, and smiles, acquire their reinforcing properties when they become signals for additional reinforcement.

At birth, infants are oblivious to these stimuli, but whenever anything "good" happens to them, such as being fed, held, or rocked, a caretaker is present. The caretaker's presence, characteristics, and behaviors are repeatedly paired with, and therefore become signals for, the gratification that follows. Eventually, the caretakers themselves become powerful reinforcers whose presence and attention can reinforce new learning.

Children learn many "attention-getting" responses because they can't get the "good stuff" (primary reinforcers) until they get our attention first. Approval becomes a particularly powerful social reinforcer because people who approve of us are very likely to reinforce us in other ways. Stimuli such as criticism, frowns, and raised voices acquire their negatively reinforcing properties by setting the occasion for either punishment or the loss of positive reinforcers. In other words, people who signal their disapproval are less likely to give us what we want (reinforcers). Children gradually learn to behave in ways that avoid such disapproval. Most parents, like me, need practice in accentuating the positive.

Mark #4

"Daily, I've been trying to show Mark that I notice his efforts, but my attempts seem feeble. Sometimes it's because I can't think of any positive feedback to give him. 'You got an A— on your safety test for Industrial Arts—ALL RIGHT!'; 'Only one wrong—that's excellent.' 'I knew that if you listened in class, you'd do well.' 'I bet you feel good about that . . . ' He'd answer affirmatively, saying, 'It was easy.' "

Notice that Mark's mother's approval was directed at Mark's behavior rather than at Mark. That's good, because we want to encourage competent behavior, not make Mark dependent on other people's approval. The use of social reinforcement is more desirable than that of tangible, extrinsic reinforcers because social reinforcers are more natural. It makes more sense to teach children that good behavior pleases other people than to teach them to behave well to get a cookie or a toy. Of course, there are usually better reasons for behaving well than just pleasing others, but for children, this is a useful place to begin.

In motivating responsible behavior in children, we move hierarchically. We go from tangible, extrinsic reinforcers, such as gold stars, food, and toys, to social and other conditioned reinforcers, such as smiles, "thank yous," and grades. Eventually, children's behavior will be guided by intrinsic and natural consequences inherent in the activity itself.

Activity Reinforcers

Some activities, such as rocking and sucking, are innately reinforcing to the infant. Most activities acquire reinforcing properties by being paired with already existing reinforcers. Children's activities and play behavior result in in-teresting sensory stimulation (e.g., drawing), gratification of some need (e.g., achievement), a desirable social consequence (e.g., winning a game), or some combination of the three. As a result, the activities themselves become reinforcing (fun).

David Premack (1962) pointed out in his famous "Premack Principle" that more-preferred activities can be used to reinforce less-preferred activities ("After your room is clean, you can watch TV"). Reversing the contingency ("OK, you can watch TV first, but make sure you clean your room afterwards") lessens or eliminates its motivational impact. Most parents have learned that their children will work hard to gain valued reinforcers.

Tangible or Token Reinforcers

Token reinforcers are "things" that have acquired reinforcing properties, such as money, toys, grades, prizes, or gold stars. Most 2-year-olds, if offered a choice of a fifty-dollar bill or five shiny new pennies, would probably choose the coins. It doesn't take long for children to learn, however, that the green paper can be exchanged for other reinforcers, such as toys, ice cream, baseball cards, and comic books. In this way, the funny green paper acquires reinforcing properties of its own, and children will ask (and work) for it. Tangibles are low-level reinforcers and should be used sparingly, or when higher-level, social or natural reinforcers are not available or effective. Food, a powerful primary reinforcer, is generally not appropriate for motivating new learning. If food is misused as an incentive, faulty eating patterns may be learned.

USING REINFORCERS JUDICIOUSLY

Natural consequences (discussion follows) are preferred to those ordinarily contrived by parents and teachers. In many situations, however, social and activity reinforcers are the natural consequences of appropriate behavior.

When used judiciously, tangible rewards can be a powerful teaching tool.

In any case, thoughtfully arranged consequences are a powerful teaching tool. Hundreds of studies and everyday observation demonstrate that primary and secondary reinforcers can be used successfully to motivate the learning of new behavior and to motivate the performance of established behavior patterns in children of all ages.

Optimal use of reinforcement requires knowledge of several learning principles. Importantly, reinforcement is most effective when it is delivered immediately following the desired response, particularly during new learning. Similarly, reinforcement is more effective when it occurs after every correct response. Once the new response is established, reinforcers can be administered more occasionally and with some delay. It is during this period that contrived reinforcers can be replaced with natural outcomes. Even after the behavior is quite ingrained, however, occasional reinforcement encourages its persistence.

NATURAL AND LOGICAL CONSEQUENCES

Study Question What natural consequences might follow if

1. *Tom refuses to brush his teeth?*
2. *Adriana borrowed Dad's radio without his permission and broke it?*

3. Tracy makes a lot of noise and keeps getting out of her seat in a restaurant?

As children mature, parental regulation of their behavior becomes less necessary. Most adolescents do not need and, in fact, would probably resent the regulation of their behavior through parental rewards and punishments. Adults take showers, brush their teeth, go to bed at a reasonable hour, and dress appropriately on cold days because of the natural consequences of these actions. That is, we feel fresh, clean, alert, and comfortable as we move around the community.

The concept of natural and logical consequences is associated with Rudolf Dreikurs (Dreikurs & Grey, 1970). Dreikurs encouraged parents to give their children the opportunity to experience the effects of their choices, good or bad (Berns, 1989). Rather than rewarding or punishing children's behavior, which makes the parents responsible for the child's behavior, children should be allowed to make their own decisions. When their judgment is good, they reap the benefits. If their judgment is poor, they will suffer the consequences. In this way, children's behavior and judgment will become more adultlike, guided by their natural outcomes rather than by parental reactions.

For example, if Carlos is late for dinner, his meal will be cold or not there at all. If he is hungry, he will prepare his own food and perhaps eat alone. This should not be conceived of as punishment. Carlos is suffering from the natural consequences of his tardiness, not from some contrived parental penalty. If Susan doesn't want to wear a hat or gloves when the windchill factor is minus 12, why not let her experience the consequences of this decision? This is not done to punish her but to give her the opportunity to learn how to dress sensibly.

With the best intentions, parents often try to protect their children from such negative outcomes. Pointing out such consequences before they occur and helping the child to see his alternatives is good parenting. Arguing, shouting, and using coercion make little sense when natural, though unpleasant, outcomes lead to faster learning.

Obviously, we would never allow a child to put himself into a dangerous situation to "teach him a lesson." For example, if Donna runs into the street to get her ball, we will not wait for a trip to the emergency room for her to learn greater caution during play. When a natural consequence is inappropriate, we use what Dreikurs calls a logical consequence, one that "fits" the situation (Dinkmeyer & McKay, 1982). If we cannot trust David when he is outside, he will have to play inside. This should not be construed or communicated as a punishment, because it is not an arbitrary penalty. Rather, it is connected in a logical way to David's careless behavior.

Natural and logical consequences are generally preferable to rewards and punishments. They allow parents to avoid power struggles while giving children the opportunity to learn the real-life consequences of good and bad choices.

Eric's "Sick Day"

When my younger son Eric was 4 years old, in an angry moment, he refused to go to nursery school. I was not willing to force him to go to school. That would be a power struggle. Since I had no obligation to be elsewhere, I said "Fine, but remember you only stay home from school when you are sick." This is a logical consequence. He put on his pajamas and stayed in bed all day (because he was "sick"). There is no TV in his room, and I couldn't play with him because I didn't want to catch whatever he had. For lunch, he had toast and jelly. You get the point. He had an extremely boring day playing sick, and he learned something about making threats.

"The purpose of allowing natural consequences to occur and of designing logical consequences is to encourage children to make responsible decisions, not to force their submission. This mode of discipline permits a child to choose and then to be accountable for the decision, whether it turns out well or not. Most children, when permitted to make poor decisions, learn from the consequences" (Dinkmeyer & McKay, 1982, p. 73).

DISCOURAGING SELF-RELIANCE

Parents often do things for children that children could do for themselves. This is not necessarily bad, but such episodes represent lost learning opportunities for the child. Children who are able to should dress themselves, make their own meals, do their own homework, and solve their own problems. Sometimes the parent's motive is to "save the child from himself." Should parents step in and save a child from the unfortunate consequences of his own actions?

A. Fischer (1985) quotes one parent as saying, "You have mixed reactions because you don't want your children relying on you all the time, but you don't want them to fail either. Against my better judgment, I've typed term papers for my children, saved their jobs by making deliveries, made phone calls to cancel appointments when they forgot." Such parental rescue missions, by preventing children from experiencing the aversive consequences of their irresponsibility, may encourage further thoughtless behavior. Of course, if the child is "in over his head," abandoning him to catastrophe would not constitute good parenting.

When staring in the frightening face of failure, children gain more by having their parents help them clarify how they "messed up" and what they can do about it. "If your child claims to be incapable of the work, it's much more helpful to look for the reasons why. Giving a child advice on time management or

making an appointment together to see a teacher is a far cry from sitting at a child's side and supplying half the sentences for a term paper" (Lopez, quoted by A. Fischer, 1985).

According to Dr. Lopez, if the child is capable of doing a job but procrastinates to the point of failure, "let him fail. This is difficult for parents to swallow. But if Tommy's grade gets lowered, or he's fired from his part-time job, there's a better chance the next time he'll do his own homework assignment or keep his personal life from interfering with his working hours. It's part of a child's training to take on responsibilities, to deal with the conflicts and to experience what happens if the job doesn't get done . . . By rushing to the rescue they're not giving their children the motivation or the inner resources to succeed independently."

Mark # 5

"With my busy schedule of full-time work and part-time schooling, I found it 'easier' to do things for Mark rather than explain to him how and why. Very often, especially while he was small, I'd dress him before I woke him. Rather than argue with him about chores, I'd keep his room neat, pick up after him, make his bed and exempt him from regular chores. Now and then over the years, I'd establish some mild expectations and request his cooperation. But as my attention wandered, I let things drop.

[2 weeks later] "One interesting observation Mark made this week is 'Why don't you ever do things for me anymore?' I was refreshed to see that he noticed and that he didn't seem angry about it. At the time he had asked me to tie his sneakers, because his shirt would come out of his pants, if he did it. I had teased him by whistling and then said, 'Well, I guess you can just put your shirt back in again.' I explained that it was 'good' for him to learn to do things for himself; that he was old enough now to be responsible for himself; and that our lives are very busy now and I need all the help he can give me.

"P.S. He's still not making his bed nor feeding his fish (without 3 reminders), nor flushing the toilet in the morning. On that last one, I stopped nagging him, so yesterday for once he did it. So I was able to praise him instead for a change (today he didn't flush again)."

OBSERVATIONAL LEARNING

Study Question *Analyze Mark's mother's initial motivation to do things for him that he could do for himself. Describe the factors that seem to discourage her efforts to modify Mark's behavior.*

Child-rearing techniques, by definition, are strategies parents adopt to change their children's behavior. Rewards, natural consequences, punishment, and thoughtful communication methods (described in chapter 7) exemplify such strategies. Observational learning refers to an often unintentional mode of learning in which someone learns a new behavior by watching another person (a model) engage in that behavior.

"The observer sees the model perform the behavior but does not engage in overt responses himself or receive any consequences" (Kazdin, 1984, p.18). If the model's behavior is reinforced, the observer is more likely to imitate the model's behavior. Albert Bandura emphasizes the role of observational learning in what he initially called social learning theory (Bandura, 1977b) and now calls social cognition theory (Bandura, 1986). The term observational learning encompasses other processes, including imitation and identification.

Although new learning may occur from simply observing the model's behavior, the likelihood that the behavior will be *performed* depends upon many factors. These include the model's prestige, status, perceived similarity to the observer, the number of models, the child's age and intelligence, the activity being observed, and the consequences of the model's behavior (Berns, 1989). Parents are usually high status models and have many opportunities to reward children for "matching" their behaviors.

It seems likely that much of what children learn from their parents is learned *not* through formal instruction or through the use of incentives but rather by watching and listening to what their parents do and say. We often hear young children make comments they could not possibly understand, only to find out they were repeating ideas expressed by their parents. Children are also very likely to observe and then imitate the behaviors of their siblings, peers, teachers, and popular culture heroes.

It is fortunate that children can learn through observation. It is usually easier to teach by example than to have to explain or instruct. Parents can say, "Watch what I do and then you try it." Children's moral reasoning and rule-following behavior are also very susceptible to the influence of models (Toner, Moore, & Ashley, 1978; Toner & Potts, 1981).

PUNISHMENT

Observe parents in the company of their young children. What do you hear them say? "No!," "Stop that," "Don't you do that again," "Keep your hands to yourself," "That's not nice to say," and "Sit still." Parents often expend greater effort discouraging misbehavior than they do promoting good behavior. What we call socialization largely refers to the inhibition of undesirable behaviors.

Parents are frustrated by their children's misbehaviors. Frustration may be accompanied by aggressive feelings and behaviors. It is not surprising that parents, when annoyed, raise their voices and show threatening facial expressions and gestures. Many parents strike their children when they are in this aroused emotional state. Young children are weak and not likely to retaliate. (In my early days of parenting, my unintentionally loud or harsh rebukes were punished when they inadvertently elicited sadness or crying in my children. I found myself in the awkward, but necessary, position of apologizing for my overreaction to their misconduct.)

The frequency of misbehavior can be so high that some parents believe their children are being deliberately provocative ("looking for trouble"). This increases their frustration and anger. We can easily understand why frustrated parents adopt punitive strategies to "correct" their children's behavior. Punitive methods are intended to discourage unacceptable behaviors by following them with unpleasant outcomes.

Mark #6

"All was going as well as could be expected until I decided to look at his homework. Then I exploded. 'What kind of crap-writing is this? You're supposed to be an artist and your circles look like they were done by someone who's retarded!' I was terrible. I angrily told him he had better clean up his act.

"Okay, so I lost it. Now I'm sorry and realize how damaging that type of response can be. It's overwhelming how frustrating parenting can be. If I am not constantly vigilant in my attempts to parent my son lovingly and firmly, my chances of success are unlikely. So I will try again . . . relentlessly, because I love him."

Parental "hurting" responses can escalate into conflicts of major proportions. Giving young children this type of power over our emotional reactions is counterproductive. It encourages "power struggles" between parents and children. Parental responsiveness to children's behavrs   can encourage either new patterns of interpersonal skills or patterns of spiteful defiance.

Defining Punishment

Behavioral psychologists consider a stimulus a punisher if its presentation following a response suppresses the response; that is, a stimulus is only considered a punisher if its presentation weakens the response. If a child continues to tell lies after a spanking, the spanking does not satisfy the definition of punishment.

Parents sometimes wonder why punishment "doesn't work." According to the present definition, if it doesn't work, it's not punishment. Many factors influence children's behavior in addition to rewards and punishments. Children may continue to misbehave following a spanking because the incentives for misbehaving are stronger than the punishment. Continuing to misbehave may also constitute "retaliation" for the punishment.

Psychologists have defined two types of punishment. *Positive punishment* describes the presentation of an aversive stimulus following a specific response and the subsequent weakening of that response. If Mom's frown following Pete's fresh answer leads to a reduction in freshness, then Mom's frown is a punisher (in that instance). If her frown has no effect or, indeed, encourages "an attitude," it is not a punisher.

Negative punishment is defined by the removal of a positive reinforcer (usually some privilege) following the misbehavior, leading to a reduction in its occurrence. After grabbing and pulling his sister's hair, John is penalized by having to leave the dinner table and go without dinner. John no longer mistreats his sister. Thus, his banishment constitutes negative punishment. A frequently used negative punishment technique is time out from reinforcement (see Spotlight: Time Out from Reinforcement).

There are two types of punishment. The more common consists of following a misbehavior with an aversive stimulus, such as a reprimand or criticism. One can also punish by withholding opportunities for reinforcement following misbehavior. Children may forfeit their dessert or the opportunity to go outside to play. This latter practice is called "grounding." Strictly speaking, grounding a child or sending him to his room does not eliminate access to all positive reinforcers. Most children have an abundant supply of reinforcers in their rooms.

Kazdin (1984) defines time out from reinforcement as "the removal of all positive reinforcers for a certain period of time . . . The crucial ingredient of time out is delineating a time period in which reinforcement is unavailable" (p. 131). Like other punishers, time out is most effective when it is applied during or immediately following a transgression.

The punishing stimulus is the child's removal from a reinforcing activity. Short time out intervals (3 to 5 minutes) seem to work as well as longer intervals. If children resist by shouting or kicking, we can tell them that the time out does not begin until they are quiet. We should praise children for the first appropriate response after time out (Dangel & Polster, 1988).

Many schools have time out rooms or booths that isolate misbehaving children from social and other reinforcers in the classroom. Brief isolation is appropriate when a child behaves aggressively toward another or engages in a response that a parent will not tolerate.

As a punishment procedure, time out from reinforcement is effective, brief, and it does not involve pain. Therefore, it is less punitive than spanking. Like most punitive methods and extinction, time out in itself is not likely to teach more appropriate behavior. Hence, it should be combined with positive reinforcement methods. In addition, isolating or removing a child from a given setting requires preparation, and the child might resist. Time out can be a powerful way of discouraging misbehavior, but it should not be used excessively.

Punishers can be verbal statements (threats, warnings, reprimands, criticisms), a loud or angry voice, facial expressions (frowns, glaring looks), physical or corporal punishment (spanking, slapping), or poor grades. If the occurrence of any of these outcomes discourages a behavior, the definition of punishment is satisfied. Note that a stimulus such as a reprimand can serve as a reinforcer or a punisher depending upon its effect on behavior.

Negative punishers include the removal of opportunities for positive reinforcement, such as losing the chance to watch TV, to use the family car, or being "grounded." The latter eliminates opportunities for out-of-house reinforcers, including interactions with friends and outdoor play activities.

It can be seen from the definitions of positive and negative punishment that punishment does not teach children good behaviors. It only teaches children what *not* to do. The use of punishment, particularly corporal punishment, in discipline is controversial, and it should be. Most psychologists discourage its use, preferring instead positive methods. Removing reinforcers is more desirable than presenting aversive stimuli. Aversive stimuli, such as spankings or criticism, generally increase a child's arousal (seen as crying, sadness, fear, or anger) and might produce "side effects" (see "Side Effects of Punishment").

Now let us discuss how to punish effectively. I do not advocate punishment, because, excessively used, punishment does not support our four parenting goals. However, its use is widespread,* and, when used sparingly, it can be an effective discipline method. Parents who choose to punish should be aware of the principles as well as the risks of punishment.

Using Punishment Effectively

Punishers are most effective when they immediately follow the misbehavior. Like reinforcers, punishers are weakened by delayed presentation. Children who are exposed to frequent punishments seem to adapt to aversive stimuli ("Hit me, I don't care"). They become less susceptible to its effects. Some children may learn that after they are punished, their parents feel guilty and offer reinforcers. This "mixed message" could encourage rather than discourage misbehavior (Kazdin, 1984).

Frequent and predictable punishment of the offending behavior is more effective than occasional punishment. Parents should encourage an acceptable alternative to the punished behavior that produces equal or greater reinforcement. For example, instead of drawing on the wall, children would be encouraged to draw on a board or easel.

Punishers should routinely be preceded by warnings and statements of relevant rules. Following a warning, noncompliance brings the designated punishment. In this way, warnings acquire aversive properties and may discourage misbehavior in their own right. "If you treat the baby roughly again, you will have to sit in the time out chair for 5 minutes." It is crucial that parents follow through. Idle threats will be ignored and weaken parental credibility. State rules that help children learn the relationship between their misbehavior and subsequent penalties.

---

*In December, 1988, Louis Harris and Associates polled (by telephone) 1,250 United States citizens regarding their attitudes about corporal punishment. About 86 percent of those sampled approved of physical discipline, down from 90 to 95 percent in previous studies. Seventy-one percent of the women and 30 percent of the men admitted that they spank their children frequently (*New York Times,* August 16, 1989).

Side Effects of Punishment

Study Question What possible side effects might discourage parents from using punishment?

Both research and conventional wisdom suggest that using punishment indiscriminately can lead to undesirable or harmful side effects (Toner, 1986). Intense physical punishment may lead to serious physical injury or emotional disturbance. Even if the punishment is not extreme, it may upset children enough to interfere with the learning of more adaptive behavior. If children are intimidated, the parent-child relationship may suffer.

Physical punishment also models a "might makes right" philosophy of social influence (Kazdin, 1984). There is a famous cartoon of a father spanking his son, and the caption reads, "This will teach you to hit your sister." It probably will! The parent who often punishes runs the risk of becoming an aversive stimulus. The child may come to fear, hate, or at least resent the indiscriminately punitive parent, rendering him or her less effective in that role (Toner, 1986).

Similarly, the setting in which punishment occurs, school or home for example, may also acquire aversive properties leading to avoidance through disruptive behavior, truancy, or running away. Because the misbehavior may momentarily cease following punishment, the parent may be misled into believing that a temporary change is permanent. Finally, parents may become "dependent" on punishment as a way of achieving immediate compliance instead of using methods that support our parenting goals.

"Parents who use punishment a lot often complain that their children trap them into using more and more punishment by acting indifferent about mild punishment and provoking them into making punishment tougher. For example, a boy who is spanked holds back his tears, rather than letting his father see how much pain he feels" (Blechman, 1985, p. 15).

Many children learn, when they feel they are being unfairly treated, to not give the punisher the "satisfaction" of seeing their pain. And parents therefore increase the intensity of their punishments in an escalating power struggle with their child.

Learning to Avoid Detection

Study Question If a child admits to misbehaving and is then punished, for what is the child being punished?

Children may learn to reduce the likelihood of punishment by not getting caught. In other words, they become more deceptive, and some learn to lie. If a child admits to misbehaving and is then punished, it may be the admission that is being punished rather than the misbehavior. Some children (and adults) put more energy into "not getting caught" than into learning socially acceptable behavior.

M. L. Hoffman (1967) observed that children of parents who use a power-assertive discipline style demonstrate higher levels of rule-breaking behavior when they are away from home. This suggests that these children may be learning to discriminate between situations on the basis of the probability of punishment. In other words, such children may become more likely to break rules in situations where punishment of rule-breaking behavior is improbable.

Overcorrection

Kazdin (1984) considers overcorrection punishment by compulsory effort. Overcorrection is a type of logical consequence wherein restitution must be made for the unacceptable behavior. This is followed by extensive positive practice of a more appropriate response. Restitution means correcting the consequences of one's actions. For example, Phillip has to help the boy he pushed down stand up, and then he must apologize to him.

A variation requires that the child restore the environment to a "better-than-original state" (Jenson, Sloane, & Young, 1988). A child who throws his clothes on the floor might be required to not only pick up his clothes but to vacuum the carpet and dust the furniture. Positive practice requires the repeated performance of behaviors that are preferred alternatives to the misbehavior. Rachel has to practice asking politely for something she wants rather than grabbing and pushing.

"Although overcorrection consists of restitution and positive practice, the constituent procedures sometimes are combined and other times used alone, depending upon the behaviors that are to be surpressed" (Kazdin, 1984, p. 136). If, for example, a situation cannot be corrected, positive practice is used alone. Repeating a pattern of correct behavior presumably has aversive properties that can be avoided by behaving well.

In the past, teachers may have had children write, "I will not be late again" a hundred times, certainly an aversive task, but writing it is not the same as doing it. Unlike most punitive methods, positive practice teaches desirable behavior, an important advantage (Kazdin, 1984). Learning when and how to use overcorrection, while avoiding physical confrontation with the child, requires practice. Other less restrictive procedures should be tried first (Jenson et al., 1988).

SHOULD PARENTS PUNISH?

The more we learn about punishment, the more aware we become about how it can be misused. Parents often use punishment prematurely without understanding its possible side effects. I try to avoid using punishment when disciplining my children, and I hope I would never strike them. There are too many alternatives for encouraging good behavior and discouraging misbehaviors. Parents who do punish usually don't punish well. The misbehavior continues.

There are times when judiciously administered punishers can be used to discourage persistent, annoying, self-destructive, or dangerous actions that cannot be tolerated. Swift punishment may be appropriate when children run into traffic, play with matches, or hang out a window. The occasional use of brief reprimands has been found to be effective when the child's name is spoken with eye contact, neutral facial expression, and neutral tone of voice. If the reprimand is not effective, time out follows. If the reprimand is effective, the desirable behavior is praised (Jenson, et al., 1988). Toner (1986) suggests as alternatives to punishment "appeals to reason tailored to children's cognitive levels, exposure to rule-following models, provision of rewards for rule-following behavior, and provision of guidelines for resisting temptation" (p. 27).

"Used judiciously, punishment can be quite effective in suppressing unwanted behavior, without adversely affecting desirable behaviors. This excludes extremely severe punishment, and that which is administered by a hostile and rejecting caretaker. What we are referring to is punishment used by a responsible and concerned person in teaching acceptable behavior" (Walters & Grusec, 1977, p. 176–177).

SUMMARY

New parents are often unsure about how to comfort a distressed infant without "spoiling" it. For most of the first year, infants cry reflexively, and parents should provide comfort by feeding or holding them or taking other appropriate actions. Toward the end of the first year, parents should become more discriminating about how and when they respond. When infants misbehave, brief, firm statements and physical restraint are appropriate. Arranging a safe and stimulating environment with minimal opportunity for mischief is an excellent precaution. As always, patience is the key to good parenting.

Responsive parents place limits on children's behavior. Children naturally test these limits. By the age of 2 years, most children can learn to inhibit actions that elicit disapproval. Having a few, simple, clearly stated rules fosters internalization of parental standards. Parental inconsistency and permissiveness encourage defiance. Parental coercion may lead children to take parents seriously but possibly at the expense of our parenting goals.

Human behavior is very much influenced by its consequences. Parents gain from understanding how to use positive reinforcers to encourage desirable behavior. Stating rules and applying appropriate reinforcement contingencies is a powerful combination of strategies. Some critics question the strategic use of rewards, because there are usually better reasons for behaving well than "getting something." Nevertheless, incentives provide a powerful means of teaching and motivating new behaviors until more natural or intrinsic outcomes can exert their influence.

In changing children's behavior, parents should address one problem at a time in small steps. They should create a flexible plan that will motivate a positive change in behavior. They should also arrange immediate positive outcomes (particularly social reinforcement) for improvement. Parents should ignore misbehavior when possible. A gradual shift from contrived to natural consequences is helpful.

When parents perform tasks or solve problems for their children, they are doing them a disservice. They are depriving them of the opportunity to learn self-management and other skills that increase their autonomy and enhance their self-esteem. Although it is sometimes difficult to watch our children falter, experience is an excellent teacher. We should avoid interfering with natural outcomes.

Extinction consists of withholding those stimuli that may be reinforcing the misbehavior. Very often, parental attention to the undesirable action encourages its repetition. Children will learn to nag, whine, or complain if such annoying behaviors get them what they want. Parents may inadvertently shape such obnoxious behaviors as tantrums by making the child nag or cry for longer and longer periods before giving in.

Parents who lack realistic expectations about their children, or who are short in patience, may discipline when they are frustrated and angry. They may develop a punitive parenting style. Parents who become emotionally aroused when children misbehave often fall into a power struggle of escalating, provocative interactions with their children.

Parents who use punishment excessively may encourage undesirable personality and behavioral patterns in their children, including resentment and anger toward the parent. Such children may behave aggressively toward other children. Parents who decide to use punishment should learn to punish strategically. Removing privileges contingent upon misbehavior is preferable to presenting aversive stimuli. The latter provokes intense emotional reactions in children, including anger and hostility. Punishment should always be preceded by a warning.

Overcorrection requires that the child make restitution for his misbehavior and that he extensively practice more desirable behavior. Time out from reinforcement consists of removing a child from reinforcing activities for a brief time for misbehaving. Punishment can be used successfully to suppress unwanted behavior, but it does not teach a child correct behavior. The possible side effects of excessive punishment should motivate parents to use more thoughtful discipline strategies.

CHAPTER SEVEN

Communication and Relationships in Families

OBJECTIVES

After studying chapter 7, students should be able to

1. Analyze the importance of the following in child rearing:
   a. Parental sensitivity
   b. Parental responsiveness
   c. Parental understanding
   d. Parental acceptance
   e. Parental patience
2. Describe the characteristics of "motherese"
3. List the steps that parents can take to encourage infant speech
4. Discuss several common pitfalls in parent-child communication
5. Define and describe the role of each of the following parental communication skills, and give one example:
   a. Attention
   b. Sympathetic listening
   c. Acknowledging feelings
   d. Nonverbal communication skills
   e. Descriptive praise
   f. Giving constructive feedback
   g. Exploring alternatives
   h. Problem ownership
   i. I messages
   j. Apologizing
6. Discuss the nature of the infant's attachment to its caretakers
7. Define secure and insecure attachment and the conditions of rearing associated with each
8. Describe stranger anxiety and separation distress
9. Describe the potential advantages and disadvantages of small and large families
10. Discuss the research findings regarding the effects of birth order and spacing between siblings
11. Compare only children to children with siblings
12. Explain why the term "sibling ambivalence" is more appropriate than "sibling rivalry"
13. Discuss how parents can best handle sibling conflict

INTRODUCTION

Mark #7

"It was close to dinnertime so I called down to my 9-year-old son. He answered me back sharply stating 'not now.' He and his friends were in pursuit of a mouse. The boys were very excited, trying to corner it on our front lawn. I yelled for them to keep their voices down. Within moments, the tension and excitement climaxed. One boy all along had been arguing to 'leave the mouse be.' Other boys were enjoying the terrorism. My son, torn between peer approval and good judgment, got so wound up that in an attempt to restrain the mouse by stepping on its tail ended up crushing him.

"In the flood of mixed reactions, I spied what I perceived as a smirk of self-satisfaction on Mark's face. Immediately I went down to 'set him straight.' I scolded him in front of his friends, explaining that he should be ashamed of himself, that it was a very cruel and heartless thing to do, etc., etc., etc. I added that his behavior made me ashamed of him and that he'd be punished the rest of the week!

"During dinner, Mark had to leave the table because he could not restrain himself. (He had gone to his room, closed the door and hid his crying until dinner. Once at the table a few moments he began crying again.) I asked him to tell me what was bothering him because I wasn't sure whether he was angry about the punishment, embarrassed in front of his friends by the scolding, or sorry for his actions. He went into his room again,

crying very hard. I tried to hold him, comfort him, and encourage him to talk to me about it. Eventually, he explained that he was very upset about the 'poor mouse' and how 'he must be suffering' and how this was the first time he had ever killed anything.

"I continued to try to hug and hold him, wipe his tears, and explain to him that the mouse was dead and out of pain. I told him that we're all human and all make mistakes and that with all the excitement 'things just got out of hand,' that God would understand and forgive him if he was truly sorry. We talked for a long time and he was upset for hours, but I think we both learned something from the experience. I learned not to be so rash but rather to remove him from the situation, calmly, and privately ask him to explain his behavior before I unjustly blurt out a punishment. (By the way, I revoked the punishment after all, when I realized how sorry he was.) Mark learned (I hope) to have more respect for living creatures."

This journal entry brings to our attention several likely phases of parent-child communications during conflict: a crisis; a "flood of mixed reactions" from the parent and the child; confusion and misinterpretation; a scolding or lecture that provokes strong reactions in the child, including crying and guilt; perhaps an attempt to communicate with caring; the expression of strong feelings; acknowledgment of the child's feelings; and some type of resolution.

In her journal, Mark's mother wondered whether Mark, the "new kid on the block," may have been trying to be the "tough guy by standing up to me and talking back" and by being the one who captured the mouse. By trying to understand his motivations and actions, she was taking an important first step in improving her parenting skills. She was learning to withhold, or temper, her immediate, angry reactions in favor of more thoughtful and caring communications.

In this chapter, we examine parent-child communication and the nature of relationships in families. The material we cover applies to all four parenting goals, but particularly goal #3— good parent-child relationships. Poor communication is almost always a factor in poor family relationships and interpersonal conflict. Successful, caring relationships require effective, direct communication.

This chapter also describes several parental communication skills that encourage children not only to express themselves freely but to behave well. The communication skills include descriptive praise, constructive feedback, sympathetic (active) listening, I messages, and how to "own" a problem.

"Once a human being has arrived on this earth, communication is the largest single factor determining what kinds of relationships he makes with others and what happens to him in the world about him. How he manages his survival, how he develops intimacy, how productive he is, how he makes sense, how he connects with his own divinity—all are largely dependent on his communication skills" (Satir, 1972, p. 30).

PARENTAL SENSITIVITY AND RESPONSIVENESS

Study Question What role do parental sensitivity and emotional responsiveness play in parent-child interactions?

Parental sensitivity and responsiveness can be observed when a mother, while preparing dinner, glances toward her seated infant. With eye contact and a smile, she asks the child a question. If the infant drops her bottle, is fretting, or is about to tip over in her seat, the mother's watchfulness allows her to assess the situation quickly and respond appropriately.

Such contingent responding teaches infants that their sounds and actions have effects (Symons & Moran, 1987). It also encourages reciprocal response patterns. This basic sequence of parental alertness and appropriate responding exemplifies a fundamental component of good parenting.

Parents closely monitor the needs and actions of their young children. Over the course of evolution, children of less-vigilant parents were probably less likely to survive. Genes encouraging greater parental sensitivity and responsiveness would have proliferated. As we saw in chapter 4, similar evolutionary processes led to "cute" facial features and appealing behaviors that keep parents interested in and close to their infants.

Immediate, appropriate (contingent) responsiveness in parents encourages sustained interactions between parent and child. Face-to-face interactions with positive emotional tone seem to be especially critical to children's emotional growth. These face-to-face, affective interactions, in turn, provide the basis for initial socialization (J. S. Watson, 1981). Infrequent positive emotional expressions, in particular, may increase the risk status of children in multiproblem families (Cohn & Tronick, 1989).

A mother's ability to adjust her attentional and emotional reactions to her infant's rhythms contributes to the quality of their relationship (Kaye, 1982). Children exhibit more distress when their mothers fail to adjust their responses to the child's patterns (Cohn & Tronick, 1989). We recall that infants of depressed mothers are generally less responsive and express fewer positive emotions than infants of healthy mothers. Similarly, mothers who are distressed often miss important signals in their children's behavior (Wahler & Dumas, 1989).

PARENTAL UNDERSTANDING, ACCEPTANCE, AND PATIENCE

Mark #8

"Mark was given a mimeographed sheet of questions and multiple-choice problems as science homework. All week long he has been proudly relating what he was learning about photosynthesis. Now when it came time to put it in writing, he decided to 'display inadequacy.' Mark sat and stared into space. When I impatiently prodded him to 'get started!' he heaved a sigh of resignation and began to read over the paper. Repeatedly, he'd complain he didn't understand the question, couldn't read a word, had no idea of the answer, was too tired, etc. This complaining and whining went on and on.

"As I was doing the dishes, I started to sense that he was purposely 'playing dumb.' I made some suggestions that he re-read the pages and start 'using his head.' As time went on, I got angrier and angrier and began to threaten him. I told him that I was getting angry enough to 'beat him' (although he's never experienced a 'beating' from me yet—only smacks now and then), that he'd better re-read all of it if necessary. I threatened that we'd stay in and stay up late every night until he developed good study habits in school and at home.

"He continued to whine, slouch, moan, fake cry and stutter over words he'd normally never have trouble with. I finally got my emotions so out of control that I smacked him, once over the head and three times on his back and shoulders. He immediately went off crying to his room, closing the door. Right away I felt

frightened that I had gotten so angry and sorry that I'd lost my good sense. I still felt that in some way I had to convey to him that I would not fall prey to his manipulations, that I wouldn't give him the answers or let him 'skip it.' My reaction was completely out of line, but my pride got in the way so I told him that he had 5 minutes to finish his homework.

"His next reaction was positive. When he did come out, he was more willing and attentive. I, in turn, was more patient, loving, instructional, and encouraging. I hinted on how to decide what sections needed to be re-read in the book, looking for key words in the paragraphs and using the glossary. By the time we were through, he had even done additional work."

Needless confrontations between frustrated parents and discouraged children occur all too frequently. As we follow the sequence of "communications," we notice that something is wrong. Parental expectations are being frustrated at every turn. Impatience gives rise to anger and even violence. Mark's mom assumed he was "playing dumb." One suspects that if she had interpreted the situation differently (as she eventually did), she would have responded more sympathetically.

Study Question *In this encounter, what assumptions did Mark's mom make about his behavior?*

What information about children do we need to help us interpret such encounters more constructively? It helps to remember that children are different from adults physically, emotionally, and cognitively. Their thinking is less logical and more intuitive, and they are less informed. They have shorter attention spans and are more easily frustrated. They also have relatively few coping mechanisms, which leaves them emotionally vulnerable. As we have seen, they are very much controlled by immediate gratification. Despite the beliefs of our ancestors, they are anything but miniature adults!

What children say and do usually makes sense to them, if not always to us. As Piaget emphasized, they have difficulty grasping our adult perspective. As parents, we have the opportunity to appreciate their unique, if limited, perspectives, to try to see (and feel) things as they do, and to respond accordingly. This willingness to consider their perspective rather than to impose our own can make a big difference in discipline encounters.

I do not advocate that parents yield to a child's point of view. Rather, children need help clarifying their issues, understanding our perspective, and seeking a resolution between the two. The alternative to problem solving is usually conflict and anger. Negative emotional expressions disrupt the problem-solving process (Forgatch, 1989).

The better we understand children, the easier it becomes to accept them as they are. Understanding is a prerequisite to patience and, therefore, to subsequent change. In the incident just cited, Mark's mother initially did not know how to handle him as a stubborn student, and so she reacted punitively. Eventually she changed her perspective, accepted his plight, and supported him through it.

Mark #8 Addendum

"Both incidents ended with us both pleased to have the task behind us. I tucked him in, said his prayers with him and snuggled a little and teased him by tickling him to make him laugh. I'm sure I did these things to reaffirm my love and to regain an equilibrium in our relationship." (See Spotlight: Parental Support and Expressions of Physical Affection.)

Physical affection and verbal caring can be powerful tools for behavior change. "When a child has misbehaved, the father or mother moves physically close to him, to offer him support. This will help the offending child to overcome his fear and guilty feelings, and make the best use of the teaching the parent is about to offer" (Satir, 1972, p. 16).

LANGUAGE ACQUISITION

Study Question What roles do biology and rearing play in preparing children to learn language?

Speech is one of the last human traits to have evolved, and it is probably the most distinctively human. It is through language that we communicate thoughts and information, organize our ideas, plan for the future, express our feelings, and regulate our behavior. There are few milestones in development that are as exciting to parents as their child's first words. It is remarkable that our most complex ability, understanding and speaking words, begins to emerge during infancy. Ironically, the word infant means "without language."

By the time children are 3 or 4 years old, they can effortlessly create and comprehend an almost infinite variety of grammatical and meaningful sentences. "Acquiring their first language is the most impressive intellectual feat many people will ever perform" (Miller & Gildea, 1987, p. 94), but we still do not fully understand how children acquire language.

We do know that language acquisition is a process that reflects the interaction between inherited dispositions and prolonged exposure to a particular language system (Hoff-Ginsberg & Shatz, 1982). The relative contribution of both factors is still disputed. Language centers present in the human brain at birth predispose children to notice and copy speech sounds and relate them to objects and events. There is good reason to believe that the prevalence of language disorders in childhood, such as dyslexia, reflects the still incomplete evolution of language ability in our species (Skinner, 1987).

First Sounds

The first sounds that infants utter (grunts, gurgles, burps, hiccups, cries, and, eventually, cooing) are prelinguistic. There is no intention to communicate, and the sounds lack symbolic meaning. Nevertheless, these sometimes mechanical and sometimes emotionally expressive vocalizations do communicate in that they elicit important reactions from caretakers. There is an unintended communication of need without language, and parents respond accordingly.

Motherese (Adult-to-Child Language)

Study Question   In what ways do we adjust our speech when we talk to very young children?

People automatically adjust their speech to the audience they are addressing, for example, speaking more loudly to a large group or to a person at a distance. Even 4-year-olds have been observed "talking down" to 2-year-olds (Sachs & Devin, 1976). The way in which we unconsciously adjust our speech when talking to infants has been labeled "motherese" (as in Chinese, Japanese) and occurs in almost all language groups (Ferguson, 1977; Grieser & Kuhl, 1988). Studies confirm that mothers, when reading to their preschool children, adjust their speech according to the children's cognitive and language skills (e.g., Goodsitt, Raitan, & Perlmutter, 1988).

These adjustments help infants make out unfamiliar sounds and also increase their emotional responses and attention (Fernald, 1985; 1989; Reich, 1986). It is not clear, however, whether motherese facilitates language acquisition (Scarborough & Wyckoff, 1986). When we speak to infants, we typically (Reich, 1986)

1. Use shorter sentences that correspond to the child's linguistic ability, with fewer verbs and modifiers
2. Raise the pitch of our voice
3. Speak louder and slower, with distinct pauses between sentences
4. Give greater emphasis to and enunciation of important words or exaggerated intonation to parts of words (e.g., "gooood")
5. Speak in the present tense about present activities
6. Use exaggerated facial expressions
7. Ask lots of questions to encourage dialog
8. Use special "words" with repetitive sounds that infants can hear and pronounce more easily, like mommy, daddy, bow-wow, doggy
9. Expand the infant's telegraphic utterances, filling in appropriate words (e.g., the infant's "daddy go work" brings the parental response "yes, that's right, daddy has gone to work")

10. Focus on the truth of the infant's statement rather than on its grammatical correctness (e.g., "I falled down and hurted my knee" brings the response "Yes, you fell down and hurt your knee"). The parent confirms the validity of the child's assertion, while modeling correct grammatical form.*

Encouraging Infant Speech

Because speech is a fundamental skill (like walking and reading), the early development of language skills gives children a head start in cognitive and social development. Language problems may lead to other problems. "A child who cannot communicate well may have trouble getting along with other children and may be inclined to use physical rather than verbal means for getting a message across. Many such children are chronically frustrated because they are so often misunderstood or are unable to perform as expected" (Brody, 1987b).

The key environmental factor influencing word acquisition in infancy and childhood may be the occurrence of several repetitions of the spoken sound in the presence of an object or event (Miller & Gildea, 1987). The child's ability to use the context in which the word is spoken (or read) is critical. Responsive parents take advantage of context and motivation by speaking the proper word while engaging the child's attention with the object. Then they pause to hear the child's response. Surprisingly, cross-cultural studies have found that children learn language normally even when their mothers hardly speak to them at all (Schieffelin & Ochs, 1983).

Consistent with this observation is the limited effectiveness of language instruction and correction. Most parents eventually discover that correcting a child's pronunciation or grammar is fruitless. Parents do respond differently to grammatical and ungrammatical utterances. They modify, expand, or ask for clarification of ungrammatical utterances more frequently than for grammatical utterances. They comment on the topic being discussed more frequently after grammatical utterances (Bohannon & Stanowicz, 1988; Penner, 1987). It is not clear whether children's speech benefits from this differential feedback. Parental expansion of children's utterances may be beneficial.

Modeling correct usage in normal conversation, elaborating children's utterances, and speaking on their level (though not using "baby talk") seem to be far more powerful teaching strategies than instruction and correction. Giving children frequent opportunities to talk and asking them lots of questions also may encourage language development (Smolak, 1986). The quality and timing of "conversations" is probably more important than their quantity (Symons & Moran, 1987).

The presence of siblings may slow language development either because parental attention is divided among the children, or because the younger child is spoken to more by the less-articulate sibling than by the parent. When older siblings are present, mothers are less sensitive to the younger child's speech. Nevertheless, they provide more stimulation to the younger sibling (Woollett, 1986). Let us dedicate this section to Albert Einstein, who, it is said, did not speak until he was 4 or 5 years old, when he was good and ready.

COMMUNICATION SKILLS

It is ironic that many adults treat their friends more kindly than they treat their children. If a child spills his drink, he may hear, "What's wrong with you? Why can't you be more careful? Now clean this mess up right now!" If an adult friend of the same parent spills a drink, he might hear, "Oh, don't worry about it. It's O.K.,

---

*Peter A. Reich, *Language Development,* © 1986, pp. 88–105. Adapted by permission of Prentice-Hall, Inc., Englewood Cliffs, New Jersey.

really, I'll clean it up in a second." How would the adult friend have responded to the first parental reaction? Why don't adults adopt at least the same standards of sensitivity, kindness, and respect in communicating with their children as they do with each other?

Our four parenting goals are supported by good communication. Children will probably practice the same communication skills modeled by their parents. When we speak kindly to our children, they feel cared for and understood. They learn to value our concern and participation in their lives. As Carl Rogers taught, when we communicate acceptance to children, they can accept themselves more and like themselves more.

The communication skills that are described in the following sections are not easy to learn. Good communication requires thoughtfulness and patience, scarce parental resources. Parents or caretakers who practice these skills are likely to find that, over time, their relationships with their children will become richer and more satisfying.

Mark #9

"More often than not, at school and in the after-school program, Marks seems to be vying for attention. Teachers have stated on his report card that he 'interrupts a lot.' Counselors have told me again and again that he has to be reprimanded for talking and misbehaving. Usually the accounts that are told to me are ones in which he's playing the 'class clown.' The past few days or so he's begun mimicking and mocking me and others. First, I'd tell him how that 'isn't very nice' and that 'it's rude' but then I'd just drop it because he'd continue or make a joke of it.

"When I try to discuss with him how he might feel if he was the one being mocked, he squirms and says untruths such as he'd feel okay, it wouldn't bother him. At that point, I feel frustrated and drop the subject."

Attention

Good communication begins with careful attention to the signals a child conveys, verbally and nonverbally. Young children wear their emotions on their sleeves. They have not yet learned to disguise or hold back their real feelings. By adolescence, many children have learned to mask their true feelings. Perhaps this is because these feelings were not understood or respected by their parents or peers. Many children learn that it is not safe to express powerful emotions such as fear, hatred, or sexual feelings. People's reactions to such expressions are unpredictable and often unsupportive.

Sensitive parents show interest when their children are upset, disappointed, frightened, or angry. They may set aside a special time to discuss these feelings. Observant parents, despite their busy schedules, notice facial expressions, tone of voice, body postures, and gestures that convey uncomfortable feelings. They attempt to discover what is "behind" them (Ginott, 1965). By observing, by listening, and by encouraging their children to clarify their feelings and seek solutions to their problems, parents model good communication skills.

Mark #10

"At least twice this week I lost my cool (confession time). When he admitted for the umpteenth time that he forgot to write down his homework assignment, I said, "Can I ask you a question? Not to be mean, but how far do you think you can push your teachers before they decide to keep you back?" I asked him, did he want to stay back? After some sarcasm, he admitted he did not. I told him, if any teachers approach me and suggest keeping him back, that I wouldn't put up a fight. I told him his life could be so much easier if he'd stop being so stubborn.

"The other incident was when he was fumbling through his math homework. I had already explained it calmly three times and

showed him that the examples in the book also explained it. He said he still didn't understand and I went 'off.' 'If you're going to continue to play dumb, you'd better plan on being a garbage man. The only art you'll be able to do is that on the side of your truck—for free!' (Remember, he's gifted in art.) Well, he answered back in sarcasm, 'Good! I'll be a garbage man and my truck'll look great.' Later, when I calmed down, I explained the math to him again, and kept telling him, 'I knew you could do it.' The long way around . . . geez!''

Sympathetic (Active, Reflective) Listening

Study Question   What role does good listening play in communication?

It is not helpful to tell our children how they should or should not feel. It is helpful to gently solicit their actual feelings. How do we do it? By asking good questions and *listening* to their answers. Active listening means really trying to hear what children are saying. When parents listen sympathetically, they listen for the often hidden or disguised messages conveyed by their children's verbal and nonverbal behaviors (Ginott, 1965).

Parents often take their children's comments or complaints at face value. Discovering their actual meanings often requires a little digging. When a young girl says, "I hate boys; they're so mean," she is summarizing an entire episode in one short sentence. The average parent might say, "Oh, boys aren't so bad." A more sensitive parent will combine good questions with attentive and thoughtful listening. "What happened at Judy's party? . . . How did it make you feel?"

"How can we help a child to know his feelings? We can do so by serving as a mirror to his emotions. A child learns about his physical likeness by seeing his image in a mirror. He learns about his emotional likeness by hearing his feelings reflected by us" (Ginott, 1965, p. 40).

By reflecting (or repeating) the key ideas and feelings being expressed by the child, parents serve as a "sounding board." At the same time, they show that they care and that they are really interested and concerned. When they are listening sympathetically, parents are trying to find out what happened, how the child really feels about what happened, and how they can help him clarify his options. However, sympathetic listening is not always appropriate or desirable. A child who asks a direct question should get a direct answer. If children do not want to talk, we should respect their right not to have to.

Mark #11

"I tried reflective listening the other night but ended up lecturing. Mark had commented that 'the counselors stink like they just fell into some fish water' and that he hates them. I said he sounded angry because he felt embarrassed at having been scolded and punished. He said 'no,' that he really did hate them because 'talking once is no reason to pull me off an activity for a week.'

"I should *have* reflected that he was feeling the 'unfairness' of it all and drawn him out from there. But instead I reminded him that three times already I have been told of his misbehaving and subsequent punishment, that didn't he think three warnings were enough? I went on to explain how responsible and difficult a job it must be for the counselors as it was, without any added trouble. Anyway, as you can assume, the subject was dropped, probably the moment I began my spiel. So I learned that that type of halfhearted attempt at reflective listening is as good as none."

Acknowledging Feelings

Young children initially express their positive and negative feelings freely unless they are taught not to do so. If a child asserts, "I look ugly," the immediate parental reaction is often, "You're not ugly; don't say that." Dismissing such negative feelings does not help a child resolve them. A more helpful response might be, "You're unhappy about the way you look." Notice that this acknowledgment of the child's utterance and the feeling behind it conveys caring and respect. It invites the child to continue expressing himself. The first parental reaction, "Don't say that," accomplishes the opposite result. The child sees there is no point in continuing to express himself because what he is saying is upsetting his parent.

Study Question *Identify the feelings behind the following children's assertions, and specify a helpful parental response:*

1. *"Nobody at school likes me."*
2. *"I'm dumb at spelling."*
3. *"I'm going to kill Paul if he teases me again."*

Encouraging Emotional Expressiveness

Parents exert considerable influence over how children view and express their "private" feelings. Although children's feelings often motivate their behavior, they usually have minimal awareness of, or at least interest in, their internal states (unless they "hurt").

Parents can support the development of such awareness by noticing the child's facial expressions, verbal and nonverbal responses, and the child's interpretation of a situation. They can then label the child's probable feeling state. "Katie, are you disappointed that Grandma's not coming?" Using the correct emotional label in an appropriate situation helps the child to not only learn the label but also apply it to her current feeling state. Mothers encourage their young daughters, more than their sons, to communicate their feelings, perhaps setting the stage for the greater emotional expressiveness we observe in females later in life (Dunn, Bretherton, & Munn, 1987).

Some parents do not take their children's feelings seriously. This may reflect the fact that children occasionally express emotions in a manipulative fashion (as in "fake" crying) to get what they want. By dismissing true expressions of fear, anger, or disappointment, parents can discourage the expression of these feelings and eventually the child's awareness of them.

Many psychologists contend that human behavior can be influenced by motives and feelings that are outside of our awareness and that this is not always to our advantage. Parents can encourage children to be in touch with their internal states and motives by acknowledging and labeling these events appropriately. They also provide the child with a useful emotional vocabulary.

Parents occasionally ignore, dismiss, or discourage children's behavior that makes them uncomfortable. Sometimes we advise people who are distressed, "Don't be upset." Is this really helpful? We are probably communicating, "When you're upset, I become uncomfortable." By placing our needs ahead of theirs and not taking their distress seriously, we risk further discouraging them, and we convey a lack of caring.

Three-year-old Tony falls and scratches his knee. He cries, but Father proclaims, "Oh Tony, that doesn't hurt." How is Tony to interpret that pain in his knee that he thought did hurt? By contradicting his son's immediate experience, Tony's father confuses him and impedes the development of his self-awareness. Parental responsiveness to children's distress, as well as encouragement of emotional expressiveness, predicts children's competence in preschool (Roberts & Strayer, 1987).

Parents may also displace their frustrations and hostilities onto their children, who cannot suspect the real causes of their parents' upset. "Because the mother is usually home with the young child . . . the slightest provocation from the child, usually a violation of one of the mother's standards, can release the parent's anger in yelling, physical punishment, or, less commonly, physical abuse . . . Because mothers typically rationalize their punishment to the child as having been provoked by the violation of a standard, and, therefore, as being in the service of the child's development, the child with an excessively punitive mother is likely to believe he is bad" (Kagan, 1984, pp. 269–270).

Young children may perceive themselves as responsible for their parents' strong feelings, particularly parental anger. They also believe that they can help change their parents' feelings (Covell & Abramovitch, 1987). Parental conflict usually upsets children; as they get older, they may attempt to intervene in increasingly sophisticated ways (McCoy & Masters, 1985). Children appear to be particularly sensitive to anger, particularly chronic anger, which E. M. Cummings (1987) calls "background anger." He hypothesizes that such anger distresses children and is distinguished from other background emotions.

Sensitive parents take their children's (and their own) emotional expression seriously. They encourage the honest expression of strong positive *and* negative, even embarrassing, feelings. When they are apparent, feelings can be addressed. Mothers who take the time to discuss feeling states with their children, usually have children who do the same (Dunn et al., 1987).

When a child is troubled, we support our parenting goals through active, sympathetic listening to their view of the problem, helping them clarify how they feel, why they feel that way, and what they can do about it. Similarly,

when parents are upset, they can model sensitive ways of expressing strong feelings honestly and directly. Children gain not only by seeing how adults express their sadness, frustration, and anger but also by seeing them express physical affection and concern.

Such parental modeling gives children the opportunity to view the facial expressions and hear the words that accompany strong positive and negative feelings. Modeling empathic behavior motivates them to express caring and concern to someone they perceive as distressed (Zahn-Waxler, Radke-Yarrow, & King, 1979). Abused toddlers, on the other hand, lacking these experiences, become distressed when they are with peers who are upset. They may even attack them verbally and physically (Main & George, 1985).

Although parents often attempt to shield their children from strong emotional arousal and upset, hiding strong feelings from them is counterproductive. "A child who sees strong emotions openly acknowledged is less likely to misinterpret those emotions than one whose parents try to cover things up. By admitting that you are angry or frustrated or sad, you are providing a context for your child to understand what you are doing and saying. Perhaps more important, you are showing your child that it is O.K. for him to express emotions, too" (Kutner, 1988b). A healthy emotional climate in the home is supported by taking children's emotional expressions seriously, by sympathetic listening, asking good questions, appropriately labeling emotions for young children, and modeling supportive and caring interpersonal skills.

Nonverbal Communication

"It is not so much what you say, it's how you say it." This cliché suggests the importance of nonverbal signals in communication. Nonverbal messages can be so powerful that they

Facial expressions, posture, and tone of voice are important elements of parent-child communication.

can contradict the accompanying verbalization. For example, if we say to someone, "you're wonderful," in a sarcastic tone of voice, we are really expressing the opposite sentiment. Rolling one's eyes with a shake of the head requires no further comment. When we communicate, our facial expressions, eye contact, gestures, body contact, affectionate touching (touch, hug, and smile), body stance, distance from the child, vocal loudness, silence, and general emotional tone speak volumes and should be consistent with what we are saying in words.

Study Question *A parent is comforting a child with a splinter in her finger. For each of the* *nonverbal behaviors mentioned in the preceding paragraph, describe how the parent can provide optimum reassurance (e.g., reassuring tone of voice).*

Another cliché, "actions speak louder than words," suggests that what we express verbally should be consistent with our subsequent behavior. Our credibility as parents partially depends upon our willingness to keep our word and to follow through on promises and warnings.

Since there is considerable variation in how people express themselves nonverbally, the meaning of nonverbal behavior is sometimes difficult to interpret. Children, like adults, eventually come to depend on nonverbal cues to understand and convey information (Silberman & Wheelan, 1980). Some children suffer socially because they are insensitive to the nonverbal feedback they receive from other children. They may not realize when they are being annoying or hurtful. Such children may require special help in learning how to interpret other children's facial expressions, gestures, and other nonverbal behaviors (Nowicki & Oxenford, 1989).

Descriptive Praise

Study Question   Give examples of descriptive praise that can be offered when a child

1. *Shares a toy*
2. *Finishes her homework*
3. *Answers the phone politely*

One of the discipline practices implied by operant conditioning is "catching the child being good." Rather than falling into the all too common "criticism trap," parents can better support a child's efforts through the use of positive, contingent descriptions of desirable behaviors (Dangel & Polster, 1988). The effectiveness of descriptive praise has been established by many research studies and clearly supports our four parenting goals.

Criticism usually does not specify what the child should be doing. Descriptive praise emphasizes positive behavior. Because there is no criticism, the child does not have to maintain a defensive posture ("I didn't do it"). Descriptive praise is delivered in a sincere, pleasant voice. It specifies what the child did that the parent liked in a way that does not embarrass the child (Wagonseller & McDowell, 1979). "Thank you for helping your sister. It makes me feel good to know that you take care of her when I'm away." "I really liked the way you read that poem at assembly. I feel proud when you make the effort to do a good job."

Constructive Feedback

Nobody likes being criticized, yet everyday life requires that we must sometimes give negative feedback. It is possible to provide feedback without threatening or humiliating the recipient. At the beginning of this chapter, we read how Mark's mother scolded him in front of his friends. She later realized that she had just made matters worse. Among other things, her timing lacked sensitivity. Because parents give their children so much feedback, it is important that the intensity of the communication be proportional to the seriousness of the transgression. Some parents respond to spilled milk as though it were nuclear war. This dilutes the effectiveness of their more serious communications.

Silberman and Wheelan (1980) suggest that we refrain from giving children negative feedback when they are in a "weak" position, that is, when they are feeling bad about themselves. They also suggest that we postpone talking until the strong feelings pass. Parents should avoid interpreting children's behavior ("You're just saying that to get attention"). Rather, describe what it is they did or didn't do that we object to. Feedback can usually be given in positive terms. It should describe what we would like to happen rather than what it was that disappointed or annoyed us. Poorly given feedback, at best, is a waste of time. Parents would be better off saying nothing than criticizing or humiliating their child.

Exploring Alternatives and Owning Problems

Dinkmeyer and McKay (1982) discourage parents from giving advice. They believe advice is not helpful in teaching children problem-solving skills. They encourage exploring alternatives, which means assisting children in "identifying and considering the options available to solve a problem" (p. 57). In helping children come up with specific courses of action, they suggest using sympathetic listening to help children understand what is really upsetting them.

They advocate exploring alternatives through the technique of brainstorming (generating several possible solutions without judging them). Helping children select a possible solution to the problem, discussing the likely effects of the decision, obtaining a commitment, and agreeing to evaluate the plan after trying it out are good problem-solving strategies.

Helping children solve their problems this way is predicated on the decision of problem ownership. In his book *Parent Effectiveness Training* (1970), Thomas Gordon defines problem ownership the following way. If the child's need is not being satisfied, and he or she is upset or unhappy, then it is the child's problem. If the child is satisfying his or her own need, but is also annoying his or her parent, then it is the parent's problem. When the child owns the problem, the parent can use sympathetic listening. The parent does not "solve" the child's problems, but supports the child's problem-solving skills by helping him or her explore alternatives. If the parent owns the problem, I messages are appropriate (Dinkmeyer & McKay, 1982).

I Messages

Yes, parents have feelings, too, and we know what happens if we ignore them or if we let them build up. How can we communicate our adult feelings to children without overwhelming them? An I message naturally begins with the word "I" and expresses how the parent feels about the child's actions. "I am getting annoyed because I cannot rest when you make so much noise." A less helpful you message might be a shouted, "You are so inconsiderate! You never give me a minute's peace!" Notice that I messages can convey strong feelings but in a nonaccusatory way.

A you message, on the other hand, "lays blame and conveys criticism of the child. It suggests that the child is at fault. It is simply a verbal attack . . . An I-message delivered in anger becomes a You-message conveying hostility" (Dinkmeyer & McKay, 1982, p. 59). Usually, when we begin a sentence with the word "you," particularly if we are communicating displeasure, the person we are addressing becomes defensive and may counterattack. I messages defuse the situation by asserting *my* annoyance or disappointment rather than *your* "nastiness" or "badness."

I messages usually have three components: (1) the child's behavior ("When you . . .), (2) how the parent feels about the behavior ("I feel . . ."), and (3) the consequence of the behavior ("because . . ."). "*When you* don't call or come home after school, *I worry* that something might have happened to you, *because* I don't know where you are" (Dinkmeyer & McKay, 1982, p. 60). Notice how I messages convey caring by explaining why the parent is feeling upset and what the child can do to correct the situation.

Thomas Gordon (1970) also describes appreciative I messages (earlier referred to as descriptive praise). They balance the occasional criticisms and preventative I messages that anticipate and attempt to avoid problems. An example of the latter is, "I would appreciate your having showered before you go to bed so that I don't have to wait to use the bathroom in the morning."

Apologizing

People in authority probably have as many interpersonal "lapses" as anyone else, but some may not feel comfortable acknowledging their mistakes. Employers and parents sometimes fall into this category. Rationalizing or denying our errors rather than admitting them not only gives children an inaccurate view of our fallibility, but it also prevents them from learning how to apologize. Children who bellow, "It's not my fault" when they are (at least partly) responsible for an incident are revealing an important lesson they may have learned from their parents: "Don't get caught messing up."

"Parents who have the most difficulty admitting they've been wrong come from families where their own parents were authoritarian. They're afraid they will lose control and that their children will think they're weak" (Cleminshaw, quoted by Kutner, 1988d). In fact, the opposite seems to be true. We tend to admire more those who "own up" to their mistakes.

Children benefit from having realistic expectations about themselves and their parents and by understanding human frailty. Acknowledging rather than denying our fallibility facilitates the development of positive self-esteem. By accepting our fallibility, we do not have to go through life pretending to be perfect.

COMMUNICATION PITFALLS

Parents who have not developed effective communication skills generally talk too much to their children. They nag, whine, lecture, suggest, advise, explain, reexplain, plead, criticize, blame, remind, threaten, ridicule, preach, judge, analyze, and speak sarcastically (Dinkmeyer & McKay, 1982). Some parents act as though they always "know better" than their children. They convey negative feedback, impatience, even hostility, and a lack of respect for the child's thoughts and feelings. Most adults would never communicate this way to their friends. If they did, they wouldn't have friends.

Criticism

Children who are repeatedly criticized or who are not heard at all eventually become discouraged. As a family therapist, I often get to meet such children. They have little to say, it seems, and have learned that it is pointless to seek their parents' counsel when they have problems or feel troubled. Such children often have low self-esteem. They have learned to anticipate disapproval from their parents (and others), and they feel rejected. (Some children receive so much criticism and disapproval that they become desensitized to it, though their self-esteem will probably suffer.)

One 14-year-old high school freshman, a sweet, bright boy, told me his mother hated him and thought he was crazy. His mother didn't really hate him, but acted as if she did when he wasn't doing well in school. She seemed to have absolutely no understanding of or sympathy for his unhappiness. Though she was an intelligent woman, she lacked the insight or personal resources to help her son. In her frustration, she became a punitive parent.

"Everything a parent says and does for the child communicates an attitude toward her. Hopefully, all parental communication has at base one central message: the parent loves the child and cares about her world . . . Unfortunately, most children hear more negative than positive comments about themselves" (Wagonseller & McDowell, 1979, p. 28).

RELATIONSHIPS

Study Question   In what ways might our early family relationships influence our later relationships outside of our immediate family?

Most people derive considerable satisfaction from their relationships. Parents are particularly concerned about their relationships with their children for at least two reasons. First, parents' psychological well-being reflects partially the quality of the parent-child relationship (Umberson, 1989; Umberson & Gove, 1989). Parents who report satisfying interactions with their children report being happier than parents who have a negative view of their relationships with their children. Secondly, parents feel responsible for teaching their children how to have good relationships.

"The person I admire most is my oldest brother Ronnie. Ever since I was allowed to go outside, I would always follow him around because I thought he was the greatest, and he still is in my eyes. I used to dress like him, listen to the same music, and I always tried to talk like him. In fact, I still use certain phrases that I learned from him many years ago. I admired him so much because he understood everything I was going through. I've always wanted to be just like him when I grew up, and I think I am" (freshman college student).

As the preceding quote suggests, families are "training grounds," particularly for having relationships. Whatever we learn (or fail to learn) about getting along with and caring for our own family members will probably be evident in our future relationships outside the family. Relationship patterns, once established, are fairly resistant to change and are usually repeated, with some variation, over one's lifetime.

Sroufe and Fleeson (1986) suggest three ways in which early relationships influence later relationships: (1) early relationships, particularly those between the infant and its caretakers, influence personality formation; (2) early relationships, such as those with siblings, shape our expectations about how relationships work, how available other people will be to us, and what is considered acceptable relationship behavior; and (3) early relationships leave us with basic relationship skills, or deficits. Our understanding of relationships changes through the positive and negative reactions we get from others.

The infant's first relationships are with its caretakers, usually its biological parents. Of course, the infant will also spend time with and become attached to many other people. Children interact with siblings, cousins, teachers, baby-sitters, pediatricians, grandparents, family friends, and neighbors. Children do not only learn about relationships by participating in them. They have many opportunities to observe relationships between others, in and out of their families.

ATTACHMENT

Most of us would not select as a companion someone who cries, burps, drools, lacks toileting skills, and sleeps most of the day. And yet, many of us not only enjoy the company of such individuals, we experience intense love and caring for them. As discussed in chapter 4, intense emotional ties bind parents to their children. These powerful feelings of affection and devotion are at the heart of the parenting process. They motivate parents to be close to and care for their children. Hence, they are of great interest to psychologists. The term *attachment* is used to describe the strong feelings that children have toward their parents and other caretakers and the behaviors that accompany these feelings.

Strong feelings are invisible to the watchful eyes of researchers. Psychologists, therefore, define and measure attachment using the following observable behaviors: (1) the caretaker's ability to comfort a distressed infant; (2) infant distress in the presence of unfamiliar people or settings; (3) infant distress when separated from its caretakers; (4) joyful sounds and facial expressions of infants when greeting or playing with a caretaker; and (5) other measures of proximity, contact, exploration, and social interaction.

Theorists have made many assumptions about attachment. They have assumed that it is a unitary phenomenon, that it is reciprocal, that it is present at birth or soon after, and that it is permanent. Theorists have also hypothesized that if attachment is not secure, the child's emotional and cognitive development may be threatened. Let's examine these assumptions.

Is Attachment a Unitary Phenomenon?

Is the emotional bond we call attachment "one thing," or does it consist of a combination of distinct psychological processes? It is not likely

For many families, dinnertime is one of the few opportunities for all family members, regardless of their hectic schedules, to join together in a common activity and enjoy each other's company (no, I'm not being sarcastic). "Regardless of how frustrating or disappointing it is, dinner is supposed to be the quintessential family experience. Indeed, surveys show that while the number of American families who usually eat dinner together has declined over the past decade, most families still manage to dine together often. Such rituals as a regular dinnertime provide families with a sense of security and identity . . ." (Rubenstein, 1988b). Other "rituals" might involve family gatherings for vacations, holiday celebrations, bedtime stories, or Sunday picnics.

A 1976 Roper poll of over 2,000 families found that 72 percent of families with children reported eating together frequently. In 1986, only 63 percent reported doing so. Hectic family schedules are a major

reason for the decrease; convenience foods, microwave ovens, TVs and VCRs also take their toll. However, most family members seem to believe that eating together at dinnertime is a good idea. It is an opportunity for them to "share" their daily experiences while participating in a common activity. Parents have the chance to ask their children about their schoolwork and other activities, plan for future family events, make decisions, and discuss problems.

Vuchinich, Emery, & Cassidy (1988) videotaped 140 families at dinnertime and found that mothers talk more to children than do fathers and ask children more questions. When conflict arises, it is usually between siblings, unless parents are busy correcting their children's manners. Vuchinich and his colleagues found that fathers, usually the more powerful parental figures, are least likely to be attacked by other family members, and that mothers typically play the role of peacemaker.

Dinnertime has become one of the rare opportunities that families have for spending time together.

that attachment is a unitary, underlying emotional state that is equally directed to all caretakers (Kagan, 1984; Sroufe & Fleeson, 1986). It is more likely that the infant's social responsiveness reflects the history and the quality of its relationship *with particular caretakers* (Smith & Pederson, 1988). The infant's attachment to one parent is probably different in intensity and kind from its attachment to the other parent, to its siblings, and to its grandparents. Another distinctive form, children's attachment to soft, inanimate objects such as blankets and stuffed animals, is generally considered to be healthy and beneficial (Passman, 1987).

Is Attachment Inevitable and Reciprocal?

Bowlby (1969) and others have suggested that there is an instinctive tendency on the part of infants to form a strong emotional bond with their caretakers. This belief is consistent with and probably based upon the observation that virtually all children do so. Even children of abusive parents become strongly attached to them, although the attachment may be insecure (see "Secure versus Insecure Attachment").

Not all parents, however, become bonded to their children. There is a category of parents, known as neglecting parents (discussed in chapter 14), whose caretaking and attachment behaviors are extremely weak or nonexistent. Neglecting parents typically have serious emotional problems. As we shall see, children of neglecting, unresponsive caretakers eventually stop sending distress and other signals. They are likely to suffer emotionally and cognitively from parental neglect.

It is therefore risky to assume that all adults are disposed by nature to be loving and caring parents. There are too many exceptions to this generalization today and throughout human history. Those adults raised by abusive or neglecting parents often have difficulty becoming attached to their own children. Some parents of children who are unwanted or difficult to care for may have ambivalent or even negative feelings about them. But let's not overreact to extreme cases. Fortunately, most parents of children who are hard to care for provide quality caretaking, and most of these children develop healthy attachments to their parents (e.g., Easterbrooks, 1989).

Onset of Attachment

As previously noted, the bonding process begins before birth. Most pregnant women experience nurturant feelings toward and express concerns about their unborn children. The attachment process may begin prenatally. Third-trimester fetuses hear their mothers' voices and apparently become familiar with their acoustic properties (DeCasper & Spence, 1986).

The newborn is not capable of distinguishing between person and nonperson, caretaker and noncaretaker, or between who is familiar and who is not. Therefore, a strong emotional bond to a particular caretaker will not be evident until the cognitive structures allowing for such distinctions develop. Between birth and approximately 3 months of age (the preattachment phase), the infant's social responsiveness is indiscriminate. Infants can be comforted when distressed by almost anyone. Between the ages of 3 and 7 months, infants begin to display preferences for familiar people. After 7 months, we observe clear attachment to family members and other caretakers. Infants stay close to their caretakers and protest when they depart.

Is Attachment Permanent?

Bowlby (1982) assumed that the attachment bond is permanent; that is, once affectional bonds are established, they endure. Since the infant's attachment to its caretakers is most adaptive during the first 2 years of life, when it is most vulnerable, it is also plausible that infantile attachment differs in form from subsequent attachments to parents, siblings, friends, and, eventually, sexual partners (Ainsworth, 1989; Kagan, 1984).

Although strong feelings about one's parents last a lifetime, it is unlikely that these feelings reflect the same attachment processes manifested during infancy. As children's cognitive and language abilities evolve, the manner in which they work with and relate to their parents changes. Enhanced motor skills allow a child to "venture farther away from his or her secure base to explore an expanded world and to connect with playmates and generally with a wider variety of people, including strangers" (Ainsworth, 1989, p. 710).

Some children, particularly adolescents, develop strong, negative feelings about their parents. Ambivalence seems to be present in almost all close relationships. There are even children who avoid contact with, abuse, or kill their parents (Kagan, 1984). Nevertheless, most of us grieve when our parents die, demonstrating that the attachment bond persists over the life span (Ainsworth, 1989). These observations suggest that the affectional bonds we call attachment are lifelong, but that they change in form over the course of development.

A child's reactions following temporary separation from a parent reflect the quality of the child's attachment to the parent.

Secure versus Insecure Attachment

Ainsworth, Blehar, Waters, and Wall (1978) studied attachment by observing infants in a so-called "strange situation" test. One-year-old infants were exposed to a series of eight increasingly stressful situations in an unfamiliar playroom with a one-way window. They were observed at different times alone with their mothers, together with their mothers and a stranger, alone with the stranger, reuniting with their mothers, and so on.

The infants' reactions were studied in each condition. The researchers measured infants' exploratory behavior, their response to being separated from their mothers, reactions to the stranger, and how the infants responded when reunited with their mothers (Ainsworth et al., 1978). (Bowlby had assumed that infants' distress to strangers indicates a secure attachment to their parents. Recent research suggests that an infant's ability to be consoled by a parent after separation is a better indication of secure attachment than the infant's reaction to a stranger.)

Based on their observations, Ainsworth and her colleagues distinguished infants according to the quality of their attachments to their mothers. Infants designated as securely attached (about 70% of Ainsworth's sample) used their caregiver as a base for exploration and for coping with unpredictable or stressful events.

Between the ages of 5 and 12 months, infants, when in the presence of strangers, display intense distress behaviors such as crying, clenching their fists, and quickly crawling to a parent. The infant's distress signals are adaptive in this potentially dangerous world. They are disturbing, however, to visiting grandparents and family friends who approach the infant for the first time during this period.

The intensity of the infant's response, to some extent, depends on the setting, whether a familiar caretaker is present, the stranger's appearance, and how the stranger approaches the child. Although it may be difficult for visiting grandparents, for example, to delay holding their grandchild, gradual approach reduces the infant's distress. Wariness of strangers continues throughout the preschool years (Greenberg & Marvin, 1982). Under "secure" conditions, children will sometimes relate well to strangers.

Separation distress consists of an intense emotional reaction precipitated by separation from primary caretakers, usually parents. It peaks between the ages of 14 to 20 months and gradually lessens throughout the preschool years. When infants see their parents getting ready to leave home without them, they usually become distressed, creep or run to a parent, and cling for dear life. Although parents are often disturbed by both types of distress reactions, keep in mind that they are adaptive. Infants are generally safer in the presence of familiar people than in their absence or in the presence of strangers. When leaving an infant with a new babysitter, parents can ease the separation distress by having the babysitter spend some time with the infant while they are present. Optimally, this would be done before the first time the parents leave the infant alone with the sitter. Not surprisingly, parents also suffer from separation anxiety (Hock, McBride, & Gnezda, 1989; McBride & Belsky, 1988).

They became upset when their mothers separated and greeted them affectionately when they returned. They were friendly to strangers when their mothers were present. Mothers of securely attached infants typically responded appropriately and caringly to them. These mothers were more loving, more helpful, and more playful.

Two types of insecurely attached infants were identified. Infants designated as anxious resistant (about 10% of the sample) also became upset when their mothers separated. When their mothers returned, however, they acted as though they resented the mother for leaving in the first place. They remained by the mother but resisted contact and were difficult to console. They were wary of strangers when their mothers were present. This type of attachment is likely to occur when caretakers respond inconsistently.

Anxious-avoidant infants (about 20% of the sample) did not get upset when their mothers separated; however, they avoided contact upon their return. They ignored strangers when their mothers were not present and were generally less compliant. Erikson would point out that both types of insecurely attached infants appear to "distrust" their mothers. Mothers of securely attached infants appear to enjoy their children more than the mothers of infants designated as insecurely attached. Mothers of anxious infants are more impatient, rejecting, and less appropriate in their responses.

Kagan (1984) has suggested that the strange-situation test measures infant temperament rather than the quality of attachment. Ainsworth and Belsky disagree. They contend that infant behavior in the strange situation reflects the quality of the caregiving that infants are used to. Securely attached infants do seem to have mothers who are particularly sensitive and responsive to their needs (Isabella, Belsky, & von Eye, 1989; Smith & Pederson, 1988). A child's temperament, per se, does not seem to predict a child's attachment status (Vaughn, Lefever, Seifer, & Barglow, 1989).

Kagan's hypothesis is also contradicted by the fact that infants may show a secure attachment to one caregiver but not to another. Additionally, the quality of a child's attachment may show a positive change when the caregiving improves (Thompson, Lamb, & Estes, 1982). Research tentatively supports the conclusion that it is primarily the quality of caregiving that determines the nature of the infant's attachment (Belsky, Rovine, & Taylor, 1984; Goldberg, Perrotta, Minde, & Corter, 1986).

Attachment Theory

The essence of attachment theory (Ainsworth, 1989; Ainsworth et al., 1978; Bowlby, 1982) is that there is a biologically rooted behavioral system (attachment behavior) in infants that keeps them near their caretakers. Attachment behaviors such as crying and smiling evolved because of their survival value. "At first, these attachment behaviors are simply emitted, rather than being directed toward any specific person, but gradually the baby begins to discriminate one person from another and to direct attachment behavior differentially" (Ainsworth, 1989, p. 710).

Toward the middle of the first year of life, the infant develops motor behaviors that allow it to maintain or seek contact with its primary caregivers. Cognitively, the infant becomes able to mentally represent familiar people and, therefore, recognize those who are unfamiliar (i.e., strangers). Distress reactions then occur in the presence of strangers or upon separating from a familiar caregiver (Ainsworth, 1989).

Attachment to one's mother, for example, develops within the context of cumulative, mother-infant interactions. Based on its experience of its mother, the infant develops expectations about her availability and responsiveness. Secure attachment is enhanced by maternal sensitivity. As previously noted, sensitive mothers are attentive to their infants' signals and interpret them accurately. They participate in "well-timed, synchronous, and mutually rewarding interactions" (Isabella et al., 1989, p. 12). They are also more affectionate and tender (Ainsworth et al., 1978).

Insensitive mothers, according to attachment theory, have insecurely attached infants. These mothers are less attentive to their infants' signals or misinterpret them. Their interactions with their infants are usually "ill-timed, asynchronous, and perhaps mutually unsatisfying" (Isabella et al., 1989, p. 12). Mothers who were themselves insecurely attached as infants may be less sensitive and responsive to their own infants. They are more likely to have infants who are also insecurely attached, perhaps mediated by the mother's somewhat impaired relationship skills (Crowell & Feldman, 1988) and by marital problems (Howes & Markman, 1989).

As influential as the mother's interactional style may be in the attachment process, the infant's characteristics, including irritability and sociability, cannot be ignored. It is likely that maternal characteristics, maternal interaction style, and infant characteristics interact with each other. "Infants who are less sociable may be less interactive with their mothers, and this interactive pattern may produce an insecure attachment relationship" (Lewis & Feiring, 1989, p. 831). These investigators found that the infant's sociability at 3 months of age is a better predictor of later attachment than maternal behavior.

A woman's ability to deliver "high-quality mothering" and, therefore, promote secure attachment in her infant is influenced by her social support system (Crockenberg & McCluskey, 1986). It is important to provide mothers with the social support necessary for them to develop optimal mothering skills, particularly if their infants are difficult to care for.

Attachment and Development

One of the most widespread assumptions about child development (encouraged by Freud) is that certain, specific experiences during infancy and early childhood can have a profound and lasting influence on a child's development and personality. Because attachment may be the emotional cornerstone of development during infancy, the quality of an infant's attachment to its primary caretakers would be expected to predict significant aspects of the child's development. Many studies report a relationship between the quality of attachment and children's social and cognitive development (e.g., Bus & van Ijzendoorn, 1988; Jacobson & Wille, 1986; van Ijzendoorn & van Vliet-Visser, 1988).

Nevertheless, it is difficult to draw conclusions about the relationship between attachment and development because mothers of securely attached infants probably differ in other important ways from mothers of insecurely attached infants. Kagan (1984) contends that it is not the quality of attachment that influences children's development. Rather, he suggests, it is the quality of the day-to-day parent-child relationship that determines both the quality of attachment *and* other important aspects of development.

We can conclude, tentatively, that responsive caregiving promotes secure attachment in the infant. Both high-quality caregiving and secure attachment are associated with a variety of positive outcomes in emotional, social, and cognitive development. Securely attached children appear to be more sociable, more compliant, and more competent than less securely attached children (Cohn, 1990).

CHILDREN IN FAMILIES

Unfortunately for researchers, families are very complex and varied. It is not easy performing studies that isolate one factor at a time, such as family size or amount of parental education, to determine its effect on children's behavior and

THE FAR SIDE By GARY LARSON

"Bob and Ruth! Come on in .... Have you met Russell and Bill, our 1.5 children?"

development. In families, many factors covary, such as socioeconomic status, parental employment, and the quality of marital and parent-child relationships. The diversity of families precludes simple generalizations about the effects of these variables. In this section, we examine research findings on family size, birth order, only-child status, spacing of sibling births, and sibling conflict.

Family Size

Study Question In what ways might the size of a family influence the nature of relationships between family members?

To some extent, deciding how many children to have reflects parents' own family histories. Parents who were only children sometimes

Children in larger families have more frequent opportunities to learn about relationships.

regret their lack of a sibling and choose to avoid that status for their children. There may also be constraints such as infertility, financial pressures, and dual-career issues that discourage parents from having more than one child. Families in the United States are getting smaller, with an average in the late 1980s of not quite 3 children per family.

There are potential advantages and disadvantages for both large and small families. These will be mediated by many other important family characteristics. Let's consider some differences between large (i.e., more than 4 children) and small (1 or 2 children) families.

The larger the family, the greater the number of relationships. There are 3 relationships with 3 family members (mother-father, mother-child, father-child), 6 relationships with 4 family members, and 10 relationships with 5 family members. As family size increases, children participate in more relationships and have the opportunity to observe more relationships. Whether this is beneficial, of course, depends upon the nature of the interactions they participate in and observe.

In larger families, older siblings, particularly females, will spend more time caring for their younger siblings. The total amount of attention each child receives increases with family size. However, the amount of parental attention diminishes with each additional child (Zajonc & Markus, 1975). Depending upon the age spacing, older children may benefit from the greater amount of attention they received when they entered the initially smaller family unit. Thus, children in small families participate in and observe fewer family relationships than children in large families, but may enjoy more parental attention.

Research reveals that children from small families perform slightly better on intelligence and other standardized tests, get more schooling, and achieve more academically and occupationally than children from large families. "In larger families, child rearing becomes more rule ridden, less individualized, with corporal punishment and less investment of resources" (Wagner, Schubert, & Schubert, 1985, p. 65). A balanced view recognizes several advantages and disadvantages for children in both types of family configurations.

Birth Order

The relationship between birth order and personality has been hotly debated for most of this century, fueled by the writings of Alfred Adler (1928). Adler described the distinct socialization processes associated with each birth position. Firstborns have the most privileged position, because parental attention does not have to be shared, at least initially. The special attention parents bestow on their firstborns is evidenced by the "diminishing snapshot effect." Parents accumulate hundreds of photographs of firstborns, dozens of secondborns, and about twelve each of laterborns.

The major hazard confronting the firstborn, according to Adler, is "dethronement" or the loss of privilege and the sharing of parental attention with the arrival of a younger sibling. This can engender hostility and resentment toward the parents, who are perceived as fa-

voring the newborn. Adler allowed that if parents handle the birth of a new sibling sensitively, the firstborn will probably adjust well and become caring and protective of the baby.

Firstborns have been depicted as high achievers, leaders, verbally aggressive, obedient, responsible, and more self-confident than their younger siblings. Children in the middleborn position were characterized by Adler as ambitious, rebellious, and envious, but better adjusted than the older or younger sibling. The lower self-esteem often associated with middleborn children is attributed to this birth position being the "least special." Though Adler characterized the youngest child as spoiled, the contemporary depiction of the lastborn is likable, sociable, cuddly, friendly, popular, disobedient, physically aggressive, and having low self-esteem.

Is there any truth to these stereotypes? Is Adler's basic premise correct, that the different birth positions are associated with different socialization patterns? Firstborns (and only children, who are similar to firstborns in some ways) are overrepresented in high-achieving groups, such as those listed in Who's Who, presidents of the United States, astronauts, and the graduate school population (Goleman, 1985b). Parents probably do have higher expectations and set higher standards for their older children. Firstborns may also receive more criticism.

Laterborns almost certainly receive less parental attention and have to cope with occupying the least powerful position in the family. "The status tactics, bossiness, and dominance of firstborns are typical of the powerful members of any social system—those who are larger and have greater ability; the appeals of laterborn children to their parents for support are typical of the weak members of social groups and are encouraged by the greater indulgence and comfort offered to laterborn children by their parents" (Dunn, 1985, p. 71).

Steelman and Powell (1985), in a relatively well-controlled study of birth order, analyzed data from two nationally representative samples of United States children and found no correlation between birth order and academic achievement. They do report a significant relationship between birth order and social success (favoring laterborns), defined by "such social skills as outgoingness, getting along with others, popularity, and ease in making friends . . ." (p. 117). Birth order predicted leadership skills for males (favoring laterborns, not firstborns!), but not for females. The research on birth order suggests that its influence on development has probably been exaggerated when compared to other parent-child, sibling, and family-related characteristics.

Only Children

About 22 percent of families in the United States with children under the age of 18 years have only one child. Despite the negative attitudes traditionally directed toward this family configuration, the single-child family is becoming more common and more accepted (Collins, 1984b). Only children (and sometimes their parents) have been stereotyped as being more lonely, selfish, spoiled, and maladjusted than children with siblings. Many parents have had a second child just to prevent stigmatizing their firstborn (Kutner, 1988q). Baskett (1985) found that adults expect only children to be more academically oriented and higher achievers. They also stereotype them as more self-centered and not very likable.

Actually, only children resemble firstborns, as described previously, without the experience of dethronement. They resemble lastborns in that they will never get the opportunity to help (or torment) younger siblings. As onlyborns, they are automatically special and may be raised more permissively than children with siblings. Falbo and Polit (1986) confirm that only children are very similar to firstborns.

Both groups are particularly susceptible to adult influence. They are as popular, and as adults they are as happy and satisfied as peers with siblings.

Importantly, they are born into an adult intellectual environment that will not be "diluted" by the presence of younger siblings. Therefore, it is not surprising that, compared to children with siblings, only children score higher on intelligence tests, show more developed abstract reasoning and problem-solving skills, and have higher academic aspirations. They also get about 3 years more schooling and achieve higher occupational prestige and higher income than children with siblings (Blake, cited by Cunningham, 1985; Falbo, 1984; Falbo & Polit, 1986).

It is clear, then, that the negative stereotypes associated with only children (and their parents) are false. In terms of intellectual and social development, only-child status is, if anything, an advantage. This is probably due to the special relationship only children have with their parents.

Spacing

What is the optimal spacing between children's births? Most children are born within 2 or 3 years of their siblings' births. Research suggests that this is the least optimal spacing pattern, although parental decisions about when to have children should not be overly influenced by this finding (Goleman, 1985b). Working mothers, for example, might not want to prolong their child-rearing years by spacing children several years apart.

There do seem to be benefits in spacing intervals of either less than 2 years or more than 5 years. Short intervals between births minimize the dethronement factor because infants cannot really appreciate the possible threat of a new sibling to their special position. Resentment and rivalrous feelings are more likely after 2 years of age when the child might miss the

Eric Jaffe

ample parental attention to which he has become accustomed. Five- and six-year-olds are usually sufficiently autonomous to avoid these feelings (Goleman, 1985b).

Another advantage of longer spacing intervals (more than 4 years) is that parents will treat the newborn as specially as they treated the firstborn. Middleborns, too, seem to feel more special when there are longer intervals between them and their siblings. "A spacing of about five years is apparently optimal. It frees the parent from having to meet the demands and pressures of two children close together in age, thus allowing parents and children more time in one-to-one interactions for a more supportive and relaxed relationship" (Kidwell, quoted in Goleman, 1985b).

Let's remember that spacing probably interacts with many other factors, including birth order and family size, in its influence on development. The quality of the individual parent-child relationships is probably more powerful than these other factors, even in combination.

Siblings

Study Question In what ways might siblings contribute to each other's development?

Adults choose their partners and together decide whether to have children. Children do not choose their parents ("I didn't ask to be born") or their siblings ("Can't we take her back to the hospital?"). Ironically, the involuntary sibling relationship, experienced by 80 percent of all children, is probably the most enduring in life.

Young siblings, particularly those spaced closely in age, probably spend more time with each other than they do with anyone else, including their parents. This often encourages a closeness, even intimacy, not found in other types of relationships. Given the frequency of daily sibling interactions, it would be naive to wonder whether siblings influence each other.

There are few easy generalizations to be made about how siblings influence each other. Age, spacing, birth order, sex of each sibling, temperament, personality differences, the emotional climate of the family, and parent-child relationships all play some role in how siblings relate. Because siblings spend so much time together in varied settings, they develop a unique understanding of each other. They become better able to predict what will please and what will annoy. They learn to adjust their own behavior accordingly.

As friends, companions, playmates, and occasional rivals, children have countless opportunities, through modeling, identification, attachment, and reinforcement, to influence each other's development. Children with younger siblings are more likely to adopt a leadership role with their peers and display more prosocial *and* aggressive behavior. Berndt and Bulleit (1985) found that, at home, preschoolers with older siblings did, indeed, play often with them and were exposed to more aggressive and prosocial behavior than were preschoolers who did not have older siblings. Even preschoolers differ from each other regarding their effectiveness as teachers for their younger siblings (Dunn, 1988; Stewart, 1983).

The birth of a new sibling, with the accompanying lessening of maternal attention, is generally considered a traumatic event for a child. However, various studies have found all of three possible outcomes: (1) distress and misbehavior, (2) no change, or (3) improvements in behavior problems. Most children become upset by the "intruder," particularly when the mother's attention is less available. They also show considerable interest in and caring for the newborn.

Sibling Ambivalence/Conflict

Study Question   What are the roots of "sibling ambivalence"?

The term "sibling rivalry" is too one-sided. *Sibling ambivalence* is a more appropriate characterization of the older child's mixed feelings about the birth of a brother or sister. When overt hostility occurs, it can be directed toward the mother or the infant. When a mother is preoccupied with her infant, the older sibling is likely to display such "naughty" behaviors as crying, clinging, throwing things, and other attention-getting, annoying behaviors. More disturbing changes, such as difficulties involving sleep, toileting, and aggression toward the mother, usually disappear by about 8 months after the birth. The development of strong fears and the tendency to withdraw may persist much longer and are indicative of a more serious problem (Dunn, 1985).

Stewart, Mobley, Van Tuyl, and Salvador (1987) interviewed 41 middle-class families at 5 intervals, from one month preceding birth to 12 months following birth. They found "more problems with toilet habits, demands for bottles, clinginess and other anxiety displays, and increased confrontations and aggression" following the birth of a sibling. Such "regressive" acts may be imitative of the infant's behavior, or reflections of increased anxiety in general. One month following birth, children's reactions to the new sibling were either imitations of the infant or confrontations with either the mother or the infant. At 4 months after birth, there were more anxiety reactions but fewer imitations or confrontations.

FIGHTING | BEING NICE

SIBLINGS

Justin Jaffe

Same-sexed siblings had more problems than opposite-sexed siblings, perhaps because of competition for gender-related reinforcers. Mothers spent much less time with the first-born child after birth, but fathers' interactions remained stable over time. Fathers also became more involved in child-care activities (Stewart et al., 1987). Decreased maternal attention and sensitivity to the older child's interests following the birth of a sibling were also reported by Dunn and Kendrick (1980).

Poor adjustment to the birth of a new sibling can be minimized by providing extra (but not excessive) attention to the older child. Fathers can increase their involvement with the older sibling; parents can emphasize how much the infant will enjoy his older sister or brother and give the older sibling "grown-up" responsibilities in caring for and feeding the infant. If the mother brings the older sibling into her care-taking transactions with the infant ("Look, he's smiling at you, he really likes it when you help me dress him"), she can foster feelings of affection and pride (Howe & Ross, 1990).

Melson and Fogel (1988), studying the development of nurturant behavior in boys and girls, found that adult expectations play a major role in young boys and girls demonstrating nurturant behavior toward infants. Young boys and girls demonstrated comparable knowledge about what babies are like and how to care for them. When mothers of infants encouraged preschool children to help them with their babies, "boys and girls were equally responsive to the mother's encouragement and were equally interested in the male and female infants" (p. 44). Without such explicit encouragement from the mother, however, boys' involvement tended to be inhibited.

Melson and Fogel suggest that if parents encourage their sons' involvement with their younger siblings, particularly by fathers' modeling nurturant behavior, they will foster their development of sensitivity, nurturance, and empathy. "Meaningful, adult-guided care-giving may be as important as play and formal education in developing nurturant skill" (p. 45). How parents, particularly mothers, relate to their children, children's individual temperaments, and the age of the younger sibling also influence sibling relationships (Stocker, Dunn, & Plomin, 1989).

"Though they clearly love each other, my children are constantly bickering. The younger provokes the older, the older overreacts, the younger one comes crying to me. The older one loves teasing his little brother. In fact, they seem to enjoy tormenting each other. Usually the little one gets hurt. When I try to figure out what happened, I always hear the same thing from both, 'He started it.' When they are fighting, and I get angry, I usually make things worse" (father of two sons).

Sibling relationships are often stereotyped as conflict ridden. There is more than a grain of truth to this generalization. Parents often complain that managing conflict between siblings is a major family problem. Virtually all sibling relationships are characterized by conflict *and* caring. The balance between these two varies widely from family to family. Because this balance exists, it is more accurate to talk about "sibling ambivalence" than sibling rivalry.

Siblings are good for each other. They encourage strong feelings, positive and negative, and therefore give children the opportunity to learn to cope with such feelings. Siblings provide each other with countless opportunities to practice relationship skills such as sharing, comforting, cooperating, and helping.

Parents often intercede prematurely when their children are fighting, weakening the children's incentive to work things out themselves. Obviously, if a child is in danger of being hurt or cannot possibly cope with a sibling's verbal or physical attack, swift intervention is appropriate. For most conflicts, however, children benefit from the opportunity to sharpen their social (and coping) skills.

If parents do intervene, they can express empathy and concern for the "victim" and ignore the aggressor. When things quiet down, a review of the events might be helpful. The aggressive child can be helped to empathize with his sibling ("How do you think she felt when you grabbed her crayon?"). Sibling disputes are more likely to center around the possession of objects than any other cause. Parents can anticipate and possibly minimize such conflict by establishing rules regarding possessions. They can encourage such prosocial behaviors as sharing and requesting objects rather than taking them. From personal experience, I know that such skills develop quite gradually over childhood.

SPOTLIGHT: Family Arguments

Occasional conflict between family members is common, inevitable, and healthy. Rebellious behavior may reflect children's desire for autonomy. It usually peaks during the "terrible twos" and again during early adolescence. Verbal conflict is particularly likely in groups, such as families, where there is frequent contact and intense emotional bonds (Vuchinich, 1985).

Many family arguments begin when someone's expectations are not fulfilled. Perhaps children do not perform their chores, eat their dinner, brush their teeth, or complete their schoolwork. Occasionally during verbal conflict, family members express "true feelings" that had previously been suppressed. This may "clear the air" or provoke further strong feelings. Conversely, during conflict, we may express thoughts or feelings that, while felt in the moment of anger, are not representative of our real feelings.

Verbal attacks usually elicit counterattacks, both often taking the form of "disagreements, insults, corrections and challenges. They are often characterized by negative remarks . . . shouting or exaggerated ways of speaking and gestures" (Vuchinich, 1985, p. 42). The conflict may become more heated and personal as it progresses. Vuchinich found that family arguments usually end in one of four ways: (1) withdrawal (leave the room, stop talking); (2) submission (giving in); most frequently, (3) standoff (dispute ends without resolution); or, preferably, (4) compromise (individual or mutual concessions).

Third-party involvement in conflicts between two family members can make things better or worse. Vuchinich, Emery, and Cassidy (1988) observed routine family arguments during dinnertime. They found that when two family members were in conflict, additional family members joined in about one-third of the time. When they did, "they were equally likely to attempt to end or to continue the conflict, they formed alliances about half the time, and their intervention strategies were related to the outcome of the conflict as well as its patterning" (p. 1293).

Girls were more likely than boys to intervene, particularly as peacekeepers, unless it was a marital dispute. Mothers and fathers supported each other when either intervened in an ongoing dispute. Parents rarely took sides against each other. This is fortunate given the importance of a "unified parental front" in child rearing. Fathers used authority strategies, and mothers preferred a mediational approach. Children, reflecting their lower power status, often used distraction to end disputes. Standoffs were the most frequent outcome, compromises the least frequent.

Parents should not overlook misbehavior or unsatisfactory performance just to avoid conflict; but escalating feelings, verbal attacks, sarcasm, shouting matches, threats, and instilling guilt rarely improve a bad situation. Some parents adopt authoritarian discipline strategies during conflict. They issue commands or use coercion. They may overreact when their children challenge their authority. This may provoke defiance in their children. Frequent, intense arguing and conflict "can disrupt social interaction, erode family bonds and leave painful emotional residues" (Vuchinich, 1985, p. 40).

The communication skills described earlier in this chapter offer an alternative to shouting matches and hurt feelings. Discussion, negotiation, and problem solving are more promising methods of resolving conflict than fighting or giving in. "Parents who use direct commands or force are more likely to have children who are openly defiant. Parents who use suggestions and explanations have children who learn to negotiate" (Kuczynski, quoted by Kutner, 1988b).

Resolving an argument is similar to other problem-solving skills in that we agree on what the problem is, express our points of view, brainstorm possible solutions, and then select the most promising alternative. We try it and see what happens.

The mere occurrence of conflict should not discourage parents. Conflict between siblings can be beneficial (Kutner, 1990). It gives children the opportunity to learn how to express and cope with intense feelings such as anger, how to negotiate, and how to compromise—in other words, how to resolve differences. It is not the occurrence of conflict between siblings that determines the interpersonal competencies that children eventually achieve. Rather, children's conflict resolution skills reflect how parents manage the conflict, including strategic *non*intervention and the modeling of empathy and concern. (See Spotlight: Family Arguments.)

Training parents not to intervene leads to lower rates of sibling conflict. Kendrick and Dunn (1983) found that firstborn sons expressed *more* hostile behavior at the age of 14 months when their mothers had intervened and prohibited quarreling with their younger siblings 6 months earlier. The older the firstborn child, the more likely the mother was to intercede on behalf of the younger sibling.

Perceived Favoritism

"Most of the time, I try not to show favoritism. But there have been times when one will say, 'Oh look what she did and she got away with it.' I can't treat them the same all the time" (mother of three).

Children typically resent younger siblings because they perceive them as receiving special parental treatment. Baskett (1985) found that adults (parents and nonparents) have higher expectations for older, compared to younger, children. Parents should be wary, however, of always holding the older sibling responsible for conflict. Older children may "take out" their resentment on the younger sibling rather than expressing it directly to the parents.

The harsh treatment received by the older sibling during parental intercession may be partially responsible for future occurrences of sibling conflict. This is particularly true if the older sibling perceives the younger sibling as receiving preferential treatment ("You always take his side"). Thus, strategic nonintervention dictates that parents avoid premature involvement when possible, particularly if they find themselves always siding with one child.

Harris and Howard (1985) questioned adolescents from intact families with at least one sibling about perceived parental favoritism. About half the subjects, girls more often than boys, reported that one or both parents demonstrated favoritism. The subjects perceived the youngest child in the family as being the favorite of the mother, and they perceived the middle child as being least likely to be a parental favorite. "Subjects who perceived a sibling as being favored evidenced increased anger and depressive feelings as well as identity confusion. This latter effect was most pronounced when a parent of the same sex favored a sibling of the same sex as the subject" (p. 45).

When children accuse parents of being unfair, parents can respond, "We try to be fair, but you are not the same people and there is no way you can or should be treated exactly the same" (Brody, 1987g). Empathic and altruistic responses are encouraged when parents draw children's attention to the effects of their aggressive behaviors. It is not only whether but also how parents intercede that encourages or discourages sibling conflict (Dunn & Munn, 1986). Parents can also discourage sibling competition by treating each child as an individual—not fostering resentment through comparison—and mostly by modeling appropriate ways of resolving conflict (Faber & Mazlish, 1987). "Talking to each child about the other, explaining feelings and actions, emphasizing in a consistent way the importance of not hurting the other—all these appear to be linked to the development of a more harmonious relationship" (Dunn, 1985, p. 167).

Evaluation of Sibling Influence

Considerable space in this chapter is devoted to the sibling relationship. This reflects the substantial influence siblings can exert on each other's development. Research suggests that the emotional quality of the sibling relationship sets the tone for other modalities of sibling influence. Sibling influence may be so pervasive that it can support or compete with parental influence.

Dunn (1988) suggests that the quality of the children's relationship with each other is linked to their relationship with their parents. By taking the time to explain each child's behavior to the other and emphasizing the importance of not hurting each other, parents can promote a more harmonious relationship between them. When children interpret their parents' interventions as being one-sided, the frequency of sibling conflict is likely to increase, particularly in distressed families.

SUMMARY

All four parenting goals are supported by skilled parental communication. Unfortunately, parents often communicate poorly when they are upset, angry, or frustrated. Many children receive more than their share of criticism, which may gradually erode their self-esteem. Given children's emotional vulnerability and relative paucity of coping resources, it is particularly important that parents adopt a supportive stance in communication and discipline.

Parents interested in improving their communication skills can tone down their lecturing, nagging, reminding, criticizing, demanding, and sarcasm. Good communication begins with careful attention to the child's verbal and nonverbal signals. Sensitive parents notice nonverbal cues that indicate that a child is upset. They inquire about the child's feelings, using appropriate questions. Communication improves when parents listen sympathetically for the real, often hidden, meanings of their children's behavior. When parents acknowledge and repeat the key feelings being expressed, children feel cared for and understood.

The thoughtful use of descriptive praise and constructive feedback allows parents to avoid the "criticism trap." Rather than solving children's problems for them by giving advice (which they typically ignore) or telling them what to do, parents can help their children explore alternative solutions.

I messages allow parents to express their frustrations, annoyances, and disappointments in a constructive way. They give information about what the child did, how the parent feels about it, and why the parent feels that way. This form of expression is much more useful than simple criticism or venting.

The infant's first relationships are with its caretakers, with whom infants form strong emotional bonds. It is in the context of the infant's attachment to its caretakers, usually its parents, that socialization occurs. Attachment allows parents to serve as a basis for exploration and security for the infant. Attachment is usually a reciprocal phenomenon. Infants inevitably form attachments to familiar caretakers. Almost all parents develop strong attachments to their infants. Most children remain attached to their parents for life, but the nature of the attachment changes as children mature.

High-quality parenting promotes the development of secure attachment. Less responsive or neglectful parenting encourages insecure attachment. Many studies have confirmed the beneficial effects of secure attachment in development, particularly in the domain of social competence. During infancy, virtually all infants display marked distress in the presence of unfamiliar people, objects, or settings and upon being separated from a caretaker. Both types of intense emotional reactions are adaptive. Parents should display sensitivity when children become distressed in these situations.

There are advantages and disadvantages for children as members of small or large families, most of which depend upon other family characteristics. Generally, children in large families benefit from the large number of relationships they can observe and participate in. Children in small families benefit from the greater amount of parental attention available to them. Compared to other family variables, birth order and spacing between births seem to have a minor influence on development.

The sibling relationship is distinctive in its complexity, intensity, and duration. It encourages a closeness not often found in other types of relationships. The term "sibling rivalry" emphasizes only one part of sibling relationships. Sibling ambivalence is a more appropriate way of characterizing the "love-hate" pattern that both impresses and depresses parents. Sibling conflict is normal and helpful to children's development of coping and conflict-resolution skills. Strategic nonintervention by parents allows children the opportunity to improve their social competence.

Occasional conflict between family members is common and, if handled properly, healthy. Parents often provoke conflict unnecessarily when it could be defused. Since conflict is inevitable, parents should model proper ways of disagreeing and resolving disputes sensitively. Punitive parents tend to overreact when children are defiant and end up modeling the very behaviors they criticize.

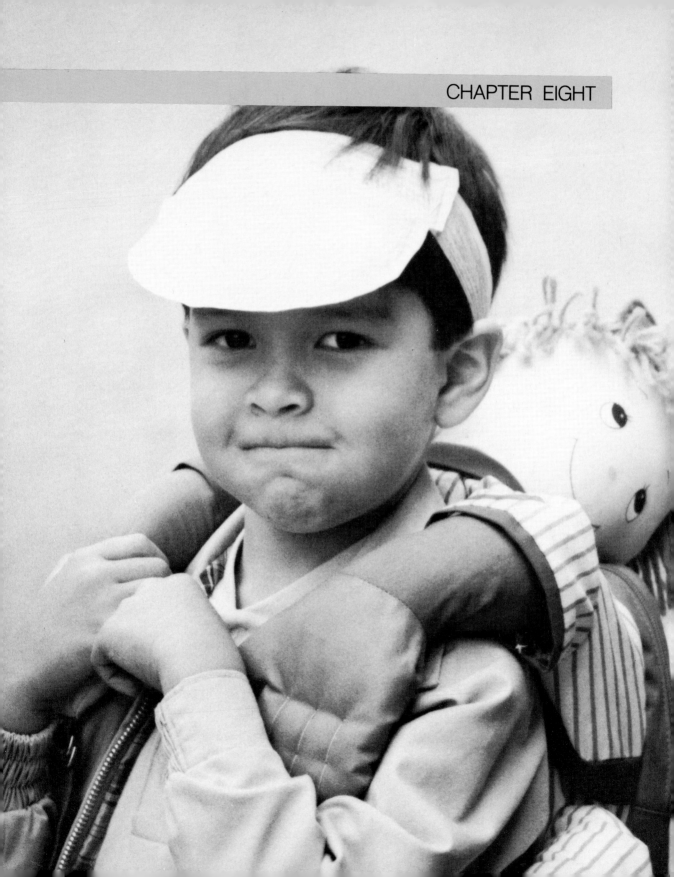

CHAPTER EIGHT

Self-Concept, Self-Esteem, and Sexual Identity

OBJECTIVES

After studying chapter 8, students should be able to

1. Briefly describe the development of self-concept in young children
2. Discuss how parents can encourage the development of empathic and altruistic behavior in their children
3. Briefly describe the development of self-esteem in young children
4. Summarize the findings of Coopersmith's study of self-esteem in preadolescent boys
5. Compare the following theorist's models of the development of self-esteem:
   a. Erikson
   b. Coopersmith
   c. Rogers
   d. Bandura
6. Explain Bandura's distinction between self-efficacy and self-esteem
7. Describe how self-efficacy is related to the following:
   a. The initiation of behavior
   b. The generalization of behavior to new situations
   c. Persistence
   d. Choice
   e. Emotional reactions
8. Describe the characteristics of individuals with low self-esteem, and parental strategies that discourage self-reliance in children
9. Describe research findings concerning differences between males and females
10. Describe some of the ways parents might raise their daughters differently than their sons
11. Describe the issues that surround children's performance of chores around the house
12. Describe the development of sexual identity in young children, according to
    a. Maccoby and Jacklin
    b. Kohlberg
    c. Bandura

INTRODUCTION

Mark #12

"In the past, when Mark wanted to attempt something I thought he couldn't handle or possibly master, I'd tell him outright. Voicing my doubts and lack of confidence in him now seems inappropriate. Our parenting class has made me realize that I have encouraged my child to display inadequacy and end up self-critical, suffering from a lack of self-worth. Rather, I should practice encouraging him to approach situations more realistically. Ideally, he will look at them as challenges and be willing to 'take risks,' knowing he doesn't have to be perfect."

It would probably never occur to a young child to evaluate herself, to ask, "How am I doing with these blocks?" or even, "What am I doing with these blocks?" Young children have little reason to evaluate themselves or their own behavior.* Rather, they accumulate a variety of evaluations from other people. Children receive daily feedback about their behavior from their parents, siblings, teachers, and peers: "What a good girl you are"; "What's wrong with you?"; "You are being so helpful today"; "You wimp."

---

*Self-evaluation probably begins when parents express conditional contingencies such as, "If you are good, then we can go to the toy store." A child might then monitor her own behavior: "Am I being good?"

Most preschool children receive enough positive feedback to balance the negative reactions they may occasionally encounter (Stipek & Mac Iver, 1989). Some disapproval—for example, from older siblings—is inevitable, and, of course, children must learn to cope with occasional negative feedback. However, some children, perhaps those who are less competent or who are poorly behaved, may become overwhelmed by the harsh, persistent criticism they receive in their daily encounters. These children may come to believe, "I can't do anything right."

Children whose behavior is overly criticized may place undue emphasis on their performance to the point of obsessive worry and anxiety. Some parents, like Mark's mother, eventually realize the impact their frequent criticisms are having on their children's self-esteem and become more encouraging.

Parenting goal #4, self-esteem and self-confidence, emphasizes the role that socialization plays in the development of these desirable traits. What children come to *believe* about themselves will influence how they *feel* about themselves. Both depend heavily upon the feedback they get from others. Generally lacking in self-evaluation skills and standards, young children see themselves through their parents' and teachers' eyes. Older children may compare their achievements to those of their peers and evaluate their own behavior according to standards they have learned from their caretakers, teachers, and peers (Stipek & Mac Iver, 1989).

This chapter explores how parenting practices influence children's self-concept and self-esteem. An important part of one's self-concept is one's gender identity, that is, seeing oneself as male or female. We will consider, therefore, how parents treat their sons and daughters differently and how such differential treatment might influence children's gender identity and sex-role development.

SELF-CONCEPT

Among the most significant tasks of infancy are the formation of a concept of self and a corresponding concept of nonself, or others. There is "me," and there is "everyone else." Bandura (1986) defines self-concept as a "composite view of oneself that is formed through direct experience and evaluations adopted from significant others" (p. 409). Newborns and very young infants probably experience the world as a stream of sensory impressions. By the middle of the first year, if not earlier, they have come to realize that they exist independently of the objects and people with which they interact. Speech and other social encounters during the second year broaden their awareness of self.

There are several indications during the latter part of the second year of life that infants have a self-concept. They can recognize themselves in a mirror (18–20 months), make self-descriptive sentences about age and gender (19–24 months), emit "mastery" smiles when they accomplish something (by 2 years), and recognize themselves in pictures (by 2 years) (Smolak, 1986). Children use the word "my" to indicate possession ("my blanket") by the age of 3 or 4 years. School-age children are better able to see themselves as others see them. Their self-concepts incorporate the feedback they get from others. They also learn what attributes are valued by others (e.g., appearance, possessions, abilities) and assess themselves accordingly.

Theorists disagree about the relative importance of social interaction and cognitive changes in the development of self-concept. Both appear to be crucial. Theorists do agree that the mother (or primary caretaker) plays a significant role in shaping the child's self-concept. "It is surely clear that the mother's view of the infant will affect the way she treats the infant, which in turn will affect the way the

Mark # 13

"Mark's camp counselor told me that Mark had been cruel by laughing when another child got hurt. He said Mark laughed while the boy cried. I told the counselor I was sorry and that I'd have a talk with my son. Mark rationalized away all the implications by saying that the boy was cruel to him, had scratched him under the eye, drawing blood (there was no evidence of blood), and by explaining that the child is regularly a 'crybaby.'

"I asked Mark how he would feel if it were him and he said it wouldn't matter to him. I tried a few times to gently prod him to admit his regret and/or guilt but when he would not, I resigned. I told him I was very displeased with his attitude."

Empathy and Altruism

Two types of social behavior that develop very gradually, from a parent's point of view, are empathy and altruism. Empathy refers to the ability to understand and care about people's feelings. Altruism refers to the willingness to help someone in need, even if there is a personal cost to the helper. The learning of prosocial behavior depends upon cognitive structures that allow children to understand that other people may feel differently from them. As they mature, children become better at interpreting other people's feelings.

A primitive form of "empathy" can be seen when even a newborn infant cries in the presence of other crying infants. Some sensitivity to other people's feelings is present by the age of 2 years. Such acts as helping, comforting, sharing, and cooperating are commonly observed in 3- and 4-year-olds (Kohn, 1988). Altruistic behaviors are often observed in preschool children, but their motives are not always clear.

Presumably, empathic feelings are elicited when a child identifies with a distressed sibling ("How would I feel if that were happening to me?"). It might occur to an older child that "I know how she feels." Understanding other people's feelings is probably rooted in our ability to imagine ourselves "in their shoes." However, an empathic response may not be sufficient, in itself, to motivate helping. In fact, understanding how their actions can affect other people encourages young children, occasionally, to intentionally elicit distress, as when children tease or torment each other.

Most children eventually demonstrate concern in the presence of another child (or adult or animal) who is distressed. Whether they offer help partly depends upon their ability to interpret the situation. The major considerations may be, "Am I responsible for your distress?" and "Am I responsible for alleviating your distress, even though I didn't cause it?" When empathic responses are elicited, and a sense of responsibility is experienced, helping is likely, or at least feeling guilty for not helping (Chapman, Zahn-

---

infant views itself, its mother, and the other inhabitants of its social world" (T. G. R. Bower, 1982, p. 278).

The development of the concept of others proceeds analagously throughout infancy and early childhood. Even young infants react differently to different people. It is not until the end of the second year, however, that empathy-like responses occur, including attempts to comfort distressed others (see Spotlight: The Development of Empathy and Altruism).

SELF-ESTEEM

Study Question   How can parents encourage the development of positive self-esteem in their children?

If self-concept refers to "one's identity as distinct from others," then self-esteem refers to "the value one places on that identity" (Berns, 1989, p. 431). In a sense, self-esteem reflects how we feel about our self-concept. Most of us

Waxler, Cooperman, & Iannotti, 1987). Dunn (1987) suggests that children as young as 24 months "show some grasp of the notion of responsibility and blame in relation to feelings and to social rules" (p. 107).

Parents are often frustrated when young children do not share, help, or offer comfort to someone in need. They are even more disturbed if their children make the "victim" feel worse ("You're a crybaby"). A parental display of anger is counterproductive when trying to teach empathic skills.

Promoting Empathy and Altruism in Children

Parents encourage the development of empathy and altruism by teaching young children sensitivity toward other people's feelings. Showing seems to work better than telling. Perhaps the best opportunity to model these interpersonal skills is when the child herself is upset or irritable. The parent can then demonstrate patience and caring rather than irritation. Parents can also model altruistic behavior for someone in distress (perhaps a sibling) in the child's presence and then give the child the opportunity to help too.

When parents observe their child behaving in a noncaring or abusive manner, they can express disapproval. They should also ask empathy-inducing questions based on the child's actual experiences. "Do you remember when Adrianne took your book without asking? How did you feel? . . . Well, how do you think Sarah felt when you took her pail without asking?" Children like Mark, who say defiantly that it wouldn't matter to them, are displaying a defensive attitude. Children become defensive when they feel they are under attack.

Parents can calmly explain to their children how our actions influence other people's feelings, and why we should be more sensitive to how our actions make other people feel. While reading to children, parents can ask questions about how people in the story are feeling about and reacting to the circumstances being depicted. With older children, parents can discuss their own life experiences or hypothetical situations with ethical or moral implications that help children explore the complexities of human motivation. Children also need instruction about how to help someone in need, according to the nature of the specific problem.

Coercing or shaming children into being "nice" is self-defeating. Eisenberg, Lundy, Shell, & Roth (1985) found that complying with adult requests or demands to be kind is not as effective, in developing empathic skills, as long-term interactions with other children. In other words, if children perceive themselves as being kind because they want to be rather than because they're being told to be, they are more likely to repeat the behavior. Nevertheless, by modeling and giving children reasons for helping, parents assist them in internalizing altruistic standards of conduct.

like certain aspects of our "selves" and dislike other aspects. In children, these mini-evaluations may change from day to day. After a victorious baseball game, my 8-year-old son thinks he's Babe Ruth. After a loss, he's convinced he "stinks" at baseball.

Self-esteem can also be defined in terms of satisfying one's expectations of oneself. Such expectations, for young children at least, are ultimately rooted in other people's expectations (Smolak, 1986). If our parents, friends, and teachers are happy with us, then we can be happy with us.

Self-concept and self-esteem appear to be linked in middle childhood by the process of self-evaluation. Parents and teachers encourage children to monitor and evaluate their own behavior ("Were you a good girl in school today?"). Eventually children monitor their own behavior using their parents' standards. My son's 8-year-old friend Mike said to me, looking at his report card, "I should have done better.

I'm disappointed in myself." Self-esteem is deflated when children do not satisfy the standards they have internalized from their parents.

Self-esteem and self-confidence also appear to be related. Children who accumulate a "track record" of success in their early years learn to expect that, if they are persistent, they will continue to be successful. They become more likely to seek challenges that allow them to demonstrate their competence. A cycle is established in which further achievement leads to a greater sense of competence, or efficacy. This, in turn, encourages them to seek further challenges. Children obviously enjoy their successes (evidenced by the "mastery smile") and the recognition they receive for their efforts. Self-esteem appears to be relatively stable over childhood, adolescence, and young adulthood (O'Malley & Bachman, 1983).

"Earned self-esteem is based on success in meeting the tests of reality—measuring up to standards—at home and in school. It is necessarily hard won, and develops slowly, but it is stable and long-lasting, and provides a secure foundation for further growth and development. It is not a precondition of learning but a product of it" (Lerner, 1985, p. 13).

Low self-esteem and self-doubt are associated with social, emotional, and academic problems in childhood. "Children who lack self-confidence are not optimistic about the outcome of their efforts. They feel incapable, inferior, pessimistic, and easily discouraged. Things always seem to go wrong; these children give up easily and frequently feel intimidated . . . Frustration and anger are handled poorly, and often turn into vengeful behavior against others or themselves. Unfortunately, their behavior typically leads others to view them as negatively as they see themselves" (Schaefer & Millman, 1981, p. 99).

Schaefer and Millman associate children's low self-esteem with faulty child-rearing practices. Parents who are overprotective prevent their children from learning self-reliance. Instead, by protecting their children from "failure," they encourage vulnerability and timidity. Neglecting parents have children who feel unworthy of being cared for. Perfectionistic and punitive parents encourage their children to feel inadequate and incapable. Children of critical and disapproving parents are likely to accept their parents' low estimation of them, but may also resent it.

Good parent-child relationships predict positive self-esteem in adolescent boys and girls. Positive self-esteem in adolescent girls is also correlated with peer support and evaluating oneself as being popular. School and athletic performance are good predictors of self-esteem in boys (Boivin & Begin, 1989; Walker & Greene, 1986). Thus, whereas positive social relations seem to boost self-esteem in girls, accomplishment is a primary determinant of self-esteem in boys. Children who are popular with their peers see themselves more positively and like themselves more than do unpopular children.

Erikson's Point of View

As described in chapter 2, Erikson's proposed eight stages of psychosocial development are represented as conflicts or crises that must be resolved for healthy personality development. The resolution of the first two crises, trust versus mistrust during the first year and autonomy versus shame and self-doubt during the second year, can have a profound impact on children's self-esteem.

Successful resolution of the first conflict requires sensitive and consistent parenting. It results in infants' ability to trust themselves and to trust their caretakers to be there when needed. Successful resolution of the second stage allows infants to believe that they can satisfy their parents' expectations, an important element of self-confidence (Smolak, 1986). Thus, the development of a sense of industry or competence depends upon the prior emergence of trust, autonomy, and initiative.

The Coopersmith Study

In reviewing the theoretical and empirical literatures on the development of self-esteem, Coopersmith (1967) identified four factors as potentially significant. They are (1) the amount of respectful, accepting, and concerned treatment that children receive from their caretakers; (2) children's history of success and the resulting recognition they receive; (3) children's values and goals, which influence how they interpret the outcomes of their efforts; and (4) children's ability to protect their self-esteem when they are criticized.

In order to assess these factors, Coopersmith investigated the relationship between parenting practices and attitudes, as reported by mothers, and the self-esteem of preadolescent middle-class boys. Coopersmith studied 85 boys who were categorized as having high, medium, or low self-esteem. The assignment of boys to these three categories was based on self-esteem inventories that they completed and their teachers' ratings of their behaviors. Their mothers were interviewed for an average of 2½ hours and completed 80-item questionnaires on their child-rearing practices.

Coopersmith concluded that children's self-esteem is essentially determined by their rearing: "The most general statement about the antecedents of self-esteem can be given in terms of three conditions: total or nearly total **acceptance** of the children by their parents, clearly defined and enforced **limits**, and the **respect and latitude for individual action** that exist within the defined limits . . . In effect, we can conclude that the parents of children with high self-esteem are concerned and attentive toward their children, that they structure the worlds of their children along lines they believe to be proper and appropriate, and that they permit relatively great freedom within the structures they have established" (p. 236). Note that Coopersmith's description of mothers of boys with high self-esteem resembles Baumrind's depiction of the authoritative or democratic parenting style.

Coopersmith also reported that "the parents of children with high self-esteem are themselves active, poised, and relatively self-assured individuals who recognize the significance of child rearing" (p. 237). They believe they have the resources to parent well, they get along well with their spouses, and they establish clear boundaries regarding authority and responsibility. Parents with high self-esteem avoid punitive discipline strategies, according to Coopersmith. They "accept and tolerate dissent within the limits that they have established" (p. 237).

People with low self-esteem, "reared under conditions of rejection, uncertainty, and disrespect, have come to believe they are powerless and without resource or recourse. They feel isolated, unlovable, incapable of expressing and defending themselves, and too weak to confront and overcome their deficiencies (p. 250) . . . By virtue of the treatment he receives and the self-attitudes he develops as a consequence, the child with low self-esteem is unlikely to believe that his personal actions can have a favorable outcome, that he can effectively cope with adversity, or that he is worthy of love and attention" (Coopersmith, 1967, p. 251).

Like Baumrind, Coopersmith found that parents who are warm *and* firm, and who encourage responsibility, have children who are self-reliant, competent, and happy. Coopersmith concluded that "definite and enforced limits" by parents are associated with children's high self-esteem. Both researchers contend that parental firmness encourages the development of "inner controls" that allow children to behave successfully. C. C. Lewis (1981) questions Coopersmith's (and Baumrind's) conclusion that firm parental control contributes positively to the development of self-esteem. Rather, he suggests, it is the child's opportunity "to shape and to alter rules" (p. 560), and not parental enforcement of rules, that is the active ingredient in the parental nurturance of self-esteem.

Rogers's Point of View

As described in chapter 2, Carl Rogers emphasized how important it is for their adjustment that children learn to appreciate themselves and others. Rogers believed that children require unconditional acceptance from their caretakers so that they can see themselves as being worthy of their parents' affection. From a parental point of view, the "unconditional" ingredient is tricky. The unconditional message asserts, "No matter what you say or do, I will always value and accept you as my child."

This is not to say that parents should condone unacceptable behavior. Rather, parents must distinguish between who the child is (which we love unconditionally) and what the child does (which may require correction, but with patience and warmth). Thus, Rogers encouraged a warm and permissive home environment. This is one in which children are encouraged to express themselves freely without fear of harsh judgment or ridicule. Parents may of course *disagree* with the child's point of view, but they respect it nonetheless.

Rogers's view is sensible. If children feel accepted by others, if they can feel "lovable," they can then accept, respect, and trust themselves, even when they "mess up." But if the prevailing message they receive is of the rejecting "bad boy/bad girl" variety, then they may come to doubt their worthiness and competence. "Every word, facial expression, gesture, or action on the part of the parent gives the child some message about his worth. It is sad that so many parents don't realize the effect these messages have on the child, and often don't even realize what messages they are sending" (Satir, 1972, p. 25).

Therapists do not get to meet many people who like and accept themselves, even among those who are deemed "successful." Some people pursue achievement partly to compensate for feelings of inadequacy induced by hard-to-please parents. Ironically, achievement in itself rarely proves satisfying. "Most of my high-achieving clients share a background in which one or both of their parents was experienced as overly critical and unsupportive. As children my clients report that they often felt like they were a disappointment and a burden to their parents. They could not say or do the right thing" (Post, 1988, p. 196).

People beginning therapy are typically anxious and depressed and have low self-esteem. They often feel worthless and hopeless, and they anticipate failure and rejection. They are usually pessimistic about their relationships and their futures. Rogers's nondirective approach to therapy provides patients with the unconditional acceptance they presumably did not enjoy in childhood.

Bandura's Model of Self-Efficacy

Study Question   What does Bandura mean by "self-efficacy," and what role does efficacy play in human personality?

According to Bandura (1977a, 1982, 1986), a major ingredient of a healthy personality is confidence in one's ability to solve a given problem or cope with a threatening situation. He refers to this ability as self-efficacy. Self-efficacy generally takes the form of judgments or expectations that one will perform well in a given situation.

These efficacy expectations play many roles in human personality. They motivate the initiation of behavior ("I can handle this"); the generalization of behavior to new situations ("Since I have succeeded before, I will probably succeed again"); persistence ("If I continue to try, I will eventually succeed"); choice ("I will take on the task I am most likely to complete successfully"); and emotional reactions ("I'm proud of my achievements"). Individuals with low self-efficacy have learned to expect negative outcomes. Their behavior becomes excessively cautious or defensive. Self-doubters give up quickly or do not try at all ("I know I will fail, so what's the use of trying?").

Bandura distinguishes between self-efficacy, a judgment of one's capabilities, and self-esteem, the evaluation of one's worth as a person. He suggests that they are not necessarily related. Nevertheless, in children, competence, self-confidence (efficacy), and positive self-esteem usually go together (Chance, 1982; Nottelmann, 1987).

"Efficacy experiences in the exercise of personal control are central to the early development of social and cognitive competence. Parents who are responsive to their infants' communicative behavior, who provide an enriched physical environment, and who permit freedom of movement for exploration have infants who are relatively accelerated in their social and cognitive development" (Bandura, 1986, p. 415). Enhancing an individual's self-confidence is associated with the alleviation of a wide range of emotional and interpersonal problems (McCleod, 1986).

Parents promote the development of children's feelings of efficacy by arranging situations in which children can perform successfully. "Successes raise efficacy appraisals; repeated failures lower them . . . After a strong sense of self-efficacy is developed through repeated successes, occasional failures are unlikely to have much effect on judgments of one's capabilities" (Bandura, 1986, p. 399).

Parents contribute to this process by teaching their children realistic standards of performance ("Do your best") rather than perfectionistic or unattainable standards ("Be the best"). Parents can also foster a child's self-esteem by valuing those abilities in which he or she excels ("I knew you could do it") rather than emphasizing weaknesses or deficits ("What's wrong with you?"). Since occasional failure is inevitable, children must learn realistic ways of evaluating themselves ("Well, nobody's perfect"). They must also understand that their worth as a person and their parents' feelings about them are not conditional on any particular achievement or failure.

We should not overlook the role of parental modeling in the development of self-esteem. Reread Coopersmith's description of parents with high self-esteem. Children of parents with low self-esteem, on the other hand, may learn that "not thinking much of yourself is natural . . . The children are not growing up in an atmosphere where positive things are felt about oneself. Parents who do not strive to do their best frequently have children who behave similarly" (Schaefer & Millman, 1981, p. 100).

SEX DIFFERENCES AND SOCIALIZATION: "IS IT A BOY OR A GIRL?"

Study Question   Other than anatomically, in what ways do boys and girls differ?

One important component of self-concept is identification with either the male or female gender and sex role. Being classified as a boy or girl at birth has a major influence on a person's life. From birth, "males and females will begin to have different kinds of experiences that to some extent will influence who and what they will become and the nature of their life courses" (J. H. Williams, 1987, p. 135).

Do parents raise sons and daughters differently? Do children identify with the same-sexed parent and adopt sex roles and personal styles accordingly? Do males and females, in fact, differ from each other? If so, how do they differ and what causes these differences? These are difficult and even controversial questions.

Everyday observation suggests that there are sex differences in behavior. For example, females are generally perceived as more expressive, warm, and sensitive to other people's feelings than males. Males are generally viewed as more assertive and competitive than females. Surprisingly, researchers have had a hard time confirming apparent differences. One reason is that girls are so different from each other, and boys are so different from each other.

SONS

DAUGHTERS

Justin Jaffe

And girls, as a group, are not that different from boys. This makes it very difficult to identify any subtle psychological and behavioral differences that might exist (J. H. Williams, 1987).

The most obvious sex differences are biological in nature, with males, on the average, being larger and weighing more. Females mature faster and live longer. Because girls mature faster, they often develop motor and other skills a little earlier than boys. The only significant physiological sex differences that have been identified are related to reproduction and health. Mortality rates are higher for males than for females at virtually every stage of life. Females' lowered susceptibility to most diseases may reflect the genetic advantages of having two identical sex chromosomes, but there are other theories (Jacklin, 1989). Nevertheless, as far as we know, males and females are much more alike biologically than they are different.

Of the hundreds of ways in which males and females could differ psychologically, few significant differences have been identified. In a somewhat controversial review of the psychology of sex differences, Maccoby and Jacklin (1974) concluded that girls have slightly greater verbal ability than boys (at least after age 11), that boys slightly excel in visual-spatial and mathematical abilities, and that boys are more physically aggressive (pp. 351–352).

Hyde and Linn (1988) performed a meta-analysis on 165 studies of gender difference in verbal abilities. They concluded that there is no such difference, at least at the present time, with the possible exception of the quality of speech production. Other recent reviews agree that if sex differences in intellectual and other abilities existed in the past, they have lessened as social roles, career, and educational opportunities have become more equitable (T. Adler, 1989c; Jacklin, 1989).

Maccoby and Jacklin (1974) rejected as "unfounded beliefs" the following: that girls are more sociable than boys (though they may differ in how they express their sociability); that girls are more suggestible than boys; and that girls have lower self-esteem or lower achievement motivation than boys. Regarding self-esteem, they concluded that the "similarity of the two sexes in self-esteem is remarkably uniform across age levels through college age" (p. 153). Females report greater self-worth in the social domain. Boys report more confidence in achievement and problem solving.

Maccoby and Jacklin felt that there was too little evidence, much of it contradictory, to draw conclusions about sex differences in anxiety, activity level, competitiveness, dominance, compliance, and nurturance. Psychologically and intellectually, males and females appear to be far more alike than they are different.

Parenting Sons and Daughters

Study Question *Do parents raise their sons and daughters differently?*

Parents might attempt to raise their sons and daughters exactly the same way, and sex differences could still emerge due to nonsocialization factors such as genetics or imitation. It is also possible that parents might treat their sons and daughters differently, and we might still find minimal sex differences. Parental influence competes with so many other forces that might encourage behavioral similarities between boys and girls.

Maccoby and Jacklin (1974) conducted an extensive review of the socialization literature to test four hypotheses regarding differential parental treatment of sons and daughters. *Their first hypothesis asserted that parents "treat children of the two sexes so as to shape them toward the behavior deemed appropriate for their sex"* (*p. 305*). The authors, in 1974, found very little evidence to support this hypothesis. They could find no clear-cut differences in the amount of parental interaction with sons and daughters; no difference in the amount of speech directed to both sexes; no differences in the expression of parental warmth; no clear demonstration of greater reinforcement for dependency in either sex; and no differences in sexual information given to boys and girls.

Although they found no consistent differences in parental restrictiveness, there was a tendency toward greater restriction of boys' behavior, but also more positive feedback given to boys. They speculated that boys may receive more positive *and* negative feedback because their behavior is more attention-getting than girls'. Maccoby and Jacklin also concluded, surprisingly, that the research literature does not support the assumption of greater permissiveness toward boys' aggressive behavior, at least by mothers.

The greatest difference in socialization between the sexes involves the encouragement of sex-appropriate behavior. (Many studies of this topic assessed toy preferences—today's boys and girls differ considerably in their play and toy preferences [C. Lawson, 1989]). Both parents, but particularly fathers, encourage sex-appropriate behavior and discourage sex-inappropriate behavior in sons more than in daughters.

Maccoby and Jacklin acknowledged the scanty evidence in some areas of this literature and the flaws in many of the studies. They concluded, nevertheless, that the "reinforcement contingencies for the two sexes appear to be remarkably similar" (Maccoby & Jacklin, 1974, p. 342). Still, we must acknowledge that parents encourage different types of play activities in their children and often assign household chores on the basis of gender (White and Brinkerhoff, 1981b). (See Spotlight: Children's Household Work.) There is also evidence that parents respond more punitively to the moral transgressions of boys compared to those of girls (e.g., Smetana, 1989b).

Parents have many questions about children's participation in household work. What chores should children perform around the house? At what age should children be expected to participate in household work? Should children be paid for their contributions? Should boys and girls perform the same tasks, or should chores be differentiated by gender? And, do children benefit from engaging in household work?

Goodnow (1988) explores these and other questions that are related to children's participation in work around the house. In the past, children's labor in and out of the home was considered a necessity. Changing conceptions of children and childhood, together with changes in family configurations, have introduced new perspectives and issues regarding the potential benefits of children's housework.

Many parents believe that participating in household work is good for children. It builds character and promotes cooperation and the development of responsibility. It encourages a sense of belonging to the family unit. Some parents (particularly single parents, those in large families, and dual-career parents) report that they really need their children's help. More than a third of parents questioned in one study reported occasionally paying their children for their help.

Household tasks are usually differentiated by role. Reviewing the findings of Thrall's (1978) study, Goodnow writes, "Mothers or children . . . set and cleared the table, but fathers did not. Fathers or children shoveled snow, but mothers did not. Mothers had fairly exclusive ties to ironing, cleaning the oven, and picking up the living room before company came. Fathers had fairly exclusive ties to fixing things around the house. Mothers or fathers might change light bulbs, but children did not" (p. 13).

Some parents believe that children should perform "tasks that teach." Others will assign any task requiring completion, regardless of its educational value. Many parents believe that children's participation in household chores promotes responsibilty and cooperation. Other parents might respond, "You're only young once," and argue that children should be relatively free of such responsibilities.

Those who advocate "domestic democracy" would require that all family members share the labor.

The age and gender of the child are important variables influencing children's participation. Age "brings changes in how much is done, what is done, how much help is expected to be given, definitions of help, offers of help and reports of satisfaction" (Goodnow, 1988, p. 13). Parents naturally take into account when assigning jobs children's abilities and the effort required to teach the child to perform a task successfully. Various tasks that might be cited for younger children, such as "picking up after themselves," would not be considered as work for older children. It is expected of them.

One study found that over 90 percent of children, by the age of 9 or 10 years, are involved in regular chores. Younger children are considered responsible only for themselves (e.g., cleaning up after themselves). As they get older, there is an increase in family work. There is also a transition from helping their parents to assuming full responsibility for certain chores (White & Brinkerhoff, 1981a).

Regarding gender, parents (particularly fathers and less-educated parents) assign jobs on the basis of the child's sex. White and Brinkerhoff (1981b) found that girls are more likely than boys to be assigned such domestics chores as cooking and cleaning. Boys are more likely to do outside work including taking out garbage, shoveling snow, and lawn mowing. Out-of-door work performed by boys was more likely to earn money.

Girls, like their mothers, are apparently being socialized "into a similar pattern of work that is 'for love.' " (Goodnow, 1988, p. 15). The implication is that females' housework, although appreciated, does not merit economic compensation. Not all tasks are differentiated by gender, including feeding pets and cleaning one's room. Parental attitudes about the sex typing of chores also reflect the number of sons and daughters available to perform these tasks (Brody & Steelman, 1985).

Parents report using a variety of techniques to motivate children to help, including rewards, punishment, social reinforcement, instruction, and "moral exhortation." Many prefer to use the principle of "minimal justification." They encourage a sense of responsibility rather than using external incentives (Goodnow, 1988). Young children are more eager to help when there is a payoff. "I hate picking up because it's so boring, and you have to keep bending down and standing up. But I want my lollipop" (Yvette, 5 years old, quoted by Foderaro, 1987).

When conflict arises regarding chores, the issue is typically the choice of task and time limits set by parents for task completion. Children tend to accept parental authority regarding the assignment of tasks, but they may argue about the details of their execution (Montemayor, 1983).

Promoting Cooperation in Household Work

It is not clear how, or even whether, children benefit from housework. More research is needed. Studies generally have not discovered impressive differences in responsibility or dependability between children who perform housework and those who do not. However, children may benefit cognitively by learning useful skills if they are given chores with potentially educational value.

It seems likely that children could benefit more from their participation if parents attend as much to the process of participation as they do to the outcome of the child's efforts. This includes helping children understand why they are being asked to help, how their efforts are contributing to the family, and that their efforts are appreciated.

With young children, parents can begin to promote cooperative skills by selecting a particular domain to work on, such as "keeping your room neat." Parents of young children can promote the learning of basic "tidying" skills by arranging the child's room in such a way that cleaning up becomes a manageable task for a toddler with a lot of stuff. Providing them with safe open-top storage boxes, oversized colorful buckets, hangers with the likeness of a cartoon character, or wicker hampers in the shape of a duck motivate their participation.

"To entice a child to tidy up, storage items with cheerful associations may help. A wise parent sets up a child's room so that straightening it up is not only possible but almost pleasurable" (Louie, 1987).

Performing household chores promotes children's self-esteem and sense of belonging to the family.

The natural consequences of not being able to find a favorite toy or a needed baseball glove also encourage neatness.

Young children may need specific instructions about how to perform a task that the parent takes for granted. "A 5-year-old might not know what to do if you say, 'clean your room.' Break the task down into specific actions like 'put your clothes in the dresser and your toys in the basket.' To a toddler, pushing all of his toys into a pile in the middle of the room seems an appropriate way to clean the room. It meets his needs, even if it doesn't meet those of his parents" (Kutner, 1987c). Rather than arbitrarily assigning tasks, parents can also arrange family meetings and assign chores democratically.

Their second hypothesis was that, due to innate characteristics, "boys and girls stimulate their parents differently and hence elicit different treatment from them" (Maccoby & Jacklin, 1974, p. 305). For example, temperamental differences between boys and girls in their ability to be comforted may elicit different patterns of handling by their parents. These, in turn, affect the child's behavior. Such "circular" patterns of interaction could have a profound effect on how boys and girls are raised. If boys are more noncompliant, parents may respond with less nurturance and greater restrictiveness, leading to more anger in their sons, and so on.

Maccoby and Jacklin concluded, based on their analysis of the literature, that "there are probably not very many initial biologically based behavioral differences, at least not many that are strong enough to elicit clear differential reactions from caretakers" (p. 343). Studies have indicated that male infants sleep less and cry more than female infants, and that mothers are more likely to respond to irritability in female infants. But overall, "mothers are equally warm, nurturing, and accepting of boy and girl babies" (J. H. Williams, 1987, p. 171).

Maccoby and Jacklin's third hypothesis was that parents "base their behavior toward a child on their conception of what a child of a given sex is likely to be like" (p. 305). Parents might compensate for "natural weaknesses" such as aggressive behavior in their sons. They might accept as inevitable such behaviors ("Boys will be boys"). Or they might overreact to behaviors they believe to be unusual for a boy or girl.

Maccoby and Jacklin concluded, based on the limited evidence available, that parents do not advocate different values for how boys and girls should behave. Parents do perceive their sons and daughters as different, regarding how rough, noisy, competitive, defiant, and helpful they are. There are very few differences, however, in the values that guide their raising of their sons and daughters.

Parental expectations may influence socialization soon after birth if parents view their newborns in sex-typed ways (Sweeney & Bradbard, 1988). "Girls are rated as smaller, softer, and less alert than boys despite the absence of real physical differences. Fathers of newborns rate boys as stronger and hardier . . . Such differences in perceptions may result in differential treatment of boy and girl infants" (Smolak, 1986, p. 227).

Maccoby and Jacklin's fourth hypothesis was that a "parent's behavior toward a child will depend, in some degree, upon whether the child is of the same sex as himself" (p. 306). This influence can be mediated by the parent's modeling behavior considered appropriate for his or her child, or by falling into stereotypical male-female roles (e.g., a mother acting submissively to her son). Parents may also identify with the same-sex child, with stronger empathic reactions to that child. Again, the authors could not find support for this hypothesis, although "fathers appeared to be more tolerant of aggression from a daughter, mothers from a son (p. 347) . . . We cannot conclude that either sex is dealt with more leniently, on the whole" (p. 348).

Despite the many limitations of the studies examined, Maccoby and Jacklin's review of the literature is remarkable in that so few differences could be found in the ways parents socialize their sons and daughters. One theme that did emerge, unexpectedly, was that boys "seem to have more intense socialization experiences than girls. They receive more pressure against engaging in sex-inappropriate behavior, whereas the activities that girls are not supposed to engage in are much less clearly defined and less firmly enforced. Boys receive more punishment but probably also more praise and encouragement. Adults respond as if they find boys more interesting and more attention-provoking than girls" (p. 348).

Boys may receive more punishment because they are not as quick to comply as girls are, or because they do more things of which their

Do children identify with their same-sexed parent?

parents disapprove. Parents may also see girls as being more fragile (J. H. Williams, 1987).

Summarizing, there is little evidence of psychological or behavioral differences between boys and girls. The slight differences that do exist may be due not to innate differences in ability and not to differential rearing patterns but rather to powerful cultural and environmental forces, including sexual stereotypes (Freedman, Sears, & Carlsmith, 1981) and parental expectations.

Parents themselves may accept sex stereotypes but usually do not apply them to their own children! People are more likely to stereotype those they do not know well. Since parents are quite familiar with their children, they treat them as individuals rather than as members of a group. Others with less information may view children stereotypically (Turkington, 1984a).

Study Question Do children identify with their same-sexed parent?

One long-standing assumption in the developmental literature is that girls become like their mothers and boys become like their fathers. Psychoanalytic theorists assume that children unconsciously identify with the same-sexed parent. This process would be more powerful for females, because "a young girl's identification with her mother continues throughout life, whereas a young boy's identification with his mother is broken and switched to his father . . . A daughter continues to identify with her caregiving mother, thereby maintaining the mother-daughter relationship while establishing her identity. A son, however, must begin to seek his identity with his more absent father, an emotional maneuver that disengages him from the intensity of the mother-child relationship. Because of their prolonged identification with their mothers, daughters often perceived themselves as more 'like' their mothers than sons are 'like' their fathers" (Boyd, 1989).

Social learning theories also predict that children will resemble the same-sexed parent more than the opposite-sexed parent, but for different reasons. They cite modeling and reinforcement for sex-appropriate behavior as mechanisms of influence. It is assumed that parents, often in subtle ways, treat their sons and daughters differently.

Parents do treat children of their own sex more harshly. J. H. Williams (1987) suggests that the father-son interaction reflects a struggle for male dominance. "That is, the father is reacting to the son as a male who is challenging him, whereas a daughter is no such threat" (p. 194). This is supported by Barber and Thomas's (1986) observation that, unlike mothers, fathers express much less physical affection to their sons than daughters. Mothers' greater tolerance for their sons' behavior may reflect the fact that women "are accustomed to using moderation in their reactions to male threat, and perhaps this conditioning comes into play when they are confronted with boys' flouting of their authority" (J. H. Williams, 1987, p. 194).

Mothers and fathers may occasionally treat their sons and daughters differently, but nevertheless, sex differences in children and adolescents are hard to find. To shed light on some of the issues already cited, current research is focusing on possible differences between all four parent-child gender combinations: mother-son, mother-daughter, father-son, and father-daughter (Boyd, 1989; Steinberg, 1987d).

Sexual Identity and Sex Typing

Study Question *In what ways might parents encourage "sex-appropriate" behavior in their children?*

Sexual identity refers to perceiving oneself as male or female. Most children label themselves correctly (as "boy" or "girl") by the age of 2½ or 3 years. Young children base their gender labels on superficial characteristics such as name, clothes, or hair length rather than on sex organs (Beal & Lockhart, 1989). They also know there are two sexes and that they "belong" to one (Emmerich, Goldman, Kirsh, & Sharabany, 1977). Once children define themselves as boy or girl, they use these labels to guide their behavior.

Sex typing refers to the psychosocial processes by which children acquire, value, and perform sex-typed behavior patterns, those considered appropriate for their sex (Mischel, 1976). Sex-typed behaviors, such as toy and clothing preferences, emerge during the preschool years, as do beliefs about what is considered masculine and what is considered feminine (Huston, 1983). Traditionally, males and females have been distinguished by their anatomy, clothes, roles, occupations, and other behaviors.

Learning Models

Different models of sex typing exist. A simple learning model based on rewards and punishments suggests that parents reward sex-appropriate traits and behaviors. They reward displays of bravery and independence in boys. They reward nurturance and warmth in girls. Parents do not encourage, and often punish, sex-inappropriate behavior, such as playing with dolls for boys and playing with guns for girls. Parents do encourage sex-appropriate play, especially for boys (Snow, Jacklin, & Maccoby, 1983).

Parents, particularly fathers, are concerned about their sons' preferences in toys. "We can assume that this concern is communicated to children in indirect and subtle ways; even if specific rewards and punishments are not given, the children are reinforced by smiles, frowns, and other expressions of approval or disapproval that can be even more powerful" (Freedman et al., 1981, p. 494).

Boys become more concerned about gender-role identity than girls. According to learning models, this is because boys are more likely to be ridiculed for displaying "feminine" traits than girls are for showing "masculine" characteristics. There is no question but that reinforcement influences children's patterns and preferences, but the effects appear to depend on who is providing the reinforcers. For example, children are more susceptible to reinforcers coming from same-sexed, rather than opposite-sexed, peers (Fagot, 1985). In a form of "self-socialization," boys reinforce each other for "masculine" behaviors and girls reinforce each other for "feminine" behaviors (Jacklin, 1989).

Learning models of sex typing, however, have not been able to account for the rate, scope, and endurance of sex typing and sex-role acquisition. Even though parents treat boys and girls similarly, in most domains, stereotyped toy preferences are displayed before 2 years of age! Parental concern about sex-appropriate play may be expressed more through the room decor and selection of toys than through direct reward and punishment of sex-appropriate behavior (Fling & Manosevitz, 1972).

"The decor and objects in the rooms of boys are different from those typically found in girls' rooms . . . Boys are more likely to be given trucks, construction sets, and sports equipment. Girls' toys are more likely to include dolls and their accompanying paraphernalia" (Smolak, 1986, p. 227). An editor of *Ms. Magazine* recalled buying a basketball hoop for her infant son. "He was 2 years old. The girls were 5, and very athletic. My husband said, 'Why are you putting this in *his* room?' It was a moment of truth for me. After that, I looked at everything in a whole new way" (Pogrebin, quoted by C. Lawson, 1989).

Additionally, masculine and feminine toys elicit different patterns of parent-child interaction. Parents play differently with their young children according to the child's sex-stereo-

Toy preferences appear to be influenced by family and cultural expectations about what is masculine and feminine.

typed toy choices. Parents (mothers and fathers) express greater enthusiasm for a toy that is stereotyped for the child (and parent's) gender (Caldera, Huston, & O'Brien, 1989).

Kohlberg's Model

Kohlberg's (1966) cognitive-developmental model contends that children learn by about the age of 3 years to label their own sexual identity as boy or girl. They then learn to recognize the gender of other people. Children evolve masculine and feminine stereotypes as oversimplified rules (e.g., men are doctors; women are nurses; all people with long hair are girls). These rules are learned through exposure to distinctive behavior patterns or traits associated with males or females. With experience, their beliefs about gender become more flexible. For example, "All married women are mothers" becomes "Not all married women have children."

Once they grasp the permanence of their own maleness or femaleness, by about the age of 5 or 6 years, they automatically come to value and try to learn those behaviors that they perceive as consistent with their gender identity. According to Kohlberg, until they are about 5 years old, children lack the cognitive structures necessary for grasping the permanence and irreversibility of gender.

Kohlberg's model is contradicted by the fact that children much younger than 5 or 6 show sex-appropriate preferences and behavior patterns (Freedman et al., 1981; Ruble & Ruble, 1980). Recent research (Bem, 1989) also confirms that preschool children can show "gender constancy," that is, they can understand that one's sex does not change when one's appearance (e.g., hair length, clothing) changes. The key is grasping that gender is defined by one's genitals, not one's appearance (Beal & Lockhart, 1989).

Bandura's Model

Maccoby and Jacklin (1974) and Kohlberg (1966) downplayed the role of social learning and modeling in the development of gender identity and sex roles in favor of biological or cognitive predispositions. Bandura (1986) and Bem (1981) advocate a "gender-schema" model of sex typing that incorporates both cognitive change and social learning. Bandura suggests that children acquire a gender identity by cognitively processing their own experiences and by watching other people. They learn about sex roles by extracting rules about what behaviors are considered appropriate for members of their own sex and the opposite sex.

Children are subject to direct reinforcement of sex-appropriate behaviors by their caretakers. They also learn about sex roles vicariously by observing same-sex models in their family, on TV, or in books and movies. We see direct socialization of sex roles in children's play when parents select different toys or play equipment for their sons and daughters. We observe vicarious socialization in educational materials and books that portray boys as more active and inventive and girls as more dependent and passive.

Unlike Kohlberg's model, in Bandura's view, gender conceptions do not automatically motivate the learning of appropriate sex-role behavior patterns. Girls, for example, do not automatically display same-sex modeling, particularly when "masculine" behavior is more highly valued by society. In middle childhood, girls exhibit a marked preference for the advantaged masculine role. They express ambivalence toward the traditionally subservient feminine role. There exist fewer sanctions for cross-sex preferences for females than for males, encouraging this ambivalence.

Bandura suggests that gender-role learning is an "ongoing process" that is not confined to early childhood (p. 98). Socialization processes do begin at birth, with distinctions based on the sex of the child being made regarding clothing, color schemes of rooms, and children's names. Toward the end of infancy, many children can identify their sex. They have already acquired verbal labels for what is male or female, such as boys, girls, mommy, daddy, man, woman, and so on.

Gender identity broadens, according to Bandura, to include behavioral, social, and vocational distinctions. Since men today are so different from each other, as are women, it is difficult for children to acquire consistent information about sex roles. They still are susceptible to stereotypical formulations. Valid distinctions are facilitated when large numbers of same-sex models exhibit similar behavior patterns. For example, on "Super Sunday," most of the men are watching football on TV and most of the women are conversing in the kitchen. Children have many such opportunities to view sex-stereotyped behaviors in their parents and on TV.

It is likely that children learn about gender roles in several ways: observation of same-sexed models, direct or subtle parental reinforcement of sex-appropriate behavior, and through the acquisition of rules based on observation. "It is probable that all these processes are involved in the emergence of [gender-related behavior], in different degrees of importance, depending on the situation and the age of the child" (J. H. Williams, 1987, p. 180).

Cross-Gender Behavior

Roberts, Green, Williams, and Goodman (1987) suggest that none of the current models of gender identity can account for people who have problems with their sexual identity. There are people who "have an intense, apparently irreversible conviction of belonging to the other sex and who trace the onset of this cross-sex identity to early childhood" (p. 544). They usually report that as children, they role-played being of the opposite sex. They preferred dressing like the opposite sex, avoided same-sex playmates and toys and games typical of their sex, and wanted to be of the opposite sex.

These researchers compared families of boys exhibiting cross-gender behaviors with families of boys displaying typically masculine behaviors. They found that boys living without their fathers were more "feminine" than boys whose parents had intact marriages. Femininity in boys was predicted by the mother's approval of cross-gender behavior at an early age and the father's desire for a girl when the woman was pregnant with her son. The dynamics of gender identity appear to be different in such families. These researchers suggest that the father's availability and possibly biological dispositions may determine whether boys' gender identity is typical or atypical.

Androgyny

Living in a time when sex roles are becoming more flexible, it is difficult to maintain stereotypical role distinctions based on sex or even to talk about "sex-appropriate behavior." A majority of mothers work, and some men are choosing to stay home and raise their children, at least part time. More men are becoming nurses and secretaries, and more women are becoming doctors and lawyers.

Rejecting the idea that masculinity and femininity are opposite ends of a continuum, or that certain behaviors should be expected of children on the basis of their gender, Bem (1974) has introduced the concept of androgyny. Androgynous traits represent the most desirable characteristics of both sexes. According to Bem, parents should encourage such attributes as warmth, assertiveness, independence, and competence in all children, regardless of their gender. People should have the choice of pursuing the career or life-style that best suits their personal needs and preferences rather than one that conforms to their chromosomal and genital makeup.

Sexual Preference

The origins of sexual preferences are not well understood. Some theorists contend that biological factors such as prenatal hormonal imbalances determine sexual preference; others suggest that social learning experiences are the key (M. Hoffman, 1977a). Different types of homosexuality appear to have different causes. Both biological and social learning factors are probably involved, perhaps to a different degree for each type of sexual preference (Bell, Weinberg, & Hammersmith, 1981).

Evidence does not support the belief that homosexual men are raised by ineffective fathers and domineering mothers. It is also unlikely that painful experiences with the opposite sex or seduction by a member of one's own sex precipitates homosexual preferences.

Play activities and toy preferences of children are certainly not related to eventual sexual preference. A poor relationship with one's father, however, may be a factor for both male and female gays (Bell, Weinberg, & Hammersmith, 1981).

Parents should not feel responsible for their children's eventual sexual preferences. There seems to be little that parents can do to influence their children's sexuality one way or another. Even though a poor relationship with one's father is often mentioned by gays, most people who have such relationships are heterosexual.

Tragically, some parents reject their children because of their sexuality. Like skin color and gender, children do not choose their sexuality. It's just there. As painful as it might be for some parents to discover that their children are not heterosexual, their love for their children can help them overcome the irrational prejudices that otherwise divide and destroy families.

SUMMARY

To a large extent, young children's self-concept and self-esteem depend upon the feedback they get from other people and the performance standards they are encouraged to meet. Self-esteem can be defined as the value one places on one's self-concept. Self-esteem reflects children's ability to satisfy others and, eventually, themselves.

Children with a track record of success usually develop a sense of "efficacy" that encourages them to seek new challenges and to take risks. Children who have overprotective, punitive, neglecting, perfectionistic, or disapproving parents may develop negative self-esteem. They learn to avoid or fear situations where their competence is being evaluated.

Coopersmith relates children's self-esteem to a variety of parenting practices, including parental acceptance of the child, clearly defined and enforced limits, and flexibility. Baumrind, Rogers, and Erikson have described parenting practices for promoting self-esteem that are very similar to those advocated by Coopersmith. Bandura describes the critical role that self-efficacy (self-confidence) plays in personality development.

Research on sex differences has confirmed that males and females are much more similar than different. Biological differences are related to reproduction and health. The only clear-cut behavioral sex difference is that boys behave more aggressively than girls. If differences in abilities have existed in the past, they are lessening, possibly because males and females are being treated more equitably.

Although parents generally raise their sons and daughters similarly, subtle differences in expectations, beliefs, and values may encourage the slight sex differences that exist in achievement and self-esteem. Parents socialize their sons somewhat more intensely than their daughters, perhaps believing that boys require firmer limits on their behavior.

Parents do encourage what they consider to be sex-appropriate behaviors in their children. Household chores are often assigned on the basis of a child's gender. Parents are more offended by "effeminate" behavior in boys than by "masculine" behaviors in girls. Partly as a result, boys are usually more rigid in the distinctions they make about what is considered appropriate sex-role behavior.

Children learn about sex roles from their parents, their peers, and from the media. Television continues to portray sex roles stereotypically. Parents who are aware of the limitations that sex roles impose upon their children may choose to encourage desirable ("androgynous") characteristics in their children, regardless of their gender.

Adjustment, Stress, and Coping

OBJECTIVES

After studying chapter 9, students should be able to

1. Describe how parents can encourage honest behavior in their children
2. List several of the common stressors of childhood
3. Describe how parents can help their children cope with strong emotions
4. Describe the general characteristics of shy children, and how parents can help children overcome their social anxieties
5. Describe how children attempt to cope with displays of anger
6. Discuss how parental reactions to and modeling of anger may influence children
7. Distinguish between jealousy and envy, and describe the conditions under which children might express each
8. Define "learned helplessness" and the conditions that foster its development
9. Describe the development of various coping styles in children and how they vary with age
10. Identify the characteristics of "resilient" children and the factors that promote their ability to adjust to very stressful life events
11. Describe children's understanding of death, and describe the roles that experiences with death, cognitive development, and religious intruction play in the development of their understanding
12. Describe how parents can help children cope with the death of a loved one

INTRODUCTION

June 14, 1989

To Whom It May Concern,
I began working with Rosa and her mother during the summer of 1987. I have had over 30 counseling sessions with them over the past two years, and I have observed Rosa in her classroom. I was originally consulted because Rosa was having difficulty getting along with the other children in her special preschool class. Because of her aggressive behaviors (screaming, biting, pinching, scratching) and her teasing, the other children were avoiding her.

Her teachers reported that Rosa was often uncooperative, stubborn, and defiant. She was almost constantly testing their authority. Occasionally, she would have a tantrum or pinch or bite a teacher, and she would have to be physically restrained. Her teachers and the school's child study team reported that Rosa has a short attention span and is mildly hyperactive. She also has speech problems and poor listening skills. Her parents' troubled relationship and eventual separation has exposed her to additional stresses.

Rosa has good and bad days, good and bad weeks. Eventually, the director of her special program felt that they could not handle Rosa because her presence was too disruptive, and she had to leave the program. Her teachers had tried various behavior modification procedures with Rosa, including time out and daily report cards, with some degree of success. Teachers who were firm with Rosa usually had better results than teachers who were permissive.

As long as Rosa continues to be placed in settings where her special needs are addressed, I would expect to see progress both academically and in her social skills. At the present time, her adjustment to her parents' separation and her father's lessening involvement in her life are my greatest concerns. If I can be of further help, please let me know.

I wrote this letter to a judge to support Rosa's mother's request for additional financial support from her ex-husband. Rosa's mother, an elementary school teacher, was having difficulty finding proper day care because of Rosa's behavior problems and special needs. The letter describes some of the adjustment problems 5-year-old Rosa had been having in school.

Recent surveys suggest that as many as one in five children suffer from emotional or behavioral problems that impair their lives. Many of these children are born to drug-addicted or teenage mothers, and many have been abused or neglected. Despite the fact that the field of infant "psychotherapy" is growing rapidly, only a small percentage of these children ever receive treatment (Goleman, 1989a; 1989b).

Children with serious emotional problems typically function poorly in social and academic settings. Maladjustment in childhood predicts adjustment problems in adolescence and adulthood (Schaefer & Millman, 1981). A small number of preschoolers (typically unwanted children who were abused or neglected) have suicidal thoughts and even attempt to end their lives (Rosenthal & Rosenthal, 1984).

Parents like Rosa's mother try to protect their children from serious emotional distress. Rosa was apparently unaware of her parents' longstanding marital problems until her father left. Because of her age, she could not understand why her parents no longer loved each other and why they could no longer live together. Children like Rosa—in fact, all children—must develop skills and personal resources that will allow them to solve common life problems, as well as cope with those that cannot be quickly resolved. Rosa will have to cope with her father's lessening availability.

Many children experience insoluble problems, such as parental divorce or sexual abuse, that overwhelm their ability to cope. These stressors may precipitate a wide range of maladaptive behaviors, ranging from nervous habits to suicide attempts. Children who experience chronic (long-term) stressors may develop fears, phobias, and depression. They often do poorly in school, have difficult relationships with their peers and family members, and may exhibit antisocial behaviors such as bullying and lying (see Spotlight: Encouraging Honest Behavior). Childhood aggression like Rosa's, if untreated, may lead to continued adjustment problems during adolescence (Lerner, Hertzog, Hooker, Hassibi, & Thomas, 1988).

HAPPINESS

Study Question   How can parents encourage "happy" behaviors in their children?

Parents value their children's happiness. Children's sad faces and crying are disturbing. They motivate most parents to "correct" the circumstances that led to the distress. Children's smiles and happy behaviors reinforce sensitive, nurturant caregiving. In a very important sense, then, children's emotional reactions (positive and negative) gradually shape more effective parenting responses. Happy, affectionate children are a good sign that parents are doing something right. Children's expressions of joy also elicit pleasurable emotions in parents that probably strengthen the parent-child bond.

Negative emotions usually receive more parental attention than expressions of joy and happiness. This may encourage children to express negative feelings manipulatively, for example, by crying to get something they want. Giving children what they want simply because they are distressed may encourage manipulative emotional expressions. The parental communication skills described in chapter 7 are excellent tools for handling children's distress.

Parents should notice and reinforce children's expressions of positive feelings by responding in kind. We can assume that children will learn to model parental expressions of

Like most other aspects of development, children's perception of "reality" changes over time. What adults call "lies" for toddlers may be nothing more than a failure to distinguish between reality and fantasy. "At first, the lies children tell seem to be an effort to remake reality so that it conforms to a more desirable state of affairs. It appears that when children first tell lies they are trying as hard to deceive themselves as other people. By age four, however, children seem really to be trying to deceive their parents" (Stone & Church, 1984, p. 371).

Most parents probably indulge young children's misstatements, understanding that a child's motivation is not malicious. For children, lying is a normal and even a healthy sign of development. "Psychologists who are studying how and why children learn to lie are finding that certain lies play positive roles in a child's emotional development. A child's first successful lie, for instance, is seen by some researchers as a positive milestone in mental growth" (Goleman, 1988a).

Usually the false statements of toddlers are so preposterous that parents gently accept or question the assertions rather than criticize them. As children get older, they may learn that lying is an easy way to impress someone. Lying is more commonly used to avoid blame and, thus, punishment ("I didn't do it").

Lying is considered a serious problem for about 3 percent of all children, typically those who are getting in trouble for other reasons. Children who are chronic liars are at risk for committing criminal offenses later in life (Goleman, 1988a). Stouthamer-Loeber and Loeber (1986) found that chronic lying is significantly related to delinquency, theft, and fighting in boys. "Subjects who lied were more likely to come from families where mothers poorly supervised their children and rejected them and where parents did not get along well or did not live together" (p. 551).

Society generally condemns lies that are told for personal gain. So-called "white lies" that are told to avoid hurting someone's feelings may be condoned, or at least tolerated, by adults. The intention is to protect rather than deceive another person. Children who observe their parents telling lies of convenience may imitate this behavior. However,

when asked, they will acknowledge that such lying is wrong or bad. In other words, a child can learn that an action is bad but still engage in it. Similarly, a child may ask a parent a question about ethics ("Is cheating a sin?") and be given a practical answer that seems to address the question but that really doesn't. The child may stop asking such questions.

When parents catch their children lying for personal gain, they may be quick to criticize or punish this behavior. This is unfortunate because parents, in effect, may be punishing the child for "getting caught" rather than for lying. If children successfully cover up their misbehavior and thereby avoid punishment, future deceptive behavior is encouraged (Blechman, 1985). For this reason, punishing lying may be counterproductive. It is clear that with proper parental "training," children can become very good liars. Children who learn that lying is "too risky" may instead invent excuses to lessen their responsibility in a difficult situation.

Thoughtful parents discourage deceptive behavior by discussing rather than punishing misbehavior. Young children know lying is bad, but they may not understand why. When my children were younger, I tried to help them appreciate the relationship between honesty and credibility by using a natural consequence. Children enjoy telling their parents about their accomplishments. If one of my sons lied to me and at a later time told me about an achievement, I would question the truthfulness of their account. I wanted to believe them, but how did I know that this was not just another lie? Distrust is a natural consequence of dishonest behavior and very frustrating to a child who is seeking credit for an actual achievement.

Honesty is promoted when parents reinforce children for telling the truth about their misbehavior. "Make sure that honesty has a bigger payoff than dishonesty. If your child is honest about misbehavior, praise your child's honesty, while still letting the child suffer the consequences of his behavior" (Blechman, 1985). Punishing truth-telling or ignoring honest behavior are common parental pitfalls. Demonstrating integrity and owning up to one's mistakes are also powerful ways of encouraging such behaviors in children.

happy behaviors. I do not believe that happy parents necessarily have happy children, but I suspect there is some correlation. The opposite is also probably true. As noted in chapter 4, children of depressed mothers show fewer positive emotions than children of nondepressed mothers.

This is not to suggest that children, or anyone, can always feel happy. Responsive parents support whatever emotional state the child is expressing, whether it is positive or negative. Ginott (1965) and others have noted that some parents overreact when their children are upset. They try too hard to make everything all right. A mother I am seeing in family therapy cannot bear to see her children quarrel or show distress. When they do, she feels compelled to find a "quick fix," even though that is not usually helpful or possible. Her older son, not surprisingly, is also overly sensitive during conflict.

Again, when children are upset or angry, the parental communication skills discussed in chapter 7 can help them clarify their problem and find a possible solution. We all must learn how to accept and cope with negative feelings. Parents should be aware that they are models for expressing both positive and negative feelings. In this chapter, we concentrate more on negative than on positive emotions. This entire book, however, is dedicated to promoting parenting skills that encourage cheerful, affectionate relationships between parents and children.

CHILDHOOD FEARS

On May 20, 1988, in Winnetka, Illinois, an 8-year-old boy was shot to death by a psychologically disturbed woman who had entered his school with a gun. In the weeks following the tragedy, many children in that town, some of whom attended the school where the boy was killed, exhibited their distress in a variety of ways. "Five- and six-year-olds are afraid to leave their homes or let their parents out of sight. A third-grade boy tells his mother he will take a bazooka to school to protect himself. A 10-year-old talks incessantly about blood splattering on the floor. Even teen-agers have trouble sleeping" (Kutner, 1988r).

The random nature of the violence in a classroom setting taxed the coping abilities of many of the town's children. Unlike their parents, who have learned to cope with traumatic events through rationalization and denial, many of the children "coped" with their anxieties by developing psychosomatic symptoms that lasted for weeks or months (Kutner, 1988r). Most children, fortunately, do not have to cope with events as traumatic as random violence in a school setting. Fear, however, is very much a part of every child's existence.

Infants generally show little fear until about 6 or 7 months after birth. They then begin to display the facial expressions that indicate fear when they are in the presence of strangers or when they are separated from their caretakers (Kagan, 1984). A fear of heights emerges by 6 months, when infants are beginning to explore their environments by crawling. As children learn more about the world, they develop fears of dangerous situations like fire, falling, and becoming separated from their parents. Because their interpretive abilities are limited, they are also susceptible to learning irrational fears. These usually diminish as children's cognitive abilities expand.

The Development of Childhood Fears

Study Question How do childhood fears develop?

Fearfulness appears to have moderate heritability (Marks, 1987), presumably because fear is adaptive. Children are predisposed to fear unfamiliar people, settings, and situations. Childhood fears can also be learned. Children can learn to be afraid in at least three ways: through (1) conditioning, (2) modeling, or (3) instruction. Children may learn to fear painful events and objects, such as injections

Justin Jaffe

and hot stoves, through conditioning. Occasionally, children might experience painful bowel movements, and then become constipated. They have associated toileting with pain.

Many children who experienced northern California's "World Series" earthquake lost their homes, saw neighbors who had been injured, and felt hundreds of aftershocks. Some said they had never seen their parents so frightened (*New York Times,* October 24, 1989).

When parents exhibit fear of an event or object ("Eek . . . there's a spider on you"), children are likely to model their apprehension ("Get it off, get it off"). Through instruction or modeling, parents can teach children to fear dangerous situations, such as being in an open field during a thunderstorm. Children can also be taught to fear harmless situations, such as using a public lavatory.

All children, even those raised in secure and supportive families, develop fears. Common childhood fears include fear of the dark, strange noises, supernatural beings, animals, doctors, burglars, kidnappers, thunder, and getting lost or being separated from one's parents. Quite a few childhood fears are school-related. Many children report being afraid of bullies, tests, and speaking or performing in public. Some fears, such as fear of animals, blood, or injury, may persist into adulthood (Marks, 1987), but most childhood fears disappear over time. Debilitating fears and phobias occur in a small percentage of children. They merit professional attention so that children can learn to cope with their fearfulness (Goleman, 1989b).

Adolescents may worry about death, nuclear war, and being rejected by the opposite sex (not necessarily in that order). Some studies report sex differences in fearfulness. Lentz (1985) found that girls are more concerned about bodily injury than boys. Aho and Erickson (1985) report that girls express more and stronger body-related fears than boys, including a fear of losing their attractiveness. Boys and girls expressed fear of losing body parts, dying, removing clothing in public, needles, and causing their parents to worry.

A recent survey of 1,814 children in 6 countries, grades 3 through 9, asked the children to rate the stressfulness of common, everyday situations (Yamamoto, Soliman, Parsons, & Davis, 1987). The survey results revealed commonalities across cultures in children's perceptions of what is stressful. The death of a parent and going blind were the two most threatening possibilities. Fear of being humiliated was ranked much higher than the birth of a sibling or having an operation. Young adolescents report being concerned about school, friends, parents, and boy/girl friends (Stark, Spirito, Williams, & Guevremont, 1989).

Dibrell and Yamamoto (1988) held face-to-face, informal conversations with 46 school-age children in California. They asked these children to "talk to me about some of these things that make you feel sad or worried or upset or angry." After initially denying that they had unpleasant experiences, the children described fears of being lost or abandoned by their parents, being hospitalized, fear that their parents would hurt each other while arguing, and parental divorce. One 10-year-old said he was afraid of what his parents might do when they were fighting. "Like they might hit each other . . . they might get a divorce. I feel sad right here [pointing to his chest] and then it goes up to the eyes, and then you just want to hold it in, and so you hold it in" (p. 22).

"In listening to children, it is difficult not to be touched by the profound sense of vulnerability among them. They are afraid of being left alone, apprehensive of what lies ahead, and uncertain of what they can do. They are so fundamentally dependent upon adults as to be almost powerless in the face of upsetting events and unpredictable developments. Often they wait—wait until something happens, wait until an adult intervenes . . . Too often they must persevere and persist alone in the face of the unknown and overwhelming" (Dibrell & Yamamoto, 1988, p. 22).

Parental Handling of Children's Fears

A recent study found that about 40 percent of students age 5 to 12 years worried about nuclear war. One of the great frustrations of parenting is that we cannot protect our children fully from these concerns (Collins, 1988). However, by modeling parental thoughtfulness about these problems and by teaching children what we can do collectively or as individuals to reduce the nuclear threat, children's fears can be lessened. Children are less distressed by these problems when they believe people are doing something about them.

Dibrell and Yamamoto (1988) suggest that parents provide their children with suitable explanations for anticipated events that may upset them, such as hospitalization. Children of different ages show their distress differently, but they should be encouraged to express their feelings. Parents can use sympathetic listening to help children clarify their fear and also to convey parental acceptance of those feelings. Studies of children who are good copers find that their parents do not indulge or overprotect them. Rather, they encourage, reward, and reassure them. We can also help young children cope with their fears by using drawings, puppets, role playing, and story telling.

SHYNESS

Study Question   How can parents discourage shy behaviors in their children?

About 42 percent of people in the United States consider themselves to be shy, and about 80 percent report either being shy or having been shy at some point in their lives (Zimbardo & Radl, 1981). Children in grade school who characterized themselves as shy also considered themselves to be less friendly, more fearful, more passive, more introverted, and less tolerant of others than their nonshy peers. They also liked themselves less. Zimbardo notes that their intolerance reflects the tendency of shy people to be critical of others.

At the root of shyness and other types of social anxiety is the fear of social evaluation, criticism, closeness, or rejection. Parents who judge their children's worth on the basis of their behavior or accomplishments render what Carl Rogers called conditional acceptance. The child feels accepted only when he satisfies the parents' standards of acceptable performance, which may occur rarely.

Although there are innate dispositions toward sociability or cautiousness (see chapter 3), some psychologists believe that shyness reflects experiential factors to a greater degree than innate tendencies. This assumption may not apply to the very inhibited children studied

For many children, shyness may reflect low self-esteem and deficiencies in social skills.

by Kagan and his colleagues. For most children, however, shyness seems to reflect deficits in the skills that enable sociable people to interact confidently and effectively.

According to Zimbardo and Radl (1981), shy people dislike being alone. Some become so dependent on the company of others that, despite (or because of) their fears, they come on too strong in social interactions. This scares off potential companions. Zimbardo associates the development of children's shyness with the authoritarian or punitive style of parental discipline. He suggests that shyness can be corrected by parents adopting an authoritative or democratic parenting style.

Parents can discourage the development of bashful behavior by "modeling appropriate social behaviors, giving the shy lots of practice in socializing, providing constructive, non-threatening feedback that helps refine the shy person's social skills, and most of all by rewarding all attempts at trying to be a social being" (Zimbardo & Radl, 1981, p. 14).

Some children hide behind their parents when they are being introduced to someone, or they may not respond to someone's question. Rather than being critical, parents can help their children develop social skills and self-confidence by role-playing social interactions with them. For example, they might say, "Let's pretend we are meeting for the first time. You say hello to me, and I'll say hello to you. Then we'll shake hands. OK?" Children can be taught what to say when meeting or greeting someone, how to speak in a loud voice while maintaining eye contact, and so on. When children successfully display these behaviors, parents can socially reinforce their efforts.

ANGER

Study Question How do children cope when their parents quarrel?

In this section, we examine how children cope with anger expressed by others and how parents can support children's healthy expressions of anger. Even young children are sensitive to displays of anger by others and may subsequently behave aggressively. E. M. Cummings (1987) refers to displays of anger observed by children in families as "background anger," which seems to emotionally arouse and distress them. "I know she doesn't like it when we argue, because she cries and gets extremely upset when I'm upset. The worst thing is when she pushes him [the father] away. She thinks he's upsetting me. She can't help it. She has to realize people do fight. It doesn't mean they don't love each other" (mother of a 3-year-old girl).

Lacking coping resources, some children may become overwhelmed by frequent and intense displays of parental anger.

Given the prevalence of chronic arguing in dysfunctional families, it is important to assess its possible effects on children. Children of divorce appear to suffer more from witnessing hostile confrontations between their parents than from the parental separation itself. Intense hostility that is not openly expressed also takes its toll on children, but verbal and physical expressions of anger are perceived most negatively. Parental anger arouses more angry feelings in boys than in girls, and boys are more likely to react with hostility. Girls are more likely to propose solutions to the problem or to become involved in mediating the dispute (Cummings, Vogel, Cummings, & El-Sheikh, 1989).

Intense conflict between parents can frighten or upset children. Such distress is seen in children as young as one year of age. Some children, believing they are responsible for parental anger, feel guilty and blame themselves. By the age of 5 or 6 years, many children try to intervene when parents fight, perhaps attempting to alleviate their parents' distress (Covell & Abramovitch, 1987).

In one study (Jenkins, Smith, & Graham, 1989), 71 percent of the children interviewed reported that they intervened when their parents quarreled. The researchers concluded that since intervention is so common, it should be considered normal behavior. "Children may feel that by intervening in a quarrel they gain some direct control over an event that otherwise would make them feel helpless" (p. 187). Children also dealt with their own distress by approaching their siblings or approaching their parents. "Experiencing family disharmony, although clearly a serious risk to the development of many children, may also provide some children with the opportunity to develop empathy and the ability to comfort others and show other prosocial behaviors that may be useful to them in subsequent relationships" (p. 187).

Most children can cope with occasional displays of parental anger, but when overt hostility persists, children may become either disposed to emotional outbursts themselves or fearful of expressing anger (Goleman, 1985a). "Angry confrontations between parents, which go on for many years, create a negative emotional climate that can undermine a child's psychological development. It can spill over into problems the child has with playmates, which can be among the early signs of trouble" (Radke-Yarrow, quoted by Goleman, 1985a). Many studies have found correlations between marital disharmony and behavioral, social, emotional, and even health problems in children (e.g., Gottman & Katz, 1989).

Study Question *What coping styles do children adopt after witnessing hostile interactions?*

E. M. Cummings (1987) and his colleagues (El-Sheikh, Cummings, & Goetsch, 1989) studied how 4- and 5-year-old children cope with background anger. They exposed pairs of children, with their mothers present, to adult strangers (trained actors) who engaged in positive or angry verbal interactions in a nearby room. This was followed by a "no emotion" period without the strangers. Children's immediate emotional responses to other people's anger and their subsequent aggression toward a friend were assessed.

Children demonstrated "greater distress, social sharing, preoccupation, and positive affect, concurrent with exposure to background anger. Increased verbal aggressiveness in play occurred in the period following exposure" (E. M. Cummings, 1987, p. 976). Thus, children "coped" with their exposure to anger in a variety of ways, some more adaptive than others.

Children were categorized into three styles of coping. (1) Concerned emotional responders (46% of the children) showed negative emotions during the exposure and later said they felt sad and wanted to intervene. (2) Unresponsive children (15%) did not show emotion but later reported feeling angry. (3) Ambivalent responders (35%) showed intense arousal during exposure and were the most likely to behave aggressively when playing with a friend.

Thus, witnessing angry interactions between adults clearly arouses and disturbs children, particularly when there is no resolution to the problem. Older children in particular are relieved when their parents apologize to each other after an angry confrontation (Cummings, Vogel, Cummings, & El-Sheikh, 1989). "Whether verbal conflicts are typically resolved may be more important than the frequency of verbal conflict in the home" (Cummings, Pellegrini, Notarius, & Cummings, 1989, p. 1042).

Observing angry confrontations elicits a variety of coping attempts (including aggressive behavior) to reduce children's distress. That children responded and coped in different ways is an important finding. Some children coped adaptively through social sharing and expressing positive emotions or minimizing the seriousness of the interaction. Others responded maladaptively through aggressive behavior.

Crockenberg (1987) found that angry and punitive adolescent mothers had children who were angry and noncompliant. These children also showed diminished self-confidence regarding their ability to cope with challenging problems. Particularly, infants who were irritable to begin with, showed these characteristics. This highlights the potentially explosive combination of angry mother and irritable infant. Crockenberg (1985) also found that toddlers display more self-concern and angry defiance toward others and less concern for others who are distressed when their mothers express anger rather than other negative emotions.

It appears that children who witness chronic displays of anger in their families, or who are recipients of intense emotional outbursts, suffer and attempt to cope in a variety of ways. There is a tendency for children to attribute their anger, but not their happiness or sadness, to their family (Covell & Abramovitch, 1987).

Expressions of anger are inevitable, even in the most harmonious families. Children (and their parents) benefit when they can accept their angry feelings and express them assertively rather than aggressively (Schaefer & Millman, 1981). Anger that is not expressed may accumulate until it reveals itself explosively or self-destructively.

Children, to some extent, learn how to express their intense emotions by watching other people do so. If they observe their frustrated parents intentionally hurting each other, children may learn that this is an acceptable means of expressing strong feelings. If children observe parental expressions of anger that lead to violence, they might learn to associate the two.

Miller and Sperry (1987) studied the role that language plays in the early socialization of anger and aggression in an urban, working-class community. Mothers in the community experienced many episodes of anger and violence and talked about them to their children. They taught their children that retaliation is justifiable when another person initiates a transgression. Thus, mothers socialized their children's anger and aggression by exposing them to "narratives" about highly emotional events the mothers experienced and by differentially reacting to the children's displays of anger and aggression.

"Anger was valued insofar as it supported the goal of self-protection, impelling the child to act quickly and decisively to defend herself" (p. 26). Children who failed to respond with anger and aggression when attacked were considered sissies. Children who initiated angry or aggressive acts were regarded as spoiled. Anger and aggression were deemed justifiable in self-defense, but not under other conditions.

Mothers' responses to their children's displays of anger were consistent with this philosophy. They tolerated such displays when they felt their children were justified, as when a parent teased them. However, when unprovoked, the mothers disapproved of their children's expressions of anger. Thus, an important consideration in conflict becomes who is at fault. This accounts for the predictable childhood defense, "He started it."

Even by age 2½ years, children were able to justify their anger in terms of another child's instigation. "The children also learned how to communicate anger and aggression. They responded with verbal refusals, protests, threats, insults, and assertions . . .'' (p. 28). Even though the children were becoming adept at justifying their actions, they generally lacked an emotional vocabulary. Miller and Sperry concluded that these children were learning that expressions of vulnerability and sadness are less acceptable than expressions of anger and aggressiveness.

Parental response to children's anger also appears to be an important determinant of their coping ability. Young children who tell their parents that they hate them are demonstrating their frustration in dramatic fashion (Kutner, 1988b). Parents who respond angrily (''Don't you ever talk to me that way again'') encourage this type of expression. ''If you hurt me, I will hurt you back.'' Demonstrating concern and caring, particularly in the face of strong emotion, usually removes fuel from the child's emotional fire. It models a more sensitive approach to handling strong feelings (''You're angry at me. Do you want to talk about it?''). And, as previously noted, apologies and solving the problems that lead to angry exchanges are optimal ways of resolving discord.

JEALOUSY

Harry Stack Sullivan (1956/1973) characterized jealousy as a ''horribly unpleasant mental state'' (p. 138). It is evoked when an individual perceives intimacies between other people that he wishes he could experience. Jealousy, a stress reaction similar to anxiety (Brody, 1987g), is distinguished from envy. Sullivan defined envy as ''an acute discomfort caused by discovering that somebody else has something that one feels one ought to have'' (p. 129). Thus, jealousy occurs when an individual desires, or fears losing, intimacy with another person. Envy refers to one's desire for another's possession.

Many investigators, including Sullivan, suggest that both jealousy and envy reflect feelings of insecurity and inadequacy. Presumably, having desired relationships or possessions proves one's worthiness. Conversely, lacking these things proves one's unworthiness. Jealousy can be so intense that it drives some to violence. Most instances of wife battering apparently involve jealous husbands (Brody, 1987g).

Young children are often jealous of their siblings. Perhaps the classic example is the proverbial reaction to the birth of a new sibling, ''Can't we send her back?'' Not understanding that Mom and Dad have enough love and attention for two or more children, youngsters assume that sharing parental resources means less for them. Most children gradually learn how to share parental time and attention. They understand that they will not be ''shortchanged'' in the long run. Children do not like to share because it usually does mean less for them in the short run. Socialization teaches children that sharing is beneficial because their generosity will be reciprocated (usually).

Many preschool children attempt to interfere when their mothers are nursing or otherwise caring for younger siblings. They may demand immediate attention and even display tantrum behavior. Parents should try to not overreact or become angry. This adds fuel to the resentful child's fire. Rather, the parent can explain, ''This is the time I spend with the baby. If you leave us alone, I will spend time with you when I am finished.''

Naturally, parents should not reinforce jealous behavior; the insecurity behind it should be addressed. ''Parents who cannot stand to see the child even momentarily unhappy risk rearing a self-centered child. These 'spoiled' children dread any sense of deprivation and tend to become inordinately demanding of attention and affection'' (Brody, 1987g).

Children also express jealousy when they perceive their parents showing favoritism. "No fair!" exclaim older children when their younger siblings receive a disproportionate amount of parental attention or patience. "No fair!" exclaim younger children when their older siblings enjoy the privileges of age.

Expressions of jealousy should be taken seriously by parents. They can practice sympathetic listening and other communication techniques described in chapter 7. "You wish you were older, don't you, so that you could stay up late like your sister." Parents try to be fair, but it is not possible or appropriate to treat siblings identically.

SHAME, EMBARRASSMENT, AND PRIDE

Research suggests that shame emerges at about the age of 18 months, and pride by 2 years of age. "Feelings of shame begin to emerge in the second year of life, at the very formation of the infant's sense of self . . . As the infant realizes that he is a separate person, he is first able to understand that others are directing emotional messages to him. Pride and shame appear—pride at pleasing others and shame at displeasing them" (Goleman, 1987f).

Presumably, the specific cognitive constructs that underlie these emotions must be present. To experience these emotions, children must be able to interpret other people's reactions and understand that these reactions are directed toward them and related to something they did. Children also have to learn the cultural guidelines that dictate how these feelings are labeled. Emotional labels play a major role in structuring emotional experience.

Parents facilitate the learning of these labels by using the context of a situation to infer the child's experience and then tentatively labeling it. "You must be so proud of yourself for getting such a good report card." Ultimately, feelings of pride or embarrassment come to serve as powerful reinforcers for new learning. Young children may feel pride when they use the toilet successfully, or feel shame when they have an accident.

The experience of pride apparently requires the ability to take personal responsibility for actions one can control. One can take pride in an inherited characteristic, such as ethnic group membership, but one cannot consider it an achievement. Older children may experience pride or embarrassment even in the absence of another person when they compare their performance to someone else's.

Personal responsibility is also not required for feeling embarrassed. Simply having attention drawn to oneself for any reason may be sufficient to precipitate this feeling (Seidner, Stipek, & Feshbach, 1988). When my younger son was about 4 years old, I attended a program at his nursery school. He looked uncomfortable standing among the other children, and he didn't show much enthusiasm in his singing. Later, when I asked about his apparent discomfort, he said being in front of all those people was "embarrassing." This was the first time I had heard him use that word. It reminded me that children may be uncomfortable being the center of attention. Such discomfort is probably related to shyness and to social-evaluation anxiety.

Seidner, Stipek, and Feshbach (1988) interviewed adults and 5-, 7-, 9-, and 11-year-old children about what made them feel proud, embarrassed, happy, and sad. They found that most 5-year-olds "understood that feelings of pride and, to a lesser extent, embarrassment result primarily from outcomes controlled by and contingent on one's own behavior or characteristics" (p. 357). All age groups implied that the presence of an audience is important for experiencing both pride and embarrassment, but especially embarrassment.

LEARNED HELPLESSNESS

Martin Seligman (1975) and his colleagues have described a pattern of helpless behavior that is associated with a variety of psychological disorders, including depression. Humans (and other animals) who are initially exposed to uncontrollable events learn to avoid taking steps to improve their situation. In a sense, the individual learns, "No matter what I try, it makes no difference. I may as well not try at all." Bandura (see chapter 8) would describe this attitude as revealing low self-efficacy.

Feelings of helplessness predict lower initiative and lower persistence in problem situations. Cognitive and emotional deficits, including sadness and lowered self-esteem, also characterize the learned helplessness syndrome (Nolen-Hoeksema, Girgus, & Seligman, 1986). Helplessness is associated with a faulty explanatory style that discourages an individual from believing he can improve a bad situation. Some students, for example, attribute academic failure to their own stupidity; others attribute their success to good luck. Both attributions imply a lack of control over life problems.

Children who explain positive and negative outcomes in ways that belittle their abilities are more depressed and are lower achievers than children who view their abilities realistically (Nolen-Hoeksema et al., 1986). Children who take credit for their successful efforts, and who correctly assess the relationship between effort, ability, and outcome, typically are not depressed and do not have achievement problems.

It is possible that children who experience unfortunate, uncontrollable life events, such as the death of a parent, might experience helplessness. They often show the motivational, cognitive, and emotional deficits mentioned above. A maladaptive explanatory style may emerge from such a pattern, leaving the child vulnerable to depressive episodes in the future (Nolen-Hoeksema et al., 1986).

It is not clear whether faulty explanatory styles lead to depression, or whether depression encourages the development of faulty explanatory styles. Nevertheless, children who learn realistic ways of appraising their efforts, and who learn to put failure in perspective, are much less susceptible to depression.

STRESS

Stress and coping are vague concepts. There is no consensus about their definitions or the processes that they refer to. Psychologists often define stress as the body's physiological response to a challenge or demand (Selye, 1976). When the brain perceives an emergency or a challenge, the body's energy resources are mobilized for immediate action. It is not helpful to perceive stress as being good or bad. It is an inevitable consequence of being alive. The response to negative stressors is sometimes referred to as distress.

Despite the variety of stressful childhood experiences, there is surprisingly little research on this topic. "The degree of neglect is puzzling in the light of evidence that, in a world of heightened stress, children are frequently among the most affected victims of a range of threatening events" (Garmezy, 1988, p. 51). In this section, we will examine some common stressors of childhood and how children cope with them. We will also discuss the characteristics of "resilient" children who adjust well despite extremely stressful life circumstances.

Study Question *What types of life events are stressful for children?*

We have seen that, in infancy, the presence of strangers or the absence of one's caretakers can elicit marked distress. Infants' responses that promote the return of their mothers may be the earliest coping behaviors (Compas, 1987). Depending upon a child's age, negative stressors may also include the following: the birth of a sibling; harsh toilet training; observing intense family disharmony or violence; living in poverty; homelessness; natural disasters; moving to a new neighborhood and school system; visits to a doctor or dentist; serious illness and prolonged hospitalization; pressure to perform well in school or school failure; parental divorce or death; racial or ethnic slurs; and rejection from peers.

Note that some of these stressors are chronic. That is, they persist over long periods. Chronic stressors usually change over time, and therefore require a variety of coping mechanisms. It is also possible that early exposure to negative stressors alters a child's sensitivity to future stressors and his general manner of coping with stress (Compas, 1987). Distress can be reciprocal in parent-child relations. Just as parental distress will affect children, a "distressed, disorganized child imposes additional stresses upon caretakers" (Maccoby, 1988, p. 220).

Children seem to be most vulnerable to either long-term, chronic stressors or accumulating short-term stressors. Sensitive parents notice changes in their children that indicate serious distress. They notice sadness; impulsive, acting-out behaviors; problems in school; reports of bodily symptoms such as headaches and stomach problems; and talk about hurting themselves. The particular behavior problems and symptoms usually depend upon the type of stressor. For example, children respond differently to parental death than they do to parental divorce.

It is unlikely that mild stressors alter the course of a child's development. In fact, mild stressors provide opportunities for learning coping strategies. Drastic conditions, however, such as extreme abuse or neglect, increase the risk of serious disturbance in all but the most resilient children. Three examples of stressors that may produce at least short-term difficulties are hospitalization, the birth of a sibling, and parental divorce. (Coping with the death of a close relative is discussed in a separate section.)

Hospital Admission

Illness can have beneficial effects on children's development (Parmelee, 1986). Nevertheless, the separation from parents that accompanies admission to a hospital can be a major stressor for young children. Hospital stays of longer than one week may produce disturbances that last for several months. This is particularly true of preschool children. They are the most threatened by interference with their parental attachments. It is not just separation that upsets hospitalized children. Their parents' attitudes and anxiety about the events related to the hospitalization and the medical and hospital routines are also possible sources of distress (Rutter, 1988).

Birth of a Sibling

Most preschool children are both excited and disturbed by the birth of a sibling. They may develop sleep and toileting problems and show an increase in clinging and oppositional behavior. Some behavior problems seem to reflect changes in the patterns of family interaction (particularly the mother-child relationship) to which the older child had been accustomed. As previously discussed, parents can compensate for these changes, to some extent, by maintaining familiar routines and by giving special attention to the older sibling. They can also point out the advantages of having a younger sibling and request the child's assistance in caring for the newborn (Rutter, 1988). There are even classes offered by hospitals that teach children how to be older siblings (Kutner, 1989b).

Parental Divorce

As we will see in chapter 12, much of the distress experienced by children of divorce reflects the long-standing and intense hostility expressed by their parents before, during, and following their separation. Following parental divorce, children are exposed to a wide range of potential stressors that may tax their ability to cope (Irion, Coon, & Blanchard-Fields, 1988).

COPING

For almost everyone, daily living is at least mildly stressful. People's sense of well-being seems to reflect, more than the type or amount of stress they experience, their ability to cope with everyday stressors. Kagan (1988) defines coping as "a reaction to a stressor that resolves, reduces, or replaces the affect state classified as stressful" (p. 196). Coping ability varies with many factors, including the child's history and temperament, the type of stressor, social support, and the number of stressors concurrently experienced.

Children's coping resources and style usually are best understood in a social context. Patterson (1988) suggests that chronic stress directly threatens not children but, rather, the family system. Certain negative life events, such as parental unemployment, do not directly affect a child. Rather, children are affected by the distressed reactions of family members. Children suffer when their distressed parents cannot provide them with adequate nurturance and support.

"Fathers who respond to economic loss with increased irritability and pessimism are less nurturant and more punitive and arbitrary in their interventions with the child. These fathering behaviors increase the child's risk of socioemotional problems, deviant behavior, and reduced aspirations and expectations. The child may also model the somatic complaints of the father" (McLoyd, 1989, p. 293). It is not the economic problem itself but the father's response to it that harms the child. Children may also suffer when family economic distress leads to marital friction or divorce.

Coping Ability

What we call coping ability refers to at least two processes: (1) the ability to define a problem in a way that leads to constructive action and (2) the ability to regulate the emotional distress caused by the stressor (Rutter, 1988). Most people use both types of coping when confronted with daily stressors. Strong feelings can be regulated by avoiding stressors or by thinking about them constructively (Compas, 1987).

How children react to stressful events will depend partly on their interpretation of the situation (Kopp, 1989). Children who are teased because of their nationality or race will be less angry if they can attribute the attack to the other child's prejudice rather than their own characteristics (Kagan, 1988). A realistic appraisal of the stressor combined with an understanding of what can be done about it is associated with successful coping. Parents can encourage such coping skills using the communication skills outlined in chapter 7.

Highly aroused infants can be soothed by swaddling and pacifiers (Campos, 1989). Older infants and toddlers, slightly less dependent on their parents for relief from distress, find security in a soft blanket, doll, or cloth. "Transitional objects" that provide security are particularly valued at bedtime. (Not all young children have the ability to comfort themselves with such objects.)

Older children develop more sophisticated ways of coping with distress. Adolescents cope differently than younger children and adults (Blanchard-Fields & Irion, 1988). "Young children are likely to become fearful of stressors, while older children are likely to become angry" (Kagan, 1988, p. 196). Distressed adults utilize "primary coping." They attempt to improve the situation that is causing distress. Adults may also engage in "secondary coping." They try to adjust to the stressor, perhaps by accepting it. Or adults may simply relinquish control, that is, ignore the stressor, neither pursuing solutions nor adjusting to the situation (Band & Weisz, 1988).

Band and Weisz asked 6-, 9-, and 12-year-old children to recall episodes involving 6 different types of stressful life situations, such as being separated from parents or school failure. They were asked to describe their reactions to each. Interestingly, only 3.5 percent of all episodes involved relinquished control. This suggests that even young children have accepted the cultural rule against "giving up" when they have a problem.

Styles of coping varied according to age and situation. As the investigators hypothesized, self-reports of primary coping (i.e., problem solving) decreased with age. Secondary coping strategies (i.e., handling distress) increased. This was particularly true when there was little the child could do to improve the circumstances, as when they were getting vaccinated. Younger children were as likely to use primary coping (e.g., screaming) to avoid getting a shot as they were to use secondary coping (e.g., distracting themselves). Older children accepted the inevitability of the medical procedure and attempted to cope with it.

It is possible that older children have learned something that younger children haven't. Improve the situation when possible. If you can't improve it, accept it. Cognitive strategies appear to work better in the latter case (Campos, 1987). Parents can encourage both types of coping strategies by modeling them or encouraging children to explore their alternatives when confronted with stressors ("What can you do to make it better?").

Humor and Coping

A sense of humor is an important coping mechanism. Most children enjoy playing with words and ideas. They quickly learn that saying or doing funny things brings them attention.

Freud (1916) speculated that humor or wit is a socially acceptable way of relieving pent-up emotions, including sexual and aggressive impulses. Many top comedians report that during their childhoods, humor was a helpful way of coping with family conflict, isolation, and deprivation. Humor provided both an escape from suffering and a defense for handling anxiety (McGhee, 1979).

"Jokes told by children during therapy sessions offer support for the view that humor is often used to help cope with conflict. For example, many of the anxieties felt by children concern parent-child relationships in some way. When children are asked to tell their favorite jokes during therapy, the jokes often center on parent conflicts or other sources of family dissension" (McGhee, 1979, p. 230).

McGhee cautions that a preoccupation with jokes could prevent children from dealing with their strong feelings and life problems. "The possession of a good sense of humor increases the odds of a person's being well adjusted, but emotional difficulties may also develop that cannot be mastered by means of humor . . . although humor may be effective in dealing with certain sources of anxiety and distress, there is no evidence that it is a cure-all for all emotional difficulties that children encounter" (p. 238). In other words, humor helps, but don't overdo it.

Resilient Children

Study Question *Some children manage to "survive" extreme conditions of deprivation and neglect during childhood. How do they do it?*

Children vary considerably in both their susceptibility to life stressors and in their resiliency or ability to cope. Most children raised by neglecting, addicted, impoverished, or mentally ill parents will have adjustment problems. And each additional stressor increases their risk.

Werner (1989a), for example, found that two-thirds of the Hawaiian children he studied who experienced four or more risk factors (such as poverty and parental divorce) by the age of 2 years, developed serious learning or behavior problems by the age of 10. Some resilient children, however, survived under the same awful conditions that emotionally devastated others. One out of three of the children in Werner's high-risk sample "grew into competent young adults who loved well, worked well and played well" (p. 108).

Researchers wonder "what the protective factors are in these children and in their care-giving environments that ameliorate, or buffer, their responses to stressful life events" (Werner, 1989b, p. 72). Are there innate factors that insulate these children from their stressful surroundings? Do they survive by reaching out to an adult who can provide them with the support and nurturance they require?

Resilient children do show "protective" traits even in infancy (Farber & Egeland, 1987; Werner, 1989b). Such children are easygoing and have a high frustration tolerance. They seek help from adults, recover quickly from upsets, and are easier to care for than high-risk infants who eventually develop serious problems. Resilient children are able to distance themselves emotionally from their parents when necessary.

Resilient children often enlist the aid of a "substitute parent," perhaps a supportive, caring teacher who will serve as a role model. This caring adult offers them comfort and hope. Sometimes these children have a special ability or interest, such as swimming or dancing, that distracts them from their misfortune and enhances their self-confidence (Goleman, 1987i).

Studies of competent black children growing up in the urban ghettos revealed three factors that predicted adjustment to the stressful ghetto environment (Garmezy, 1988). (1) Dispositional attributes of the child such as friendliness, positive self-esteem, and a sense of personal power were associated with positive adjustment. (2) Affection and family togetherness provided emotional support. And (3) an external (nonfamily) support system reinforced these children's abilities and determination to survive. Werner (1989a; 1989b) identified these same three protective factors in his longitudinal study of high-risk, resilient Hawaiian children.

UNDERSTANDING AND COPING WITH DEATH

"I asked Noah [age 6½ years] what he thought it meant when someone died. He said, 'You never get to see someone again, but you get to keep your happy memories.' We talked a little bit about Aunt Gladys and then I told him that Grandpa's doctor said it was likely that Grandpa was so sick he would die. (Later when I told Seth [age 3½ years] that Grandpa was going to die, Noah protested that before I had said it was 'likely'.) Noah asked me why I told him something that made him so sad. Then he asked me if I talked to all of Grandpa's doctors and whether they all thought he would die. Then he asked if there was any medicine that would work and how could someone die who was at home, not in the hospital?

"Noah's lips trembled and he asked to change the subject. A few minutes later (he was processing the information) he said, 'Is that why you've been yelling at me so much?' He's right, I have been. We went upstairs and Seth told me that his goldfish died. When I said that Grandpa was very sick, Seth told me that Grandpa was so sick he was going to die—end of discussion.

"Noah told me that he was so sad that he wasn't sure he could live without Grandpa. A few minutes later when Grandma Sarah came over, Noah told her he was sad, but not what he was sad about." (J.W.)*

*Reprinted with permission of Jeri Warhaftig.

Children's earliest contacts with death usually occur with the death of a grandparent, a classmate's parent, or a pet. But death is also "very much a part of the fantasy thought of children. It is also part of a child's everyday life—the games he plays, the stories he hears, the books he reads, television programs he watches, and the movies he sees" (Bluebond-Langner, 1974, p. 171).

When children bring their questions about death to their parents, they get different reactions. These depend partly on how prepared the parent feels to discuss this profound, and possibly intimidating, topic. Even parents who are accepting of their own mortality may not know what to tell a child. They may not know how to give good information without upsetting or frightening the child.

Death is a fact of life, but parents' first impulse might be to protect their child (and themselves) from its harsh reality (Brody, 1987j). Like adults, children must eventually adjust to the death of a loved one, the inevitable deaths of their parents, and their own mortality. Unfortunately, many children do this on their own without proper support (Vianello & Lucamante, 1988).

Children's Limited Understanding of Death

"I thought Seth had totally forgotten what I had told him about Grandpa. Today he asked Brig whether her daddy had died. When she said yes, he wanted to go to ShopRite to get her another one. Brig tried to explain that you don't buy dads in stores but he was persistent." (J.W.) *

Childrens' understanding of death changes as they mature. It reflects both their direct experiences with death and dying and their ability to understand the implications of mortality. Asking young children basic questions about

Young children usually do not understand that death is inevitable and irreversible.

death usually reveals their intuitive, sometimes magical, perceptions of what causes death, who or what can die (e.g., Berzonsky, 1987), whether death is permanent, and what happens after death. Children may believe that they are responsible for the death, particularly if they have had hostile thoughts and feelings about the deceased. If a parent dies, young children should be reassured that they (and the surviving parent) are in no way responsible for the death.

Stambrook and Parker (1987) reviewed the literature on the development of children's concept of death. They considered the influence of death experiences, religious instruction, cognitive development, and life circumstances. Upon discovering death in their very early years, children may become alarmed and try to cope with it in a variety of ways, particularly through denial. Noah wanted to believe that Grandpa could only die if he were

---

*Reprinted with permission of Jeri Warhaftig.

in a hospital. Seth wanted to believe that Grandpas are replaceable. Young children seem to "experiment" with different forms of coping, seeking adult confirmation for their attempts. It is not clear at what age children are able to grasp that death is inevitable and permanent, although preschool children apparently view death as "temporary, reversible, and a diminution of function" (Stambrook & Parker, 1987, p. 139).

Children as young as 3 years have definite ideas about what death means. "Some children have been described as perceiving death to be a separation or departure, like sleep, where there is a possibility of a return to life if the correct measures are taken . . . For other children, death is believed to be life under changed circumstances . . . For example, the dead in coffins can still sense what is happening in the environment but cannot move. Although death is seen as temporary and/or partial, the child is very curious to know and understand the practical and concrete aspects of all that surrounds death (e.g., the rites of burial, what happens to the body)" (Stambrook & Parker, 1987, p. 138). Brody (1987j) quotes her 4-year-old son's reaction to finding a worm, the preferred food of their dead pet lizard Iggy. "Let's save it for when Iggy isn't dead anymore."

There is reason to believe that children who are exposed to religious instruction develop beliefs about death somewhat consistent with the ideas they have been taught. Some children aged 6 to 8 years may personify death (e.g., death man, angel of death) or believe that death results from the actions of bad or careless people (e.g., murderers, bad drivers) or disease. Children in this age range see death as final but not inevitable. If they are good or lucky, death will not come looking for them. Many children in this age group know that everybody dies, including themselves, but they prefer to believe that only old people die (Stambrook & Parker, 1987).

"Noah says its not fair that I got to know Grandpa for 32 years and he only got 6. So exactly a miniature version of my reaction! Last night we went to Grandma's and Noah sat in her lap and they both cried. Noah said, 'I am so sad, I can't possibly imagine how sad you must be' and Grandma said (very wisely, it seems to me), 'You can't measure sadness, we are both as sad as we can possibly be.'

*"We went up to see Daddy and I told him, in a loud voice, that Noah was there to see him. His eyes flickered with recognition and he took his hand out from under the sheet for a little wave. Noah climbed on a chair, kissed him on the nose and said, 'Grandpa is too sick, I'm too sad to stay here' so we said bye and went down. Then we visited awhile and Grandma told him that even sad people can joke and laugh. With Noah's dry humor he said, 'Oh? and when did anyone here say anything worth laughing at?' I left it up to Noah whether he goes to see Grandpa. He said he didn't want to mention to Grandpa that he was dying, because 'it would be insulting to him.' When I agreed that it might make Grandpa sad, Noah said Grandpa couldn't possibly be as sad as Noah. Noah told me he understood that I was telling him about Grandpa so it wouldn't be a 'surprise' but that he wished I hadn't done it because it made him so sad." (J.W.)**

"Grieving parents often try to protect their children from death, hiding their emotions and barring their children from memorial services. Confused and afraid, their children retreat to a magical world peopled by sick-monsters, seeking answers to questions they can't ask" (Turkington, 1984e). Direct experiences with dying appear to facilitate children's understanding of the process and its implications, at

*Reprinted with permission of Jeri Warhaftig.

least for children between the ages of 3 and 6 years. Older children's conceptions do not seem to be as influenced by directly experiencing the death of someone close to them. "Older children usually see death as an internal biological process that operates according to natural laws" (Stambrook & Parker, 1987, p. 147).

As they develop, children come to understand that, although illness may be caused by external factors, illness and death primarily reflect internal biological dysfunctions. Children 9 to 12 years, like much younger children, continue to express curiosity about the rites and rituals surrounding death. It is not clear how many children this age accept the finality of death. Again, religious training may influence children's beliefs about and attitudes toward death.

*"This morning Daddy died at about 9:45. While he was slowly gasping and fading in his hospital bed, Jonah was two feet away, sound asleep on the regular bed. When we told Noah and Seth, Noah was very sad. He said he couldn't remember anything about Grandpa except the sadness. Seth walked around explaining that Grandpa was dead and that Grandma could get another Grandpa at the 'Grandpa Store.'" (J.W.)**

Helping Children Cope with Death

A variety of reactions have been observed in bereaved children, including denial of death, reunion fantasies, feelings of anger and sadness, phobias, and refusal to attend school. Most children will demonstrate initial grief reactions of crying, sadness, and irritability, and various behavioral changes, including poor appetite, difficulty sleeping, and withdrawal.

---

*Reprinted with permission of Jeri Warhaftig.

Children's ability to grieve partly depends upon the grief responses they observe in their parents or surviving parent. "It isn't possible for a child to fully mourn without guidance by parents" (Turkington, 1984e). Children with depressed mothers are more likely to have persistent behavioral dysfunctions (Black & Urbanowicz, 1987). Possibly the best predictor of a child's adjustment to the death of a parent is the quality of his relationship with the surviving parent (Goleman, 1988c).

In the past, when most people died at home, children received greater exposure to the entire process of dying and death. These days, "most deaths occur in hospitals or nursing homes, places rarely visited by children, and relatives may be buried before anyone even tells young children that they are dead. Thus, it is even more important today to help children develop a realistic understanding of death and its many causes, as well as to help them express their grief, their questions and their anxieties" (Brody, 1987j). Rosenheim and Reicher (1985) found that children who were informed about a parent's terminal illness were significantly less anxious than children not so informed. The anxiety of the latter group was related to the child's age.

Kutner (1988e) describes four tasks that a child must accomplish following the death of a friend or family member: (1) understanding the cause of death, (2) grieving for and then (3) commemorating the deceased, and (4) getting on with life. Children should be given truthful explanations of the causes of death at a level they can understand. Fox (quoted by Kutner, 1988e) suggests that parents describe death to children as "what happens when the body stops working."

Parents can be guided by children's questions. Young children need special reassurance that it is very unlikely that their parents or they will die before they are very old. "Explain the nature of death in a matter-of-fact fashion to young children. Tell them that the dead person no longer eats or talks or breathes, that he has been buried in a special place and cannot return, and that he feels no pain" (Brody, 1987j).

Children should be given the choice of attending memorial services or not (Weller, Weller, Fristad, Cain, & Bowes, 1988). If they decide to attend, they should be given realistic expectations about the proceedings, including that many people will probably be crying because they're sad. Children should be told that they can leave whenever they want. If a parent has died, children should be reassured that the remaining parent will take care of them as long as needed (Brody, 1987j) and that expressing sadness, loneliness, fear, and anger is appropriate when someone you love dies (Turkington, 1984e). Young children are fairly likely to misbehave as an expression of strong grief.

"This morning was the funeral. Noah was with us every step of the way. He was very attentive during the service. He held Mommy [Grandma] and cried through the graveside service—so did she. I'll never forget the way Mommy asked everyone to leave her alone at the grave for a minute, and, as everyone was walking away, Noah put his arms around Mommy and said, 'I'll wait here with Grandma.' When we went back home, Noah was totally normal and happy. Seth, on the other hand, has started acting out over everything. Bedtime has become a major battle. It's a hard time to try and muster extra patience.

[5 days later] "Over the course of the week the boys joined us at Mommy's house for dinner and then went home to bed. Noah has been warm and compliant and content—all of which makes me feel like we've helped him through in the 'right way.' Seth, however, grew crazier and more frenetic as the week went on. His behavior was very naughty. He has been daring me to punish him. He seems

to desire negative attention. Instead, we've been trying to give him individual attention and praise. It seems to be working since his behavior was a lot better yesterday and today. Plus, earlier this week he was wetting his pants and that has stopped again. He was also acting very fearful (bugs, wind, dogs) and that's stopped too.

"Seth must be slowly processing Daddy's death. Today he called Mommy to ask her why 'grandmas don't die.' After all, he has two grandmothers and three great-grandmothers, so logically, at least to him, only grandfathers die. [One week later] Seth has been totally obnoxious. He is disobedient. Twice this weekend we caught him turning off the computer! Yesterday he asked his father, out of the blue, 'Can kids die?' " (J.W.)*

Girls under 11 who lose their mothers and adolescent boys who lose their fathers may exhibit an intense grief reaction more like an adult's (Garmezy, 1988). "Adolescents often feel more comfortable grieving with their peers than with adults. They may view the death of someone in their family as embarrassing and may try to hide it from outsiders" (Kutner, 1988e). Gray (1987) found that adolescents' positive adjustment to the death of a parent was associated with a high level of social support following the loss, a good relationship with the surviving parent before the loss, and religious beliefs. Talking about the deceased seems to help children of all ages.

When a Child Dies

Study Question   How do parents cope when a child dies?

As previously noted, mortality rates for children throughout human history have been depressingly high. Some historians have argued that parents did not allow themselves to

---

*Reprinted with permission of Jeri Warhaftig.

become attached to their children at least until the child was in middle childhood and had a reasonable chance of reaching adulthood.

In this modern era of immunizations, antibiotics, and enlightened child-care practices, we expect almost all children to survive birth, infancy, and childhood. It is difficult to imagine a greater loss than the death of a child (Vuillemot, 1988). Each year in the United States, approximately 400,000 parents of children under the age of 25 lose a child as the result of illness, accident, murder, or suicide (Brody, 1983).

"No other loss, with the possible exception of the death of a spouse, extracts the heavy outpouring of anguish that loss of a child elicits . . . For some parents, years pass before they are able to resume their normal lives. Others never seem to find their way out of the turmoil and disorganization of bereavement . . . The sorrow, sadness, despair, depression, anger and bitterness are long-lasting and debilitating and exceedingly difficult to resolve" (Knapp, 1987, p. 60).

Knapp interviewed 155 families who had recently lost a child through terminal illness, suicide, murder, or whose children died suddenly and unexpectedly. He found 6 significant similarities in how they reacted to the deaths: (1) the desire never to forget the child and a need to talk about their tragic experience and about their memories of the child; (2) a loss of hope, with no way to justify their lives or continue to live without their child; (3) an attempt to find some reason or justification for the loss to make it meaningful; (4) a significant change in values, giving up worldly ambitions and searching for personal satisfaction; (5) a sense of vulnerability regarding life and death and greater tolerance of and sensitivity toward other people; and (6) the existence of "shadow grief," grief that is never totally resolved, an emotional dullness that prevents a person from responding fully and completely to outer stimulation. Knapp considers these reactions normal for parents who have lost a child.

Even parents who lose children after prolonged illness, which seemingly would give them time to prepare for the loss, often carry a burden of guilt for not preventing their child's death (Gaylin, 1985). Guilt is also a common reaction when a child dies suddenly and unexpectedly, as in Sudden Infant Death Syndrome (see chapter 4). Parents wonder, or obsess about, whether they could have prevented the death. Common reactions following unbearable loss include shock; denial; loneliness; depression; loss of appetite; insomnia; feelings of guilt, anger, and hostility; lack of energy; perpetual grief; and an inability to resume a normal life-style (Gaylin, 1985).

"Compounding the tragedy of losing a child are friends and relatives who say the wrong things or who try to avoid the issue altogether; death-denying medical professionals who remain aloof from the emotional turmoil or compound it with their callousness; and the parents themselves, whose different responses to a child's death may lead to misunderstanding, resentment, and distance at a time when mutual support is most crucial" (Brody, 1983).

Parental acceptance of a child's death is facilitated by social support and understanding from others, giving grieving parents the opportunity to share their strong feelings (when they're ready) and allowing them to express their grief totally. It would not be helpful to suggest that "you can always have another," to suppose "it's all for the best," or to criticize the child's medical care, if he died as the result of illness or accident. Being available, sorry, attentive, patient, and caring are important forms of support. Common pitfalls to avoid include staying away from the bereaved, changing the subject when a parent needs to discuss the death, and trying to find something positive to say about the loss (Blakeslee, 1988; Gaylin, 1985).

Although most parents never fully recover from the loss of a child, even one who lived only for a few hours, they do eventually "learn

Dear Daddy,

I lie in bed at night composing eloquent messages i wish to send you. Then, in the cold light of the morning I invariably dismiss my nighttime thoughts as melodramatic, morbid, or at the very least, irrelevant. And yet, every night, I am flooded by pressing images and ideas that I feel I must convey. I am finally crying "uncle" and giving in to my nighttime self. Feel free to stop reading here . . .

First, I am astonished that you are dying. That probably comes as no big surprise since it's not exactly something you anticipated either. Nonetheless, I am talking about early shattering mind boggling astonishment that makes me feel constantly breathless. Life has caught me off-guard both because you have cancer and in the way it makes me feel.

Once, years ago when we lived in Hackensack, and you and Mommy were in a rough time in your marriage, you admonished me to refrain from becoming overly involved in other people's lives and problems. You told me that my blessing and my curse was my ability to stand totally in someone else's shoes and to experience their emotions. Yes, that means that I suffer for more than just myself. Too often I stand in the shoes of your wife, grandsons, son-in-law, parents-in-law and other children. After all, why just wallow in my own misery when I

can really indulge in someone else's! On the other hand, I walk around tallying all of the people I know who have lost a parent, or even more accurately a father, and survived. I see that some have survived better than others. I try to visualize myself "standing in the shoes" of the heartiest survivors . . . just in case.

I think that what awakens me at night (aside from Noah, Jonah and Seth of course) is something that Carol once told me about her father's sickness and death. She said that by the time her father had died, he had been dead for her for quite some time. As he underwent progressively more strenuous forms of chemotherapy, he was unable to maintain contact with her. All of his emotional and psychological strength was needed just to stay alive. I am so afraid that I will have left something unsaid.

You told me that you and I have nothing to say to one another. I took that as a sort of compliment. There is nothing left to say, we each are fully aware of and embraced by the extent of our love for one another. But, but, but the unspoken message haunts me (I told you there would be melodrama if you read this far). I think perhaps that the unspoken message is that you are more to me than you could possibly know. It is not our love that is unclear. You father, me daughter, I get that. It is our

Reprinted with permission of Jeri Warhaftig.

to get on with life, to laugh again, take pleasure without guilt and remember without grief" (Brody, 1983). The most intense mourning occurs within a year or two of the loss, with recurring episodes on anniversaries, birthdays, or other special days that bring the child to mind.

Many marriages become unstable following a tragedy. Men and women cope differently with their sorrow: women grieve intensely; men

return to work. Women may misperceive their husbands' lack of visible grieving as a lack of caring. "Surviving brothers and sisters also suffer when a child dies, but parents in pain may overlook the siblings' anguish, anxiety and guilt. A surviving sister may think the same thing will happen to her. A child may think he somehow caused his brother's death" (Brody, 1983). There are many support groups and family therapists that specialize in helping families accept and grieve the loss of a child.

relationship that is so incredibly expansive as to defy definition. Never mind that you are my friend, adviser, confidant, and companion. That is apparent to mere strangers. There is something else, something special, even unique that I feel we share. There are parts of you that will remain with me and in me for the rest of my life. Will I ever find a job or career that I love? Will I ever abandon pacifism? Will I ever make TONS of money? (Will I ever learn to type?) It's not so much that I share your views as that knowing yours has permanently shaped mine. After all, I believe in God (sort of) and you don't.

Remember when Carol's father was dying and Cheryl wouldn't bring her kids to visit him anymore because she didn't want them to remember him like that? You told me that you understood her actions because to a young child there would be no difference between someone passing out of their lives at age 3 as compared with age 3¼. Actually, that should be more true of an adult since a few weeks or months represent a far smaller fraction of an entire adult lifetime. I have to confess that although that sounds good in theory, I have dug my heels in against the passing of time and grab at the minutes of each day as they slip from my grasp. (If you have read this far you're entitled to a little poetry!)

When I sit with you, or more accurately, doze next to you, I always feel that you know what is in my heart. But in the middle of the night when you are not around I am clenched by the fear that I assume too much. I do not know what the course of your illness will be. Whatever the future holds for us all, I want you to know that your life fills me with admiration for a man who is honest, courageous, loving, and above all, consistent. You are my hero and my role model. This would not be a good time to tell me the emperor is wearing no clothes.

I know that, especially now, I fulfill a certain function in your life and in Mommy's. I will try not to let either of you or, I guess, myself, down. A very long time ago, in a department store, Mommy asked me to stop calling her "Mommy" at the top of my lungs because it sounded so childish coming from a grown up of nineteen years old. For some reason, that request, which I hardly ever honored and which now she herself would probably deem nonsensical, comes to mind almost daily. I LOVE YOU, DADDY (get the message?).

(Jeri Warhaftig's father died about 3 weeks later. Her eulogy is reprinted in chapter 14, and her journal entries are found throughout this section.)

Adult's Loss of a Parent

The loss of a parent can occur at any age, and is, of course, more likely in adulthood than childhood. Each year, in this country, about 12 million adults lose a parent. Parental loss is therefore the most common source of bereavement. Sometimes death comes gradually, and sometimes suddenly, without any opportunity to say those things that we would like (or need) to say to feel complete in our relationship (see Spotlight: Letter to a Dying Father).

"No chance to say, 'Goodbye Daddy—I love you,' 'Thanks for all you have given me and my children,' 'I'm sorry for all the times I must have hurt you' " (Brody, 1987a). Some people who have lost parents find that writing a letter or speaking to the deceased in one's mind can create a sense of completion.

When children grow up and perhaps become parents themselves, their relationships with *their* parents remain intense, unique, and irreplaceable. The loss can be devastating. "Even when parents are old and have lived fulfilling lives, or when death terminates a prolonged illness and might be a welcome relief, the pain felt by children can be surprisingly intense. And even when children had a hostile or ambivalent relationship with their parents they might grieve for might-have-beens, the rapport they never experienced'' (Brody, 1987a).

Some adult children feel guilty for not having done enough for their parents. Many feel anger toward a wide range of targets, including the parent who died and abandoned them, doctors and siblings who didn't show enough caring, and toward life, for its harsh realities. Like most life experiences, losing a parent can serve as a vehicle for emotional growth. ''Some learn not to postpone the frills of life—vacation trips, visits and other pleasures. Some are spurred to restore lost contacts with friends and relatives or establish a closer relationship with their own children. Some simply become more sensitive, more aware of the needs of others and more willing to give of themselves, even without being asked'' (Brody, 1987a).

SUMMARY

Stress is normal and inevitable for children and adults. All people benefit from having coping skills that allow us to identify and solve problems that can be solved and accept and adjust to those problems that can't be. Children cannot always be happy. It is important that parents learn how to support the expression of both positive and negative emotions in their children.

Positive adjustment is encouraged by parental support and understanding when children are afraid, shy, angry, or embarrassed. Mild stressors encourage the development of coping skills, but some children become overwhelmed by extreme circumstances such as intense parental conflict, abuse, or neglect. These children may develop maladaptive behaviors that persist throughout childhood, adolescence, and even adulthood.

Most adults find their mortality intimidating, and children are no different. Children's understanding of death changes over time. Older children come to understand that death is inevitable and irreversible. Children initially deny these realities and then desperately search for a way to cope with them. The inevitable death of their parents and other loved ones intensifies children's natural fears of being abandoned. Direct experiences with dying people and the death of loved ones, including pets, may facilitate their understanding of the process.

Parents can support their children's grieving by answering their questions truthfully at a level they can understand and by modeling their own expressions of grief. Children should be given choices regarding participation in the rites and rituals for the deceased. Talking about the loss, asking children sensitive questions, and giving them thoughtful answers to their own questions is good parenting. Parents who lose a child and adult children who lose parents also require special understanding and support.

Competence and Achievement

OBJECTIVES

After studying chapter 10, students should be able to

1. List several home and family factors that predict children's achievement
2. Describe how the following family factors can encourage children's achievement:
   a. Verbal interaction between parent and child
   b. Parental expectations about achievement
   c. Good parent-child relationship
   d. Parental beliefs and attributions concerning the child
   e. Parental style of discipline
3. Describe the issues involved in the "superkid" controversy
4. Analyze the high achievement of Asian-American students
5. Describe the special efforts made by Japanese mothers to promote their children's achievements
6. Explain why reading and writing are considered fundamental skills and discuss how parents can promote their development
7. Describe how parental involvement in their children's schooling benefits children
8. Describe how parental pressure may inadvertently discourage achievement
9. Describe how parents can promote children's cognitive development and creativity through play and expressive activities
10. Describe how television may influence children's behavior and what parents can do to guide their children's viewing

INTRODUCTION

Mark #13

"On Thursday, I had a conference with Mark's homeroom teacher, and I was given his grades. During the semester, parents were sent a progress report. On that he seemed to be doing OK but nothing I'd settle for happily. Purposely, I reserved my opinion and asked what he thought of his grades. He said, 'OK' I asked did he feel he had done his best and when he said 'yes' what could I do? So I said 'OK' if he felt he was doing his best then how could I ask for more?

"When I spoke to Mr. B, I wasn't surprised that all the teachers felt Mark needed better class preparation (including homework), participation and concentration. 'He's easily distracted' was a common comment. In Math and English he got Bs, Social Studies a C, Science a D, Art 'outstanding,' Health Satisfactory—and Gym, Satisfactory. I reserved comment as long as I could and deeply pondered how to broach the subject. Finally, after I asked him the usual questions and got the usual answers, I told him that I know he's got to make more of an effort to pay attention in class and in doing his homework.

"I asked him to think of ways he can improve and ways that I can help. What we came up with was that he'd bring home his homework pad nightly for starters. On each page I wrote his subject names. I suggested that all he had to do each day is write in the assignment page numbers and which books (notebook, textbook, workbook) to bring home. He agreed to try.

"So far he's brought the pad home both days. One day he wrote in both assignments but forgot the second subject's book. The next day he remembered the books but not to write the assignments down. Both times I tried to suggest how he could avoid these problems next time and I encouraged him to solve each problem."

Children's first schools are their homes, and their parents are their first teachers. Infants and toddlers typically display an intense curiosity and wonder about their environment ("What's this?"). We also observe children's desire to manipulate objects and make interesting events happen ("Look what I can do"). These natural tendencies can be enhanced or diminished by the specific experiences they have at home, in school, or anywhere else.

Most parents, like Mark's mother, have had no training as educators. Though they may value achievement and competence, it is not obvious how they can encourage their children's abilities. Despite her frustration with Mark's performance in school, his mother is learning to be patient and understanding in helping him become better organized.

Parenting goal #2, competence, encompasses not only teaching children problem-solving skills but also encouraging an appreciation of this remarkable world and children's ability to study and understand it. Many parents view competence and achievement as the school-related areas of their children's development. By the time children enter an educational setting, however, they have already developed an orientation to learning that will influence their future academic and intellectual accomplishments. The preparation for learning that children receive at home is as important to their education as what happens in the classroom.

In this chapter, we explore the roots of competence. We focus on family resources that appear to promote achievement and the process of schooling. We consider how high-achieving children differ from low-achieving children, examine parenting styles that encourage competence and achievement, and note the influence of cognitive and affective variables on these phenomena.

HOME AND FAMILY FACTORS IN ACHIEVEMENT

Traditional models of cognitive growth have assumed that high-achieving parents provide their children with an enriched and stimulating environment. R. White (1959) suggested that play and exploratory behavior produce feelings of efficacy (or mastery) in children, which serve to intrinsically reinforce these behaviors. A motivational cycle results that fosters the development of competent behaviors. Parents support this cycle by providing their children with frequent opportunities to make interesting things happen.

Children who are raised under economically impoverished conditions, particularly if education is not highly valued, may not master basic literacy skills (Samuels, 1986). "Unable to achieve in school, these children begin to see academic success as unattainable, and so they protect themselves by deciding school is unimportant . . . Such children are at risk for dropping out, teen-age pregnancy, drug abuse and crime" (Comer, 1988a, p. 46).

Yet the children of poor and illiterate Jewish and Chinese immigrants who settled in this country excelled academically. This may reflect the "reverence for education which these groups had and which their children accepted and adopted . . . What seems important in the cognitive development of children, then, is not the social class or race of the family, but the lifestyle and culture in the home" (Samuels, 1986, p. 8). Even mothers of disadvantaged children who are considered at risk for becoming mentally retarded have been trained successfully to enhance their children's cognitive skills (Slater, 1986).

Few would deny that the home environment is a major factor in children's school performance. Many theorists have emphasized the influence of children's **early** home environment on their achievement. It is plausible that parental sensitivity and nurturance early in life promote social and cognitive skills that encourage academic achievement. Kagan (1984), however, contends that the influence of early environment on achievement has been exaggerated. He suggests that it is a child's **contemporary** home environment that is the key to understanding achievement.

A problem in distinguishing between these two models is that children who were fortunate enough to have enjoyed a nurturant early home environment are also more than likely to have a stimulating contemporary home environment. A third model of achievement emphasizes the **cumulative** effects of a stable and nurturant home environment over childhood.

Bradley, Caldwell, and Rock (1988) compared these three models of home influence on school performance. They examined the home environments of 42 demographically diverse children when the children were infants and again during middle childhood. Although all three models received some support, the children's contemporary environment was the best predictor of their classroom behavior and achievement. The researchers concluded that "all three models of environmental action seem useful in explaining parts of the results obtained. However, none of the three models is adequate to explain all of the data" (p. 865).

Rutter (1985b) hypothesizes that stimulation by itself does not promote cognitive growth. Rather, growth is enhanced by "the reciprocity of the parent-child interactions, the variety and meaningfulness of their content, and the active role taken by the child" (p. 686). Rutter suggests that when spending time with their children, parents should minimize background noise that might distract and confuse the child. Parents are encouraged to provide a variety of opportunities for active rather than passive participation in parent-child play and conversation.

Like other theorists, Rutter emphasizes the importance of parental nurturance, sensitivity, and responsiveness to the child's verbal and nonverbal signals. In teaching children how to learn, parents should provide interesting and meaningful experiences and many opportunities for discovery and experiment. The extent to which any one of these factors promotes a child's cognitive development may depend upon the child's age. For example, physical contact may be particularly important early in infancy, and responsiveness to nonverbal signals may increase in importance during the second year.

Hess and Holloway (1984) identified five family factors that predict school achievement: (1) verbal interaction between mother and child, (2) parental expectations about achievement, (3) a good parent-child relationship, (4) parental beliefs and attributions concerning the child, and, especially, (5) parental style of discipline. Home background variables, including the parents' educational level, income, and number of books in the home, have been shown to be related to children's achievement.

Verbal Interaction

Given the critical role that language plays in cognitive and social development, verbal interaction between parent and child can easily be appreciated as an influence on competence and achievement. Five- to fifteen-year-olds speak approximately 20,000 words a day, resulting in about 2 to 3 hours of pure speaking time (Wagner, 1985). Parents can create endless opportunities for verbal interaction and, in the process, stimulate children's curiosity and expressiveness.

Rutter (1985b) suggests that the slightly higher academic achievement and verbal intelligence levels observed in firstborn and only children may be attributable to the fact that parents interact with and talk more to their firstborns. Many studies have related characteristics of mothers' speech to the rate of language acquisition in their children (e.g., Harris, Jones, Brookes, & Grant, 1986).

Children who frequently talk out loud to themselves are the most socially advanced and brightest preschoolers (Berk, 1986). Such private talk appears to foster the development of internalized private speech. Children need learning environments that "permit them to be verbally active while solving problems and completing tasks" (Berk, 1986, p. 42).

Parents can promote children's intellectual development by serving as models for good language skills (Samuels, 1986). Parents can provide work spaces for children to read and to do their homework. They can provide children with stimulating reading materials, take them to museums and libraries, and "establish a model of the parent as one who reads and respects scholarship" (Samuels, 1986, p. 8).

Parental Expectations about Achievement

Parents of high-achieving children typically have high expectations about their children's abilities. More importantly, they set *realistic* standards that the child will not only be able to satisfy but will also find challenging. Parents of low-achieving children may not model success-oriented behavior or teach achievement-related values. Parents who set standards that are too high or too low create unnecessary obstacles to their children's achievement.

When parents establish unrealistically high (or perfectionistic) standards, children are being set up for failure. Eventually, they may exhibit a fear of failure that discourages intellectual risk-taking. Such children give up prematurely and avoid challenging tasks (see "Too Much Too Soon?: Creating Superkids"). Parents whose standards are too low may not provide adequate opportunities for learning.

What constitutes a realistic expectation partially depends upon the child's *readiness* to address and master a problem-solving task. Parents of infants and toddlers can challenge a child who is ready maturationally, behaviorally, and motivationally. For a child to perform successfully on a task, whether toilet training or reading, she must be biologically mature enough to learn the skill, have the prerequisite behavioral skills, and be willing to accept the challenge. While parents have little to say about biological readiness (other than by simply waiting), there is much that they can do regarding prerequisite skills and motivation.

Some children exaggerate the significance of the negative feedback they occasionally receive and end up underestimating their competence. It is important that children learn how to perceive failure realistically, not in personal terms but with a task orientation. Rather than believing, "I made a mistake, I am stupid," children can learn to reason, "I made a mistake, perhaps I am working too quickly. Let me try again."

Although the United States is as a culture notably achievement-oriented, parents differ substantially in their achievement standards. Middle-class parents typically encourage a future orientation in their children, advocating delay of gratification skills. Middle-class children gradually learn to be guided by the more fulfilling, long-term consequences of their behavior. Less-educated parents often encourage an orientation toward the present. The meaning of an action lies in the immediate reward or punishment it produces. Children who become

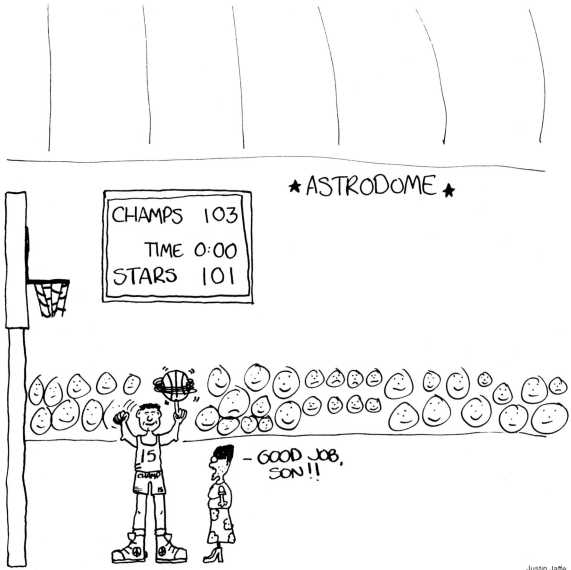

Justin Jaffe

"dependent" on rewards and punishments are less susceptible to the intrinsic rewards inherent in achievement behavior (Santrock, 1988).

Research and clinical observation (e.g., Bandura, 1977b) confirm that children accept and eventually adopt their parents' standards, realistic or not. During the early school years, children will also compare their performance to that of their peers. Thus, children's standards eventually reflect a combination of personal, parental, and peer influences.

Good Parent-Child Relationship

High-achieving children often come from homes that are more like learning centers. These homes are not cold and sterile but rather warm, inviting, interesting environments. They are safely arranged to encourage free exploration and equipped not with expensive toys but with objects that teach. Such children have responsive parents to whom they are securely attached. These parents encourage stimulating interaction and share the excitement of exploration and discovery with their children.

B. L. White (1988) summarizes the recommendations of the Harvard Preschool Project for developing young children's intelligence as follows: "Newly crawling infants should be allowed to practice their climbing and other emerging motor skills. For most of their waking hours, they should have easy access to people who have a very special love for them. Those people should talk to them about what they are focusing on at the moment, using ordinary language to expand ideas and introduce new ideas. They should lavish affection, encouragement, and enthusiasm on the babies, thereby intensifying their interest and excitement in learning. They need not make use of elaborate educational toys or programs" (pp. 18–19).

Estrada and her colleagues (1987) performed a longitudinal study of 67 mothers and their children. The children were observed when they were 4 and 12 years old. The study revealed a significant correlation between the affective quality of the mother-child relationship and the child's mental age at 4 years, readiness for school at ages 5 to 6 years, IQ at age 6, and the child's school achievement at age 12 (Estrada et al., 1987).

The parent-child relationship thus provides a major context for encouraging children's cognitive development (Bretherton, 1985). "Children who are securely attached as infants subsequently approach cognitive tasks in ways conducive to cognitive development. Their problem-solving style is characterized by more curiosity, persistence and enthusiasm, and less frustration than less securely attached infants. Securely attached children also appear to use adult direction and attention in ways that promote cognitive and social development. They

are more able to benefit from maternal assistance during problem-solving tasks and to interact effectively with teachers" (Estrada et al., 1987, p. 210).

Parental Beliefs and Attributions Concerning the Child

Parental beliefs about development and child rearing, rooted in parents' education or their everyday experiences, influence their child-rearing practices and, therefore, their children's cognitive development (Ladd & Price, 1986; S. A. Miller, 1988; Sameroff & Feil, 1985). Parental beliefs are also influenced by a child's development (Johnson & Martin, 1985). Thus, there is an ongoing reciprocal interaction between parental beliefs and children's behavior.

Parental beliefs can influence children's intellectual development. Beliefs are manifested through "the organization of the home, the types of toys and activities provided, selection of geographical location of the home and school" (McGillicuddy-De Lisi, 1985, p. 8), and through beliefs directly communicated to the child, verbally and nonverbally.

Certain parental beliefs are associated with the family's socioeconomic level and children's performance on a variety of tasks. "Middle-class parents may foster independence, activity, intellectuality, and achievement to a greater extent than do lower SES [socioeconomic status] parents in part because of social class differences in parental knowledge and beliefs about child development and about what is considered important in child development according to the latest standards" (Johnson & Martin, 1985, p. 39).

Parental Style of Discipline

Dornbusch, Ritter, Leiderman, Roberts, and Fraleigh (1987) reported that children of parents who practiced the authoritative (democratic) parenting style had better grades than children whose parents were authoritarian (punitive) or permissive. Children of parents who scored highest on authoritative parenting had the best grades. Children of "inconsistent" families that combined punitive parenting with other styles had the worst grades. These findings applied to males and females, five different age groups, five different types of family structure, and three different levels of parental education.

Baumrind also observed a relationship between the authoritative style of parental discipline and children's achievement (see chapter 5). What do children learn from authoritative parents that enhances their achievement motivation or cognitive development? The authoritative style of parenting apparently promotes the development of self-reliance, positive self-esteem, and realistic standards of performance. Parents who are accepting and encouraging, who avoid placing children under pressure by equating their self-worth with their achievement, and who model problem-solving skills may be providing their children with the essential ingredients of achievement motivation. Authoritative parents appear to be more effective teachers of their children than are nonauthoritative parents (Pratt, Kerig, Cowan, & Cowan, 1988).

The question remains, what specific aspects of the authoritative parenting style contribute to children's academic success? What do children gain from their warm, yet firm parents that allows them to excel academically? Steinberg, Elmen, and Mounts (1989) tested the hypothesis that specific elements of the authoritative parenting style *facilitate* rather than simply accompany academic success.

These researchers collected data on family relationships (by interviewing the adolescents) and adolescents' school grades and scores on standardized achievement tests. Data were collected for 120 white, middle-class families with a firstborn child between the ages of 11 and 16 years.

They found that "adolescents who describe their parents as treating them warmly, democratically, and firmly are more likely than their peers to develop positive attitudes toward, and beliefs about, their achievement, and as a consequence, they are more likely to do better in school" (p. 1433). The researchers tentatively concluded that authoritative parents encourage a healthy sense of autonomy in their children, and a willingness to work hard. These attributes contribute to their school success. Similar findings were reported by Grolnick and Ryan (1989).

Summarizing Family Influences

Parents can promote their children's cognitive development within the broad limits set by heredity. They do so by arranging a safe and interesting environment that encourages free exploration and the manipulation of objects. Parents of high-achieving children convey realistic expectations regarding their child's cognitive development. They provide assistance with everyday problems and schoolwork as needed.

These children are encouraged to use their senses to notice interesting features of their home and neighborhood settings. Musical instruments, records, and tapes encourage them to listen and to hear. Children who accompany their parents out of the house on walks, trips, or shopping excursions are exposed to rich combinations of meaningful experiences that contribute to their understanding of the world.

Children who observe their parents performing household tasks or who participate in such chores as food preparation or caring for younger siblings or even pets have the opportunity to develop a variety of competencies that serve their development. In the process of these ordinary, everyday experiences, children develop attentional skills, persistence, and enthusiasm for discovery—in effect, they learn how to learn.

The most promising sources of enriching experiences for young children are pleasurable parent-child interactions that occur in the context of a close, emotionally supportive relationship. Examples of such interactions are conversations, story telling, and playing games that challenge the child's imagination while teaching basic skills (e.g., Freund, 1990).

Parents of high-achieving children provide a nurturant and supportive learning environment and establish the child's readiness and willingness to learn. They seek to present a task in a way that is optimally meaningful and challenging, taking advantage of the child's motivation to participate and to succeed.

Children have greater opportunity for such challenges and more frequent one-to-one interactions with adults in the home environment than they do in school, where teachers generally work in a group setting (Tizard & Hughes, 1985). Children have more frequent, more complex, and longer conversations at home than at school and are asked more interesting and more complex questions at home.

Parents of children who become high achievers generally model achievement behaviors, express lots of encouragement, reward accomplishment, and foster independence and creativity of thought. Positive self-esteem has the self-fulfilling effect of encouraging children to take intellectual and social risks.

The sequence becomes clear whereby achievement breeds more achievement. Challenge leads to intellectual risk taking, which may lead to success. This encourages further risk taking and persistence. Occasional failure is seen in a positive light as the inevitable by-product of risk taking. Taking on new challenges becomes a sign of personal growth. The parental contributions to high achievement are not mysterious; rather, they reflect nurturant and stimulating styles of rearing that encourage children to appreciate and expand their abilities.

TOO MUCH TOO SOON?: SUPERKIDS

Study Question Do children benefit from very early schooling?

United States culture is very competitive. More, faster, and sooner are often equated with better. We are tempted to judge people by their "successes" rather than by their characters. In the past, parents hoped that their children would be normal. Many parents today expect their children to excel. They worry that their children will not get into the right preschool or kindergarten program. They seek a competitive advantage for their children academically.

Psychologist David Elkind (1987a) has criticized parents who either "hurry" or "miseducate" their young children. Hurrying children to grow up, Elkind surmises, alleviates some of the inconveniences and stresses of raising dependent preschool children. Miseducating children, or exposing them to formal instruction during the "preschool" years, satisfies parents' need to provide their children with academic advantages while proving their own talent for parenting.

"Parents today believe they can make a difference in their children's lives, that they can give them an edge that will make them brighter and abler than the competition. Parents who started out in the seventies hurry their children; parents of the eighties are miseducating them. Parents who started in the seventies need mature children, while parents of the eighties want superkids" (Elkind, 1987a, p. xiii).

The so-called "superkid" syndrome is essentially a middle-class phenomenon. Parents who highly value achievement and equate it with success and happiness read books like *Give Your Child A Superior Mind, Raising Brighter Children,* and *How To Have A Smarter Baby.* They seek out special enrichment or accelerated learning environments for their children (Collins, 1985a; Elkind, 1987b).

Young children benefit from a low-pressure, informed preschool setting.

Young children are instructed not only in academic subjects but also foreign languages, music, dance, swimming, gymnastic activities, and competitive sports. As their children are learning to walk, some parents have visions of Princeton, Stanford, or an Olympic gold medal. Elkind cautions that parents should examine their own motives for placing children in high-pressure learning environments. Whose needs are being addressed?

To some extent, parental excitement about preschool enrichment programs may reflect the successes of early intervention programs like Head Start and the Brookline Early Education Project. These projects, however, were directed at culturally and economically disadvantaged children. They targeted families rather than individual children. It has not been demonstrated that middle-class children benefit, in the long run, from such interventions. They generally receive enough stimulation and encouragement during the course of their daily lives.

Research has not revealed clear-cut long-term benefits of early preschool or even full-day kindergarten. Early schooling clearly benefits economically disadvantaged children, but "middle-class children gain little, if anything, from exposure to early education" (Bennett, 1985). "Certainly parents play a crucial role in the lives of individuals who are intellectually gifted or creatively talented. But this role is not one of active instruction . . . Rather it is the support and encouragement parents give children and the intellectual climate that they create in the home which seem to be the critical factors" (Elkind, 1987a, p. 21).

Educators and developmental specialists contend that young children benefit from participating in low-pressure, relaxed, interesting, and unstructured activities with their caretakers. Most preschool and nursery school programs also provide a comfortable, nurturant setting for children, with activities that are appropriate for the children's ages and interests.

Elkind refers to early, formal instruction as miseducation, not so much because such training is ineffective, but because it may be harmful. Placement in high-pressured, structured preschool learning environments may create unnecessary stress for children (Elkind, 1987a). Other risks of exposing children to challenges that are beyond their capabilities include achievement anxiety and fear of failure. The optimal formula is for parents to have high expectations and set appropriate goals for their children but to avoid being pushy and critical (K. Fisher, 1989).

"If we have reared a well-mannered, good and decent person, we should take pleasure and pride in that fact. More likely than not, if we have achieved those goals, the child's success will take care of itself. Each child has a unique pattern of qualities and abilities that makes him or her special. In this sense, every single child is a superkid" (Elkind, 1987b, p. 61).

EARLY SCHOOLING

Historically, preschool programs and day-care programs have had quite different origins. Until recently, the two have remained distinct entities (Scarr & Weinberg, 1986). Today, the two services are merging as working parents search for the most beneficial arrangements for their children.

It is not so much education as child care that concerns many working parents. They must choose a preschool program for their child from the increasing variety of available day-care and early-schooling arrangements. "Today's parents want professionals to care for their young children because they do not have the time to do so themselves" (Elkind, 1988, p. 22).

Mary Futrell (1987), president of the National Education Association, contends that public schooling should be available for 4-year-olds. Schools should not be a place of refuge for neglected children, but rather they should provide an opportunity for children to take their first steps toward lifelong learning.

Educators seem to agree as long as children will participate in "developmentally appropriate activities" for their age group and not formal academic instruction. "Structured play—play that enlivens the imagination and exercises the intellect—is the indispensable prerequisite for the development of the critical thinking skills fundamental to academic achievement. That fact by itself suggests the content of a 'curriculum' for four-year-olds" (Futrell, 1987, p. 252).

Modern preschools reflect the influences of Maria Montessori, Jean Piaget, and John Dewey. They involve children in a variety of individual and group activities that encourage them to develop their motor, perceptual, and social skills through play rather than through instruction. Teachers read stories, and children sing songs, pile up blocks, paint pictures, and talk about their families and themselves. Teachers, aware of a given child's readiness to learn, provide materials and activities that will stimulate and challenge him or her. Aware of children's developing but still limited social skills, teachers promote peer interactions in small groups and remind children to "keep your hands to yourself."

"Teachers at the preschool level must do more comforting, more limit setting, more crisis intervention than teachers at the higher

A stereotype is an overgeneralized belief about a group of people. It emphasizes one trait or characteristic that the members of the group presumably share. Stereotypes ignore the usually considerable differences among group members. The image of Oriental "whiz-kids," model students living trouble-free lives, has been popularly presented in national magazines and newspapers. The image ignores the real struggles of immigrant children trying to adapt to an alien culture (Fischer, 1988).

About 80 percent of these children are Chinese (from Hong Kong), Filipino, Japanese, Vietnamese, or Korean. About 60 percent live in California, Hawaii, or New York (Population Reference Bureau estimates, 1985). Many of their families live below the poverty line and depend on public assistance.

Some Oriental children, particularly those who came to the United States in the late 1960s and early 1970s, and those who arrived after the Vietnam war in 1975 are exceptional achievers. Their parents are "mostly middle- to upper-income professional people who were fairly well-educated and who passed on to their children an abiding interest in education and a strong work ethic . . . While Asians make up just 2.1% of the U.S. population, last fall's freshman class at Harvard was 14% Asian American; at the Massachusetts Institute of Technology, 20%; and at the University of California at Berkeley, 25%. Of the 70 students who've won scholarships in the Westinghouse Science Talent Search since 1981, 20 have been of Asian descent. In 1986, Asians won all five top scholarship awards from Westinghouse . . . An Asian student's average math SAT score is 518 out of 800—43 points above the national average" (Fischer, 1988, pp. 14–15).

In 1988, 11 of the 14 Westinghouse finalists in New York City were Asian, four of them female. Ironically, their successes are giving rise to discriminatory attempts to limit the number of Asians in the best universities and to rejection from their non-Asian peers who resent their hard work and achievement.

These data arouse our curiosity—why do Asian children succeed when so many of their native-born peers in the United States languish? High school teachers in Queens, New York, were asked to rank their students according to ethnic or national group membership. The Asian students were "ranked highest for motivation and blacks the lowest, with blacks given highest marks for physical ability and Asians the lowest. 'Nature' did not dictate that this be so. If it had, there would be no explaining the great Asian successes in the Olympics. Nor did 'nature' intend blacks to be 'athletic'; had that been the design, blacks from Africa would invariably beat the competition from other continents" (Graubard, 1988).

It is tempting to compare Oriental school systems with ours to seek reasons for the high achievement of many Asian children. Most observers credit the Oriental mother more than the school for encouraging their children to value high achievement (See Cultural Perspective: The Japanese Mother). "Japanese mothers play a prominent role in their children's education. And while opinion polls here show that American parents want their children to succeed in school, studies of family life suggest that most parents are too stressed, tired or self-absorbed to support and encourage their youngsters' academic endeavors during after-school hours . . . The strains of divorce and single parenthood, and the stress of juggling two wage earners' work schedules have made it all but impossible for American parents to keep up their end of the bargain" (Steinberg, 1987e).

Stevenson (1985) administered a battery of 10 cognitive tasks and achievement tests in reading and math to 1,440 Chinese, Japanese, and American children in grades 1 and 5. Children in the 3 cultures were similar in their cognitive abilities. The Chinese children surpassed Japanese and American children in reading scores, and both Chinese and Japanese children produced higher math scores than American children. Stevenson concluded that

Are some cultures or ethnic groups more successful at promoting academic achievement than others?

the superior performance of the Asian children could not be attributed to higher intellectual abilities and, therefore, must reflect home and school experiences.

Oriental youngsters also provide each other with considerable peer support for achievement, compared to children in the United States who may not value social and material gains more than academic success. Many high school students in the United States work part time, which is unheard of in Japan during the school year. "No one would argue that the intense do-or-die pressure to succeed felt by Japanese adolescents is a healthy state toward which our youngsters should be pushed. But there surely is an appropriate middle ground between being neurotically obsessed with an important exam and being riveted to MTV" (Steinberg, 1987e).

The best predictors of children's academic achievement are related to their mothers or primary caretakers. They include maternal level of education, maternal involvement in child rearing, and most of all, the quality of the mother-child relationship. As previously noted, the outstanding success of Asian-American children is usually attributed to their mothers. Asian women typically stay home with their young children rather than pursue a career. They help their children do their schoolwork and create a home environment that fosters achievement.

"The Japanese mother spends hours reading stories to her children and playing what we would call educational games. She breaks each task into small steps, lavishes praise on the children as they master each one and seldom resorts to punishment . . . The mother forms an alliance with her child; they work together to conquer educational challenges" (Chance, 1987a, p. 80).

Japanese mothers, so described, resemble the parents described by Professor Bloom (in chapter 3) whose children became the best in their fields. Like Professor Bloom, Japanese mothers do not believe that achievement is rooted in innate ability.

They value, instead, a commitment to excellence, selflessness, and hard work. "Until her child goes to school, the Japanese mother devotes herself to the rearing of the child. In verbal and nonverbal ways, she reminds the child of her deep, deep, warm feelings and that the child is the most important thing in the world to her" (Kagan, quoted by Garfinkel, 1983, p. 56). Japanese mothers discipline their children gently, often by patiently expressing their displeasure.

Japanese and Chinese schoolchildren surpass their American counterparts virtually across the board academically, but particularly in science and mathematics. Oriental children spend more time in school than American children and spend more time after school in school-related activities, including homework. They also receive more help from family members (Chen & Stevenson, 1989; Stevenson, Lee, & Stigler, 1986).

As we have seen, there is no reason to assume they are innately brighter or that they get an earlier start in their schooling (Stevenson, 1987). The size of their classes are larger, not smaller, than American classes. Japanese teachers are more highly

grade levels. But they are also helping children acquire the fundamental concepts of space, time, number, causality, relations, and nature-concepts that form the essential data base for all later learning" (Elkind, 1988, p. 23). Teachers should give children freedom to decide when to pursue a particular activity, Elkind suggests, but much less freedom to decide what curricular areas to pursue.

Parents who are seeking a safe and healthy environment for their preschoolers should consider the student-teacher ratio, the qualifications of the teaching staff, and the physical layout of the school. Most important are the school director's child-care philosophy and the child's reactions to the school (Shell, 1989).

Should advantaged children attend preschool? Elkind (1988) responds ". . . if parents do not have the commitment, the time, the energy, and the resources to provide young children with an environment that approaches that of the good early childhood program, then it *does* matter whether the child attends a preschool . . . The issue then is not whether preschool is important, but rather to what extent home schooling can duplicate what preschool has to offer" (p. 26).

paid, more enthusiastic in the classroom, and much more respected than their American counterparts.

Japanese students attend school 240 days a year, compared to 178 days for American children. Japanese first graders worked an average of 233 minutes a week on homework, compared to 79 minutes for American first graders (Garfinkle, 1983). Importantly, Chinese and Japanese elementary school-children are as happy and well-adjusted as their American counterparts (Stevenson, 1987).

One critical difference between Oriental and American mothers is their level of expectations about their children's progress in school. "American children had to do less well than Japanese and Chinese children for their mothers to be satisfied and much worse before their mothers expressed dissatisfaction with their academic performance. Such high evaluations of ability and achievement by the American children and their mothers cannot be conducive to a child's diligent study" (Stevenson, 1987, p. 30). As previously noted, parents with low expectations about achievement usually do not encourage their children to fulfill their potential. Sadly, this is characteristic of many American families, de-

spite the fact that the American curriculum is less demanding than the Oriental.

Cross-cultural comparisons help us put into perspective our own society's assumptions, expectations, and practices. We can appreciate that there are distinctive cultural values regarding dependency, harmony, obligation, conformity, and perserverence that influence how Japanese and American children are viewed and treated by their parents and teachers. But American children have fallen behind their Oriental peers academically, and we can identify several relevant factors. These include a less demanding curriculum, less time spent in class, low parent and teacher expectations about children's ability, the lack of a work ethic, and less stable domestic environments in America.

On a daily basis, young Japanese children seem to benefit, in terms of their achievement and self-efficacy, from their mothers' intense involvement in their lives. It seems that the attitudes and behaviors inculcated at home during and following the preschool years prepare Oriental children for levels of effort and achievement that are beyond the expectations of most American parents.

THE PROCESS OF SCHOOLING

Mark #14: The Book Report
"The weekend was a toughy. Mark had almost half of his library book to finish so he could write his book report for Wednesday. Saturday wasn't feasible because we had to spend it with the family for an 'early Thanksgiving.' Sunday Mark procrastinated the whole day. As it began to drive me insane, I prayed, kept my cool, and offered my help.

"For example, as soon as he began to read, he squawked that he didn't have any idea what 'they' were talking about. (There were some new characters already involved in a conversation.) So I had him read it aloud and I explained how the sentences should be read. I told him that books are like that at times, and we have to read on until we can figure out what's happening. He wouldn't settle for that and kept complaining and trying to get me involved. As I would not get perturbed or

help any more, he eventually threw a tantrum (which I ignored) and then stormed to his room.

"Later when he decided to approach me again he was calmer. He did attempt to finish the chapter again and when he told me that he now understood, I told him, 'I knew you would.'"

The 10,000 or so hours that children spend in classrooms by the time they graduate from high school account for a significant part of their socialization. School influence is probably second only to that of the family environment as a factor in personality and cognitive development. Teachers and schools can make a big difference in children's development (Good & Weinstein, 1986; Linney & Seidman, 1989), but there is widespread agreement that academic environments could be and should be more effective.

In addition to time spent in classrooms, most children will devote thousands of hours to homework, special projects, and school-related activities. Perhaps the key factor determining how much value children will derive from schooling is their interest in learning. Achievement motivation is very susceptible to home influences (Hess & Holloway, 1984).

Parental encouragement and involvement can increase the value of a school's curriculum and of school assignments, particularly when children become frustrated by their lack of progress or understanding. Parents like Mark's mother must find the fine line of encouraging and helping without actually doing the assignment for or further discouraging the child.

Reading and Writing

Reading

A telephone poll of 1,000 parents by the Roper organization (*New York Times,* May 25, 1988) reported that only 44 percent of the parents polled said that their children read for pleasure every day. Girls were reported to read more than boys; younger schoolchildren read more than older. Children of well-educated parents read more than those of less-educated parents.

Ninety-one percent of the parents felt that reading well is important to their child's success. One-third reported not being satisfied with how well their child read. Only a bare majority of the parents said that their children were very interested in reading, with a big drop in interest following the fifth grade.

Reading is a fundamental skill; so many other skills depend upon reading ability. Children who can read by the time they are four or five years old have an academic advantage in the first grade, when most of their peers are just beginning to master basic literacy skills. But more importantly, early readers can begin to explore new worlds and appreciate the richness of written language. They can enjoy the classic children's literature and acquire interesting information about their environment.

Since reading and writing emerge from more general language and communication skills, talking and reading to children are optimal ways of promoting these skills. A national survey (Jackson, 1977) revealed that most of the top students in the first grade had parents who read to them almost daily. Parents who evidenced the greatest interest in reading had children who were good readers.

Reading stories to children, asking them to tell the story in their own words, using the pictures as guides, and possibly drawing pictures based on the story all foster verbal and motivational skills that encourage early reading ability. Conversations that provide children with opportunities to describe their experiences and their feelings also sharpen language skills (Jackson, 1977).

Conventional wisdom suggests that children are not ready to learn how to read until they are at least 6 years old, but many educators disagree. Literacy-related skills, such as oral communication, begin to emerge during early childhood (W. S. Hall, 1989). Two-year-olds know what a story is, and how to hold a book, and they understand that adults "get" a story from the pages of a book. At this age, children may believe that each letter stands for a word, that each page tells a whole story, or that the parent is "reading" the picture.

Three-year-olds know that the story is in the text, not in the pictures, and they can usually recite part of the alphabet, recognize some letters, and distinguish word sounds (thank you, "Sesame Street"). Many 3- and 4-year-olds "read" in the sense that they associate a group of letters with a particular word and understand that particular letters correspond to specific sounds. Many children may be ready to learn to read by the age of 5 years, and some even earlier.

We can conceive of reading as a set of skills that gradually emerge during the preschool years. Children are ready to begin to learn these skills when they show interest in stories that are being read to them and when they show willingness to learn words that are associated with pictures. A good way to encourage the development of reading skills is to read interesting stories to children frequently. We can ask them questions about the story and answer their questions. When children are being read to, they are learning far more than just the story. Attentional, perceptual, memory, and other cognitive abilities are exercised (Beck & Carpenter, 1986; W. S. Hall, 1989).

When teaching children to read, they should have the background knowledge required to understand the story they will be reading. They should also be given frequent opportunities to read out loud. If they make many errors, the selection they are reading is too difficult. Mistakes should generally be ignored, because correcting them detracts from the child's train of thought and comprehension.

"The emphasis during reading lessons should be on understanding and appreciating the content of the story. Lessons in which the children do little else but take turns reading the story, and the teacher does little else but correct reading errors, are ineffective" (R. C.

Anderson, 1985, p. 29). Silent reading is also an important component of the more successful reading programs and should usually precede oral reading. In a classroom or home environment, a discussion following the child's reading motivates higher level thinking (R. C. Anderson, 1985).

Should parents teach their children to read? If a child is interested in learning to read, if he can recognize letters and identify their corresponding sounds, and if parents can make learning to read fun for the child, there is no reason not to try. "No roadblocks of any kind should be put in the way of children who want to read on their own . . . You can never miseducate children by responding appropriately to their demands for information" (Elkind, 1987a, pp. 184–185).

Writing

Because writing involves motor skills that require considerable practice, writing ability emerges later than reading. Initially, children may believe that each letter stands for a word and may write sentences like URVRE NIS (you are very nice). Early writing involves the composition of sentences reflecting an understanding of the relationship between letters and words, between words and sentences (Wells, 1988).

Hayes and Flower (1986) analyze three major writing processes: (1) planning (generating and organizing ideas), (2) sentence generation (producing formal sentences), and (3) revision (improving the first draft). Older models of reading and writing that stressed the importance of maturation refuted the possibility that very young children could learn these skills. Newer models allow for the early emergence of these capabilities. They emphasize activities that parents can arrange to promote literacy skills.

Writing letters, preparing book or movie reviews, creating stories, and keeping a journal are but a handful of writing activities that can motivate children to sit down with pencil in hand and compose. Computer technology, particularly word processing, can make writing more fun for children. It gives them immediate feedback regarding their compositions, with the opportunity to edit, revise, and print out a "hard copy" when desired.

Parental Involvement in Schooling

Schooling can make an enormous contribution to children's development, particularly when parents become involved in the educational process. Do parents understand the potential value of their participation? What can school systems do to bring parents into the educational system?

In 1987, 22,000 teachers from all 50 states participated in a survey (*New York Times,* December 12, 1988). Ninety percent of the teachers reported that the lack of parental support at their schools was a problem. My home state, New Jersey, with the help of generous corporate contributions, has been promoting a large-scale, three-year public-relations campaign ("Partners in Learning") to increase parents' involvement in their children's education (*New York Times,* November 15, 1987). Through the use of television and radio commercials, McDonald's place mats, Johanna Farms milk cartons, oil bills, and paychecks, parents will be reminded of six ways to improve their children's performance in school.

It is suggested that parents check that homework is done each day; make sure their children get a good night's sleep; provide a quiet place and time for children to study; have children arrive at school on time; talk to children about their daily school experiences; and read with them, or encourage them to read, at least 15 minutes a day. In addition, schools that make exemplary efforts to promote parental involvement will receive special recognition from the state. Grants will be available for pilot projects that foster home-school partnerships.

Parental support of children's efforts in school encourages both greater achievement and more positive attitudes toward school. It helps parental decision making about school-related matters and improves communication between parents and teachers (*NJEA Review,* May, 1988; A. S. Wells, 1987). Stevenson and Baker (1987), for example, observed that the children of parents who are involved in school activities perform better in school than children of less-involved parents.

Children from low-income families benefit the most when their parents become actively involved in their education (Wells, 1987). "The failure to bridge the social and cultural gap between home and school may lie at the root of the poor academic performance of [disadvantaged minority] children (Comer, 1988a, p. 43). "A child from a poor, marginal family . . . is likely to enter school without adequate preparation. The child may arrive without ever having learned such social skills as negotiation and compromise. A child who is expected to read at school may come from a home where no one reads and may never have heard a parent read bedtime stories . . . In some families a child who does not fight back will be punished. And yet the same behavior will get the child into trouble at school" (p. 45).

Some parents feel uncomfortable in school settings, perhaps reflecting difficult times in their own educational history. Other parents report they just hear from school personnel when their children are in trouble. These parents often become suspicious or resentful of the school staff. "And those individuals under great stress, with their own personal problems and failures, often view the school problems of their children as yet another failure. Thus, many parents stay away from schools or interact with school people in angry, defensive, and confrontational ways" (Comer, 1988a, pp. 37–38).

School personnel may react defensively and view such parents as part of the problem rather than seeing that they could be part of the solution. And even if they succeed at bringing the parents in, few principals or teachers have been adequately trained in developing parents' skills and teaching them how to work with their children at home" (A. S. Wells, 1987).

Comer (1988a) describes a successful program for improving the school performance of poor minority children. "We developed a program that involved parents at three levels: shaping policy through their representatives on the governance and management team, participating in activities supporting the school program, and attending school events" (p. 47). As a result of these and other interventions, behavior problems in the school declined, parent-staff relations improved, and children's achievement increased.

Handling School-Related Problems

Parents and teachers, as part of a "team," need to learn how to be assertive with each other. When they misunderstand each other or miscommunicate, it is the child who suffers. "If your child has a problem, begin by trying to resolve it with a teacher before going to the principal or the school board. Offer specific solutions. Keep the conversation focused on what you want for your child, not what you think the teacher or school is doing wrong" (Kutner, 1988m).

Getting visibly upset or upsetting a child about poor grades and report cards is another parenting pitfall. Punishing children for poor performance or offering them material rewards for improvement are not generally effective strategies. "What *does* work is the low-key, positive response—offering praise for the positive aspects of a child's performance, encouraging the child to do better with those things that aren't going so well and offering to help" (Dornbusch, quoted by Collins, 1986c).

Any gesture that encourages the intrinsic motivation to achieve is more likely to be helpful than offering extrinsic rewards or punishments. Expressing negative emotions is usually counterproductive. "In focusing on bad grades, parents can say things like, 'I know you can do better if you just put out a little more effort' " (Dornbusch, quoted by Collins, 1986c). Low-key encouragement is not likely to help children who are performing poorly across-the-board. Such children need the attention of sympathetic school personnel who are willing to work with them on a one-to-one basis.

Achievement and Underachievement in Adolescents

The Case of Peter

Peter, a bright, articulate 14-year-old high school freshman, was sitting before me in my office. His mother was characterizing him as a disrespectful, "pathological liar." He did nothing in school, did no homework, and was "getting away with murder." Clearly Peter was as unhappy as his mother. He felt frustrated, depressed, and discouraged. When I spoke to Peter alone, he told me, "My mother thinks I'm crazy."

He acknowledged that he lied to her about his schoolwork because he was afraid of telling her the truth. He had been "grounded" for almost the entire previous year—he could not leave his house after school. He was not allowed to watch TV or listen to the radio because of his poor performance in school. The major effect of these punishments was to further discourage him. Rather than addressing the causes of Peter's underachievement in school, his mother was attempting to coerce him into achievement. This is not an unfamiliar scene for family therapists.

Metcalf and Gaier (1987) suggest that middle-class parents like Peter's may inadvertently encourage underachievement in their children by overstressing school achievement. Their children may resent this pressure and rebel by not working up to their capacity. If too much is expected of them, they become discouraged. "Children may be unaware that they are working below capacity, and may offer irrelevant excuses when the problem is pointed out. They may claim the teacher is unfair, that the subjects are uninteresting, or that other children do better because they cheat. By the time they reach high school, the pattern of underachievement is habitual and difficult to change" (p. 920).

Metcalf and Gaier compared four different parenting patterns regarding their relationship to adolescent academic underachievement: (1) upward striving, (2) overprotective, (3) indifferent, and (4) conflicted. The upward-striving pattern of middle-class parenting, in which parents criticize and nag their children to get good grades so that they can get into a superior college, was associated with underachievement in adolescents.

"Perhaps this is why the adolescents react by disliking school and thus work below their capacities. When they encounter constant criticism and seemingly fail to live up to their parents' standards, they begin to become anxious and develop feelings of inadequacy which then may be manifested in hostility toward parents and school or a sense of futility—discouraging them from making a full effort" (Metcalf and Gaier, 1987, p. 926).

Metcalf and Gaier's model is supported by the findings of Eskilson, Wiley, Muhlbauer, and Dodder (1986). They interviewed 161 high school and 155 junior high school students to investigate the relationship between parental pressure to succeed and adolescents' self-esteem and deviant behavior. Students who reported that their parents pressured them to succeed had lower assessments of their ability to meet their parents' goals. They also had lower self-esteem and displayed more frequent deviant behavior.

Parents who emphasize the materialistic benefits of education may be sabotaging their children's achievement motivation. Nicholls, Patashnick, and Nolen (1985) interviewed ninth and twelfth graders about the relationship between their personal goals, their view of success, and the general purposes of education. "The view that school should enable students to enhance their wealth and status was less likely than any other view to be associated with a commitment to learning for its own sake and more likely to be associated with academic alienation" (p. 683).

Encouraging Creative Expression

Study Question *How can parents encourage creative behavior in their children?*

What did children do before TV? They played, they read, they explored the world, and they interacted with other people. They spent considerably more time than children today engaged in creative and stimulating tasks. Creativity is not the same as intelligence. Although there is no widely agreed upon definition of creativity, originality and flexibility are considered two measurable attributes of creative behavior.

Children's creative expression and imagination reflect at least three abilities. They must be able to (1) generate new possibilities, (2) appreciate unusual outcomes, and (3) be willing to take risks. Unlike many other abilities, creative expression appears to be inhibited by incentives and competition (Kohn, 1987a).

Teresa Amabile's research on children's creative behavior demonstrates that factors that limit children's flexibility, such as deadlines and evaluations, undermine their interest in a project and suppress creative behavior. Self-direction, encouragement and support from supervisors, access to proper resources, constructive feedback, and enough time to complete a project enhance creative expression (Amabile, 1989). Amabile encourages her daughter's accomplishments by reinforcing her interest in a project instead of evaluating the finished product. "Gee, how neat! You tried something very different from what you did before" or "You look like you're having fun over there!" (quoted by Kohn, 1987a).

Parents can encourage creative thinking in their children by responding to their "unusual" questions in a thoughtful way and by asking unusual, even provocative, questions themselves. Language is the richest medium for creative expression. Most young children enjoy playing with words and ideas. Unfortunately, taking creative risks may be discouraged by conventional schooling, which usually values correct answers more than original thinking. Enjoyable and creative interaction with computers is available even to preschool children who cannot type or read (Eltgroth, 1989; Lepper & Gurtner, 1989).

Storytelling, musical activities, and dramatic play are excellent opportunities for children to invent new ways of representing their experiences. When a child draws a picture, asking her to tell us about the picture is a more encouraging response than "What is it?" Young children are not as interested in realistic depictions in their art as are older children. "Because preschool children are unconcerned with realism, their drawings are free, fanciful and inventive. Suns may be green, cars may float in the sky . . . The older child's drawing may be more realistic, neat and precise, but, in my opinion, it is also less imaginative and less striking" (Winner, 1986, p. 35).

PLAY

Study Question *What are the "functions" of child's play?*

A child sits in a sandbox pouring sand from one receptacle to another while a sibling climbs a jungle gym. An infant raps her rattle against a bar on her crib. Three 8-year-olds are competing to accumulate expensive properties in Monopoly. Two toddlers sit side by side piling one block upon another until the entire structure collapses.

Play is by far the most common activity of waking children. Children will play in the crib, on the floor, at the breakfast table, in a bath, in the park, and when they are supposed to be getting dressed. Impatient parents assert, "There's a time and a place for everything," but for children, play naturally occurs whenever the situation allows.

Although it is not easy to define play, researchers agree that play is an enjoyable, spontaneous, and voluntary activity that is performed for its own sake. Consequences that would normally follow "forbidden" behaviors like fighting or teasing are withheld when these behaviors occur as play. Play behavior is also commonly observed in human adults and animals.

"Play is a primitive activity through which animals and humans cooperate and communicate their desire to deal with such potentially dangerous behavior as chasing and escaping, attacking and defending. In play they can express these desires safely, because they give each other signals showing that they do not really mean what they are doing. Monkeys use a play face, dogs wag their tails and children say, 'I'm just pretending' " (Sutton-Smith, 1985, p. 64).

It has been said that "play is the work of the child" because play behavior serves virtually every domain of development. Physical play provides children with exercise and sharpens both gross and fine motor coordination. Pretend, dramatic, and creative play stimulate children's imaginations and help them distinguish between reality and fantasy. Play helps children appreciate the countless possibilities that exist in any situation. Children play for fun but, in the process, develop competencies that prepare them for school.

Playing with other children sharpens communication and interpersonal abilities and dispositions, including conflict-resolution skills, sharing, empathy, and cooperation. Play also can be a form of coping, as when children act out fearful situations. Play can also serve as an outlet for frustration and anger. Observing children in play gives parents an excellent opportunity to assess their children's perceptions of the world and of themselves.

In the past, play was much more of a communal pastime than it is today. Modern children are more likely than their ancestors to spend their time in solitary play—perhaps alone in their bedrooms or playrooms— watching TV, playing a video game, or playing with an electronic toy or action figure. "The shift in play has been steady: a taming of most violence; mechanization of toys, increasingly electronic in character; symbolization in games of language, information and strategy, which have largely replaced rough physical play; decreasing differentiation between the play of boys and girls; increasing remoteness from direct experience through fantasy; and most significantly, isolation" (Sutton-Smith, 1985, p. 64).

Parents as Playmates

Research reveals that during play, more-competent parents interact with their children differently than less-competent parents. Mondell and Tyler (1981), for example, observed parents and children participate in a semi-structured problem-solving/play task. They reported that more-competent parents "treated the child as being more capable and resourceful, showed generally warm and positive feelings, and were more helpful with problem-solving" (p. 73).

Stevenson, Leavitt, Thompson, and Roach (1988) observed that parents are able to provide a structure to play interactions with very young children that would not be present when young siblings play with each other. Hence, if a parent is present, a preschooler might initiate play behavior that requires a partner. If a young sibling is present, the child would be more likely to play with a toy. These investigators concluded that parents, not young children, determine the course of a play interaction.

Parents naturally simplify their play behaviors with very young children. Even infants enjoy bouts of "pat-a-cake" and "peek-a-boo." "These and other games introduce infants to the rules of social behavior. Being highly repetitive with simple roles for both parent and infant, these games help infants learn such things as the rules of give-and-take during conversations" (Trotter, 1987b, p. 31).

Parents naturally adjust their play behaviors to a child's age and level of maturity. Power (1985) videotaped mothers and fathers playing with their boys and girls at ages 7, 10, and 13 months. He found that parents of the older children were more likely to "encourage pretend, turn-taking, and relational behavior and less likely to direct infant attention. Moreover, parents of older infants were more likely to use verbal techniques alone and less likely to physically perform behaviors for their children" (p. 1514).

Ross and Lollis (1987) had parents participate in a variety of "baby games" with their infants. The parents were then instructed to *not* take their turn and sit quietly for several seconds. "When the adults failed to participate, the infants showed considerable independent understanding of the games they played." Through sounds and gestures, the infants appeared to be signaling their parents to take their turn. The older the infants, the more signals they displayed, encouraging their parents to continue.

Given the potential value of interactive play in children's development and the tendency for today's children to isolate themselves in their fully equipped electronic bedrooms or play-rooms, parents should consider making inter-active play a priority when helping a child decide how to spend his day. Solitary play can be valuable, too, but a balance should be struck between both types of play.

Sex Differences in Play and Toy Preferences

Some parents, usually fathers, assume that the toys children play with can influence their sexual identity. Research, however, demon-strates that children's gender identities and eventual sexual preferences are in no way in-fluenced by their toys. Mothers are more likely to give children of either sex the freedom to play with whatever toys they desire.

Bradbard (1985) asked the parents of 47 pre-school children to list the toys their children received at Christmas. Although the children requested an average of 3 or 4 toys, they re-ceived an average of 11 to 12 toys. Boys ask for and receive vehicle toys (e.g., cars, airplanes) and "spatial-temporal" toys (e.g., building blocks) whereas girls are more likely to re-quest and receive "domestic" toys (e.g., dolls, toy dishes). Other types of toys (e.g., books, stuffed animals) are given equally to boys and girls. Ironically, it is the parent's attitude toward a child's choice of toys that is associated with later school adjustment and friendship pat-terns. In infancy, children arc already demon-strating preferences for toys that are associated with their gender.

Generally, mothers play differently with children than do fathers. Mothers are more verbal with infants and preschoolers; fathers are more physical. Power (1985), in the study cited previously, reported that as children aged, mothers of girls became more directive in play

and mothers of boys became less directive. In most other respects, mothers and fathers are similar in their play behavior. They adjust their reactions according to the situation and modify their play behavior according to their chil-dren's age.

TELEVISION

Study Question   Should parents regulate their children's television viewing?

For almost 40 years, serious questions have been raised about television's impact on chil-dren. Parents and psychologists wonder whether televised violence or the portrayal of other antisocial behaviors "toughen" children or desensitize them to real-life violence. Do televised portrayals of women, the elderly, and minorities encourage unflattering stereotypes about these groups? What are the effects, if any, of exposing children to television's steady diet of sexual innuendo and activity? Are children manipulated by misleading commercials that present distorted or exaggerated claims about products? (Liebert & Sprafkin, 1988).

We also must ask whether children should be spending so much of their time so passively. Television watching has become the default activity for most people in the United States. It is what we do when there is "nothing else worth doing." Parents encourage this habitual pattern in children by using TV as a baby-sitter instead of encouraging more active and chal-lenging pursuits.

A survey published by *Weekly Reader Mag-azine* in May, 1988, confirms that watching television is children's favorite leisure activity. Reading has become the least popular, at least for children in grades 4 to 6. In addition to dis-tracting children from more beneficial play and social experiences, television is a teacher. Children in the United States watch an average of 25 hours of TV a week, which accumulates

Television watching competes with other activities that might be more likely to promote children's social and cognitive development.

to about 15,000 hours by the time they graduate from high school. Compare that figure to the 11,000 hours they spend in classrooms. Lawrence (1986) reported that adolescents watch an average of 17 hours of TV a week.

Most children (and some adults) are not aware that the purpose of TV programming is to get viewers to watch the commercials. Young children do not understand that the purpose of a commercial is to get them to buy a product. In fact, young children may not distinguish between the program and the commercial! Further, many children's toy commercials are followed by disclaimers ("partial assembly required") that children do not understand. Food commercials directed at children offer heavily sugared, nonnutritious junk food (Liebert & Sprafkin, 1988).

"In the course of their viewing, they will see perhaps 350,000 commercial messages, many for unhealthful foods and other products that are not conducive to health. The social messages are often no better: sex without affection or regard to the risk of pregnancy or disease; frequent consumption of alcohol and drugs; misrepresentations of women, minorities, the elderly and the handicapped; unrealistically easy solutions to complex problems; and countless depictions of violence" (Brody, 1987e). Cable movies and video rentals increase children's possible exposure to graphic, sadistic violence and tasteless, sexually explicit material.

A study conducted for the Planned Parenthood Federation of America concluded that there are 65,000 sexual references a year broadcast during prime afternoon and evening hours on the major networks. Each hour there are 9 kisses, 5 hugs, 10 sexual innuendoes, and 1 or 2 references each to sexual intercourse and "deviant" sexual practices. Comparable references to birth control, sexually transmitted diseases, and sex education are virtually nonexistent. The study estimated that Americans view almost 14,000 instances of sexual material a year in popular time slots (*New York Times,* January 27, 1988). Adolescents are more likely to understand the sexual innuendos than are preadolescents (Silverman-Watkins & Sprafkin, 1983).

Effects on Children

Television is an instrument of social learning, particularly as a provider of information (Huston, Watkins, & Kunkel, 1989). Young children, having difficulty distinguishing between fantasy and reality (Flavell, 1986), are particularly susceptible to the values, attitudes, and behaviors portrayed in the electronic media. Children as young as 14 months of age show deferred imitation of TV models, even after a 24-hour delay (Meltzoff, 1988).

It would be an oversimplification to conclude that children automatically believe everything they see and hear, or that they will imitate violent or other behaviors viewed on TV. Blaming television for children's misbehavior or underachievement is naive. Japanese adolescents watch as much TV as adolescents in the United States do, yet score higher on standardized tests. "Television is not the culprit behind low scores . . . a more likely culprit is the little time Americans give to intellectual tasks outside their classrooms" (Fischman, 1986).

Children who are already aggressive may be attracted to more violent TV programming and may behave more aggressively following such viewing (Josephson, 1987). Most children who have incorporated many of their parents' values, and who have learned how to inhibit their antisocial impulses, are not likely to blindly copy behaviors viewed on TV (Abelman, 1985). The research literature examining the effects of violent TV watching on aggressive behavior is extremely inconsistent (K. Fisher, 1983). Liebert and Sprafkin (1988) conclude, tentatively, that TV violence is one of many possible causes of aggressive behavior for some children. When all possible causes are considered, televised violence may not be one of the most influential.

Studies do suggest that children who are heavy viewers of television perform more poorly in school. Tucker (1987) interviewed 406 male teenagers about their life-style and TV viewing habits. He found that adolescents who were light viewers were "more physically fit, emotionally stable, sensitive, imaginative, outgoing, physically active, self-controlled, intelligent, moralistic, college bound, church oriented, and self-confident" than their peers who were heavy viewers (p. 415).

Light viewers also reported feeling less troubled and less frustrated and used drugs less frequently than moderate and heavy TV watchers. Preadolescents who were heavy watchers performed more poorly on a test of imaginative problem solving compared to light or moderate watching peers (Peterson, Peterson, & Carroll, 1986). This finding is consistent with observations made of preschoolers' imaginative play.

Tucker (1986) also studied the relationship between amount of TV viewing and physical fitness. He found that light viewers performed better on a wide variety of fitness measures, including push-ups, pull-ups, sit-ups and jog-walking. There was no difference between groups in weight, however. Tucker suggests that, on behalf of good physical fitness, children watch no more than one hour of TV daily.

What's a Parent to Do?

Television is here to stay. Over 99 percent of United States homes have TV sets. A majority of homes have more than one set. Most parents are probably not aware of how much time their children spend watching TV. Keeping track of viewing time is probably a good first step. If you judge that your children spend too much time viewing low-quality programming, consider setting time limits on their viewing.

Attempts to keep offensive programming off the air conflict with our free-speech tradition. Concerned parents, therefore, must monitor and guide their children's selections of TV programs. There is a considerable amount of programming, particularly on cable TV, that is just not appropriate for children (Meyer, 1989; Singer, 1989). Parents should note the ratings of movies and use them as a starting point. If the parent has not seen the movie, he or she should be guided by the rating.

When my children were of preschool age, I directed them to the higher-quality children's programs, such as "Sesame Street," "Captain Kangaroo," and "Mr. Rogers." "Sesame Street," incidentally, was intended to narrow the intellectual gap between advantaged and disadvantaged preschool children. Ironically, the show is watched more often by advantaged than disadvantaged children, perhaps widening the gap.

Families with VCRs can rent or tape quality programs of interest to children, so that when they sit down to watch, they are not limited to programs currently being broadcast. Parents can establish rules about what children can watch, when, and how much. "Together, establish some reasonable rules, such as limits on viewing time or no television until homework assignments are completed or none during meals . . . Each week, review the television listings with your children, and write down which programs each child can watch" (Brody, 1987e).

Parents can watch TV with their children, making comments, asking questions, and explaining content that may confuse children. Children can be taught to be television-literate. Dorr, Graves, and Phelps (1980) developed a curriculum to teach children how to watch television. Children are taught that what they are watching is not real. They learn that the plots are fabricated, and that the characters are actors and actresses reading scripts. The settings are constructed, children are told, and commercials are shown to make money. Children can gain insight about TV production methods by creating their own videotapes of original material.

SUMMARY

Children's achievement is highly correlated with their parents' achievement. Children raised under economically deprived conditions are at risk for low achievement and even illiteracy. It is not poverty, per se, that inhibits intellectual development but rather a lack of stimulating and meaningful parent-child interactions during infancy and toddlerhood.

Parents can encourage the development of competent behavior in children by arranging safe and interesting environments and activities. They can stimulate verbal interaction and have realistic expectations about their children's achievement. They can also practice the authoritative parenting style, offering affection and support. Ultimately, the key factor in competence is the reciprocal patterns of parent-child interaction and parental involvement in learning. Japanese mothers are excellent examples of this phenomenon.

Some parents push their young children into activities for which they are not prepared. This can discourage them, damage their self-esteem, and encourage negative attitudes about the activity or even about learning in general. Young children seem to benefit most from low-pressure, relaxed, unstructured activities.

Culturally disadvantaged children show clear gains from attending preschool programs such as Head Start. Such programs compensate for the inadequate stimulation they may receive at home. Advantaged children do not benefit academically from preschool programs, but they may benefit socially.

Many school systems are encouraging parents to become more involved in their children's schooling. Parental support of children's schooling is predictive of greater achievement and more positive attitudes toward school. Some parents feel uncomfortable in schools or believe that they do not belong there. Given the amount of time children work in and out of school, parental involvement and support can dramatically enhance their education.

The topic of early schooling is controversial. Most educators agree that 4- and 5-year-old children should not be exposed to formal education. Preschool programs should accommodate individual children's readiness to participate in particular activities. They should also provide appropriate play materials and activities that will stimulate and challenge but not overwhelm.

Through unstructured play, children gain in virtually every domain of development. Modern children play differently than children in the past. They prefer more solitary activities. Given the potential benefits of play behavior, parents should encourage children's exploration of the environment, manipulation of objects, and interactions with other children. By playing with their children in thoughtful and challenging ways, parents can encourage a wide range of useful skills. Parents can also encourage creative expression in children by reinforcing risk-taking and original behaviors.

Children spend more time watching television than in any other waking activity. Television can be a powerful instrument of social learning, and there are excellent programs available. Children who are heavy viewers may do more poorly in school and are less physically fit. Parents can limit the amount of children's viewing and help them avoid inappropriate or offensive programs. They can also establish rules about viewing and watch TV with their children, helping them put what they view into perspective.

Parenting Adolescents

OBJECTIVES

After studying chapter 11, students should be able to

1. Describe the characteristics of adolescence as a stage of development
2. Describe some stereotypes of adolescence, such as the defiant, antisocial teenager, and explain why they are false
3. List the most common causes of conflict between adolescents and their parents
4. Describe the characteristics of formal operational thought and its role in adolescent development
5. List the most common worries and concerns of adolescents
6. Describe the ways in which teenagers display their need for independence
7. Describe how parents react when their young adult children leave home to live independently
8. Evaluate the effects of part-time employment on adolescents
9. Identify the factors that promote "risk-taking" behaviors in adolescents
10. Describe what parents and educational institutions can do to discourage adolescent pregnancy
11. Discuss the issues that surround teenage pregnancy, the availability of birth control devices, and abortion
12. Describe how parents can address the topic of sexuality with their children
13. Identify the factors that promote drug abuse in teenagers
14. Describe personal and family factors that are associated with adolescent suicide

INTRODUCTION

Sitting uneasily before me was Kenny, a bright, 16-year-old eleventh grader. His mother, Annie, was telling me that her relationship with her husband was being destroyed by their problems with Kenny. Kenny's father, Steve, no longer wanted Kenny in his house. He rarely spoke to him unless to criticize or argue.

Kenny's parents voiced the following complaints: He drove his parents' car without their permission. He had 11 cavities because of his candy-laden diet. He was extremely uncooperative. He never washed or put away his dirty clothes. He left his schoolbooks on the kitchen table despite his parents' repeated protests. He occasionally missed school because he woke up too late for the bus. He performed poorly in school. He talked back to his parents, cursed in their presence, and even had fist fights with his father. As a result, Kenny was not allowed to use the family car, his television, or the family phone. These punishments, in turn, enraged Kenny, and he responded with greater defiance.

Kenny's father, Steve, admitted that he did not handle Kenny's defiance well. He claimed that he "goes crazy" when Kenny provokes him, and that he often hated his son. He yearned to have Kenny move out. He also reported feeling guilty about their terrible relationship. He was now struggling to show good faith and hoped they could learn to get along. He also felt that his wife was too sympathetic to Kenny. His own "strategy," he realized, was to hurt Kenny as much as Kenny was hurting him. Ironically, Kenny felt that his father was a "good guy" but unable to overcome their years of perpetual antagonism.

Annie agreed that Kenny was trying harder than her husband to improve their relationship. With tears streaming down her face, she told me that she was being torn apart by their endless displays of hostility toward each other. Steve, in his own frustration, was doing very little to improve what was certainly his own greatest personal failure. Kenny's behavior was certainly "obnoxious," but not that unusual for someone his age. I was sure that this bit of information would not help Steve be more patient with his son.

Kenny and his father were caught in an escalating, sometimes violent, pattern of mutual distrust and animosity. They had reached a point where they could barely communicate with each other. Fortunately, in most families with adolescents, parent-adolescent conflict does not reach this level of intensity.

In this chapter, we address the fascinating challenge of parenting adolescents. We will emphasize the family environment as the primary social context for adolescent growth and maturation. We will also consider some of the potential hazards of adolescence, including unwanted pregnancy, drug abuse, impulsive risk taking, and suicide.

ADOLESCENCE AS A STAGE

Study Question   What is adolescence?

Prior to the late nineteenth century, those whom we today call adolescents were considered adults. Adolescence as a sheltered phase of development had not yet been "invented." Today, we view adolescence not only as a period of transition between childhood and adulthood but also as a stage of development that is important in its own right. We consider teenagers too old to be treated like younger children, but too young to be given full adult responsibilities.

Adolescence has been stereotyped as a time of stress and emotional turmoil. Freud, Erikson, and other theorists in the psychiatric tradition assumed that intense emotional reactions and maladjustment are inevitable (and therefore normal) during adolescence. The emotional strains we commonly observe in families with adolescents presumably reflect the challenges of the teenage years: becoming less dependent on one's parents, establishing one's personal identity, and, ultimately, trying to separate from one's family (Powers, Hauser, & Kilner, 1989).

Research has not supported the stereotype of adolescents as maladjusted and unpredictable. Individual adolescents respond to the challenges of this stage in extremely varied ways. "Changes that may challenge and stimulate some young people can become overwhelming and stressful to others. The outcome seems to depend on prior strengths and vulnerabilities—both of the individual adolescents and their families—as well as on the pattern, timing and intensity of changes" (Peterson, 1987, p. 32).

If there is any one theme that does run through this special stage of development, it is adjustment to change. Adolescence is a period of remarkable change, with relatively rapid physical growth, unparalleled sexual development, a substantial broadening of the social network, and the expansion of cognitive abilities (Pestrak & Martin, 1985). Adolescents must adjust to the increasing responsibilities and challenges of school and family life, including rising parental expectations. They begin to make decisions that could have life-long consequences.

Study Question   What special challenges confront parents of adolescent children?

Parents naturally become concerned when their children's physical and sexual maturity precedes the development of corresponding cognitive, judgmental, and emotional resources (Hamburg & Takanishi, 1989). It would be a mistake, however, to assume that today's adolescents experience severe identity crises or perpetual emotional distress. Parents should take comfort in knowing that the "vast majority of these teenagers function well, enjoy good relationships with their families and friends, and accept the values of the larger society" (Offer, 1987). Changes that occur in adolescents and their parents may temporarily destabilize families, but this is "natural, expected and healthy" (Steinberg, 1987b, p. 77).

Raising adolescents evokes a variety of strong emotions in parents. Baldwin (1986) describes the following: (1) *fear* about what the secretive child will do next; (2) a deep sense of *helplessness* when their teens are in emotional turmoil but refuse their parents' offers of help or comfort; (3) high levels of *frustration and anger* when adolescents confront their parents verbally, and when they violate rules and test limits; (4) *awareness of loss* as the adolescent withdraws from the family and the parents recognize that their teenage children will eventually leave the family unit; and (5) *personal hurt and rejection* when teens do not show appreciation and gratitude for the parents' support.

Erikson (1968) viewed this stage of life as a time when adolescents search for a personal identity. Parents are well aware of adolescents' attempts to assert or even demand their independence of parental authority. Today's adolescents are pressured to grow up quickly and to emulate adult values and practices. Some compromise their health and safety in doing so. Middle and late adolescents (and many young adults) also confront the major developmental task of separating from their parents, a particularly difficult task for females (Frank, Avery, & Laman, 1988).

FAMILY RELATIONSHIPS AND CONFLICT

Communication between parents and young adolescents may become increasingly strained. Parents come to expect more "adultlike" behavior, and adolescents begin to question parental authority. Adolescent strivings for autonomy sometimes clash with parental attempts to regulate their behavior. This may set the stage for intergenerational conflict and occasional heated confrontation, as between Kenny and his father.

Before industrialization, many children were sent away from their families at the onset of puberty to work and live under the authority of adults who were not their parents. (Steve's wanting Kenny out of the house reminded me of this tradition.) "Placing out," as this practice is called, still exists in many nonindustrialized societies. It also resembles emigration patterns observed in other primates, such as monkeys and apes. In primate communities, male and female "adolescents" leave their natal group and seek mates elsewhere. In primates, this practice improves reproductive fitness by minimizing inbreeding and promoting genetic diversity (Steinberg, 1987a).

Steinberg suggests that conflict between parents and teens "may be a vestige of our evolutionary past, when prolonged proximity between parent and offspring threatened the species' genetic integrity" (p. 38). Many studies have confirmed that the onset of puberty is correlated with strained family relationships, particularly between adolescents and their mothers. Perhaps this is because mothers usually play a greater role in socialization. Adolescents with personal problems are more likely to seek assistance and comfort from mothers than from fathers. Given that mothers are usually more sympathetic and nurturant than fathers, it is not surprising that adolescents also report feeling closer to their mothers (LeCroy, 1988).

Although biology may play a role in family conflict, adolescents and their parents also have differing views about what constitutes acceptable behavior. Smetana (1989a) refers to adolescents' "minor but persistent conflict with parents over the everyday details of family life" (p. 1052).These include "doing the chores, getting along with others, regulating activities and interpersonal relationships, appearances, and doing homework" (p. 1063). Other common issues in parent-adolescent conflict include possessions, family obligations, use of time, emotional support, dating, and ideology (J. A. Hall, 1987; Hill & Holmbeck, 1987).

Conflict is most likely to occur when adolescents are noncompliant or violate their parents' expectations about behavior. Teenagers believe that they should have the right to privacy and the right to reach their own decisions about personal matters. Parents might agree, but differ on which decisions are considered personal. The larger conflict is between the adolescent's desire for personal autonomy versus the parents' intention to maintain their authority and an orderly family system. The important point is that adolescents view family conflicts differently than do their parents (Smetana, 1989a).

Over the course of adolescence, parents gradually relinquish control over their children's behavior. Male and female adolescents adopt different conflict-resolution strategies. Males are generally more controlling, especially with their mothers. Both sexes prefer to negotiate with their mothers rather than with their fathers. In the process, they develop a more diverse "arsenal of strategies" to use with mothers (White, Pearson, & Flint, 1989). Negotiation replaces confrontation as adolescents and parents become more sensitive to each other's points of view. Toward the end of this stage, parents and children are more likely to treat each other as equals.

Parents (particularly mothers) of adolescents report "lower levels of life satisfaction, less marital happiness and more general distress than parents of younger children" (Steinberg, 1987a, p. 36). Silverberg and Steinberg (1987) found that parental sense of well-being is related to the degree of emotional independence displayed by their same-sexed adolescent children. Not surprisingly, mothers report greater peace of mind when they get along well with their teenage children.

Families with poor communication and poor conflict-resolution skills experience more intense parent-adolescent conflict. They encounter more physical and verbal aggression and have adolescents who are at greater risk for drug abuse, running away, school failure and delinquency (J. A. Hall, 1987). Families that can provide mutual support and a sense of belonging on the one hand, while allowing increasing autonomy on the other, have the fewest intergenerational conflicts.

Parents are more likely to indulge inappropriate or annoying behavior in preschoolers, because young children are perceived as being relatively helpless and naive. In the process of asserting their independence, adolescents act defiantly in ways that parents find difficult to overlook. Some parents, like Kenny's father, are too easily provoked into verbal confrontations. One of the "secrets" of parenting adolescents is overlooking as much obnoxious behavior as possible. It's not easy, but criticism, sarcasm, and conflict almost never improve family relationships.

Newman (1985) suggests that parents and teachers find adolescents exasperating because adults lack awareness of the "incompetencies of adolescents that lead to their obnoxious behavior" (p. 635). We think they should know better, but they really don't! Some adults expect adolescents to be defiant and hostile, and perhaps overreact to mild provocations (J. A. Hall, 1987). Stefanko (1987) contends that parents and adolescents see each other stereotypically. Both groups expect to be viewed in a distorted way by members of the other group.

Research, however, does not confirm negative, stereotypical characterizations of adolescents (Adelson, 1980). Preadolescents (Thompson, 1985) and teenagers generally accept and agree with their parents' values. They are also quite similar to their parents in other ways. "Taken as a whole, adolescents are *not* in turmoil, *not* deeply disturbed, *not* at the mercy of their impulses, *not* resistant to parental values, *not* politically active, and *not* rebellious" (Adelson, 1979, p. 37).

Youniss and Ketterlinus (1987) asked ninth and eleventh graders how well their parents knew them and how much they cared about what their parents thought about them. Sons and daughters felt their mothers knew them fairly well. Daughters believed their fathers did not know them so well. Sons and daughters expressed concern about what both parents thought of them.

Puberty and Family Relationships

Study Question Does the onset of puberty change the way children relate to their parents?

Steinberg (1987c) investigated the relationship between the onset of puberty and family relations. He studied 204 families with a firstborn child between the ages of 10 and 15 years. He found that the onset of puberty is associated with increased emotional distance between parents and children, but also greater adolescent autonomy (particularly for late maturers).

The onset of puberty, according to the study, is accompanied by increased adolescent-mother conflict, though the pattern differs for boys and girls. Early-maturing boys have increased conflict with their mothers, compared to later-maturing boys. For girls, the increase in conflict is not related to the timing of puberty. Steinberg suggests that adolescent-mother conflict may be more likely when puberty occurs before a certain chronological age. Since girls mature, on the average, about two years before boys, their "on-time" maturation may be early enough to provoke mother-daughter conflict.

An equivalent increase in conflict with fathers was not found. Steinberg suggests four possible reasons: (1) mothers are perceived as having a lower status than fathers; (2) adolescents have a greater need to separate from the mother; (3) mothers are more active in disciplining their children; and (4) the emotional quality of adolescents' relationships with their mothers may be stronger than with their fathers. Overall, there are surprisingly few differences between male and female adolescents in their family interaction patterns (Steinberg, 1987d).

Steinberg (1988a) longitudinally studied 157 male and female firstborn adolescents and their parents. He confirmed that biological maturation increased adolescent autonomy but also increased conflict between parents and children and reduced parent-child closeness. Maturation thus accelerates the development of autonomy in adolescents. Perhaps this occurs by increasing parent-child distance and encouraging parent-child conflict. Studies suggest that less mature, and therefore younger, teens experience greater friction with their parents than more mature teenagers.

In late adolescence and young adulthood, males and females differ in the way they relate to their parents. There is evidence that males move in the direction of greater autonomy, or increased separateness, from their parents. Females maintain high levels of "connectedness" with their parents, particularly with their mothers (Frank, Avery, & Laman, 1988). "As adults, women develop a greater capacity for closeness and empathy than men, but they also remain more entangled in and preoccupied with their family relationships. In particular, the mother-daughter relationship continues to be especially close, but the daughter's unresolved, ambivalent struggle for greater separateness often tinges this relationship with strong emotional conflict" (p. 730). Intimacy with fathers may be a better predictor of adolescent adjustment than intimacy with mothers (LeCroy, 1988).

Peer Group Influence and Support

Healthy families support their adolescents' striving for autonomy rather than resist or discourage it. The peer group provides one of the best opportunities for "distancing" from the family. Peer groups give adolescents the opportunity to learn how to participate in adult-like relationships. Peer relationships also give parents the opportunity to observe their children's social behaviors outside of the family.

Gold and Yanof (1985) found that girls who have positive relationships with their mothers emulate their mothers' relationship skills in their close peer relationships. Girls who identified their mothers' parenting style as democratic reported greater mutual influence in their friendships.

Not surprisingly, the influence of peers on adolescents can be positive or negative. When family ties are strained, adolescents become more susceptible to peer pressure and perhaps at greater risk for peer-related adjustment problems. Hunter (1985) found that peers are often better listeners than parents. As they get older, adolescents are more likely to discuss personal issues with friends than with parents.

While adolescents are more likely to discuss their current problems with their same-sexed friends, they are more likely to discuss decisions about education, vocation, money, and marriage with their parents (Wilks, 1986). "Adolescents will seek their parents' advice and opinions for longer-term, important, and difficult decisions, whereas friends' opinions and feelings will be more important for decisions in short-term, less important, and less difficult areas" (p. 333).

COGNITIVE DEVELOPMENT

Study Question *Do changes in adolescents' thinking abilities alter their views of their families and themselves?*

Piaget labeled the fourth and final stage of cognitive development "formal operations." Formal operational thought (see chapter 2) is usually achieved by the age of 15 years by those who have appropriate educational experiences. Formal operational thought allows adolescents to think logically about abstract and hypothetical situations. It is the type of thinking that is necessary for complex problem solving and planning for the future. It also enables adolescents to think more realistically about family issues and other family members.

Although adolescents have a better grasp of "how the world works" than younger children, their thought remains egocentric (self-centered). Adolescent egocentrism is different from that of younger children. It is characterized by idealism, skepticism about society's rules, exaggerated self-consciousness, and believing that their experiences and insights are unique. Many adolescents construct an "imaginary audience" that they believe to be as preoccupied with their appearance and behavior as they are themselves. They may also create "personal fables," elaborate fantasies in which they star (Elkind, 1978). These changes in how adolescents view the world and themselves color almost every aspect of adolescent personality.

Smetana (1988) and others propose that such cognitive changes underlie the family tensions in households with adolescent children. Adolescents come to view adult authority and their own roles and responsibilities in a new light. Their skepticism about rules and their ability to challenge adult authority make many parents uncomfortable. Conflict becomes less likely if parents respond sensitively to adolescents' challenges rather than viewing them simply as "rebelliousness."

Researchers have questioned whether the cognitive stage of formal operations, as described by Piaget, can be used to explain other normative aspects of adolescents' personalities

(Blasi & Hoeffel, 1974; Buis & Thompson, 1989). One important line of evidence points to large numbers of normal adolescents and even young adults who show the characteristic changes associated with adolescence, but who have not achieved formal operational thought.

ADJUSTMENT

Study Question   What are some common adjustment problems of adolescence?

Most adolescents appear to adjust well to the changes we have been describing, particularly if their family relationships are supportive (Powers, Hauser, & Kilner, 1989). Researchers have generally found positive changes in self-concept, self-esteem, and everyday functioning during the transition from childhood to adolescence (Nottelmann, 1987).

Although a child's transition to adolescence usually increases family tensions, most families cope well. Hill (1985) suggests that families are able to adapt because the gradual nature of adolescent development gives parents time to adjust their rearing strategies. As adolescents become more sophisticated, both parents and children learn how to avoid unnecessary confrontations.

The most common adjustment problems for adolescents involve temporary worries and anxieties about their handling of awkward situations, occasional mild depression, and loneliness. Williams and Campbell (1985) asked over 700 12-year-olds and their parents to complete questionnaires regarding their attitudes about the coming teenage years. The children were concerned about social relationships, their physical appearance, and their desire to achieve independence. Their parents worried about parent-child communication and peer pressure.

About 20 percent of all adolescent high school students are in need of mental health care (Offer, 1985; 1987). Boys reveal their adjustment difficulties "through external behavior, such as being rebellious and disobedient, whereas girls [are] more likely to show internal behavior, such as having depressed moods" (Peterson, 1987, p. 33). Adolescent girls report feeling more attached to their family and friends than do boys, but boys are more confident in their ability to cope (Offer, 1985).

Normal adolescent moodiness should not be mistaken for severe depression. Even drastic mood swings seem to be a normal part of adolescent life. Adolescents whose moods change the most report being as happy, as in control, and as well-adjusted, as their less moody peers (Csikszentmihalyi & Larson, 1984). Not all instances of adolescent depression are temporary and benign, however, particularly for adolescents with low self-esteem whose parents are critical and rejecting (Robertson & Simons, 1989).

Some adolescents experience a temporary reappearance of the anxiety-related problems they had as young children, particularly during times of stress. These include nail-biting, bruxism (tooth grinding), and bed-wetting. "The mood swings and testiness often lead to family arguments and rebellion at school. One critical battle . . . occurs at home. Adolescents want more of a say in decisions that affect them and the family, yet may not know how to express that adult need in an adult manner. They may ask to come home at 2 A.M. on a school night, or mention that they admire another teenager's shaved head. Parents, who expect power struggles at this time, often react poorly" (Kutner, 1988s).

Investigators are studying whether adolescents are particularly vulnerable to cumulative major life transitions. This is likely to be true during early adolescence when children experience the complex changes and increased autonomy associated with puberty. Many begin dating, and some move from elementary schools to much larger, and more impersonal,

"In some ways I can't imagine the children not being here—in this house. It will seem like a totally useless place, except for them to come back to" (mother, quoted by Galinsky [1981, p. 286]). If we review the reasons we desire children (see chapter 1), it is not surprising that many parents dread the day their youngest child departs to live elsewhere.

I am not immune to these feelings. A major part of my identity is "father of two sons." I do not look forward to the time that I will have to redefine my identity as "father of two grown sons who live elsewhere." As I write, my older son has been at sleep-away camp for two weeks. (Sleep-away camps help parents build up empty-nest antibodies by providing an opportunity to adjust to relatively short-term separations.) My younger son is on his way home from day camp. I miss them, but I'm comforted by the knowledge that in about 45 minutes, my younger son will ask, "Can we have a catch?" I am comforted when I know that there is a son, a faithful companion, in the next room, waiting to spring into action.

Of course, there are moments when I feel they cannot leave soon enough. Like many parents, I am ambivalent about the profound, and probably inevitable, changes that will occur in my family when my children are grown. I understand that at some future time, my children will probably not live at home. Separating from one's parents and from one's children is normal and healthy. It is also a bit scary. I must reassure myself that the so-called empty nest will give me a freer life-style, fewer responsibilities, and more time (and money) to spend with my wife. Studies confirm that most parents, particularly mothers, respond to the empty nest with relief, not depression (e.g., Rubin, 1979). But who will laugh at my stupid jokes or tell me theirs? I guess that is why they invented grandchildren.

Parents who have careers, hobbies, and interests other than caretaking are in the best position to adjust to the empty nest. Women who have devoted their adult lives to child care are the most vulnerable to depression when their children leave (Powell, 1977). "What have their years of motherhood prepared them for? To start back at the beginning of the career ladder? That can be a painful thought, especially when their friends (men and women) who have stayed in the job market are rungs ahead, seemingly reaching the pinnacle of success" (Galinsky, 1981, p. 291).

Return to the Nest

In the past, most children, particularly daughters, lived at home until they married. Families today still discourage their daughters' premarital independence, at least compared to sons'. Nevertheless, delaying marriage to pursue educational and other goals has increased the tendency for young adults to live away from home before marriage (Goldscheider & Goldscheider, 1989). These researchers had previously found that most adolescents expect to live independently before marriage, and most of their parents agree. The average age of first marriage for men is now 26, and for women is 24, higher for both sexes than it's been for almost a century (A. L. Cowan, 1989).

This delay in marriage, together with high divorce rates and the high cost of housing, has led to the "return to the nest" phenomenon. About half of single men in their early twenties and about one-third of single women this age live with their parents. Ironically, adult children of affluent parents are more likely to return home, not being able to duplicate their parents' living standards. Very few parents expect their children to pay for their room and board. Parents vary in their response to returning adult children, but most encourage their children to become more independent (Cowan, 1989). Me, I'm going to go have a catch, while I still can.

junior high schools. Some children also have to endure their parents' marital conflicts or moving to a different residence.

Young adolescents (particularly girls) who are coping with one life transition find it difficult to cope with simultaneous stresses. Most children benefit from more gradual change and from having positive life changes that balance the stressors (Simmons, Burgeson, & Carlton-Ford, 1987). Girls cope better with stress when they simultaneously experience enjoyable life events that balance the negative stressors (Cohen, Burt, & Bjorck, 1987).

PREPARING FOR INDEPENDENCE

Viewing adolescence as a transition stage between childhood and adulthood helps us appreciate the importance of preparing adolescents for their inevitable separation from their parents and family. Living on one's own successfully requires a number of decision-making, self-help, and problem-solving skills that can best be learned while adolescents still live at home. "The expression of independence is more readily observed among the male children, who say they are more likely to make decisions on their own. This is also recognized by the children as being modeled more clearly among their fathers than among their mothers. At the same time, the achievement of new levels of independence at age 17 is accompanied by feelings of loss of parental closeness and understanding by the children and a decline in satisfaction with the parental role for the parents . . . Daughters and mothers seem to have an easier time preserving closeness during this period because they value it in relationships and they involve each other in decision making more than do fathers and sons" (Newman, 1989, pp. 922–923).

Striving for autonomy is *not* a process of detachment from one's parents; rather, it is a new step in the attachment process. Adolescents who are securely attached to their parents can usually expect them to be emotionally accepting and supportive of their quest for independence (Ryan & Lynch, 1989).

It may be difficult for some parents to encourage greater independence in older adolescents, partially because of the parent's mixed feelings about separation. So much of our lives revolves around our children that some parents fear reaching the stage when we are no longer needed. We become accustomed to our children's dependency on us, and we find ourselves reluctant to play a less important role in their lives (see Spotlight: Empty Nests That Do Not Always Remain Empty).

Nevertheless, children benefit when parents define the responsibilities they will keep and those they will delegate. It is destructive of an adolescent's self-concept and self-esteem when overprotective parents encourage their children's dependence through the adolescent years. "One goal of being an effective parent is to teach your child not to need you" (Kutner, 1987a).

OLDER ADOLESCENTS' GOALS AND VALUES

Study Question Do today's adolescents have different goals and values than adolescents of the 1960s?

Adolescent subcultures, with distinctive values, behaviors, and preferences, emerged in the 1950s, both influenced by and reflected in the popular music, movies, language, and dress of that time. The major themes of teenage subculture were alienation and rebelliousness. In the 1960s, these themes persisted but broadened into more general and more intense social criticism and conflict.

Today, "youth culture" is big business, yet so diverse it is difficult to describe. Teenagers from urban, rural, and suburban communities are more different from each other than they are from their parents. The adolescents of the 1950s and 1960s have become the parents of

Bachman (1987) reported that three-quarters of the high school seniors surveyed had part-time jobs, worked an average of 16 to 20 hours a week, and earned more than $200 a month. Most of those interviewed did not find the work challenging, and almost half said that it interfered with their social lives. Only a quarter said that work interfered with their school work or family lives.

Most spent their money on such "teen luxuries" as stereos, records, cars, and clothes, which Bachman views as poor preparation for adult financial responsibility. Greenberger and Steinberg (1986) contend that many teens spend as fast as they earn, sometimes buying drugs or gambling, and their schoolwork and school attendance suffer from their part-time jobs. Gottfredson (cited in Walton, 1984) reported that teenagers with jobs were not less committed to school or their families, and that senior high boys who worked showed less dependency on their parents.

The "work-and-spend" ethic is very common today in adolescents. They are more materialistic than their predecessors and find that their parents are unwilling to supply them with the money they feel they need to purchase clothes and records and to attend movies and other forms of entertainment. Bachman reported that only 5 percent of students who work contribute most of their income to their families.

Greenberger and Steinberg (1986) report that fewer than 20 percent of teenagers who work attempt to save more than a few dollars from their paycheck. Many teens who work in clothing and music stores spend a substantial part of their paycheck where they work. Teenage jobs tend to be routine, nonchallenging activities that provide minimum opportunity to learn or practice cognitive skills.

Parents and researchers are concerned about the effects of part-time employment on high school students. They wonder whether adolescents benefit from their financial independence through enhanced self-esteem and financial responsibility or whether their schoolwork is suffering and they are not spending enough time with their families and

For most adolescents, part-time jobs represent a trade-off between greater financial independence and less time for school and friends.

friends. Steinberg contends that work experience helps children become more responsible. He suggests, however, that parents set limits on their children's spending and encourage enforced savings. Parents can also help their children select part-time work that is relevant to their career goals or that benefits society.

For most adolescents, part-time work is a mixed blessing. Part-time work decreases adolescents' dependence on their parents and enhances their self-esteem. On the other hand, it reduces the amount of time available for studying, spending time with their peers, and being involved in extracurricular activities at school. If adolescents spend as quickly as they earn, are they not mirroring the conspicuous consumption of their parents and society?

the 1980s and 1990s. Much of what was considered "underground" or counterculture back then has become mainstream. Many children of the sixties, now the parents of the nineties, complain about the materialism and "yuppiness" of their children, an interesting parent-child role reversal from the past. Today's adolescents seem to be much more accepting of their parents than were those of 20 years ago.

The stereotype of the defiant, antisocial teenager has not been supported by research. Offer (1985) interviewed large numbers of adolescents. He found that normal adolescents (80% of the total) "did not perceive any major problems between themselves and their parents. They did not present any evidence of major intergenerational conflict. The generation gap so often written about was not in evidence among the vast majority of subjects we studied" (p. 36).

A national study of 300 teenagers in 1983 found that teenage children's values are much more influenced by their parents' values than by their peers' (Ianni, cited in Collins, 1984d). Adolescents do depend upon their peers for support, and youth culture does influence their attitudes. However, there is greater consistency in attitudes between parents and children than between teenagers and their peers.

A nationwide survey of thousands of high school seniors (Johnston, Bachman, & O'Malley, 1985) found that the vast majority expect to marry and have children. There is increasing acceptance of working mothers and wives, but today's teens don't feel mothers of young children should work full time. Fewer of today's teenagers approve of the use of drugs, and most believe their personal values are similar to their parent's.

RISK-TAKING BEHAVIOR

Study Question In what ways are adolescents particularly vulnerable to life-threatening activities?

Many of the parents of adolescents I know keep their fingers crossed. They hope that their children won't follow in their collective footsteps in the kinds of risk-taking behaviors that became part of adolescent subculture in the 1960s. At the same time that they are thinking, "I hope my children won't do what I did," they may also think "but I'm glad I had the experience." Do we detect a double standard?

Under the guise of social protest or spiritual liberation, the counterculture of the 1960s advocated a hedonistic philosophy revolving around "drugs, sex, and rock 'n' roll." For the last 25 years, adolescents have had to make hard choices about whether to experiment with the legal and illegal drugs that are so prevalent in our society. At the same time, they have had to balance their strong sexual drive against the constraints placed on their sexual activity by the possibility of sexually transmitted diseases and the risk of pregnancy. They must make these difficult decisions at a time when their judgment is someplace between that of a child's and that of an adult's.

Psychologists have come to refer to such behaviors as "risk taking." These are potentially self-destructive behaviors that violate society's conventions and good judgment. In addition to the use of drugs, risk-taking behaviors include unsafe sexual practices, reckless use of vehicles and weapons, suicide, and violent behavior (Landers, 1988g).

"From acrobatics on skateboards to sex without contraceptives, teenagers are notoriously reckless. Research suggests a combination of hormonal factors, an inability to perceive risks accurately and the need to impress peers helps explain all this. All of these influences seem to peak in the years between 10 and the mid-20s" (Goleman, 1987g). Some risk-taking behavior can have life-threatening consequences. "Delayed consequences include cancer and cardiovascular disease in adult life, illnesses that are made more likely by high-calorie, high-fat dietary patterns, inadequate exercise, heavy smoking or alcohol use" (Hamburg & Takanishi, 1989, p. 826).

Many adolescents are prone to risk-taking, self-destructive behaviors.

Diana Baumrind (cited by Goleman, 1987g) contends that many of the characteristics associated with risk-proneness are actually normal, even healthy, factors in adolescent development. She distinguishes between growth-enhancing risk taking, which is desirable, and health-compromising risk taking, which is not. Baumrind suggests that prevention efforts should be aimed at problem drinking, a precursor for many other self-destructive acts.

As Baumrind notes, growth-enhancing risk taking is one way in which teens assert their independence. Unfortunately, they have not yet achieved a level of cognitive development that allows an accurate assessment of the risk involved. ". . . By age 10 or so, they enter a risky period when they do lots of exploring at a time when their cognitive development has not yet reached the point where they can make judgments that will keep them out of trouble. They cannot really comprehend laws of probability.

And they also have ideas of invulnerability that persuade them that they can safely take a known risk" (Hamburg, quoted in Goleman, 1987g).

Nancy Adler, a health psychologist in California studied girls 11 to 14 years old attending inner-city schools in San Francisco and developed a profile of "bad" girls. "She found that such girls had already started smoking and experimenting with drugs and were exposed to other risks—such as riding in cars going too fast—far more than other girls their age. Other risks . . . included drinking, fighting, hitchhiking, arguing with strangers, seeking entertainment in high-crime areas and carrying a knife [and their intention] to become sexually active in the next year" (Goleman, 1987g).

Common risk-taking activities in "macho" boys were "drinking, smoking cigarettes and marijuana, riding on motorcycles and getting knocked unconscious." Researchers hope that teenagers can learn to recognize actual risks and feel confident enough to say "no" when confronted with a foolish challenge. Health education should include efforts to help adolescents recognize and avoid dangerous situations. Parental supervision is a necessity for many young adolescents.

ADOLESCENT SEXUALITY

Sexual prohibitions have gradually weakened in our society over the course of this century, largely due to the availability of safe and effective birth control technologies. We still confront serious problems, including sexually transmitted diseases, such as AIDS, and adolescent pregnancies. Healthier attitudes about sexuality have been evolving, fostered by an increase in sexual knowledge, though not necessarily among adolescents.

Research confirms that girls are more sexually conservative than boys, less sexually impulsive, and more relationship-oriented. This should not be interpreted to mean that females have a weaker sex drive than males, or that

Adolescent pregnancies are occurring at epidemic proportions in the United States.

social and cultural factors play minimal roles in discouraging female sexual expression. Children, particularly daughters, in families with parental supervision, good communication, and close relationships usually become sexually active later than children in troubled families (Jessor & Jessor, 1977). Family stability, economic security, religious affiliation, and sex education predict sexually responsible behavior (Forste & Heaton, 1988).

Adolescent Sexual Activity and Pregnancy

Study Question Given the tragic consequences of adolescent pregnancy out of wedlock, why do so many teens avoid using contraceptives during sexual intercourse?

About half of United States adolescents are sexually experienced by age 19, with age of first intercourse averaging about 16 years. About half of those who are sexually active do not use contraceptives (Faulkenberry, Vincent, James, & Johnson, 1987; Lewin, 1988c). As a result, adolescent pregnancy is occurring at epidemic proportions.

Each year, over one million teenage girls become pregnant. About half a million continue their pregnancies to birth, and about half have abortions (*New York Times,* February 20, 1986). Recent Supreme Court decisions are likely to make it more difficult for adolescent girls, and all women, to have abortion on demand. Only 4 percent of unwed teenage mothers give up their infants for adoption (*New York Times,* July 16, 1989). Teens in the United States are not more sexually active than those in western Europe, yet the incidence of adolescent pregnancy is much higher in this country. The major reason is poor contraceptive use (Brooks-Gunn & Furstenberg, 1989).

The 385,000 children born to adolescent mothers in 1985 will receive at least $6 billion in welfare benefits over a 20-year period. In 1984, the federal government spent $16.5 billion in welfare costs to support families started by teenage mothers. This figure does not include such services as housing, special education, child protection, foster care, day care, and other social services (*New York Times,* February 20, 1986). This enormous financial expenditure is but one of many costs to society for careless sexual behavior.

Adolescent pregnancies are considered high-risk for both the mother and child. Children born to adolescents typically have lower birth weights. They are more likely to suffer from a variety of neurological problems. They are more susceptible to childhood illnesses, largely due to the poor prenatal care received by their mothers. These children may have lower IQs than those born to older mothers and are at greater risk for child abuse (Stark, 1986).

Children, particularly boys, born to teenage mothers show cognitive and psychosocial deficits that predict later academic and social problems (Furstenberg, Brooks-Gunn, & Chase-Lansdale, 1989). Given that adolescent pregnancy precipitates a crisis in most families, professional intervention should be considered (Baptiste, 1986; Black & DeBlassie, 1985).

Why do so many teenage girls keep their babies rather than give them up for adoption? Many feel it is their responsibility, having conceived and born an infant, to raise it. Girls' families typically oppose adoption as an alternative. The status of "unwed mother" has also become more acceptable over time (Folkenberg, 1985).

Half of all black adolescent females conceive before marriage (Conger, 1988; Hayes, 1987) and most opt to keep their babies. Perhaps they understand the difficulty in finding homes for minority infants and fear that their infants would otherwise be placed in orphanages or institutions. Many of their families are tolerant of early sexual behavior and pregnancy (Stark, 1986).

Teenage girls are not aware of how drastically pregnancy and, particularly, motherhood will change their lives. Adolescent mothers are twice as likely to drop out of school and to become economically dependent on welfare. Lacking high school diplomas and job skills, they are likely to raise their child or children in poverty. One 18-year-old mother said, referring to pregnant adolescents, "I go to school, take care of my baby and go to sleep. If they understand that there is no time for parties or even going to a shopping mall, it might help them" (J. F. Sullivan, 1987).

Adolescent mothers usually are caring, but not very competent, as parents (Garcia Coll, Hoffman, & Oh, 1987; Reis & Herz, 1987; but also see Buchholz & Gol, 1986). Parenting education programs and enrichment programs like Head Start have been successful in improving both teenagers' parenting practices and their children's development. Child care that allows parents to complete their education and then job training benefit these young parents and their children (Furstenberg, Brooks-Gunn, & Chase-Lansdale, 1989).

Given the serious and often tragic consequences of adolescent pregnancy, it is preferable that such pregnancies be prevented. Teenage girls underestimate their fertility and, like teenage boys, are poorly informed about conception and the timing of intercourse. They also highly value spontaneity rather than preparation in sexual activity (Stark, 1986). Pregnant teens often report that they did not think they could get pregnant.

Many adolescents apparently have sex to satisfy emotional needs that are essentially nonsexual. "Adolescents have sex when, in fact, they primarily want and need something else, such as affection, to ease loneliness, to confirm masculinity or femininity, to bolster self-esteem, to express anger or escape from boredom. In short, during adolescence, sex becomes a coping mechanism to express and satisfy nonsexual needs" (Hajcak & Garwood, 1988, p. 755).

Some want to become pregnant. "For those who feel isolated, the prospect of a baby offers the possibility of someone to love. Pregnancy also brings attention to a girl who may be feeling neglected. The ploy of entrapping a reluctant suitor may motivate some teenagers. Others may see pregnancy as a way to assert their independence from their parents, to become their mothers' equal. Some may want to keep up with their pregnant girlfriends" (Stark, 1986, p. 30).

Teenage Fathers

Teenage males are often happy when their girlfriends become pregnant, even those who may have no intention of caring for the infant (Stark, 1986). It is a blow to their masculinity when, due to family pressure, their girlfriends have abortions. Contrary to the popular stereo-type of the opportunistic teenage boy looking only for sexual gratification, teenage fathers are often emotionally attached to their girlfriends and want to be involved in supporting and caring for the infant (Robinson & Barret, 1985).

They usually do not marry the mother and face contempt from her family. Their feelings and opinions are almost never considered when the infant is aborted, born, or put up for adoption. A study done by the Bank Street College of Education of 395 teenage fathers showed that 82 percent maintained daily contact with their children and 72 percent provided financial support. Fewer than 10 percent married their child's mother.

Teenage fathers often want babies as much as teenage mothers do, for many of the same reasons. A child may be the first "possession" in their young lives that seems truly theirs. "For those performing poorly in school, caring for a baby may be their first tangible accomplishment. For those reared in troubled homes, the infant may be the first human from whom they can receive love" (Robinson & Barret, 1985, p. 68). Unfortunately, like teenage mothers, they do not have realistic expectations about the cost of supporting a child. When their funds are depleted, they are likely to terminate all involvement with the infant and its mother.

Prevention of Adolescent Pregnancy

Clearly, there is a great need for accurate sex education, not the kind of sexual misinformation and casual portrayals of sex often seen on television. In this era of AIDS, experimenting with sex has become potentially life-threatening, particularly among risk-taking adolescents.

A broad-based sex-education campaign is needed. "First, we need age-appropriate, family-life education, including sex education from the early school years through adolescence for all children and adolescents. Adolescents, in particular, need the facts not only

about sexuality and parenthood, but even more important, they need help in learning to integrate this information into their thinking about themselves and their future" (Conger, 1988, p. 297).

Most parents favor "family-life" or sex education in the schools. However, a national poll revealed that almost half of the parents surveyed reported that sex education is not available in their children's schools. About half of the 15-year-old girls who are sexually active have never taken such a course, despite research evidence that such courses discourage promiscuity. Sweden, the world leader in sex education, has one of the lowest rates of unwanted pregnancy; the United States has one of the highest (Lohr, 1987).

Many sexually active teens are "contraceptive risk takers." McCormick, Izzo, and Folcik (1985) surveyed rural New York County high school students and found that more than one-fifth of the nonvirgins "relied exclusively on such ineffective contraceptives as withdrawal, trusting in luck, and douching" (p. 385). Faulkenberry and his colleagues (1987) reported that both early (16 or younger) and late (17 to 20 years old) initiators of intercourse scored very low on a test of basic reproductive knowledge. Late initiators made better use of contraception and were more committed in their relationships with their initial sex partners. Many female teens, particularly those with low self-esteem, feel pressured by peers or by their boyfriends to be sexually active. They are usually reluctant to approach parents with their concerns.

This point is confirmed by a girl who became pregnant when she was 15. When asked about what she had learned in her sex-education class, she responded, "Sex-ed didn't instill morals or give you enough reasons not to get pregnant. No one told us how much diapers, formula and food would cost. No one said people might be disappointed in us and that we might not make it to college. They talked about the pill and stuff like that. My teachers tried to teach all the right things. But there should have been more talk about love, commitment and values. I guess they figured we learned all that from our parents" (Scott, 1988).

Poverty, racism, and sexism are as important as ignorance in perpetuating teenage pregnancies (S. Gordon, 1986). Drug use also typically accompanies the early onset of adolescent sexual activity. Girls who use drugs are more likely to become pregnant than sexually active girls who don't use drugs. Ninety percent of those who become pregnant had been drinking the first time they were sexually active (Cordes, 1986).

Adolescents, Parents, and Birth Control

Study Question   Should adolescents have the right to obtain birth control devices without their parents' permission or knowledge?

The controversial topic of adolescent sexuality has given rise to many difficult questions, including whether adolescents should have rights to obtain birth control information, birth control devices, and even abortions without their parents' knowledge or consent. Some argue that parents have the right to be notified about any transaction that could affect their children's health. Others contend that adolescents should have the same rights to confidentiality that adults enjoy. If adolescents are not guaranteed confidentiality, it is maintained, they will avoid contraception but not sexual activity. This will lead to high rates of adolescent pregnancy. Those who advocate abstinence ("Just say no") are not being realistic, given current statistics.

When these matters have been litigated, courts have generally supported adolescent rights to obtain birth control and abortion without parental approval (Brozan, 1982). Nevertheless, about half the states have passed legislation requiring some notification of, or consent from, parents or a judge before a minor can obtain an abortion. These laws have been challenged by such groups as the American

Civil Liberties Union (Bishop, 1987). The Supreme Court appears to be moving in the direction of greater restrictions on abortion and adolescents' rights.

"Everyone Else is Doing It": Guidelines for Parents Teaching Sexual Responsibility

It is desirable for parents to provide sexual knowledge in an accepting and matter-of-fact way to their children. Most parents do not do so. Most children (about 60%) therefore acquire sexual information (and misinformation) from their friends (Planned Parenthood Poll, 1986). "Young people want to know about homosexuality, penis size, masturbation, female orgasm, and the answers to such questions as how can I tell if I'm really in love, what constitutes sexual desire, what is the best contraceptive, when are you most likely to get pregnant, and various questions about oral and anal sex" (S. Gordon, 1986, p. 24).

Effective sex education also includes discussions of dating and relationships, beliefs, life goals, and values (Stark, 1986). Being able to discuss sexuality with children in a matter-of-fact way (without preaching) is an important parental resource. And the earlier the better, because children are more comfortable talking to their parents about sex before they are sexually active.

"Keep in mind that children learn at least as much from context as they do from content; your child will learn and remember more from how you present things than from what you say. If you are upset and uncomfortable discussing sexual issues with your child, your child will feel uncomfortable discussing his own sexuality" (Kutner, 1988n).

Most parents have not had the benefit of sex education themselves and may be misinformed about sexual matters. Many parents (fathers give the facts-of-life talk less frequently than mothers) are uncomfortable discussing sex and will shy away from any direct dialogue about sex with their children. These parents can give their children reading materials that are appropriate for their age and perhaps volunteer to answer any questions they might have after their reading. If parents are inhibited about such matters, it is helpful for them to admit it to the child rather than try to hide it. "Children appreciate honesty and easily see through hypocrisy" (Brody, 1986b).

Giving children good information about sexuality and reproduction before they are sexually active is essential, even though they learn more about the parents' values than about sex (T. D. Fisher, 1986; Moore, Peterson, & Furstenberg, 1986). During and after puberty, adolescents have strong sexual feelings that they may not be able to manage successfully without support. Helping them see that fantasy and masturbation are satisfying, low-risk alternatives to intercourse is an example of such support. Almost all people derive gratification from genital self-stimulation. Such behavior should be viewed as normal, but private. Many boys also worry about nocturnal emissions ("wet dreams") and spontaneous erections. They can be reassured that emissions are normal and diminish with age.

"Tell the boys not to worry about penis size. You can't tell the size of the penis by observing its detumescent state. (Freud got it wrong—men are the ones with penis envy.) Reassure girls about their vaginas—one size fits all . . . Sexual orientation is not a matter of choice. It's not OK to be antigay" (S. Gordon, 1986, p. 26).

Parents should also help children view sexuality as an expression of love and as a source of pleasure within an intimate relationship. "Instead of sitting a child down for an awkward 'heart to heart' talk, it is usually easier to let conversations about sex emerge naturally from shared events, such as a movie, television program, sexy advertisement, even a pop song with sexual messages" (Brody, 1986b).

Threatening children or otherwise inducing sexual fears are self-defeating strategies that simply communicate to children that they will have to act deceptively. Brody suggests the following appeal: "We hope that you won't have sex until you are much older, but if you do, we want you to know what it's all about and especially how to avoid unwanted consequences."

Many teens who would otherwise refuse sexual advances find they lack the assertiveness skills to do so. They do not know what to say or do in the face of intense pressure from peers or boyfriends. "Teenagers should be urged to consider whether sexual intercourse is something they are ready for and want for themselves, not because their partners are pushing them into it" (Brody, 1986b). Children must learn that they can say "no" and learn how to recognize and avoid situations in which pressure might be applied to weaken their resistance.

ADOLESCENT DRUG USE

Drug abuse remains one of the most serious health problems in the United States. It is not at all surprising that adolescents are particularly susceptible. Drugs (the term includes alcohol) provide a convenient, fast, and relatively inexpensive way of altering one's mood, an appealing combination to temperamental teens.

Like cigarette smoking, drinking gives adolescents the impression that they are more adultlike. Peer pressure to consume alcohol or other drugs may be irresistible to teens who have not learned how to say no. TV advertising and movies sometimes glamorize the drug experience. Tucker (1985) investigated the relationship between the amount of TV viewing and alcohol consumption. He found that heavy TV viewers consumed alcohol significantly more often than did light and moderate viewers.

Beschner (1985) reported that in 1983, one out of every 18 high school seniors smoked marijuana daily. About 57 percent had experimented with marijuana, 27 percent had used stimulants, and 93 percent had tried alcohol.

According to the National Institute on Drug Abuse (1987), half of young adolescents regularly smoke and drink. Preteens report using drugs too. The American Council for Drug Education claims that 100,000 elementary school children report getting drunk on a weekly basis (Barron, 1988).

Adolescent drug use appears to reflect parental attitudes about illicit drug use, peer use (Klinge & Piggott, 1986), and, to a lesser extent, parental use. Parental style of discipline and closeness correlate with adolescent drug use (e.g., Coombs & Landsverk, 1988). Once teenagers begin to use drugs, parental influence lessens and peer influence increases (Halebsky, 1987). "Most use of drugs occurs as a result of social influences, whereas abuse of drugs is more strongly tied to internal, psychological processes" (Newcomb & Bentler, 1989, p. 244).

The good news that illicit drug abuse is gradually decreasing in adolescents (Landers, 1989) is countered by the bad news that alcohol use remains high. Many teenagers (and adults) do not consider alcohol a drug. They drastically underestimate its ability to impair their ability to function, particularly when they are driving (Barron, 1988). As we learn more about the debilitating effects of alcohol, we become more cautious about its availability to minors. All states now have a minimum drinking age of 21 years. Many schools have instituted alcohol-education programs. Some schools advocate total abstinence, a stronger position than that adopted by most parents.

Parents, of course, should advocate responsible use of alcohol, although it is not always easy to describe what constitutes responsible use. The need for drug education is as important as that for sex education so that children can learn how drugs affect the body and the mind and can learn to view drug use realistically.

Unfortunately, providing information to adolescents about drugs and drug abuse has not had impressive results. Adolescents like to experiment. Adolescents who have never tried cigarettes or alcohol might be considered deviant by their peers. Fortunately, most teens who occasionally use drugs do not develop drug problems (Newcomb & Bentler, 1989).

ADOLESCENT SUICIDE: A PERMANENT SOLUTION TO A TEMPORARY PROBLEM

Jody White, age 17 years, shot himself in his bedroom on May 9, 1977. "In the year before his death he had been expelled from school for lying about his participation in minor vandalism in the library and transferred to a new school; he regularly used marijuana and told his mother he needed it to concentrate on his studies; he took unreasonable risks with his motorcycle and had gone through a turbulent romance. In fact, he had told his girlfriend that unless they repaired their relationship, he would kill himself. Two and a half years earlier, in November, 1974, his father, John O'Donnell White, also killed himself at home. After several separations, the Whites had been divorced eight months earlier. Mr. White returned for one more attempt at reconciliation. When his wife refused, he kissed her goodbye and shot himself" (Brozan, 1986).

A recent survey by the U.S. Department of Health and Human Services of 11,419 eighth and tenth graders found that 42 percent of the girls and 25 percent of the boys had seriously considered ending their lives. Eighteen percent of the girls and 11 percent of the boys claimed that they had attempted suicide (Dismuke, 1988). About 14 adolescents accomplish their fatal mission each day.

The estimates for suicide attempts among people aged 15 to 24 years vary from 50,000 to 500,000 a year, and the number of successful suicides averages about 5,000 a year. This number may be an underestimate, as many suicides are not recognized as such. In the United States, almost 50,000 young people in this age range took their lives in the 1970s (*New York Times,* February 22, 1987). This is roughly the same number of United States soldiers who died in the Vietnam war.

Suicide is the third major cause of death for adolescents, after accidents and murder. "The typical adolescent suicide victim is white, male, and from the middle class. Guns are the means often used, and the most common reason is depression over the loss of loved ones or status" (Santrock & Yussen, 1984, p. 398). About 90 percent of those who attempt suicide are female (who typically try to poison themselves with prescription drugs), but 75 percent of those who succeed are male (guns are more lethal than pills). Most successful attempts at suicide are preceded by several unsuccessful attempts.

Many adolescents who attempt suicide, like Jody White, report serious family problems. These include parental divorce and conflict, poor parent-child communication (excessive criticism, arguing), unrealistic parental expectations, school pressures, and problems with peers (Neiger & Hopkins, 1988). Parental alcoholism may be a more potent factor than adolescent alcohol use (Allen, 1987). Children of parents who have committed suicide are also considered at high risk. Like Jody, they are likely to model this extreme way of coping with problems.

Personal factors associated with attempted suicide also include low self-esteem, drug use, loss of boy- or girlfriend, poor academic performance, having been sexually abused, and loss of a confidant. "When friends kill themselves on different occasions in close order, loss of a confidant may be the important factor" (Allen, 1987, p. 273). Some psychologists believe that adolescents do not fully appreciate the irreversibility of death. "They see this as an easy way out of their troubles, a way to get even with people they have a grudge with, 'I'll die and you'll be sorry' " (Eron, quoted by Barron, 1987b).

Signs of Suicide: "I Might As Well Be Dead"

It is no surprise that suicidal adolescents are usually depressed. Garfinkel (cited by Swartz, 1987) found that only 12 percent of the suicidal adolescents he studied were not depressed. Depressed behaviors, such as crying and hopelessness, and statements about wanting to die are considered "signs" of suicide, that is, "signals emitted by the person which 'telegraph' an impending act of self-destruction" (Allen, 1987).

Other signs include previous suicide attempts, drug use, recent suicide of a loved one, preoccupation with death, giving away personal belongings, changes in eating and sleeping patterns and school performance, and unusual personality changes. Families of suicidal adolescents often deny the reality of the problem, block out the threat, dissociate themselves from it, or are unsympathetic (Allen, 1987).

Jody White's mother explained that he "was screaming with problems, though he was not talking about them. His appearance was different, he stopped caring about his clothes or his hair, and he was no longer concerned about making plans for the future. He did once ask another boy what it was like to be in therapy, but he didn't want to worry me by asking me" (Brozan, 1986).

There is no simple way of protecting children from the stresses and pressures of life. We can, as parents, attempt to prepare them for life's inevitable problems by teaching them problem-solving and coping skills. Parents can also provide them with the emotional support that we all require in difficult circumstances. Most problems have several possible solutions, but these may not occur to some adolescents or younger children. Fortunately, the vast majority of adolescents have learned to deal effectively with their problems. The signs of suicide we have indicated are not subtle; parents would have to exercise extreme denial to not notice them. It happens every day.

SUMMARY

There are many stereotypes of adolescence and adolescents, but few capture the diversity we observe in children during this special stage of development. Adolescence is a time of change and, therefore, of adjustment. Some adolescents adjust better than others, and the same can be said of their parents.

Conflict between parents and teenagers is to be expected and is normal. Living with adolescent children is associated with diminished life satisfaction for middle-aged parents, particularly mothers. Families with poor communication skills are most likely to suffer through their children's changes.

As puberty takes its course, most adolescents strive to assert their independence. They attempt to establish a personal identity separate from, but consistent with, their family associations and values. They are doing so in an era in which children are pressured to grow up quickly. They are expected to take on adult responsibilities while showing good judgment and consideration of others.

Most adolescents satisfy these expectations, despite the challenges of physical growth and sexual development. With physical maturity comes the long-anticipated lessening of parental control and increased susceptibility to peer influences. The latter can be helpful or harmful. Some parents find their teenager's desire for autonomy threatening. Some do not know how to gradually lessen their involvement in their child's daily lives. Most parents are relieved when their young adult children leave home and are disappointed if they return home as dependents.

Even adolescents with good family relationships will occasionally argue with their parents over homework, schoolwork, personal grooming, family obligations, or many other issues. Parents who understand their adolescent's concerns and social deficits are more likely to be patient and caring in the face of inappropriate behavior. The more life stresses confronted at a given time by the teenager, the greater the adjustment necessary to maintain normal functioning.

There is disagreement about the value of "risk-taking" behavior in adolescents, whether such behaviors are inherently destructive or whether they are "growth enhancing." Many adolescents take risks by being sexually active and not taking proper precautions.

Over one million adolescent girls become pregnant each year, and over half eventually deliver their infants. Being unmarried, unemployed, and poor does not lead to a satisfying life-style or good parenting. Children born to adolescent mothers are at risk for a variety of problems, largely due to the immaturity of their mothers' reproductive systems and poor prenatal care.

Teenage pregnancy is usually a painful experience for the mother, the father, and their families. Parents and schools can do more to prevent irresponsible sexual behavior in teenagers. Many parents are uncomfortable discussing sexuality with their children. Even school sex-education programs fall short of providing teenagers with the information and assertiveness skills they need to make good choices.

Drug and alcohol use among adolescents is a serious health problem. Adolescent drug use appears to be associated with parental and peer attitudes about drugs and, to a lesser extent, parental drug use. While adolescents seem to be using fewer illicit drugs than in the past, alcohol use is still high.

Suicide is the third major cause of death among teenagers, after accidents and homicide. Most adolescents who attempt suicide have serious family problems, low self-esteem, and may be experiencing a crisis for which they can see no solution. Most suicidal teenagers communicate their desperation in many ways before attempting to take their lives, but they may not be heard in time.

CHAPTER TWELVE

Divorce, New Family Configurations, and Fathering

OBJECTIVES

After studying chapter 12, students should be able to

1. Discuss some of the factors that have contributed to the high divorce rate
2. Describe three common custody arrangements and their implications for children's adjustment following parental separation
3. Discuss why noncustodial fathers usually have minimal contact with their children following divorce
4. Discuss the conditions under which joint custody is most likely to be successful
5. Analyze the effects of divorce on children in general and according to a child's age
6. Describe the stages of the divorce process
7. Describe how boys and girls adjust to parental separation
8. Distinguish between how men and women view intimate relationships
9. Describe the special burdens of the single parent
10. Describe why stepfamilies are the most complex and varied family configuration
11. Describe the special problems that confront children and adults living in stepfamilies
12. Describe recent trends toward increased father involvement in child care and factors that have promoted these changes
13. Analyze the obstacles that currently discourage father involvement in child care
14. Describe some of the special concerns and fears experienced by expectant fathers
15. Compare the parenting styles of mothers and fathers regarding
    a. Division of labor
    b. Play
    c. Interaction with children
    d. Discipline

INTRODUCTION

"Being the sole custodian of my daughter, I can honestly say that I do think a custody arrangement like mine can be in the best interest of the child. For example, Laurie's (my five-year-old daughter) father didn't want joint custody. It wasn't even considered. He did not share much in the responsibilities of raising her when we lived together, and he was not interested in taking on any additional responsibility when we separated.

"I had always taken care of Laurie and continued to do so after we separated. It takes a lot of patience and effort (and love) to raise a child successfully on your own, but I was willing to do it and worked hard at it, reaping the obvious rewards such as her deep, unconditional love. My daughter is relatively well-adjusted and a happy child in spite of the mountains we have scaled" (Laurie's mother).

Perhaps no family-related change has a more devastating and enduring impact on children than parental separation. About one out of 3 schoolchildren in the United States has experienced parental divorce. Thirty percent of them have become members of stepfamilies. The rest, like Laurie, live in a single-parent household. When parents separate and divorce, children lose the most stabilizing force in their lives—daily contact with both parents.

From the mid-nineteenth century to the mid-twentieth century, the nuclear family was the basic social unit. It was headed by a working father and a caretaking mother. When their father was away at work, young children could count on their mother's presence and her active involvement in their daily lives. Grandparents and other relatives usually lived nearby and had frequent contact with young family members.

Changes since the middle of this century have led to a proliferation of nontraditional family configurations and life-styles that, compared to the nuclear family, make it more difficult for parents to provide guidance, support, and stability to their children. Mothers are not as available to their young children as they used to be. Grandparents often retire to places far away from their grandchildren. And large numbers of parents are having difficulty staying in love with their partners.

Ironically, it would never occur to young children that one of their parents could, or would even want to, permanently leave home. This realization can make parental separation that much more jolting. Many children experience a double loss when their now single mother (mothers are usually the custodial parent) seeks full-time employment to compensate for the financial strains that follow separation.

It takes approximately 2 to 3 years for most families to reorganize following the disruption and turmoil of divorce (Gray & Coleman, 1985). Parental separation becomes just the first of a series of transitions that challenge the coping resources of parents and children alike (Hetherington, 1989; Wallerstein & Blakeslee, 1989). Even the extramarital affairs that sometimes precede parental separation take their toll on children, whose welfare becomes a lower priority to the preoccupied parent (Brooks, 1989; A. Lawson, 1988). Most divorced parents eventually remarry, giving rise to stepfamilies, the most distinctive and complex of the various family configurations. There is much distress when families fragment, and sometimes when they reconstitute.

In this chapter we consider the effects of parental divorce on children. Additionally, we examine two family configurations that have become increasingly common in our society as a result of the high divorce rate: single-parent families and stepfamilies. We also discuss the changing role of fathering.

SEPARATION AND DIVORCE

Study Question *Why are divorce rates so high in western industrialized countries?*

It is well known, though still disturbing, that the divorce rate in western industrialized nations has stabilized at close to 50 percent. Second marriages have an even higher divorce rate. Children are involved in about 60 percent of all divorces. In the United States, over a million children experience their parents' divorce each year. About one-fifth of them, alas, will experience a second parental divorce, and some a third (Brody, Neubaum, & Forehand, 1988). Half of all United States children will live with a single parent for at least part of their childhood.

Why is divorce so common? Are people today unhappier in their relationships? Have relationships become more difficult to maintain? These questions are not easy to answer. The divorce rate reflects the stability of marriages, not their quality. There are poor marriages in which individuals will not consider divorce. There are successful marriages in which couples separate for reasons having nothing to do with their relationship (Belsky, Lerner, & Spanier, 1984).

It doesn't seem likely, however, that the quality of relationships has changed much in this century (See Spotlight: Two Styles of Marriage: Male and Female). Rather, there has been an easing of the constraints that in the past discouraged unhappy spouses from separating.

Divorce used to be viewed as a shameful act. Unhappy spouses were expected to stay together for the "sake of the child." Today, we understand that parents in a hopelessly unsatisfying marriage are probably not doing their children a favor by staying together. This is particularly true when children witness frequent hostile, sometimes violent, exchanges between their parents. No-fault divorce laws instituted in 1970 represent society's acknowledgment that individuals must retain "freedom of relationship," despite the hardships and suffering that result.

Women are twice as likely as men to initiate divorce proceedings (*New York Times,* June 15, 1989). In the past, when women left their husbands, they had to return to their parents, often with children in hand. Most women today would not find this alternative palatable. Valuing their independence, many women would rather seek or increase the amount of their employment and work toward self-sufficiency.

Divorce is painful for everyone involved. Sometimes, it is the only solution to a hopeless marital situation. The intended effect of divorce is to relieve marital distress and reduce the suffering of family members that might result from continuing animosity between the parents (Wallerstein, 1988).

"The decision to divorce or remarry may be made on the basis of the possibility for improved well-being of the parent, in many instances with little or no consideration for the concerns of the child. Few children wish for their parents' divorce, and many children resent their parents' remarriages" (Hetherington, Stanley-Hagan, & Anderson, 1989, p. 303). Divorce is the price that children pay for their parents' failure to get along (Wallerstein & Blakeslee, 1989).

Adjustment to divorce is a lifelong process for all family members, although the spouse who initiates the divorce usually adjusts better than the one who separates reluctantly (Wallerstein & Blakeslee, 1989). Most parents and children eventually learn to accept the divorce, but new stressors continually arise. "The children are often neglected. In the first couple of years after the divorce, children have less regular bedtimes and mealtimes, eat together as a family less, hear fewer bedtime stories, and are more often late for school. Discipline is less

consistent, positive and affectionate. And perhaps most salient of all, the aftermath of divorce brings economic disaster for most mothers and children" (Clarke-Stewart, 1989, p. 61).

The following sequence of events, occurring over a period of years, is not unusual for large numbers of children: parental conflict, parental extramarital affairs, parental separation, bitter divorce and custody proceedings, single-parent family, moving to a new community and school, maternal employment, parental remarriage into a stepfamily with new stepparent and stepsiblings, and perhaps, stepfamily conflict and another divorce. The events following parental divorce may tax children's coping abilities more than the initial separation (Hetherington, 1989).

Study Question   *Should unhappy spouses stay together for the sake of their children?*

Long and Forehand (1987) observed that it is not divorce per se, but rather the displays of hostility between parents that most stress children. They questioned teachers about 40 adolescents' academic and social performance. Half of the teens had parents who recently divorced, and half belonged to intact families. Teachers could not distinguish between those students from broken homes and those from intact families on the basis of their behavior in school. However, they could distinguish between those children whose parents displayed high levels of conflict and those children whose parents got along. Thus, it is parental conflict rather than parental separation that is most associated with poor adjustment in children.

Child Rearing after Divorce: "Best Interests of the Child"

Ironically, until the mid-nineteenth century, fathers almost always were awarded sole custody of their children (and the home) when their marriages dissolved. This was partly due to their superior financial status. Women generally had no independent means of support. Children in those days were considered the property of their fathers. Single fatherhood is not new. Many men became single parents following the death of their wives during childbirth.

Subsequently, courts decided that mothers and children have rights of their own and usually awarded sole custody to mothers. Such rulings were based on the assumption that women are more nurturant than men and better able to care for young children. Fathers could only gain custody by proving the mother unfit. In sole custody proceedings, this bias is still common. In the last decade, however, the joint custody arrangement has been proposed as a way of avoiding bias in either direction (Greif, 1985).

Furstenberg and Nord (1985) sampled representative households across the country to study relationships among parents, stepparents, and children following separation and divorce. They found that "coparenting among formerly married couples is more of a myth than a reality . . . marital disruption effectively destroys the ongoing relationship between children and the biological parents living outside the home in a majority of families. Nearly half of all children have not seen their nonresident fathers in the past year" (p. 902).

Study Question *Why do children in their mothers' custody rarely see their fathers following divorce?*

Following divorce, some children almost never see their fathers. Visitation, letters, phone calls, and child support usually decline within two years of the divorce, and children often feel rejected and unlovable (Loewen, 1988; Seltzer, Schaeffer, & Charng, 1989). Mothers who are bitter cite father absence to children as evidence that he is uncaring. Naturally, children do not benefit from hearing one parent denigrate the other.

Children usually miss their absent father and desire contact with him. Research confirms that nonvisitation fathers suffer too. Many cite the emotional strains of visitation, particularly uncooperative and hostile ex-spouses, as the major reason for their absence (Teyber & Hoffman, 1987). Eventually, most fathers remarry. The relationship between an ex-spouse and a remarried couple is a powerful determinant of life in the stepfamily and therefore in children's eventual adjustment (Giles-Sims, 1987).

When noncustodial parents do visit their children, it is often more of a social ritual than an opportunity for closeness. Parent and child spend time together, but it is not a conventional parent-child interaction where the parent is assisting or nurturing the child. It is more likely to be sitting in front of the TV watching a rented tape. Noncustodial parents "typically give up decision-making authority, and exercise little direct influence over their children's upbringing" (Furstenberg & Nord, 1985, p. 903). These researchers reported that custodial parents complained about the lack of involvement and support they received from the absent parent. Over half reported that they did not discuss their child rearing with their ex-spouse to avoid the possibility of conflict.

Furstenberg and Nord suggest three reasons why nonresident parents (usually fathers) lessen their involvement with their children following divorce. (1) They are unwilling to provide child support, (2) they are reluctant to interact with their ex-spouse, and (3) many fathers assume parenting responsibilities with their new families. Additionally, children who live with "substitute" parents, such as stepparents or adoptive parents, have less contact with their noncustodial biological parents (Seltzer & Bianchi, 1988). Of course, many nonresident parents do remain very involved with their children, but they are the exception.

Joint Custody

Study Question *If you were a judge, what would you want to know about a case before assigning custody?*

There are three common custody arrangements. When *sole custody* is granted, one parent is given sole responsibility and the other parent is given visitation rights. *Split custody* occurs when each parent is given sole custody of one or more children. *Joint custody* gives both parents legal custody of a child, requiring shared parenting responsibilities and decision making (Hanson, 1988).* Joint custody ensures fathers' visitation rights when mothers have physical custody. It also allows them to participate in decision making and other significant parenting roles. However, many nonresident parents do not take advantage of the rights granted them.

The joint custody arrangement was initially considered an optimal way of providing children with continuing access to both parents, therefore avoiding the anguish associated with father nonvisitation. Most states have mandated joint legal *and* physical custody, if both parents agree, unless the court decides it is not in the best interests of the child (Hanson, 1988).

Joint custody is increasingly being granted. However, recent studies have found that other factors are better predictors of children's adjustment than the custody arrangements (Buie, 1988b; Isaacs, Leon, & Kline, 1987; Kline, Tschann, Johnston, & Wallerstein, 1989). These include the quality of each parent-child relationship, parental psychological functioning, and the working relationship between the ex-spouses.

*Joint legal custody does not necessarily mean that both parents will share physical custody of the child. Joint physical custody does require that a child reside with both parents some of the time.

Wallerstein (1987) found that children of parents who maintained an amicable relationship following their divorce were not affected by the type of custody arrangement. However, if the parents bitterly contested the divorce, children were psychologically disadvantaged when joint physical custody was imposed. (Ironically, frequent access to both parents following divorce may harm a child. The parents' contact with each other is increased, and, if they are hostile, their children are exposed to more conflict [Johnston, Kline, & Tschann, 1989].) For joint custody to work to the child's advantage, a degree of cooperation between parents is required that is not often present in postdivorce relationships (Camara & Resnick, 1989; Felner, 1985). Wallerstein cautions that these findings do not suggest that joint custody is harmful, but neither should it be viewed as the optimal arrangement for all children of divorce.

Wolchik, Braver, and Sandler (1985) compared children in maternal and joint custody and found no differences in psychological symptoms between the two groups. However, children in joint custody reported more positive experiences than children in maternal custody. They also demonstrated higher levels of self-esteem and had more frequent contact with the noncustodial parent. Many studies have confirmed that the continued participation of both parents in the lives of their children following divorce is important to children's eventual adjustment, especially when the parents get along with each other. Nonadversarial forms of mediation are needed to arrive at custody arrangements that are suited to particular families (Coller, 1988).

Stages of the Divorce Process

Wallerstein (1988) has distinguished three stages in the divorce process, although they are not inevitable. The *acute phase* begins with the formal separation of the marital partners (filing for divorce) and a parent's (usually the father's) departure from the household. Most children recall vividly, perhaps for the rest of their lives, both being told about the divorce and the day their parent left. Much of the stress of this period reflects the fact that the decision to separate is usually not mutual.

The acute phase lasts from several months to over a year. Disruptive parental behaviors include "verbal accusations, threats, and rage accompanied by violence, and depression which may include a preoccupation with suicide (p. 276) . . . Children are rarely protected from witnessing the angry scenes and, in fact, in some families the fighting only occurs when the children are present" (p. 279).

Perhaps out of guilt, custodial parents soften their discipline. Children may be exposed to inconsistent, even contradictory, standards from day to day. During the year following the separation, "the custodial parent tends to be less competent as a parent, less able to maintain the structure of the household, and less available to the children. The youngsters are irritable, edgy, and often accusatory and rebellious" (Wallerstein, 1988, pp. 277–278).

The second or *transitional phase* "spans a period of several years, during which adults and children embark on unfamiliar roles and relationships within the new family structure" (p. 275). This may involve a change in residence, life-style and a reduced standard of living. The third or *stabilizing phase* finds the family reorganized and functioning well. The custodial parent may remarry, and the family will continue to face new challenges.

Effects of Divorce on Children

"Divorce is a different experience for children and adults because the children lose something that is fundamental to their development—the family structure. The family comprises the scaffolding upon which children mount successive developmental stages, from infancy into adolescence. It supports their psychological, physical, and emotional ascent into maturity. When that structure collapses, the children's world is temporarily without supports" (Wallerstein & Blakeslee, 1989, p. 11).

Their parents' divorce and the conflicts leading up to and following it can have lifelong effects on children (Wallerstein & Blakeslee, 1989). A significant number of children, but still a minority, develop serious emotional disorders and aggressive behaviors that may require professional attention (Brady, Bray, & Zeeb, 1986; Kalter, 1987). Less extreme problems—involving behavior problems, performance in school, and psychological distress—are quite common in children following parental divorce (Allison & Furstenberg, 1989; Bisnaire, Firestone, & Rynard, 1990).

The specific effects of parental divorce depend upon several factors (Kalter, Kloner, Schreier, & Okla, 1989). These include the child's temperament and personality, the quality of both parent-child relationships before the divorce, the quality of the absent parent's relationship with the child, the quality of life in the custodial parent's household, the custodial parent's postdivorce adjustment, and the parents' postseparation relationship (usually poor) with each other (Fishel, 1987; Hetherington, 1989; Wallerstein, 1988).

The greater the number of stressors and the poorer the child's coping and other resources, the greater the risk for serious adjustment problems. The impact of the child's age on his or her postseparation adjustment may also be mediated by the number of major life events or stressors experienced (Stolberg & Bush, 1985). At a time when grieving children need extra attention and reassurance, their parents become less available and less supportive (Wallerstein & Blakeslee, 1989).

Study Question How do children respond emotionally to their parents' divorce?

Children of divorce experience a variety of intense feelings (Wallerstein & Blakeslee, 1989). These include fear and insecurity regarding their future, including a fear of being abandoned by the remaining, custodial parent; loneliness due to the minimal support they usually receive; anger toward the parent they hold responsible for the separation; depression and helplessness about their plight; and, occasionally, guilt regarding their perceived role in the marital breakup. Keep in mind that children's immediate reactions to parental divorce do not predict their long-term adjustment.

"In the period immediately following divorce, children may grieve for the absent parent, may respond with noncompliance and aggression to parental conflict and family disorganization, and may become confused by and apprehensive of changing relationships with parents" (Hetherington, Stanley-Hagan, & Anderson, 1989, p. 304). Many children experience conflicting loyalties regarding each parent or feel rejected by the absent parent. Problems in school and with peers are common.

Children might think that their parent left because they were bad or because the parent no longer cares about them. It is therefore important for separating parents to reassure their children that the divorce had nothing to do with their feelings about the child, whom they both will always love. It is not helpful for children to hear that their parents no longer love each other, even though it is true.

Very few children of divorce report that a sympathetic parent or adult spoke to them caringly during their times of distress (Wallerstein & Blakeslee, 1989). McCoy (1984) describes how sensitive parents told their young child about their decision to separate. "They told her Mommy and Daddy couldn't get along anymore and had trouble living together, so they had decided, after a lot of

thought and trying, to get a divorce. This meant, they said, that Mommy and Daddy would live in different houses. She would live with Mommy most of the time, but Daddy wouldn't live far away, and she would visit him at his new house soon. They explained that this divorce was something between Mommy and Daddy and that they would always love her and be her parents. She would still go to the same school and see her friends" (p. 112).

Usually, when children suffer intense and threatening feelings, their parents provide comfort and reassurance. When the parents themselves are preoccupied by their own needs, children require additional support from relatives and other concerned adults. Some adults, during separation, look to their children for emotional support. Following divorce, these parents may eventually become involved with new partners, distracting them from their child-care responsibilities. For some, their children may represent a reminder of failure (Brooks, 1986).

Children who adjust the most poorly to divorce typically come from homes that are characterized by conflict, punitive parenting, and poor conflict-resolution skills. The fathers or stepfathers of many maladjusted boys are unavailable or rejecting (Hetherington, 1989).

Effects of Children's Age When Their Parents Separate

It has been suggested that the younger children are when their parents divorce, the greater its impact on their development (Allison & Furstenberg, 1989; Emery, 1988). After all, younger children are more dependent upon their parents than older children. They also lack coping mechanisms that would allow them to adjust to the prolonged disruption of their lives.

Wallerstein's longitudinal study (1987; 1988) of 60 predominantly white California families of divorce found, however, that preschool children, although initially the most frightened, eventually showed the *best* long-term adjustment. Children who were very young at the time of separation had limited understanding and recall of the predivorce drama that traumatizes older children.

After 18 months had passed, the young children's distress worsened. Boys in particular were disruptive at school and home. Even 5 years after the separation, the younger children were showing signs of maladjustment. However, by 10 years after the separation, the youngest children seemed to have adjusted, many claiming they could not even remember their lives before the divorce. Tentatively, it appears that children who are very young when their parents divorce show the poorest short-term adjustment and the best long-term adjustment.

Nevertheless, young children are very parent-dependent and usually suffer greatly from the loss of the absent parent. Working at the developmental task of separation, they are vulnerable to new fears of abandonment. They are likely to regress behaviorally. They may develop sleep disturbances and be irritable and aggressive. Many children feel personally responsible for the separation (Wallerstein, 1988).

When Wallerstein (1987) performed the 10-year follow-up study, most of the children were finishing high school or starting college. About three-quarters were in the custody of their mothers, and the rest lived with their fathers. "Feelings of sadness, of neediness, of a sense of their own vulnerability, were expressed by a majority of these young people. Although two thirds of their lives have been spent in the divorced or remarried family, they spoke sorrowfully of their loss of the intact family and the consequent lack of opportunity for a close relationship with the father . . . Anxieties about relationships with the opposite sex, marriage, and personal commitments ran very high" (p. 210).

Ten years following the divorce, the younger children were still fantasizing that their parents would get back together. The children who lived with their mothers revealed a strong desire to contact their natural fathers as they approached adolescence. They would write to these men, even if their letters were not answered. The younger children were generally optimistic about their future relationships. Older siblings anticipated continued loss and betrayal in their lives. Adolescent girls in particular showed a delayed or sleeper effect, with lower self-esteem and increased anxiety about having relationships with men (Wallerstein & Corbin, 1989).

Adjustment to divorce comes slowly and sometimes not at all. "We found that although some divorces work well—some adults are happier in the long run, and some children do better than they would have been expected to in an unhappy intact family—more often than not divorce is a wrenching, long-lasting experience for at least one of the former partners. Perhaps more important, we found that for virtually all the children, it exerts powerful and wholly unanticipated effects" (Wallerstein, 1989, p. 19).

A weakness in Wallerstein's study is the absence of a control group of intact families with which to compare the families undergoing divorce. Some of the reported "effects of divorce" may turn out to be characteristic of intact families, too. Additionally, children who are identified as "troubled" following parental separation may have had problems beforehand. Generally, studies of the effects of divorce on children have serious methodological flaws (Demo & Acock, 1988), and we should consider our understanding of these effects tentative.

Adolescents Adolescents are in a better position than younger children to understand the causes of divorce. They are less parent-dependent, and they can find emotional support outside of the family when necessary. Forehand, Middleton, and Long (1987) questioned 58 young adolescents and their teachers. About half of the children were from intact families, and about half had parents who were recently divorced. They found that the level of adolescent functioning was related to the number of stressors.

Adolescents who experienced three stressors (parental divorce, poor relationship with their mothers, and poor relationship with their fathers) functioned more poorly than adolescents who experienced zero, one, or two of these stressors. A good relationship with at least one of their parents is an important protective factor for children of divorce. Adolescents are also less likely to have problems in school when their mothers are adjusting well to their separation and when there are low levels of family conflict (McCombs & Forehand, 1989).

Adolescents who have experienced parental divorce often become wary of entering new relationships (Wallerstein & Corbin, 1989). They also may resent either parent attempting a social life of his or her own. Raising adolescent sons is more difficult in divorced families than in intact families (Borduin & Henggeler, 1987).

Young Adults About a fifth of all divorces terminate marriages that have lasted over 15 years. Usually the children are grown. If they are over 18 years old, custody and support issues don't apply. While it has been assumed that young adults are much less vulnerable to their parents' divorce than children and adolescents, recent evidence suggests otherwise.

Cooney, Smyer, Hagestad, and Klock (1986) interviewed undergraduates between the ages of 18 and 23 years whose parents had divorced within the past 3 years. Sixty-two percent of the women and 42 percent of the men reported emotional problems early in the divorce proceedings, with about one-third reporting subsequent relief. More than half of their 39 subjects reported that their emotional health had suffered.

These students were so moved by their parents' plight that they felt as though they were experiencing the divorce themselves. Many of the students found that their relationships with their parents (particularly mothers) improved following the divorce, presumably due to their involvement in the crisis. There was least relationship improvement between fathers and daughters, with daughters expressing considerable anger toward their fathers. Those who were already having difficulty with their own separation from their parents became the most distressed by the parental divorce.

Fine, Moreland, and Schwebel (1983) reported that college students from divorced families perceived their relationships with their parents, particularly with their fathers, more negatively than students from intact families. The poorest relationships were reported by those who were younger than 11 years old when their parents divorced. As a group, the children of divorce reported that their relationships with their parents were average in quality. Proulx and Koulack (1987) found no differences in undergraduates from separated and intact families in the personal conflict they experienced when leaving home for college.

Divorce is difficult for children of all ages. Each age group is working on different developmental tasks. They respond to the divorce according to their current level of understanding and with the coping resources that are available. Even within age groups, children differ widely in their ability to adjust. "Many children eventually emerge from the divorce or remarriage of their parents as competent or even enhanced individuals" (Hetherington, Stanley-Hagan, & Anderson, 1989, p. 310).

Sex Differences in Adjustment

Study Question Do boys suffer more from parental divorce than girls?

Although early studies suggested that divorce is more traumatic for boys than for girls, some recent studies (e.g., Allison & Furstenberg, 1989) challenge this belief. We have good reason to hypothesize, however, that boys and girls respond differently to marital dissolution, and that different measures of adjustment will reflect at least modest sex differences (Wallerstein & Corbin, 1989).

SPOTLIGHT: Two Styles of Marriage: Male and Female

Marriage continues to be a popular institution in the late twentieth century. However, there remains a basic destabilizing force in each marriage: one partner is male and one is female. Research and clinical observation reveal that men and women bring quite different needs to marriage and different expectations of what marriage entails.

Women desire and expect greater intimacy or closeness in relationships than do men. "Men are much more likely to be either satisfied with the status quo or seeking changes that would provide them with greater distance and autonomy" (Jacobson, 1989, p. 30). Whereas men often complain about their sexual advances being spurned, women complain that men are too aggressive sexually. Many men see women as moody and self-absorbed, whereas women often view men as condescending and inconsiderate. Not surprisingly, the poorer the relationship, the longer the list of complaints (Buss, 1989).

Ted Huston, a psychologist at the University of Texas at Austin, interviewed 130 couples concerning their view of the marital relationship. He observed that men and women differ regarding their interpretations of what constitutes emotional intimacy in a close relationship. "For the wives, intimacy means talking things over, especially talking about the relationship itself. The men, by and large, don't understand what the wives want from them. They say, 'I want to do things with her, and all she wants to do is talk' " (Huston, quoted by Goleman, 1986b).

Dr. Huston found that men are much more likely to accommodate their partners' desire for intimacy during courtship than during marriage. As marriage proceeds, men come to prefer spending more time at work or with their friends. If there is a wide discrepancy between their partners' behavior during courtship and then after marriage, women become disappointed or angry. Marital conflict may ensue, particularly if differing intimacy expectations result in sexual miscommunications and sexual anger (Jacobson, 1989).

Women may not know how to explain to their spouses that they look to them for emotional support. Unfortunately, many men have difficulty satisfying this need and may become angry when confronted with their "inadequacy." Dr. Huston says, "You can't force intimacy. It has to arise spontaneously from shared activities." Many women eventually resign themselves to getting emotional support from their female friends or from their mothers. Husbands who are capable of satisfying their wives' needs for intimacy and emotional support are likely to have more stable relationships (Jacobson, 1989).

Ironically, men seem to need marriage more than women do. Their physical and social needs are more likely to be satisfied in marriage than are their wives' needs. Men generally report greater satisfaction with marriage than women. It is not surprising, therefore, that men evaluate almost all aspects of marriage more positively than do their wives. They are more satisfied regarding sex, money, relationship with parents, romance, and communication. Women are less satisfied with their marriages, complain more about them, and suffer more within them. Perhaps this helps us understand why women are twice as likely as men to file for divorce. Women's psychological health, more than men's, seems to depend upon the quality of the marital relationship (J. M. Lewis, 1988a).

We can better understand the high divorce rate when we can identify fundamental differences in how men and women view close relationships. Clearly, men and women have a lot to offer each other in intimate relationships. However, women usually have a stronger social orientation than men, and they tend to be more giving (DeAngelis, 1989). This ultimately may be at their own expense in marriage. Parents who value intimacy and caring in relationships can make a special effort to instill these relationship skills in sons and daughters alike.

How boys and girls adjust to parental divorce depends largely upon their personal characteristics and their postdivorce circumstances. For example, temperamentally difficult boys have the most serious adjustment problems (Hetherington, 1989). When the absent parent is the father, boys appear to be more vulnerable. This is particularly true if they live with an unmarried mother and have limited contact with their fathers after the separation. Boys appear to do better when their mothers remarry.

The fact that fathers are more involved in the rearing of their sons has been used to explain the observation that parents of sons have a somewhat lower risk of separation or divorce, compared to parents of daughters. Mothers and fathers apparently agree that sons need their fathers more than daughters do. This may even serve as a deterrent to divorce. On the other hand, if unhappy parents with sons stay married longer, they expose these boys to longer periods of marital strife.

In Wallerstein's (1987) study, the quality of the relationship with the father, particularly for boys, was a major predictor of postdivorce adjustment. Many boys attempted to increase their contact with their fathers during adolescence, despite poor relationships with them. Wallerstein notes that the children of fathers who do not respond appropriately to their overtures may experience intense disappointment, and some may need professional help. It is likely that sons of abusive or otherwise incompetent or uncaring fathers will *benefit* from father absence, even though the child may still be distressed at his departure (Wallerstein, 1988). Girls may adjust more poorly following divorce if they live with a stepfather, are in the custody of their father, or if their mothers remarry (Zaslow, 1989).

SINGLE PARENTING

Study Question What special burdens confront parents without partners?

"As a single mother, I made financial sacrifices. I assumed full responsibility for my children's growth and development. I had no one to depend on for emotional support. I made all decisions alone. I had sole responsibility for providing home, security, love, discipline, and religious training" (single mother of three children).

Parenting young children is a full-time job. The duties usually shared by two parents include earning a living, making good decisions about child care, and solving everyday problems. Parents must also purchase goods and services, prepare meals, clean house, and launder clothing. Parents transport children, participate in and supervise play activities, help with schoolwork, teach life skills, and much, much more.

When these responsibilities are shared by two adults, even if both are employed, they are usually manageable. Of course, this depends upon how well the parents work together, their ability to afford child-care assistance, how many children they have, and so on.

What happens when these "chores" must be accomplished by one parent with limited financial resources? What if the parent is employed in a relatively low-paying job? What if the parent is coping with the stress of recent separation or divorce, a hostile or uncooperative ex-spouse, and distressed children? "One parent can model only one gender role, give only so many hugs, offer so much discipline, and earn so much money" (Clarke-Stewart, 1989b, p. 61). Welcome to the plight of the single parent.

About half of all children born in the 1970s and 1980s will spend some time (an average of 6 years) in a single-parent family. Fathers are awarded custody about 11 percent of the time. Most single parents with custody are women who become the heads of their households following divorce and who bear the full responsibility for raising their children.

There are over 8 million women raising their children without the assistance of a partner, two-thirds as a result of divorce or separation. Never-married women, about half of them adolescents, women over 30 having children on their own, and widows also contribute to the single-parent category. The median income of these families is about one-third the national average (*Dollars and Sense,* September, 1983).

Incredibly, about a fifth of United States households are headed by single parents. In the United States, approximately one-quarter of children under the age of 18 years (15 million children) are living with single parents. More than half of all black children (53%) and almost one-third of Hispanic children live with a single parent (Cordes, 1984; *New York Times,* January 28, 1988).

To make ends meet, over two-thirds of single mothers seek employment. Lacking work experience or higher education, most must settle for unskilled, low-paying jobs with little opportunity for advancement or promotion. Those with preschool children either work part time or spend a significant part of their salary for child care. Many of their children receive an inadequate amount of parental supervision. We can hope that as this constituency increases in size, society will recognize their plight and provide economic relief.

Only about half of fathers who are required to pay child support actually contribute the full amount. A quarter pay some of the designated amount, and a quarter pay nothing, even

About one out of 5 families in the United States are headed by single parents.

though most could afford to. Lack of custody may be a factor that discourages many men from voluntary support. Fathers with joint custody remain involved with their children long after noncustodial fathers have ceased visitation and support (Meredith, 1985).

Children of Single Parents

It is difficult to untangle the effects of living with a single parent from the effects of having experienced parental conflict, separation, and divorce. For most children, it is a "package deal." It has been estimated that about a third of the children who have lived through their parents' divorce develop serious problems. As Wallerstein notes, children experience more stress in the joint custody of two belligerent parents than they do living in the sole custody of one of them.

Santrock and Warshak (1986) report that children do better living with the same-sexed parent. "Children living with opposite-sexed parents tend to be more immature and dependent, and to show higher levels of anxiety and lower levels of self-esteem . . . While I think boys do need their fathers and girls their mothers, I also think boys need their mothers and girls their fathers . . . it's important for a child to maintain a relationship with both parents" (Warshak, quoted by Meredith, 1985).

Children are usually ambivalent when their custodial parent dates. They may worry that the new man in Mom's life will replace them in her affections, and boys in particular may act "protectively" toward their mother. Adolescent boys may also wonder whether their mother is sexually involved with her friend. Children who feel threatened by their parent's relationship may attempt to sabotage it, one way or another. Most children appear to accept their parents' need for companionship and a social life. Sometimes, children become more emotionally involved with a parental friend than does the parent, so parents should be thoughtful about when they introduce their new friends to their children.

Mullis, Mullis, and Markstrom (1987) questioned single and married mothers about their children's behavior. Married mothers reported better relationships with their children than did single mothers, who rated their sons less favorably in independence and obedience. Better-educated mothers had better-behaved children. Wadsworth, Burnell, Taylor, and Butler (1985) compared British children from single-parent, step-, and nuclear families on a variety of measures. They found that, on the average, children from single-parent families scored worst and children from nuclear families scored best on tests of behavior, vocabulary, and visuomotor coordination. Children from single-parent families were also perceived as more antisocial and slightly more neurotic than children from two-parent families. Studies generally do not find differences in sex role development for girls according to father absence versus presence. Small effects for boys are sometimes found (e.g., Stevenson & Black, 1988).

Webster-Stratton (1989) confirmed that single mothers are more critical and demanding than married mothers and that their children are more deviant and noncompliant. A national survey (Gelles, 1989) revealed that poor single mothers are more likely to behave violently toward their children than mothers who live with their partners. The rate of severe violence toward children was even higher for single fathers (particularly poor single fathers) than for single mothers. Given the number of children being raised by single parents, these findings are very disturbing.

STEPPARENTING

Study Question *What types of problems would you anticipate if you were marrying someone who already had children?*

"Can stepfamilies ever really blend? Before my husband and I got married sixteen months ago I thought, definitely yes—we will easily blend—no problem. However, we are still working on blending and I am confident that we will be for some time to come. At first, I felt guilty about the minor difficulties we were experiencing—where was the 'perfect blend' we expected? But I have come to realize that it is going to take a lot of perseverence, love, communication, and *time*.

"Our problems, to name a few, are: one child resenting attempts by the stepparent to impose discipline; having to deal with my feelings of not having been the first (but the third, after his first wife and child) to share my husband's life; having to raise my husband's child, of whom he has joint custody; and something we are both guilty of, favoring our own child over our spouse's. We suppress it at every opportunity, but it is difficult not to favor your own flesh and blood. We may never feel the same kind of love for the stepchild, but as long as we keep that hidden deep inside of our hearts, that is the best we can do. As far as they are concerned, we love them both" (a new stepmother).

There are over a million divorces each year in this country. Four out of 5 adults remarry within 3 years of their divorce. Along the way, children of divorce become children of remarriage. So-called remarried or blended families are becoming increasingly common. There were over 4 million stepfamilies in 1987, containing almost 9 million children. It has been estimated that by the year 2000, stepfamilies will be the most common type of family unit in this country (Kutner, 1989a).

We have already seen that the transition from nuclear family to single-parent family disrupts family functioning. It places a significant number of children at risk for serious emotional and behavioral problems. The transition from single-parent to stepfamily also requires a substantial adjustment for all family members, sometimes including noncustodial biological parents and their families as well.

Stepfamilies provide us with perhaps the most varied and complex family configuration. A single mother or father may marry another single father or mother, or they may marry a childless adult who may or may not have been previously married. New partners may bring children into the stepfamily. One partner or both may also have natural (biological) children who are living with an ex-spouse. (Imagine how confusing this must be to children.)

Most often, a man (who, if he has children, may or may not have sole or joint custody of them) marries a woman with custody of her children. "In these instances, while the mother and her children share common background,

history, and cultural values, the new stepfather has a different background and history, and his values may differ considerably from those of his new stepfamily. Thus, the new stepfather is often in the position of trying to break into a unit of mother and children, whose bonds predate the association between the spouses" (Santrock, Sitterle, & Warshak, 1988, p. 145).

People who are not familiar with stepfamilies are often amazed at the degree of adjustment and organization required just to allow routine family functioning. First of all, the newly married couple must adjust to their new relationship. "Researchers believe that partners drag into the new marriage all of the insecurities and personality problems that disrupted the old one. And with one divorce under their belt, they feel less hesitant about obtaining a second one when trouble appears" (Turkington, 1984d). In fact, remarriages are more likely to end in divorce than first marriages (Brody, Neubaum, & Forehand, 1988).

Coleman and Ganong (1987) noted that marital conflict in stepfamilies influences how children perceive and feel about their stepparents (particularly their stepfathers). When parents are in conflict, children remain loyal to their biological parent and will line up against their stepparent or stepsiblings. As in nuclear families, stepfathers' relationships with children are more affected by marital conflict than are stepmothers' relationships with children. Relationships in stepfamilies are typically more fragile than those in nuclear families. Low levels of marital conflict encourage positive feelings among family members.

Stepparent Family Research

Santrock and his colleagues (1988) have reviewed the literature on stepfathering. Stepfathering results when a man marries and lives with a divorced, widowed, or never married woman who has custody of her children. A child's age when the stepfather marries into the family is an important factor in a stepfather-stepchild relationship. Children younger than nine years appear to be more likely than older children to accept and form a warm relationship with a stepfather.

Stepfathers report that they are unprepared for the challenges and conflicts that arise when they remarry into an established family. "He is expected to master many roles in a hurry. He is expected to quickly win the respect and caring of the stepchildren. He must meet the needs and expectations of his new wife and himself as a loving husband. And he must come across as an affectionate parent to her children even though they may resent him" (E. Visher, quoted by Brooks, 1988).

Common problems for new stepfathers include communicating with their stepchildren, deciding how much authority to assume in their role as father ("You're not my real father"), and coping with discomfort about their loyalty to their natural children living with their ex-spouse. They may also be unhappy with how their new spouses discipline their own children (particularly sons).

Stepfathers may be wary of their stepchildren's ongoing relationship with their natural father. Children in remarried households often experience a conflict of loyalty between their natural parents and their stepparents. Clingempeel and Segal (1986) observed that the more frequently girls visited their nonresident natural mothers, the poorer their relationship with their resident stepmother.

Gaining the acceptance of their stepchildren is the key factor in stepfathers' adjustment to their new family. Children usually resent being disciplined by anyone but their "real" parent. The parental role should not be assumed too quickly. Many experienced stepfathers advise new stepparents to "move slowly and be patient, emphasizing that developing a relationship with the stepchild takes time. It seems gradual participation in the parenting process by the stepfather may often be the best answer" (Santrock et al., 1988, p. 155).

Stepparents who have not previously raised children feel the most awkward when joining an established family. They have unrealistic expectations about how quickly they will be accepted by their acquired family. When hostile children treat them as intruders, they take it personally. They do not know how to react. Stepfathers usually have more difficulty with daughters, particularly adolescent girls who might view the stepfather as competing with them for their mother's companionship.

Contradicting the "wicked stepmother" stereotype of children's fables and fairy tales, stepmothers are typically accepted more quickly by children than are stepfathers. They have a closer, warmer relationship and are more involved in their stepchildren's daily lives. In fact, stepmothers have been found to be as involved with their children as are mothers in intact families.

"It seems that remarriage may have a positive and stabilizing effect on custodial mothers, which is then reflected in their relationship with their children. More money is available for child support and other aspects of running a household than was likely the case as a single parent. Also, stepfathers are available to help with family work and, perhaps more important, to offer nurturance and support to their wives . . ." (Santrock et al., 1988, p. 161).

Stepmothering resentful children leaves many women very dissatisfied, particularly with minimal support from their husbands. When communication is very poor between children and their stepparents, children may run away or ask to live with their noncustodial natural parents.

An early study by Bowerman and Irish (1962) found that relationships in stepfamilies were characterized by more stress and ambivalence than those in nonstepfamilies. Ganong and Coleman (1987) wondered whether these differences continue to exist, given the demographic changes of the past 25 years. They used the same questions as Bowerman and Irish to examine the attitudes of 126 adolescent stepchildren about their stepmothers or stepfathers, depending upon the family configuration.

Modern stepchildren reported feeling at least moderately close to their stepparents. They did not report feeling more distant from stepfathers than from stepmothers. Stepsons and stepdaughters perceived their stepparents similarly. As previously noted, the stepdaughter-stepfather relationship is usually the least emotionally close of the stepparent-child relationships (Fischman, 1988b).

Almost half of the females reported that they did not feel close to their stepfathers, compared to only 11 percent of the males. Most of the females reported feeling much closer to stepmothers than stepfathers. Length of time in the stepfamily did not affect closeness in the Ganong and Coleman study, but Clingempeel and Segal (1986) found that the longer stepdaughters lived with their stepmothers, the more positive the relationship.

Fortunately, most recent studies, like Ganong and Coleman's (1987), confirm that relationships in stepfamilies are reasonably good. Mothers and children in stepfamilies usually report being as happy as their counterparts in nondivorced families. Stepchildren perceive themselves as happy, successful, and achieving as children from nuclear families. Living in stepfamilies compensates for many of the negative effects of divorce and father absence (Visher & Visher, 1988).

Does it help for the remarried couple to have a child together? How do stepchildren feel about the birth of a sibling? Younger children seem to be more accepting of new siblings in a blended family, but the addition of a new family member can also destabilize the fragile stepfamily system. Remarried couples in blended families who give birth to "mutual" children do not appear to differ in the strength or quality of their relationships from remarried couples who choose not to have additional children (Ganong & Coleman, 1988).

Sexuality is usually a visible element in new stepfamilies in several ways. The newlywed parents are in the honeymoon phase of their relationship. Opposite-sexed adolescent stepsiblings may experience sexual attraction toward each other or toward their opposite-sexed stepparent. Young girls in stepfamilies are at greater risk for sexual abuse by their stepfathers than girls in nuclear families are by their natural fathers. The situation is complicated by occasional false accusations of abuse (Visher & Visher, 1988). Biological mothers should be properly vigilant (without being unduly suspicious) about inappropriate displays of affection between family members.

Parenting Stepchildren

The primary task of the remarried family is for the new marriage partners to strengthen their relationship, which is the backbone of the reconfigured family. The new stepparent should proceed slowly and sensitively when interacting with stepchildren. The stepparent should support but not replace the biological parent as the primary family authority. This may be more difficult for men, as the traditional role of a father is to lead rather than to support one's spouse.

Young children will accept stepparents more quickly than older children. The latter may require up to 4 or 5 years before they treat the stepparent as equal to the biological parent. Children should be given the choice of how to address a stepparent. The discipline and communication methods discussed in previous chapters are particularly useful in stepfamilies (Dinkmeyer, McKay, & McKay, 1987).

Following their parents' divorce, most children hope for and fantasize about reconciliation. When either parent remarries, it becomes clearer that the divorce is irrevocable. Children may direct their anger to the person they perceive as being responsible, usually the intruding stepparent. Many children report that it is helpful to see both of their biological parents together occasionally being nice to each other. If family interactions become strained, professional help may be necessary (Visher & Visher, 1988).

"After several complaints from Laurie's preschool teacher, I began to realize that she was going through a difficult time in her development. She had lived with me (and slept in the same bedroom) for 2½ years after her father and I separated. She didn't have to compete with anyone else for my attention. All at once I got married and acquired a husband and stepdaughter, and Laurie acquired a stepfather and stepsister.

"Her stepfather slept in the same room with Mommy, she didn't. She was attending a new school and was living in a new house. All of this change was too much for her. Her way of getting my attention was to misbehave in school. Once we figured out the problems and communicated our support and concern for her, she got over her problems in school, and, with time, she has adjusted remarkably well to her new life" (Laurie's mother).

Who benefits when fathers become more involved in child rearing?

FATHERING IN PERSPECTIVE

Study Question What changes in society are encouraging men to become more involved in their role as father?

Today we know that fathers can be excellent caretakers if they want to be (Risman, 1989), and more and more men want to be. However, centuries of rigid sex-role definitions and cultural practices discouraged male parents from participating in the daily routines of child rearing. Recently, traditional assumptions about men as primary caretakers have begun to be challenged.

Over the last century, several factors have contributed to changes in our conceptions of parenting in general and fathering in particular. One relatively recent change (discussed in chapter 1) is the dual-career family. When mothers stayed home to care for their children, fathers retained the "freedom" to pursue financial ambitions and other forms of personal fulfillment away from their families. Now that so many mothers work, the situation is ripe for greater father involvement.

"When I was a child, my father often told me that he would like to be a beachcomber when he grew up. Perhaps that is why I have only a hazy understanding of how he made a living during my formative years . . . he really was just a beachcomber in training. In retrospect, I see that my father was a beachcomber on the beach of life. He revered every aspect, from the tiny grain of sand to the giant tidal wave. He stopped to notice, appreciate, and catalog all of the treasures that came his way. He was buffeted by the elements and came away slightly worn and battered but willing to stroll along the next stretch of beach.

"My father taught me a great deal about making one's way through life. He taught me that the entire educational system was one giant game to be played and won. Perhaps it is because he had mastered one game that my father never desired to play any others.

"I most clearly recall three of Daddy's maxims. As I recall them, I also notice that he was less than successful at adhering to them on his own behalf. First, never learn how to type or you can be sure that someone will ask you to type something for them. Second, if you don't have enough money, make more. And third, never die before anyone you love.

"You each must know why Jack Warhaftig was special to you. I only know why he was special to me. He liked me exactly as I am. He loved me like a daughter. He was my father, advisor, confidant, confessor, business partner, friend and hero. He showed me how to keep sight of the sweetness of life when mired to the waist in bullshit. He was a man who could cry and sometimes did. He collected wooden pulleys, typewriters, cameras, and bicentennial quarters, just because he liked them. He derived indescribable pleasure from knocking down a tile wall with the help of his grandsons.

"My father believed that he was supremely lucky to have found his one true love. He knew that there was only one match for him, only one possible soulmate. As a result, he lived his life in gratitude for the fortuitous waves that had thrown him into my mother's arms and carried them along for many years. My father never took my mother, or his love for her, for granted. Their love and their marriage is a lesson unto itself.

"I cannot summarize in words Daddy's total experience of his three grandsons. He incorporated them into his life until the very end and they worship and adore him. Daddy was an integral part of a loving circle of brothers and sisters, nieces and nephews. That circle has now been broken and must draw closer and re-form.

"Months ago, when Daddy knew he was dying, we spent many languid days together, lying on the bed, side by side, barely able to see the TV screen over my blossoming belly. Once, I turned to him and said, 'I can't help but feel that there is something I should want to say to you, some last important secret we should share.' He said to me, 'There is nothing unsaid between us.' And he was right." (J.W.)

Reprinted with permission of Jeri Warhaftig.

Eric Jaffe

Contemporary mothers, particularly those who work, are becoming less willing to bear the full burden of child care. Politically, feminism has led to a gradual increase in the democratization of relationships. Psychologically, males and females are gradually becoming more androgynous, that is, more flexible in their sex roles. Males and females today have many more choices than their ancestors regarding life-style, professional aspirations, and even personality traits.

It is becoming more acceptable for males to be nurturant, sensitive, and affectionate (e.g., Kaye & Applegate, 1990), and for females to be assertive, independent, and achieving. There are also increased opportunities for women to fulfill their personal goals. More adults are viewing marriage as a partnership rather than as a monarchy. Women prefer to see their husbands as partners in sharing the seemingly endless chores of parenting.

Thus, many women are becoming more assertive in bringing their partners into the caretaking fold. Some wives, however, are ambivalent about increasing their husband's family work load. To some, increased participation from their husbands may imply their own inadequacy as homemakers. Others may feel threatened when their husbands intrude upon their areas of competence. Or they may be afraid their husbands will become resentful of additional responsibilities (Baruch & Barnett, 1981).

More fathers *are* becoming more involved in the day-to-day raising of their children (Radin & Goldsmith, 1983). On the other hand, their time spent caring for children is still a fraction of that of mothers'. We also cannot assume that increases in father involvement always translate into improved quality of fathering (Grossman, Pollack, & Golding, 1988). Fathers who are "coerced" into greater participation by their working wives may not display high-quality caretaking (L. W. Hoffman, 1983).

Factors That Encourage or Discourage Father Involvement

Study Question Why are some fathers more likely than others to participate in family work and child care?

It is tempting to assume that fathers would be more involved in child care if not for such obstacles as rigid sex-role attitudes, long working hours, and unsympathetic employers. We would like to believe that fathers want to provide their working wives with the shared parenting they so desire and deserve. The reality is much more complicated (Barnett & Baruch, 1988). Men differ considerably from each other in their actual involvement in child care. They

also differ in their willingness to be involved and in their ability to allocate time and other resources to child rearing.

Perhaps the most long-standing obstacle to increased paternal involvement is the persistent cultural stereotype that women are inherently more nurturant and sensitive than men. Child care is still perceived as a feminine domain. Our culture supported this view in the past by excluding fathers from delivery rooms. Even at the birth of their children, men were seen only as a nuisance or as a source of infection.

Social institutions in general either "neglect the father's care-giving role, or in many cases actually work against widespread father involvement" (Power, 1984, p. 324). The implication is clear—women are naturally better with children. Men are too rough, too insensitive, or too stupid to care for a child. It is true that some men are less interested in caring for children than others, but the same can be said of women. There are women who choose not to bear children because they perceive themselves as lacking in nurturant qualities. Many men have at least some interest in caretaking. This interest could be encouraged to the critical point where interest leads to greater participation in a self-perpetuating cycle of increasing involvement.

A mother's sex-role attitudes, her feelings about her marital relationship and particularly about her own father's availability, may be the most important factors influencing the degree of her husband's involvement (Baruch & Barnett, 1981). Radin and Goldsmith (1985), for example, observed that in families with daughters, mothers who had negative views of their own fathers' availability had spouses who were more involved.

"The mother seems to function much as a gatekeeper, regulating the father's involvement with the infant, and she continues to influence his relationship with the infant even when he is not at home, in the way she refs to him in his absence . . . in marriages filled with conflict, spouses may attempt to undermine the partner's parenting role" (Yogman, Cooley, & Kindlon, 1988, p. 61). Less-motivated fathers may see child care as work, which is easily delegated to the more interested mother. Thus, the mother may "conspire" with her husband to view the infant's care as her sphere of influence.

"He's never changed a diaper in his life. He's even afraid to change her clothes. He's a big man—he's afraid he's going to hurt her. He will feed her, now that she's older" (mother of a 3-year-old, referring to her husband).

Early paternal involvement during delivery and then in infant care encourages continued participation (Palkovitz, 1985). The father-child bond can begin to develop immediately. Early involvement becomes self-perpetuating. The father gets "hooked" and is involved because he cares too much about his children not to be. Early paternal involvement is also fostered by maternal illness, a cesarean or a premature birth. It can be discouraged by job loss or job insecurity (Yogman et al., 1988), although unemployed fathers with working wives increase their involvement (Radin & Harold-Goldsmith, 1989).

Another major obstacle to greater father involvement is the fact that in our culture, for men, work is considered a higher priority than child care. Many men find that their employers are not very sympathetic when it comes to their missing work because their children are performing in a school assembly program or even because they are ill. It is harder for men to miss work, partially due to employer attitudes and partially due to self-imposed constraints. Many men view being a good provider as a higher family value than involvement in child care. They are reluctant to jeopardize their employment status.

The least painful type of child-care involvement for fathers appears to be time spent with children while mothers are present. Some fathers dislike time spent being solely in charge of children. "When alone with their children, fathers, not surprisingly, are vulnerable to the boredom, fatigue, and tension so familiar to mothers" (Baruch & Barnett, 1986a, p. 991).

Family variables associated with father involvement include the sex, age, and number of children. As children age and become more independent, fathers spend less time with them. Fathers may spend more time with sons than daughters because of similar interests ("male bonding"). Fathers with larger families spend more time interacting with their children than fathers in smaller families. Generally, fathers spend relatively little time alone with their children. When they do, they are helping out their wives rather than taking primary responsibility for the activity. Wives still plan and supervise their husbands' caretaking activities (Barnett & Baruch, 1988; Baruch & Barnett, 1986b; Radin & Goldsmith, 1985).

Fathering Quality and Quantity

Although fathers seem to be increasing their involvement in child care and rearing, the best fathers do not necessarily spend the most time with their families. Several investigators (e.g., Easterbrooks & Goldberg, 1984; Grossman, Pollack, & Golding, 1988) have found that the quality and quantity of fathering are not necessarily related!

"Men who enjoy and value their own capacities for separateness and closeness appear able to encourage both of these dimensions in their children . . . Men who enjoyed their work also had sensitive and responsive interactions with their 5-year-old children. The inevitable conflict is that satisfying, demanding careers leave relatively little time for such family interactions, and, indeed, the men in this study with such careers did not spend much time with their children" (Grossman et al., 1988, pp. 88–89).

Thus, those fathers who liked their jobs and were generally the most satisfied felt better about themselves and had good relationships with their children. Their jobs, although satisfying, were demanding, leaving them little time to spend with their families.

Interestingly, the husbands of older, more educated women with higher status occupations spent less time with their children. The researchers speculate that "warm and nurturing mothers might be said to have preempted the father-child relationship with their firstborn, or at least rendered the father's involvement less salient." However, "the more skillful the mothers were with their children, the more skillful the fathers were as well" (Grossman et al., 1988, p. 89). This suggests that competent mothers "create" competent fathers.

On Becoming a Father

Study Question How do expectant fathers differ from expectant mothers in the adjustments they must make to parenting?

Pregnant women occupy a special status in our society. Given their vulnerability and the contribution they are making, they certainly deserve the support and consideration they usually receive. What about "expectant" fathers? In the past, husbands were supposed to get their wives to the hospital on time for the delivery and then anxiously pace while waiting for the blessed event. Fathers were rarely involved in the delivery. Given the gradual shift in the fathering role, men today experience increasing pressure during their wives' pregnancies (Shapiro, 1987b).

"He shows no physical signs of pregnancy, but in some ways, emotionally and psychologically, he is as pregnant as she is. This is particularly true in America today, where society expects fathers to play an increasingly large role during pregnancy and birth . . . From the moment he knows of the pregnancy, a man is thrust into an alien world. He is encouraged, instructed and cajoled to be part of the pregnancy and birth process, something he knows little about. He is expected to become the coach or supporter for his wife, who has the leading role in the drama. He has no role model, since his own father almost certainly didn't do what he is expected to do" (Shapiro, 1987a, pp. 36–38).

Shapiro (1987a) interviewed 227 expectant and recent fathers. They ranged in age from 18 to 60 years and were from a wide variety of backgrounds. Shapiro observed a "cultural double bind." Men are encouraged to become fully involved in the pregnancy and birth process. At the same time, they are given the message that they are outsiders. Any negative feelings they have, such as fear, anger, or sadness, should be kept to themselves, lest their wives be upset. The pregnancy process caters to the concerns of the mother-to-be. The "father-to-be has neither the support systems nor the cultural sanctions for what he experiences" (p. 38).

Shapiro's male subjects expressed several concerns. They feared queasiness about the birth itself and were apprehensive about increased financial pressure. They were uncomfortable accompanying their wives to obstetrical examinations. Some men expressed doubts about really being the child's father, fear of losing their spouse or child during the delivery, and fear of being replaced by the infant in their wives' affections. Some felt a greater responsibility to remain alive and healthy to take care of their families.

Most of the fathers felt they could not share these concerns with their wives, out of fear of upsetting them. Most kept their worries to themselves (an unfortunate male trait). The intensity of the fears increased when wives were unavailable emotionally, physically, and sexually. These men had no substitute support system to compensate for their loss of spouse support. They wondered whether they would be strong enough to handle their concerns alone. Men who were able to share their concerns with their wives benefited from the closer and deeper relationship that resulted.

Following birth, husbands who feel particularly close to the infant may view themselves as competing with their wives. They may feel excluded when, for example, their wives are breast-feeding the newborn. "Husbands of nursing mothers have described feelings of inadequacy, envy, and exclusion, and the competition may actually undermine the mother's attempts at breast-feeding, unless these feelings are addressed . . . The effects of these feelings on *fathers'* involvement with their infants, however, have not yet been addressed" (Yogman et al., 1988, p. 61). Adjustment to the birth of an infant goes more smoothly when the parents are older, have been married longer before the birth, and conceive after marriage (Belsky, 1981).

Daniels and Weingarten (1988) interviewed 72 couples who had their first child at different times in their life cycles. Regardless of age, all of the women in the study had to readjust their life-styles for motherhood. Most reported drastically reducing their nonfamily work loads. Only one of the 72 fathers, however, had to make extensive readjustments in educational plans, professional ambitions, or personal goals. Fathers of all ages reported their work commitments were "insulated from the daily cares of hands-on parenting" (p. 39). Almost all of the fathers reported believing that being a good father meant primarily being a good provider.

A few parents reported that parenting came naturally. For most, however, "skill and sensitivity in dealing with their children had to evolve, competence in child care had to be learned, confidence in the 'goodness' of one's parenting had to be earned" (p. 42).

House-Husbands: Fathers As Primary Caregivers

Study Question Do women have a natural advantage over men in the domain of nurturing and rearing a child?

Men serving as primary caregivers (so-called "house-husbands") have received considerable media attention. However, most men who adopt this role do so for relatively short durations. Single fathers aside, there are very few fathers in nuclear families who provide long-term primary care for their children (Radin, 1988).

Radin (1988) and her colleagues studied primary caregiving fathers in families with at least one preschool child, living in Ann Arbor, Michigan, a university community. A follow-up study was performed 4 years later, allowing them to compare families that persisted in primary father care with families that reverted back to primary mother care.

They found that men who become primary caregivers are typically somewhat older, better educated individuals with flexible working hours. They have small families and are generally satisfied with their wives' employment status and the child-care arrangements. Many have negative views of their own fathers' lack of involvement in child rearing. Some of their wives were raised in homes with working mothers and had positive views of their fathers.

When the parents were asked why they selected father-care, they gave several reasons. Many felt that children should be left with a parent, not with a baby-sitter. One wife commented, "It's a comfortable arrangement that we fall into naturally, and my husband won't quit child care even if there is a change in his job status." Radin suggests that there are so few house-husbands because "it is difficult to find the combination of conditions which may be necessary for a family to withstand the powerful societal pressures on those who try to create new parental patterns of behavior" (p. 140).

Children benefited cognitively from high father involvement in their rearing. This may be attributable to the special way fathers interact with their children. "They tend to be more physical, more provocative, and less stereotyped in their play than mothers . . . primary caregiving fathers spend more time than do traditional fathers in cognitively stimulating activities with children, particularly with daughters" (p. 140). Having a working mother and primary care father may encourage boys and girls to seek nontraditional careers and lifestyles.

Single Custodial Fathers

Almost a million fathers are raising over a million children in the United States today. Hanson (1988) reviewed the characteristics and motivations of single fathers who have gained legal custody of their children. Single fathers generally are better educated, make more money, and have a higher-status job than fathers in nuclear families. Recent trends suggest that increasing numbers of working-class men will be joining their ranks. Remember, most men who have become single fathers are highly motivated to parent. They have special resources, particularly job flexibility, that allow them to accept this role.

Many single fathers seek neither divorce nor custody, but accept both reluctantly if the situation requires it. They do not adjust as quickly to the fathering role or parent as skillfully as fathers who actively seek custody. Given their comfortable financial situation, custodial fathers usually do not have to move to another home or community. Thus, they can maintain stability in their children's daily life (Hanson, 1988).

Fathers who have been involved in their children's care since infancy are more likely to seek custody and are better prepared to become primary caretakers. They also report feeling closer to their children and believe that they are doing a good job. Single-custodial parents generally have positive motives for seeking custody. They consider themselves the better parent and certainly love their child. Some fathers adopt this role because the mother refused to accept custody (Greif, 1985; Hanson, 1988).

Fathers are more likely to gain custody of adolescents and boys than younger children or girls. Nevertheless, almost half of custodial fathers raise daughters ranging in age from infancy to young adulthood. Children being raised by the same-sexed parent appear to be better adjusted than those being raised by opposite-sexed parents. Hanson reported that children raised by single fathers rated their fathers as more nurturing than children from nuclear families rated either parent.

Single fathers usually share homemaking chores with their children, and the latter seem to benefit from the responsibility. Children in single-father homes appear to be happier and better behaved than children in single-mother homes (Ambert, 1982). Single fathers report that they do not have enough time to spend with their children or to create a satisfying social life for themselves.

Studies of single fathers confirm that highly motivated men can provide their children with high-quality parenting (Risman, 1989). This is reassuring as their ranks appear to be growing. "Most fathers were happy with their decision to have sought or consented to custody, and they felt that they were clearly the better choice of parent. Children reported happiness with this arrangement, and there did not appear to be much yearning to live with the noncustodial parent" (Hanson, 1988, p. 185).

COMPARISONS OF FATHERS' AND MOTHERS' PARENTING STYLES

Study Question In what ways do mothers and fathers display different styles of parenting?

Researchers have compared extensively the parenting styles of mothers and fathers. The most important general finding is that fathers and mothers are equally competent at caregiving. Perhaps because fathers are usually less interested in providing care, mothers spend far more time caring for young children than fathers do. Mothers provide care to infants and toddlers; fathers play with them (Berk & Berk, 1979; J. P. Robinson, 1977).

Division of Labor

Mothers and fathers typically adopt a division of labor in which mothers perform most caretaking duties. Fathers, when available, serve as both playmates to their children and as helpers to their wives. Caretaking is considered the mother's job. The fathers serve as helpers when needed. "When and if the father does participate, it is presumed to be under the mother's direction" (Larossa & Larossa, 1989, p. 144).

J. P. Robinson (1977) found that mothers spend 7 times as much time caring for infants and toddlers as fathers do. Half of the time fathers spend with their young children is play time, compared to one-tenth of mothers' time spent in play. Other than play, the average father provides only about one-tenth of an infant's total care (Larossa & Larossa, 1989).

Some fathers sabotage their own child-care efforts by displaying incompetence, perhaps not intentionally. They forget to change diapers, they give up trying to feed the baby, or they do a mediocre job giving the baby a bath. If they do an adequate job, they expect enormous gratitude. Larossa and Larossa (1989) also note that play, fathers' preferred activity, is "cleaner" than the forms of baby care provided by mothers (e.g., changing diapers, feeding). It is also less demanding and requires less parental attention. "Fathers, in other words, may choose play over work because play 'eats' less into their own free time" (p. 141).

Play

Play behavior is an important modality of potential father influence, particularly with sons. "When distressed, infants tend to direct more attachment-related behaviors (e.g., proximity and contact seeking) toward the mother; when

not distressed, however, they tend to direct more playful distal behaviors toward the father than the mother . . . The father, as socializer and playmate, provides the infant with cognitive and social stimulation that is qualitatively distinct from that provided by the mother" (Bridges, Connell, & Belsky, 1988, pp. 92–93).

Many studies have compared father and mother play. Almost all have found that father play is less conventional and less verbal than mother play (particularly with preschoolers). Father play is "more proximal, vigorous, arousing, and state-disruptive than mother's play" (Yogman et al., 1988, p. 57). Father play is more tactile and physical. Mother play is more visual. Anyone visiting a playground and observing parents interact with young children will find that, compared to mother play, father play is more rough-and-tumble, occasionally eliciting protests from anxious mothers.

"I would do more physical things with Dan than with his sister—be a little rougher in our play. We had a pool with our first house. We have photographs of me tossing Dan way up into the sky, and he'd fall back in the water. We also liked to wrestle on the floor" (father of 2).

The father-child relationship may be particularly influential regarding the child's non-family relationships. "Fathers, in essence, teach their children how to 'get along' with friends and strangers outside of the family" (Bridges et al., 1988, p. 99).

Interest and Interaction

A father's interest in his children is revealed by his presence and participation during birth and his desire to hold and gaze at the newborn. It is also evident in his descriptions of his elated feelings and pride following birth. There is a remarkable similarity between the feelings expressed by mothers and fathers following birth.

In chapter 4, we saw that mothers who have extended contact with their infants at birth demonstrate greater attachment even a year later. Similarly, fathers who have extended contact at birth interact more with their infants and become more involved in caretaking responsibilities (Keller, Hildebrandt, & Richards, 1985). The greater the caretaking responsibilities of mothers or fathers, the sooner both respond to a crying infant (Donate-Bartfield & Passman, 1985).

Yogman and his colleagues videotaped mothers and fathers interacting with their young infants. They found that fathers are "capable of skilled and sensitive social interaction with young infants" (Yogman et al., 1988, p. 56). They observed that "by three months of age, infants successfully interacted with both mothers and fathers with a similar, mutually regulated, reciprocal pattern, in which both partners rhythmically cycled to a peak of affective involvement and then withdrew . . . Mothers and fathers were equally able to involve the infant in games" (p. 56).

New fathers bottle-feed their infants about the same amount of milk as mothers. They are equally sensitive to such cues as mouth movements, coughs, spitting up, and sneezes. They adjust their speech to infants and report feeling as attached to their infants as mothers do (Parke & Suomi, 1983). Fathers are quite interested in their children, though they often show more interest in sons than daughters (Bronstein, 1988b). In general, however, mothers appear to enjoy their relationships with infants more than fathers do. Fathers are more likely than mothers to care for a child out of obligation than out of enjoyment (Larossa & Larossa, 1989).

Discipline

To compare the mother's and the father's role in disciplining their young children, Yogman and his colleagues (1988) provided slightly frustrating tasks to male and female toddlers and observed parent-child interactions. One task was a 2-minute prohibition episode, during which 2 attractive objects (a toy frog and a tape recorder) were presented, one of which was designated "off limits." The researchers videotaped the parents' attempts to promote compliance with their instructions that the child not touch the tape recorder.

They found that the fathers' and mothers' interactions with the toddlers (male and female) were much more similar than different. They were alike in who gave the first directive, the number of directives given, and the compliance elicited in the child. Mothers did verbalize more often than fathers. The investigators concluded that the stereotype of fathers as family disciplinarian was not supported by their observations. Similarly, Power and Parke (1986), during naturalistic observations of families at home, noted that mothers attempted to enforce more rules than did fathers. In other ways, however, mothers and fathers adopted comparable discipline strategies.

Russell and Russell (1987) interviewed parents of school-age children and observed them interacting with their children at home. They observed that mothers interacted more with their children and were more directive and more involved in caregiving. Fathers interacted primarily in the context of play. The investigators did not find differences between fathers and mothers in parental sensitivity or reactions to misbehavior. Fathers were not found to be more negative or restrictive. In fact, fathers were observed engaging in more physical affection, warmth, and playful joking with children than were mothers!

Brachfeld-Child (1986) observed parents teach their infants to place a cube in a cup. She found that mothers and fathers generally spent the same amount of time and used the same types of strategies directing the infants' activities. Fathers talked more to the infants, and, unlike the fathers in the 3 previously cited studies, did set more limits.

McLaughlin (1983) videotaped parents attempting to achieve compliance verbally in their preschool children during free play at home. He observed that mothers and fathers behaved similarly, but fathers did use more commands. Children complied equally with mothers' and fathers' suggestions and questions. These studies are typical in revealing basic similarities in discipline strategies adopted by mothers and fathers.

Differential Treatment of Sons and Daughters

Do parents interact differently with their sons and daughters? The research literature is mixed on this question. No one has suggested, for example, that fathers love their sons more or less than their daughters. However, many have observed that traditional fathers distance themselves more from their sons in terms of displays of emotion or affection. Fathers play more with their sons, but perhaps in ways that communicate the traditional message, "This is how men interact—competently, with courage, and with minimal expression of tenderness."

"Fathers' higher level of physical activity in their play with sons may communicate to children that boys are better equipped to handle and enjoy the challenges of the physical world. Girls, for their own safety, had best be more cautious. And of course, as they are communicating different attitudes to and about girls and boys, fathers are differentially imparting skills in these areas, so that they may in fact be creating self-fulfilling prophecies" (Bronstein, 1988a, p. 119).

The different ways that parents interact with boys and girls may convey traditional gender-based expectations about how males and females conduct themselves (Power & Shanks, 1989). This may reinforce aggression in boys, "while providing them with less opportunity to learn cooperation and empathy. In treating sons more instrumentally and less sociably than daughters, fathers may be providing their sons with less opportunity to learn the interpersonal skills necessary for establishing and maintaining intimate relationships, while also

providing an early model of a traditional male-male relationship—of *doing* things together, rather than verbally connecting in a more intimate way" (Bronstein, 1988a, p. 119).

Frankel and Rollins (1983) asked parents to play with their 6-year-old children using a jigsaw puzzle and to teach them to remember picture cards. Mothers and fathers did not differ in their instructional behaviors. Both were "more directive and more approving or disapproving of their sons than of their daughters." Parents were more performance- and task-oriented with sons. They "interacted with their daughters in a more cooperative, concrete and specific fashion, and daughters were given more feedback about their performance" (p. 694). The investigators found that both mothers and fathers were "very effective" in teaching their children.

SUMMARY

Demographic, social, and economic changes in the late twentieth century have given rise to a variety of family configurations. They differ substantially from either the traditional extended family or the nuclear family. Large numbers of children experience a very stressful sequence of transitions: parental divorce, single-parent family, and then stepfamily.

Parental separation and divorce and the turmoil that accompanies them can overwhelm children's coping ability. It takes at least 2 to 3 years for most children (and parents) to recover from the impact of family disorganization. In a real sense, the parties involved may never fully recover. Nevertheless, unhappy parents in poor marital relationships are not doing their children a favor by staying together "for the sake of the child."

Custody battles usually increase children's suffering. This is particularly true when parents continue their hostilities after custody is decided. Usually, the mother is granted sole custody, and the father receives visitation rights and support obligations. Divorce mediation and joint custody are becoming more common. Both attempt to minimize the pain of divorce for children and their parents. Joint custody usually increases fathers' participation in their children's lives following divorce. Joint custody is likely to fail unless the ex-spouses can maintain a good working relationship with each other.

Children in the sole custody of their mothers usually have little contact with their fathers. Fathers claim that they want to spend time with their children, but hostile ex-spouses discourage their involvement. More important than custody arrangements are the ongoing relationships children maintain with both parents, including the noncustodial parent. Children also benefit when their divorced parents get along with each other.

Children's ability to cope with parental divorce depends upon many factors. These include their age, sex, parental support, their predivorce adjustment, and their personal coping resources. Even under optimal conditions, parental separation causes children much pain and severely disrupts their lives. Its effects may continue throughout childhood, adolescence, and even adulthood.

About one out of 5 households in the United States are headed by single parents. They raise about one-quarter of all United States children under the age of 18. Almost 90 percent of these parents are women. Their median income is about one-third the national average. About one million fathers have sole custody of their children, and they seem to be doing well. Single fathers usually seek and receive more cooperation from their children regarding household chores and are typically regarded highly by their children. Research generally suggests that children benefit from living with the same-sexed parent.

Stepfamilies are very varied and complex family configurations. Adults entering stepfamilies usually do not have realistic expectations about the stepparent role. Stepchildren may resist their authority and resent their intrusion into the family. Gaining their acceptance may take time and patience. Stepmothers are usually accepted more quickly than stepfathers, possibly because they become much more involved in their stepchildren's lives. Generally, children in stepfamilies report being as happy as children in other family configurations.

Mothers and fathers are equally competent at caregiving and have similar parenting styles. Mothers, however, spend far more time with children and in different types of activities. Mothers provide care and nurturance; fathers play. Most fathers spend relatively little time caring for their children. When they do, they are typically providing assistance to their wives. There are real obstacles to increased father participation in family life. These include long-standing stereotypes about what constitutes masculine and feminine behavior, long working hours, and unsympathetic employers.

It is gradually becoming more acceptable for males to be nurturant, sensitive, and affectionate, and for females to be assertive, independent, and achieving. These changes encourage men to adopt closer and more satisfying relationships with their children. They allow women to exercise greater choice about how they will balance their personal, occupational, and educational goals. In the long run, children will probably benefit from both of these trends.

CHAPTER THIRTEEN

Special Children, Special Parents

OBJECTIVES

After studying chapter 13, students should be able to

1. Describe what is meant by the term "special children"
2. Describe, generally, how parents react to the birth of a disabled or handicapped child
3. Describe the family life-cycle model as it applies to families of disabled children
4. List the special stressors confronting families with disabled or ill children
5. Evaluate the special problems of chronically ill children and their parents
6. Discuss the nature of home interventions that allow parents of Down syndrome children to learn language and other skills
7. List the characteristics of autistic children and family interventions that have contributed to their development
8. Describe the characteristics that define a child as "learning disabled" and steps that parents can take to promote LD children's adjustment
9. Discuss how the three types of prevention apply to physical and psychological disorders
10. Describe the cultural bias toward blaming mothers for their children's disorders

INTERVIEW WITH PARENTS OF A DOWN SYNDROME CHILD

Q. Why did you decide to have children?

Mother I love kids. When I was in high school, I baby-sat a lot. I was an art counselor for two years. I taught arts and crafts.

Q. With Charles, I understand that you discovered he had a problem the day after he was born?

Mother Yes, that night they didn't tell me. They should have waited until my husband arrived. I was beside myself. The doctor said, "I'm sorry, your son is not right. He has Down syndrome. Take him home and love him." No encouragement. I went bananas. They had to calm me down with tranquilizers. Thank God I found this woman, a social worker with a Down syndrome child much older than mine. She came to my home and told me about a program her son was in, how far he had come, that there was hope. She gave me encouragement.

My parents said, "Put him in an institution." I had no support from my parents at all. But my husband's family advised us to keep him at home. I was torn. The social worker convinced me that there was hope for these children. So I started a program, giving him stimulation, when he was 2 or 3 months old. They would take him to a room and work with him physically. And they would teach me. I would have him on the changing table, and move his legs up and down, move his arms, blow in his face, give him all types of stimulation.

We had rap sessions with the other parents. That's what really saved me. Knowing that I wasn't alone. It was therapy for me. I stayed in the group, but I changed doctors. I was so turned off by his attitude. They are not trained to support parents.

Father You have to realize that when a child like this is born, a first child, there is a lot of guilt on the part of the parents, thinking we caused it in some sense. We went for genetic counseling, and they determined that it was not genetically caused. Once we understood that it was not inherited from us, we were able to put aside our feelings of guilt. Because my mother was ill, she could not help us. The lack of support from my wife's parents was the worst. To this day, I have not forgiven them. Now, they pay lip service to Charles's development. I despise them for their total lack of interest in this child.

We eventually discovered that Charles had a congenital heart defect, which is common in Down syndrome children. He also had respiratory problems, hearing problems, lots of physical problems besides mental retardation. He had open heart surgery when he was 10 years old, and still has a leaky valve. But Charles is the one child of our three that is the least complaining. We never hear from him unless he is in considerable pain. He also has Tourette's syndrome, a second affliction, which has made his ability to function more difficult.

He's bused to camp in the summer; he loves it. He has music, arts and crafts, rowing; he occasionally goes on trips. In the fall, he goes to school in a TMR class [training for the mentally retarded]. Next year he'll be 13, and he will go to junior high. As parents, we have the choice of what school he'll attend in New Jersey. Parents have become aware of our right to make decisions regarding our children.

I don't think Charles is aware that he's retarded. He is very content. He does not feel rejected. He does not know anything but love. He does not have the capacity to hate; his inner feelings are always positive. Some Down children are more loving than others. We must constantly watch him because of his outgoing nature. He would go anywhere with anyone. Nobody could be mean as far as he's concerned. This is our greatest worry . . .

Mother I bought him a bike, put on training wheels, and made him get on it. My husband said, "He's not going to do it." But he did it in two days.

Father I was negative. He is obstinate. He does not want to be challenged by us. He'll fight us, but we fight harder. He's perfect in the sense of what he had to overcome. His siblings are proud of his achievements, but like any other siblings, they also resent him. As we were teaching him, they would help us with his lessons. My other son would say, "Come on, Charles, you can do it." My wife and I were also totally supportive of each other.

We have minimal expectations. We're being realistic. He can only go a certain distance mentally. We only hope he can go the furthest that we can bring him, that he will be a functional human being. When we pass away, we know he'll have some kind of venture in life. We have never instilled in our other children the burden of responsibility for him. Only to care about him. We're responsible for him. We know his brother and sister are very proud of him; they're good to him and very supportive.

INTRODUCTION

In this chapter, we examine a special topic— parenting children whose development is not typical. Because the topic of this book is not developmental disabilities, we will not dwell on childhood disorders per se. We will focus, instead, on the problems confronting parents raising children with developmental, intellectual, or emotional problems.

One particular hazard we confront in addressing uncommon children is seeing them as an accident or as a tragedy rather than seeing them as children. A mother of a child with serious kidney problems writes, "For a time, I almost stopped seeing him as a child, a separate person, and saw only a disease, a handicap, a collection of symptoms" (Weatherly, 1985, p. 10). Physically handicapped, learning disabled, chronically ill, and dying children must be viewed as children first. The alternative is to see them through a veil of labels, sympathy, and fear, which encourages them to do the same.

Today, expectant parents have the luxury of anticipating a normal birth and a healthy infant. Over 95 percent of the time, this is the case. However, each year, tens of thousands of new parents are shocked to discover that their infant or child has a serious emotional, intellectual, perceptual, or behavioral problem or some combination (see Spotlight: What It Means to Have Juliet). Physical impairments are usually apparent at birth. Psychological and neurological disorders may not be identified until a child is of school age or, occasionally, much older.

We have previously noted that new parents have many images or expectations of what their child will be like and what parenting will be like. Fortunately or unfortunately, the reality is usually quite different from the image. This is particularly true when children are born less than perfect.

"When a child's health is impaired, parents can be confronted harshly and abruptly with a reality that allows little or no hope for fulfillment of their dreams. A child with muscular dystrophy is not likely to become a pro football player; a child with Down syndrome is not likely to win a Nobel prize. So the fantasied child is lost and a process of grieving begins" (A. T. McCollum, 1985, p. 3).

WHO IS SPECIAL?

Almost all parents consider their children special, and they, of course, are right. All children are unique. What constitutes being "special,"

to some extent, is dictated by our beliefs about what constitutes normality. The labels "special" and "exceptional" are relative terms. They are usually defined on the basis of children's attributes or the circumstances of their life situation in comparison to those of more "typical" children (Lewis & Rosenblum, 1981).

Children considered special on the basis of their psychological or biological characteristics might be labeled developmentally disabled, learning disabled, autistic, emotionally disturbed, antisocial, handicapped, or chronically ill. Children may also be considered special on the basis of characteristics that are not considered impairments. Exceptionally bright and gifted children are special, too, with distinctive needs and problems (See "Gifted Children" later in this chapter).

Children who become special because of their life circumstances include abused and neglected children; children of addicted, depressed, or mentally ill parents; and children raised in nonconventional families. Similarly, parents may be considered "special" on the basis of their personal characteristics or their life circumstances (Lewis & Rosenblum, 1981).

PARENTING CHILDREN WITH SPECIAL PROBLEMS

Study Question   What obstacles confront parents raising special children?

First-time parents have little basis for comparing their infant's development with that of other children. They suspect that something is not quite right, but they attribute this uneasy feeling to their lack of knowledge about normal development or to a lack of parenting experience. For example, they may view hyperactivity and a short attention span as disobedient or defiant behavior rather than as being symptomatic of a hidden organic or emotional problem.

For certain disabilities, the parent-infant bonding process may suffer. The infant may be very difficult to care for and may provide few cues during social encounters. "Social interactions with disabled babies are often less spontaneous, less fun, require more effort, and even become less frequent than with 'easier' babies" (J. McCollum, 1985, p. 6).

Handicapped infants may not emit the sounds and gestures exhibited by nonhandicapped infants. They may not smile or greet a parent with anticipation. Blind and deaf infants are less likely to provide their parents with the kinds of pleasing interactions that foster the bonding process in other families. Some parents have to learn how to accept and care for children who have unusual appearances and behaviors (J. McCollum, 1985, p. 6).

There is some commonality across families in initial reactions to a dreaded diagnosis, the disability's disorganizing effect on family functioning, and the ways in which family members cope with the disability. Denial and grief are common first reactions. "After the facts of the disease became clear, Will and I went through a period of vacillating between grief and denial. We spent many nights crying and holding on to each other, feeling completely helpless. At other times we refused to acknowledge that Jesse had muscular dystrophy, hoping that if we did not give it a name, it might go away. Why think about it since nothing could be done anyway?" (Gamble, 1985, p. 16).

With less clear-cut disabilities, parents (usually mothers) eventually seek diagnostic services to help resolve their apprehensions. This is more of a coping response than an act of denial. "In reflecting over their initial reactions to the diagnosis [of learning disability] the majority of mothers described feeling relief on confirmation of their suspicions, not defensive reactions" (Faerstein, 1986, p. 9). Of course, the parents' reactions will reflect their understanding of the diagnosis and the prognosis they are given for their child's future development.

Handicapped children will confirm that people's (particularly other children's) reactions to their disability can be as much a source of stress or pain as the disability itself. They have to learn to adjust not only to their disability but to its social and emotional consequences. Being "different" is one of the most difficult problems for disabled (or any) children. Many children with special needs are ashamed of their handicaps and have low self-esteem. Even teachers sometimes treat children with physical disabilities as though they were mentally handicapped. Children adjust better when they can communicate to their parents their strong feelings about people's insensitivity (Gamble, 1985; Rousso, 1985).

Case History

Harris and Powers (1984) describe in a case history a couple's reaction when they discovered that their son was autistic:

"By the time the boy was 18 months old it was impossible to turn away from the problems; he was not developing as he should. There were no indications that he was going to talk, he seemed quite indifferent to other people, and appeared content to be left alone. At first, his parents wondered if he were deaf, but since he would respond to the soft rustling of a candy wrapper this hardly seemed likely. By 24 months of age, their anxiety was acute and they began to push their pediatrician for more information. It was at that point that they were referred for a complete assessment at a special child evaluation center of the local hospital. Shortly before their son was 30 months of age the parents received a definitive diagnosis: their boy was autistic.

"His parents recall vividly the sickening impact of that first conference in the pediatric neurologist's office. A feeling in the stomach of dread and fear that remained for weeks and still, after all these years, returns when they talk about that day.

"Abruptly, the woman and the man underwent a transformation in their view of themselves and their child. They were the parents of a defective child. This child, made of their body and their love, was irreversibly damaged. A child who would never be normal. A child whose future was radically different from all they had envisioned. Their sense of normalcy, of belonging in a snug niche in the community around them, was rudely shaken. They were different and

life would never be the same for them. Their dreams were shattered and they hardly knew what to do."

Waisbren (1980) confirms that many parents of developmentally delayed infants see themselves more negatively and express ambivalent or negative feelings about the child.

Family Life-Cycle Model

Study Question   How does raising a child with special needs affect a parent's development and life style?

Harris and Powers (1984), applying the family life-cycle model described in chapter 2, view family adjustment as a series of tasks, conflicts, or challenges. All families experience these challenges. Since families with handicapped children are more similar to other families than different, they confront similar challenges (Harris & Bruey, 1988). Nevertheless, the presence of a handicapped child magnifies the obstacles they must confront in each phase of the family's life cycle.

For example, two young people enter into an intimate marital relationship and anticipate the birth of a healthy child. They are learning to settle their problems through mutual accommodation. They look forward to seeing themselves as a threesome rather than as a couple. They begin to consider how, with a child, they will protect the boundaries of their marital relationship. Their lives are going smoothly. They become comfortable viewing themselves as mother and father, as well as wife and husband. They are then shocked to find themselves raising a child diagnosed as autistic (Harris & Powers, 1984).

Many profound questions occur to these parents in their confusion and pain. Can they love this child? How will they cope? What do they have to offer him as parents? How will his pres-

ence affect the family, their marital relationship, and other siblings? Will he be dependent upon them for the rest of their lives? If so, who will care for him when they cannot? Where can they find help?

Strong feelings usually accompany these thoughts. Parents report sadness about their child's prospects and their own. They may feel angry at the child or at his problem. They feel disappointed that their anticipated normal child is not there to enrich their lives. Most report guilt about having these "awful" feelings. Some couples cannot adjust to this profound change in their lives and eventually separate. "At a time when mutual support may be vital, individuals may withdraw from one another or turn their pain outward and become hurtful to each other" (Harris & Powers, 1984). Worse, they may withdraw from the child.

Perhaps the primary challenge of parents in this phase is to accept the reality of their child's status and to not sacrifice their relationship to child care. Couples often report that marital tensions increase following the birth of a handicapped child. Marital conflict and parental stress increase according to the severity of the handicap (Kazak, 1986). The presence of a handicapped child brings some couples closer together and separates others. The status of the relationship before the birth is a good predictor of which of these outcomes is more likely (Byrne & Cunningham, 1985).

As the child grows, the nature of the challenges confronting the family changes. Even when reaching school age, the special child still requires an inordinate amount of attention and care. "Over the years a number of mothers have shared with us their sense of entrapment about their lives. They fear that they will never be free to define the space of their own existence. This sense of helplessness and burden can produce feelings of depression" (Harris & Powers, 1984).

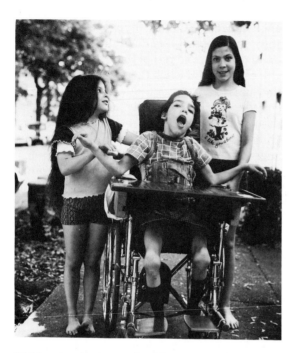

Children tend to have mixed feelings about their disabled siblings.

Study Question *How are siblings affected by the presence of a disabled sister or brother?*

"We don't have a normal family. Ronnie has a lot of respiratory problems. He will need intense medical care for at least one more year. The kids are resentful of him at times because he needs so much care. He's so prone to infections that they have to be isolated from him.

"He has changed our lives alot. You love him so much because of all he's gone through. There's a special bond that I'll never have with the other two because of what he's gone through and what we've gone through with him. You can't give up on him because if it wasn't for us fighting for him he wouldn't be here.

"The hard part is helping his sisters understand that he will get better. They ask, 'Is he going to die?' They are resentful of him but

they've learned a lot from having him as a brother. It's just hard to promote a bond between them when they've been separated so much. I find myself saying to them, 'You can't touch the baby until you've washed your hands.' The three of them need us in such different ways" (mother of three).

Siblings of handicapped children may develop behavior problems of their own (Lavigne & Ryan, 1979). They typically report strong, ambivalent feelings about their disabled sibling. Sisters of disabled siblings in particular often become discouraged by the burdens of caring for and coping with their disabled brother or sister. They have more conflict with their mothers (McHale & Gamble, 1989). Siblings must also adjust to other people's, including their friends', reactions.

"In my family, we were not allowed to discuss our feelings about Bonnie. After all, she was retarded and if we said anything negative, we might hurt her feelings. Well, what about my feelings? Who was concerned about how I felt? I hated my sister for ruining my life . . . I lay awake at night praying that God would forgive me for having such thoughts about my sister. The range and intensity of emotions were too much for me to handle. My parents never sat me down and said, 'This is the problem. This is what's wrong with her . . .' I remember several times trying to tell my Mom how I felt and she would say, 'Your feelings are wrong and you'd better change them' " (Ellifritt, 1985, p. 46).

Family Stressors

Lipsky (1985) discusses the unique stresses that befall parents of disabled children. As both a researcher and a parent of a teenager with spina bifida, she resents that our culture focuses "solely on the negative emotional aspects of raising children with handicapping conditions. [Professionals] give little attention to the resilience shown by the many parents and families who do well in spite of having experienced a form of stress often thought to carry a substantial risk of adverse outcome" (p. 614).

Many parents with disabled children report that inadequate professional support provides additional stress. Lipsky criticizes the double messages that professionals sometimes give parents. On the one hand, they view parents as crucial to their child's growth and development. On the other hand, parents are told they are ill-equipped to meet their children's emotional and other needs.

Some professionals treat parents of handicapped children as obstacles to treatment or as the cause of the child's adjustment problems (see Spotlight: Blaming Mothers for Children's Problems, later in this chapter). Such attitudes increase parental distress. "It is essential that parents and professionals attempt to understand and make others aware that stress is most often not a factor of psychological dysfunction, but, rather, the absence of a sympathetic social or economic support system" (p. 617). The bitterness expressed at the beginning of this chapter by Charles's parents toward his unsupportive grandparents reinforces this point.

Parents of children with cystic fibrosis report coping successfully. However, during interviews, they expressed having difficulty in adjusting to the hospitalization of their children. They also complained about strained marital relationships. Many found it hard to accept their child's illness. Some felt they weren't doing enough for their child. Many parents were concerned that the siblings of the ill child were being neglected or deprived (Phillips, Bohannon, Gayton, & Friedman, 1985).

Supportive social networks are associated with positive personal and family adjustment and positive child behavior outcomes (Dunst, Trivette, & Cross, 1986). To a large extent, a family's adjustment will reflect the support they receive from their relatives and from support services available in their community. "We found other parents who had children with muscular dystrophy and met with them on a regular basis. This told us more about the disease than any book, doctor, or social worker we had previously encountered" (Gamble, 1985, p. 17).

Parents who bear a developmentally disabled child generally have ambivalent feelings about the child, in addition to their sadness and disappointment. Most parents marshall their personal and family resources and do what must be done. Raising disabled or chronically ill children can be a challenging, but very rewarding, experience. After parents adjust to the initial shock, denial, anger, and guilt, they usually find they have a delightful child who is very difficult to care for. Most of these children will eventually participate fully in the adult world.

"There are thousands of Americans with disabilities who are leading satisfying lives. Disabled people are husbands, wives, and stamp collectors. They are members of virtually every profession. Time and time again, disabled individuals have proven that anatomy is not destiny" (Blumberg, 1985, p. 129).

CHILDREN WITH ACUTE AND CHRONIC ILLNESS

Study Question *What special stresses confront parents of chronically ill children?*

About 2 percent of all children are chronically ill. They may suffer from cancer, kidney problems, cystic fibrosis, spina bifida, sickle cell anemia, diabetes, or heart disease. They are "for the most part, normal children in different situations. Nevertheless, such children as a group have a higher rate of significant emotional and social difficulties. Separation from parents, missed days from school, painful medical procedures, complex medical regimens and changes in body appearance are just some of the stresses they may face" (Hurley, 1987, p. 34).

Since many chronically ill children died in the past, there were few services available to prepare those who lived for returning to a more normal daily existence. Today, most of these children survive. Together with their families, they require extensive medical and social support for their full recovery. Most children with debilitating illnesses have medical, social, and educational needs that are not likely to be met.

Children's reactions to their serious illness and to the separation from their parents that accompanies hospitalization depend upon many factors. These include the type and length of illness, their level of maturity, their ability to communicate about their distress, and the quality of their family relationships (Hurley, 1987; Thunberg, 1981).

Some chronically ill children must learn to cope with painful treatment procedures, such as spinal taps. Unlike adults, children have little influence over the course of these events. In addition to their confusion and distress, they may feel helpless and discouraged. Young children might interpret hospitalization and separation from their family as abandonment or punishment. They sometimes regress to a lower level of functioning. "Thus, an already verbal child may decide to stop speaking, or a toilet-trained child . . . may begin wetting or soiling himself. Initial protest of separation may be followed by withdrawal behavior with depressed affect" (Thunberg, 1981, p. 175).

Hospitalization obviously intensifies children's fears. Parental expression of fear, dramatic hospital encounters, and painful diagnostic procedures carried out by insensitive personnel also contribute to a child's distress. If the hospitalization is brief, the impact on the child's development will probably be minor or nonexistent. Chronic or long-term hospitalization requires considerably greater coping from both children and parents.

Ruth Stein, founding director of the Pediatric Home Care program at Bronx Municipal Hospital Center, suggests there are two levels of support for chronically ill children. The first is good medical care. "The second is help in living a complicated life under difficult circumstances, and that kind of help is the same for most illnesses. The parents have day-to-day problems like finding baby sitters who can understand the child's illness, explaining the illness to the child's schoolteacher, dealing with economic burdens and handling their own worries" (quoted by Hurley, 1987, p. 36). Social and psychological care not only benefit the children but also their parents and siblings. They are all profoundly affected by the illness and sometimes more in need of support than the ill child.

The impact on family life of having a chronically disabled child depends upon several factors. These include the severity of the disability, the child's age, and any medical complications that accompany the disability. The family's coping resources, particularly marital satisfaction and the quality of family life, are important predictors of adjustment (Friedrich, Wilturner, & Cohen, 1985).

Studies have suggested that mothers of chronically ill children are vulnerable to depression, and that fathers tend to withdraw from child-care responsibilities. Some siblings of ill children may suffer adjustment problems, while others seem to benefit from the experience. Family stress appears to be related to the type of disability and is greater when children have multiple problems or handicaps. Educated parents, having higher aspirations for their child, report more child-related stress than parents who are less educated (Palfrey, Walker, Butler, & Singer, 1989).

Open and honest communication and expression of feelings among all parties appear to be crucial for successful adjustment. Many psychologists have noticed that these trying circumstances often bring family members closer together. "Resiliency is the rule rather than the exception. And if you talk with enough parents and children, they're likely to emphasize how the illness brought them in touch with each other. Facing common adversity forces some families to work together more effectively. It sounds horrible to say that there are benefits to chronic childhood illness. No one would choose to have the illness, but psychological benefits can happen as a result" (Drotar, quoted by Hurley, 1987, p. 43).

DOWN SYNDROME CHILDREN

Approximately one in 800 infants is born with Down syndrome, a form of mental retardation caused by an extra chromosome. Down syndrome children have characteristic facial features. Unfortunately, their appearance has encouraged the stereotypes that they are all alike, and that they cannot be educated. Isolating them in institutions where they experience impoverished environments has led to self-fulfilling, tragic outcomes that mask their true potential.

Down syndrome children like Charles, whose parents are interviewed at the beginning of this chapter, are typically multihandicapped, with heart and other organ abnormalities. They usually have problems with their motor coordination, hearing, and seeing. They do not seem to hear and recognize words normally and may speak in incomplete sentences. Most are mildly retarded, but they differ extensively in their intellectual potential (Kolata, 1987b; Turkington, 1987).

Most developmentally delayed infants require extra stimulation from their caretakers. For some types of developmental disability, children's infrequent initiations of interactions may discourage parental responsiveness. How parents respond to their children's initiations may be the crucial factor in remedial play (Berlin & Critchley, 1989; McConachie & Mitchell, 1985).

The development of social interaction usually depends upon infant-generated signals that stimulate reactions in the parent. Retarded infants, however, are less responsive and less verbal than normal infants. They also show fewer attentional and emotional responses.

Parents may also fail to notice or respond to the signals the infant is providing (McConachie & Mitchell, 1985). Parents of disabled children can learn to compensate for their lowered responsiveness by using more commands. They also learn to become more active in general, prompting the child to behave more (Hanzlik & Stevenson, 1986).

Certain infant characteristics and behaviors may also inhibit parent-child bonding (Fraser, 1986). Retarded children are less likely to smile and to initiate pleasurable interactions. They also cry more often than nonretarded children (Levy-Shiff, 1986).

Today there are successful early intervention programs that teach parents how to encourage social and other responses in their disabled children (e.g., Breiner, 1989; Riley, Parrish, & Cataldo, 1989). These programs arose in the wake of the Education for All Handicapped Children Act of 1975. This law requires that disabled children receive an education in the least restrictive environment allowable, preferably classrooms. Most programs show parents of children like Charles how to provide their handicapped children with enriched and stimulating home environments. With intensive training, retarded children can acquire skills that develop more naturally in children of average intelligence.

Educators and parents have discovered that many Down syndrome children can achieve after all (Turkington, 1987). Parent training programs are critical for these children's development. Child-rearing strategies exert a greater influence on mildly retarded children's conduct than do organic factors (Richardson, Koller, & Katz, 1985).

Parents of Down syndrome children have also been trained to help them acquire language skills. For example, a 5-year study called EDGE (Expanding Developmental Growth through Education) attempted to improve communication skills by teaching parents how to play with their children. About two-thirds of the subjects, when tested at the age of 5 years, scored in the educable range. Only half of the subjects who did not receive special lessons accomplished this criterion.

Although mothers and fathers are similar in their interactions with their mentally handicapped children, differences have been observed. The differences correspond to those described between mothers and fathers of nonhandicapped children. Fathers of retarded children may be more similar to their counterparts in families with normal children than are mothers. Fathers seem to be less distressed by the burdens of rearing a disabled child (Levy-Shiff, 1986). Perhaps this is because they are less involved in caretaking.

Mothers usually react more successfully and show greater flexibility. Fathers may elicit more negative responses. Dominating fathers may have less-compliant children. Most professionals who train parents work with mothers, but fathers also benefit from professional guidance (McConachie & Mitchell, 1985). Siblings are sometimes involved in training programs. They learn how to become more accepting and caring of their retarded brother or sister.

At least half of Down syndrome children who are raised at home by middle- and upper-class parents will be educable when they start school. They will read at or above the second grade level in elementary school (Turkington, 1987). Unfortunately, many school districts resist mainstreaming these children, and many parents remain unaware of their children's true potential.

AUTISTIC CHILDREN

Autism, previously known as childhood schizophrenia, is a severely debilitating disorder, the causes of which remain unknown. New evidence suggests that autism probably has a variety of causes, including a genetic defect (*New York Times,* August 24, 1989).

Older theories attributing autism to inadequate parental care have been discarded (Plienis, Robbins, & Dunlap, 1988).

A rare disorder that occurs in about 5 out of 10,000 live births, autism usually emerges by the age of 2½ years. It is far more common in males. In the film *Rain Man,* Dustin Hoffman movingly portrays an autistic adult with astonishing mathematical abilities. The portrayal is generally realistic. However, most autistic people are retarded; only some are of normal intelligence.

Virtually all autistic individuals are withdrawn and generally nonresponsive to other people, including their parents (Plienis, Robbins, & Dunlap, 1988). Most either do not speak at all or mechanically repeat whatever is said to them (echolalia). Repetitive behaviors, such as rocking back and forth, and self-destructive behaviors are common. A 5- or 10-year-old autistic child might behave like a normal one-year-old, requiring constant, long-term supervision (Lovaas, 1987; Lovaas, Koegel, & Schreibman, 1979; Lovaas & Smith, 1989).

The demands of raising an autistic child can seriously strain a family's resources. DeMyer and Goldberg (1983) report that family relationships, the emotional well-being of the parents, family recreation, and finances are adversely affected. Mothers, in particular, report feeling guilty and inadequate (DeMyer, 1979).

In *Rain Man,* the autistic man throws a tantrum that allows him to avoid having to fly on an airplane. Research with autistic children suggests that their bizarre behavior may be a learned way of expressing, "I don't want to do this. If you try to make me do this, I'll act crazy until you stop" (Carr & Durand, 1987, p. 63). Autistic children apparently learn to punch, bite, kick, or scratch themselves or others so that they can have their way.

The concept of bizarre behavior as a form of communication brings together interpretational approaches to abnormal behavior and

The practice of mainstreaming has led to increased numbers of handicapped children attending classes with those who are not handicapped. Today's public classrooms may contain children with physical, emotional, and learning disabilities, or children with cancer or AIDS. All children seem to benefit when exposed to those who are different from them, even though many children require some adjustment (Kutner, 1988i).

Mainstreamed children benefit from the opportunity to interact with and compete with nonhandicapped children. The latter benefit from learning how to relate to and understand human disability. "Helping able-bodied children understand what has happened to someone who is sick, scarred or disabled can be complex. As children develop, they respond to different cues and have very different concerns from those of their parents" (Kutner, 1988i).

Toddlers tend to disregard physical differences in their peers, but preschoolers judge other children on the basis of their appearance and behavior. Older children may express their curiosity in ways that would embarrass adults. Teenagers appear to be the most uncomfortable with individual differences. Most people, children and adult, have not learned how to relate comfortably to handicapped or disabled people. Focusing on the disability prevents us from seeing the person "inside." This can be quite painful to the disabled child who is struggling to accept, but not to identify with, his impairment.

When children make insensitive comments about disabled or disfigured individuals, parents should withhold judgment about the child's remark. They

Parents can help their children become more accepting of their children's disabled peers.

should ask questions that will help the child understand his own feelings about the individual. "Do the scars scare you? Are you frightened by how the other children might treat him? Do you worry that this might happen to you?" (Kutner, 1988i). Parents can help their children avoid the common human pitfall of equating people with their appearance or behavior, and see instead that people are basically similar despite outward appearances.

behavior modification models that emphasize the powerful influence of consequences on behavior. Carr and Durand (1987) taught autistic children better ways of communicating their desires, for example, by saying "Help me" or "Look at what I've done." After training, the children had fewer severe behavior problems.

Unresponsive to traditional psychoanalytic therapies, autistic children have shown remarkable progress through the use of behavior modification techniques and parent training programs (Harris & Bruey, 1988; Lovaas & Smith, 1989; Marcus & Schopler, 1989). Children treated in a program at U.C.L.A. received

40 hours of training a week from a behavior modification specialist. They were then treated at home by their parents and by teachers in special preschool programs.

"The therapy puts a huge demand on the child's family, as the parents must be alert to the child's behavior to be able to respond appropriately. The responses include praising appropriate speech or actions, ignoring bizarre behavior, putting a child who became aggressive in a room alone for a time-out period, or responding to undesirable behavior with a loud 'no'" (Goleman, 1987e).

Lovaas (1987) observed that autistic children who live with their parents after training continue to make progress, whereas children who are returned to institutions regress. Children receiving the most intensive treatment gained an average of 30 IQ points. "The training only really works if you get the parents involved" according to Lovaas (quoted by Goleman, 1987e). Some researchers question the wisdom of exposing families to the considerable burden of working with their autistic children, particularly when the results are uncertain (B. Bower, 1989). Lovaas contends that mainstreaming autistic children is the optimal treatment for this impairment. Parents must become part of the therapy team if their children are to progress.

As with other serious childhood disabilities, "unless parents push for change, they may never become free of their role as caretaker and the child may remain so dependent that when the parents die there is little choice but institutional care" (Harris & Powers, 1984).

UNDERACHIEVING CHILDREN: LEARNING DISABILITIES

Some of us know children of normal intelligence or even bright children who learn to read, write, or do math only with great difficulty. Such children express intense frustration when trying to master certain basic skills. As a result of repeated failure, they misbehave in school, get along poorly with their peers, and suffer from low self-esteem. Some eventually develop an aversion to school, the scene of their embarrassing failures. Some drop out of school before completing their high school education.

It is estimated that 5 to 10 percent of all children have problems learning, many more boys than girls. Attention deficit disorder (ADD), characterized by impulsive behavior and an inability to concentrate, occurs 10 times more frequently in boys than in girls. By 1987, almost 2 million children had been identified as learning disabled (LD), almost half of the nation's special education students (Bales, 1985; Landers, 1987b). Unusual patterns of brain growth during prenatal development may be responsible for certain types of learning disabilities (T. Adler, 1989a).

Who are the learning disabled? There is still considerable controversy about this designation (Gallagher, 1985). The label refers to children who show a significant deficit in some academic area but who score in the normal range on standardized intelligence tests. They show no major emotional or sensory impairments. In other words, children are classified as learning disabled if their achievement in some academic area is less than what would be expected based on their intelligence.

"Learning disabled children are often reported to be poorly coordinated in both gross and fine motor activities. They are likely to have trouble catching a ball, tying shoelaces, or writing with a pencil. Some learning disabled children have speech difficulties. Others may suffer from memory problems, difficulties in coordinating vision and action, or defective ability to process information and make sense of what they see or hear. They can be either overactive or lethargic" (Stone & Church, 1984, p. 554).

Parenting LD Children

As with other disorders, parents of very young LD children suspect that something is wrong. Years may elapse, however, between the onset of parental suspicions (at about age 2½ years) and an actual diagnosis of learning disability (at about age 6 years, on the average). This delay in diagnosis is unfortunate. The earlier LD is diagnosed and treated, the better the child's eventual adjustment.

In Faerstein's (1986) study, a majority (58%) of the mothers reported feeling responsible in some way for the disability. Many reported that raising an LD child, particularly one that is hyperactive, is extremely frustrating. LD children, like other children who are difficult to care for, are at greater risk for child abuse. "The mothers in this study found that society does not accept them or their child because they are unable to demonstrate that their child is ill. The children are not seen by the community as having a physical problem but rather as being bad or different and therefore undesirable" (p. 11).

Once parents understand the problem, there is much that they can do to help their children compensate for their disability. An article by the parents of an LD child and cowritten by the child (McWhirter, McWhirter, & McWhirter, 1985) describes retrospectively how the family helped their son build his self-esteem and focus on his strengths rather than becoming overwhelmed by his disability.

"We used many strategies with Robert to build his self-esteem. These included educating him about his specific disability, the identification and emphasis on his strengths, the use of I-messages and ego-inflating terms, the minimization of criticism, and others" (p. 315). Having graduated from his college's Honors Program with a magna cum laude designation and being on the Dean's honor roll, Robert's achievements support his family's and his own efforts.

GIFTED CHILDREN

No widely accepted definition of giftedness exists. It is not clear whether giftedness is simply high intelligence or something qualitatively different. Gifted children have superior intelligence. They are usually highly motivated to learn and to achieve. They are more likely to fulfill their potential in special, supportive learning environments (Sternberg & Davidson, 1986).

Intellectually gifted children are sometimes stereotyped as poorly adjusted, socially inept individuals who get lost in their scholarly pursuits. Research does not support this portrait. Gifted children are usually not only very intelligent and high achieving but also emotionally stable, popular, skilled as social leaders at school, and happy. Nevertheless, very bright individuals who are teased by their peers or who feel they don't fit in may experience stress and adjustment problems.

Some children's exceptional talents go unrecognized because of parental or societal indifference or due to lack of opportunity to develop their potential. The children may be at risk for academic, social, and emotional maladjustment (Freeman, 1985). Etlin (1988) describes the "gifted underachiever" as having high intelligence but also as being insecure and having low self-esteem, poor social skills, and less persistence than other students. "Paradoxically, the students with the highest intelligence often suffer from the lowest self-image and the most severe emotional and behavioral problems."

Parents of the gifted may have difficulty disciplining their precocious children, who are so adept at getting their way. It is important that parents of gifted children set limits and delegate responsibilities just as parents of less talented children do.

Psychologists Paula Caplan and Ian Hall-Mc-Corquodale observe a tendency in the clinical literature to blame mothers for their children's problems. A survey of 125 articles in major clinical journals revealed 72 kinds of psychopathology attributed to mothers. Examples include agoraphobia, arson, bedwetting, and hyperactivity.

Eighty-two percent of the articles attributed at least part of a child's pathology to the mother (Caplan & Hall-McCorquodale, 1985a; 1985b). In more than three-quarters of the articles, research or therapy addressed the mother-child relationship rather than the father-child relationship or just the child.

"In the articles we reviewed, not a single mother was ever described as emotionally healthy, although some fathers were, and no mother-child relationship was said to be healthy, although some father-child ones were described as ideal. Far more space was used in writing about mothers than about fathers. Furthermore, fathers were often described mostly or only in terms of their age and occupation, whereas mothers' emotional functioning was usually analyzed (and nearly always deemed essentially 'sick')" (Caplan, 1986, p. 70).

Freud was one of the first psychologists to emphasize the mother's role in the development of neurosis. More recently, we hear about "overprotective mothers," "maternal deprivation," and "schizophrenogenic mothers" (Caplan, 1986). Mothers, more than fathers, are blamed for children's problems because they are more visible to therapists. "It's easier to blame the person in the waiting room than to explore arduously what—and who—else might contribute to the child's problems" (Caplan, 1986, p. 71).

Caplan contends that viewing mothers as the only or main cause of children's psychopathology is destructive to mothers, children, society, and the discipline of psychology. It encourages mothers to feel guilty about their children's problems. It discourages researchers from searching for the many factors that contribute to children's disorders.

Mothers may indeed inadvertently encourage poor adjustment, but so may fathers, siblings, peers, and others. Some children may be so vulnerable that they adjust poorly despite excellent parenting. "Mothers, despite their anxiety and guilt, manage to raise millions of reasonably well-adjusted kids. They deserve far more credit for this than they get" (Caplan, 1986, p. 71).

PREVENTION OF PSYCHOLOGICAL PROBLEMS

Study Question   What types of interventions allow society to prevent rather than having to treat psychological problems in children?

It is remarkable how many of society's resources are directed toward treatment and remediation and how few to preventing serious problems from occurring in the first place.

Given the cost to society of treating mental and physical health problems and the human suffering involved, a greater allocation of resources to preventative practices makes sense (Offord, 1987).

Primary prevention consists of reducing the frequency of new cases of a disorder by eliminating its cause (Offord, 1987). Good examples of effective primary prevention include good prenatal care for pregnant women, nutritional counseling, and vaccinating children.

Immunizations have almost eliminated new cases of potentially devastating childhood illnesses (Bumpers, 1984). Parents who are mentally ill, retarded, teenage, poor, or abusive may place their children in jeopardy through faulty rearing practices. Programs that identify special, particularly "hard-to-reach" parents, and provide effective early interventions exemplify primary prevention (Finney & Edwards, 1989; Jaffe, 1990; Kessler, 1988).

Secondary prevention refers to the early detection and treatment of existing physical or psychological problems. Early intervention is more likely to be successful than remediating a problem after it has become firmly ingrained. Most children, prior to entering kindergarten, are routinely screened for speech, visual, and hearing problems. Those who are identified as having problems are treated. This allows them to benefit fully from their school attendance.

Recent successful interventions focus on the "mother-child system," rather than on just the child. Routine psychological screening of preschool children (and their parents) could be useful. Some infants who are at risk for developmental problems can be treated as early as infancy. Early treatment increases the likelihood that intervention will succeed (Turkington, 1984c).

So-called *tertiary prevention* involves intervention in the form of rehabilitation or remediation of established problems to limit their harmful effects (Offord, 1987). Such interventions emphasize a child's resources. Their goal is to achieve as normal a life-style as possible. Most children needing such attention are not receiving it. Of the 7.5 to 9.5 million children needing mental health services, less than one-third are being helped. Many of these problems could be successfully treated or prevented (K. Fisher, 1987b).

Clearly, primary prevention is the most cost efficient and humane of the three prevention strategies. Such programs have enormous potential that is, as yet, unfullfilled. Obstacles include identifying children or families who are at high risk for psychological or physical disorders. Poor, young families are particularly vulnerable (Halpern, 1990). Sometimes, resistant parents have to be persuaded to participate in prevention programs (Greenspan, Wieder, Nover, Lieberman, Lourie, & Robinson, 1987). Programs will be more effective when parents and teachers coordinate their efforts in minimizing the effects of the child's disability.

SUMMARY

Families with disabled or chronically ill children are more similar to than different from ordinary families. Parenting ordinary children is not easy. Parents of children with special needs confront a host of additional obstacles that sometimes seem insurmountable. The nature of the obstacles depends partly upon the specific disability and its severity. The child's age and family and personal resources are also important factors. A critical family resource, as always, is a strong marital relationship.

Typical stressors in families with disabled children include frustrating interactions with professionals and inadequate professional support. Financial problems, finding appropriate educational resources and child care, and marital discord are additional challenges. Because of the added stressors, good communication skills are particularly helpful. Parents adjust best when they have realistic expectations about their children's development and about their own ability to care for their children.

As disabled children mature, the nature of the challenges and tasks facing the family changes. The school-age child may still require an inordinate amount of care. Mothers may fear that they will never be free to pursue their own life goals. Brothers and sisters may have ambivalent feelings about their disabled sibling. They may develop behavior problems of their own.

Fortunately, there are many intervention programs that teach parents how to provide their handicapped children with enriched and stimulating home environments. Support groups help parents cope with their ambivalent feelings about their child. Mainstreaming helps disabled children learn to interact and compete with nonhandicapped children. Nonhandicapped children also benefit from this contact. They become more empathic and sensitive to individual differences.

Unfortunately, theorists and researchers sometimes hold mothers responsible for their children's disorders. Although some mothers may, indeed, encourage poor adjustment, so may fathers and siblings. The optimal approach to psychological and physical disorders is to prevent their occurrence when possible. Primary prevention, eliminating the causes of these disorders, is the most cost-effective and humane strategy.

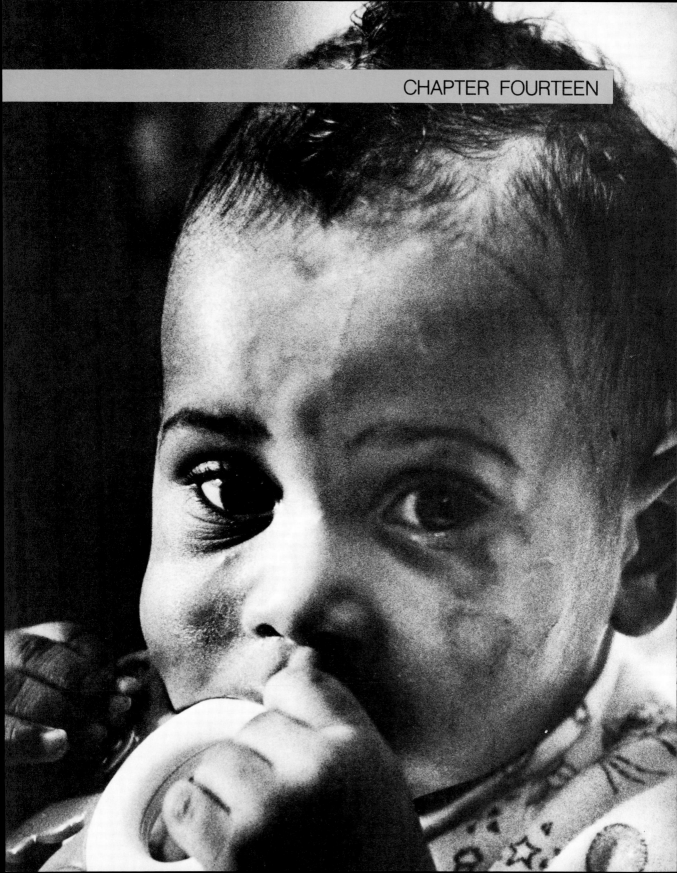

CHAPTER FOURTEEN

Family Violence, Child Abuse, and Neglect

OBJECTIVES

After studying chapter 14, students should be able to

1. Describe the various forms of family violence and their prevalence in United States society
2. Describe the characteristics of violent husbands, battered wives, and their children and the situational factors that are associated with family violence
3. Discuss the two identified types of maritally violent families
4. Distinguish between physical abuse, psychological maltreatment (emotional abuse), sexual abuse, and neglect
5. Profile the "typical" abusive parent and the life circumstances that increase the risk of child abuse
6. Describe the effects of physical abuse on children's emotional development
7. Describe the various forms of psychological maltreatment (emotional abuse)
8. Evaluate the interventions that treat and prevent physical and emotional child abuse
9. Describe the effects of sexual abuse on children
10. Discuss steps that parents can take to protect their children from being sexually abused
11. Describe the characteristics of neglecting parents and neglected children
12. Describe the characteristics of families with children at risk for becoming delinquents, including their style of discipline
13. Describe the distinctive psychological profiles of bullies and their victims
14. Analyze the possible role of playing with guns in the development of aggressive behavior

INTRODUCTION

The 36-year-old single, unemployed father was describing how he had tied the hands of his defiant 9-year-old stepdaughter and "kicked her butt." He told me he had smacked her on the face and body several times and hit her with a belt. His attack left visible bruises on her body. Her 10-year-old sister, the father's biological daughter, observed the beating. (The girls' mother, never married to the father, had long ago fled to California.)

The day following the incident, the abused girl, in considerable pain, visited the school nurse. The nurse reported the incident to the Division of Youth and Family Services. The father was subsequently arrested for child endangerment and abuse. He pleaded guilty. The two girls were placed in the temporary custody of their aunt and uncle. The agency referred the father to me for counseling.

The father told me he had beaten the girl because she had misbehaved in school. She had been bouncing a ball in the school building and had talked back to a teacher. He believed the only alternative to beating her was to "give her away." In other words, he felt that unless he beat her, she would not take him seriously and he couldn't continue to raise her. He told me that he wanted to regain custody of his biological daughter. He said that he had learned his lesson. In his mind, apparently, that meant not getting arrested again.

Almost everyday, in newspapers and on TV, we hear startling accounts of parents turning on their children. We hear reports of child neglect, sexual abuse, beatings, stabbings, shootings, and worse. Family violence and brutality take many forms. Husbands batter their wives or children; children attack their parents or grandparents; parents sell their children for drugs.

There are about one million episodes of child abuse and neglect reported each year in this country. Experts suggest that most incidents are not reported. Thus, the number of actual incidents of abuse is probably much higher (though the rate of severe abuse may actually be declining [Gelles & Straus, 1987]). Almost 2 million women are battered by their husbands each year. The FBI reports that about 20 percent of all murders are committed by family members. Emotional abuse and neglect leave scars as deep and enduring as battering.

It is risky to make general statements about those who commit family violence; they are a varied lot. Nevertheless, the situational and psychological factors associated with family violence have been studied. In this chapter, we consider these factors and review what is known about the psychological effects of family violence on children.

As we shall see, the same parents who practice violence within their marital relationship are likely to be abusive when "disciplining" their children. Children who are victims of abuse may subsequently display violent behaviors with siblings or peers. In this final chapter we examine the darker sides of family life. We attempt to understand the irrational, destructive behavior that is all too common in families.

FAMILY VIOLENCE

***Study Question** What factors predict violent behavior in children?*

We observe violence and conflict at all levels of society in all social classes. Children are exposed daily to violence in movies, on TV news programs and dramas, and, for some children, on the streets where they live and in their own homes (Landers, 1990).

Theorists have suggested many models of aggressive behavior. Some contend that aggressive behavior is instinctive; others suggest it is learned. Some view aggression as a response to frustration; others appeal to the arousing effects of group pressure or aggressive models. Many studies confirm that aggressive behavior sometimes results from the temporary weakening of an individual's ability to control his or her aggressive impulses. The truth probably encompasses all these factors and others. Profiles of violent parents suggest a combination of personality dispositions and stressful life and situational factors. These lead to a loss of control, violent behavior, and, usually, feelings of guilt.

Many children witness the violent domestic disputes of their parents. Some are victims of violence themselves. Children, particularly boys, who observe repeated domestic violence may suffer from emotional disturbance, behavior problems, and social maladjustment. Children who run away from home usually report that physical violence and verbal abuse were common occurrences between parents or between parent and child (Ek & Steelman, 1988).

Boys who are not abused but who are exposed to repeated family violence resemble abused boys in their pattern of adjustment problems (Jaffe, Wolfe, Wilson, & Zak, 1986). Thus, exposure to family violence may be as harmful as abuse itself. Both groups of children, however, may have other situational factors in common that could account for their adjustment difficulties. These include family stress, inadequate child management, and parental separations. About 40 percent of the boys in this study both witnessed family violence and were abused themselves. Children who are both victims and observers of family violence are most prone to psychological problems (Kalmuss, 1984).

"I can still remember him in vivid detail: the edge in his voice as he taunted his victims, the delight in his face, even his name, though I won't say it here. I always gave him a wide berth and so avoided his aggression, but other kids, not so lucky, were his constant victims. You probably remember him, too, by a different name. He's the schoolyard bully" (Roberts, 1988, p. 52).

Most children at one time or another will find themselves, reluctantly, confronted by a bully. It has been estimated that about 20 percent of school-age boys become involved in ongoing aggressive confrontations. Half are bullies and half are victims (Olweus, cited by Collins, 1986e). A survey by the National Association of Secondary School Principals revealed that 25 percent of the students polled considered the possibility of being bullied a major worry. Most children have not been taught how to handle such threatening situations. They are therefore susceptible to intimidation, fear, embarrassment, and guilt.

Recently, researchers have addressed the psychology of the bully and of his victim. Interestingly, the new models of bullying behavior support Alfred Adler's contention that the aggressive, controlling behavior of bullies is an attempt to compensate for their feelings of inferiority and inadequacy.

Research confirms that aggressive children come from aggressive families. Parents who were bullies themselves as children are likely to have children who follow in their footsteps. Females are rarely bullies, but those who are, bully other girls. They harass them verbally rather than physically. Very aggressive girls may become the mothers of bullying sons. About half of all victims of bullying are girls (Perry, Kusel, & Perry, 1988).

Parents of bullies are typically punitive, critical, and sarcastic with their children (and each other).

They model aggressive and confrontational behavior for their children (Kutner, 1988j). "A bully at school is often a victim at home . . . Often bullies have been abused, or have witnessed the parent beat up his spouse or other children in the home" (Floyd, quoted by Collins, 1986e). They respond in unpredictable ways and appear to have little interest in their children.

As a result of their rearing, these children may feel inadequate and worthless. Lacking opportunities to develop prosocial skills at home, bullies have distorted, even paranoid, perceptions of other children's behavior. They might interpret a harmless encounter, such as an ambiguous facial expression, as an intentional provocation and feel justified in striking back (Goleman, 1987h).

Feeling inadequate, they cannot tolerate teasing or even harmless comments from other children. They overreact and eventually alienate their peers and teachers. As we have seen, such antisocial behavior patterns elicit reactions in other people (particularly avoidance) that perpetuate the self-defeating pattern and prevent the learning of more adaptive social skills.

Eron (cited by Goleman, 1987h) has profiled the "typical" bully. By the age of 8, he initiates fights for no reason. He has a quick temper and takes other people's possessions. He is a poor student, and, because of his brutality, he becomes a social outcast. His parents punish him harshly for his behavior but otherwise show little interest in him. He is defiant with his teachers and therefore disliked.

By age 19, he has probably dropped out of school. He is 3 times more likely than his nonaggressive peers to have been in trouble with the law and is generally viewed as a troublemaker. By age 30, his wife, who also has a quick temper, views him as abusive. He continues to get into trouble, perhaps for drunken driving or violent behavior. He is a punitive parent, probably raising a bully of his own.

The Victims of Bullies

Researchers have discovered that the victims of bullies have their own distinctive profile. Like some rape victims, they blame themselves. Because of their shame, they are reluctant to seek the counsel of their teachers or parents. "The child who is bullied often will hide his predicament out of shame. He will mention it to his parents only obliquely, testing the home waters for an emotional chill. It is better to pay the money and go without lunch than to risk being called a coward or a failure" (Kutner, 1988j).

Such children may feign illness to avoid having to be "picked on" at school. They may become truants or even commit suicide or kill their tormentors (Roberts, 1988). Some victims provoke aggression; some passively submit to it.

"A dance goes on. It is as if they court each other, and often it seems as if neither can leave the other alone. Bullies seem to need a victim, and may work hard to create a victim, even if there isn't one there . . . When these bullies see kids they perceive as vulnerable, they are threatened because it reminds them of the shame and humiliation of their own victimization. In the bully's constant teasing and aggression, it is as if he is desperately trying to get the victim to say no, so that the bully himself will feel less threatened" (Floyd, quoted by Collins, 1986e). Both bullies and victims are usually rejected by their peer groups. They may end up with each other because of this exclusion (Perry, Kusel, & Perry, 1988).

Intervention programs teach aggressive children social skills. They also teach potential victims how to handle aggressive confrontations. There is some agreement among experts that children should be encouraged to approach an authority figure and report the harassment. If no adults are available, the child can attempt to ignore the bully's taunts. Victims can be taught to act assertively by demanding that he cease his harassment.

Children can also learn various strategies of "disarming" the bully. Whether children should be encouraged to return violence with violence depends upon their parents' values. Some parents teach their children to hit back; other parents discourage such behavior. Perhaps children should be given the option of fighting back, acting assertively, ignoring the bully if possible, or seeking help from an adult.

The optimal strategy for handling bullying is prevention. This strategy requires working with the parents of bullies, teaching them parenting skills that will promote prosocial behavior in their children. Psychologists have been successful in working with parents. "We assume that the parents we're working with have out-of-control kids because they're out of control themselves. We teach parents to talk to their children the way they would talk to a neighbor: with respect and dignity" (Horne, quoted by Kutner, 1988j).

Aggressive children are usually victims themselves. They can be taught social skills, nonaggressive conflict-resolution skills, and other prosocial behaviors. They can learn these skills through group discussion, role-playing, watching videotapes of confrontational encounters, and assertiveness training. Their victims can learn assertiveness skills. It is important that they understand their unique contribution to the destructive bully-victim relationship.

Over 200 incarcerated juvenile offenders from New Jersey were interviewed for a federal study of child abuse and neglect (Geller, 1984). Investigators found that about 70 percent of these children had been beaten with a belt or extension cord. About half were beaten with a stick, 12 percent were attacked with a weapon, and a third were beaten so severely that bruises resulted. A quarter were beaten until they bled. A quarter saw their mothers being punched by their fathers. Almost 10 percent saw their mothers beaten so severely that they had to be hospitalized.

Most of these juvenile offenders "had a history of violent behavior, of offenses like assault and rape and even murder. But, in general, the more violent their homes, the more violent were the offenders themselves" (Geller, 1984). This is the first lesson in family violence. Children who witness brutality at home often imitate their violent parents or siblings when they leave their homes (See Spotlight: Bullies and Their Victims). Domestic violence is worsened by many situational factors. These include financial problems, job stress, unemployment, poor money management, illness, conflict over child care, and poor communication.

Families With Marital Violence

Violent husbands are usually impulsive, excessively dependent upon their wives, and irrationally jealous. Their most common emotional expression is anger. Battered women are typically unassertive, submissive, and quiet. Perhaps this reflects their "learned helplessness" (discussed in chapter 9). Children from maritally violent homes are typically aggressive underachievers. They have low self-esteem, psychosomatic and sleep disorders, and may display antisocial behaviors (Gullette, 1987).

Gullette (1987) interviewed and observed parents and children from maritally violent families and interviewed professionals who work with such families. She was able to identify two types of violent families, labeled Type

1 and Type 2. In *Type 1* families, marital violence "served as a method of establishing hierarchy and maintaining control of family members" (p. 122). Violence was inflicted by the father, whose role it was to keep order in the family. Fathers stated rules, and mothers enforced them. In *Type 2* families, anyone could be violent when expressing anger or reacting to stress. Mothers and fathers competed for the role of "decision maker." Children felt helpless, not knowing with which parent to side. They risked punishment if they made the wrong decision.

Children from Type 1 families became violent when the controls were absent. They used violence as a means to an end or to accomplish a goal. "Teenagers, replicating their fathers' behavior, frequently directed violence against their mothers" (p. 127). Children in Type 2 families used violence to express anger, as a response to stress, or when they lost control. Violence was used to intimidate. "Teenagers frequently directed their violence against their fathers, as an escalation of a disagreement with the father or to protect the mother from the father's violence" (p. 127).

The effects on children of their parents' marital violence were mediated by the quality of the parent-child relationships. Many fathers in the study reported not knowing how to get close to their children. Like the abusive father described at the beginning of this chapter, they believe that force is the only way to get their children to take them seriously.

Parental Discipline

Aggressive behavior in children has been shown to be associated with various features of the punitive (authoritarian) parenting style. These include parental rejection, inconsistent discipline, and the use of forceful methods. Through coercive parent-child interactions, children can become either instigators or victims of aggressive behavior.

Aggressive children are training and being trained by their parents to use power in a mutually escalating pattern of violence (Patterson, 1982). Harsh physical punishment and inconsistent discipline predict a range of antisocial behaviors. Children raised in violent families often display antisocial behavior, criminality, drug abuse, depression, and alcoholism (e.g., Holmes & Robins, 1988). Coercive parents are teaching their children that aggressive behavior is appropriate and even desirable (McCord, 1988b).

CHILD ABUSE

Study Question   Are parents ever justified in hitting or beating their children?

"If you messed up, you got hit, sometimes with a belt, sometimes with a switch . . . My father was real strict with us—real strict . . . My father would kill me, just tear me up" (Michael Jackson, in his autobiography, *Moonwalk*).

Most parents have probably experienced "dark urges" to strike out at their children (Ungar, 1988). "I'm going to kill them" is not an unusual parental aside. As we have seen, raising children can be extremely frustrating. If one is having a bad day, has no support from one's partner, or has had too much to drink, aggressive impulses may spill over into violent behavior.

Most parents apparently have dark urges but do not act on them for a variety of reasons. Perhaps our enduring love of our child is stronger than our momentary anger. Maybe we anticipate the terrible guilt we would be feeling a few moments later. Certainly we know it's wrong for a big person to intentionally hurt a little person. Some parents, however, cannot always inhibit their aggressive impulses, and they lash out at a helpless, frightened child.

It is helpful to distinguish between physical abuse, psychological maltreatment (emotional abuse), sexual abuse, and neglect. Definitions of these terms vary according to the nature of the abusive act, its effects on the victim, the intentions of the perpetrator, relevant situational factors, and community standards (Emery, 1989).

Physical abuse is said to occur when children are intentionally injured, leaving bruises, wounds, or burns. As long as spanking is considered acceptable, however, it will be difficult to tell when parents have exceeded the limits set by society on the use of corporal punishment. *Psychological maltreatment* occurs when parents continually berate, ridicule, or ignore their children, when "parents are inconsistent in their talk, rules or actions, when they have unrealistic expectations of their children, when they belittle and blame their children, when they do not take an interest in any of their activities, or when they do not ever praise them" (Berns, 1989, p. 450).

Sexual abuse occurs when children are inappropriately held or fondled or encouraged or forced to engage in sexual activities. Sexual contact between family members is called incest. *Neglect* occurs when children are "abandoned, lack supervision, are not fed properly, need medical or dental care, are frequently absent or late for school, do not have appropriate or sufficient clothing, are unclean, or live in unsafe or filthy homes" (Berns, 1989, pp. 449–450).

Physical Abuse

"I became terrified that when I started hitting my son, I couldn't seem to stop. I kept hitting and hitting him without ever thinking about how hard I was slapping him. Actually, it was my bottled rage that was coming out on him, but I didn't know what to do or who to talk to about it" (mother, quoted by Zigler & Rubin, 1985, p. 102).

Over 2 million suspected cases of abuse or neglect were reported in 1987, 20 percent more than in 1986, and 100 percent more than reported in 1983. Some of the increase is probably due to greater public awareness of the problem and greater willingness to report suspected family violence. Between 1,000 and 1,500 children die each year from being physically maltreated (Pitt, 1988).

These statistics raise many questions about the identification, causes, prevention, and treatment of physical abuse. Should abused children be taken away from their parents? Can abusive parents be trained to become more understanding and patient with their children? How reliable is young children's testimony about abuse? Are therapists working with families obligated to report incidents of abuse, voiding their obligation of confidentiality and possibly discouraging abusive parents from seeking help?

Accusations of child abuse create tremendous strains on courts and agencies. These institutions must respond quickly to possibly life-threatening situations. They must also respect the rights of all individuals involved, including the accused adult. In 1974, the United States federal government enacted the Child Abuse Prevention and Treatment Act. This law led to the establishment of the National Center on Child Abuse and Neglect. Before this time, the ancient practice of battering children received very little research and clinical attention. In the nineteenth century, battered children were rescued by the Society for the Prevention of Cruelty to Animals! (Kessler, 1988).

Although abusive parents have become the focus of research and treatment, the primary victims of physical abuse are, of course, children. Being so dependent upon their parents leaves children vulnerable to the vagaries of human emotion and parental fallibility. Infants who are the "wrong" sex, mentally retarded, have minor physical problems, or are born prematurely are at increased risk for abuse. In other words, children who are unwanted or generally difficult to care for will be more likely to evoke aggressive behaviors from their frustrated caretakers.

Although no "abusive personality syndrome" has been discovered, correlates of abuse are known (Emery, 1989). The profile of abusive parents depicts them as emotionally troubled, undereducated, and socially isolated. Their lives are very stressful. They have limited child-rearing skills. They often are in unsatisfying relationships and have limited financial resources.

Abusive parents typically suffer from low self-esteem and have unrealistic expectations about their infants or children. They do not understand why their young children misbehave. With their low tolerance for frustration, abusive parents have difficulty inhibiting their angry, violent impulses. When in pain or under stress, they strike out. Kropp and Haynes (1987) report that abusive parents do not know how to interpret their children's emotions correctly. They may even believe that they are not capable of exerting a positive influence on their children (Bugental, Blue, & Cruzcosa, 1989). Therefore, they respond coercively when their children are "annoying" or distressed.

Many abusive parents have been abused or witnessed abuse as children. Like the mother described at the beginning of this section, abusive parents are "troubled, isolated individuals, often as much a victim as the child" (Zigler & Rubin, 1985). The role of alcoholism and other drugs, such as cocaine and crack, in the maltreatment of children, should not be overlooked (Famularo, Stone, Barnum, & Wharton, 1986; Kerr, 1988).

Trickett and Susman (1988) found that compared to nonabusive families, abusive parents enjoyed their children less, found child rearing more difficult, and were generally isolated. They observed a suppression of positive emotions such as affection and satisfaction but frequent expression of conflict, anger, and anxiety. Abusive mothers believed more strongly in the value of spanking than did abusive fathers or nonabusive parents and reported more frequent verbal and material punishment.

Abusive parents did not report using physical punishment more frequently than control parents. They were more likely to report using such harsh punishments as striking a child's face, hitting children with objects, and pulling their hair. They do not usually believe that reasoning is an effective discipline strategy (Trickett & Kuczynski, 1986). Trickett and Susman (1988) emphasize the importance of broadening the social and educational supports of abusive parents. They need good information about child rearing. They must be encouraged to adopt more nurturant and realistic discipline strategies.

Clearly, most of these young (and often impoverished) parents love their children. However, they have difficulty caring for and nurturing them, and some are weakly bonded. Most incidents of abuse follow ineffective attempts to discipline or control crying or defiance. Let's not forget that even nonabusive parents experience frustration and occasional aggressive feelings when their children are misbehaving.

Mothers who are likely to abuse their children report more behavior problems in their children, although they may have biased perceptions (Reid, Kavanagh, & Baldwin, 1987). Those who lack child management skills or suffer intense family conflict become involved in coercive interaction cycles that escalate into abusive episodes (Stringer & la Greca, 1985).

A popular, although somewhat simplistic, model of abuse suggests that to the insecure, abusive parent, the child's crying or defiance signifies rejection. This enrages the frustrated parent, who, rather than comforting the infant, provokes additional crying, perhaps by shouting at or threatening him. When the child continues to cry, the mother's frustration builds. This cycle escalates until the parent loses control. Clearly, any plausible model of child abuse must take into account the *interaction* between parent characteristics, child characteristics (particularly temperament), and situational factors.

Effects of Abuse on Children

In his review of the child-abuse literature, Emery (1989) emphasizes two important points. "First, there is no single behavioral or emotional reaction that has been found to characterize abused children. Second, the experience of being a victim of violence may not be the principal factor responsible for many of the psychological difficulties that have been found among abused children. Other aspects of the child's psychological environment that often accompany physical abuse may be more psychologically damaging" (p. 324). For example, abused children often witness violent fights between their parents (Jouriles, Barling, & O'Leary, 1987). The combination of being abused and witnessing abuse is more destructive emotionally than simply witnessing abuse (Hughes, 1988).

Compared to nonabused children, those who are abused are more aggressive, less compliant, and less empathetic (Main & George, 1985). They are less competent, have lower self-esteem, and have more difficulty getting along with their peers (Kaufman & Cicchetti, 1989). Their language and cognitive development may suffer (Coster, Gersten, Beeghly, & Cicchetti, 1989). The greater the abuse, the more extreme its effects. We still do not know whether these differences between abused and nonabused children are partly dispositional or reflect their history of abuse or their parents' deficient child-rearing practices (Emery, 1989; Trickett & Susman, 1988).

Not surprisingly, abused infants and toddlers are insecurely attached to their caretakers (Aber & Allen, 1987; Carlson, Cicchetti, Barnett, & Braunwald, 1989). Growing up in an emotionally unpredictable and sometimes violent environment leaves children fearful and inhibited. They are wary of relationships in and out of their family.

Other studies have found that abused children exhibit more frustration, aggression, and negative emotions in problem-solving situations. A few abused children develop multiple personalities, with only one or two subpersonalities being aware of previously abusive encounters. Perhaps this is their way of protecting themselves from remembering their physical and emotional pain.

Not all abused children are infants or toddlers. Almost half of abused children are between the ages of 12 and 17 years. Most of these children are white females whose parents do not conform to the profile already described. Their parents are better educated and financially secure.

Fathers and Abuse

Most research on child abuse has focused on mothers, despite the fact that paternal neglect may be the most common form of child maltreatment. Historically, fathers have been more physically and sexually abusive and neglectful of children than mothers. Fathers have also been more likely to "abandon" their children following marital separation or divorce. Additionally, lack of partner support is one of the prime risk factors for abusive mothers. Biller and Solomon (1986) include as instances of father neglect paternal unavailability, rejection, disinterest, and excessive criticism.

Psychological Maltreatment (Emotional Abuse)

Study Question In what ways might parents emotionally abuse their children?

Many psychologists contend that psychological maltreatment or emotional abuse is at least as destructive to children's development as physical abuse (Hart & Brassard, 1987). Emotional abuse is probably more common, though harder to identify. It may precede physical abuse. Both types of abuse often occur together (Garrison, 1987).

It is estimated that there are about 200,000 cases of maltreatment a year. The absence of precise definitions of what constitutes maltreatment makes such estimates tentative. Child welfare advocates argue that children's observing parental violence, parental drug use, and parental neglect are forms of psychological maltreatment (Rosenberg, 1987).

Children differ in their sensitivity to harsh parental communications. Some children cry when their parents raise their voices. Other, more resilient children become accustomed to daily criticism and disapproval. Some children are threatened with parental abandonment. "If you do that again, I'll leave you here and you'll never see me again." Insensitive parents can reject, terrorize, ridicule, and otherwise intimidate their children in countless ways.

A national media campaign on emotional abuse has expressed the following message: "Words hit as hard as a fist. Next time, stop and listen to what you're saying. You might not believe your ears" (Denton, 1987). Assessing emotional abuse is a problem. Physical abuse leaves visible scars, but verbal attacks and emotionally unavailable parents do not. Children may also be emotionally abused by a teacher (Denton, 1988).

Breaking the Cycle of Abuse

Although it is popularly believed that abused children inevitably become abusive parents, Kaufman and Zigler (1987) refute this notion. They argue that two-thirds of the people who are physically or sexually abused or neglected as children do not abuse their own children but provide them with adequate care. "Although it is true that most parents who abuse their children were themselves maltreated, this group of parents are a minority of all individuals who were maltreated as children" (Kaufman, 1987). Thus, most abused children do not become abusive parents, but most abusive parents were, indeed, abused as children.

Kaufman indicates that the likelihood that abuse will be transmitted across generations depends upon many factors. These include the parents' social support system, the quality of the marital relationship, the number of stressful life events, and whether the individual was abused by one or both parents. A third of those who have been abused become abusive parents themselves. It is important, however, that those who have been victims not believe that they must inevitably continue the cycle.

Women who were abused as children but who did not abuse their own children were more likely than abusive mothers to have received emotional support from a caring adult in childhood. They were more likely to have been in therapy at some point in their lives and were likely to have an emotionally supportive, satisfying relationship with a mate. Most mothers who were abused as children declare that they would never abuse their own children, but a substantial number do. These women report considerable life stress and are more anxious, dependent, immature, and depressed (Egeland, Jacobvitz, & Sroufe, 1988).

Many of the mothers who broke the cycle of abuse had a relationship with a supportive and nonabusive adult during their childhood or with a therapist. Such a relationship "may have enhanced the abused parent's self-esteem and helped them realize that others can be emotionally available in time of need . . . Emotional support from a partner may help provide parents with the emotional resources necessary to give adequate care to their children" (Egeland, Jacobvitz, & Sroufe, 1988, p. 1087).

Prosecuting or punishing parents who abuse their children or separating children from their abusive parents may not always be in the best interests of the child. It certainly does not rehabilitate the parent (Melton & Davidson, 1987). Children may end up in foster homes, group homes, or institutions that do not provide adequate rearing conditions.

Punitive actions may also discourage abusive parents from seeking help (Denton, 1987). However, children should never be left in the custody of their parents if they are in danger of being sexually or physically abused or neglected. We still have difficulty knowing when removing children from abusive households is ultimately in their best interest (Emery, 1989).

Should citizens report suspected incidents of abuse to local social service agencies? Definitely! An official investigation will be conducted, and all involved parties will be interviewed. Not getting involved may condemn an innocent child to years of terror. Eighteen states require bystanders to report suspected cases of abuse (*New York Times,* January 8, 1989).

The Child Abuse Prevention Act provided funds for research programs aimed at preventing future cases of abuse. This is best accomplished by training parents to use effective, positive forms of discipline. Parents can also learn, through stress management procedures, to control their aggressive impulses. Parents Anonymous was founded in 1970 as a support group for abusive parents. This organization gives parents the opportunity to share their frustrations with other parents and work out healthier ways of relating to their children (Berns, 1989).

Studies show that abusive parents can be treated successfully through counseling or parent training programs (e.g., Wolfe, Edwards, Manion, & Koverola, 1988). More effective interventions are needed. If necessary, foster care and crisis nursery placements are available to provide temporary shelter. Providing parent training for high-risk families is probably the best preventive measure. Unfortunately, poverty and drug abuse increase the risk of child abuse, and there are few, if any, practical solutions to these problems.

Sexual Abuse

Study Question *How common is sexual abuse in the United States today?*

Incest is not a new phenomenon. Parents and relatives have sexually exploited children over the ages. Incest taboos, universal across human cultures, evolved to protect both the vulnerable child and the community from inappropriate sexual expression. Despite the severity of the crime and the trauma involved for the child victim researchers and the public have given minimal attention to this serious problem until recently.

Many of Freud's female patients reported painful sexual trauma suffered in early childhood. Their accounts led Freud to suggest his "seduction theory." He contended that the neurotic syndrome known as hysteria was precipitated by incestuous advances by his patients' fathers. Within a year, partially based on his clinical observations, he began to question his theory. He eventually abandoned it. Instead, he interpreted his patients' reports as unconscious incestual *fantasies* (Rosenfeld, 1987). In other words, he no longer took their reports literally. In what has since been called "blaming the victim," Freud interpreted their accounts as Oedipal wish fulfillments. He believed these women unconsciously longed to have sexual relations with their fathers.

"In the period in which the main interest was directed to discovering infantile sexual traumas, almost all my women patients told me that they had been seduced by their father. I was driven to recognize in the end that these reports were untrue and so came to understand that hysterical symptoms are derived from phantasies and not from real occurrences. It was only later that I was able to recognize in this phantasy of being seduced by the father the expression of the typical Oedipus complex in women" (Freud, 1933/1965, p. 120).

Note that Freud felt "driven to recognize" that his female patients' reports of abuse were false. Rather than pursue the possibility that father-daughter incest was common, he devised the female Oedipus complex, partially to justify his patients' disturbing accounts. If Freud had considered the possibility of widespread incest within families, child sexual abuse might have been taken seriously as a societal problem much earlier.

Today we confront sensational news headlines about incest, reports of day-care center scandals, and TV dramas and talk shows focusing on child sexual abuse. They all attest both to the scope of the phenomenon and society's willingness, finally, to acknowledge that some families sexually exploit their children. Sexual molestation includes exhibitionism, pornography, fondling, and sexual intercourse. Fondling and exhibitionism are the most common forms. Since the research in this area is relatively new, the statistics cited in this section should be treated cautiously.

In 1984, there were more than 123,000 reports of sexual abuse of children, believed to be the tip of the iceberg (*New York Times,* February 17, 1985). A study published by the *Los Angeles Times* in August, 1985, based on a national telephone poll of 2,627 randomly selected adults, found that 22 percent of those interviewed (27% of the women and 16% of the men) reported being sexually abused. A 1984 Gallup poll of 2,000 Canadians confirmed the 22 percent figure. The number almost doubles when sexual advances not reaching sexual contact are included (Kohn, 1987b). Inappropriate sexualized attention to or stimulation of young children may be a precursor to sexual abuse (Haynes-Seman & Krugman, 1989).

David Finkelhor, associate director of the Family Violence Research Program at the University of New Hampshire (Collins, 1983) studied 521 Boston families as part of a study on the prevalence of child sexual abuse. This study was conducted for the National Center for the Prevention and Control of Rape. Nine percent of the parents reported that their children had been victims of abuse or attempted abuse. Forty-seven percent of the parents reported knowing of a child who had been sexually abused. Dr. Finkelhor estimates that the actual number of sexually abused children might be double the 9 percent reported. Many, perhaps most, abused children do not report the incident. They may fear being blamed, punished, or not being believed.

In the *L.A. Times* study, one-third of the victims reported never telling anyone. Some researchers have estimated that as many as 34 percent of all girls and 9 percent of all boys have been molested. Apparently, over one million women in the United States have had incestuous relations with their fathers. About 16,000 new cases occur each year. In Finkelhor's study, 94 percent of the abusers were men, usually relatives. Father-daughter abuse is the most common variation, estimated at 75 percent of sexual abuse incidents that take place at home (Trotter, 1985). Stepfamilies, families where the mother has a live-in male companion, and families with marital problems may be at greater risk for child sexual abuse.

Dr. Finkelhor found that 15 percent of the women and 6 percent of the men interviewed had themselves been sexually abused as children. Many parents expressed false beliefs about abuse. For example, some believed that abusers are usually strangers. In fact, 60 to 75 percent of cases of sexual abuse are committed by relatives, neighbors, or acquaintances of the child. Only a minority (29%) of the parents had talked to their children about sexual abuse. This was particularly true for children under the age of 9 years, even though young children are the most vulnerable to sexual advances. About 10 percent of all victims are younger than 5 years old when first molested.

Many parents who did talk to their children used kidnapping as a metaphor for sexual abuse. This approach is not helpful because two-thirds of abusers are not strangers to the child. Children are least likely to report abuse if a relative is involved. Clearly, parents are uncomfortable bringing up a sexually related topic. Many expressed a need for help in bringing this problem to their children's attention.

Effects of Sexual Abuse

The ages at which sexual abuse and incest are most likely to occur are between 9 and 12 years. Disclosures are most likely in the 12- to 15-year-old group. Older children seem to be harmed more than younger because they understand and are ashamed of the sexual nature of the assault (Farrell, 1988; K. Fisher, 1985). Abuse is not usually limited to a single encounter. Incest, in particular, usually persists for years and is probably underreported. Pregnancy and venereal disease are sometimes the only indications of incest. The psychological impact of incest increases with the age of the child, the child's closeness to the abuser, and the number of abusers (Farrell, 1988).

Sexually abused children typically show immediate disturbances in eating and sleeping, social withdrawal, anger, guilt, and fear (Kohn, 1987b). "Two additional signs show up so frequently that experts rely upon them as indicators of possible abuse when they occur together. The first is sexual preoccupation: excessive or public masturbation and an unusual interest in sexual organs, sex play and nudity . . . The second sign consists of a host of physical complaints or problems, such as rashes, vomiting and headaches, all without medical explanation" (p. 56).

Signs of abuse also include clinging to parents, refusal to leave the house, school phobias, and frequent crying (Swartz, 1984). The types of behavior problems exhibited by abused children are predicted by a host of abuse-related factors (Friedrich, Urquiza, & Beilke, 1986).

The long-term effects of child sexual abuse are still being investigated. Researchers at Boston City Hospital studied 66 children who had been sexually exploited by pornography and sex rings. They found severe and long-lasting psychological problems (*New York*

Times, May 6, 1984). Many of the 6- to 16-year-old children experienced flashbacks of the abuse, nightmares, bedwetting, insomnia, and aggressiveness.

Some reported vivid nightmares in which the offender returns to carry out threats. About 25 percent of the children studied adjusted well, realizing they were not to blame. Children who are victimized by more than one adult are particularly at risk. The use of force during abuse, repeated occurrences, and the abuser being a relative also increase the likelihood of serious adjustment problems (K. Fisher, 1985; Kohn, 1987b).

"At least 50% of women who were abused do not suffer long-term ill effects" (Bagley, quoted by Kohn, 1987). However, a quarter of them do develop serious psychological problems. Other studies report that abused women feel isolated and are distrustful of men. They see themselves as unattractive and generally feel bad about their families. Bagley suggests that the many studies that report lower self-esteem in women may be tapping the effects of the prevalent sexual abuse of females.

Panelists at the annual meeting of the American Orthopsychiatric Association in May, 1987 (K. Fisher, 1987c) confirmed that sexually abused children have flashbacks and distorted self-images. They describe having difficulty in forming relationships. Many also have problems accepting their own bodies and see themselves as asexual.

Eliana Gil, one of the panelists, described a 3-year-old patient who drew a picture of a gingerbread man with a line through his waist. Pointing to the top half, the child said, "That's the part of me that's awake." Pointing to the bottom half, he said, "and that's the part that's asleep when daddy hurts me." Such children eventually have trouble finding stable relationships. They have learned that "people who love you may also hurt you."

Panelists Williams and Fuller reported that many of the adult victims of intense child abuse they studied were overweight. More than half were completely asexual, and almost all had sexual problems. Twenty-two percent of their patients had multiple personalities, 84 percent had attempted suicide, and 88 percent had totally repressed memories of the incidents. Most of their patients had not told anyone of the incidents.

Even when they did, no actions were taken. Most felt they were to blame for initiating or not stopping the incidents and felt guilt and shame. Anger was expressed toward the parent who did not protect them. One study found that fewer than half of the mothers of daughters reporting paternal incest were consistently supportive throughout the crisis (Everson, Hunter, Runyon, Edelsohn, & Coulter, 1989). A quarter of the mothers sided with their husbands or boyfriends, the alleged perpetrators of the incest. This is particularly disturbing because children count on their parents' support when they are in emotional turmoil. If one parent (or partner of a parent) causes the turmoil, and the other parent withdraws or sides with the offender, the child's coping resources become overwhelmed. How can the abused child ever trust anyone again?

Thus, if a child is sexually abused, parental support and understanding play a critical role in the child's adjustment. Wyatt (cited by K. Fisher, 1985) found that 55 percent of female victims who received positive support from their parents showed no negative effects of abuse. Most of the research on this topic suggests that sexual abuse does predispose children to psychological problems.

Dr. Finkelhor tentatively describes the processes that partly determine children's adjustment to sexual abuse. Traumatic sexualization varies according to the child's understanding of sex and the intensity of the abuse. It can lead to subsequent problems in sexuality. Betrayal results from children being harmed by those they trust and on whom they depend. This may lead to adjustment problems in adult relationships. Powerlessness reflects the extent to which the abuse is repeated and the child's body space is invaded against his will. This can produce later "real world" adjustment difficulties. Stigmatization occurs when children believe themselves to be guilty or bad because of what happened. This may precipitate low self-esteem, drug abuse, and antisocial behavior (Finkelhor, Araji, Baron, Browne, Peters, & Wyatt, 1986; K. Fisher, 1985).

Causes of Sexual Abuse

Dr. Finkelhor proposes that father-daughter incest reflects inadequate socialization of men, many of whom seek emotional fulfillment through sex. They may consider as attractive someone who is smaller, younger, and less powerful than they are. Men who participate more fully in raising their children become more caring and are less willing to inflict pain on their children through sexual advances (Swartz, 1984).

This is supported by Parker and Parker's (1986) observation that incestuous fathers are weakly bonded to their own parents. They also maintain low levels of involvement in their daughters' socialization. This reflects faulty bonding with their daughters. Almost half of these abusers were stepfathers. Daughters are more likely to be sexually abused by stepfathers than by their biological fathers. However, abusive biological fathers are more likely than stepfathers to subject their daughters to intercourse (Gordon & Creighton, 1988). It may be stepfathers' lack of involvement in raising their young daughters rather than their lack of blood relationship that predicts abuse.

Child Care and Sexual Abuse

Despite the widespread publicity about child abuse at day-care centers, children are at less risk of abuse at the centers than they would be at home, according to a study by Dr. Finkelhor (*New York Times,* March 22, 1988). This federally financed study of large day-care centers found that for every 10,000 children enrolled in day care, 5.5 were sexually abused each year compared to 8.9 per 10,000 who were abused at home. (Both figures may underrepresent the actual incidence of abuse.)

Approximately two-thirds of the victims were girls. Ninety-three percent of the children were penetrated by a finger, object, or genital. Forty percent of the day-care abusers were women, and 50 percent of the abusers had some college education. These data contradict popular stereotypes of perverted janitors luring naive children into broom closets. Very few of the male abusers were teachers. Most were support staff, boyfriends, or relatives of staff. Most of the abusers were married and had children. Parents, noticing suspicious symptoms, most often reported the abuse. The major short-term effects of the abuse on children were fears and sleep disturbances.

The study found that there were 4 allegations of abuse for every substantiated case. Some of the unsubstantiated cases may have been actual abuse. In a 2-year period, 1,639 children in child care were found to be sexually abused. Although any incidence of abuse is unacceptable, this number should be considered in the context of the millions of children in child care in the United States. The study concluded, "Although a disturbing number of children are sexually abused in child care, the large numbers coming to light are not an indication of some especially high risk to children in child care. They are simply a reflection of the large numbers of children *in* child care and the relative high risk of sexual abuse to children in all settings."

Parents still need to be vigilant about day-care facilities. They should interview the staff, make surprise visits, and encourage their children to report incidents of abuse. One unfortunate side effect of this problem is that teachers are becoming reluctant to express physical affection (e.g., hugging, embracing) to their preschool and elementary schoolchildren. They worry that overly vigilant observers will mistake such expressions for fondling (Chance, 1987b).

Assessment of Sexual Abuse

In assessing abuse in children, investigators are learning the importance of sensitivity and reassurance. If suspicions exist, children should be interviewed alone by a competent and caring person, preferably using anatomically correct dolls. Abused children "often become very graphic in their play, demonstrating vaginal, anal or oral sex. Once the child has played with the dolls in this way, the therapist may ask specific questions, such as 'Has anyone ever done this to you' or 'Show me what they did' " (Swartz, 1984). We will not pursue the topic of treatment for abuse (see Damon, Todd, & Macfarlane, 1987). Families suffer tremendously when accusations are made against relatives. Children must provide evidence against those who should be protecting and nurturing them.

Children's Testimony

One of the most difficult issues in the sexual abuse field is the credibility of young children's testimony that they have been sexually abused. On the one hand, such accusations must be taken very seriously, despite children's limited ability to express themselves directly and consistently. On the other hand, many individuals (particularly fathers involved in custody battles) have been falsely accused, and their lives have been devastated. The rights of children and adults must be protected. This is not easy to accomplish, as children and adults sometimes give false testimony (Mantell, 1988). Children's testimony is best corroborated by physical evidence of abuse, witnesses, or admissions by the abusers. Physical evidence, however, is not usually present and does not identify the abuser. Abuse usually occurs in secrecy without witnesses (Faller, 1988).

Prevention of Sexual Abuse

Children as young as 2 months can be abused. Children between the ages of 6 and 8 years are the most vulnerable. Since parents are usually reluctant to talk to their preadolescents about this topic, young children do not expect nor know how to refuse a sexual advance. After all, they are taught to obey adults!

Molesters look for vulnerable targets. Parents can teach children how to assertively refuse sexual advances and how to identify who they could ask for help (Brody, 1987f). Young children do not automatically know who is a "stranger" or how to refuse a sexual advance. Parents should rehearse these situations with their children. Parents can teach them how and when to say, "No, I'm not going to do that" or "I'm going to tell my father."

The optimal strategy in the area of child abuse is prevention. Prevention of child abuse begins when we provide children with accurate information about their bodies and about their sexuality. With young children, the best approach is to answer their questions about sexual matters. Children need to know how boys and girls differ. They can be given information about reproduction at a level they can understand. In addition to answering questions, parents can visit libraries with their children and borrow books on sexuality. With older children, parents can discuss *in a matter-of-fact way* such topics as masturbation, pregnancy, menstruation, and birth control.

Prevention is also fostered through films, plays, books, board games, family discussions, and other media that warn children of the danger. Children should be encouraged to resist any attempts to touch them without their permission ("bad touching"). They should be told how to escape from the offender and to persist in reporting any such attempts until they are believed. Naturally, the offender tells them that what they are doing is fine or threatens to hurt them or their parents if they tell.

Sexual abuse prevention programs are becoming increasingly available. But are they effective? It has not been demonstrated that preschool children, after being "trained," remember what they have been taught. It has not been shown that having the proper information will translate into appropriate behavior in a threatening situation. It is still not clear whether preschool children are even capable of protecting or defending themselves from being sexually abused by an adult (Reppucci & Haugaard, 1989).

Even older children differ in their ability to conceptualize the meaning of sexual abuse (Wurtele & Miller, 1987). They may have difficulty making the most important distinction, that between good touching and bad touching (deYoung, 1988). Parents, assuming their children have been properly trained may become less vigilant (Bales, 1988). Unfortunately, prevention programs might lead children to associate being tickled or bathed with sad feelings. Some have criticized efforts to educate young children about sexual abuse. They worry that large numbers of children are needlessly being frightened and confused, and may falsely accuse innocent adults who are simply showing affection. Parents must decide whether such prevention efforts justify the possibility of disturbing their children.

A behaviorally based prevention program aimed at 5- to 7-year-old children used instructions, modeling, rehearsal, and social reinforcement (requiring 1½ hours of intervention). It was found to be effective at a 7-week follow-up (Harvey, Forehand, Brown, & Holmes, 1988). A similar program aimed at 4-year-olds is described by Wurtele (1990). Neither program led to harmful side effects, such as increased fearfulness. Parent education leading to child education is also essential. As we have seen, most parents are misinformed about child sexual abuse. They are reluctant to address this difficult topic with their children (Swartz, 1984).

Neglected children are at high risk for psychological and emotional problems.

CHILD NEGLECT

Study Question   How is child neglect different from child abuse?

Even more common and more damaging than child abuse is child neglect. Approximately one and a half million children are victims of parental neglect (Brenner, 1985). Unfortunately, abuse and neglect are rarely distinguished as separate forms of psychological maltreatment.

They are two distinct problems with very different causes. They have dissimilar effects on children and require different interventions.

"While abusive parents may simultaneously love and hate their children, neglectful parents have little or no feeling for them. Unwilling or unable to become involved with their children, these mothers and fathers are emotionally absent. They don't talk to their sons and daughters or teach them the simplest life skills. They stay away from home for days at a time and make no provision for the youngster's care or safety. They neither see nor hear distress, however loudly it is expressed, even when in the same room with their children . . . Social workers find neglected babies lying silently in their cribs, covered with feces, with bottles of soured milk beside them. They see 3- and 4-year-olds who have never been outside to play or to go to a store, children who sleep on bare mattresses amidst garbage, who go hungry and lack appropriate clothing" (Brenner, 1985, p. 47).

Naturally, children living under these conditions are vulnerable to a host of emotional, physical, and intellectual disorders. They have difficulty expressing emotions. They are often withdrawn or depressed, overactive, and aggressive. They may display a large number of antisocial and incompetent behaviors. "By late adolescence a disproportionate number are mentally ill or have serious emotional and physical handicaps that make them dependent on mental-health and welfare agencies" (Brenner, 1985, p. 48). Some of their intellectual problems reflect a history of malnourishment and school failure. An additional burden for some is having to act as a parent surrogate for an even younger sibling.

Attempts to help the parents of these children usually fail. Neglecting parents have serious psychological problems and usually resist offers of assistance. "Typically they are lonely, yet hostile and mistrustful of all outsiders. Many live in poverty or have unpredictable incomes.

A significant number try to escape through alcohol or drugs or by sleeping away long hours of each day. Mental illness, especially chronic depression, and borderline intellectual functioning are common. Frequently they are outcasts in their communities. They are isolated even from their own relatives, with no support from family or friends. Many had troubled childhoods, marked by delinquency, failure in school and parental divorce" (Brenner, 1985, p. 48). Inadequate child care is only one aspect of these disturbed individuals' chaotic life-style (Polansky, Chalmers, Buttenwieser, and Williams, 1981).

Given the difficulty of working with such individuals, social service agencies prefer to work directly with the children. The earlier in the child's life outside support is offered, the better the child's prospects. As previously noted, resilient children, with the nurturance of at least one caring adult, can overcome extremely difficult life situations.

FAMILY, ANTISOCIAL BEHAVIOR, AND DELINQUENCY

Study Question   How do some families train their children to behave antisocially?

The label "juvenile delinquent" usually applies to adolescents who are caught engaging in illegal activities. Delinquency, particularly violent crimes, has been increasing over the past 15 years. The FBI estimates that at least 2 percent of United States teenagers have been involved in juvenile court proceedings (Santrock, 1988).

Violence toward parents and family members is also increasing. Over 1,500 participants in a national survey of white, male high school students in 1966 were asked how often they hit either parent and other questions about their family life. Eleven percent reported hitting their fathers and 7 percent hitting their mothers. Parental use of power, the level of family cohesion, and the child's religiosity predict child-to-parent violence (Peek, Fischer, & Kidwell, 1985).

Many possible causes of delinquency have been suggested. These include biological factors, such as genetic susceptibility to stress, and inadequate socialization of children. Certain types of psychological maltreatment of children are also associated with delinquent behavior (Doerner, 1987). Family characteristics, such as marital discord and poor parent-child relationships, are likely influences. Family and peer influences apparently encourage different aspects of delinquent behavior (DiLalla, Mitchell, Arthur, & Pagliocca, 1988). We will focus on family factors.

Children at risk for delinquent behavior generally receive inadequate supervision and management of their activities from their families. A national study by the justice department revealed that almost 3 out of 4 juveniles in correctional institutions were from broken homes. Almost half were using drugs or alcohol when committing their offenses. Nearly three-quarters reported not growing up with both parents. More than half said a family member had also been in trouble with the law (*New York Times,* September 19, 1988).

Parents of children at risk for delinquency often do not know where their adolescent is, what he is doing, or with whom he is doing it. They may use ineffective discipline methods, and they may not encourage the development of prosocial behaviors. "When rule-breaking behavior occurs, such parents are less likely to provide punishment, such as loss of a privilege, work detail, or loss of allowance. If they react to such information at all, it often is in the form of lecturing, scolding, or barking out a threat—abrasive overtures usually not backed up by effective consequences" (Santrock, 1988, p. 609).

Patterson, DeBaryshe, and Ramsey (1989) have described a developmental model of antisocial behavior that emphasizes the primary

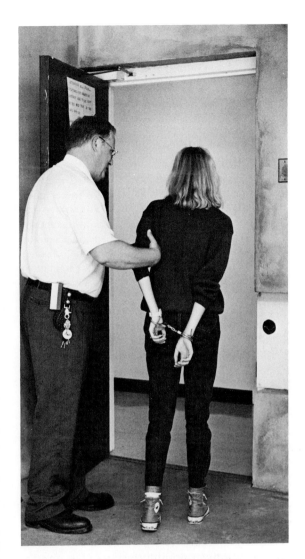

Ineffective parental discipline and inadequate parental supervision are among many family predictors of delinquent behaviors.

role of ineffective parental discipline. Patterson's major premise is that "family members directly train the child to perform antisocial behaviors . . . The parents tend to be noncontingent in their use of both positive reinforcers for prosocial and effective punishment for deviant behaviors. The effect of inept parenting

SPOTLIGHT: Do Toy Guns Encourage Aggression?

Children in the United States, particularly boys, have always enjoyed playing with toy guns. Whether playing cowboys and Indians, G.I. Joe, or Star Wars, children have mimicked the violent behavior of their elders, to the dismay of many parents and child welfare advocates.

Toy makers, of course, justify the sale of war toys. Wayne Charness, vice-president of the company that makes G.I. Joe toys, asserts: "We believe that today's action figures like G.I. Joe provide a modern extension of the role of toys in enhancing children's play experiences. And the reality is that children have played fantasy games involving the triumph of good over evil for centuries" (*New York Times,* June 16, 1988).

Some researchers have found that children do indeed behave more aggressively after playing with guns. Dr. Thomas Radecki, a psychiatrist and executive director of the National Coalition on Television Violence, observed that antisocial and violent behavior doubled after children played with war toys. "The evidence is quite strong that we are transmitting an unhealthy message encouraging children to have fun pretending to murder each other" (*New York Times,* June 16, 1988).

Some researchers distinguish between playful and violent aggression. They contend that access to war toys and guns may encourage healthy "rough and tumble" play. Such play lets children express their aggressive impulses in a socially acceptable way. They point out that many children who are deprived of toy guns invent their own out of sticks, clothes hangers, or even food.

Philosophically, I align myself with psychologist Dr. Helen Boehm: "I don't like toy guns. But ultimately children don't learn values from toy guns and G.I. Joe. It's parents and other role models who have the most important influence on a child's behavior" (*New York Times,* June 16, 1988).

practices is to permit dozens of daily interactions with family members in which coercive child behaviors are reinforced [directly] by family members" (p. 330).

The parent intrudes in an aggressive manner, the child responds in kind, and the parent then withdraws. The child learns that reacting aggressively "works." The parent learns to avoid confrontations by not interfering in the child's activities (Patterson, 1982). These parents also use violent discipline methods. Their children learn that aggressive behavior is an acceptable way of retaliating or of getting their own way. Coercive family interactions escalate into "high-amplitude" behaviors, including physical attacks.

Children thus learn that they can control other family members through threats and coercion. Prosocial behaviors are either ignored or responded to inappropriately. Away from home, their antisocial behaviors lead to peer rejection and academic failure. They may eventually be accepted by deviant peer groups whose members encourage further antisocial or delinquent behavior. ". . . About half of the antisocial children become adolescent delinquents, and roughly half to three-quarters of the adolescent delinquents become adult offenders" (Patterson et al. 1989, p. 331).

Prevention and Treatment

Unfortunately, traditional prevention and treatment programs for delinquent and antisocial behaviors have shown minimal success. Most programs attempting to work directly with antisocial teenagers have not been effective. Approaches such as institutionalization, therapy, casework, and community programs generally fail to reduce delinquent children's contacts with police or keep them in school.

It is currently hoped that parent management programs can train parents to dispense positive reinforcers for prosocial behaviors rather than resort to coercive or violent interactions (Landers, 1988b). Studies support the effectiveness of such interventions. Training parents of younger antisocial children has been the most successful approach (Kazdin, 1987).

Parents can be taught how to monitor their children's behavior and to use the authoritative discipline style described in chapters 5 and 6. According to Patterson, successful programs teach child management skills to parents, teach children prosocial skills, and rectify children's academic deficiencies. Placing antisocial boys in groups with prosocial children rather than grouping them with other antisocial boys has also proven to be effective (Hurley, 1985).

SUMMARY

It is difficult for those of us who have been raised by supportive parents to appreciate the daily terror confronting children living in violent families. Even nonviolent parents, under frustrating circumstances, occasionally experience "dark urges" to hurt their children. Many adults with violent family histories, drug problems, or extraordinary life stresses are unable to control their destructive impulses and attack their children. Most adults, fortunately, have acquired strong inhibitions against hurting children.

Children suffer whether they witness violence between their parents or are victims of such violence themselves. Family violence appears to be intergenerational, that is, passed on from one generation to the next. Life stresses that tax the coping resources of vulnerable parents include financial problems, job stress, drug abuse and alcoholism, unemployment, and marital conflict. Unwanted children or those who are difficult to care for are at greater risk for abuse.

Violent husbands are impulsive and jealous. Their battered wives are usually submissive and passive. Their children end up being aggressive and underachieving in school. They are also at risk for delinquency. Violent husbands are typically violent fathers. Using coercive discipline methods, misguided parents train their children to use threats or violence to get what they want.

Abusive parents are typically emotionally immature, poorly educated, socially isolated, and insecure. They lack effective parenting skills and adopt punitive discipline methods. They usually love their children, but they have difficulty caring for them. When frustrated, they lack the controls necessary to inhibit violent behavior. Adults who have been able to break the cycle of abuse usually have had a supportive, caring relationship with an adult when they were children.

Nearly a quarter of all people in the United States may have been sexually abused as children. Apparently, most instances of sexual abuse are never reported. Children are unwilling or unable to implicate the family members involved. Incest usually persists over a period of years. It may only be discovered through the occurrence of pregnancy or venereal disease.

Sexually abused children show many symptoms, including sexual preoccupation, physical complaints, and fears. As adults, they have difficulty forming trusting relationships and may suffer from sexual dysfunctions. It is important that children be told that they are not to blame for the encounters. Parental support of the abused child plays a major role in adjustment. Fathers who are weakly attached to their daughters are at higher risk for committing incest.

It is not clear whether preschool children can protect themselves from sexual abuse. Parents and teachers therefore play a particularly important role in ensuring their safety and welfare. Older children can benefit from instruction and rehearsal in recognizing and refusing inappropriate sexual advances from others.

Child neglect is more common and potentially more destructive than abuse. It is difficult and painful to imagine children growing up without any adult support and nurturance. Children raised under social and emotional deprivation are at very high risk for a wide range of psychological disorders. By adolescence, a disproportionate number are mentally ill or emotionally handicapped. Whereas abusive parents love their children, neglecting parents are usually indifferent and unavailable. At-

tempts to help neglecting parents usually fail. Working with neglected children can overwhelm social service agencies, which must take over parental responsibilities.

Juvenile delinquents usually come from broken homes where they may repeatedly observe parental violence, criminality, and drug abuse. Parents of delinquent children usually lack effective parenting and discipline skills. They use coercive methods that encourage violent interactions. Traditional prevention and treatment programs have not been successful in helping such children. Behavioral techniques that emphasize positive outcomes for prosocial behavior have been more promising.

Epilogue

We have come a long way in our study of the parenting process. Textbooks contain so much information that it is easy to become overwhelmed by details and somehow overlook the main points. Therefore, I would like to summarize some of the key themes and ideas presented in this book.

1. The best reason for having children is to enjoy raising them.
2. The best way of studying development and the parenting process is through systematic, controlled observation. We also gain important information by observing children and parents in their natural settings and by interviewing children and their caregivers. The conclusions we draw based on research are always tentative.
3. What we call the environment consists of hundreds of factors that can influence children's development. Many of these factors interact with each other to produce complex, unanticipated outcomes.
4. Children's development reflects the interaction of biological factors and the conditions of rearing. Inherited dispositions may lead children to select or create mini-environments for themselves that reinforce the dispositions.
5. Depending upon the amount of parental involvement and the competence of the parent, parental influence may be strong or weak. Strong parenting practices can often modify inherited dispositions.
6. The family is the basic unit of society and, potentially, the most important source of influence on children. Children raised in the same family have quite different experiences.
7. The marital relationship is the key relationship in any family. Children benefit directly and indirectly when their parents support each other's caretaking efforts.
8. Siblings are good for each other. They provide children with countless opportunities to learn social skills and to develop emotional and coping resources.
9. Children's development is affected by a multitude of factors. Some can be controlled by parents (e.g., style of discipline), some cannot be controlled (e.g., inherited dispositions, chance encounters), and some may compete with parental influence (e.g., deviant peer influence).
10. Children who are securely attached to their caretakers usually show more positive developmental outcomes than children who are insecurely or anxiously attached.
11. Parental bonding to a child and the parent-child relationship are primarily determined by the minute-by-minute reciprocal interactions that occur throughout childhood ("small moments" model).
12. Children, even those in the same family, vary considerably in their needs, personal resources, and vulnerabilities.

13. The core conditions of competent parenting include patience, acceptance, sensitivity, flexibility, realistic expectations, good communication skills, and good information about child development.
14. The authoritative parenting style is associated with more positive social, emotional, and cognitive outcomes than the permissive or punitive styles.
15. Positive child outcomes ("parenting goals") that might guide one's parenting orientation include good behavior, competence, a good parent-child relationship, and positive self-esteem and self-confidence.

References

Abelman, R. (1985). Styles of parental disciplinary practices as a mediator of children's learning from prosocial television portrayals. *Child Study Journal, 15*(2), 131–146.

Aber, J. L., & Allen, J. P. (1987). Effects of maltreatment on young children's socioemotional development: An attachment theory perspective. *Developmental Psychology, 23*(3), 406–414.

Adams, J. W., & Tidwell, R. (1988). Parents' perceptions regarding the discipline of their hearing-impaired children. *Child: Care, Health and Development, 14*(4), 265–273.

Adelson, J. (1979, February). Adolescence and the generation gap. *Psychology Today,* pp. 33–37.

Adelson, J. (1980). *Handbook of adolescent psychology.* New York: John Wiley.

Adler, A. (1928). Characteristics of first, second, and third children. *Children, 3,* 14–52.

Adler, T. (1989a, November). Brain's language area is abnormal in disabled. *APA Monitor,* p. 7.

Adler, T. (1989b, July). Future still uncertain for preterm infants. *APA Monitor,* p. 12.

Adler, T. (1989c, March). Sex-based differences declining, study shows. *APA Monitor,* p. 6.

Aho, A. C., & Erickson, M. T. (1985). Effects of grade, gender, and hospitalization on children's medical fears. *Journal of Developmental and Behavioral Pediatrics, 6*(3), 146–153.

Ainsworth, M. D. S. (1989). Attachments beyond infancy. *American Psychologist, 44*(4), 709–716.

Ainsworth, M. D. S., Blehar, M., Waters, E., & Wall, S. (1978). *Patterns of attachment.* Hillsdale, NJ: Erlbaum.

Allen, B. P. (1987). Youth suicide. *Adolescence, 22*(86), 271–286.

Allison, P. D., & Furstenberg, F. F., Jr. (1989). How marital dissolution affects children: Variations by age and sex. *Developmental Psychology, 25*(4), 540–549.

Amabile, T. M. (1989). *Growing up creative: Nurturing a lifetime of creativity.* New York: Crown Publishers.

Ambert, A. (1982). Differences in children's behavior toward custodial mothers and custodial fathers. *Journal of Marriage and the Family, 44,* 73–86.

Anderson, K. E., Lytton, H., & Romney, D. M. (1986). Mothers' interactions with normal and conduct-disordered boys: Who affects whom? *Developmental Psychology, 22,* 604–609.

Anderson, R. C. (1985, Winter). What we know about learning to read: The report of the commission on reading. *American Educator,* pp. 24–29.

Andersson, B. (1989). Effects of public day-care: A longitudinal study. *Child Development, 60,* 857–866.

Aries, P. (1962). *Centuries of childhood.* New York: Random House.

Asher, J. (1987, April). Born to be shy? *Psychology Today,* pp. 54–64.

Azrin, N. H., & Foxx, R. M. (1976). *Toilet training in less than a day.* New York: Pocket Books.

Bachman, J. G. (1987, July). An eye on the future. *Psychology Today,* pp. 6–8.

Baldwin, B. A. (1986, October). Puberty and parents: Understanding your early adolescent. *Pace Magazine,* pp. 15–19.

Baldwin, J. D., & Baldwin, J. I. (1986). *Behavior principles in everyday life* (2nd ed.). Englewood Cliffs, NJ: Prentice-Hall.

Bales, J. (1985, January). Attention disorders need better measures and theory. *APA Monitor.*

Bales, J. (1988, June). Child abuse prevention efficacy called in doubt. *APA Monitor,* p. 27.

Band, E. B., & Weisz, J. R. (1988). How to feel better when it feels bad: Children's perspectives on coping with everyday stress. *Developmental Psychology, 24*(2), 247–253.

Bandura, A. (1977a). Self-efficacy: Toward a unifying theory of behavioral change. *Psychological Review, 84,* 191–215.

Bandura, A. (1977b). *Social learning theory.* Englewood Cliffs, NJ: Prentice-Hall.

Bandura, A. (1982). Self-efficacy mechanism in human agency. *American Psychologist, 37,* 122–147.

Bandura, A. (1986). *Social foundations of thought and action: A social cognitive theory.* Englewood Cliffs, NJ: Prentice-Hall.

Baptiste, D. A. (1986). Counseling the pregnant adolescent within a family context: Therapeutic issues and strategies. *Family Therapy, 13*(2), 163–176.

Barber, B. K., & Thomas, D. L. (1986). Dimensions of fathers' and mothers' supportive behaviors: The case for physical affection. *Journal of Marriage and the Family, 48,* 783–794.

Barglow, P., Vaughn, B. E., & Molitor, N. (1987). Effects of maternal absence due to employment on the quality of infant-mother attachment in a low-risk sample. *Child Development, 58,* 945–954.

Barnett, R. C., & Baruch, G. K. (1988). Correlates of father's participation in family work. In P. Bronstein & C. P. Cowan (Eds.), *Fatherhood today: Men's changing role in the family.* New York: John Wiley.

Barron, J. (1987a, Summer). Learning the facts of life. *New York Times,* Education Section, pp. 16–19.

Barron, J. (1987b, April 15). Suicide rates of teenagers: Are their lives harder to live? *New York Times.*

Barron, J. (1988, Summer). The teen drug of choice: Alcohol. *New York Times,* Education Section, pp. 41–44.

Baruch, G. K., & Barnett, R. C. (1981). Fathers' participation in the care of their preschool children. *Sex Roles, 7*(10), 1043–1055.

Baruch, G. K., & Barnett, R. C. (1986a). Consequences of fathers' participation in family work: Parents' role strain and well-being. *Journal of Personality and Social Psychology, 51*(5), 983–992.

Baruch, G. K., & Barnett, R. C. (1986b). Fathers' participation in family work. *Child Development, 57,* 1210–1223.

Baskett, L. M. (1985). Sibling status effects: Adult expectations. *Developmental Psychology, 21*(3), 441–445.

Baumrind, D. (1966). Effects of authoritative parental control on child behavior. *Child Development, 37,* 887–906.

Baumrind, D. (1967). Child care practices anteceding three patterns of preschool behavior. *Genetic Psychology Monographs, 75,* 43–88.

Baumrind, D. (1968). Authoritarian vs. authoritative parental control. *Adolescence, 3,* 255–272.

Baumrind, D. (1971). Current patterns of parental authority. *Developmental Psychology Monographs, 4* (1, Pt. 2), 1–103.

Baumrind, D. (1975). *Early socialization and the discipline controversy.* Morristown, NJ: General Learning Press.

Baumrind, D. (1978). Reciprocal rights and responsibilities in parent-child relations. *Journal of Social Issues, 34*(2), 179–196.

Beal, C. R., & Lockhart, M. E. (1989). The effect of proper name and appearance changes on children's reasoning about gender constancy. *International Journal of Behavioral Development, 12*(2), 195–205.

Beck, I. L., & Carpenter, P. A. (1986). Cognitive approaches to understanding reading: Implications for instructional practice. *American Psychologist, 41*(10), 1098–1105.

Becker, W. C. (1964). Consequences of different kinds of parental discipline. In M. L. Hoffman & L. W. Hoffman (Eds.), *Review of child development* (Vol. 1). New York: Sage Foundation.

Bell, R. Q. (1968). A reinterpretation of the direction of effects in socialization. *Psychological Review, 75,* 81–95.

Bell, R. Q. (1979). Parent, child, and reciprocal influences. *American Psychologist, 34,* 821–827.

Bell, R. Q., & Harper, L. V. (1977). *Child effects on adults.* Hillsdale, NJ: Erlbaum.

Bell, R. Q., Weinberg, M. S., & Hammersmith, S. K. (1981). *Sexual preference: Its development in men and women.* Bloomington: Indiana University Press.

Belsky, J. (1981). Early human experience: A family perspective. *Developmental Psychology, 17*(1), 3–23.

Belsky, J. (1984). The determinants of parenting: A process model. *Child Development, 55,* 83–96.

Belsky, J., Lang, M., & Huston, T. L. (1986). Sex typing and division of labor as determinants of marital change across the transition to parenthood. *Journal of Personality and Social Psychology, 50*(3), 517–522.

Belsky, J., Lerner, R. M., & Spanier, G. B. (1984). *The child in the family.* Reading, MA: Addison-Wesley.

Belsky, J., & Rovine, M. J. (1988). Nonmaternal care in the first year of life and the security of infant-parent attachment. *Child Development, 59,* 157–167.

Belsky, J., Rovine, M. J., & Taylor, D. G. (1984). The Pennsylvania Infant and Family Development Project, III: The origins of individual differences in infant-mother attachment—maternal and infant contributions. *Child Development, 55,* 718–728.

Bem, S. L. (1974). The measurement of psychological androgyny. *Journal of Consulting and Clinical Psychology, 42,* 155–162.

Bem, S. L. (1981). Gender schema theory: A cognitive account of sex-typing. *Psychological Review, 88,* 354–364.

Bem, S. L. (1989). Genital knowledge and gender constancy in preschool children. *Child Development, 60,* 649–662.

Benin, M. H., & Agostinelli, J. (1988). Husbands' and wives' satisfaction with the division of labor. *Journal of Marriage and the Family, 50,* 349–361.

Bennett, D. (1985, November). Early preschool benefits are few. *APA Monitor,* p. 3.

Berk, L. E. (1986, May). Private speech: Learning out loud. *Psychology Today,* pp. 34–42.

Berk, R. A., & Berk, S. F. (1979). *Labor and leisure at home.* Beverly Hills, CA: Sage Publications.

Berlin, I. N., & Critchley, D. L. (1989). The therapeutic use of play for mentally ill children and their parents. In C. E. Schaefer & J. M. Briesmeister (Eds.), *Handbook of parent training.* New York: John Wiley.

Berndt, T. J., & Bulleit, T. N. (1985). Effects of sibling relationships on preschoolers' behavior at home and at school. *Developmental Psychology, 21,* 747–760.

Berns, R. M. (1985). *Child, family, community.* New York: Holt, Rinehart & Winston.

Berns, R. M. (1989). *Child, family, community* (2nd ed.). New York: Holt, Rinehart & Winston.

Bernstein, R. (1988, February 29). Twenty years after the Kerner Report: Three societies, all separate. *New York Times.*

Berzonsky, M. D. (1987). A preliminary investigation of children's conceptions of life and death. *Merrill-Palmer Quarterly, 33*(4), 505–513.

Beschner, G. (1985). The problem of adolescent drug abuse: An introduction to intervention strategies. In A. S. Friedman & G. Beschner (Eds.), *Treatment services for adolescent substance abusers* (pp. 1–12). Washington, DC: U.S. Government Printing Office.

Bettelheim, B. (1987). *A good enough parent.* New York: Knopf.

Biller, H. B., & Solomon, R. S. (1986). *Child maltreatment and paternal deprivation: A manifesto for research, prevention, and treatment.* Lexington, MA: Lexington Books.

Bishop, K. (1987, November 1). Getting permission to have an abortion. *New York Times.*

Bisnaire, L. M. C., Firestone, P., & Rynard, D. (1990). Factors associated with academic achievement in children following parental separation. *American Journal of Orthopsychiatry, 60*(1), 67–76.

Black, C., & DeBlassie, R. R. (1985). Adolescent pregnancy: Contributing factors, consequences, treatment, and plausible solutions. *Adolescence, 20*(78), 281–290.

Black, D., & Urbanowicz, M. A. (1987). Family intervention with bereaved children. *Journal of Child Psychology and Psychiatry, 28*(3), 467–476.

Blackwelder, D. E., & Passman, R. H. (1986). Grandmothers' and mothers' disciplining in three-generational families: The role of social responsibility in rewarding and punishing grandchildren. *Journal of Personality and Social Psychology, 50*(1), 80–86.

Blakeslee, S. (1988, September 8). New groups aim to help parents face grief when a newborn dies. *New York Times.*

Blanchard-Fields, F., & Irion, J. C. (1988). Coping strategies from the perspective of two developmental markers: Age and social reasoning. *Journal of Genetic Psychology, 149*(2), 141–151.

Blasi, A., & Hoeffel, E. C. (1974). Adolescence and formal operations. *Human Development, 17,* 344–363.

Blechman, E. A. (1985). *Solving child behavior problems at home and at school.* Champaign, IL: Research Press.

Bluebond-Langner, M. (1974). Meanings of death to children. In H. Feifel (Ed.), *New meanings of death.* New York: McGraw-Hill.

Blumberg, L. (1985). The right to live—Disability is not a crime. *The disabled child and the family: An exceptional parent reader.* Boston, MA: The Exceptional Parent Press.

Bogat, G. A., & Gensheimer, L. K. (1986). Discrepancies between the attitudes and actions of parents choosing day care. *Child Care Quarterly, 15*(3), 159–169.

Boggiano, A. K., & Main, D. S. (1986). Enhancing children's interest in activities used as rewards: The bonus effect. *Journal of Personality and Social Psychology, 51*(6), 1116–1126.

Bohannon, J. N., & Stanowicz, L. (1988). The issue of negative evidence: Adult responses to children's language errors. *Developmental Psychology, 24*(5), 684–689.

Boivin, M., & Begin, G. (1989). Peer status and self-perception among early elementary school children: The case of the rejected children. *Child Development, 60,* 591–596.

Borduin, C. M., & Henggeler, S. W. (1987). Post-divorce mother-son relations of delinquent and well-adjusted adolescents. *Journal of Applied Developmental Psychology, 8*(3), 273–288.

Bowen, M. (1978). *Family therapy in clinical practice.* New York: Jason Aronson.

Bower, B. (1988, October 1). From here to maternity. *Science News,* 220–221.

Bower, B. (1989). Remodeling the autistic child. *Science News, 136,* 312–313.

Bower, T. G. R. (1982). *Development in infancy* (2nd ed.). San Francisco, CA: W. H. Freeman.

Bowerman, C., & Irish, D. (1962). Some relationships of stepchildren to their parents. *Marriage and Family Living, 24,* 113–121.

Bowlby, J. (1951). *Maternal care and mental health.* Geneva, Switzerland: World Health Organization.

Bowlby, J. (1969). *Attachment and loss* (Vol. 1). New York: Basic Books.

Bowlby, J. (1982). *Attachment and loss* (2nd ed., Vol. 1). New York: Basic Books.

Boyd, C. J. (1989). Mothers and daughters: A discussion of theory and research. *Journal of Marriage and the Family, 51*(2), 291–302.

Brachfeld-Child, S. (1986). Parents as teachers: Comparisons of mothers' and fathers' instructional interactions with infants. *Infant Behavior and Development, 9*(2), 127–131.

Bradbard, M. R. (1985). Sex differences in adults' gifts and children's toy requests at Christmas. *Psychological Reports, 56,* 969–970.

Bradley, R. H., Caldwell, B. M., & Rock, S. L. (1988). Home environment and school performance: A ten-year follow-up and examination of three models of environmental action. *Child Development, 59,* 852–867.

Brady, C. P., Bray, J. H., & Zeeb, M. A. (1986). Behavior problems of clinic children: Relation to parental marital status, age and sex of child. *American Journal of Orthopsychiatry, 56*(3), 399–412.

Brazelton, T. B. (1986). Issues for working parents. *American Journal of Orthopsychiatry, 56*(1), 14–25.

Breiner, J. (1989). Training parents as change agents for their developmentally disabled children. In C. E. Schaefer & J. M. Briesmeister (Eds.), *Handbook of parent training.* New York: John Wiley.

Brenner, A. (1985, May). Wednesday's child. *Psychology Today,* pp. 46–50.

Bretherton, I. (1985). Attachment theory: Retrospect and prospect. *Monographs of the Society for Research in Child Development, 50* (1–2, Serial No. 209).

Bridges, L. J., Connell, J. P., & Belsky, J. (1988). Similarities and differences in infant-mother and infant-father interaction in the strange situation: A component process analysis. *Developmental Psychology, 24*(1), 92–100.

Brody, C. J., & Steelman, L. C. (1985). Sibling structure and parental sex-typing of children's household tasks. *Journal of Marriage and the Family, 47,* 265–273.

Brody, G. H., Neubaum, E., & Forehand, R. (1988). Serial marriage: A heuristic analysis of an emerging family form. *Psychological Bulletin, 103*(2), 211–222.

Brody, G. H., Pellegrini, A. D., & Sigel, I. E. (1986). Marital quality and mother-child and father-child interactions with school-aged children. *Developmental Psychology, 22*(3), 291–296.

Brody, G. H., Stoneman, Z., & Burke, M. (1987). Family system and individual child correlates of sibling behavior. *American Journal of Orthopsychiatry, 57*(4), 561–569.

Brody, J. E. (1982, December 22). Early intervention programs can help children born with Down's syndrome. *New York Times.*

Brody, J. E. (1983, February 16). Helping parents to cope with tragedy, the death of a child. *New York Times.*

Brody, J. E. (1985, November 6). Parents play a major role in determining children's patterns of alcohol usage. *New York Times.*

Brody, J. E. (1986a, September 10). For children in day care, a new study assesses the risks and costs of illnesses. *New York Times.*

Brody, J. E. (1986b, April 30). Guidelines for parents of teen-agers who are, or are about to be, sexually active. *New York Times.*

Brody, J. E. (1986c, November 12). Parents can often teach a baby who cries at night how to stay asleep till morning. *New York Times.*

Brody, J. E. (1987a, September 23). Adults can be emotionally and physically devastated by the death of a parent. *New York Times.*

Brody, J. E. (1987b, May 5). Child development: Language takes on new significance. *New York Times.*

Brody, J. E. (1987c, August 26). For children of alcoholics, a life of fear, humiliation and broken promises. *New York Times.*

Brody, J. E. (1987d, June). Give children enough to eat, but not too much, and avoid any sort of food deprivation. *New York Times.*

Brody, J. E. (1987e, January 21). Guidelines for parents on children's TV viewing. *New York Times.*

Brody, J. E. (1987f, February 18). How parents can prevent, or, if necessary, deal with the sexual abuse of a child. *New York Times.*

Brody, J. E. (1987g, December 3). Jealousy: A complex and powerful emotion that can be positive as well as negative. *New York Times.*

Brody, J. E. (1987h, May 27). Parents' attitudes toward diet can contribute to obesity in children and adolescents. *New York Times.*

Brody, J. E. (1987i, March 24). Research lifts blame from many of the obese. *New York Times.*

Brody, J. E. (1987j, August 12). Shielding a child from the reality of death can make it only more fearsome. *New York Times.*

Brody, J. E. (1987k, May 5). Talking to the baby: Some expert advice. *New York Times.*

Brody, J. E. (1988a, March 3). Keeping tabs on teen-age bodies. *New York Times.*

Brody, J. E. (1988b, March 3). Trip across adolescence is just as risky as ever. *New York Times.*

Brody, J. E. (1989, August 10). As breast-feeding is more widely applied in U.S., recent studies shatter myths. *New York Times.*

Bronstein, P. (1988a). Father-child interaction: Implications for gender role socialization. In P. Bronstein & C. P. Cowan (Eds.), *Fatherhood today: Men's changing role in the family.* New York: John Wiley.

Bronstein, P. (1988b). Marital and parenting roles in transition: An overview. In P. Bronstein & C. P. Cowan (Eds.), *Fatherhood today: Men's changing role in the family.* New York: John Wiley.

Brooks, A. (1986, July 28). Divorced parents and the neglected child. *New York Times.*

Brooks, A. (1988, December 1). For stepfathers, trust comes slowly. *New York Times.*

Brooks, A. (1989, March 9). Experts find extramarital affairs have a profound impact on children. *New York Times.*

Brooks-Gunn, J., & Furstenberg, F. F., Jr. (1989). Adolescent sexual behavior. *American Psychologist, 44*(2), 249–257.

Brown, S. (1988). *Treating adult children of alcoholics: A developmental perspective.* New York: John Wiley.

Browne, M. W. (1987, September 1). Relics of Carthage show brutality amid the good life. *New York Times.*

Brozan, N. (1982, March 8). Adolescents, parents and birth control. *New York Times.*

Brozan, N. (1986, January 13). Life after a son's suicide: One family's struggle. *New York Times.*

Brozan, N. (1987, March 14). Success in preventing teen-age pregnancy. *New York Times.*

Buchholz, E. S., & Gol, B. (1986). More than playing house: A developmental perspective on the strengths of teenage motherhood. *American Journal of Orthopsychiatry, 56*(3), 347–359.

Bugental, D. B., Blue, J., & Cruzcosa, M. (1989). Perceived control over caregiving outcomes: Implications for child abuse. *Developmental Psychology, 25*(4), 532–539.

Buie, J. (1988a, January). Divorce hurts boys more, studies show. *APA Monitor.*

Buie, J. (1988b, November). Joint custody advantages doubted. *APA Monitor,* p. 25.

Buis, J. M., & Thompson, D. N. (1989). Imaginary audience and personal fable: A brief review. *Adolescence, 24*(96), 773–782.

Bumpers, D. (1984). Securing the blessings of liberty for posterity: Preventive health care for children. *American Psychologist, 39*(8), 896–900.

Bus, A. G., & van Ijzendoorn, M. H. (1988). Attachment and early reading: A longitudinal study. *Journal of Genetic Psychology, 149*(2), 199–210.

Buss, D. M. (1989). Conflict between the sexes: Strategic interference and the evocation of anger and upset. *Journal of Personality and Social Psychology, 56*(5), 735–747.

Butterfield, F. (1981, January 5). How China raises its well-behaved children. *New York Times.*

Byrne, E. A., & Cunningham, C. C. (1985). The effects of mentally handicapped children on families—A conceptual review. *Journal of Child Psychology and Psychiatry, 26*(6), 847–864.

Cain, V. S., & Hofferth, S. L. (1985). Parental choice of self-care for school-age children. *Journal of Marriage and the Family, 51,* 65–77.

Caldera, Y. M., Huston, A. C., & O'Brien, M. (1989). Social interactions and play patterns of parents and toddlers with feminine, masculine and neutral toys. *Child Development, 60,* 70–76.

Callan, V. J. (1986). The impact of the first birth: Married and single women preferring childlessness, one child, or two children. *Journal of Marriage and the Family, 48,* 261–269.

Camara, K., & Resnick, G. (1989). Styles of conflict resolution and cooperation between divorced parents: Effects on child behavior and adjustment. *American Journal of Orthopsychiatry, 59*(4), 560–576.

Campos, R. G. (1987). *Soothing pain-elicited distress in infants with swaddling and pacifiers.* Unpublished doctoral dissertation, University of Denver.

Campos, R. G. (1989). Soothing pain-elicited distress in infants with swaddling and pacifiers. *Child Development, 60,* 781–792.

Cantor, C. (1988, March 13). SIDS: We don't know why your baby died. *New York Times.*

Caplan, P. J. (1986, October). Take the blame off mother. *Psychology Today,* pp. 70–71.

Caplan, P. J., & Hall-McCorquodale, I. (1985a). Mother-blaming in major clinical journals. *American Journal of Orthopsychiatry, 55*(3), 345–353.

Caplan, P. J., & Hall-McCorquodale, I. (1985b). The scapegoating of mothers: A call for change. *American Journal of Orthopsychiatry, 55*(4), 610–613.

Carlson, V., Cicchetti, D., Barnett, D., & Braunwald, K. (1989). Disorganized/disoriented attachment relations in maltreated infants. *Developmental Psychology, 25*(4), 525–531.

Carr, E. G., & Durand, V. M. (1987, November). See me, help me. *Psychology Today,* pp. 62–64.

Carter, B., & McGoldrick, M. (Eds.). (1988). *The changing family life cycle: A framework for family therapy* (2nd ed.). New York: Gardner Press.

Caspi, A., Elder, G. H., & Bem, D. J. (1987). Moving against the world: Life-course patterns of explosive children. *Developmental Psychology, 23*(2), 308–313.

Caspi, A., Elder, G. H., & Bem, D. J. (1988). Moving away from the world: Life-course patterns of shy children. *Developmental Psychology, 24*(6), 824–831.

Chadez, L. H., & Nurius, P. S. (1987). Stopping bedtime crying: Treating the child and the parents. *Journal of Clinical Child Psychology, 16*(3), 212–217.

Chance, P. (1982, January). Your child's self-esteem. *Parents Magazine.*

Chance, P. (1987a, July). Asian studies. *Psychology Today,* p. 80.

Chance, P. (1987b, May). A touching story. *Psychology Today,* p. 14.

Chapman, M., Zahn-Waxler, C., Cooperman, G., & Iannotti, R. (1987). Empathy and responsibility in the motivation of children's helping. *Developmental Psychology, 23*(1), 140–145.

Chase-Lansdale, P. L., & Owen, M. T. (1987). Maternal employment in a family context: Effects on infant-mother and infant-father attachments. *Child Development, 58,* 1505–1512.

Chen, C., & Stevenson, H. W. (1989). Homework: A cross-cultural examination. *Child Development, 60,* 551–561.

Chin, Ann-Ping. (1988). *Children of China.* New York: Knopf.

Christenson, A. (1983). Intervention. In Kelley, H. H., Bersheid, E., Christenson, A., Harvey, J. H., Huston, T. L., Levinger, G., McClintock, E., Peplau, L. A., & Peterson, D. R. (Eds.), *Close relationships.* New York: Freeman.

Clarke-Stewart, K. A. (1989a). Infant day care: Maligned or malignant? *American Psychologist, 44*(2), 266–273.

Clarke-Stewart, K. A. (1989b, January). Single-parent families: How bad for the children? *NEA Today,* pp. 60–64.

Cleverley, J., & Phillips, D. C. (1986). *Visions of childhood: Influential models from Locke to Spock* (rev. ed.). New York: Teachers College Press.

Clingempeel, W. G., & Segal, S. (1986). Stepparent-stepchild relationships and the psychological adjustment of children in stepmother and stepfather families. *Child Development, 57,* 474–484.

Cohen, L. H., Burt, C. E., & Bjorck, J. P. (1987). Life stress and adjustment: Effects of life events experienced by young adolescents and their parents. *Developmental Psychology, 23*(4), 583–592.

Cohn, D. A. (1990). Child-mother attachment of six-year-olds and social competence at school. *Child Development, 61,* 152–162.

Cohn, J. F., Campbell, S. B., Matias, R., & Hopkins, J. (1990). Face-to-face interactions of postpartum depressed and nondepressed mother-infant pairs at 2 months. *Developmental Psychology, 26*(1), 15–23.

Cohn, J. F., & Tronick, E. (1989). Specificity of infants' response to mothers' affective behavior. *Journal of the American Academy of Child and Adolescent Psychiatry, 28*(2), 242–248.

Coleman, M., & Ganong, L. (1987). Marital conflict in stepfamilies. *Youth and Society, 19*(2), 151–172.

Coller, D. R. (1988). Joint custody: Research, theory and policy. *Family Process, 27,* 459–469.

Collins, G. (1983, February 2). Child sexual abuse prevalent, study finds. *New York Times.*

Collins, G. (1984a, May 21). Charting teen-agers' moods and days. *New York Times.*

Collins, G. (1984b, August 13). Dispelling myths about the only child. *New York Times.*

Collins, G. (1984c, February 13). New studies on "girl toys" and "boy toys." *New York Times.*

Collins, G. (1984d, February 6). Study says teen-agers adopt adult values. *New York Times.*

Collins, G. (1985a, November 4). Children: Teaching too much, too soon? *New York Times.*

Collins, G. (1985b September 30). Children and video games. *New York Times.*

Collins, G. (1986a, September 26). A survey of parents' views. *New York Times.*

Collins, G. (1986b, February 26). Children of alcoholics: Strength in numbers. *New York Times.*

Collins, G. (1986c, March 3). Parents' reactions to bad marks. *New York Times.*

Collins, G. (1986d, Summer). Preparing for the first day of school. *New York Times,* Education Section, pp. 27–30.

Collins, G. (1986e, May 12). Studying the behavior of bully and victim. *New York Times.*

Collins, G. (1987a, November 25). Day care for infants: Debate turns to long-term effects. *New York Times.*

Collins, G. (1987b, October 14). Latchkey children: A new profile emerges. *New York Times.*

Collins, G. (1987c, June 15). Marriage is still popular. *New York Times.*

Collins, G. (1988, May 19). The fears of children: Is the world scarier? *New York Times.*

Comer, J. P. (1988a, November). Educating poor minority children. *Scientific American,* pp. 42–48.

Comer, J. P. (1988b, January). Is "parenting" essential to good teaching? *NEA Today,* pp. 34–40.

Compas, B. E. (1987). Coping with stress during childhood and adolescence. *Psychological Bulletin, 101*(3), 393–403.

Conger, J. J. (1988). Hostages to fortune: Youth, values, and the public interest. *American Psychologist, 43*(4), 291–300.

Coombs, R. H., & Landsverk, J. (1988). Parenting styles and substance use during childhood and adolescence. *Journal of Marriage and the Family, 50,* 473–482.

Cooney, T. M., Smyer, M. A., Hagestad, G. O., & Klock, R. (1986). Parental divorce in young adulthood: Some preliminary findings. *American Journal of Orthopsychiatry, 56*(3), 470–477.

Coopersmith, S. (1967). *The antecedents of self-esteem.* San Francisco: Freeman.

Cordes, C. (1984, August). The rise of one-parent black families. *APA Monitor,* pp. 16–18.

Cordes, C. (1985, November). Type A children anxious, insecure. *APA Monitor.*

Cordes, C. (1986, April). Drug use and pregnancy link sought. *APA Monitor,* pp. 28–29.

Costanzo, P. R., & Woody, E. Z. (1985). Domain-specific parenting styles and their impact on the child's development of particular deviance: The example of obesity proneness. *Journal of Social and Clinical Psychology, 3*(4), 425–445.

Coster, W. J., Gersten, M. S., Beeghly, M., & Cicchetti, D. (1989). Communicative functioning in maltreated toddlers. *Developmental Psychology, 25*(6), 1020–1029.

Cotton, S., Antill, J. K., & Cunningham, J. D. (1989). The work motivations of mothers with preschool children. *Journal of Family Issues, 10,* 189–210.

Covell, K., & Abramovitch, R. (1987). Understanding emotions in the family: Children's and parents' attributions of happiness, sadness, and anger. *Child Development, 58,* 985–991.

Cowan, A. L. (1989, March 12). "Parenthood II": The nest won't stay empty. *New York Times.*

Cowan, G., & Avants, S. K. (1988). Children's influence strategies: Structure, sex differences, and bilateral mother-child influence. *Child Development, 59,* 1303–1313.

Cowan, P. A. (1988). Becoming a father. In P. Bronstein & C. P. Cowan (Eds.), *Fatherhood today: Men's changing role in the family.* New York: John Wiley.

Cox, M. J., Owen, M. T., Lewis, J. M., & Henderson, V. K. (1989). Marriage, adult adjustment, and early parenting. *Child Development, 60,* 1015–1024.

Cranley, M. S., Hadahl, K. J., & Pegg, R. J. (1983). Women's perspectives of giving birth: A comparison of vaginal and cesarean deliveries. *Nursing Research, 32,* 10–15.

Crockenberg, S. (1985). Toddlers' reactions to maternal anger. *Merrill-Palmer Quarterly, 31*(4), 361–373.

Crockenberg, S. (1987). Predictors and correlates of anger toward and punitive control of toddlers by adolescent mothers. *Child Development, 58*(4), 964–975.

Crockenberg, S., & McCluskey, K. (1986). Change in maternal behavior during the baby's first year of life. *Child Development, 57*(3), 746–753.

Crowell, J. A., & Feldman, S. S. (1988). Mothers' internal models of relationships and children's behavioral and developmental status: A study of mother-child interaction. *Child Development, 59,* 1273–1285.

Csikszentmihalyi, M., & Larson, R. (1984). *Being adolescent: Conflict and growth in the teen-age years.* New York: Basic Books.

Cummings, E. M. (1987). Coping with background anger in early childhood. *Child Development, 58,* 976–984.

Cummings, E. M., Vogel, D., Cummings, J. S., & El-Sheikh, M. (1989). Children's responses to different forms of expression of anger between adults. *Child Development, 60*(6), 1392–1404.

Cummings, J. S., Pellegrini, D. S., Notarius, C. I., & Cummings, E. M. (1989). Children's responses to angry adult behavior as a function of marital distress and history of interparent hostility. *Child Development, 60,* 1035–1043.

Cunningham, S. (1985, August). Scientists debate impact of spacing on child's abilities. *APA Monitor,* pp. 46–48.

Cutrona, C. E., & Troutman, B. R. (1986). Social support, infant temperament, and parenting self-efficacy: A mediational model of postpartum depression. *Child Development, 57,* 1507–1518.

Dadds, M. R. (1987). Families and the origins of child behavior problems. *Family Process, 26,* 341–357.

Damon, L., Todd, J., & Macfarlane, K. (1987). Treatment issues with sexually abused young children. *Child Welfare, 66*(2), 125–137.

Dangel, R. F., & Polster, R. A. (1988). *Teaching child management skills.* Elmsford, NY: Pergamon Press.

Daniels, D. (1986). Differential experiences of siblings in the same family as predictors of adolescent sibling personality differences. *Journal of Personality and Social Psychology, 51*(2), 339–346.

Daniels, D., Dunn, J., Furstenberg, F. F., & Plomin, R. (1985). Environmental differences within the family and adjustment differences within pairs of adolescent siblings. *Child Development, 56*(3), 764–774.

Daniels, D., & Plomin, R. (1985a). Differential experience of siblings in the same family. *Developmental Psychology, 21*(5), 747–760.

Daniels, D., & Plomin, R. (1985b). Origins of individual differences in infant shyness. *Developmental Psychology, 21*(1), 118–121.

Daniels, P., & Weingarten, K. (1988). The fatherhood click: The timing of parenthood in men's lives. In P. Bronstein & C. P. Cowan (Eds.), *Fatherhood today: Men's changing role in the family.* New York: John Wiley.

Deal, J. E., Halverson, C. F., Jr., & Wampler, K. S. (1989). Parental agreement on child-rearing orientations: Relations to parental, marital, family, and child characteristics. *Child Development, 60,* 1025–1034.

DeAngelis, T. (1986, November). Twins: Mirror image more than skin deep. *APA Monitor,* p. 21.

DeAngelis, T. (1987, October). Kids' peer groups have mixed impact. *APA Monitor,* p. 18.

DeAngelis, T. (1989, November). Men's interactional style can be tough on women. *APA Monitor,* p. 12.

DeCasper, A. J., & Spence, M. J. (1986). Prenatal maternal speech influences newborns' perception of speech sounds. *Infant Behavior and Development, 9*(2), 133–150.

DeChick, J. (1988, July 19). Most mothers want a job, too. *USA Today.*

Deci, E. L. (1985, March). The well-tempered classroom. *Psychology Today,* pp. 52–53.

Demo, D. H., & Acock, A. C. (1988). The impact of divorce on children. *Journal of Marriage and the Family, 50,* 619–648.

DeMyer, M. K. (1979). *Parents and children in autism.* New York: John Wiley.

DeMyer, M. K., & Goldberg, P. (1983). Family needs of the autistic adolescent. In E. Schopler & G. B. Mesibov (Eds.), *Autism in adolescents and adults.* New York: Plenum.

Denton, L. (1987, June). Emotional abuse hardest to evaluate. *APA Monitor,* p. 22.

Denton, L. (1988, January). School—cause or cure for abuse? *APA Monitor,* p. 29.

deYoung, M. (1988). The good touch/bad touch dilemma. *Child Welfare, 67*(1), 60–70.

Dibrell, L. L., & Yamamoto, K. (1988). In their own words: Concerns of young children. *Child Psychiatry and Human Development, 19*(1), 14–25.

Dick-Read, G. (1933). *Childbirth without fear: The principles and practices of natural childbirth.* New York: Harper & Row.

Dickstein, S., & Parke, R. D. (1988). Social referencing in infancy: A glance at fathers and marriage. *Child Development, 59,* 506–511.

DiLalla, L. F., Mitchell, C. M., Arthur, M. W., & Pagliocca, P. M. (1988). Aggression and delinquency: Family and environmental factors. *Journal of Youth and Adolescence, 17*(3), 233–237.

Dinkmeyer, D., & McKay, G. D. (1982). *The parent's handbook—STEP—Systematic training for effective parenting.* Circle Pines, MN: American Guidance Service.

Dinkmeyer, D., McKay, G. D., & McKay, J. L. (1987). *New beginnings: Skills for single parents and stepfamily parents.* Champaign, IL: Research Press.

Dismuke, D. (1988, November). Reducing suicides. *NEA Today,* p. 21.

Dix, T., & Grusec, J. E. (1985). Parental attribution processes in the socialization of children. In I. E. Sigel (Ed.), *Parental belief systems* (pp. 201–233). Hillside, NJ: Erlbaum.

Dix, T., Ruble, D. N., Grusec, J. E., & Nixon, S. (1986). Social cognition in parents: Inferential and affective reactions to children of three age levels. *Child Development, 57*(4), 879–894.

Dix, T., Ruble, D. N., & Zambarano, R. J. (1989). Mothers' implicit theories of discipline: Child effects, parent effects, and the attribution process. *Child Development, 60*(6), 1373–1391.

Dodge, K. A. (1990). Developmental psychopathology in children of depressed mothers. *Developmental Psychology, 26*(1), 3–6.

Doerner, W. G. (1987). Child maltreatment seriousness and juvenile delinquency. *Youth & Society, 19*(2), 197–224.

Donate-Bartfield, E., & Passman, R. H. (1985). Attentiveness of mothers and fathers to the baby's cries. *Infant Behavior and Development, 8*(4), 385–393.

Dornbusch, S. M., Ritter, P. L., Leiderman, H., Roberts, D. F., & Fraleigh, M. J. (1987). The relation of parenting style to adolescent school performance. *Child Development, 58,* 1244–1257.

Dorr, A., Graves, S. B., & Phelps, E. (1980). Television literacy for young children. *Journal of Communication, 30*(3), 71–83.

Dreikurs, R., & Grey, L. (1970). *Guide to child discipline.* New York: Hawthorn.

Dunn, J. (1985). *Sisters and brothers.* Cambridge, MA: Harvard University Press.

Dunn, J. (1987). The beginnings of moral understanding: Development in the second year. In J. Kagan & S. Lamb (Eds.), *The emergence of morality in young children.* Chicago, IL: University of Chicago Press.

Dunn, J. (1988). Sibling influences on childhood development. *Journal of Child Psychology and Psychiatry, 29*(2), 119–127.

Dunn, J., Bretherton, I., & Munn, P. (1987). Conversations about feeling states between mothers and their young children. *Developmental Psychology, 23*(1), 132–139.

Dunn, J., & Kendrick, C. (1980). The arrival of a sibling: Changes in patterns of interaction between mother and first-born child. *Journal of Child Psychology and Psychiatry, 21,* 119–132.

Dunn, J., & Munn, P. (1985). Becoming a family member: Family conflict and the development of social understanding. *Child Development, 56,* 480–492.

Dunn, J., & Munn, P. (1986). Sibling quarrels and maternal intervention: Individual differences in understanding and aggression. *Journal of Child Psychology and Psychiatry, 27*(5), 583–595.

Dunst, C. J., Trivette, C. M., & Cross, A. H. (1986). Mediating influences of social support: Personal, family, and child outcomes. *American Journal of Mental Deficiency, 90*(4), 403–417.

Dworetzky, J. P. (1984). *Introduction to child development.* St. Paul, MN: West Publishers.

Easterbrooks, M. A. (1989). Quality of attachment of mother and father: Effects of perinatal risk status. *Child Development, 60,* 825–830.

Easterbrooks, M. A., & Goldberg, W. A. (1984). Toddler development in the family: Impact of father involvement and parenting characteristics. *Child Development, 55,* 740–752.

Easterbrooks, M. A., & Goldberg, W. A. (1985). Effects of early maternal employment on toddlers, mothers and fathers. *Developmental Psychology, 21*(5), 774–783.

Egeland, B., Jacobvitz, D., & Sroufe, L. A. (1988). Breaking the cycle of abuse. *Child Development, 59,* 1080–1088.

Egeland, B., & Sroufe, L. A. (1981). Attachment and early maltreatment. *Child Development, 52,* 44–52.

Eiger, M. S., & Olds, S. W. (1986). *The complete book of breastfeeding* (2nd ed.). New York: Bantam.

Eisenberg, N., Lundy, T., Shell, R., & Roth, K. (1985). Children's justifications for their adult and peer-directed compliant (prosocial and nonprosocial) behaviors. *Developmental Psychology, 21*(2), 325–331.

Ek, C. A., & Steelman, L. C. (1988). Becoming a runaway: From the accounts of youthful runners. *Youth and Society, 19*(3), 334–358.

Elkind, D. (1978). Understanding the young adolescent. *Adolescence, 13,* 127–134.

Elkind, D. (1987a). *Miseducation: Preschoolers at risk.* New York: Knopf.

Elkind, D. (1987b, May). Superkids and super problems. *Psychology Today,* pp. 60–61.

Elkind, D. (1988, January). Educating the very young: A call for clear thinking. *NEA Today,* pp. 22–27.

Ellifritt, J. (1985). Life with my sister—Guilty no more. *The disabled child and the family: An exceptional parent reader.* Boston, MA: The Exceptional Parent Press.

El-Sheikh, M., Cummings, E. M., & Goetsch, V. L. (1989). Coping with adults' angry behavior: Behavioral, physiological, and verbal responses in preschoolers. *Developmental Psychology, 25*(4), 490–498.

Eltgroth, M. B. (1989, January). Starting them young. *PC/Computing,* pp. 257–259.

Emery, R. E. (1988). *Marriage, divorce, and children's adjustment.* Beverly Hills: Sage.

Emery, R. E. (1989). Family violence. *American Psychologist, 44*(2), 321–328.

Emmerich, W., Goldman, K. S., Kirsh, B., & Sharabany, R. (1977). Evidence for a transitional phase in the development of gender constancy. *Child Development, 48,* 930–936.

Entwisle, D. R., & Doering, S. G. (1981). *The first birth: A family turning point.* Baltimore, MD: Johns Hopkins University Press.

Erikson, E. H. (1963). *Childhood and society* (2nd ed.). New York: Norton.

Erikson, E. H. (1964). *Insight and responsibility.* New York: Norton.

Erikson, E. H. (1968). *Identity: Youth and crisis.* New York: Norton.

Eskilson, A., Wiley, M. G., Muhlbauer, G., & Dodder, L. (1986). Parental pressure, self-esteem and adolescent reported deviance: Bending the twig too far. *Adolescence, 21*(83), 501–515.

Estrada, P., Arsenio, W. F., Hess, R. D., & Holloway, S. (1987). Affective quality of the mother-child relationship: Longitudinal consequences for children's school-relevant cognitive functioning. *Developmental Psychology, 23*(2), 210–215.

Etlin, M. (1988, April). Is there a gifted underachiever? *NEA Today,* pp. 10–11.

Evans, O. (1989, February 16). For infants, quiet and a warm bath. *New York Times.*

Everson, M. D., Hunter, W. M., Runyon, D. K., Edelsohn, G. A., & Coulter, M. L. (1989). Maternal support following disclosure of incest. *American Journal of Orthopsychiatry, 59*(2), 197–207.

Faber, A., & Mazlish, E. (1987). *Siblings without rivalry.* New York: W. W. Norton.

Fabes, R. A., Fultz, J., Eisenberg, N., May-Plumlee, T., & Christopher, F. S. (1989). Effects of rewards on children's prosocial motivation: A socialization study. *Developmental Psychology, 25*(4), 509–515.

Faerstein, L. M. (1986). Coping and defense mechanisms of mothers of learning disabled children. *Journal of Learning Disabilities, 19*(1), 8–11.

Fagot, B. I. (1985). Beyond the reinforcement principle: Another step toward understanding sex-role development. *Developmental Psychology, 21,* 1097–1104.

Falbo, T. (1984). *The single-child family.* New York: Guilford Press.

Falbo, T., & Polit, D. F. (1986). Quantitative review of the only child literature: Research evidence and theory development. *Psychological Bulletin, 100*(2), 176–189.

Faller, K. C. (1988). Criteria for judging the credibility of children's statements about their sexual abuse. *Child Welfare, 67*(5), 389–400.

Famularo, R., Stone, K., Barnum, R., & Wharton, R. (1986). Alcoholism and severe child maltreatment. *American Journal of Orthopsychiatry, 56*(3), 481–485.

Farber, E., & Egeland, B. (1987). *The invulnerable child.* New York: Guilford Press.

Farrell, L. T. (1988). Factors that affect a victim's self-disclosure in father-daughter incest. *Child Welfare, 67*(5), 462–470.

Farson, R. (1974). *Birthrights.* New York: Macmillan.

Faulkenberry, J. R., Vincent, M., James, A., & Johnson, W. (1987). Coital behaviors, attitudes, and knowledge of students who experience early coitus. *Adolescence, 22*(86), 321–325.

Felner, R. (1985). Child custody: Practices and perspectives of legal professionals. *Journal of Clinical Child Psychology, 14*(1), 27–34.

Ferguson, C. (1977). Baby talk as a simplified register. In C. Snow & C. Ferguson (Eds.), *Talking to children: Language input and acquisition.* Cambridge: Cambridge University Press.

Fernald, A. (1985). Four-month-old infants prefer to listen to mothercese. *Infant Behavior and Development, 8*(2), 181–195.

Fernald, A. (1989). Intonation and communication intent in mothers' speech to infants: Is the melody the message? *Child Development, 60,* 1497–1510.

Fine, M. A., Moreland, J. R., & Schwebel, A. I. (1983). Long-term effects of divorce on parent-child relationships. *Developmental Psychology, 19*(5), 703–713.

Finkelhor, D., Araji, S., Baron, L., Browne, A., Peters, S. D., & Wyatt, G. E. (1986). *A sourcebook on child sexual abuse.* Beverly Hills, CA: Sage.

Finney, J. W., & Edwards, M. C. (1989). Prevention of children's behavior problems. *The Behavior Therapist, 12*(8), 183–186.

Fischer, A. (1985, November). Should parents assume a child's duty? *New York Times.*

Fischer, B. (1988, March). "Whiz kid" image masks problems of Asian Americans. *NEA Today,* pp. 14–15.

Fischman, J. (1986, October). The children's hours. *Psychology Today,* pp. 16–18.

Fischman, J. (1988a, January). Exercise: Getting your head in shape. *Psychology Today.*

Fischman, J. (1988b, November). Stepdaughter wars. *Psychology Today,* pp. 38–45.

Fishel, A. H. (1987). Children's adjustment in divorced families. *Youth and Society, 19*(2), 173–196.

Fisher, K. (1983, February). TV violence. *APA Monitor,* pp. 7–9.

Fisher, K. (1985, November). Parental support vital in coping with abuse. *APA Monitor,* p. 12.

Fisher, K. (1987a, November). Cigarette ads aimed at youth. *APA Monitor.*

Fisher, K. (1987b, March). Kids' services work; too few receive them. *APA Monitor,* p. 26.

Fisher, K. (1987c, June). Sexual abuse victims suffer into adulthood. *APA Monitor,* p. 25.

Fisher, K. (1989, July). Pushing preschoolers doesn't help, may hurt. *APA Monitor,* p. 9.

Fisher, T. D. (1986). Parent-child communication about sex and young adolescents' sexual knowledge and attitudes. *Adolescence, 21*(83), 517–527.

Flavell, J. H. (1986). Really and truly. *Psychology Today,* pp. 38–44.

Fleming, A. S., Ruble, D. N., Flett, G. L., & Van Wagner, V. (1990). Adjustment in first-time mothers: Changes in mood and mood content during the early postpartum months. *Developmental Psychology, 26*(1), 137–143.

Fling, S., & Manosevitz, M. (1972). Sex typing in nursery school children's play interests. *Developmental Psychology, 7,* 146–152.

Foderaro, L. W. (1987, November 19). Voices of the counterculture. *New York Times.*

Folkenberg, J. (1985, May). Teen pregnancy: Who opts for adoption? *Psychology Today,* p. 16.

Forehand, R., Middleton, K., & Long, N. (1987). Adolescent functioning as a consequence of recent parental divorce and the parent-adolescent relationship. *Journal of Applied Developmental Psychology, 8*(3), 305–315.

Forgatch, M. S. (1989). Patterns and outcome in family problem solving: The disrupting effect of negative emotion. *Journal of Marriage and the Family, 51,* 115–124.

Forste, R. T., & Heaton, T. B. (1988). Initiation of sexual activity among female adolescents. *Youth and Society, 19*(3), 250–268.

Framo, J. (1976). Family of origin as a therapeutic resource for adults in marital and family therapy: You can and should go home again. *Family Process, 15,* 193–210.

Frank, S. J., Avery, C. B., & Laman, M. S. (1988). Young adults' perceptions of their relationships with their parents: Individual differences in connectedness, competence, and emotional autonomy. *Developmental Psychology, 24*(5), 729–737.

Frankel, M. T., & Rollins, H. A., Jr. (1983). Does mother know best? Mothers and fathers interacting with preschool sons and daughters. *Developmental Psychology, 19*(5), 694–702.

Fraser, B. C. (1986). Child impairment and parent/ infant communication. *Child Care, Health and Development, 12*(3), 141–150.

Freedman, J. L., Scars, D. O., & Carlsmith, J. M. (1981). *Social psychology* (4th ed.). Englewood Cliffs, NJ: Prentice-Hall.

Freeman, J. (Ed.). (1985). *The psychology of gifted children: Perspectives on development and education.* Chichester, England: John Wiley.

Freud, S. (1916). *Wit and its relation to the unconscious.* New York: Moffat Ward.

Freud, S. (1965). *New introductory lectures on psychoanalysis.* New York: Norton. (Original work published 1933)

Freund, L. S. (1990). Maternal regulation of children's problem-solving behavior and its impact on children's performance. *Child Development, 61,* 113–126.

Friedrich, W. N., Urquiza, A. J., & Beilke, R. L. (1986). Behavior problems in sexually abused young children. *Journal of Pediatric Psychology, 11*(1), 47–57.

Friedrich, W. N., Wilturner, L. T., & Cohen D. S. (1985). Coping resources and parenting mentally retarded children. *American Journal of Mental Deficiency, 90*(2), 130–139.

Furstenberg, F. F., Jr., Brooks-Gunn, J., & Chase-Lansdale, L. (1989). Teenaged pregnancy and childbearing. *American Psychologist, 44*(2), 313–320.

Furstenberg, F. F., Jr., & Nord, C. W. (1985). Parenting apart: Patterns of childrearing after marital disruption. *Journal of Marriage and the Family, 47,* 893–905.

Futrell, M. H. (1987). Public schools and four-year-olds. *American Psychologist, 42*(3), 251–253.

Galambos, N. L., & Dixon, R. A. (1984). Toward understanding and caring for latchkey children. *Child Care Quarterly, 13*(2), 116–125.

Galinsky, E. (1981). *Between generations: The six stages of parenthood.* New York: Times Books.

Gallagher, J. J. (1985). Unthinkable thoughts—Reexamining the concept of learning disability. *The disabled child and the family: An exceptional parent reader.* Boston, MA: The Exceptional Parent Press.

Gamble, M. (1985). Helping our children accept themselves. *The disabled child and the family: An exceptional parent reader.* Boston, MA: The Exceptional Parent Press.

Ganong, L. H., & Coleman, M. M. (1987). Stepchildren's perceptions of their parents. *Journal of Genetic Psychology, 148*(1), 5–17.

Ganong, L. H., & Coleman, M. M. (1988). Do mutual children cement bonds in stepfamilies? *Journal of Marriage and the Family, 50,* 687–698.

Garcia Coll, C. T., Hoffman, J., & Oh, W. (1987). The social ecology and early parenting of Caucasian adolescent mothers. *Child Development, 58,* 955–963.

Gardner, H. (1983). *Frames of mind: The theory of multiple intelligences.* New York: Basic Books.

Garfinkel, P. (1983, September). The best "Jewish mother" in the world. *Psychology Today,* pp. 56–60.

Garmezy, N. (1988). Stressors of childhood. In N. Garmezy & M. Rutter (Eds.), *Stress, coping, and development in children.* Baltimore, MD: Johns Hopkins University Press.

Garrison, E. G. (1987). Psychological maltreatment of children: An emerging focus for inquiry and concern. *American Psychologist, 42*(2), 157–159.

Gaylin, J. (1985, February). When a child dies. *Parents,* pp. 80–83.

Geller, M. (1984, May 20). Family violence: The price we pay is dear. *Newark Star Ledger.*

Gelles, R. J. (1989). Child abuse and violence in single-parent families: Parent absence and economic deprivation. *American Journal of Orthopsychiatry, 59*(4), 492–501.

Gelles, R. J., & Straus, M. A. (1987). Is violence toward children increasing? A comparison of 1975 and 1985 national survey rates. *Journal of Interpersonal Violence, 2,* 212–222.

Gerson, K. (1986, November). Briefcase, baby or both? *Psychology Today,* pp. 30–36.

Gesell, A. L. (1928). *Infancy and human growth.* New York: Macmillan.

Giles-Sims, J. (1987). Parental role sharing between remarrieds and ex-spouses. *Youth and Society, 19*(2), 134–150.

Ginott, H. G. (1965). *Between parent and child.* New York: Macmillan.

Ginsburg, H. P., & Opper, S. (1988). *Piaget's theory of intellectual development* (3rd ed.). Englewood Cliffs, NJ: Prentice-Hall.

Gold, M., & Yanof, D. S. (1985). Mothers, daughters, and girlfriends. *Journal of Personality and Social Psychology, 49*(3), 654–659.

Goldberg, S. (1983). Parent-infant bonding: Another look. *Child Development, 54,* 1355–1382.

Goldberg, S., Perrotta, M., Minde, K., & Corter, C. (1986). Maternal behavior and attachment in low-birth-weight twins and singletons. *Child Development, 57,* 34–46.

Goldscheider, F. K., & Goldscheider, C. (1989). Family structure and conflict: Nest-leaving expectations of young adults and their parents. *Journal of Marriage and the Family, 51,* 87–97.

Goldsmith, H. H. (1983). Genetic influences on personality from infancy to adulthood. *Child Development, 54,* 331–355.

Goleman, D. (1985a, June 25). Chronic arguing between parents found harmful to some children. *New York Times.*

Goleman, D. (1985b, May 28). Spacing of siblings strongly linked to success in life. *New York Times.*

Goleman, D. (1986a, October 21). Child development theory stresses small moments. *New York Times.*

Goleman, D. (1986b, April 1). Two views of marriage explored: His and hers. *New York Times.*

Goleman, D. (1987a, August 31). Black child's self-view is still low, study finds. *New York Times.*

Goleman, D. (1987b, July 28). Each sibling experiences different family. *New York Times.*

Goleman, D. (1987c). Girls and math: Is biology really destiny? *New York Times,* Summer Supplement on Education.

Goleman, D. (1987d, June 9). Personality: Major traits found stable through life. *New York Times.*

Goleman, D. (1987e, March 10). Research reports progress against autism. *New York Times.*

Goleman, D. (1987f, September 15). Shame steps out of hiding and into sharper focus. *New York Times.*

Goleman, D. (1987g, November 24). Teen-age risk taking: Rise in deaths prompts new research effort. *New York Times.*

Goleman, D. (1987h, April 7). The bully: New research depicts a paranoid, lifelong loser. *New York Times.*

Goleman, D. (1987i, October 13). Thriving despite hardship: Key childhood traits identified. *New York Times.*

Goleman, D. (1988a, May 17). Lies can point to mental disorders or signal normal growth. *New York Times.*

Goleman, D. (1988b, April 5). New scales of intelligence rank talent for living. *New York Times.*

Goleman, D. (1988c, December 1). Nurturing can offset the trauma of loss in childhood, study says. *New York Times.*

Goleman, D. (1988d, June 2). Psychotherapists zero in on making too much of failure. *New York Times.*

Goleman, D. (1988e, March 17). What do children fear most? Their answers are surprising. *New York Times.*

Goleman, D. (1988f, April 14). When a baby cries: Researchers seek clues to potential problems. *New York Times.*

Goleman, D. (1989a, March 23). Infants in need of psychotherapy? A fledgling field is growing fast. *New York Times.*

Goleman, D. (1989b, January 10). Pioneering studies find surprisingly high rate of mental ills in young. *New York Times.*

Goleman, D. (1989c, June 13). Study defines major sources of conflict between sexes. *New York Times.*

Good, T. L., & Weinstein, R. S. (1986). Schools make a difference: Evidence, criticisms, and new directions. *American Psychologist, 41,* 1090–1097.

Goodnow, J. J. (1988). Children's household work: Its nature and functions. *Psychological Bulletin, 103*(1), 5–26.

Goodnow, J. J., Knight, R., & Cashmore, J. (1983). Adult social cognition: Implications of parents' ideas for approaches to development. In M. Perlmutter (Chair), *Minnesota Symposium on Child Development,* Minneapolis.

Goodsitt, J., Raitan, J. G., & Perlmutter, M. (1988). Interaction between mothers and preschool children when reading a novel and familiar book. *International Journal of Behavioral Development, 11*(4), 489–505.

Gordon, M., & Creighton, S. J. (1988). Natal and non-natal fathers as sexual abusers in the United Kingdom: A comparative analysis. *Journal of Marriage and the Family, 50,* 99–105.

Gordon, S. (1986, October). What kids need to know. *Psychology Today,* pp. 22–26.

Gordon, T. (1970). *Parent effectiveness training.* New York: Wyden.

Gottman, J. M., & Katz, L. F. (1989). Effects of marital discord on young children's peer interaction and health. *Developmental Psychology, 25*(3), 373–381.

Graubard, S. G. (1988, January 29). Why do Asian pupils win those prizes? *New York Times.*

Gray, M. M., & Coleman, M. (1985). Separation through divorce: Supportive professional practices. *Child Care Quarterly, 14*(4), 248–261.

Gray, R. E. (1987). Adolescent response to the death of a parent. *Journal of Youth and Adolescence, 16*(6), 511–525.

Green, R. (1987). *The "sissy boy syndrome" and the development of homosexuality.* New Haven, CT: Yale University Press.

Greenberg, M. T., & Marvin, R. S. (1982). Reactions of preschool children to an adult stranger: A behavioral systems approach. *Child Development, 53,* 481–490.

Greenberger, E., & Goldberg, W. A. (1989). Work, parenting, and the socialization of children. *Developmental Psychology, 25,* 22–35.

Greenberger, E., & Steinberg, L. (1986). *When teenagers work.* New York: Basic Books.

Greenspan, S. I., Wieder, S., Nover, R. A., Lieberman, A. F., Lourie, R. S., & Robinson, M. E. (Eds.). (1987). *Infants in multirisk families: Case studies in preventive intervention.* Madison, CT: International Universities Press.

Greif, G. L. (1985). Single fathers rearing children. *Journal of Marriage and the Family, 47,* 185–191.

Gretarsson, S. J., & Gelfand, D. M. (1988). Mothers' attributions regarding their children's social behavior and personality characteristics. *Developmental Psychology, 24*(2), 264–269.

Grieser, D. L., & Kuhl, P. K. (1988). Maternal speech to infants in a tonal language: Support for universal prosodic features in motherese. *Developmental Psychology, 24*(1), 14–20.

Grolnick, W. S., & Ryan, R. M. (1989). Parent styles associated with children's self-regulation and competence in school. *Journal of Educational Psychology, 81*(2), 143–154.

Grossman, F. K., Pollack, W. S., & Golding, E. (1988). Fathers and children: Predicting the quality and quantity of fathering. *Developmental Psychology, 24*(1), 82–91.

Guidubaldi, J., & Nastasi, B. K. (1987). *Home environment factors as predictors of child adjustment in mother-employed households: Results of a nationwide study.* Paper presented at the biennial meeting of the Society of Research in Child Development, Baltimore, MD.

Guillen, M. A. (1984, December). The first cause. *Psychology Today,* pp. 72–73.

Gullette, L. C. (1987). Children in maritally violent families: A look at family dynamics. *Youth & Society, 19*(2), 119–133.

Gustafson, G. E., & Harris, K. L. (1990). Women's responses to young infants' cries. *Developmental Psychology, 26*(1), 144–152.

Hajcak, F., & Garwood, P. (1988). Quick-fix sex: Pseudosexuality in adolescents. *Adolescence, 23*(92), 755–760.

Halebsky, M. A. (1987). Adolescent alcohol and substance abuse: Parent and peer effects. *Adolescence, 22*(88), 961–968.

Haley, J. (1976). *Problem solving therapy.* San Francisco: Jossey-Bass.

Hall, C. S., & Lindzey, G. (1978). *Theories of personality* (3rd ed.). New York: John Wiley.

Hall, E. (1987, July). China's only child. *Psychology Today,* pp. 45–47.

Hall, J. A. (1987). Parent-adolescent conflict: An empirical review. *Adolescence, 22*(88), 767–789.

Hall, W. S. (1989). Reading comprehension. *American Psychologist, 44*(2), 157–161.

Halpern, R. (1990). Poverty and early childhood parenting: Toward a framework for intervention. *American Journal of Orthopsychiatry, 60*(1), 6–18.

Hamburg, D. A., & Takanishi, R. (1989). Preparing for life: The critical transition of adolescence. *American Psychologist, 44*(5), 825–827.

Hanson, S. M. H. (1988). Divorced fathers with custody. In P. Bronstein & C. P. Cowan (Eds.), *Fatherhood today: Men's changing role in the family.* New York: John Wiley.

Hanzlik, J. R., & Stevenson, M. B. (1986). Interactions of mothers with their infants who are mentally retarded, retarded with cerebral palsy, or nonretarded. *American Journal of Mental Deficiency, 90*(5), 513–520.

Harris, I. D., & Howard, K. I. (1985). Correlates of perceived parental favoritism. *Journal of Genetic Psychology, 146*(1), 45–56.

Harris, M., Jones, D., Brookes, S., & Grant, J. (1986). Relations between the non-verbal context of maternal speech and rate of language development. *British Journal of Developmental Psychology, 4*(3), 261–268.

Harris, S. L., & Bruey, C. T. (1988). Families of the developmentally disabled. In I. R. H. Falloon (Ed.), *Handbook of behavioral family therapy.* New York: Guilford Press.

Harris, S. L., & Powers, M. D. (1984). Behavior therapists look at the impact of an autistic child on the family system. In E. Schopler & G. Mesibov (Eds.), *The effects of autism on the family.* New York: Plenum.

Hart, S. N., & Brassard, M. R. (1987). A major threat to children's mental health: Psychological maltreatment. *American Psychologist, 42*(2), 160–165.

Harvey, P., Forehand, R., Brown, C., & Holmes, T. (1988). The prevention of sexual abuse: Examination of the effectiveness of a program with kindergarten-age children. *Behavior Therapy, 19*(3), 429–436.

Hayes, D. (Ed.). (1987). *Risking the future: Adolescent sexuality, pregnancy, and childbearing* (Vol. 1). Washington, DC: National Academy Press.

Hayes, J. R., & Flower, L. S. (1986). Writing research and the writer. *American Psychologist, 41*(10), 1106–1113.

Haynes-Seman, C., & Krugman, R. D. (1989). Sexualized attention: Normal interaction or precursor to sexual abuse? *American Journal of Orthopsychiatry, 59*(2), 238–245.

Henshaw, C. V. (1988, July 10). The baby has arrived. Now what? *New York Times.*

Hertz, R. (1987). *More equal than others: Women and men in dual-career marriages.* Berkeley, CA: University of California Press.

Hess, R. D., & Holloway, S. D. (1984). Family and school as educational institutions. In R. D. Parke (Ed.), *Review of child development research* (Vol. 7, pp. 179–222). Chicago: University of Chicago Press.

Hetherington, E. M. (1989). Coping with family transitions: Winners, losers, and survivors. *Child Development, 60,* 1–14.

Hetherington, E. M., Stanley-Hagan, M., & Anderson, E. R. (1989). Marital transitions: A child's perspectives. *American Psychologist, 44*(2), 303–312.

Hill, J. P. (1985). Family relations in adolescence: Myths, realities and new directions. *Genetic, Social and General Psychology Monographs, 111*(2), 233–248.

Hill, J. P., & Holmbeck, G. N. (1987). Disagreements about rules in families with seventh-grade girls and boys. *Journal of Youth and Adolescence, 16*(3), 221–246.

Hiller, D. V., & Dyehouse, J. (1987). A case for banishing "dual-career marriages" from the research literature. *Journal of Marriage and the Family, 49,* 787–795.

Hock, E., McBride, S., & Gnezda, M. T. (1989). Maternal separation anxiety: Mother-infant separation from the maternal perspective. *Child Development, 60,* 793–802.

Hoff-Ginsberg, E., & Shatz, M. (1982). Linguistic input and the child's acquisition of language. *Psychological Bulletin, 92*(1), 3–26.

Hoffman, L. W. (1974). Effects of maternal employment on the child—A review of the research. *Developmental Psychology, 10*(2), 204–228.

Hoffman, L. W. (1983). Increased fathering: Effects on the mother. In M. Lamb & A. Sagi (Eds.), *Fatherhood and social policy.* Hillsdale, NJ: Erlbaum.

Hoffman, L. W. (1989). Effects of maternal employment in the two-parent family. *American Psychologist, 44*(2), 283–292.

Hoffman, L. W., & Manis, J. D. (1979). The value of children in the United States: A new approach to the study of fertility. *Journal of Marriage and the Family, 41,* 583–591.

Hoffman, M. (1977). Homosexuality. In F. A. Beach (Ed.), *Human sexuality in four perspectives.* Baltimore: Johns Hopkins University Press.

Hoffman, M. L. (1967). Power assertion by the parent and its impact on the child. In G. Medinnus (Ed.), *Readings in the psychology of parent-child relationships.* New York: John Wiley.

Hoffman, M. L. (1970). Moral development. In P. H. Mussen (Ed.), *Carmichael's manual of child psychology* (Vol. 2). New York: John Wiley.

Holden, C. (1985, January). Genes, personality and alcoholism. *Psychology Today,* pp. 38–44.

Holden, C. (1987, September). Genes and behavior: A twin legacy. *Psychology Today,* pp. 18–19.

Holden, G. W. (1988). Adults' thinking about a child-rearing problem: Effects of experience, parental status, and gender. *Child Development, 59,* 1623–1632.

Holden, G. W., & West, M. J. (1989). Proximate regulation by mothers: A demonstration of how differing styles affect young children's behavior. *Child Development, 60,* 64–69.

Holmes, S. J., & Robins, L. N. (1988). The role of parental disciplinary practices in the development of depression and alcoholism. *Psychiatry, 51,* 24–32.

Hopkins, J., Marcus, M., & Campbell, S. B. (1984). Postpartum depression: A critical review. *Psychological Bulletin, 95,* 498–515.

Hostetler, A. J. (1988a, May). Rethinking how personality flowers. *APA Monitor,* pp. 12–13.

Hostetler, A. J. (1988b, May). Why baby cries: Data may shush skeptics. *APA Monitor,* p. 14.

Houseknecht, S. K. (1979). Timing of the decision to remain voluntarily childless: Evidence for continuous socialization. *Psychology of Women Quarterly, 4,* 81–96.

Howe, N., & Ross, H. S. (1990). Socialization, perspective taking, and the sibling relationship. *Developmental Psychology, 26*(1), 160–165.

Howes, C., & Stewart, P. (1987). Child's play with adults, toys, and peers: An examination of family and child-care influences. *Developmental Psychology, 23,* 423–430.

Howes, P., & Markman, H. J. (1989). Marital quality and child functioning. A longitudinal investigation. *Child Development, 60,* 1044–1051.

Hughes, H. M. (1986, March–April). Research with children in shelters: Implications for clinical services. *Children Today,* pp. 21–25.

Hughes, H. M. (1988). Psychological and behavioral correlates of family violence in child witnesses and victims. *American Journal of Orthopsychiatry, 58*(1), 77–90.

Hunter, F. T. (1985). Adolescents' perception of discussions with parents and friends. *Developmental Psychology, 21*(3), 433–440.

Hurley, D. (1985, March). Arresting delinquency. *Psychology Today,* pp. 63–68.

Hurley, D. (1987, August). A sound mind in an unsound body. *Psychology Today,* pp. 34–43.

Huston, A. (1983). Sex-typing. In P. Mussen (Ed.), *Handbook of child psychology* (4th ed., Vol. 4). New York: John Wiley.

Huston, A. C., Watkins, B. A., & Kunkel, D. (1989). Public policy and children's television. *American Psychologist, 44*(2), 424–433.

Hyde, J. S., & Linn, M. C. (1988). Gender differences in verbal ability: A meta-analysis. *Psychological Bulletin, 104*(1), 53–69.

Irion, J. C., Coon, R. C., & Blanchard-Fields, F. (1988). The influence of divorce on coping in adolescence. *Journal of Youth and Adolescence, 17*(2), 135–145.

Isaacs, M. B., Leon, G. H., & Kline, M. (1987). When is a parent out of the picture? Different custody, different perceptions. *Family Processes, 26,* 101–110.

Isabella, R. A., Belsky, J., & von Eye, A. (1989). Origins of infant-mother attachment: An examination of interactional synchrony during the infant's first year. *Developmental Psychology, 25*(1), 12–21.

Jacklin, C. N. (1989). Female and male: Issues of gender. *American Psychologist, 44*(2), 127–133.

Jackson, S. A. (1977, October). Should you teach your child to read? *American Education.*

Jacobson, A. L., & Owen, S. S. (1987). Infant-caregiver interactions in day care. *Child Study Journal, 17*(3), 197–209.

Jacobson, J. L., & Wille, D. E. (1986). The influence of attachment pattern on developmental changes in peer interaction from the toddler to the preschool period. *Child Development, 57,* 338–347.

Jacobson, N. S. (1989). The politics of intimacy. *The Behavior Therapist, 12*(2), 29–32.

Jaffe, M. L. (1990). Counseling parents in child management skills. *New Jersey Psychologist, 40*(1), 15–16.

Jaffe, P., Wolfe, D., Wilson, S., & Zak, L. (1986). Similarities in behavioral and social maladjustment among child victims and witnesses to family violence. *American Journal of Orthopsychiatry, 56*(1), 142–146.

Jenkins, J. M., Smith, M. A., & Graham, P. J. (1989). Coping with parental quarrels. *Journal of the American Academy of Child and Adolescent Psychiatry, 28*(2), 182–189.

Jenson, W. R., Sloane, H. N., & Young, K. R. (1988). *Applied behavior analysis in education.* Englewood Cliffs, NJ: Prentice-Hall.

Jessor, R., & Jessor, S. L. (1977). *Problem behavior and psychosocial development.* New York: Academic Press.

Johnson, J. E., & Martin, C. (1985). Parents' beliefs and home learning environments: Effects on cognitive development. In I. E. Sigel (Ed.), *Parental belief systems: The psychological consequences for children.* Hillsdale, NJ: Erlbaum.

Johnson, S. (1988a, April 3). Learning the art of bringing up baby. *New York Times.*

Johnson, S. (1988b, July 21). To smoke or not: Among teen-agers, parents lead the way. *New York Times.*

Johnston, J. R., Kline, M., & Tschann, J. M. (1989). Ongoing postdivorce conflict: Effects on children of joint custody and frequent access. *American Journal of Orthopsychiatry, 59*(4), 576–592.

Johnston, L. D., Bachman, J. G., & O'Malley, P. M. (1985, January 4). News and Information Services Release, Institute of Social Research, University of Michigan, Ann Arbor.

Jones, D. A. (1987). The choice to breast feed or bottle feed and influences upon that choice: A survey of 1,525 mothers. *Child: Care, Health, and Development, 13*(2), 75–85.

Josephson, W. L. (1987). Television violence and children's aggression: Testing the priming, social script, and disinhibition predictions. *Journal of Personality and Social Psychology, 53*(5), 882–890.

Jouriles, E. N., Barling, J., & O'Leary, K. D. (1987). Predicting child behavior problems in maritally violent families. *Journal of Abnormal Child Psychology, 15*(2), 165–173.

Kagan, J. (1978, August). The parental love trap. *Psychology Today,* pp. 54–91.

Kagan, J. (1981). *The second year.* Cambridge, MA: Harvard University Press.

Kagan, J. (1984). *The nature of the child.* New York: Basic Books.

Kagan, J. (1988). Stress and coping in early development. In N. Garmezy & M. Rutter (Eds.), *Stress, coping, and development in children.* Baltimore, MD: Johns Hopkins University Press.

Kagan, J., Reznick, J. S., & Gibbons, J. (1989). Inhibited and uninhibited types of children. *Child Development, 60,* 838–845.

Kagan, J., Reznick, J. S., & Snidman, N. (1987). The physiology and psychology of behavioral inhibition in children. *Child Development, 58,* 1459–1473.

Kagan, J., Reznick, J. S., Snidman, N., Gibbons, J., & Johnson, M. O. (1988). Childhood derivatives of inhibition and lack of inhibition to the unfamiliar. *Child Development, 59,* 1580–1589.

Kalmuss, D. (1984). The intergenerational transmission of marital aggression. *Journal of Marriage and the Family, 47,* 11–19.

Kalter, N. (1987). Long-term effects of divorce on children. A developmental vulnerability model. *American Journal of Orthopsychiatry, 57*(4), 587–600.

Kalter, N., Kloner, A., Schreier, S., & Okla, K. (1989). Predictors of children's postdivorce adjustment. *American Journal of Orthopsychiatry, 59*(4), 605–618.

Kanfer, F. H., & Schefft, B. K. (1988). *Guiding the process of therapeutic change.* Champaign, IL: Research Press.

Kaplan, P. S. (1988). *The human odyssey.* St. Paul, MN: West.

Kaufman, J. (1987, June 23). From abused child to good parent. Letter to Editor, *New York Times.*

Kaufman, J., & Cicchetti, D. (1989). Effects of maltreatment on school-age children's socioemotional development: Assessments in a day-camp setting. *Developmental Psychology, 25*(4), 516–524.

Kaufman, J., & Zigler, E. (1987). Do abused children become abusive parents? *American Journal of Orthopsychiatry, 57*(2), 186–196.

Kaye, K. (1982). *The mental and social life of babies.* Chicago: University of Chicago Press.

Kaye, L. W., & Applegate, J. S. (1990). Men as elder caregivers: A response to changing families. *American Journal of Orthopsychiatry, 60*(1), 86–95.

Kazak, A. E. (1986). Families with physically handicapped children: Social ecology and family systems. *Family Process, 25,* 265–281.

Kazdin, A. E. (1984). *Behavior modification in applied settings* (3rd ed.). Homewood, IL: Dorsey Press.

Kazdin, A. E. (1987). Treatment of antisocial behavior in children: Current status and future directions. *Psychological Bulletin, 102,* 187–203.

Keller, W. D., Hildebrandt, K. A., & Richards, M. E. (1985). Effects of extended father-infant contact during the newborn period. *Infant Behavior and Development, 8*(3), 337–350.

Kendrick, C., & Dunn, J. (1983). Sibling quarrels and maternal responses. *Developmental Psychology, 19*(1), 62–70.

Kennedy, J. F., & Keeney, V. T. (1988). The extended family revisited: Grandparents rearing grandchildren. *Child Psychiatry and Human Development, 19*(1), 26–35.

Kerr, P. (1988, June 23). Addiction's hidden toll: Poor families in turmoil. *New York Times.*

Kessen, W. (1975). *Children in China.* New Haven, CT: Yale University Press.

Kessler, J. W. (1988). *Psychopathology of childhood* (2nd ed.). Englewood Cliffs, NJ: Prentice-Hall.

Klass, P. (1988, October 23). Survival odds. *New York Times Magazine,* pp. 56–57.

Klaus, M., & Kennell, J. H. (1976). *Maternal-infant bonding.* St. Louis: Mosby.

Kline, M., Tschann, J. M., Johnston, J. R., & Wallerstein, J. S. (1989). Children's adjustment in joint and sole physical custody families. *Developmental Psychology, 25*(3), 430–438.

Kline, P. (1972). *Fact and fantasy in Freudian theory.* London: Methuen.

Klinge, V., & Piggott, L. R. (1986). Substance use by adolescent psychiatric inpatients and their parents. *Adolescence, 21*(82), 323–331.

Knapp, R. J. (1987, July). When a child dies. *Psychology Today,* pp. 60–67.

Kochanska, G., Kuczynski, L., & Radke-Yarrow, M. (1989). Correspondence between mothers' self-reported and observed child-rearing practices. *Child Development, 60,* 56–63.

Kohlberg, L. (1966). A cognitive-developmental analysis of children's sex-role concepts and attitudes. In E. E. Maccoby (Ed.), *The development of sex differences.* Stanford, CA: Stanford University Press.

Kohn, A. (1987a, September). Art for art's sake. *Psychology Today,* pp. 52–57.

Kohn, A. (1987b, February). Shattered innocence. *Psychology Today,* pp. 54–58.

Kohn, A. (1988, October). Beyond selfishness. *Psychology Today,* pp. 34–38.

Kojima, H. (1986). Japanese concepts of child development from the mid-17th to mid-19th century. *International Journal of Behavioral Development, 9*(3), 315–329.

Kolata, G. (1987a, November 10). Alcoholism: Genetic links grow clearer. *New York Times.*

Kolata, G. (1987b, December 22). The poignant thoughts of Down's children are given voice. *New York Times.*

Kolata, G. (1988a, May 12). Confident obstetricians discovering new frontiers of prenatal diagnosis. *New York Times.*

Kolata, G. (1988b, May 10). When the baby is late: Obstetricians search for the safest approach. *New York Times.*

Kopp, C. B. (1989). Regulation of distress and negative emotions: A developmental view. *Developmental Psychology, 25*(3), 343–354.

Kropp, J. P., & Haynes, O. M. (1987). Abusive and non-abusive mothers' ability to identify general and specific emotion signals to infants. *Child Development, 58,* 187–190.

Kuczynski, L., Kochanska, G., Radke-Yarrow, M., & Girnius-Brown, O. (1987). A developmental interpretation of young children's noncompliance. *Developmental Psychology, 23*(6), 799–806.

Kutner, L. (1987a, December 30). Preparing a child for independence must begin early. *New York Times.*

Kutner, L. (1987b, December 3). Temper tantrums: It helps to realize they're just a stage. *New York Times.*

Kutner, L. (1987c, November 19). What's really important is responsibility rather than neatness. *New York Times.*

Kutner, L. (1988a, January 21). A preschooler's lie may be a normal reaction to conflict. *New York Times.*

Kutner, L. (1988b, February 18). Arguing is a skill, and parents can be the best teachers. *New York Times.*

Kutner, L. (1988c, August 4). Child-rearing classes can ease parental frustration. *New York Times.*

Kutner, L. (1988d, May 12). Children can benefit when parents learn to apologize. *New York Times.*

Kutner, L. (1988e, March 10). Death's no friend, so use care in introducing him. *New York Times.*

Kutner, L. (1988f, March 17). Empathy must be learned, just like any other skill. *New York Times.*

Kutner, L. (1988g, June 30). For children and stepparents, war isn't inevitable. *New York Times.*

Kutner, L. (1988h, November 3). Friendship as testing ground. *New York Times.*

Kutner, L. (1988i, August 25). If a youngster is distressed by another's disabilities. *New York Times.*

Kutner, L. (1988j, May 5). In dealing with bullies, solutions start at home. *New York Times.*

Kutner, L. (1988k, August 18). In teasing, children learn their social boundaries. *New York Times.*

Kutner, L. (1988l, April 7). It isn't always a tough life with a single parent. *New York Times.*

Kutner, L. (1988m, February 11). Keep a cool head to resolve conflict with a teacher. *New York Times.*

Kutner, L. (1988n, June 23). Open talk on sex is more important than ever. *New York Times.*

Kutner, L. (1988o, May 19). Parents may miss signals of depression. *New York Times.*

Kutner, L. (1988p, February 4). Searching for the best in day care. *New York Times.*

Kutner, L. (1988q, April 14). Should every child have a brother or sister? Not really. *New York Times.*

Kutner, L. (1988r, June 2). The fears that follow violence. *New York Times.*

Kutner, L. (1988s, March 3). The stresses and power plays of adolescence. *New York Times.*

Kutner, L. (1988t, June 16). Visited by ghosts of parents' fury. *New York Times.*

Kutner, L. (1988u, January 14). What you don't tell your child *can* hurt him. *New York Times.*

Kutner, L. (1988v, April 21). When parents wish their children would go away. *New York Times.*

Kutner, L. (1989a, January 5). In blended families, rivalries intensify. *New York Times.*

Kutner, L. (1989b, September 14). Prepare children early for the new baby's arrival. *New York Times.*

Kutner, L. (1990, February 1). Sibling fights can actually help children later on. *New York Times.*

Ladd, G. W., & Price, J. M. (1986). Children's cognitive and social competence: The relation between parents' perceptions of task difficulty and children's perceived and actual competence. *Child Development, 57,* 446–460.

Lamaze, F. (1972). *Painless childbirth: The Lamaze method.* New York: Pocket Books.

Landers, S. (1986a, December). Alternatives to self-care "dotted across landscape." *APA Monitor,* pp. 6–7.

Landers, S. (1986b, December). Latchkey kids. *APA Monitor,* pp. 1, 6.

Landers, S. (1986c, November). Youthful thefts called no pranks, no "phase." *APA Monitor,* p. 17.

Landers, S. (1987a, April). Homeless families. *APA Monitor,* pp. 1–4.

Landers, S. (1987b, December). LD definition disputed. *APA Monitor,* p. 35.

Landers, S. (1988a, May). Abuse education efforts abstract to preschoolers. *APA Monitor,* p. 34.

Landers, S. (1988b, July). Delinquency knowledge "in disarray." *APA Monitor,* p. 41.

Landers, S. (1988c, May). Early testing: Does it help or hurt? *APA Monitor,* p. 37.

Landers, S. (1988d, July). Lack of TLC harming AIDS boarder babies. *APA Monitor.*

Landers, S. (1988e, April). National plan forged for service to families. *APA Monitor,* pp. 25–26.

Landers, S. (1988f, January). Study finds "latchkey kid" alarm to be exaggerated. *APA Monitor,* p. 28.

Landers, S. (1988g, November). Survey verifies teen risk-taking. *APA Monitor,* p. 30.

Landers, S. (1989, May). High school seniors' illicit drug use down. *APA Monitor,* p. 33.

Landers, S. (1990, January). Increase in violence scars urban children. *APA Monitor,* p. 24.

Larossa, R., & Larossa, M. M. (1989). Baby care: Fathers vs. mothers. In B. J. Risman & P. Schwartz (Eds.), *Gender in intimate relationships: A microstructural approach.* Belmont, CA: Wadsworth.

Laupa, E., & Turiel, M. (1986). Children's conceptions of adult and peer authority. *Child Development, 57,* 405–412.

Lavigne, J., & Ryan, M. (1979). Psychological adjustment of siblings of children with chronic illness. *Pediatrics, 63,* 616–627.

Lawrence, F. C. (1986). Adolescents' time spent viewing television. *Adolescence, 21*(82), 431–436.

Lawson, A. (1988). *Adultery.* New York: Basic Books.

Lawson, C. (1989, June 15). Toys: Girls still apply makeup, boys fight wars. *New York Times.*

Leboyer, F. (1975). *Birth without violence.* New York: Knopf.

LeCroy, C. W. (1988). Parent-adolescent intimacy: Impact on adolescent functioning. *Adolescence, 23*(89), 137–147.

Lee, C. M., & Gotlib, I. H. (1989). Maternal depression and child adjustment: A longitudinal analysis. *Journal of Abnormal Psychology, 98*(1), 78–85.

Lefkowitz, M. M., & Tesiny, E. P. (1984). Rejection and depression: Prospective and contemporaneous analyses. *Development Psychology, 20,* 776–785.

Lentz, K. A. (1985). Fears and worries of young children as expressed in a contextual play setting. *Journal of Child Psychology and Psychiatry and Allied Disciplines, 26*(6), 981–987.

Lepper, M. R. (1981). Social control processes, attributions of motivation, and the internalization of social values. In E. T. Higgins, D. N. Ruble, & W. W. Hartup (Eds.), *Social cognition and social behavior: Developmental perspectives.* San Francisco: Jossey-Bass.

Lepper, M. R., & Gurtner, J. (1989). Children and computers: Approaching the twenty-first century. *American Psychologist, 44*(2), 170–178.

Lerner, B. (1985, Winter). Self-esteem and excellence: The choice and the paradox. *American Educator,* pp. 10–16.

Lerner, J. V., Hertzog, C., Hooker, K. A., Hassibi, M., & Thomas, A. (1988). A longitudinal study of negative emotional states and adjustment from early childhood through adolescence. *Child Development, 59,* 356–366.

LeVine, R. A. (1974). Parental goals: A cross-cultural view. *Teachers College Record, 76,* 226–239.

Levy-Shiff, R. (1986). Mother-father-child interactions in families with a mentally retarded young child. *American Journal of Mental Deficiency, 91*(2), 141–149.

Lewin, T. (1988a, March 27). Despite criticism, fetal monitors are likely to remain in wide use. *New York Times.*

Lewin, T. (1988b, April). Family support efforts aim to mend two generations. *New York Times.*

Lewin, T. (1988c, March 20). Fewer teen mothers, but more are unmarried. *New York Times.*

Lewis, C. C. (1981). The effects of parental firm control: A reinterpretation of findings. *Psychological Bulletin, 90*(3), 547–563.

Lewis, J. M. (1988a). The transition to parenthood: I. The rating of prenatal marital competence. *Family Process, 27,* 149–165.

Lewis, J. M. (1988b). The transition to parenthood: II. Stability and change in marital structure. *Family Process, 27,* 273–283.

Lewis, J. M. (1988c). The transition to parenthood: III. Incorporation of the child into the family. *Family Process, 27,* 411–421.

Lewis, M., & Feiring, C. (1989). Infant, mother, and mother-infant interaction behavior and subsequent attachment. *Child Development, 60,* 831–837.

Lewis, M., & Rosenblum, L. A. (Eds.). (1974). *The effect of the infant on its caregiver.* New York: John Wiley.

Lewis, M., & Rosenblum, L. A. (Eds.). (1981). *The uncommon child.* New York: Plenum.

Liebert, R. M., & Sprafkin, J. (1988). *The early window* (3rd ed.). Elmsford, NY: Pergamon.

Linney, J. A., & Seidman, E. (1989). The future of schooling. *American Psychologist, 44*(2), 336–340.

Lipsky, D. K. (1985). A parental perspective on stress and coping. *American Journal of Orthopsychiatry, 55*(4), 614–618.

Loehlin, J. C., Willerman, L., & Horn, J. M. (1987). Personality resemblance in adoptive families: A 10-year follow-up. *Journal of Personality and Social Psychology, 53*(5), 961–969.

Loewen, J. W. (1988). Visitation fatherhood. In P. Bronstein & C. P. Cowan (Eds.), *Fatherhood today: Men's changing role in the family.* New York: John Wiley.

Lohr, S. (1987, Summer). Swedes instill a sense of responsibility. *New York Times,* Education Section, p. 19.

Long, N., & Forehand, R. (1987). The effects of parental divorce and parental conflict on children: An overview. *Journal of Developmental and Behavioral Pediatrics, 8*(5), 292–296.

Lorenz, K. Z. (1943). The innate forms of possible experience. *Zeitschrift fur Tierpsychologie, 5,* 233–409.

Louie, E. (1987, November 19). Teaching habits that help. *New York Times.*

Lovaas, I. (1987). Behavioral treatment and normal educational/intellectual functioning in young autistic children. *Journal of Consulting and Clinical Psychology, 55,* 3–9.

Lovaas, I., Koegel, R. L., & Schreibman, L. (1979). Stimulus overselectivity in autism: A review of research. *Psychological Bulletin, 86*(6), 1236–1254.

Lovaas, I., & Smith, T. (1989). A comprehensive behavioral theory of autistic children: Paradigm for research and treatment. *Behavior Therapy and Experimental Psychiatry, 20,* 17–29.

Lovko, A. M., & Ullman, D. (1989). Research on the adjustment of latchkey children: Role of background/demographic and latchkey situation variables. *Journal of Clinical Child Psychology, 18*(1), 16–24.

Luepnitz, D. A. (1988). *The family interpreted: Feminist theory in clinical practice.* New York: Basic Books.

Luster, T., Rhoades, K., & Haas, B. (1989). The relation between parental values and parenting behavior: A test of the Kohn hypothesis. *Journal of Marriage and the Family, 51,* 139–147.

Maccoby, E. E. (1980). *Social development: Psychological growth and the parent-child relationship.* New York: Harcourt Brace Jovanovich.

Maccoby, E. E. (1988). Social-emotional development and response to stressors. In N. Garmezy & M. Rutter (Eds.), *Stress, coping, and development in children.* Baltimore, MD: Johns Hopkins Press.

Maccoby, E. E., & Jacklin, C. N. (1974). *The psychology of sex differences.* Stanford, CA: Stanford University Press.

Maccoby, E. E., & Martin, J. A. (1983). Socialization in the context of the family: Parent-child interaction. In E. M. Hetherington (Ed.), *Handbook of child psychology: Vol. 4. Socialization, personality, and social development* (4th ed.). New York: John Wiley.

Maeroff, G. I. (1985, October 2). Training parents helps toddlers, experiment finds. *New York Times.*

Main, M., & George, C. (1985). Responses of abused and disadvantaged toddlers to distress in agemates: A study in the day care setting. *Developmental Psychology, 21*(3), 407–412.

Mantell, D. M. (1988). Clarifying erroneous child sexual abuse allegations. *American Journal of Orthopsychiatry, 58*(4), 618–621.

Marcus, L. M., & Schopler, E. (1989). Parents as co-therapists with autistic children. In C. E. Schaefer & J. M. Briesmeister (Eds.), *Handbook of parent training.* New York: John Wiley.

Margolis, M. (1984). *Mothers and such: Views of American women and why they changed.* Berkeley, CA: University of California Press.

Marks, I. (1987). The development of normal fear: A review. *Journal of Child Psychology and Psychiatry, 28*(5), 667–697.

Martinez, G. A., & Krieger, F. W. (1985). The 1984 milk-feeding patterns in the United States. *Pediatrics, 76,* 1004–1008.

McBride, S., & Belsky, J. (1988). Characteristics, determinants, and consequences of maternal separation anxiety. *Developmental Psychology, 24*(3), 407–414.

McCartney, K., & Galanopoulos, A. (1988). Child care and attachment: A new frontier the second time around. *American Journal of Orthopsychiatry, 58*(1), 16–24.

McCleod, B. (1986, October). Rx for health: A dose of self-confidence. *Psychology Today,* pp. 46–50.

McCollum, A. T. (1985). Grieving over the lost dream. In M. J. Schleifer & S. D. Klein (Eds.), *The disabled child and the family: An exceptional parent reader.* Boston, MA: The Exceptional Parent Press.

McCollum, J. (1985). Parenting an infant with a disability—A practical guide for interaction. In M. J. Schleifer & S. D. Klein (Eds.), *The disabled child and the family: An exceptional parent reader.* Boston, MA: The Exceptional Parent Press.

McCombs, A., & Forehand, R. (1989). Adolescent school performance following parental divorce: Are there family factors that can enhance success? *Adolescence, 24*(96), 871–880.

McConachie, H., & Mitchell, D. R. (1985). Parents teaching their young mentally handicapped children. *Journal of Child Psychology and Psychiatry, 26*(3), 389–405.

McCord, J. (1988a). Alcoholism: Toward understanding genetic and social factors. *Psychiatry, 51,* 131–141.

McCord, J. (1988b). Parental behavior in the cycle of aggression. *Psychiatry, 51,* 14–23.

McCormick, N., Izzo, A., & Folcik, J. (1985). Adolescents' values, sexuality, and contraception in a rural New York County. *Adolescence, 20*(78), 385–395.

McCoy, C. L., & Masters, J. C. (1985). Children's strategies for the social control of emotion. *Child Development, 56,* 1214–1222.

McCoy, E. (1984, November). Kids and divorce. *Parents.*

McGhee, P. E. (1979). *Humor: Its origin and development.* San Francisco: W. H. Freeman.

McGillicuddy-De Lisi, A. V. (1985). The relationship between parental beliefs and children's cognitive level. In I. E. Sigel (Ed.), *Parental belief systems: The psychological consequences for children.* Hillsdale, NJ: Erlbaum.

McHale, S. M., & Gamble, W. C. (1989). Sibling relationships of children with disabled and nondisabled brothers and sisters. *Developmental Psychology, 25*(3), 421–429.

McLaughlin, B. (1983). Child compliance to parental control techniques. *Developmental Psychology, 19*(5), 667–673.

McLoyd, V. C. (1989). Socialization and development in a changing economy: The effects of paternal job and income loss on children. *American Psychology, 44*(2), 293–302.

McQuarrie, H. G. (1980). Home delivery controversy. *Journal of the American Medical Association, 243,* 1747–1748.

McWhirter, J. J., McWhirter, R. J., & McWhirter, M. C. (1985). The learning disabled child: A retrospective review. *Journal of Learning Disabilities, 18*(6), 315–318.

Melson, G. F., & Fogel, A. (1988, January). Learning to care. *Psychology Today,* pp. 39–45.

Melton, G. B., & Davidson, H. A. (1987). Child protection and society: When should the state intervene? *American Psychologist, 42*(2), 172–175.

Meltzoff, A. N. (1988). Imitation of televised models by infants. *Child Development, 59,* 1221–1229.

Meredith, D. (1985, June). Mom, dad and the kids. *Psychology Today,* pp. 60–67.

Metcalf, K., & Gaier, E. L. (1987). Patterns of middle-class parenting and adolescent underachievement. *Adolescence, 22*(88), 919–929.

Meyer, M. (1989, April). Locking out sex and violence on cable. *Video Magazine,* pp. 61–62.

Meyerhoff, M. K., & White, B. L. (1986, September). Making the grade as parents. *Psychology Today,* pp. 38–45.

Miller, G. A., & Gildea, P. M. (1987, September). How children learn words. *Scientific American,* pp. 94–99.

Miller, P., & Sperry, L. L. (1987). The socialization of anger and aggression. *Merrill-Palmer Quarterly, 33*(1), 1–31.

Miller, S. A. (1986). Parents' beliefs about their children's cognitive abilities. *Developmental Psychology, 22*(2), 276–284.

Miller, S. A. (1988). Parents' beliefs about children's cognitive development. *Child Development, 59,* 259–285.

Mills, R. S. L., & Rubin, K. H. (1990). Parental beliefs about problematic social behaviors in early childhood. *Child Development, 61,* 138–151.

Minuchin, S. (1974). *Families and family therapy.* Cambridge, MA: Harvard University Press.

Mischel, W. (1976). *Introduction to psychology* (2nd ed.). New York: Holt, Rinehart & Winston.

Mohar, C. J. (1988). Applying the concept of temperament to child care. *Child & Youth Care Quarterly, 17*(4), 221–238.

Mondell, S., & Tyler, F. B. (1981). Parental competence and styles of problem-solving/play behavior with children. *Developmental Psychology, 17*(1), 73–78.

Montemayor, R. (1983). Parents and adolescents in conflict: All families some of the time and some families all of the time. *Journal of Early Adolescence, 3,* 83–103.

Moore, K. A., Peterson, J. L., & Furstenberg, F. F. (1986). Parental attitudes and the occurrence of early sexual activity. *Journal of Marriage and the Family, 48,* 777–782.

Mulhern, R. K., & Passman, R. H. (1981). Parental discipline as affected by the sex of the parent, the sex of the child, and the child's apparent responsiveness to discipline. *Developmental Psychology, 17*(5), 604–613.

Mullis, R. L., Mullis, A. K., & Markstrom, C. (1987). Reports of child behavior by single mothers and married mothers. *Child Study Journal, 17*(3), 211–225.

Murray, A. D., Dolby, R. M., Nation, R. L., & Thomas, D. B. (1981). Effects of epidural anesthesia on newborns and their mothers. *Child Development, 52,* 71–82.

Muuss, R. E. (1982). *Theories of adolescence* (4th ed.). New York: Random House.

Myers, B. J., Jarvis, P. A., & Creasey, G. L. (1987). Infants' behavior with their mothers and grandmothers. *Infant Behavior & Development, 10*(3), 245–259.

Neal, A. G., Groat, H. T., & Wicks, J. W. (1989). Attitudes about having children: A study of 600 couples in the early years of marriage. *Journal of Marriage and the Family, 51*(2), 313–328.

Neiger, B. L., & Hopkins, R. W. (1988). Adolescent suicide: Character traits of high-risk teenagers. *Adolescence, 23*(90), 469–475.

Newcomb, M. D., & Bentler, P. M. (1989). Substance use and abuse among children and teenagers. *American Psychologist, 44*(2), 242–248.

Newman, B. M. (1989). The changing nature of the parent-adolescent relationship from early to late adolescence. *Adolescence, 24*(96), 915–924.

Newman, J. (1985). Adolescents: Why they can be so obnoxious. *Adolescence, 20*(79), 635–646.

Nicholls, J. G., Patashnick, M., & Nolen, S. B. (1985). Adolescents' theories of education. *Journal of Educational Psychology, 77*(6), 683–692.

Nolen-Hoeksema, S., Girgus, J. S., & Seligman, M. E. P. (1986). Learned helplessness in children: A longitudinal study of depression, achievement, and explanatory style. *Journal of Personality and Social Psychology, 51*(2), 435–442.

Nottelmann, E. D. (1987). Competence and self-esteem during transition from childhood to adolescence. *Developmental Psychology, 23*(3), 441–450.

Nowicki, S., Jr., & Oxenford, C. (1989). The relation of hostile nonverbal communication styles to popularity in preadolescent children. *Journal of Genetic Psychology, 150*(1), 39–44.

Offer, D. (1985, Summer). A portrait of normal adolescents. *American Educator,* pp. 34–37.

Offer, D. (1987, February 3). Smooth adolescence (quote). *New York Times.*

Offord, D. R. (1987). Prevention of behavioral and emotional disorders in children. *Journal of Child Psychology and Psychiatry, 28*(1), 9–19.

Oldershaw, L., Walters, G. C., & Hall, D. K. (1986). Control strategies and noncompliance in abusive mother-child dyads: An observational study. *Child Development, 57*(3), 722–732.

O'Malley, P. M., & Bachman, J. G. (1983). Self-esteem: Change and stability between ages 13 and 23. *Developmental Psychology, 19*(2), 257–268.

Palfrey, J. S., Walker, D. K., Butler, J. A., & Singer, J. D. (1989). Patterns of response in families of chronically disabled children: An assessment of five metropolitan school districts. *American Journal of Orthopsychiatry, 59*(1), 94–105.

Palkovitz, R. (1985). Father's birth attendance, early contact, and extended contact with their newborns: A critical review. *Child Development, 56*(2), 392–406.

Parke, R. D. (1969). Effectiveness of punishment as an interaction of intensity, timing, agent nurturance and cognitive-structuring. *Child Development, 40,* 213–235.

Parke, R. D. (1973). Explorations in punishment, discipline and self-control. In P. Elich (Ed.), *Social learning.* Bellingham, WA: Western Washington State Press.

Parke, R. D., & Suomi, S. (1983). Adult male-infant relationships: Human and nonhuman primate evidence. In K. Immelmann, G. Barlow, M. Main, & L. Petrinovitch (Eds.), *Behavioral development: The Bielefeld interdisciplinary project.* New York: Cambridge University Press.

Parker, H., & Parker, S. (1986). Father-daughter sexual abuse: An emerging perspective. *American Journal of Orthopsychiatry, 56*(4), 531–549.

Parmelee, A. H. (1986). Children's illnesses: Their beneficial effects on behavioral development. *Child Development, 57,* 1–10.

Passman, R. H. (1987). Attachments to inanimate objects: Are children who love security blankets insecure? *Journal of Consulting and Clinical Psychology, 55*(6), 825–830.

Patterson, G. R. (1982). *A social learning approach to family interventions: Vol. 3. Coercive family process.* Eugene, OR: Castalia.

Patterson, G. R. (1988). Stress: A change agent for family process. In N. Garmezy & M. Rutter (Eds.), *Stress, coping, and development in children.* Baltimore, MD: Johns Hopkins Press.

Patterson, G. R., DeBaryshe, B. D., & Ramsey, E. (1989). A developmental perspective on antisocial behavior. *American Psychologist, 44*(2), 329–335.

Peek, C. W., Fischer, J. L., & Kidwell, J. S. (1985). Teenage violence toward parents: A neglected dimension of family violence. *Journal of Marriage and the Family, 47,* 1051–1060.

Penner, S. G. (1987). Parental responses to grammatical and ungrammatical child utterances. *Child Development, 58,* 376–384.

Perry, D. G., Kusel, S. J., & Perry, L. C. (1988). Victims of peer aggression. *Developmental Psychology, 24*(6), 807–814.

Pestrak, V. A., & Martin, D. (1985). Cognitive development and aspects of adolescent sexuality. *Adolescence, 20*(80), 981–987.

Peterson, A. C. (1987, September). Those gangly years. *Psychology Today,* pp. 28–34.

Peterson, C., & Peterson, R. (1986). Parent-child interaction and daycare: Does quality of daycare matter? *Journal of Applied Development Psychology, 7*(1), 1–15.

Peterson, C. C., Peterson, J. L., & Carroll, J. (1986). Television viewing and imaginative problem solving during preadolescence. *Journal of Genetic Psychology, 147*(1), 61–67.

Peterson, L. (1989). Latchkey children's preparation for self-care: Overestimated, underrehearsed, and unsafe. *Journal of Clinical Child Psychology, 18*(1), 36–43.

Pettit, G. S., & Bates, J. E. (1989). Family interaction patterns and children's behavior problems from infancy to 4 years. *Developmental Psychology, 25*(3), 413–420.

Phillips, D., McCartney, K., & Scarr, S. (1987). Child-care quality and children's social development. *Developmental Psychology, 23*(4), 537–543.

Phillips, S., Bohannon, W. E., Gayton, W. F., & Friedman, S. B. (1985). Parent interview findings regarding the impact of cystic fibrosis on families. *Journal of Developmental and Behavioral Pediatrics, 6*(3), 122–127.

Piaget, J. (1954). *The construction of reality in the child.* New York: Basic Books.

Pines, M. (1982, March 30). What produces great skills? Specific pattern is discerned. *New York Times.*

Pitt, D. E. (1988, March 15). New program to combat child abuse. *New York Times.*

Plienis, A. J., Robbins, F. R., & Dunlap, G. (1988). Parent adjustment and family stress as factors in behavioral parent training for young autistic children. *Journal of the Multihandicapped Person, 1*(1), 31–52.

Plomin, R. (1989). Environment and genes: Determinants of behavior. *American Psychologist, 44*(2), 105–111.

Plomin, R., McClearn, G. E., Pedersen, N. L., Nesselroade, J. R., & Bergeman, C. S. (1988). Genetic influence on childhood family environment perceived retrospectively from the last half of the life span. *Developmental Psychology, 24*(5), 738–745.

Polansky, N. A., Chalmers, M. A., Buttenwieser, E., & Williams, D. P. (1981). *Damaged parents: An anatomy of child neglect.* Chicago: University of Chicago.

Post, R. D. (1988). Self-sabotage among successful women. *Psychotherapy in Private Practice, 6*(3), 191–205.

Powell, L. (1977). The empty nest, employment, and psychiatric symptoms in college-educated women. *Psychology of Women Quarterly, 2,* 253–265.

Power, T. G. (1984). Life with father: New directions for family policy. Review of M. E. Lamb & A. Sagi (Eds.). (1983). *Fatherhood and family policy.* Hillsdale, NJ: Erlbaum. In *Contemporary Psychology, 29*(4), 324–325.

Power, T. G. (1985). Mother- and father-infant play: A developmental analysis. *Child Development, 56*(6), 1514–1524.

Power, T. G., & Chapieski, M. L. (1986). Childrearing and impulse control in toddlers: A naturalistic investigation. *Developmental Psychology, 22*(2), 271–275.

Power, T. G., & Parke, R. D. (1986). Patterns of early socialization: Mother- and father-infant interaction in the home. *International Journal of Behavioral Development, 9*(3), 331–341.

Power, T. G., & Shanks, J. A. (1989). Parents as socializers: Maternal and paternal views. *Journal of Youth and Adolescence, 18*(2), 203–220.

Powers, S. I., Hauser, S. T., & Kilner, L. A. (1989). Adolescent mental health. *American Psychologist, 44*(2), 200–208.

Pratt, M. W., Kerig, P., Cowan, P. A., & Cowan, C. P. (1988). Mothers and fathers teaching 3-year-olds: Authoritative parenting and adult scaffolding of young children's learning. *Developmental Psychology, 24*(6), 832–839.

Premack, D. (1962). Reversibility of the reinforcement relation. *Science, 136,* 255–257.

Price, R. H., & Lynn, S. J. (1986). *Abnormal psychology* (2nd ed.). Chicago: Dorsey Press.

Proulx, J., & Koulack, D. (1987). The effect of parental divorce on parent-adolescent separation. *Journal of Youth and Adolescence, 16*(5), 473–480.

Radin, N. (1988). Primary caregiving fathers of long duration. In P. Bronstein & C. P. Cowan (Eds.), *Fatherhood today: Men's changing role in the family.* New York: John Wiley.

Radin, N., & Goldsmith, R. (1983). *Predictors of father involvement in childcare.* Paper presented at the biennial meeting of the Society for Research in Child Development, Detroit.

Radin, N., & Goldsmith, R. (1985). Caregiving fathers of preschoolers: Four years later. *Merrill-Palmer Quarterly, 31*(4), 375–383.

Radin, N., & Harold-Goldsmith, R. (1989). The involvement of selected unemployed and employed men with their children. *Child Development, 60,* 454–459.

Reich, P. A. (1986). *Language development.* Englewood Cliffs, NJ: Prentice-Hall.

Reid, J. B., Kavanagh, K., & Baldwin, D. V. (1987). Abusive parents' perceptions of child problem behaviors: An example of parental bias. *Journal of Abnormal Child Psychology, 15*(3), 457–466.

Reinhold, R. (1987, October 4). California tries caring for its growing ranks of latchkey children. *New York Times.*

Reis, J. S., & Herz, E. J. (1987). Correlates of adolescent parenting. *Adolescence, 22*(87), 599–610.

Reppucci, N. D., & Haugaard, J. J. (1989). Prevention of sexual abuse: Myth or reality. *American Psychologist, 44*(10), 1266–1275.

Richardson, S. A., Koller, H., & Katz, M. (1985). Relationship of upbringing to later behavior disturbance of mildly mentally retarded young people. *American Journal of Mental Deficiency, 90*(1), 1–8.

Riley, A. W., Parrish, J. M., & Cataldo, M. F. (1989). Training parents to meet the needs of children with medical or physical handicaps. In C. E. Schaefer & J. M. Briesmeister (Eds.), *Handbook of parent training.* New York: John Wiley.

Risman, B. J. (1989). Can men "mother"? Life as a single father. In B. J. Risman & P. Schwartz (Eds.), *Gender in intimate relationships: A microstructural approach.* Belmont, CA: Wadsworth.

Roberts, C. W., Green, R., Williams, K., & Goodman, M. (1987). Boyhood gender identity development: A statistical contrast of two family groups. *Developmental Psychology, 23*(4), 544–557.

Roberts, M. (1988, February). Schoolyard menace. *Psychology Today,* pp. 52–56.

Roberts, W., & Strayer, J. (1987). Parents' responses to the emotional distress of their children: Relations with children's competence. *Developmental Psychology, 23*(3), 415–422.

Robertson, J. F., & Simons, R. L. (1989). Family factors, self-esteem, and adolescent depression. *Journal of Marriage and the Family, 51,* 125–138.

Robinson, B. E., & Barret, R. L. (1985, December). Teenage fathers. *Psychology Today,* pp. 66–70.

Robinson, J. P. (1977). *How Americans use time: A social-psychological analysis of everyday behavior.* New York: Praeger.

Rodman, H., Pratto, D. J., & Nelson, R. S. (1985). Child care arrangements and children's functioning: A comparison of self-care and adult-care children. *Developmental Psychology, 21,* 413–418.

Rodman, H., Pratto, D. J., & Nelson, R. S. (1988). Toward a definition of self-care children: A commentary on Steinberg (1986). *Developmental Psychology, 24*(2), 292–294.

Rogers, C. (1961). *On becoming a person.* Boston: Houghton Mifflin.

Rosen, C. M. (1987, September). The eerie world of reunited twins. *Discover,* pp. 36–46.

Rosenberg, M. S. (1987). New directions for research on the psychological maltreatment of children. *American Psychologist, 42*(2), 166–171.

Rosenfeld, A. (1987). Freud, psychodynamics, and incest. *Child Welfare, 66*(6), 485–496.

Rosenheim, E., & Reicher, R. (1985). Informing children about a parent's terminal illness. *Journal of Child Psychology and Psychiatry and Allied Disciplines, 26*(6), 995–998.

Rosenthal, E. (1990, February 4). When a pregnant woman drinks. *New York Times Magazine,* pp. 30–61.

Rosenthal, P., & Rosenthal, S. (1984). Suicidal behavior by preschool children. *American Journal of Psychiatry, 141*(4), 520–525.

Ross, H. S., & Lollis, S. P. (1987). Communication within infant social games. *Developmental Psychology, 23*(2), 241–248.

Rousso, H. (1985). Fostering healthy self esteem. *The disabled child and the family: An exceptional parent reader.* Boston, MA: The Exceptional Parent Press.

Rowe, D. C., & Plomin, R. (1981). The importance of nonshared (E1) environmental influences in behavioral development. *Developmental Psychology, 17*(5), 517–531.

Rubenstein, C. (1988a, January 21). The American family is adjusting to teen-agers' work-spend ethic. *New York Times.*

Rubenstein, C. (1988b, May 12). The struggle to keep family time quality time. *New York Times.*

Rubenstein, C. (1989, October 8). The baby boom. *New York Times Magazine,* pp. 34–41.

Rubin, L. (1979). *Women of a certain age.* New York: Harper & Row.

Rubinstein, J., & Slife, B. D. (1984). *Taking sides: Clashing views on controversial psychological issues* (3rd ed.). Guilford, CT: Dushkin.

Ruble, D. N., & Ruble, T. L. (1980). Sex stereotypes. In A. G. Miller (Ed.), *In the eye of the beholder: Contemporary issues in stereotyping.* New York: Holt, Rinehart & Winston.

Rushton, J. P. (1986). Altruism and aggression: The heritability of individual differences. *Journal of Personality and Social Psychology, 50*(6), 1192–1198.

Russell, G., & Radin, N. (1983). Increased paternal participation: The father's perspective. In M. Lamb & A. Sagi (Eds.), *Fatherhood and social policy.* Hillsdale, NJ: Erlbaum.

Russell, G., & Russell, A. (1987). Mother-child and father-child relationships in middle childhood. *Child Development, 58,* 1573–1585.

Rutter, M. (1985a). Family and school influences on behavioural development. *Journal of Child Psychology and Psychiatry, 26*(3), 349–368.

Rutter, M. (1985b). Family and school influences on cognitive development. *Journal of Child Psychology and Psychiatry, 26*(5), 683–704.

Rutter, M. (1988). Stress, coping, and development. In N. Garmezy & M. Rutter (Eds.), *Stress, coping, and development in children.* Baltimore, MD: Johns Hopkins University Press.

Rutter, M. (1990). Commentary: Some focus and process considerations regarding effects of parental depression on children. *Developmental Psychology, 26*(1), 60–67.

Ryan, R. M., & Lynch, J. H. (1989). Emotional autonomy versus detachment: Revisiting the vicissitudes of adolescence and young adulthood. *Child Development, 60,* 340–356.

Sachs, J., & Devin, J. (1976). Young children's use of age-appropriate speech styles. *Journal of Child Language, 3,* 81–98.

St. James-Roberts, I. (1989). Persistent crying in infancy. *Journal of Child Psychology and Psychiatry & Allied Disciplines, 30*(2), 189–195.

Sameroff, A. J., & Feil, L. A. (1985). Parental concepts of development. In I. E. Sigel (Ed.), *Parental belief systems: The psychological consequences for children.* Hillsdale, NJ: Erlbaum.

Samuels, S. J. (1986). Why children fail to learn and what to do about it. *Exceptional Children, 53*(1), 7–16.

Sanders-Phillips, K., Strauss, M. E., & Gutberlet, R. L. (1988). The effect of obstetric medication on newborn infant feeding behavior. *Infant Behavior and Development, 11*(3), 251–263.

Santrock, J. W. (1988). *Children.* Dubuque, IA: Wm. C. Brown.

Santrock, J. W., Sitterle, K. A., & Warshak, R. A. (1988). Parent-child relationships in stepfather families. In P. Bronstein & C. P. Cowan (Eds.), *Fatherhood today: Men's changing role in the family.* New York: John Wiley.

Santrock, J. W., & Warshak, R. A. (1986). Development, relationships, and legal/clinical considerations in father-custody families. In M. E. Lamb (Ed.), *The father's role: Applied perspectives.* New York: John Wiley.

Santrock, J. W., & Yussen, S. R. (1984). *Children and adolescence: A developmental perspective.* Dubuque, IA: Wm. C. Brown.

Satir, V. (1972). *Peoplemaking.* Palo Alto, CA: Science and Behavior Books.

Scarborough, H., & Wyckoff, J. (1986). Mother, I'd still rather do it myself: Some further non-effects of "motherese." *Journal of Child Language, 13*(2), 431–437.

Scarr, S., & Grajek, S. (1982). Similarities and differences among siblings. In M. E. Lamb & B. Sutton-Smith (Eds.), *Sibling relationships: Their nature and significance across the lifespan.* Hillsdale, NJ: Erlbaum.

Scarr, S., & McCartney, K. (1983). How people make their own environments: A theory of genotype-environment correlations. *Child Development, 54,* 424–435.

Scarr, S., Phillips, D., & McCartney, K. (1989). Working mothers and their families. *American Psychologist, 44*(11), 1402–1409.

Scarr, S., & Weinberg, R. A. (1986). The early childhood enterprise: Care and education of the young. *American Psychologist, 41*(10), 1140–1146.

Schachere, K. (1990). Attachment between working mothers and their infants: The influence of family processes. *American Journal of Orthopsychiatry, 60*(1), 19–34.

Schaefer, C. E., & Millman, H. L. (1981). *How to help children with common problems.* New York: Van Nostrand Reinhold.

Schaffer, H. R., & Crook, C. K. (1980). Child compliance and maternal control techniques. *Developmental Psychology, 16*(1), 54–61.

Schiamberg, L. B. (1988). *Child and adolescent development.* New York: Macmillan.

Schieffelin, B., & Ochs, E. (1983). A cultural perspective on the transition from prelinguistic to linguistic communication. In R. Golinkoff (Ed.), *The transition from prelinguistic to linguistic communication.* Hillsdale, NJ: Erlbaum.

Schwartz, B. (1986). *The battle for human nature: Science, morality and modern life.* New York: Norton.

Scott, M. (1988, August 21). "How adults could have helped me." *Parade Magazine.*

Sears, R. R., Maccoby, E. E., & Levin, H. (1957). *Patterns of childrearing.* Evanston, IL: Row Peterson.

Seidner, L. B., Stipek, D. J., & Feshbach, N. D. (1988). A developmental analysis of elementary school-aged children's concepts of pride and embarrassment. *Child Development, 59,* 367–377.

Seligman, M. E. P. (1975). *Helplessness: On depression, development and death.* San Francisco: W. H. Freeman.

Seltzer, J. A., & Bianchi, S. M. (1988). Children's contact with absent parents. *Journal of Marriage and the Family, 50,* 663–677.

Seltzer, J. A., Schaeffer, N. C., & Charng, H. (1989). Family ties after divorce: The relationship between visiting and paying child support. *Journal of Marriage and the Family, 51,* 1013–1032.

Selye, H. (1976). *The stress of life* (rev. ed.). New York: McGraw-Hill.

Shapiro, J. L. (1987a, January). The expectant father. *Psychology Today,* pp. 36–42.

Shapiro, J. L. (1987b). *When men are pregnant.* San Luis Obispo, CA: Impact.

Shell, E. R. (1989, December). Now, which kind of preschool? *Psychology Today,* pp. 52–57.

Silberman, M. L., & Wheelan, S. A. (1980). *How to discipline without feeling guilty: Assertive relationships with children.* Champaign, IL: Research Press.

Silverberg, S. B., & Steinberg, L. (1987). Sex differences in family relations at adolescence. *Journal of Youth and Adolescence, 16*(3), 293–312.

Silverman-Watkins, L. T., & Sprafkin, J. N. (1983). Adolescents' comprehension of televised sexual innuendoes. *Journal of Applied Developmental Psychology, 4*(4), 359–369.

Simmons, R. G., Burgeson, R., & Carlton-Ford, S. (1987). The impact of cumulative change in early adolescence. *Child Development, 58,* 1220–1234.

Singer, J. L. (1989, April 9). Why Johnny's watching needs watching. *New York Times.*

Sirignano, S. W., & Lachman, M. E. (1985). Personality change during the transition to parenthood: The role of perceived infant temperament. *Developmental Psychology, 21*(3), 558–567.

Skinner, B. F. (1953). *Science and human behavior.* New York: Macmillan.

Skinner, B. F. (1971). *Beyond freedom and dignity.* New York: Knopf.

Skinner, B. F. (1987). *Upon further reflection.* Englewood Cliffs, NJ: Prentice-Hall.

Slater, M. A. (1986). Modification of mother-child interaction processes in families with children at-risk for mental retardation. *American Journal of Mental Deficiency, 91*(3), 257–267.

Smetana, J. G. (1988). Adolescents' and parents' conceptions of parental authority. *Child Development, 59,* 321–335.

Smetana, J. G. (1989a). Adolescents' and parents' reasoning about actual family conflict. *Child Development, 60,* 1052–1067.

Smetana, J. G. (1989b). Toddlers' social interactions in the context of moral and conventional transgressions in the home. *Developmental Psychology, 25*(4), 499–508.

Smith, P. B., & Pederson, D. R. (1988). Maternal sensitivity and patterns of infant-mother attachment. *Child Development, 59,* 1097–1101.

Smolak, L. (1986). *Infancy.* Englewood Cliffs, NJ: Prentice-Hall.

Snow, M. E., Jacklin, C. N., & Maccoby, E. E. (1983). Sex-of-child differences in father-child interactions at one year of age. *Child Development, 54,* 227–232.

Snowden, L. R., Schott, T. L., Awalt, S. J., & Gillis-Knox, J. (1988). Marital satisfaction in pregnancy: Stability and change. *Journal of Marriage and the Family, 50,* 325–333.

Sollie, D. L., & Miller, B. C. (1980). The transition to parenthood as a critical time for building family strengths. In N. Stinnett, B. Chesser, J. Defain, & P. Kraul (Eds.), *Family strengths: Positive models of family life.* Lincoln: University of Nebraska Press.

Sosa, R., Kennell, J., Klaus, M., Robertson, S., & Urrutia, J. (1980). The effect of a supportive companion on perinatal problems, length of labor, and mother-infant interaction. *New England Journal of Medicine, 303,* 597–600.

Spitz, R. A. (1946). In R. S. Eissler (Ed.), *Psychoanalytic study of the child* (Vol. 2). New York: International Universities Press.

Sprunger, L. W., Boyce, W. T., & Gaines, J. A. (1985). Family-infant congruence: Routines and rhythmicity in family adaptations to a young infant. *Child Development, 56*(3), 564–572.

Sroufe, L. A., & Fleeson, J. (1986). Attachment and the construction of relationships. In W. W. Hartup & Z. Rubin (Eds.), *Relationships and development.* Hillsdale, NJ: Erlbaum.

Stambrook, M., & Parker, K. C. H. (1987). The development of the concept of death in childhood: A review of the literature. *Merrill-Palmer Quarterly, 33*(2), 133–157.

Stark, E. (1985, August). Boys 1, girls 1. *Psychology Today,* p. 18.

Stark, E. (1986, October). Young, innocent and pregnant. *Psychology Today,* pp. 28–35.

Stark, L. J., Spirito, A., Williams, C. A., & Guevremont, D. C. (1989). Common problems and coping strategies: I. Findings with normal adolescents. *Journal of Abnormal Child Psychology, 17*(2), 203–212.

Steelman, L. C., & Powell, B. (1985). The social and academic consequences of birth order: Real, artifact, or both? *Journal of Marriage and the Family, 47,* 117–125.

Stefanko, M. (1987). Adolescents and adults: Ratings and expected ratings of themselves and each other. *Adolescence, 22*(85), 208–221.

Steinberg, L. (1987a, September). Bound to bicker. *Psychology Today.*

Steinberg, L. (1987b). Family processes at adolescence: A developmental perspective. *Family Therapy, 14*(2), 77–86.

Steinberg, L. (1987c). Impact of puberty on family relations: Effects of pubertal status and pubertal timing. *Developmental Psychology, 23*(3), 451–460.

Steinberg, L. (1987d). Recent research on the family at adolescence: The extent and nature of sex differences. *Journal of Youth and Adolescence, 16*(3), 191–197.

Steinberg, L. (1987e, April 25). Why Japan's students outdo ours. *New York Times.*

Steinberg, L. (1988a). Reciprocal relation between parent-child distance and pubertal maturation. *Developmental Psychology, 24*(1), 122–128.

Steinberg, L. (1988b). Simple solutions to a complex problem: A response to Rodman, Pratto, and Nelson (1988). *Developmental Psychology, 24*(2), 295–296.

Steinberg, L., Elmen, J. D., & Mounts, N. S. (1989). Authoritative parenting, psychosocial maturity and academic success among adolescents. *Child Development, 60*(6), 1424–1436.

Stemp, P. S., Turner, R. J., & Noh, S. (1986). Psychological distress in the postpartum period: The significance of social support. *Journal of Marriage and the Family, 48,* 271–277.

Stern, M., & Karraker, K. H. (1988). Prematurity stereotyping by mothers of premature infants. *Journal of Pediatric Psychology, 13*(2), 255–263.

Sternberg, R. J., & Davidson, J E. (Eds.). (1986). *Conceptions of giftedness.* New York: Cambridge University Press.

Stevenson, D. L., & Baker, D. P. (1987). The family-school relation and the child's school performance. *Child Development, 58*(5), 1348–1357.

Stevenson, H. W. (1985). Cognitive performance and academic achievement of Japanese, Chinese, and American children. *Child Development, 56*(3), 718–734.

Stevenson, H. W. (1987, Summer). The Asian advantage: The case of mathematics. *American Educator,* pp. 26–48.

Stevenson, H. W., Lee, S. Y., & Stigler, J. W. (1986). Mathematics achievement of Chinese, Japanese and American children. *Science, 231,* 693–699.

Stevenson, M. B., Leavitt, L. A., Thompson, R. H., & Roach, M. A. (1988). A social relations model analysis of parent and child play. *Developmental Psychology, 24*(1), 101–107.

Stevenson, M. R., & Black, K. N. (1988). Paternal absence and sex-role development: A meta-analysis. *Child Development, 59,* 793–814.

Stewart, R. B. (1983). Sibling interaction: The role of the older child as teacher for the younger. *Merrill-Palmer Quarterly, 29*(1), 47–68.

Stewart, R. B., Mobley, L. A., Van Tuyl, S. S., & Salvador, M. A. (1987). The firstborn's adjustment to the birth of a sibling. A longitudinal assessment. *Child Development, 58,* 341–355.

Stipek, D., & Mac Iver, D. (1989). Developmental change in children's assessment of intellectual competence. *Child Development, 60,* 521–538.

Stocker, C., Dunn, J., & Plomin, R. (1989). Sibling relationships: Links with child temperaments, maternal behavior, and family structure. *Child Development, 60,* 715–727.

Stolberg, A. L., & Bush, J. P. (1985). A path analysis of factors predicting children's divorce adjustment. *Journal of Clinical Child Psychology, 14*(1), 49–54.

Stone, L. J., & Church, J. (1984). *Childhood and adolescence* (5th ed.). New York: Random House.

Stoneman, Z., Brody, G. H., & Burke, M. (1989). Marital quality, depression, and inconsistent parenting: Relationship with observed mother-child conflict. *American Journal of Orthopsychiatry, 59*(1), 105–115.

Stouthamer-Loeber, M., & Loeber, R. (1986). Boys who lie. *Journal of Abnormal Child Psychology, 14*(4), 551–564.

Streissguth, A. P., Barr, H. M., Sampson, P. D., Darby, B. L., & Martin, D. C. (1989). IQ at age 4 in relation to maternal alcohol use and smoking during pregnancy. *Developmental Psychology, 25*(1), 3–11.

Stringer, S. A., & la Greca, A. M. (1985). Correlates of child abuse potential. *Journal of Abnormal Child Psychology, 13*(2), 217–226.

Sullivan, H. S. (1973). *Clinical studies in psychiatry.* New York: Norton and Co. (Original work published 1956)

Sullivan, J. F. (1987, October 29). Pregnancy task force hears from teen-agers. *New York Times.*

Sutton-Smith, B. (1985, October). The child at play. *Psychology Today,* pp. 64–65.

Swartz, J. (1984, June). Behavior clue to child abuse. *APA Monitor,* p. 23.

Swartz, J. (1987, December). Depression often missed in teens. *APA Monitor.*

Sweeney, J., & Bradbard, M. R. (1988). Mothers' and fathers' changing perceptions of their male and female infants over the course of pregnancy. *Journal of Genetic Psychology, 149*(3), 393–404.

Symons, D. K., & Moran, G. (1987). The behavioral dynamics of mutual responsiveness in early face-to-face mother-infant interactions. *Child Development, 58,* 1488–1495.

Synnott, A. (1988). Little angels, little devils: A sociology of children. In G. Handel (Ed.), *Childhood socialization.* New York: Aldine De Gruyter.

Teyber, E., & Hoffman, C. D. (1987, April). Missing fathers. *Psychology Today,* pp. 36–39.

Thomas, A., & Chess, S. (1977). *Temperament and development.* New York: Brunner/Mazel.

Thomas, A., Chess, S., & Birch, H. G. (1968). *Temperament and behavior disorders in children.* New York: New York University Press.

Thomas, A., Chess, S., & Birch, H. G. (1970, August). The origins of personality. *Scientific American, 223,* pp. 102–109.

Thompson, D. N. (1985). Parent-peer compliance in a group of preadolescent youths. *Adolescence, 20*(79), 501–508.

Thompson, R. A., Lamb, M. E., & Estes, D. (1982). Stability of infant-mother attachment and its relationship to changing life circumstances in an unselected middle-class sample. *Child Development, 53,* 144–148.

Thrall, C. A. (1978). Who does what? Role stereotyping, children's work, and continuity between generations in the household division of labor. *Human Relations, 31,* 249–265.

Thunberg, U. (1981). Clinical perspectives on the sick and dying child. In M. Lewis & L. A. Rosenblum (Eds.), *The uncommon child.* New York: Plenum Press.

Tisak, M. S. (1986). Children's conceptions of parental authority. *Child Development, 57,* 166–176.

Tizard, B., & Hughes, M. (1985). *Young children learning.* Cambridge, MA: Harvard University Press.

Toner, I. J. (1986). Punitive and non-punitive discipline and subsequent rule-following in young children. *Child Care Quarterly, 15*(1), 27–37.

Toner, I. J., Moore, L. P., & Ashley, P. K. (1978). The effect of serving as a model of self-control on subsequent resistance to deviation in children. *Journal of Experimental Child Psychology, 26,* 85–91.

Toner, I. J., & Potts, R. (1981). Effect of modeled rationales on moral behavior, moral choice, and level of moral judgment in children. *Journal of Psychology, 107,* 153–162.

Trickett, P. K., & Kuczynski, L. (1986). Children's misbehaviors and parental discipline strategies in abusive and nonabusive families. *Developmental Psychology, 22,* 115–123.

Trickett, P. K., & Susman, E. J. (1988). Parental perceptions of child-rearing practices in physically abusive and nonabusive families. *Developmental Psychology, 24*(2), 270–276.

Tronick, E. Z. (1989). Emotions and emotional communication in infants. *American Psychologist, 44*(2), 112–119.

Trotter, R. J. (1985, March). Fathers and daughters: The broken bond. *Psychology Today,* p. 10.

Trotter, R. J. (1987a, December). Project day-care. *Psychology Today,* pp. 32–38.

Trotter, R. J. (1987b, January). The play's the thing. *Psychology Today,* pp. 27–34.

Trotter, R. J. (1987c, May). You've come a long way, baby. *Psychology Today,* pp. 35–44.

Tucker, L. A. (1985). Television's role regarding alcohol use among teenagers. *Adolescence, 20*(79), 593–598.

Tucker, L. A. (1986). The relationship of television viewing to physical fitness and obesity. *Adolescence, 21*(84), 797–806.

Tucker, L. A. (1987). Television, teenagers and health. *Journal of Youth and Adolescence, 16*(5), 415–425.

Turkington, C. (1984a, April). Parents found to ignore sex stereotypes. *APA Monitor,* p. 12.

Turkington, C. (1984b, April). Project looks at stress in children. *APA Monitor,* p. 14.

Turkington, C. (1984c, December). Psychologists help spot danger in crib. *APA Monitor.*

Turkington, C. (1984d, October). Stepfamilies: Changes in the family tree can be for better or for worse. *APA Monitor,* pp. 8–9.

Turkington, C. (1984e, December). Support urged for children in mourning. *APA Monitor,* pp. 16–17.

Turkington, C. (1987, September). Special talents. *Psychology Today,* pp. 42–46.

Umberson, D. (1989). Relationships with children: Exploring parents' psychological well-being. *Journal of Marriage and the Family, 51,* 999–1012.

Umberson, D., & Gove, W. R. (1989). Parenthood and psychological well-being: Theory, measurement, and stage in the family life course. *Journal of Family Issues, 10*(4), 440–462.

Ungar, J. (1988, May 10). "Good" mothers feel dark urges. *New York Times.*

van Ijzendoorn, M. H., & van Vliet-Visser, S. (1988). The relationship between quality of attachment in infancy and IQ in kindergarten. *Journal of Genetic Psychology, 149*(1), 23–28.

Vandell, D. L., & Corasaniti, M. A. (1988). The relation between third graders' after-school care and social, academic, and emotional functioning. *Child Development, 59,* 868–875.

Vaughn, B. E., Block, J. H., & Block, J. (1988). Parental agreement on child rearing during early childhood and the psychological characteristics of adolescents. *Child Development, 59,* 1020–1033.

Vaughn, B. E., Lefever, G. B., Seifer, R., & Barglow, P. (1989). Attachment behavior, attachment security, and temperament during infancy. *Child Development, 60,* 728–737.

Ventura, J. N. (1987, January). The stresses of parenthood reexamined. *Family Relations,* pp. 26–29.

Vianello, R., & Lucamante, M. (1988). Children's understanding of death according to parents and pediatricians. *Journal of Genetic Psychology, 149*(3), 305–316.

Visher, E. B., & Visher, J. S. (1988). *Old loyalties, new ties: Therapeutic strategies with stepfamilies.* New York: Brunner/Mazel.

Vuchinich, S. (1985, October). Arguments, family style. *Psychology Today,* pp. 40–46.

Vuchinich, S., Emery, R. E., & Cassidy, J. (1988). Family members as third parties in dyadic family conflict: Strategies, alliances, and outcomes. *Child Development, 59,* 1293–1302.

Vuillemot, L. (1988, September 25). The fate of baby Amy. *New York Times,* Magazine Section, pp. 39–101.

Wadsworth, J., Burnell, I., Taylor, B., & Butler, N. (1985). The influence of family type on children's behavior and development at five years. *Journal of Child Psychology & Psychiatry & Allied Disciplines, 26*(2), 245–254.

Wagner, K. R. (1985). How much do children say in a day? *Journal of Child Language, 12*(2), 475–487.

Wagner, M. E., Schubert, H. J., & Schubert, D. S. (1985). Family size effects: A review. *Journal of Genetic Psychology, 146*(1), 65–78.

Wagonseller, B. R., & McDowell, R. L. (1979). *You and your child: A commonsense approach to successful parenting.* Champaign, IL: Research Press.

Wahler, R. G., & Dumas, J. E. (1989). Attentional problems in dysfunctional mother-child interactions: An interbehavioral model. *Psychological Bulletin, 105*(1), 116–130.

Waisbren, S. E. (1980). Parents' reactions after the birth of a developmentally disabled child. *American Journal of Mental Deficiency, 84*(4), 345–351.

Walker, L. S., & Green, J. W. (1986). The social context of adolescent self-esteem. *Journal of Youth and Adolescence, 15,* 315–322.

Wallerstein, J. S. (1987). Children of divorce: Report of a ten-year follow-up of early latency children. *American Journal of Orthopsychiatry, 57*(2), 199–211.

Wallerstein, J. S. (1988). Children of divorce: Stress and developmental tasks. In N. Garmezy & M. Rutter (Eds.), *Stress, coping, and development in children.* Baltimore, MD: Johns Hopkins University Press.

Wallerstein, J. S. (1989, January 22). Children after divorce: Wounds that don't heal. *New York Times Magazine,* pp. 19–44.

Wallerstein, J. S., & Blakeslee, S. (1989). *Second chances.* New York: Ticknor and Fields.

Wallerstein, J. S., & Corbin, S. B. (1989). Daughters of divorce: Report from a ten-year follow-up. *American Journal of Orthopsychiatry, 59*(4), 593–604.

Walters, G. C., & Grusec, J. F. (1977). *Punishment.* San Francisco: Freeman.

Walton, S. (1984, August). Get a job, stay out of trouble. *Psychology Today,* p. 11.

Watson, J. B. (1924). *Behaviorism.* New York: People's Institute.

Watson, J. S. (1981). Contingency experience in behavioral development. *Behavioral Development, 18,* 83–89.

Weatherly, J. (1985). Meeting parental needs: A never-ending dilemma. *The disabled child and the family: An exceptional parent reader.* Boston, MA: The Exceptional Parent Press.

Webster-Stratton, C. (1989). The relationship of marital support, conflict, and divorce to parent perceptions, behaviors, and childhood conduct problems. *Journal of Marriage and the Family, 51,* 417–430.

Weisz, J. R. (1980). Autonomy, control, and other reasons why "Mom is the greatest": A content analysis of children's Mother's Day letters. *Child Development, 51,* 801–807.

Weller, E. B., Weller, R. A., Fristad, M. A., Cain, S. E., & Bowes, J. M. (1988). Should children attend their parent's funeral? *Journal of the American Academy of Child and Adolescent Psychiatry, 27,* 559–562.

Wells, A. S. (1987, Summer). The parents' place: Right in the school. *New York Times,* Education Section, pp. 63–68.

Wells, M. (1988, June). The roots of literacy. *Psychology Today,* pp. 20–22.

Werner, E. E. (1989a, April). Children of the garden island. *Scientific American,* pp. 106–111.

Werner, E. E. (1989b). High-risk children in young adulthood: A longitudinal study from birth to 32 years. *American Journal of Orthopsychiatry, 59*(1), 72–81.

White, B. L. (1971, October 21–22). *Fundamental early environmental influences on the development of competence.* Paper presented at the Third Western Symposium on Learning: Cognitive Learning, Western Washington State College, Bellingham, WA.

White, B. L. (1988). *Educating the infant and toddler.* Lexington, MA: D. C. Heath.

White, K. D., Pearson, J. C., & Flint, L. (1989). Adolescents' compliance-resistance: Effects of parents' compliance strategy and gender. *Adolescence, 24*(95), 595–621.

White, L. K., & Brinkerhoff, D. B. (1981a). Children's work in the family: Its significance and meaning. *Journal of Marriage and the Family, 43,* 789–798.

White, L. K., & Brinkerhoff, D. B. (1981b). The sexual division of labor: Evidence from childhood. *Social Forces, 60,* 171–181.

White, R. (1959). Motivation reconsidered: The concept of competence. *Psychological Review, 66,* 297–333.

Wilks, J. (1986). The relative importance of parents and friends in adolescent decision making. *Journal of Youth and Adolescence, 15*(4), 323–335.

Williams, J. A., & Campbell, L. P. (1985). Parents and their children comment on adolescence. *Adolescence, 20*(79), 745–748.

Williams, J. H. (1987). *Psychology of women* (3rd ed.). New York: Norton.

Williams, L. (1989, May 25). New rallying cry: Parents unite. *New York Times.*

Winn, M. (1989, April 16). New fights over spoiling your baby. *New York Times Magazine,* pp. 27–68.

Winner, E. (1986, August). Where pelicans kiss seals. *Psychology Today,* pp. 25–35.

Wolchik, S. A., Braver, S. L., & Sandler, I. N. (1985). Maternal versus joint custody: Children's postseparation experiences and adjustment. *Journal of Clinical Child Psychology, 14*(1), 5–10.

Wolfe, D. A., Edwards, B., Manion, I., & Koverola, C. (1988). Early intervention for parents at risk of child abuse and neglect: A preliminary investigation. *Journal of Consulting and Clinical Psychology, 56*(1), 40–47.

Wolff, P. H. (1966). The causes, controls, and organization of behavior in the neonate. *Psychological Issues, 5*(1, Serial No. 17).

Woollett, A. (1986). The influence of older siblings on the language environment of young children. *British Journal of Developmental Psychology, 4*(3), 235–245.

Wurtele, S. K. (1990). Teaching personal safety skills to four-year-old children: A behavioral approach. *Behavior Therapy, 21,* 25–32.

Wurtele, S. K., & Miller C. L. (1987). Children's conceptions of sexual abuse. *Journal of Clinical Child Psychology, 16*(3), 184–191.

Yamamoto, K., Soliman, A., Parsons, J., & Davis, O. L. (1987). Voices in unison: Stressful events in the lives of children in six countries. *Journal of Child Psychology and Psychiatry, 28,* 855–864.

Yogman, M. W., Cooley, J., & Kindlon, D. (1988). Fathers, infants, and toddlers. In P. Bronstein & C. P. Cowan (Eds.), *Fatherhood today: Men's changing role in the family.* New York: John Wiley.

Young, K. T. (1990). American conceptions of infant development from 1955 to 1984: What the experts are telling parents. *Child Development, 61,* 17–28.

Youniss, J., & Ketterlinus, R. D. (1987). Communication and connectedness in mother- and father-adolescent relationships. *Journal of Youth and Adolescence, 16*(3), 265–280.

Zahn-Waxler, C., Radke-Yarrow, M., & King, R. (1979). Child-rearing and children's prosocial initiation towards victims of distress. *Child Development, 50,* 319–330.

Zajonc, R. B., & Markus, G. B. (1975). Birth order and intellectual development. *Psychological Review, 82,* 74–88.

Zaslow, M. J. (1989). Sex differences in children's response to parental divorce: 2. Samples, variables, ages, and sources. *American Journal of Orthopsychiatry, 59*(1), 118–141.

Zeskind, P. S. (1980). Adult responses to cries of low- and high-risk infants. *Infant Behavior and Development, 3,* 167–177.

Zigler, E. F., & Rubin, N. (1985, November). Why child abuse occurs. *Parents,* pp. 102–218.

Zimbardo, P., & Radl, S. (1981). *Shyness.* New York: McGraw-Hill.

Credits

CHAPTER OPENERS

Chapter 1: © H. Armstrong Roberts; Chapter 2: © Michael Siluk; Chapter 3: © H. Armstrong Roberts; Chapter 4: © James L. Shaffer; Chapter 5: © Michael Siluk; Chapter 6: © Richard Anderson; Chapter 7: © H. Armstrong Roberts; Chapters 8 and 9: © James L. Shaffer; Chapter 10: © Richard S. Orton; Chapter 11: © James L. Shaffer; Chapter 12: © Michael Siluk; Chapter 13: © Unicorn Stock Photos; Chapter 14: © Michael Hayman/Photo Researchers, Inc.

CHAPTER 1

Page 6: The Bettmann Archive; pages 17 and 21: © Elizabeth Crews/The Image Works; page 24: © Richard Hutchings/ Photo Researchers, Inc.

CHAPTER 2

Page 34 left: © Keystone/The Image Works; middle: The Bettmann Archive; right: © Frost Publishing Group; page 51: © Erika Stone/Photo Researchers, Inc.

CHAPTER 3

Page 66: © James L. Shaffer; page 71: © Barbara Rios/Photo Researchers, Inc.

CHAPTER 4

Page 84: © James L. Shaffer; page 88: © Richard Anderson; page 95: © Nita Winter/ The Image Works

CHAPTER 5

Page 116: © James L. Shaffer; page 123: © Unicorn Stock Photos; page 125: © Hella Hammid/Photo Researchers, Inc.

CHAPTER 6

Page 135: © Michael Siluk; page 144: © Unicorn Stock Photos

CHAPTER 7

Page 167: © James L. Shaffer; page 172: Hanna Schreiber/ Photo Researchers, Inc.; page 174: © Ursula Markus/Photo Researchers, Inc.; page 178: © Elizabeth Crews/The Image Works

CHAPTER 8

Pages 203 and 205: © James L. Shaffer; page 207: © Michael Siluk

CHAPTER 9

Page 220, 221, and 231: © Michael Siluk

CHAPTER 10

Page 250: © Richard Anderson; page 253: © Jean-Claude Lejeune; page 264: © James L. Shaffer

CHAPTER 11

Pages 279 and 281: © Michael Siluk; page 282: © Erika Stone/Photo Researchers, Inc.

CHAPTER 12

Page 303: © James L. Shaffer; page 308: © Elizabeth Crews/ The Image Works

CHAPTER 13

Page 328: © Arthur Glauberman/Photo Researchers, Inc.; page 333: © Bob Daemmrich/The Image Works

CHAPTER 14

Page 357: © George W. Gardner/The Image Works; page 359: © James L. Shaffer

Name Index

Subject Index

Intimacy, and isolation, 41
Involvement, and fathering, 311–12
Isolation, 25, 41

JAMA. *See Journal of the American Medical Association* (JAMA)
Japan
    and behavior, 110, 252–55
    and childhood, 8
Jealousy, 224–25
Joint custody, 296
Journal of the American Medical Association (JAMA), 84
Justification, 45

Knowing, 45–46
Kohlberg's cognitive-developmental model, 207–8

Labor, 12
    division of, 316
    and pregnancy, 81–82
    See also United States Department of Labor
Lamaze method, 83, 84
Language
    and achievement, 244–45
    acquisition, 160–62
    and communication skills, 162–70
Latchkey children, 25
Latency stage, 39
Law of effect, 109
LD. *See* Learning disabilities (LD)
Learned helplessness, 226
Learning
    disabilities. *See* Learning disabilities (LD)
    history. *See* Learning history
    models. *See* Learning models
    observational, 49, 147
    and reading and writing, 256–58
Learning disabilities (LD), 334–35
Learning history, 72–74
Learning models, and sexual identity and sex typing, 206–7
Leboyer method, 85
Lies, 216
Life-long project, 13
Listening, sympathetic (active, reflective), 164
Loneliness, 26
Los Angeles Times, 352, 353
Loss, and adolescence, 272

Maltreatment, psychological, 347, 350–51
Marriage
    and marital violence, 346
    styles of males and females, 301
Massachusetts Institute of Technology, 252

Media, 75, 263–66
Middle Ages, and childhood, 6–7
Misbehavior, analysis of, 109–10
"Mister Rogers," 266
Modification, behavior. *See* Behavior
Motherese, 161–62
Mothering, compared to father's styles, 315–18
Motivation, unconscious, 37–38

Nagging stage, 35
National Center for the Prevention and Control of Rape, 352
National Center on Child Abuse and Neglect, 348
National Education Association (NEA), 107, 251, 258
National Institute of Child Health and Human Development, 25
National Institute on Drug Abuse, 287
National Organization of Nonparents (NON), 11–12
National Parent-Teacher Association (P.T.A.), 24
Nature and nurture, 61–62
NEA. *See* National Education Association (NEA)
NEA Today, 107
Negative punishment, 148
Negative reinforcement, 136
Neglect, 347, 357–58
Negotiation, 108
Nest, empty. *See* Empty nest
New Parents as Teachers Project, 27
Newsweek, 85, 86
New York Times, 5, 9, 10, 14, 16, 25, 69, 86, 90, 92, 95, 103, 138, 150, 256, 258, 265, 282, 288, 294, 303, 332, 351, 352, 353–54, 359, 360
NJEA Review, 258
NON. *See* National Organization of Nonparents (NON)
Noncompliance, 100–127
Nongenetic biological variables, 72
Nonshared family environments, 54–55
Nonverbal communication, 166–68
Nurturing stage, of parenthood, 43

Observational learning, 49, 147
Oedipus complex, 37–38
Only children, 180
Operant conditioning, 134–42
    and punishment and extinction, 134
    reservations about, 141–42
    Skinner's model, 48
Oral stage, 39
Overcorrection, 151

Parental authority, 100–127
    and adolescents, 112
    and children, 111–12
    and internalization, 112–13
Parent and Child Education Program, 27
Parent-child conflict, 107–12
Parent-child relationships, 15–16, 246–47
Parent Effectiveness Training, 26
Parent Effectiveness Training, 169
Parenthood
    Galinsky's stages of, 42–43
    and parent-infant bonding, 87–91
    transition, 78–98
Parent-infant bonding, 87–91
Parenting
    and adolescents, 268–89
    and children's behavior, 128–53
    contemporary issues, 16–28
    domain-specific styles, 53–54, 120
    and dual careers, 16–20
    and early decisions, 4–5, 10–13
    and fathering, 283–84, 308–15
    goals of, 13–16
    and infants, 91–96
    introduction, 2–28
    and power and punishment, 120–26
    process model of determinants, 33
    and sensitivity and responsiveness, 157–58
    and single parenting, 302–4
    and special children, 320–38
    and stepparenting, 304–8
    theoretical perspectives, 30–57
    and understanding, acceptance, and patience, 158–60
Parents
    and Hoffman's model of parental power assertion, 122
    and parent-child conflict, 107–12
    and perceptions of children, 103–7
    and play, 262–63
    pleasing one's own, 12
    and realistic expectations, 104–7
    and rights, 121
Parent-support and training programs, 26–28
Parent-Teacher Association (P.T.A.). *See* National Parent-Teacher Association (P.T.A.)
Passive influence, 68
Passive noncompliance, 108
Patience, parental, 158–60
Peer groups, and adolescents, 275
Permissive parental discipline style, 117, 118, 119
Personal growth, 13

Socialization, and sex differences, 199–210
Social reinforcement, 142–43
Society for the Prevention of Cruelty to Animals, 348
Sons
    and differential treatment, 318
    and sex differentiation, 201–6
Sounds. See Language
Spanking, 149
Special children, 320–38
    and family life-cycle model, 327–28
    introduction, 323–24
Speech. See Language
Split custody, 296
Stability, 66–67
Stabilizing phase, and divorce, 297
Stagnation, and generativity, 41
Stepparenting, 304–8
Stimulus, aversive, 135
Stranger anxiety, 175
Strange situation test, 23, 174, 175
Stress, 226–28
    adjustment, and coping, 212–38
    and infants, 131
    and pregnancy, 80–81
    and stressors, and family, 328–29
Stressors. See Stress
Styles
    discipline. See Baumrind's model of discipline styles and Discipline
    marriage. See Marriage
    parenting. See Domain-specific parenting styles
Sudden infant death syndrome (SIDS), 92
    See also Death
Suicide, and adolescents, 287–88
Superego, 36–37
Superkids, 249–51
Support. See Parent-support and training programs
Sympathetic listening, 164

Talent, 70–71
Tangible reinforcers, 143
Tantrum, 138–39
Team approach, to parental discipline, 114
Teenage fathers, 283–84
Television, 75, 263–66
Temperament, 63–65
Temper tantrum, 138–39
Tertiary prevention, 337
Theory
    attachment, 176
    Bandura's social-cognitive, 48–49, 198–99
    Baumrind's method of discipline styles, 117–20
    chance encounters, 55–56
    of development, 34–35
    domain-specific parenting styles, 53–54, 120
    Erikson's psychosocial, 39–42, 196
    family systems, 49–51
    Freud's psychodynamic, 35–39
    Galinsky's stages of parenthood, 42–43
    Kohlberg's cognitive-developmental model, 207–8
    nonshared family environments, 54–55
    and parenting, 30–57
    Piaget's cognitive development, 45–47
    Rogers's self-actualization, 44–45, 198
    Skinner's operant conditioning model, 48
    small moments model, 51–52
Threats, 149
Time out, 149
Toddlers, 39, 131–34
Toilet training, 39, 94
Token reinforcers, 143
Toys
    and aggression, 360
    and sex differences, 263

Training
    parent. See Parent-support and training programs
    toilet. See Toilet training
Transition, to parenthood, 78–98
Transitional phase, and divorce, 297
Trust, and mistrust, 40–41
Twins, 69–72

Unconditional acceptance, 44
Unconditioned reinforcers, 142–43
Unconscious motivation, 37–38
Underachievement. See Achievement
Understanding, parental, 158–60
United States Department of Health, Education, and Welfare, 22
United States Department of Labor, 24
University of California at Berkeley, 252
University of California at Los Angeles, 333
University of New Hampshire, 352
University of Texas at Austin, 301
U.S. News and World Report, 10

Values, and adolescents, 278–80
Vermont Department of Health, 27–28
Violence, family and marital, 343–47

Warnings, 149
Weekly Reader Magazine, 263
Westinghouse Science Talent Search, 252
Women
    and childbearing destiny, 12
    and dual-career parenting, 16–20
Work, and adolescents, 279
Writing, and reading, 256–58